Ellis' Handbook of Mental Deficiency, Psychological Theory and Research

Third Edition

Ellis' Handbook of Mental Deficiency, Psychological Theory and Research

Third Edition

edited by

William E. MacLean, Jr.
Peabody College of Vanderbilt University

Routledge
Taylor & Francis Group
LONDON AND NEW YORK

First published 1997 by Lawrence Erlbaum Associates, Inc.

2 Park Square, Milton Park, Abingdon, Oxon OX14 4RN
711 Third Avenue, New York, NY 10017, USA

Routledge is an imprint of the Taylor & Francis Group, an informa business

First issued in paperback 2016

cover design by Teresa Horton

Library of Congress Cataloging-in-Publication Data

Ellis' handbook of mental deficiency, psychological theory and research / William E. MacLean, Jr., editor. — 3rd ed.
p. cm.
Previous ed. published as: Handbook of mental deficiency / edited by Norman R. Ellis. 1979.
Includes bibliographical references and index.
ISBN 0-8058-1407-8 (alk. paper)
1. Mental retardation. I. MacLean, William E.
RC570.H344 1996
616.85'88—dc20 95-52850
CIP

Publisher's Note
The publisher has gone to great lengths to ensure the quality of this reprint but points out that some imperfections in the original may be apparent.

ISBN 978-0-8058-1407-1 (hbk)
ISBN 978-1-138-96859-2 (pbk)

Dedicated to Norman R. Ellis, PhD

Contents

Preface to the Third Edition

More than 15 years separate the publication of this, the third edition of the *Handbook*, from the second published in 1979. That interval was witness to enormous reformation of research strategies, theoretical developments, scope and range of problems and issues investigated, technological innovation, and cross-disciplinary inquiry. An entire generation of researchers was intellectually born and bred during that interval. They not only brought a renewed vitality to the broad research enterprise, but they have substantively contributed to the changing theoretical tenor through introduction of novel conceptual approaches, incorporation of recent technological advances, and integration into their research of facts, data, and theories from diverse orientations.

Measured in sheer volume alone, research into the constellation of phenomena that together comprise the field of mental retardation has undergone a veritable revolution. In the early 1960s, under the leadership of President John F. Kennedy, major policy decisions were made at the federal level to mount a major and sustained research effort to unravel the mysteries of mental retardation, to apply the power of science to finding causes and treatments, and to enhance life's quality for children exposed to risks and who suffered the effects.

The field was until then in an embryonic stage—disorganized, and devalued both as a scientific undertaking and as a major public priority initiative. In some respects the turnabout was sudden and dramatic as a cascade of resources, concerns, advocacy, and, most importantly, the investment of careers of many talented researchers who devoted themselves to a common cause. In review of this history of almost four decades and in consideration of how barren the cache of scientific certainties was then, the growth of knowledge has been startling. We now have at our disposal methods and discoveries that could have only have been dreamt of then. The lives of many have been spared and made more full as a consequence. But this is not to say that the road to understanding has been smooth, certain, or without its jarring disappointments and disagreements, not only in our science but in our pervasively changing socialization. Perhaps in the heady atmosphere of the times, the complexities of the problems associated with mental retardation were not sufficiently appreciated and, in retrospect, one of the most significant discoveries has been a fuller and sobering realization of just how vastly complex and daunting is that multivariate constellation of biological, social, educational, psychological, and political characteristics that together form the backdrop against which we pursue our research. Many uncertainties are persistent, and sometimes it seems that each fresh insight is but a fresh frustration. Take, for example, excitement over the discovery of the metabolic perturbation associated with PKU, universal screening, and the clinical demonstration that infant dietary prophylaxis can avert the serious mental retardation that usually accompanies PKU. And in so doing, we now confront a new problem—Maternal PKU—that in a single generation can wipe out all the gains. There are other current overly optimistic claims, some of which are simply foolish and still others born of sincere and commendable hope, that do not survive careful scientific scrutiny. Many unanswered questions concerning causes, prevention, treatment, and definition await our attention. But taking the broader view and on balance, a clearing has been made and the path is open for more discovery.

Nor is this to say that the course of inquiry is not characterized by marked discontinuities. As in any other area of scientific endeavor, behavioral research into myriad aspects of mental retardation has clearly been and continues to be an evolutionary process. Many direct antecedents of the basic conceptual thrusts reflected in this volume are to be found in the first (1963) edition of the *Handbook*. Although many of the contributors to the initial book have moved on to other areas, retired, or passed away, their intellectual legacy persists.

Norman Ellis devoted nearly 40 years to behavioral research in mental retardation. His legacy includes many important and original theoretical formulations as well as critical and pioneering empirical studies. In keeping with his leadership role and in an effort to lend identification to and a forum for the relatively small group of behavioral scientists committed to mental retardation, in the 1960s he conceived and created the annual Gatlinburg Research Conference devoted to behavioral research in mental retardation. He further contributed to the field through various editorial positions and NIH peer review panels, by mentorship of many prominent research scientists, and through his editorship of volumes on mental retardation research. Through these efforts, Ellis attained a position of prominence and eminence in the field of mental retardation as both an advocate for and critic of behavioral research. He has been honored frequently and formally in recognition of his scholarly contributions. In 1968 he received the Research Award of the American Association on Mental Deficiency. In appreciation of Ellis' international scholarly status, The University of Alabama conferred on him the Burnum Distinguished Faculty Award in 1984.

The *International Review of Research in Mental Retardation* was another of his creations and has been published periodically since its inception in 1966. For many years, Ellis served as editor, and later as collaborator with Dr. Norman Bray. Publication of that highly respected series continues.

For all of his contributions, perhaps the singularly most noteworthy and influential was publication, in 1963, of the *Handbook of Mental Deficiency*. More than any other marker, this pivotal publication marks the beginning of systematic and organized behavioral theory concerning mental retardation. At the time of its publication in 1963, the *Handbook* summarized practically all that was known in the field of behavioral research in mental retardation. For the first time, all the major theories of behavior aspects of mental retardation were fully articulated and brought together in a single reference source. For many years, the *Handbook* was the most frequently cited work in the field of mental retardation research. In its time it was recognized as among the 100 most influential books in psychology. Ellis also edited the second volume. Now retired from his academic appointment at the University of Alabama, he continues to contribute to the scientific literature but at a more relaxed pace.

I am deeply grateful for the trust and confidence Dr. Ellis has shown in support of me as editor of the third edition. This volume is dedicated to him in recognition of his longstanding commitment and enduring contributions to research and theory in mental retardation.

Retaining the original title of this volume perhaps will be criticized by some as it was by reviewers of the second edition. The term *mental deficiency* has fallen into disfavor and has yielded to *mental retardation* in scientific, professional, and advocacy-related writings. My reason for retaining the title was to preserve the historical significance of the untold contributions to the field made by the two previous editions. No other volume devoted exclusively to psychological theory and research in mental retardation has had a comparable impact on the field. It represents one of the most significant milestones in the history of inquiry into mental retardation.

In the years since the publication of the second edition of this volume, psychological theory and research in mental retardation have continued to expand and extend scientific, theoretical, and clinical understanding of this most complex and challenging human condition. Explicit effort has been made to translate theory and research into useful and efficacious assessment, intervention, prevention, and policy actions. Among my reasons for pursuing publication of this third edition was to provide an opportunity to critique major conceptual developments and empirical research in an effort to stimulate further behavioral research of practical, social importance.

The *Handbook* contains 16 chapters written by prominent contributors to a major scientific endeavor that has grown by orders of magnitude in the past three decades. The chapters include extensive reviews and critiques as well as thorough compilations of existing research and theory in selected content domains. Perspectives are presented that are not addressed in previous editions, reflecting enlarging content, changing approaches, new developments, and dramatically changing social conditions. The introductory chapters on behavioral research in mental retardation and issues of definition and classification establish an important context for the subsequent chapters. The next section includes major contemporary perspectives on understanding mental retardation. In contrast to previous editions organized by particular theoretical perspectives, this section includes new syntheses of existing research emerging from a variety of theoretical and interdisciplinary approaches concerning the etiology of mental retardation. Research on cognitive processes has been a traditional strength of the *Handbook* and continues to be well represented in the current volume. Chapters focus on rigidity, strategy use, attention, cognition, response speed, and motor skills. The final section includes chapters on social, communicative, and adaptive processes such as social intelligence, personality and motivation, communication and language, family adaptation, and severe behavior problems. The challenge for each author was to identify important theoretical and empirical issues, provide a critical, selective review of exemplary research, and discuss the questions that remain unanswered in each area. In short, the goal for this third edition was to consolidate the knowledge gained over the past 30 or so years and to present a blueprint for future research in mental retardation, the broader field of learning disabilities, and other developmental disorders such as autism.

It was not possible to include every perspective and content area in a field that has grown by such proportions. Some areas have been covered recently by well-recognized scholars and these efforts are not duplicated here. Unlike the era of the earlier editions, particularly the first, there are now alternative outlets for psychological theory and research relating to intelligence and developmental disabilities. The field as a whole has clearly benefited from this growth. The book is intended to be adequately comprehensive, not encyclopedic.

In comparison with the previous two editions, several trends in the field are evident in this *Handbook*. There is no longer a separate chapter on brain damage. In the years since the second edition, there has been greater acceptance of the view that the brain is ultimately and intimately implicated in deficient intellectual and adaptive functioning. Rapproachment between behavior and biology is evident in many of the current chapters as well. Biological underpinnings of aberrant behavior, language, cognitive processes, and motor behavior are but a few examples. Tremendous advances in genetic research, brain imaging, and other biomedical technologies that now permit identification of specific etiologies have played a major role in this trend. Examples of this progress include the discovery of fragile X syndrome as the most frequent inherited cause of mental retardation (an etiology just being described at the time of the second edition). Widespread use of computerized tomography, positron emission tomography, and magnetic resonance imaging has greatly expanded understanding of neural processes, both with respect to clinical practice and to basic research on such topics as attention, language, problem solving, memory, concept formation, and information processing.

Second, the field of mental retardation is gradually being absorbed into the larger domain of developmental disabilities. Mental retardation no longer stands alone as it is now widely recognized that mental retardation is but one entity that affects adaptation and that the same precipitating and maintaining events are interlocked in many of these conditions. As this trend continues, it may be that artificial distinctions made along a continuum of intellectual and adaptive ability will become even less important.

A third trend is the adoption of a developmental life-span perspective by many authors. This perspective is manifest in the methods of study and by the disparate ages of subjects (ranging from newborns to elders) and testing the relevance and application of normative theories for people with mental retardation.

A fourth trend is the explicit attempt by many researchers to increase our understanding of mental retardation by reducing variability in the populations we study. Etiology is now recognized as an important defining characteristic and extremely heterogeneous samples, defined by a single, unitary metric, are less frequently studied. There has been longstanding interest in Down syndrome by psychologists, but behavioral approaches have now been expanded to include Prader Willi syndrome, Rett syndrome, fragile X, and Williams syndrome to name but a few genetic conditions. The same can be said of myriad acquired forms of mental retardation arising from infections, exposure to toxins, and the like. Intensive study of relatively homogeneous groups of people permits more careful, precise, and etiologic analysis of retarded development.

I wish to thank the following people, who played a central role as consulting editors and those whose efforts went beyond that of cursory reviews: Robert Arendt, Al Baumeister, Verne Bacharach, Norman Ellis, Leslie Halpern, Mark Lewis, Edward Merrill, and Wendy Stone.

Finally, I wish to express my appreciation to several people. I am grateful for the consultation that I received early on from Norman Ellis, Al Baumeister, and Carl Haywood. Their guidance on identifying potential contributors was most useful. Over the long haul, Al Baumeister and Steve Warren provided much needed moral support as did my wife, Gay. Marilyn Riggs provided crucial technical assistance in the preparation of the manuscript and indices. I very much appreciate her persistence and dedication to the project. I also want to thank Teresa Horton and Ray O'Connell of LEA for their valuable assistance in the preparation of the *Handbook*.

—William E. MacLean, Jr.

Contributors

Alfred A. Baumeister, PhD Department of Psychology and Human Development, Peabody College of Vanderbilt University, Nashville, TN 37203

Norman Bray, PhD Department of Psychology, The University of Alabama at Birmingham, Birmingham, AL 35294-0017

Cynthia L. Dulaney, PhD Department of Psychology, Xavier University, Cincinnati, OH 45207-6511

Norman R. Ellis, PhD Department of Psychology, The University of Alabama, University, AL 35487-0348

Kathryn L. Fletcher, PhD Department of Psychology, The University of Alabama at Birmingham, Birmingham, AL 35294-0017

Stephen Greenspan, PhD Department of Educational Psychology, University of Connecticut, Storrs, CT 06269

Robert M. Hodapp, PhD Department of Special Education, University of California, Los Angeles, Los Angeles, CA 90024-1521

Ann P. Kaiser, PhD Department of Special Education, Peabody College of Vanderbilt University, Nashville, TN 37203

Pippa S. Loupe, PhD Schiefelbush Center for Life Span Studies, The University of Kansas, Lawrence, KS 66045

Peter F. Love, PhD Department of Educational Psychology, University of Connecticut, Storrs, CT 06269

William E. MacLean, Jr., PhD Department of Psychology, University of Wyoming, Laramie, WY 82071

Donald L. MacMillan, PhD School of Education, University of California at Riverside, Riverside, CA 92521-0128

Ted Nettelbeck, PhD Department of Psychology, University of Adelaide, Adelaide, South Australia

Karl M. Newell, PhD Department of Exercise and Sport Science, The Pennsylvania State University, University Park, PA 16802-3903

Mary O'Callaghan Department of Psychology, University of Notre Dame, Notre Dame, IN 46556

Samuel L. Odom, PhD Department of Special Education, Peabody College of Vanderbilt University, Nashville, TN 37203

Daniel J. Reschly, PhD Department of Psychology, Iowa State University, Ames, IA 50011-3180

Stephen R. Schroeder, PhD Schiefelbush Center for Life Span Studies, The University of Kansas, Lawrence, KS 66045

Kristie Sommer Department of Psychology, University of Notre Dame, Notre Dame, IN 46556

Christopher J. Stodgell, PhD Schiefelbush Center for Life Span Studies, The University of Kansas, Lawrence, KS 66045

Zolinda Stoneman, PhD University Affiliated Program for Persons with Developmental Disabilities, The University of Georgia, Athens, GA 30602

Harvey N. Switzky, PhD Department of Educational Psychology, Counseling, and Special Education, Northern Illinois University, Dekalb, IL 60115

Richard E. Tessel, PhD Schiefelbush Center for Life Span Studies, The University of Kansas, Lawrence, KS 66045

Lee Anne Thompson, PhD Department of Psychology, Case Western Reserve University, Cleveland, OH 44106-7123

Veronica Tinsley, PhD Department of Psychology, The University of Florida, Gainesville, FL 32611

Phillip D. Tomporowski, PhD Department of Psychology, The University of Florida, Gainesville, FL 32611

Lisa A. Turner, PhD Department of Psychology, The University of South Alabama, Mobile, AL 36688

Steven F. Warren, PhD Department of Special Education, Peabody College of Vanderbilt University, Nashville, TN 37203

Thomas L. Whitman, PhD Department of Psychology, University of Notre Dame, Notre Dame, IN 46556

Carlene Wilson, PhD Department of Psychology, University of Adelaide, Adelaide, South Australia

Paul J. Yoder, PhD Department of Special Education, Peabody College of Vanderbilt University, Nashville, TN 37203

Edward Zigler, PhD Department of Psychology, Yale University, New Haven, CT 06520

› I ‹

Introduction

1

Behavioral Research: Boom or Bust?

Alfred A. Baumeister
Vanderbilt University

A LITTLE BACKGROUND

The prefaces and introductions by Norman Ellis to the first (1963) and second (1979) editions of the *Handbook* are in themselves a highly instructive encapsulation of the recent history of behavioral research and theory in the field of mental retardation. The period between those two earlier editions reflected startling growth in the amount of research reported, complexity of design, and, in some respects, increased sophistication of methods. Publication of research articles increased by virtually exponential proportions, no doubt greatly abetted by federal largess.

Equally significant was the enormous and remarkable expansion in range of problems and issues addressed, in both theoretical domains and practical terms. During the earlier period (i.e., the 1960s), most formal, theory-driven, psychological research was conducted in laboratories or at least in relatively well-controlled settings—directed at topics such as learning, memory, perception, information processing, attention, motivation, and other mainstream psychological concepts.

During the 1960s and well into the 1970s, the age of the Great Society, emphasis of the behavioral sciences was almost entirely on the environment with virtually complete disregard (even disdain) for genetics and other biological constructs (e.g., Bijou, 1966). We were apparently convinced that we could adjust intelligence by enriching or controlling environments. Early preschool intervention (e.g., Head Start) was embraced within national policy; behavior modification within educational and clinical practice.

In the next decade pragmatic and utilitarian concerns became increasingly prominent, including research on alternative living arrangements, normalization, social processes, aberrant responding, self-help and work skills, peer relations, service delivery systems, adaptive assessment, early educational intervention, applications of computer technology, brain function and disorders, language skills, and genetics. For the most part, these are topics well represented in the present edition. The focus is still primarily on psychological and educational research, although a number of chapters incorporate data and theory from biological disciplines.

Another similar text, arguably of quite equal importance and influence, is *Mental Deficiency: The Changing Outlook*, originally edited in 1958 in Great Britain by A. M. Clarke and A. D. B. Clarke, both prominent psychologists. That text has also undergone several revisions, with the fourth edition appearing in 1985. At that time the Clarkes were joined by J. M. Berg, a biomedical researcher and physician, as editor. Like those written by Ellis, the prefaces and introductions to the four editions of *Mental Deficiency: The Changing Outlook* chronicle the field in evolution from the early dominant psychometric focus that pervaded behavioral research through the seemingly endless array of studies of different topics, theoretical developments and controversies, and cross-disciplinary inquiry and focus.

Both books, in their updated editions, are markers of how research on mental retardation has progressed, both quantitatively and qualitatively. They represent the best and most thorough compilations of knowledge stretching across the horizon of the recent history of the field. It is of interest that both have also retained the term mental deficiency in their titles, despite the political-correctness frenzy that now pervades our descriptive terminology. At the same time, the editors are cognizant of the advocacy-inspired socialization process in which the word deficiency has fallen into disfavor.

One very notable difference between the two books is the much heavier emphasis in *Mental Deficiency: The Changing Outlook* on biochemical aspects, genetic determinants, epidemiology, and neurology. The *Handbook* has been, from its very inception, explicitly devoted to behavioral research, although recognizing that biology, epidemiology, and sociology are all vital to a comprehensive understanding of mental retardation. This is both a strength and a weakness. On the one hand, it provides the most complete compendium of the current status of mental retardation research in the behavior sciences. On the other, there is a growing appreciation of the need for more thorough integration of concepts and data from various disciplines, ranging from studies of the molecule through service delivery systems. The 1990s, after all, is the Decade of the Brain.

The most extensive recent endeavor to describe, integrate, and characterize psychological research concerning children with mental and physical disabilities is to be found the book *Children with Handicaps: A Review of Behavioral Research*, by Berkson (1993). Although Berkson briefly reviewed the earliest antecedents, starting with prehistoric times, he focused almost entirely on the decade of the 1980s. Taking the period 1984 to 1989, Berkson found over 5,000 published articles, excluding book chapters. Compare that with the state of the field in the 1940s when McPherson (1948) was able to list only a dozen formal experimental studies devoted to consideration of learning and mental retardation.

Even though behavioral research was certainly the major focus of Berkson's attention, he devoted considerable discussion to etiological issues, genetic and acquired. Emphasis is appropriately placed on the continuum of reproductive causality, pleiotropic effects, the multivariate nature of the phenomena, and diagnostics issues—important topics to which we return.

Berkson also connected etiology with prevention, indicating that prevention "perhaps is the ultimate treatment for disorders of development" (1993, p. 69). Perhaps? There is no "perhaps" about it—primary prevention is not only the most effective, sensible, and cost beneficial approach to treatment of developmental disabilities, but it also breaks down artificial and disciplinary distinctions about developmental problems, placing the issue squarely in the domain of public health and epidemiology (Baumeister, Kupstas, & Woodley-Zanthos, 1993). A categorical approach to the needs of children, couched within inflexible disciplinary boundaries, is, in the main, ineffective and, on a population basis, dysfunctional. Perhaps the most intractable problem is demarcation of narrow disciplinary boundaries, guarded by bureaucratic strictures, that fragment rather than coordinate.

Nevertheless, primary prevention of mental retardation has never been a major priority of researchers or policymakers for numerous reasons described by Baumeister et al. (1993).

My purpose here is to identify some of the major conceptual issues and dilemmas that continue to underlie or even plague behavioral research on the subject of mental retardation and other disorders of child development. As the foregoing discussion suggests, our research accomplishments, when measured in terms of volume, are impressive. What is less evident is the extent to which behavioral science has resolved any major uncertainties regarding conditions of aberrant development. The conclusion offered here, admittedly a generalization and one that will surely be disputed, is that we have *not* made major strides in this direction. It is not for want of effort or resources. The central thesis to my argument is that we have handicapped ourselves by reliance on inadequate, inappropriate, and inbred models of inquiry, conceptually and methodologically.

Values, Politics and the Role of Behavioral Research

Numerous factors account for the rapid emergence of mental retardation research from its embryonic stage to maturity as an established and respected area of scientific endeavor. Some influences are easier to pinpoint and track than others, nor are they entirely independent. Although there can be little doubt that the cumulative process of scientific inquiry and adventures into new theoretical territories explains some of the changing tenor of research, perhaps the most powerful influence affecting the national research agenda is to be found in expression of normative or value judgments, as reflected in policy determinations.

A view commonly held by professionals is that public policy requires science. On reflection, this proposition is audacious, because it is not only false but its converse is true. The fact is that science is not a prime determinate of public policy. Science, both as a general endeavor and in terms of priorities of problems targeted for exploration, is the product of public sentiment, formal and informal. Research in mental retardation is no exception to this generalization—in fact, on reflection is confirmation.

A study of the history of mental retardation reveals that societal regard for and treatment of those with mental retardation have been erratic, swinging between epochs of pessimism and optimism, between fear and compassion, between denial and acceptance, and between nature and nurture. Thus, in the 1950s the social pendulum began to swing back to pervasive changes with regard to compassion, hope, and advocacy for a better life and greater regard for personal and civil rights of those afflicted. The resolution was to be found in restructuring the environment through social means. Research and the wherewithal to conduct it on a large and broad scale ineluctably followed this reform movement.

With the election of President Kennedy, research about and services for persons with mental retardation became central features of domestic policy. A group of highly respected advisors (later, in 1966, to become the President's Committee on Mental Retardation) was convened to advise the president with respect to immediate policy determinations.

One major outcome of the deliberations of this advisory group was the decision to create a stable and visible mechanism to ensure large-scale and long-term support of biomedical and behavioral research to prevent and treat conditions associated with mental retardation. Thus was established the National Institute of Child Health and Human Development (NICHD)—the most concrete and substantial political expression of the commitment to address the health problems of children and their mothers. There was then, as now, divergence of views as to how best to accomplish these goals. For example, should mental retardation be considered within the wider context of developmental issues? What would be the proper relative balance of behavior and biomedical research? If the broader biomedical/developmental view prevailed, would mental retardation, so to speak, become a second-class citizen? At the time, in fact, there was considerable sentiment for designation of the Institute as the National Institute on Mental Retardation.

In any case, signing into law on October 17, 1962 Congressional authorization creating the NICHD, President Kennedy stated: "We will look to the (NICHD) for a concentrated attack on the unsolved problems of children . . . encourage imaginative research into the complex processes of human development . . . permit major advances in the conquest of those chronic conditions such as mental retardation and other congenital defects which derive from aberrations in early development" (cited in Alexander, 1992). Clearly, the intention as conveyed by this language was the mandate to address a broad range of health concerns affecting mothers and children, inclusive of but not limited to mental retardation.

Three decades and about $6 billion later there have been many important, startling discoveries that we could never have anticipated at the outset. It is important to emphasize, and worthy of further reflection, that most of the dramatic discoveries as to etiology, prevention, and treatment have come in biological spheres. Nevertheless, over the years intense criticism, mostly by psychologists, has increasingly been leveled at the Institute for alleged lack of commitment to mental retardation on the one hand and behavior research on the other.

Whether those criticisms are justified is debatable (Baumeister, in press). What is not debatable is that an enormous amount of money, millions and millions of dollars, has been and still is being awarded to behavioral scientists expressly on the subject of mental retardation through NICHD and other institutes, as well as by various federal agencies such as the Office of Special Education. We will return to the bread-and-butter issue of research support and funding trends and what may lie in store, because this concern occupies the attention of the research community at large.

How Far Have We Come? How Far to Go? How to Get There?

Notwithstanding that over the past three decades enormous dedication and resources have been directed at unraveling behavioral mysteries associated with mental retardation, the question still arises as to how far along the road to understanding, treatment, amelioration, and prevention all this sustained and sometimes systematic effort and investment has taken us. Where are the great discoveries that have been translated into demonstrably effective and cost-efficient social and health practices? What major uncertainties about mental retardation have been resolved? Through behavioral research have we significantly reduced incidence or prevalence, on a population basis, of mental retardation or any other manifestation commonly associated with this overall condition? Has behavioral research, independently of advocacy movements, improved quality of life for those afflicted with developmental disabilities and associated problems? Have efforts in the form of early education or cognitive intervention prevented mental retardation or lastingly boosted IQs in a meaningful and convincing manner? Are claims purported to have achieved breakthroughs such as in the case of early preschool intervention, skill training, and treatment of self-injurious behavior truly warranted? How does the record of behavior research stack up against biomedical research in the areas of diagnosis, evaluation, treatment, and prevention? Have the basic arguments over method, model, and mentality changed to advance our theories and approaches?

These and myriad other questions now command answers. The halcyon days of massive increments in research support are over. In fact, as we will see, there has been a decline in research support for mental retardation research. A cynical taxpayer might well ask whether the many millions of dollars spent on behavioral research produced information commensurate with the investment. Uncomfortable as it may be, that is not a frivolous question and is ignored to our collective peril.

At the beginning of the modern enterprise (i.e., when significant resources were made available to behavioral research), the optimistic (and convenient) claim could be made that the field was in its infancy and that it was necessary to establish basic and normative information that, through a cumulative process, would eventually find its way into aggressive and effective broad-based practice and policy. It is my contention that, with some notable exceptions, this has not generally happened and, furthermore, that after three decades the claim of "infancy" is no longer valid.

On the other hand, the frequent appeal to the shield of complexity is certainly understandable. There was then and, in some respects, still is a tendency to underestimate the complexities of that constellation of behavioral, biological, social, legal, economic, and ethical considerations that together form the backdrop of mental retardation. The result is not only fragmentation of services, but research as well.

This is not to say that there are not specific instances in which behavioral methods have not been successful, at least to some extent, in ameliorating effects or manifestations of mental retardation. There is evidence, of course, that basic behavioral research has produced procedures that are purportedly useful in teaching children with mild or moderate mental retardation or for controlling undesirable responding (e.g., Berkson, 1993; Brooks, Sperber, & McCauley, 1984; Clarke, Clarke, & Berg, 1985; Ellis, 1979).

But optimistic case reports, isolated and short-term intensive programs, or even well-controlled studies are not a solid basis on which to evaluate the public health successes that are allegedly produced by research. Nor is it absolutely easy to answer the question as to whether we have accomplished much of enduring value in our studies of retarded behavior, because the answer can take a variety of forms, not the least of which is that our understanding of basic psychological and intellectual processes may have been advanced. Furthermore, the case can be made, with some justification, that the lag between research discovery and application of that knowledge to practical ends is considerable. It takes time and dedication for scientific information to filter into "ordinary knowledge" (Baumeister, 1981). However, that begs the questions of what it is exactly that might be translated into practice or whether the cost–benefit trade-off is worth the investment.

Basic and Applied Research. Then there is the perpetual conflict that Ellis (and many others) addressed: the proper balance between basic and applied research. The claim has been often made by basic scientists, often defensively, that this is an arbitrary and invalid distinction. Braddock (1994) maintained that "the distinction between basic and applied research is not very useful" (p. 438). Perhaps so, but I hold that there is a useful and meaningful contrast between empirical knowledge that bears scientific or theoretical value and empirical knowledge that is of immediate social and practical significance.

In any event, it should be emphasized that research in general, but behavioral research in particular, has had little conspicuous impact on major policy initiatives. There are exceptions, but studies of information transfer indicate that policymakers are not greatly tempted by the fruits on the behavioral tree of knowledge (Baumeister, 1992). Moreover, it is frequently the case that research is selectively used to bolster a policy position (pro or con) reached in advance of the evidence (e.g., Head Start and other early intervention programs).

There is another related conflict that has been unfolding for a long time, but that is particularly salient in the current climate of federal deficits, welfare reform, prioritization, and fiscal restraint. Many scientists are taught that the quest for knowledge has its own momentum and internal sense of self-correcting direction. This value is advanced as a historically valid argument. Accordingly, social relevance is not or should not be a criterion for public support of the scientific enterprise. We, the public (and Congressional appropriations subcommittees), are implored to have patience because in due course science will pay off, as it always has.

However, in this day and time, when a swirling ocean of demands is threatening to engulf a shrinking island of resources, it seems singularly inappropriate and maladaptive to press the point that an untethered and flourishing science amply rewards the public faith—quite aside from the rewards enjoyed by scientists whose concerns are not always as pure as our public pronouncements avow. As the scale, cost, and scope of science have increased, so has the demand for a utilitarian approach. Whether we like it or not, the question of social relevance is unavoidable, as is the issue of accountability. The public trust demands that research contribute to the management of problems for which governments have responsibility and, furthermore, that publicly supported science must be responsive to the needs of society by directly addressing serious problems such as mental retardation. According to Braddock (1994), in recent years there has been a growing distance between researchers and providers, and that those researchers who fail to appreciate the various perspectives and ideologies that comprise the field of mental retardation "risk a steady slide into irrelevancy" (p. 438). He was correct.

Ecological Validity Revisited

In his introduction to the second edition of the *Handbook*, Ellis dealt with important conceptual issues that have long been the subject of a great deal of discussion and argument. These are issues that, in a very real sense, have defined behavioral research in mental retardation. The one that he elected to address most directly was the "plea for ecological validity" raised by Brooks and Baumeister (1977a, 1977b). Despite the spirited and well-articulated defense of traditional theoretically derived behavioral research offered by House (1977) in rebuttal, the problem of ecological validity will not go away and, in today's scientific and political climate, has never been more salient.

Ellis (1979) pointed out that, with the exception of behavior modification as derived from the principles of operant conditioning, there really had been little translation of basic behavioral research findings into application. Over the past 15 years the picture has changed somewhat in that cognitive psychologists, neuroscientists, and others have increasingly addressed practical issues. Other social science research has focused on such important areas as "normalization," socialization, service delivery, family stability, and educational mainstreaming.

However, there is much more to the core issue of ecological validity than the matter of direct translation of research findings to practical ends. Indeed, if the rather pessimistic conclusions presented here about the accomplishments of behavior research have any merit, one feature of failure that is central, in my view, relates to the concept of *ecological validity*—however much more broadly construed than first enunciated by Brunswick (1955).

Ecological validity should not be confused with social validity. That is a common misunderstanding. Laboratory or controlled experiments, the tasks that are employed, and the measurements obtained are not required to bear a one-to-one relationship with real-life events in order to be ecologically valid. The critical core issue is one of generality of representativeness; that is, pertaining to the structure of the environment and the individual's use of that structure in adaptations.

In a book that is unlikely to win him many friends among the staunch environmentalists, Wachs (1992) concluded that the only meaningful basis to understanding of the environment and its effects is the full external and internal context—the child's genetic makeup and place in the social order. It was his contention that isolated, univariate studies of environmental influences should be discontinued because they do not disentangle all the critical variables, including genetic and systemic influences that determine and condition intelligence—and, in my view, mental retardation.

The "one-variable rule" is still the standard of much psychological research. We control a variable in order to observe its independent effects. (This is not to say that we cannot systematically control more than one variable at a time and observe their main effects and interactions.) In our efforts to emulate "hard" science (which many domains of psychology are not), psychology has adopted methods that often limit rather than expand generalization.

Although the time-honored linear process model ostensibly makes for "clean" inferences, it also often has the effect of obliterating the natural patterns of correlations that exist between the behavior in question and the broader context in which the behavior occurs. At any time and in any situation behavior is a probabilistic function of numerous proximal and distal variables and their interactions.

If mental retardation is the historical and immediate product of complex entanglements of causes, mediators, and effects, then research strategies that rely on contrived and narrow manipulations greatly limit generality, failing to characterize and explain retarded behavior at a level commensurate with its complexity. We cannot even determine from such studies the direction of causality. A few descriptive parameters neatly studied in isolation produce untenable indeterminacy in our efforts to capture the essential essence of mental retardation in its reality and totality. If the developmental phenomena and deviations that we seek to understand, explain, and control are complex and multitiered, then our efforts to do so can be no less (Baumeister & Kupstas, 1991; Rutter, 1982; Sameroff & Fiese, 1991).

Some have suggested that we abandon laboratory research (meaning tightly controlled experiments) entirely in favor of naturalistic paradigms (e.g., Petrinovich, 1979). That is not the point. More important to ecological validity, here in the case of behavioral research in mental retardation, are metatheoretical constraints that lead us to explore phenomena in a particular manner, following time-honored but questionable assumptions, using standard methods and analyses that greatly limit the range of valid generalization. This might be termed *paradigm paralysis*.

Definitions Have Something to Do With Our Research. Consider, for instance, the very definition of mental retardation (i.e., by low IQ). There are exceptions, of course, but by convention and tradition behavioral research in the past and present has relied primarily on the venerable *g* construct for identification of groups or selection of individuals for study. Although this system of recruiting subjects for research possesses a certain practical functionality, and although not all behavioral investigators explicitly embrace the general factor theory of intelligence, the very procedure of constituting groups on this single metric means that certain theoretical assumptions about the nature of intelligence are implicitly accepted, thus further constraining representativeness. The operational definition of mental retardation, so heavily dependent on a single score, has had a procrustean effect on behavioral research.

Furthermore, research based on the traditional definition of mental retardation conditions the inferences and conclusions that follow—that is, the attribute is general, endogenous, and that mental retardation, therefore, is global. As an administrative concept, the single-score IQ may be useful for allocation of resources and services. (Even that is highly questionable.) There are exceptions, such as Sternlicht (1987), who advocated etiological rationalized special education. Others have also strongly advocated etiology-based interventions for children with known genetic disorders such as fragile X, Down, or Prader-Willi syndromes, and others (e.g., Dykens, Hodapp, & Evans, 1994). Maybe that is what the "special" in special education should be.

Nevertheless, as Rowitz (1988) and Kahn (1988) observed, special educators favor noncategorical or generic services for children with mental retardation. Baumeister and Muma (1975) attempted, without much conspicuous effect, to show just how fallacious such reasoning is. Special education research and practice seems to be more concerned with place than with process, more with generality than specificity, and more with political correctness than with biological correctness. Federal laws to achieve inclusion as central to educational custom cannot violate or override natural laws of variability and selection.

Perhaps the strongest expression of the noncategorical philosophy comes from Goodman (1990), who asserted that classification systems based on etiology lead to self-fulling prophecies that have untoward, bad social consequences. In my view, the far more irresponsible posture is to ignore scientific and clinical realities of the variable causative aspects of mental retardation, including those of biological origin and their different manifestations.

It is of considerable interest that professionals representing areas of special education, psychology, social work, and medicine differ rather substantially as to prognostic optimism concerning children with mental retardation, particularly in the moderate to severe range. Siperstein, Wolraich, and Reed (1994) speculated about the sources of this differential expression of optimism. Physicians, who are the most pessimistic, may have, as Siperstein et. al. suggested, less clinical experience over the life span of these individuals in diverse settings and therefore a narrower view as to the range of indicators. That may be so, but I think they also are less clouded by inclusionary doctrine and are more inclined to look to specific clinical indicators with a better appreciation of their significance for prognosis.

To the extent that psychological and educational research on mental retardation has become enslaved to the unitary, general, nondifferentiated factor theory of intelligence without adequate respect for myriad distinctive biological, environmental, and behavioral features, such metatheoretical restraints seriously compromise ecological validity. A group of handicapped people, defined solely in terms of an IQ score, are demonstrably variable along a host of other relevant variables associated with adaptation. In fact, if nothing else, we have repeatedly shown that a group of people with mental retardation exhibit much more inter- and intraindividual variability on dependent measures than so-called "normals."

The focus on IQ has usually blinded us to the importance of asking questions about variable demands of capricious environments and how different groups of people, so crudely constituted, differentially adapt to these demands and what coping skills are required. A taxonomy of environments is as important as a taxonomy of behavior. We have regrettably achieved neither. Until we do, our efforts will not be any more fruitful than those of the proverbial blind men who tried to study the elephant by diligent examination of its constituent parts.

Some may argue that the definition of mental retardation requires attention to deficits in adaptive behavior—implying that specific environmental constraints are to be considered as an equal partner in the diagnosis. To be sure, formal definitions of mental retardation almost universally make this bivariate distinction in principle. In practice, however, it is the IQ score that is the primary diagnostic feature. After all, a perceived deficit in adaptive behavior brings the child forward for "diagnosis." Moreover, creating lists of adaptive behaviors by consensus, without external validation, does not constitute a systematic and empirically established basis for understanding the hierarchy of demands, the adjustments required, or how they are interrelated. Formal measurement of adaptive behavior is based on time-honored normative psychometric methods and procedures derived from the flawed theory of true and error scores, with relatively little systematic regard for setting conditions and cultural variations.

The most recent definition of mental retardation promulgated by the American Association on Mental Retardation (AAMR) clings to the signal condition of "significantly subaverage intellectual functioning"—meaning IQ of 75 to 70 and below, as one of the two main defining features, along with limitations in adaptive skills (Luckasson et al., 1992). To say that this "new" definition and its associated assumptions have not come in for some heated and well-founded criticism would be a gross understatement of the intensity of the current controversy (e.g., MacMillan, Gresham, & Siperstein, 1993). Indeed, not much of substance has changed since Baumeister and Muma (1975) leveled many of the same charges, both conceptual and practical, against the older but essentially same IQ-based definition. We have a penchant for reinventing the wheel with a new spoke added here and there.

This is not the place to reiterate all criticisms. But to the extent that the prevailing definition of mental retardation continues to hold the IQ as the central determinant means that a great deal of behavioral research will continue to sail under the flag of the general intelligence construct. Specificity of function is still forced to yield to generality of accommodation.

Aside from metatheoretical restraints on ecological validity that derive from the general factor theory of intelligence (widely but not uniformly accepted), mental retardation behavioral research is, in effect, marginalized from the main stream of developmental and health research. Berkson's (1993) view, echoing that of many others, is that mental retardation research is essentially a question of human development. As reasonable as that admonition may seem, developmental inquiry is not the dominant thrust of research.

Just how valuable is the IQ as the independent variable for defining mental retardation research? How helpful is it to the biochemist who is interested in understanding perturbations of galactose-I-phosphate uridyle transferase activity to know that galactosemia is often diagnosed as mental retardation? How fruitful has been experimental research that looks on the IQ as the dependent variable and seeks predictors?

Assuming our interest is in studying IQ in an effort to draw inferences about intelligence (which is what a great deal of behavioral research in this area is about), then the standard method of comparing extreme groups—those with mental retardation versus those with "normal" IQs—is patently absurd. Given that the intent is simply to uncover group differences, the ultimate, most powerful design would be to select cohorts markedly divergent in mean IQ, with all individuals having the same IQ within groups—that is, no within-group (error) variance. The product of such a contrived strategy is wildly distorted inferences about the "effects" of IQ on any dependent measure.

A much more satisfactory and inferentially sound method for the study of the main and interactive effects of IQ on dependent variables would be to sample along the entire range of measured intelligence in direct proportion to the numbers of people represented at each point in the hypothetical distribution. It is not entirely clear to me why anyone should want to do this without a sound theoretical rationale. In any case, to my knowledge, no one of any theoretical persuasion has suggested that intelligence is distributed in a rectangular fashion, although that is implied when we constitute two or three IQ groups of equal size for study. That is the standard approach, however implicit, in much behavioral research having to do with mental retardation.

It is not uncommon to encounter statements in the literature about the "effects of intelligence" on this or that measure based on two or three extreme group comparisons with the same number of subjects in each group. To what hypothetical population can the results of such studies be generalized? (This author is no exception, by the way, to a penchant for making such ill-advised inferences.) What kinds of generalizations about intelligence are justifiable on the basis of such a crude and unrepresentative construction of the independent variable? Validity—construct, ecological, and predictive—is severely jeopardized by such a methodological approach.

If our objective is to discover something distinctive about mental retardation, then the level-of-impairment strategy typically pursued by lumping people together on the basis of a single unitary metric obscures the very essence of the phenomena under consideration. What is it that a group of children diagnosed as mentally retarded have in common? They have low IQs. Even then, there typically are large variations even on this metric—variability that is relegated to the black hole of ignorance known as the *error term*.

The Search for Processes. Numerous studies have shown that many different, relatively independent, processes underlie general intelligence (e.g., Detterman, 1986; Kranzler & Jensen, 1991). This amounts to a continuing search for information processing deficiencies experienced by people with mental retardation. One conclusion that can be drawn from this extensive body of research evidence is that people with mental retardation, both children and adults, display different profiles of cognitive processes and abilities than do their age-matched peers with normal or higher than normal IQs (Detterman, 1992).

Another consideration is that equality of overall level of performance (i.e., the same IQ or mental age) does not necessarily imply comparability of function. Early factor analytic studies of Stanford–Binet items revealed that children may achieve the same level of performance, but by different routes (Magaret & Thompson, 1950; Thompson & Magaret, 1947). They were able to identify clusters of test items that differentiated three IQ groups. Their conclusion, reached 50 years ago, is as astute and accurate now as it was then: "In effect this is to say that dull Ss differ from brighter ones not only in being less bright, but in showing other characteristics to a greater degree" (Magaret & Thompson, 1950, p. 165). Just how far have we come since then?

Both level and rate of intellectual development are a direct reflection of the efficiency and effectiveness by which an individual processes information. Cognitive behavior and deficits thereof can only be understood when these complex process are revealed and differentiated into their component elements. However, it is not fruitful any longer to focus on correlations between distinct processes and overall IQ. That reasoning is tautological and furthermore all processes are connected and interlocked. The emphasis should shift away from nonproductive efforts to decompose and predict IQ, and more toward how individuals process information in different contexts, how these processes are reflected across the entire range of intellectual functioning, how they develop, and how they matter in real life.

One of the most carefully conceived, controlled, and theoretically driven studies of information processing components and how these relate to extreme IQ differences was recently reported by Detterman et al., (1992). The model they employed was basically the old stage conception of information processing, but now accompanied by an "executive," a homunculus whose job it is to keep the stage running smoothly and on time. They found many indicators on which performance of adults with mental retardation are quantitatively and qualitatively different from college students. Although the observed deficits were not uniform, Detterman et al. concluded that on nearly every basic cognitive parameter measured in their information processing model there were differences between college students and adults with mental retardation and that these "deficits were so pervasive and so ubiquitous that it is not possible to localize a deficit to a single process" (p. 276). This implies the "everything deficit," as Detterman once described learning, memory, and information processing capabilities of people with mental retardation.

Maybe despite our efforts to decompose cognitive behavior into its component parts and, therefore, to isolate those domains where mental retardation can be most precisely described, we are forced back into the shadows of the *g* concept. Perhaps, but this may be a conclusion shaped by the very nature of the way in which the modal cognition study is conducted. That is, by grouping heterogenous subjects as if they were all alike, and by relying on mean differences between groups to draw inferences, we may be unable to detect individual differences on these parameters. The assumption, again subject to metatheoretical constraints, is that people with mental retardation are essentially alike in their overall deficient thought processes. But it is equally plausible that various psychological (including sensory, motor, and experiential) causes are implicated and that cognitive deficits, although multiple, are different for different people (Detterman, 1987). Or it could be that some specific deficit is so fundamental that it affects every event downstream in the information processing sequence. In any case, it seems that as we set out to examine one thing, we find that it is linked to just about everything else. Although this consideration is not an endorsement of "chaos" theory, it does speak to ecological validity.

In addition, etiological factors, differing manifestations, comorbidities, reinforcement history, living circumstances, and a host of other factors are usually ignored. Under these conditions, what uncertainties can be resolved about mental retardation? Nomothetic methodology applied to the study of individual differences, which is what mental retardation is about, has led us to all sorts of methodological and conceptual problems that are threats to inferential and ecological validity. We may be still be floundering in "a theoretical swamp inhabited by all sorts of conceptual and methodological monsters that have a particular affinity for experimental psychologists" (Baumeister, 1984, p. 26).

All lip service notwithstanding, researchers have failed, in the main, to accept into our studies the fact that mental retardation is a constellation of biological, behavioral, historical, and social variables that continuously interact and transact to compromise and condition physical and intellectual development. The physical–intellectual distinction used here, by the way, is an example of a crippling neo-mind/body dualism that has persistently bedeviled the field and that has been the source of unnecessary, distracting, and even harmful confrontation—especially in the argument over the sources of "mild" mental retardation. (Actually, epidemiological data reveal that we may be "curing" mild mental retardation while undergoing an epidemic of "learning disabilities"; Baumeister et al., 1993.)

The Nature–Nurture War Continues. The recent book by Herrnstein and Murray (1994), *The Bell Curve*, has engendered high-volume controversy. Herrnstein and Murray took a severe public pummeling in the media, particularly because of their genetic interpretation of the persistent racial IQ gap of about 15 points. (*Ethnic* is their choice of terms in recognition of the genetic fact that African-American and White races are not distinct populations. However, this is a distinction that seems to have gotten obscured in the book as well in the commentary that followed its publication.)

Curiously, about the same time another, much less well-publicized book appeared that painstakingly reviewed 50 years of research in human population genetics throughout the world (Cavalli-Sforza, Menozzi, & Piazza, 1994). This is a formidable synthesis that deals with the issue of human variability at a much more molecular level than twin or adoption studies—that is, the proteins that can be used to define genetic makeup by blood groups. One fundamental conclusion is that variability among individuals within groups is so much greater than variability between groups that race, aside from superficial characteristics, is not meaningful at a genetic level. The authors insisted that there is no scientific support for the assertion of genetic inferiority of one population pitted against any other. But blood groups are indirect markers. Through relatively new DNA technology a much more precise and refined analysis of human genetic diversity is proceeding under the aegis of the Human Genome Project. Regardless, the debate over inheritability of intelligence and differences between populations is likely to continue, although at the present nature seems to have the edge.

This controversy is a good example of how philosophical divisions over the nature of individual and group differences are played out in the public arena and in politics. This is also an illustration of how research data are selectively used to further or attack a position. Implications for behavior research addressing the problem of mental retardation are profound.

Research and Control of Intelligence. Research is not the dispassionate and disinterested observer in the fight over values and policies, but actually becomes a weapon in the conflict. If this controversy were merely confined to the halls of academia, with professors expounding our views in little-read professional journals or books, then not much harm could come. However, in view of the resurgent American abhorrence of welfare (for poor people) and the contemporary political adventures into reform, the lives of millions of people turn on the outcomes of these debates.

Even in those instances of mental retardation in which a specific causal agent can be identified, such as a single gene defect (of which there are many), numerous other biological, psychological, and environmental characteristics are inextricably interwoven into the fabric of a child's development and adaptations. More than any other human affliction, developmental disabilities, including mental retardation, must be studied and understood in terms of the intricate and interrelated issues of causes, etiologies, manifestations, treatment, and prevention.

Examining the past 30 years of behavior research, we should conclude that the weight of the current evidence, along with our collective inability to significantly alter the course of deviant development, shows that we are dealing here with multiple risk problems that usually do not yield to unidimensional explanatory models. Understanding of causes and effects and the design of health and educational intervention measures should be based on multifactorial perspectives and interdisciplinary strategies that systematically incorporate diverse kinds and sources of information, including that from the biological sciences and cultural patterns. We cannot solve these problems by focusing on just one thing. Rather, we are dealing here with systems within systems; that is, contextualism.

Recently, several comprehensive systems models have been proposed that, although differing in some details and emphasis, all share one common perspective: The individual is not the primary unit of analysis, but rather should be regarded as a biological system in interaction and transaction within a network of broader family, community, social, service, economic, and political systems. These models include the new morbidity (Baumeister et al., 1993), ecology of human development (Bronfenbrenner, 1977), human ecology of risk (Garbarino, 1991), and transactional regulation (Sameroff, 1983). These are all comprehensive network conceptualizations of understanding and prevention of children's disorders.

The proposition advanced here has been that prevention and treatment of child disorders is not easily accomplished. The problem is that we have attempted to employ traditional clinical concepts that focus on single causes and, accordingly, we can fix the problem by treating the child. This is not to say that conditions should not be treated as indicated, such as infectious meningitis. But if we are to prevent mental retardation and other "psychosocial" disorders, a contextual systems approach is the only way to achieve substantial gains as expressed in population terms.

EARLY EDUCATIONAL INTERVENTION—AGAIN

The IHDP. Although certainly well-intentioned in principle, early compensatory education programs typically enroll children on the basis of gross and imprecise risk indicators such as maternal IQ, education, or poverty. Although such a procedure may be high in sensitivity (because of the net so broadly cast), specificity (detection of those who will not profit from the service) is at the same time compromised. In rarer instances, the selection rationale is based on an etiological specification—most notably Down Syndrome.

Although many outcome measures are of interest, the main focus is on an index of cognitive function, usually the developmental quotient or IQ. These projects are expensive (expressed in terms of dollars per IQ point temporarily gained), considering that the outcomes generally are so distinctly unimpressive. From a research perspective, they commonly are also fraught with all manner of methodological confounds. Thus, studies that are not only experimentally sound but that also select children on the basis of their known putative risk factors are of great interest.

In this vein, a number of projects have reported purportedly demonstrating that developmental status of low birthweight (LBW) infants can be enhanced by early educational intervention. The most current, expensive, extensive, and best known of these is the Infant Health and Development Program (IHDP; 1990). The compelling rationale for IHDP is that LBW babies are known to be at greatly elevated risk for immediate and later medical, developmental, social, and educational complications.

The primary thrust of IHDP was to test effectiveness of an intensive package of early preschool and family support services, along with pediatric follow up, for reducing incidence of health and developmental problems among premature LBW infants. Randomized intervention trials with 985 infants were conducted at eight sites. All children received medical, social, and developmental assessments with service referral as indicated. About one third of the children were assigned randomly to an intervention group—home visitation, center-based education, or parents groups. The program began upon the baby's discharge from the neonatal nursery. During the first year, families in the intervention group received home visitation that included health information, family support, and a curriculum designed to promote cognitive, social, and linguistic development. A second curriculum was implemented to provide parents with skills for coping with problems they identified. In addition, parents were encouraged to attend bimonthly parent meetings during the 2 years of day care. At 12 months the intervention children were enrolled in a "high-quality" center-based early education program 8 hours per day, 5 days a week, for 2 years. Of course this does not mean that all attended or that attendance was uniform among those who did participate.

The first cut at the results revealed what one might expect—significantly higher-mean Stanford–Binet IQ scores at three years among LBW infants who received this comprehensive intervention package as compared with a control follow-up group. Infants in what was designated the "lighter" birthweight category (< 2,000 grams) scored, on the average, 6.6 points higher than did LBW infants below 2,000 grams who did not receive the intensive intervention. Those in the "higher" LBW birthweight group (2,001 to 2,500 grams) were 13.2 points above their follow-up counterparts.

The first publication summed up the major conclusion as follows: "The results of this study indicate the effectiveness of a comprehensive intervention, even for biologically vulnerable infants" (IHDP, 1990, p. 3040). The claim was subsequently made that this "intensive high-quality early intervention" resulted in an almost "nine-fold reduction in the number of low birthweight children who were mentally retarded" among those families with the highest intensity of participation (the Family Participation Index; S. L. Ramey & Ramey, 1992, p. 341). Risk of mental retardation was reduced by factors of 4.9 and 1.3 for the intermediate and low levels of participation groups, respectively.

But children with different levels of participation differed in other ways that confound these results. Furthermore, the Family Participation Index was a conglomerate measure obtained simply by summing number of home visits, attendance at parent group meetings, and days attended in the program (Ramey et al., 1992). A part of the rationale for this summative measure was that the program's efficacy was to be evaluated as a package rather than as separable contributions. Nevertheless, it also seems reasonable to ask whether these components differentially affected the outcome at 3 years. Perhaps just having support groups (parents' meetings) is all that is necessary to explain treatment effects seen at 3 years.

All this notwithstanding, ninefold reduction of relative risks of any problem, in any group, is a pretty impressive accomplishment. But in this case, relative to what? The only experimental control in IHDP for intensity was random assignment of children to intervention and follow up. Examination of the total groups suggests that the effect on prevention of mental retardation is modest at 3 years. Of the 561 children in the follow-up group who were tested on the Stanford–Binet at 36 months, 119 or 21.2% had IQs of less than 70, the conventional IQ cut-off for defining mental retardation. Of the 347 children in the intervention group tested at 36 months, 39 or 11.2% had IQs of less than 70. This is not quite a twofold relative risk—still of interest but not of such magnitude as to warrant sweeping, "premature" assertions about prevention of mental retardation based on 36-month IQ scores alone.

Division of children by birthweight for the initial analysis presented by IHDP is somewhat curious and unorthodox in that 1,500 grams is the universally accepted standard by which risks for subsequent development are accelerated. Clearly, the finding that those children in the "lighter" birthweight category did not profit to any great extent from the intensive intervention suggests that CNS involvement does make a difference and that the intervention was misdirected for these infants.

The database from this study is enormous and invites independent analysis. Together with Dr. Verne Bacharach, I did just that. Some of the main findings of our analysis were that treatment explained only 4.6% of the IQ variance, that home environment accounted for 20.3% in the first year and increased over time, and that the mother's IQ explained about 50% of child IQ variance. There was so much overlap of IQs for the treated and control children that their distributions were virtually identical.

Because we were not wedded to the all-or-nothing approach as reflected in the Family Participation Index described previously, we examined the three main components separately within a multiple regression model including "CDC Days," "Home Visits," "Parent Meetings," and "Maternal IQ." Only "Parent Meetings" was significantly related to child IQs at 3 years. Furthermore, children of parents who participated the most in meetings (range 0 to 12; mean about 4) had higher cognitive scores at 12 months (i.e., when the day care component began). In other words, there was something different about these children (i.e., those whose parents attended meetings and who showed the greatest effect of the treatment) that was present before the center program even began.

Assuming that day care makes a difference—a not unreasonable assumption in light of the main thrust of IHDP—we should expect that those children who attended the most would have better outcomes at 3 years. In fact, that is not what we found. To be sure, there is a small but significant correlation between days attended and IQ at 36 months, but those children who attended day care most frequently had also the highest DQs at 12 months—before the day-care component even began. So all we can say is that those who were smarter at the beginning were also smarter at the end. I do not believe we needed a massive program such as IHDP to alert us to that possibility.

Looked at from these perspectives, the question must be raised as to whether such an expensive educational intervention has any meaning even at 3 years. One wonders just how much each IQ point temporarily saved actually cost in dollar terms. Not only that, but there was ample reason, as reflected in the extensive literature on the subject (Baumeister et al., 1993), to be suspicious about the durability of any effects observed at 3 years among these LBW children.

Questions still remain as to whether these gains are sustainable, why those in the lower weight range did not show the same magnitude of effect, and why there were marked differences across sites. In this regard, a study by Wilson (1985) involving twins (one born smaller than the other) showed that LBW risk alone (i.e., apart from associated family status considerations) did not confer any disadvantage on long-term intellectual development. Although premature LBW was a powerful initial suppressor, LBW infants from higher SES groups recovered their IQs completely by the time they were in school (i.e., as compared with their heavier concordant twin). Wilson found what we found: Maternal competence was the far more decisive factor. Similarly, McGaughey, Starfield, Alexander, and Ensminger (1991) showed that LBW children born into high-risk social environments, but not those in moderate or low-risk environments, are much more likely to have a poor health outcome as contrasted with comparable normal birthweight children. Furthermore, this disadvantage does not appear to be outgrown during childhood—it was evident in both preschool and school-age children. The largest and longest-term longitudinal analysis of birthweight for an entire population is to be found in the 1959 British cohort study. A recent follow up of this cohort revealed that birthweight is linearly associated with socioeconomic disadvantage (Bartley, Power, Blane, Smith, & Shipley, 1994).

This is not to say that LBW children in whom brain organogenesis is disrupted do not present significant long-term delay independently of socioeconomic status (Halsey, Collin, & Anderson, 1993). In short, there are two plausible explanations, one direct and the other correlational, of the link between birthweight and later chronic illness. For one, specific etiologic processes condition neurological development, cardiovascular regulation, and other somatic processes to fix risk before other moderating factors are encountered. Second, birthweight serves as a marker for the occurrence of other causal circumstances. LBW children are thus in double jeopardy (Baumeister et al., 1993).

My contention is that the Infant Health and Development Program seriously missed the mark by focusing on gross measures of LBW and intensive education rather than on the specific risk factors that covary and interact with LBW. Yet this study has had an impact, perhaps ill-advised. For instance, the Centers for Disease Control and Prevention are funding projects (BEGIN) in 10 states to conduct intervention programs based on the IHDP/Abecedarian intervention models. In this case, children are selected on the basis of maternal educational level (i.e, less than 12 years). One may ask as to the fate of LBW as a risk factor if the results of IHDP were so startling. Extreme LBW (< 1,500 grams) is a better indicator of subsequent risk than maternal education of less than 12 years.

Here is a situation in which a little patience should have tempered enthusiasm and the collective rush to judgment in the public media and in policy determinations. Consider what happened. Follow up of these children at five years showed that the initial overall significant difference between intervention and control groups had disappeared completely (mean WPPSI IQS of 92.7 vs. 93.2, respectively; Brooks-Gunn et al., 1994). The original effects for the lighter infants (< 2,000 grams) were completely washed out, primarily because of a 9-point rebound among the control children. For the heavier group (between

2,000 and 2,500 grams), the effect size was now only about 3 WPPSI IQ points with no difference in health indicators or any of the behavior deviations that were also measured.

Clearly, there was no sustained effect of intensive day-care education for the sample as a whole or for the lighter LBW infants. Brooks-Gunn et al. (1994) claimed in the case of the heavier LBW infants that the mean effect sizes at 5 years "are modest, but educationally relevant" (p. 1260). How can anyone maintain that such a trivial mean IQ difference (about 3 IQ points, falling within the standard error of measurement) has any individual meaning, educational or otherwise? Not only that, but even this small difference will certainly disappear with later measurement as regression to the mean continues. (Measurements of these children, now at 8 years, have been collected, but because of a "policy decision" these data are not available to me at this time.)

Brooks-Gunn et al. (1994) offered a variety of tortuous explanations to explain these outcomes and justify their conclusion that early intervention (now for "disadvantaged children") is a good thing. What is meant by "disadvantage?" Are children disadvantaged because they are born small, too soon but within the range of 2,000 to 2,500 grams? Or is disadvantage the source of LBW? The lighter LBW children were not similarly disadvantaged? These investigators overlook the obvious: Gross and nonspecific educational interventions, however intense, do not overcome biological and/or social adversities. In fairness, the authors commented: "The results of the IHDP call into question the notion that providing enrichment experiences in the first few years of life can protect children against biological disadvantages over extended periods of time" (Brooks-Gunn et al., 1994, p. 1261). They are by no means the first to express such caution. But what is meant by "*biological* disadvantage," as they are using the term, given the implication that those who do not exhibit biological handicap might substantially benefit? LBW (anything less than 2,500 grams), by itself, is but a gross risk indicator involving both direct effects and indirect effects. There are many causes and correlates of LBW. Much more refined analyses associated with LBW are possible and should have been pursued to guide selection of participants, interventions, and choice of outcome measures. In any case, if LBW is strongly related to developmental outcome—the rationale for IHDP in the first place—then it seems that the appropriate prevention initiative should be to prevent LBW, especially very LBW.

However one may interpret the results of IHDP, they represent the outer limit of what can be expected from early educational intervention. No study this intense and costly has been attempted on such a large scale. Given the expense, service programs of such intensity or magnitude will not likely become a standard intervention within the larger network of services. Actually, community day programs for these infants are already available. In fiscal years 1992 and 1993, the federal government funded 93 early childhood programs scattered through 11 federal agencies and 20 offices (United States General Accounting Office, 1994). Of the "key" programs identified by GAO, 13 targeted economically disadvantaged children from birth through age 5. Consequently, a disadvantaged child could be eligible for all 13 programs. There are so many programs that they are stumbling all over themselves, at terrible cost. From a policy standpoint, it would have made greater sense to compare the IHDP children with children enrolled in available community day-care programs. From a practical point of view, it seems reasonable to ask which components of IHDP make a difference above and beyond what we are already doing.

Given that the outcomes were so disappointing at 5 years, that intrinsic factors such as maternal IQ were so overwhelming by comparison, and that children at risk for adverse outcome (those below 1,500 grams) did not benefit, the IHDP should be heralded as the project that finally lays to rest the debate over whether intense early education fundamentally changes developmental trajectory. There is always the possibility, of course, that we shall undergo a revolution in education technology that will markedly increase the educational productivity of children exposed to risks associated with LBW. However, nothing on the horizon should engender great optimism in this respect.

Placing the IHDP within the context of the broader literature on the subject of preschool interventions, we can say confidently that it squarely supports the well-documented conclusion that the effects are transitory, not enduring, and are completely overcome by the prevailing family ecology. In their characteristic way of cutting through the obfuscating jungle of words and getting to the bottom line, Clarke and Clarke (1989) stated: "The lack of enduring benefits on cognitive skills from preschool programs has been documented so many times that is scarcely needs repeating" (pp. 291–292). However, as with other matters in which we are heavily invested, controversy rages around long-term efficacy of early educational intervention. Barnett and Escobar (1987), although properly cautious, maintained that there is some credible evidence of long-term efficacy and that "much work needs to be done" (p. 387). This is the ageless "more research is needed" refrain.

Other Pedagogical Attempts to Prevent and Cure Mental Retardation. Our history is replete with grand attempts to raise intelligence and to "cure" mental retardation through pedagogical means. After all, this is the mentality that drove the creation of the Binet tests.

The most scholarly review of this checkered past was accomplished by Spitz (1986). What he so cogently showed in his detailed analysis of the best-known projects is that compensation for early cognitive disadvantage by educational means is extraordinarily difficult to do. In view of this historical background, Spitz was puzzled that there is so little curiosity about why this remarkable feat has not been accomplished in the past. Spitz contended that there is a pervasive lack of awareness of this history and that the present body of knowledge is not appreciably different from that available to the earliest dedicated workers, such as Itard and Seguin, both of whom were early interventionists using sensory training techniques that today we might call "behavior modification" (Baumeister, 1970). Seguin's "physiological method of education" was adopted by Montessori for the education of impoverished preschoolers in Rome (Crissey, 1975; Spitz, 1986). I don't think that it is so much a matter of lack of appreciation of that two centuries of history (although that assertion certainly has some validity), but rather that some of us continue to maintain faith despite evidence to the contrary. (For instance, see C. T. Ramey & S. L. Ramey, 1992, for another, much more upbeat view of the purported long-term effects on mental retardation of intensive long-term educational intervention.)

There are some less-than-generous explanations that can be given to explain some people's persistent willingness to reinvent the pedagological wheel in quest of prevention or cure of mental retardation. In any case, the leap beyond data, accompanied by exorbitant and unsubstantiated claims is, as Spitz maintained, an embarrassment to the "entire field of psychology" and that in this area we are still in the "dark ages" (Spitz, 1986, p. 218). There are those, of course, who take great umbrage over such sweeping pessimistic and negative conclusions, especially when they strike home. Giving in to what appears to be a massive dose of frustration, Ramey (1993, p. 25) brought the art of professional personalizing (e.g., "disingenuousness," "irritating," "crass style," and "misguided zealotry," among others) to a new high in his attempts to counter some of the valid criticisms persistently leveled by Spitz (1992, 1993) at claims that the Abecedarian Project prevented sociocultural mental retardation. Hurt feelings aside, the argument should turn on its soundness, not its shrillness. We certainly seem to be able to convert a small investment of fact into a huge return of conjecture.

Early Experience: Critical Periods? One rationale that persistently reappears in defense of early compensatory education is the "critical stage" conception of early development. This is rather like a "window of opportunity" proposition in that if the chance is missed to achieve some developmental milestone it is either gone forever or, at best, compensation is difficult and incomplete. A corollary proposition is that early demonstrable effects should be enduring, regardless of later social deprivation. Although that may be the case for certain highly specific developmental tasks, the universality of the critical stage theory is highly questionable—as long-forgotten experiments in infant locomotion reveal.

During the period of neonatal development, severe sensory deprivation unquestionably produces atrophy and disorganization in the particular brain system(s) deprived of stimulation. Most of this research is based on studies with rats, cats, and rhesus monkeys. It is rare that humans are ever subjected to such extraordinarily severe sensory deprivation. On the other hand, there is overwhelming evidence that neural circuitry and the behavior it mediates develop quite adequately in the absence of experience. The more critical role of experience, at least in regard to "higher-level" processes, may be for maintenance rather than induction or facilitation (Aslin, 1981).

Many of the "myths" of early experiences were exposed by Clarke and Clarke (1976). They came to "see development as a series of linkages" (p. 154) rather than as specific phases where a critical event either arrests or regresses development (Clarke & Clarke, 1992). To be sure, recent discoveries in developmental neuroscience convincingly show that subtle dendritic sprouting and synaptic development during the formative period of brain growth are affected by many factors, including experience. The ability to learn language, for instance, seems to be a behavioral attribute that is related to epochs of brain growth.

It is one thing to say that neurological differentiation and neuromaturation provide periods of opportunity for certain experiences to be maximally encoded into neural pathways. It is quite another to argue that experience fundamentally alters those pathways and, missing that critical window of opportunity, unalterable deficits are the consequence.

An extraordinary leap of faith is required to conclude that preschool teaching has anything at all to do with organogenesis at the synaptic level. How do you define a "critical period"—when does it begin, when does it end, and what behavior is mediated? Furthermore, aside from the most extremely devastating environmental circumstances, the mass of developmental research evidence reveals that we are destined to return to our preprogrammed developmental trajectory, sometimes known as "canalization." Predestination even applies in the case of premature birth and LBW as revealed through studies of monozygotic twins, one of whom is born much smaller than the other (Wilson, 1985).

Studies of human development that are basically cross-sectional in nature, typically encompassing the early years, inevitably will find that some particular stage of development matters. Indeed that is no doubt true, but when the whole of the developmental pattern is considered, there is no evidence that one stage is any more important than another. The concept of resiliency has only lately begun to compete with vulnerability for the attention of behavioral researchers. As Garmezy (1991) pointed out, many children subjected to poverty, deprivation, disabling conditions, and other challenges to development overcome such adversities of life. Perhaps they missed their "critical" period.

Not many prospective studies have been conducted to assess resilience of infants exposed to biological and/or psychosocial risk factors. The best of these is the Kauai Longitudinal Study in which children, born to impoverished and more affluent parents, were followed from the prenatal period through adulthood. Children in the impoverished birth cohort were exposed to multiple risk factors (perinatal complications, family instability, chronic poverty, and other adversities). One third exhibited learning or behavior problems during the first two decades. But about 10% of that cohort, exposed to at least four risk factors, developed into competent adults without any overt pathologies (Werner, 1991). Why? Various studies have shown that the temperament of the child together with nurturing family characteristics may overcome early threats of risks. As Sameroff, Seifer, Barocas, Zax, and Greenspan (1987) showed, the number of psychosocial risks (including family characteristics) and their combinations are prime determinants of outcome. When three or more of these risk factors are present, there seems to be a pronounced decline in preschool intelligence.

Resilience or resistance to stress is typically regarded as a characteristic of the child. This is not an absolute, but rather a relative conception in that resilience must be measured in terms of degrees of resistance to threats against some meaningful baseline. In epidemiologic terms, degree of resistance is similar to rates of *relative risk*, in that the denominator consists of those not exposed to the risk. Furthermore, as emphasized within the new morbidity model of Baumeister et al., (1993), there are numerous systemic factors beyond the child's own constitutional resilience that can either deepen or defer the risk. Any risk factor (except at the extreme), taken in isolation, is not likely to be predictive of outcome.

Some Other Variations on the Theme. "Facilitated communication" (FC) is only the latest of the almost mystical absurdities some people have unleashed without any scientific credibility (Biklen, 1993). This is a technique designed to provide impaired people with the ability to communicate their latent and suppressed thoughts and feelings through the assistance of trained "facilitators." There are those who have referred to FC as "exciting." If there is anyone who doubts that determined zealots cannot sell snake oil to an unwary public or to gullible professionals, consider that a recent court order in Iowa commands that state to offer FC to all residents in a public residential facility who display autistic-like behavior. Within the past few years FC has enjoyed increased respectability, as evidenced by widespread application in public schools and other service programs. After careful examination of the few studies purporting to support FC, numerous professional groups have formally condemned FC as an accepted, scientifically valid, and effective therapeutic intervention (e.g., Jacobson & Mulick, 1995). In the past such proclamations, although certainly warranted, have not stemmed public and even professional enthusiasm for plunging blindly ahead. Remember the old story about Hans, the clever horse?

FC is not our only adventure into promotion of "cures" without scientific justification or, rather, despite evidence to the contrary. The patterning procedures central to Doman-Delacato methods remain as an example of an unproved intervention that is sold through public relations rather than through scientific examination. Again, reservations expressed about patterning procedures by different professional organizations have not greatly diminished public ardor for this "therapy."

Another popular treatment for remediation of motor and academic problems is sensory integration (SI) therapy, as practiced by occupational therapists. Sensory integration theory and therapy was first promulgated by Ayers (e.g., 1972) and enthusiastically adopted by her followers. The treatment methods subsumed under sensory integration have evolved into an organized professional constituency and discipline.

Examination of the theoretical neurological underpinnings as well as the empirical outcome literature pertaining to individuals with mental retardation and children with learning disabilities show that SI theory is hopelessly naive and that the therapy is not only unproven, but demonstrably ineffective for treatment of learning disabilities and learning disorders (Arendt, MacLean, & Baumeister, 1988; Hoehn & Baumeister, 1994). According to the American Academy of Pediatrics' Committee on Children with Disabilities (1985), "neurophysiological retraining programs such as patterning, optometric exercises, and sensory integration therapies, although reported by some to have beneficial results in selected cases, lack value" (p. 648).

Another recent arrival into behavioral treatment territory is the "gentle teaching philosophy" for treatment of persons with behavior problems (e.g., McGee, 1992). Condemning applied behavior analysis as "culture of death" technology, the essential philosophy and key treatment element of gentle teaching is "unconditional valuing." Clearly this technique has a certain spiritual claim. Actually, the procedures borrow heavily from behavior analysis, except that contingent reinforcement and aversive stimulation are excluded because they are devaluing. There is little doubt that McGee and his associates find many sympathizers in that vein.

Just how effective is gentle teaching in reducing problematic behavior such as self-injury and aggression? The case reports by McGee and his collaborators are nothing short of spectacular, in that they have never found the procedure to fail and that the positive results can be very rapidly achieved. A few commentators have been accepting of these results. Others have been much more skeptical and critical. The few confirmatory studies have not substantiated such profound positive effects of gentle teaching and, in comparison, found that conventional behavior analysis procedures were far more effective. Of course, that only intensified the dispute. In the most thorough review of the literature on gentle teaching, including data presented by McGee and his associates, Mudford (1995) asserted that the results are not credible, that the procedure has no proven efficacy, and that, in fact, there are potential harms that may result from adoption of the philosophy.

We seem to have a constitutional penchant to search for the "holy grail" that will somehow simply overcome the inequities that are inherent in human variability and rooted in natural discordance. It is as Paul Simon said in a song about 25 years ago: A man hears what he wants to hear and disregards the rest.

The Educational Solution. In any event, huge and expensive doses of educational fix, without proper attention to all relevant antecedent and contextual factors and reliance on highly restricted outcome measures, to say nothing of administration of gross, poorly attuned, and ill-described interventions that are hopelessly confounded, cannot be continuously justified. The effects are too small, too transient, and too expensive. On a population basis, there is no one single environmental variable that has shown to have a large, consistent, and enduring effect on behavior. Despite frequent denunciations of the "inoculation" mentality inherent in early intervention enrichment programs, the search for the magic solution continues unabated. Zigler, a prime mover and advocate of the Head Start program, stated that it is unrealistic to expect such interventions to offset the experiences and health risks of children born into and reared in impoverished family circumstances (Zigler, 1992). In view of the pronounced regression that usually accompanies intense and sustained interventions, we should abandon the "vaccination" metaphor and adopt the "insulin" model in which constant injections are needed to keep the "disease" under control.

These statements should not be in any way construed to mean that people with mental retardation cannot learn and should not be taught. Nor does it mean that we should abandon the quest for better education methods grounded in etiological specificity (Hodapp & Dykens, 1991). However, hope does have rational limits and to the extent we oversell general all-purpose approaches we undermine our credibility.

These are matters of ecological validity, as the term is used here. We in the behavioral sciences have been captive to certain major theoretical issues concerning intelligence and the nature of causality. We are enslaved to traditional research paradigms that fail to capture the range of phenomena that the concept of mental retardation is intended to embrace. These are biases that have led us to arbitrarily select independent variables, restrict their range and form, and to impose on them a contrived symmetry that does not exist in the world in which people must live and cope with daily demands.

Some More Specific Methodological Research Issues. Dependent variables are typically selected, especially in more traditional group designs, on the basis of convenience or tradition, without a full appreciation of the contextual nature of behavior and relationships between responses. Our procedures, although deriving from the tenets of good research practice, actually nullify or obscure patterns of correlations and interactions between the environment and organismic variables. This is a criticism not confined to traditional group designs.

In the case of applied behavior analysis, specific responses targeted for either acceleration or deceleration typically are selected for and not by the experimenter, in that direct clinical and/or educational issues are usually the driving concern. But even here dependent measures are usually arbitrarily isolated from the complex of behavior streams and setting conditions. The underlying assumption of response separability is both logically and empirically unwarranted. Contingencies that occur in the normal environment may be and probably are only partly or coincidentally represented in the highly structured format of single-subject designs.

In their comprehensive treatment of the issue of response definition within the tradition of experimental analysis Scotti, Evans, Meyer, and DiBenedetto (1991) concluded that "such designs have limited usefulness" (p. 158). In addition, contrived environments deliberately arranged to study a restricted range of responses under rigorously controlled circumstances actually defeat understanding of the commonalities of response hierarchies and repertoires between handicapped and nonhandicapped children (Evans & Scotti, 1989). In fairness, the recent experimental analysis of behavior literature does reflect growing concern with arbitrary definitions of singular responses as the proper unit of study, given that the purpose of intervention is to improve the individual's daily quality of life.

On the other hand, a sophisticated meta-analysis of single-subject intervention research designed to alter problem behavior reveals that this research is poorly conceptualized and conducted (Scotti, Evans, Meyer, & Walker, 1991). These authors concluded: "Overall, the standards of practice revealed by the published literature can only be described as highly disillusioning" (p. 254).

Of course, this disillusionment is not universally shared. Others who have extensively reviewed some of the same literature (but not with the same degree of rigor or with the same methods) have also pointed to some conceptual and methodological problems and gaps. But they are also much more sanguine about the overall state of affairs regarding the research knowledge base and its application (Carr, Taylor, Carlson, & Robinson, 1991; Cataldo, 1991).

In pursuit of behavioral research we tend to select samples of subjects on the basis of convenience or availability. Furthermore, we emphasize replications across subjects rather than situations. These are considerations that seriously compromise representativeness and generality. Statistical significance and internal validity are commonly required for publication; social significance and external validity are less highly regarded. *P* values seem to be the currency with which we deal. In the case of the single-subject design, one can only wonder how many subjects whose baselines bounce up and down have been dismissed from study. Just how great must a departure from baseline be to show that we have accomplished something more than merely establishing some degree experimental control over a behavior?

Our research procedures, rooted in a fixed or closed system, have led us to the point that we may be able to specify possible causes of behavior, rather than likely causes. That is hardly comforting. There is still much to be done, because the fountain of knowledge about the behavioral aspects of mental retardation is a mere trickle. Whether the old, comfortable ways of gaining useful empirical information are up to this task must be seriously questioned.

What Is the Essential Nature of Mental Retardation?

Structure Versus Process. A number of conceptual issues concerning the nature of impaired performance exhibited by people with mental retardation have long been debated—or, if not always explicitly debated, have nevertheless guided research concerned with understanding and/or ameliorating behavioral deficits. Perhaps the most enduring and important of these is the distinction between *structural features* and *control processes* (Baumeister, 1984). Another, less elegant way of framing the distinction is whether attributes of intelligence, particularly those implicated in retarded behavior, are "hard" or "soft" wired.

Structural features refer to those components of behavior (e.g., information processing) that are fixed and invariant and not directly susceptible to modification through environmental means. Control processes, on the other hand, are viewed as flexible attributes that are trainable and modifiable through educational or behavioral interventions.

This distinction has not only theoretical and experimental relevance, but great social import as well. In fact, the issue of malleability or trainability of intelligence is at the core of the hubris unleased by publication of *The Bell Curve* (Herrnstein & Murray, 1994) and by others well before it. Before the birth of Christ, Homer attributed individual differences in intelligence and good looks to the gods.

Debates over the relative and/or interactive effects of genes and environment on behavior extend well beyond explanations of mental retardation. The issue goes to the very roots of class differences and inheritability of intelligence. That is, are some people poor because they are less intellectually capable or is it the other way around? Which is cause and which is effect? Are such well-established programs as Head Start futile, at least insofar as boosting intelligence is concerned? Should our current system of welfare programs be adjusted accordingly? Putting aside the dispute over racial IQ differences, the major point hammered away by Herrnstein and Murray in *The Bell Curve* was that intellectual level—not poverty, environmental circumstance, or lack of educational opportunity—is the root of a wide range of major social and medical problems—crime, low birthweight, unemployment, school dropout, injury and neglect, and many of the other New Morbidities. This is quite the opposite direction from that taken by Baumeister et al. (1993) in their analyses and recommendations for preventing the New Morbidities.

The notion that mental retardation is "essentially incurable" (the structural feature point of view) dominated the field for many years and was considered by Doll (1941) to be an essential diagnostic feature. Aside from the obvious problem that such a definition confuses diagnosis and prognosis, there are those who maintain that only structural features are meaningfully associated with intelligence. Although laypeople would probably be disinclined to use such terms, there is little doubt that the common knowledge is that retardation is incurable. On the other hand, there is a vocal faction of professionals who flatly deny that most cases of mental retardation are incurable. Others maintain that evidence for immutable structural features is tenuous and the notion that individual differences are fixed is pessimistic (e.g., Sternberg, 1981, 1984).

Optimism and pessimism aside, the centrality of the question still remains. Much comparative behavioral research in the field of mental retardation over the past three decades has been motivated by the search for stable parameters that represent immutable, fixed, and nontrainable attributes—that is, deficits or defects. Given that kind of information, the practical strategies are to circumvent the deficit rather than to correct it.

The Rebirth of Cognitive Psychology. At the same time, a great deal of research, particularly under the rubric of cognitive psychology, has been directed at understanding and training higher-order processes such as the "executive function" to overcome memory or transfer limitations. Various descriptions or derivations of this hypothetical construct—"higher-order control processes," "selecting, sequencing, and coordinating processes," "solution monitoring," "strategic behavior," and "executive control" have been proposed—along with experiments showing that it (whatever the "it" is) can be trained. This makes the conception of executive function sound suspiciously like the old-fashioned general intelligence construct. Perhaps all that we are saying is that people with mental retardation do not think as well as people without mental retardation. That is hardly a remarkable observation.

It was in the early 1970s that cognitive psychology was rediscovered (but see Bartlett, 1932) along with unabashed conceptual escalation into higher and ever higher intellectual regions. Perhaps this top-down transformation came about as a counterreaction to those information processing theorists who try to analyze learning, memory, and discrimination into bits and pieces—the bottoms-up approach. It could be, too, that radical behaviorists were gaining ground in rejecting unobservable mentalistic constructs as legitimate for study. Moreover, they were aggressively applying behavior principles and shaping methods in teaching skills, including some relevant to academic performance and socialization. Surveys were showing that behavior modification was ranked by psychologists practicing in residential facilities as their most important function (Baumeister & Hillsinger, 1984). Cognitive psychologists were having little conspicuous impact on educational or clinical practices. Maybe we were simply not getting anywhere and sought new conceptualizations to advance understanding of impaired thought processes and their remediation.

Marveling over the suddenness with which cognitive psychology came into dominance, Battig (1975) described it as "one of the most sudden and remarkable turnabouts in the entire history of a discipline" (p. 196). From the point of view of mental retardation, numerous influential psychologists (e.g., Butterfield, 1983) were avowing that cognitive deficits associated with mental retardation could be "cured" by focusing on the executive command function instead of each separate cognitive area. Thus, given the proper training and by targeting the highest-order process, intelligence can be trained among children who do not present clearly identifiable major insult to the central nervous system.

Curiously, however, even some of the most prominent leaders of this movement express caution. Campione, Brown, and Ferrara (1982) observed that it will be no easy matter to train away individual differences and, what is most revealing, is that given equal training opportunities highly intelligent people will profit more than people with less intelligence. This conclusion is consistent with the implications imbedded with the reaction range concept, in which training is shown to improve performance across different intelligence groups, but differentially according to IQ (Baumeister, 1984). There must be structurally determined limits, individually determined, beyond which training will not facilitate performance. Individual differences never will be obliterated by training or any other method. Variability is inherent in nature, human or otherwise.

In Defense of Biology. There is one critical point on which there seems to be substantial agreement. Those people with mental retardation whose condition can be traced to some organic perturbation, such as an inborn error of metabolism, are considered to have structural limitations. This leads to the well-known dichotomous expression of mental retardation as brain-damaged versus sociocultural, organic versus nonorganic, endogenous versus exogenous, and so on.

A widely held view, without much empirical support, is that about 75% to 80% of cases of mental retardation are of the cultural–familial variety and do not present hard signs of organicity. With increasing knowledge of organic causes, estimates of the percentage of those with organic manifestations have been increasing. Downsizing a bit, Zigler and Hodapp (1986) maintained that genetic, chromosomal, and environmental factors (prematurity, toxins, infectious diseases) are implicated as causative in about 50% of all individuals with mental retardation. But that still leaves those who are not "brain-damaged." It is over this group that the argument about structural difference primarily centers.

A variation of this theme can be found in the defect versus developmental controversy; that is, how best to characterize observable differences in performance. A defect or deficit refers to a deficiency in some particular cognitive process such as perception, memory, discrimination, and the like. The developmental position is that people with mental retardation (except those who are brain-damaged) follow the same stages of development of cognitive processes, but more slowly in rate and to a lower upper limit. The developmental position is embodied in the similar sequence hypothesis advanced by Weisz and Zigler (1979). From the developmental perspective, mental retardation is not regarded as discontinuous in any fundamental way, but rather reflects deviation from normal functioning as the natural expression of polygenic variability. Most people with mental retardation, then, are victims of a bad draw from the polygenic deck.

Implications for Research Strategy. This argument not only has important theoretical and educational ramifications, but it is central as to how groups are constituted for study (i.e., matching on the basis of mental age or chronological age). From the developmental perspective, people with the same mental ages should perform at the same level. If performance differences are observed, then these are attributable to nonintellectual characteristics such as reinforcement history or motivation. The defect position is typically reflected in research designs in which groups of individuals, representing different levels of intelligence, are matched (usually by group means rather than subject-by-subject matches) on chronological age. The rationale essentially is that, given equal opportunities to develop, observed group differences are attributable to cognitive defects.

From time to time there have been those who have suggested that if the intention is to learn something about mental retardation, then it makes sense to study those with mental retardation. From this perspective, comparative group research is not only irrelevant, but laden with all manner of problems (Baumeister, 1967). Judging, however, from the balance of the experimental literature, the single-group strategy is not widely adopted. We are persistent in our efforts to uncover "differences."

Berkson (1993) accepted the two-factor distinction within the context of a continuum of reproductive causality. At the same time, he pointed out that it is sometimes not possible to determine whether a handicapped person is a "normal deviation" or suffers from some frankly pathological process. The burden of proof is not equal, because unless a pathological process can be unequivocally identified, the child is assumed to be within the normal distribution. In any case, it is difficult to imagine what is "normal" about deviation. For every effect there is a cause.

Some Biological Considerations. It is time to abandon this time-honored and convenient but clearly erroneous bivariate organically couched conceptualization, particularly as applied to mental retardation. Baumeister and MacLean (1979) maintained that any such dichotomous expression about brain–behavioral relationships is inherently wrong. For one thing, there is no syndrome of brain damage that is pathognomonically characteristic of people with mental retardation. Injury to the brain is distributed over the entire range of intellectual proficiency. People cannot be neatly divided into two nonoverlapping categories. The more critical issues concern type, timing, magnitude, and locus of injury and what is expected of the individual. The integrity of the central nervous system obviously has something to do with the way we process information, think, or otherwise behave intelligently or maladaptively.

For instance, neurotransmitters, such as dopamine, are implicated in a host of disorders, some of which are known to be genetic origin, such as Lesch-Nyhan syndrome and Tourette syndrome, and many other conditions where the etiology is not well understood. The neurochemical basis of behavior is too pervasive and the evidence too persuasive to be ignored (Lewis & Baumeister, 1982). In commenting on their research investigating the role of neurotransmitters in relation to repetitive behavior, along with the implications for targeted pharmacological interventions, Bodfish, Powell, Golden, and Lewis (1995) observed that there has been little in the way of neurobiological research in the area of mental retardation, "an irony given the *necessary* organic basis of mental retardation" (p. 342; italics added).

Thus here comes the obvious: Intelligent behavior, by whatever reasonable definition one chooses, is mediated through events and processes in the central nervous system. This means that there is a biological basis for mental retardation—not an original or new observation, but one that seems to be only grudgingly acknowledged. (The mind–body dualism again.) Although a reductionistic approach to mental retardation is not necessitated by this observation, examination of the broader mental retardation research history reveals that more and more specific and vastly diverse biological etiologies and correlates are constantly being identified, relentlessly chipping away at that large percentage assumed to be "nonorganic" or of "unknown origin." The well-known "bump of pathology" is growing ever larger. The Bell Curve has a lump in its bottom.

Fragile X Syndrome as a Model. By now there are literally hundreds of known causes of mental retardation, both genetic and acquired. For instance, using mass spectrometric analytical procedures, geneticists have now identified over 200 gene defects with abnormal organic aciduria, many of which produce neurological deviations associated with developmental disabilities (Sweetman, 1991).

It used to be the case that Down syndrome was thought to be the most common inherited form of mental retardation, presenting with specific genotypes. Fragile X syndrome, fairly recently described, is, for now, the most common form of genetic mental retardation (the FMR-1 gene). In addition, fragile X syndrome reveals the subtle and intricate process (pre-mutations to full mutations by repeats of the cytosine-guanine-guanine bases in the FMR-1 gene) through which genetic disease gradually progresses across generations. Knowledge gleaned from the biological sciences is being increasingly translated into diagnostic, prevention, and treatment measures that have high sensitivity and specificity.

There are other lessons to be drawn from fragile X syndrome that are relevant to resolution of the distinction between organic and nonorganic forms of mental retardation. Typically, the assumption has been made that without evidence to the contrary, a child with mental retardation is assumed to be biologically intact. However, this is tantamount to proving the null hypothesis. There is, as suggested earlier, quite another way of looking at this matter. To the extent that behavior is impaired, defects of the central nervous system are present even though the putative cause(s) cannot be identified.

Effects of organic involvement are, then, best represented by a continuum of neural impairment, from severe to mild, even within a particular causal connection. Concepts of risk continua are hardly new. In 1902, Ballantyne recognized that all manner of threats during the antenatal and perinatal periods produce a host of adverse physical and behavioral outcomes ranging from death to subtle disturbances.

The lethargic encephalitis pandemic in the first part of this century led to many reports of a wide variety of behavioral sequelae in postencephalitic children. The continuum of effects among children all exposed to the same infectious agent included "hard" neurological signs at one end to "soft" signs at the other—in the latter case, symptoms that otherwise might not have been associated with the disease.

What has expanded most dramatically is our knowledge of diseases' processes and their effects. The examples are virtually endless. Consider, for example, fetal alcohol syndrome (FAS). The link between parental alcohol consumption and birth defects has long been known, a connection understood in very sophisticated multivariate terms (Elderton & Pearson, 1910). However, it has only been fairly recently that French and American scientists described the physical stigmata defining FAS. For every case of full-blown FAS exhibiting the distinctive dysmorphology, there are undoubtedly many more who display milder deviations known as fetal alcohol effects (FAE). The manifestations of most diseases are of a continuous nature. Although the pathogenesis of a particular disease may not be completely understood, knowing a cause is a huge step in appreciating how the condition unfolds and where intervention may be most effectively targeted to correct or at least modify the perturbations.

The fragile X syndrome is, like most other conditions, highly variable in phenotypic expression. This disease is heterogenous, often resulting in moderate to severe mental retardation. Yet fully 20% of affected males display no overt clinical symptomatology. Pleiotropy is a well-established characteristic of genes. Unlike most gender-linked disorders, 30% to 50% of fragile X carrier females are mildly affected. In addition, other physical and behavioral manifestations are common. People with this genetic mutation often present dysmorphic features including elongated face, strabismus, enlarged ears, hyperextensible joints, and enlarged testicles.

In addition to cognitive delay and age-related declining intellectual ability, other behavioral problems often include language deficits, poor eye contact, hyperactivity, attention deficits, and autistic stereotypic responding. Many of these aberrant behavioral manifestations have been reported recently in numerous studies (Lachiewicz, Spiridigliozzi, Gullion, Ransford, & Rao, 1994). Unfortunately most of these studies are retrospective and relied on questionnaires for data collection. But taken together, this research strongly indicates that when clinicians observe this particular constellation of behaviors, DNA analysis is indicated.

Although the case can be made for etiological specificity and its relevance for behavior manifestations, it is also true that we have not established a well-defined and distinct behavioral profile for fragile X syndrome or any other entity that is comparable to physical features that are distinctive for many medical conditions. For those conditions that have been much more thoroughly researched in regard to behavioral characteristics such as Down syndrome or Turner syndrome, there is some measure of consistency. But there are also many variations. From the phenotypic perspective there is not and probably never will be complete uniqueness to any condition, behaviorally or physically.

In summary, using fragile X syndrome as a model, there are several points about the behavioral–biomedical research trade-off that should be emphasized.

1. The assumption that a condition is nonorganic may be a reflection of our current scientific ignorance.

2. Phenotypic expressions of IQ or other behavioral characteristics as a result of a disease process (whether genetic or environmental induced) are usually highly variable.
3. Disease processes are systemic and typically produce numerous deviations, both physical and behavioral.
4. Understanding of the specific etiology of the disease and its pathogenesis presents the opportunity for highly targeted prevention and treatment.
5. Grouping or selecting people with mental retardation on the basis of IQ for purposes of behavioral study conceals the effects of all manner of variance attributable to etiological distinctions and manifestations.
6. Although some aspects of behavior are tied to a specific diagnostic entity, there are also developmental commonalities that cross diagnostic groupings and, even more generally, are related to degree of intellectual impairment.
7. There is a definite sequence to developmental characteristics of the human species that applies to most individuals, no matter what their intellectual status and the source of mental disability.

THE "TWO CULTURES" OF RESEARCH

Discussing some these same issues, Hodapp and Dykens (1994) referred to "two cultures" of mental retardation research, one rooted in a level-of-impairment approach, the other etiologically based. In comparison with some other controversies they see this as "quieter, less dramatic" (p. 675) but equally significant in contrast to some others that have long dominated the field. They are quite correct in their assertion of its importance, but controversy has been anything but "quiet" when placed in the context of the nature–nurture, structural feature–control process, and defect–developmental arguments.

Then there is the matter of which discipline(s) should have the major responsibility for service and research in the matter of mental retardation (not always but sometimes motivated by the desire to protect turf). The American Psychological Association (1970) strongly protested the historical role of medicine as the primary responsible agent in the diagnosis, treatment, and investigation of mental retardation. The argument is the familiar one: Because most cases of mental retardation arise from polygenetic or environmental sources and because the defining operations are psychometric, it is inappropriate that the main thrust of treatment, funding, and research should be the responsibility of medical disciplines. In any case, the research implications are clear enough. What is not quite so evident is the enormous social impact of the distinction when it comes to framing policy and generating more effective service systems.

In their approach to demonstrating the distinction between etiology-based and level-of-impairment-based research, Hodapp and Dykens surveyed publications of generic and special education journals (such as the *American Journal of Mental Retardation*) and discipline-oriented journals (such as the *American Journal of Medical Genetics*) between 1985 and 1990. Only those research articles that were directly or substantially concerned with behavioral issues and mental retardation were included in the survey. The results were not unexpected. Articles based on the level-of-impairment strategy far outnumbered etiology-based approaches in behavioral and special education journals. The outcome was just the opposite for more medically oriented journals.

Examining the question from the other direction—which journals publish behavioral research on etiological disorders—yields the same conclusion. That is, for specific syndromes we would look to the genetic and medical journals. Very few research articles dealing with distinct syndromes were found in psychology or special education journals. The major exception reported by Hodapp and Dykens to their generalization concerning the two-culture distinction was Down syndrome, about which there is a great deal of behavioral research across the two categories of periodicals. A much earlier, intensive, and sophisticated review of the medical/behavioral literature on Down syndrome (and other diseases) was accomplished by Belmont (1971), who not only showed how interesting this issue has been and continues to be, but how difficult it is from a design standpoint to conduct such research.

A Definition of Mental Retardation Research Based on Funding

As has been pointed out repeatedly, behavioral researchers tend to construe mental retardation (with humans) from an IQ orientation. This is reflected in the level-of-impairment approach, with etiology deemphasized. Biomedical researchers are more apt to be disease or pathology oriented, focusing on underlying pathological structures, functions, and processes. (These, I understand, are generalizations, and there are exceptions to the rule).

How is this distinction fed into public policy—more specifically, that policy pertaining to the national research effort? The meaning of the term "mental retardation" is critical when attempting to characterize research funding, and what is considered relevant in that regard. Thus, from the standpoint of what constitutes mental retardation research it is instructive to examine the grant portfolios of agencies mandated to support mental retardation research.

As indicated earlier, the National Institute of Child Health and Human Development (NICHD) was established with the expressed purpose of enabling a comprehensive research program to explore cause, treatment, and prevention of mental retardation. There are many other federal agencies, both within NIH and outside, that are also committed to providing research support to understand mental retardation.

Periodically, each division within NICHD prepares a report describing its research agenda and accomplishments. In addition to providing administrative information and fiscal data, these reports are a veridical reflection of the overall research thrust on particular topics and, by inference, define the area. Recently, the Mental Retardation and Development Branch (MRDD) published a progress report describing grant mechanisms, the amounts of money allocated to each, the topics researched, and a summary of scientific accomplishments (Mental Retardation and Developmental Disabilities Branch, 1993).

A very clear message in the report is that the umbrella of research support on topics related to mental retardation is very broad. The point is stressed that there are over 350 known causes of mental retardation stemming from prenatal, perinatal, and postnatal conditions. Given the diversity of phenotypic expression within conditions, clinical manifestations are much more varied than the causes. In recognition of this heterogeneity, "research efforts must be organized within a comprehensive and systematic framework that embraces a diversity of problems and approaches" (Mental Retardation and Development Disabilities Branch, 1993, p. 3). The major headings in the report subsume general areas of research supported by the MRDD, including: genetics and genetic disorders; inborn errors of metabolism; developmental neurobiology; prenatal diagnosis; exogenous and environmental factors; HIV/AIDS; learning, perception, memory, cognition, and operant methods; low birthweight at-risk infants; early environmental interventions; behavioral problems; social adaptation during childhood, adolescence, and throughout the life span; and families with retarded members. Throughout the report, much more specific discussion is given to various topics within each of these major headings.

The question still remains as to how many projects are supported within each classification as well as the corresponding level of support. For each fiscal year the Public Health Service (PHS) publishes the Computer Retrieval of Information on Scientific Projects (CRISP) *Thesaurus*—a database designed to describe research in progress supported by PHS. The *Thesaurus* is a controlled vocabulary, assigning over 12,000 indexing terms from which topic-related information may be retrieved. From this source I obtained information on mental retardation-related projects supported by NICHD in fiscal year 1994. These selected areas, along with the numbers of projects and funds, are presented in Table 1.1.

There may be some arbitrariness in this listing, but these data were supplied by officials within the Office of Program Analysis of NICHD and represent their best judgment as to the topics NICHD considers relevant to mental retardation research. The range is considerable, but clearly most of the supported research is etiological or pathogenic oriented. It is of significance that more dollars are directed to biomedical than to behavioral research (64% vs. 36%, respectively, in fiscal year 1995).

A more detailed analysis of the 1993 MRDD report reveals that although there is some overlap between biomedical and behavioral projects with respect to the level-of-impairment versus etiologic-specific research approaches, the latter predominates. Such an analysis, of course, does not answer the question as to which is the more fruitful.

That is a question that must be addressed in terms of pragmatic outcomes featuring issues such as cause and effect, treatment, and prevention. Measurement in terms of accomplishment is difficult, but, at the risk of generalization by extreme example, consider Hemophilus influenza type b (Hib). This disease is caused by an invasive bacterium that

TABLE 1.1
NICHD MR-Related Projects in Selected Areas (for fiscal year 1994)

Selected Area	*Number of Projects*	*Funds*
Inborn errors of metabolism	80	$10,534,362
Infectious diseases	19	2,363,983
Chromosomal disorders	91	13,900,475
Teratogenetic exposure	13	1,619,603
Nutrition	54	10,178,853
Molecular biology	186	14,753,238
Low birthweight	71	12,286,648
Language and communication	108	14,422,335
Early intervention	15	1,688,783
Family and community studies	24	4,045,884
Learning disabilities	65	10,097,842
Epidemiology	49	10,151,417
Socioecological processes	43	5,896,565
Prevention	47	11,043,655
Treatment (educational & medical)	83	9,661,208
Pharmacology	68	9,600,700
Destructive behavior	17	1,656,916

Note. Subprojects of program projects and center grants are counted individually.

may produce meningitis, a leading cause of mental retardation. It is also the leading bacterial child killer. About 18,000 children are infected annually, leading to about 5,000 cases with mental retardation. NICHD scientists recently developed conjugate vaccines that can protect young infants. Efficacy trials attested to these vaccines and they are now considered part of the inoculation series that all children should receive (Baumeister et al., 1993). Universal use of these vaccines will prevent mental retardation (and deafness) caused by Hib (Alexander, 1991).

Preserving the Union. The argument can be advanced that behavioral scientists deal with more complex issues, and such direct comparison is unfair and misleading. But, I ask, referring to Hib, has there been a comparable achievement of such direct and dramatic proportion from the behavioral sciences? Unfair or not, it is clear that judging from the distribution of funds by projects, more public trust is placed in the direction of biomedical/etiological considerations. Of course, nothing is quite this simple in that vested professional and advocacy interests and political pressures have a great deal to do with spending priorities, even at the level of NICHD. These considerations aside, it is at the conjunction of behavioral/biomedical research where the promise seems to be the greatest.

An excellent example is the large-scale national Maternal Phenylketonuria (PKU) Collaborative Study funded by the MRDD Branch of NICHD. PKU is an inborn error of metabolism characterized by a diminished ability to convert the essential amino acid phenylalanine (phe) into tyrosine. If a child born with PKU is untreated with a low phe diet in early infancy the phenotypic result is usually severe mental retardation. Indeed universal neonatal screening has almost eliminated PKU as a cause of mental retardation.

After brain growth has been completed, treated PKU children are commonly returned to a normal diet, usually by age 8 or 10. Although mental retardation due to elevated phe has been averted, blood serum levels of phe are again abnormally high after resuming the normal diet. Ironically and tragically this course of treatment has led to a significant public health problem in that women who had been treated with the special diet as children produce babies who are not PKU, but who are almost always seriously retarded, usually with microcephaly, frequently at low birthweight, and commonly with congenital heart disease (Lenke & Levy, 1980). That is, children born to PKU women who returned to a normal diet have been subjected in utero to a devastating teratogen—maternal phe and other metabolic by-products. Similar, although somewhat less severe, outcomes are found in offspring of women with hyperphenylalaninemia (HPA), a milder form of the disorder.

Despite what is commonly believed, PKU is a very heterogenous disease at the phenotypic level—due both to exogenous as well as genetic factors. It is now known that there are over 250 mutations and microdeletions, varying in severity, of the gene that directs phe hydroxylase.

The result of universal screening and dietary treatment of classical PKU infants is that gains made in preventing mental retardation by dietary treatment of PKU and HPA female infants will be completely erased within one generation without an intervention designed to reduce fetal exposure to elevated phe. The basic strategy of the Maternal PKU Collaborative Study (begun in 1984) now involving the United States, Canada, Germany, Austria, and Switzerland is to enroll PKU and HPA women in a dietary management program either preconceptionally or during early stages of pregnancy.

The principal thrust of this project is to prevent mental retardation as indicated by scores on IQ tests, measures of adaptive behavior, and other indices. Furthermore, SES differences are related to outcome. From this standpoint, the maternal PKU project could be considered a behavioral study based on a disease of known (although imperfectly) biological etiology. Still, it is also a biomedical project in that enrollment of mothers is based on serum phenylalanine levels and that the main intervention is nutritional prophylaxis to reduce teratogenic effects of maternal phenylalanine and other metabolic by-products. Many measures are biochemical. It would be an unnecessary exercise in futility to characterize this study as either behavioral or biomedical. Whatever one wishes to call it, this is a research project that is having a decided effect on incidence of maternal PKU and mental retardation.

The term *etiological specificity* is disarmingly simple and should not be regarded as an "either or" proposition. As an example, just where does mental retardation begin? Does it begin with a teen pregnancy, with unhealthy maternal behavior, with intrauterine infection, with premature low birthweight, with intracranial bleeds, with an impoverished home environment, with abuse or neglect, with poor school performance, or with a measured low IQ? Etiology is not always a matter of clear identification of some critical agent. Pathogenesis is best regarded as a sequence of events, the proper understanding of which will point to opportunities for interventions that optimize sensitivity and specificity. It is my contention that behavioral researchers have not properly addressed pathogenic processes that produce deviations from normal development (including mental retardation) but rather have tended to focus on the endpoint of that sequence. Take low birthweight as an example.

In their analyses of conditions that give rise to children's health disorders with a view toward prevention of infant mortality and morbidity, Baumeister et al. (1993) directed a great deal of attention to premature birth (< 37 weeks gestation) and to low birthweight (LBW—< 2,500 grams). The LBW criterion has been widely accepted by the international health community as the standard measure of risk for adverse perinatal outcome. A well-established fact is that LBW infants are at enormously increased risk for immediate medical (e.g., residual chronic lung disease, intraventricular hemorrhage, and retinopathy) and long-term disabilities including neurodevelopmental conditions, learning disabilities, cerebral palsy, autism, sensory deficits, and behavior disorders. Risks of mortality and morbidity greatly increase as birthweight decreases—similar to the dose-response effect associated with teratogenic or drug exposure.

Many of the risk factors for premature LBW have been identified such as poverty, race, maternal age, exposure to toxins, infections, poor nutrition, lack of access to prenatal care, maternal health, parental education, and genetic predispositions, among others. On the other hand, relatively little is known about effective intervention in regard to longer-term outcomes, including mental retardation, how individual differences are manifested, and what mediates these outcomes.

The NICHD, through the MRDD branch, is funding a project to follow cohorts of extremely LBW (< 750 grams), very LBW (< 1,500 grams), and full-term infants as they progress through school. Predictors include past and present neurological and medical conditions, social–familial adversity, and cognitive and behavioral problems. Longitudinal studies of LBW infants are surprisingly scarce. There are many more retrospective investigations. It was not until 1993 that the first prospective study was reported of babies weighing less than 1,000 grams at birth. Follow up of these children demonstrated how serious and long term adverse effects can be (Halsey et al., 1993). About 75% showed generalized performance lags at age 4. Brain damage was subtle, involving disruption and interruption of fetal brain organogenesis, rather than severe intracranial hemorrhage or other major neurological complications at birth.

Scientific concern over LBW reveals three issues that have bearing on the etiologic versus level-of-impairment strategies for conducting research on mental retardation. First, precise etiology of LBW is not always known, but the pathogenic processes persist and understanding this process enables interventions that are closer in time and relevance to the cause. Second, etiology and level of impairment are not or should not be competitive or alternative approaches to the study of mental retardation. Finally, and perhaps most important, this is an example among others that reveals how meaningless for scientific analysis the gross outcome condition of mental retardation has become when taken in isolation. It is not possible (or necessary) to identify which babies in a neonatal intensive care unit will have mental retardation, medical complications, cerebral palsy, any other developmental manifestation, or who will develop normally. They are at greatly elevated risk for all these problems, often in combination. Research on prevention and pathogenesis, behavioral and medical, is not furthered by isolated definitions of conditions that arise from social conventions rather than from scientific analyses that have immediate bearing on the problems at hand.

We are dealing here with multifaceted health problems that implicate biomedical, psychological, and social factors. The research program of the NICHD is predicated on an appreciation of the complex matrix of causes and effects. This is not to say that in the portfolio of research projects supported through MRDD, there are not many whose orientation is based on the level-of-impairment approach. But that is not the predominant definition of mental retardation reflected in their research funding, as revealed by analysis of the types and nature of grant-supported projects.

Recently we have seen that research on behavioral aspects of fragile X syndrome is making its way into behaviorally oriented journals as well medical publications. Nevertheless, etiological specificity is not the guiding strategy for most behavioral research—despite the fact by now there is growing evidence that different etiologies differ in such domains as linguistic attributes, frequency, and type of maladaptive behavior, as well as in developmental trajectories.

However, there is still persistent advocacy of the view that behavioral research derived from a disease orientation will not be very fruitful. After his extensive review of the causes of developmental disabilities, Berkson (1993) concluded that there "are few instances yet of specific genetic influences having highly specific behavioral effects" (p. 87). His reasoning was that messages encoded at the cellular level undergo a complex series of developmental stages and processes, reflecting the operation of other genetic as well as myriad environmental influences before the defect is phenotypically expressed as a behavioral pattern.

To be sure, there are many factors that interact to condition outcome and, furthermore, behavioral manifestations are often indistinct, variable in expression, overlapping, and crudely measured. Nor are behavioral manifestations static, but instead are ever abiding and mutable to continuing influences. However, these considerations inform us as to how biological–behavioral research should be conducted and do not make a compelling argument for a level-of-impairment approach.

In one significant respect, Berkson (1993) did make a strong case for the etiologic strategy—prevention of mental retardation. This point has been expressly argued as the most fundamental underlying basis for public health measures for primary prevention of all manner of children's health disorders, including mental retardation, by Baumeister et al. (1993). Their position was that without proper understanding of causative mechanisms and all relevant moderating and mediating influences, then sensitivity and specificity (measures essential to effective preventive intervention) are compromised and produce costly and marginally effective reliance on expensive treatment (i.e., secondary or tertiary prevention).

Not only has there been a major disregard for the relevance of research findings and methods, one for the other, but also a disdain, even antagonism, between the two camps, as Hodapp and Dykens (1994) and Belmont (1971) before them so vividly illustrated. Public displays of outrage by behavioral scientists as to the disproportionate funding support in favor of biomedical research is but one manifestation of this clash of two worlds (Baumeister, in press).

Of course, this is not to say that the gulf is never bridged and that all is conflict and no commerce. Indeed, as already noted, there is a large literature on medical–behavioral aspects of mental retardation. However, much of this has been poorly conceived, retrospective, theoretical, and opportunistic, without due regard to the pathogenesis of the particular disease. There are some highly instructive exceptions, such as the national maternal PKU project. Nevertheless, the fault lines of contention still run deep and disciplinary warfare is in no one's best interests, most notably children who are compromised.

However, the resolution is more than tacit acceptance by behavioral scientists of biomedical revelations and approaches, or even active collaboration among investigators (although that would be nice). It is a matter of learning the essentials of other disciplines, their theories, methods, and findings. Commerce between the two worlds of behavior and biology research needs to be aided and abetted. At the present we are facing a large trade deficit in favor of biology. Perhaps the best collaborative research is that which occurs within one head.

THE BREAD AND BUTTER ISSUE OF RESEARCH FUNDING

The engine that drives research may be intellectual, but the fuel is money. Practically ever since the creation of the NICHD concern has been expressed, mostly by behavioral researchers, that the institute has devalued mental research in general and behavioral research in particular. As we have seen, part of the problem inheres in the very meaning of the term *mental retardation*. We noted earlier that the American Psychological Association (1970) weighed in with the proclamation that because mental retardation is primarily a behavioral construct, without demonstrable biological causes, most federally supported research should be left to psychologists. It is doubtful whether anyone outside the choir paid any great attention to that preaching.

On the other side of this issue are those who maintain that basic research concerned with developmental and genetic processes is, by definition, relevant to mental retardation. That is, the definition as to mental retardation relevance should be a very broad one. Although the loftier explanation of these discrepant views is that they reflect honest professional expression as to the generality of science and its applicability to mental retardation, it hardly seems to be any accident that the debate became especially heated after NICHD recently adopted a mental retardation relevance criterion for support of research projects within the Mental Retardation Research Centers.

After the early 1970s, when there appeared to be a precipitous decline in mental retardation research as a proportion of the NICHD budget, the battle became heated and public. After a period of highly contentious behind-the-scenes maneuvering, psychologists took to professional journals to express their displeasure and unease. Zigler (1978) strongly condemned the NICHD leadership because of policy changes that, in his view, presaged "a crisis in mental retardation research" (p. 2). Then Baumeister and Berkson (1982) examined funding trends within NICHD over a 10-year period, finding a steady and linear decline in relative support for mental retardation research. They claimed that serious consequences would be felt if this trend were allowed to continue. Braddock (1987) conducted an extensive and comprehensive analysis of federal discretionary expenditures for mental retardation and developmental services and research. He also documented a steady decline in research support, adjusted for inflation, from 1971 to 1985, leading him to pronounce that "To describe this long-term decline as a crisis is an understatement" (p. 185). Schroeder (1991) continued this theme, claiming that "behavioral MR/DD research at NICHD . . . is a second class citizen" (pp. 11–12).

During that period of discontent, continuing to the present, researchers, mostly psychologists, also took to the political arena for help. Beginning in 1976, testimony was presented annually to the House and Senate appropriations subcommittees documenting the purported erosion of research support for mental retardation. Lobbying efforts were launched in earnest. At best, all this effort can be described as minimally effective. Given this background, what is the situation with respect to funding levels and trends? Are we in crisis? What is meant by crisis? As we have shown, the agency with the clearest mandate to support mental retardation research is NICHD, but the research mandate is very broad.

In fiscal year 1994, Congressional appropriation for NICHD was $552,145,000. The largest administrative unit within NICHD is the Center for Research for Mothers and Children (CRMC). The center received 52% of the total ($289,852,000). The Mental Retardation and Developmental Disabilities Branch (MRDD) is organizationally within the CRMC. In fiscal year 1993, the branch supported a total of 187 projects in the amount of $51,889,000. Obviously, this is a very small portion of the overall NICHD budget or even of the CMRC. At the same time, it must be stressed that a great deal of mental retardation-relevant research (using the institute's definition) is funded outside the MRDD, including other centers, branches, and the intramural program. Earlier, data were presented displaying NICHD funding by topical areas and by amount for fiscal year 1994.

The analysis presented here focuses of two major issues: funding trends for mental retardation, in general, and support for behavioral research. Three general categories are identified for purposes of this evaluation: (a) total mental retardation research support within the CRMC, (b) support by the MRDD Branch, and (c) core support for the mental retardation research centers. The reason for using the CRMC as the base rather than the NICHD is that the CRMC is the administrative unit primarily responsible for mental retardation research and that mental retardation research accounts for a relatively small proportion of the total NICHD budget—7% in 1966, 11% in 1985, and 13% in 1994. Small as that is, the relative amount devoted to mental retardation has increased over the years.

Table 1.2 presents trends in mental retardation research funding from 1972 to 1994. In terms of current dollars, there is a continuing increase in support for mental retardation. However, when inflation, as measured by the Biomedical Research and Developmental Price Index (frequently called the "Birdpie"), is factored in, investment over the past 10 years is essentially flat or even on the decline (in the case of the mental retardation research centers). The index changes from year to year and is set at 4.0% for fiscal year 1995.

A detailed discussion of the overall funding climate for research within the NIH or, more importantly, for the NICHD, is not possible here. (Baumeister, in press, has presented a more thorough analysis of research funding for mental retardation research within the context of various fiscal pressures, priorities, competition, procedures, and politics.) In any event, the general statement can be made that overall the budget of NICHD has remained essentially constant over the past several years. In this sense there does not appear to be any particular bias against mental retardation and other developmental disabilities.

Aside from more generalized economic considerations and competing interests, it is possible and appropriate to gauge the *relative* priority status of mental retardation research within NICHD. It is no great secret that we are undergoing a period of austerity and that "cost containment" has become the overriding issue of the times. In this climate, some areas of research will inevitably fall back in the pack given that hard choices will be made as to how a dwindling supply of money will be distributed among countless competing interests.

TABLE 1.2
Trends in MR Funding (millions of dollars)

Year	*Total CRMC Funds*	*Total CRMC-MR*	*MRDD*	*MRCC Core*
1972	$42,838,000	$21,365,000	$17,250,000	$5,856,000
1973	41,971,000	21,330,000	16,642,000	6,533,000
1974	51,894,000	23,886,000	18,096,000	5,761,000
1975	55,094,000	25,420,000	18,884,000	5,672,000
1976	60,161,000	27,016,000	20,423,000	5,608,000
1977	64,979,000	28,419,000	21,434,000	6,166,000
1978	73,790,000	30,298,000	23,318,000	6,455,000
1979	102,492,000	35,321,000	28,121,000	6,759,000
1980	101,154,000	34,731,000	27,559,000	6,751,000
1981	106,055,000	32,997,000	26,969,000	6,623,000
1982	105,530,000	31,768,000	25,963,000	6,549,000
1983	123,346,000	35,270,000	29,306,000	7,343,000
1984	135,489,000	35,699,000	29,263,000	7,737,000
1985	157,727,000	44,329,000	36,365,000	9,298,000
1986	158,009,000	47,008,000	36,478,000	8,378,000
1987	190,505,000	54,066,000	42,726,000	9,224,000
1988	213,398,000	59,186,000	46,700,000	9,802,000
1989	228,521,000	60,462,000	45,001,000	10,638,000
1990	245,001,000	61,757,000	47,725,000	11,267,000
1991	261,369,000	67,325,000	52,319,000	11,276,000
1992	272,615,000	68,568,000	52,154,000	10,759,000
1993	282,838,000	68,641,000	51,899,000	10,429,000
1994	289,852,000	71,511,000	54,332,000	10,925,000

Note. Source of data: NICHD, Office of Science Policy & Analysis, Program Analysis Branch.

In an effort to address this issue I converted dollars as shown in Table 1.2 to *proportions* of the total budget of the CRMC. These data are presented in Fig. 1.1.

These trend lines reveal a consistent, virtually linear erosion over time for mental retardation as a research priority. As can be seen, in 1973 mental retardation accounted for 51% of the total CRMC budget. By 1994, that proportion had dwindled to 25%. Not only does mental retardation fail to hold the same status (within CRMC) as it did two decades ago, but the downward trajectory is continuing. Funding for mental retardation research through the CRMC has kept pace neither with inflation nor with appropriations to NICHD. On the other hand, for the institute as a whole, percentage of budget devoted to mental retardation has increased over 30 years.

It would be a gross oversimplification to attribute this decline to diminished enthusiasm for mental retardation by NICHD officials, as has been claimed by others. There is evidence to the contrary. To be sure, the institute does have some discretionary latitude. But the problem, in great measure, lies with the grants review process, much of which is beyond the control of the institute. Researchers themselves are part of the problem. NIH is not an entitlement program for researchers. If we do not submit grant proposals, we will not receive funding. If the study sections that review grant proposals are harder on mental retardation-related projects, then applications will disappear in the dust of the percentile system that dictates funding.

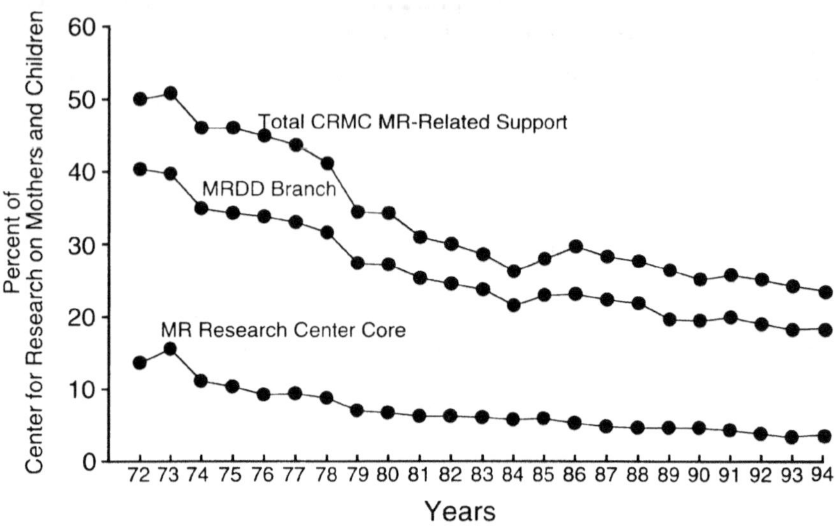

FIG 1.1. Trends in support of mental retardation research [Data supplied by NICHD (OSPA-PAB)].

Another bottom-line measure is "success rate"—defined as the number of grants awarded as a percentage of the number of applications. There are numerous categories of grants. The one that is best known and most dear to researchers is the individual grant, the RO1. I compared the success rates of mental retardation RO1 applications to the general category of RO1s funded by NICHD. In 8 of the past 10 fiscal years, the success rates of mental retardation applications has been lower than those in the general category. Thus, there appears to be a bias. But what is its source? Certainly, NICHD policy cannot be blamed entirely because, as noted earlier, the review process is conducted through a different mechanism—the Division of Research Grants. Either reviewers impose a more stringent standard on mental retardation applications, the applications are inferior, or both.

The same kinds of analyses may be applied to the question concerning the balance between behavioral and biomedical research. Critics have raised two related issues in this respect. One is that biomedical research receives the lion's share of support, and the second is that behavioral research is losing ground. This brings up, once again, the knotty question of what is behavioral and what is biomedical. Given that the data are compiled by NICHD, their definitions have to be accepted for purposes of this analysis.

What do the data reveal? Table 1.3 presents percentages for behavioral and biomedical research within the NICHD (their extramural program) from 1985 to 1995.

TABLE 1.3
CRMC Extramural MR and MR-Related Biomedical and Behavioral Support (% of total), 1985–1995

CRMC MR and MR Related	*1985*	*1986*	*1987*	*1988*	*1989*	*1990*	*1991*	*1992*	*1993*	*1994*[a]	*1995*[a]
Biomedical	62	63	61	62	61	63	65	65	66	64	64
Behavioral	38	37	39	38	39	37	35	35	34	36	36

[a]Estimated.

Clearly, biomedical research is significantly favored, roughly by a two-to-one edge. On the other hand, the percentages have remained fairly stable over the decade. There has not been, as some behavioral scientists have maintained, a steady erosion of support for behavioral research in favor of biomedical interests. And what about the documented imbalance favoring biomedical research? Does this show that the institute has an unwritten policy bias against behavioral research? The answer to the question is a qualified "no."

For one thing, there are many more biomedical applications submitted for funding. Simply on a probabilistic basis, one might reasonably expect there to be more biomedical projects funded. It is also instructive to compare mental retardation research against other programs in NICHD. In fiscal years 1993 through 1995, the percentages for all categories of behavioral research were 21%. On this basis, the argument can be made that there is a significant bias in favor of behavioral research in the field of mental retardation.

Considering the multifaceted biological nature of the condition known as "mental retardation," the complex review and funding processes, the subterranean world of politics and special interests, changing social priorities, and the national fiscal crisis, we behavioral researchers ought to stop complaining. There is still ample money available, from numerous sources, to conduct research on topics concerning mental retardation.

It is not so much that we need more research; we need better research. Our own house is in disarray. Greater effort should be made to honestly and objectively review what we have and have not accomplished, to generate a coherent and balanced plan, and to avoid placing ourselves at the margins. Perhaps we suffer from collective myopia and require new lenses to see if we cannot approach these problems from fresh perspectives.

CONCLUSION

The past three decades encompassing the modern era of behavioral research and theory have comprised a period of quite remarkable growth in concepts, issues, and productivity. Scientific inquiry has occurred within and has been conditioned by evolving and encompassing value systems, economic adjustments, and legal issues. These provide the crucial backdrop against which people with disabilities are regarded and treated within our social/moral fabric. Much of the profound change in life's circumstances for those with mental retardation that has occurred over this period stems from advocacy initiatives. Science and the technology it spawns have played a role in this process, but they are more focused on means rather than ends. That is as it should be, for truth is ultimately a moral, not a scientific test. Decisions to deinstitutionalize, to ban aversive conditioning, and to provide public assistance are the expressions of changing societal values, not of scientific revelation. Such values are always subject to change.

Although it is possible to point to some positive advances, there is a grimmer side to this generally sanguine picture. Evidence marshaled from various sources shows that economic travail, destablization of families, marked social changes, the rapid growth of the information age, the tumult surrounding public education, and a generalized public malaise have directly and adversely affected the lives of many people, particularly those at the shadowy margins of society—the poor, the disabled, and the minorities. Those at risk for mental/physical handicaps are increasingly vulnerable to all these pressures, pressures that dwarf the capabilities of our conventional scientific approaches to resolution of developmental disadvantage.

The fact can no longer be ignored that children are rapidly losing ground in some very critical health domains. This is a conclusion forced by such population-based indices as access to primary care, low birthweight, immunization rates, abuse and neglect, infectious diseases, violence, accidents, exposure to toxins, preconceptual and prenatal screening, teen pregnancy, nutrition, screening for diseases, and increasing rates of developmental disabilities. The terrible tide of new morbidities cannot be stemmed by continued and uncritical reliance on old models, old paradigms, and old disciplinary distinctions—as comfortable as these may be to those of us who are entrusted to conduct research that contributes to knowledge about diseases, their prevention, and their treatment.

To characterize the extraordinary energy, dedication, and diligent work of the legions of behavioral researchers concerned with mental retardation as trivial and inconsequential would be grossly unfair and inappropriate. But times are changing, and we confront a moral imperative to anticipate what the future holds and to respond accordingly. The fault lines of contention threaten to set a new record on the social Richter Scale. We in the behavioral sciences are indeed confronting an inexorable slide into irrelevancy.

If the battle is waged in absolute determination to subdue nature, then surely we are destined to lose. Rather, we must understand and accept nature on its terms and take advantage of every opportunity afforded in order to avert some of the awful circumstances that compromise or even destroy lives. There is another lesson conveyed by our experience with mental retardation: We shall never attain scientific perfection on a grand scale, such as eradication of mental retardation. Our scientific accomplishments must be measured in small increments of knowledge, condition by condition, and translation of that knowledge into highly sensitive and specific practices, in which costs are balanced against benefits. We must escape the well-worn calf-paths of our minds and forge new trails.

REFERENCES

Alexander, D. (1991, February). *A national strategy for addressing conditions that negatively affect mothers and children.* Keynote address at the National Summit on the National Effort to Prevent Mental Retardation and Related Disabilities, Washington DC.

Alexander, D. (1992, September). *The National Institute of Child Health and Human Development: Three decades of research accomplishments.* A report to the founders of the council, Washington, DC.

American Psychological Association. (1970). Psychology and mental retardation. *American Psychologist, 25*, 267–268.

Arendt, R. E., MacLean, W. E., Jr., & Baumeister, A. A. (1988). critique of sensory integration therapy and its application to mental retardation. *American Journal on Mental Retardation, 92*, 401–411.

Aslin, R. N. (1981). Experiential influences and sensitive periods in development: A unified model. In R. N. Aslin, J. R. Alberts, & M. R. Peterson (Eds.), *Development of Perception* (Vol. 2, pp. 45–93). New York: Academic Press.

Ayers, A. J. (1972). *Sensory integration and learning disorders.* Los Angeles: Western Psychological Services.

Ballantyne, J. W. (1902). *Manual on Antenatal Pathology: The Foetus.* Edinburgh, Scotland: William Green.

Barnett, W. S., & Escobar, C. M. (1987). The economics of early educational intervention: A review. *Review of Educational Research, 57*, 387–314.

Bartlett, F. C. (1932). *Remembering.* Cambridge, England: Cambridge University Press.

Bartley, M., Power, C., Blane, D., Smith, G. D., & Shipley, M. (1994). Birthweight and later socioeconomic disadvanatge: Evidence from the 1958 British cohort study. *British Medical Journal, 309*, 1475–1478.

Battig, W. F. (1975). Within-individual differences in "cognitive" processes. In R. L. Solso (Ed.), *Information processing and cognition* (pp. 195–228). Hillsdale, NJ: Lawrence Erlbaum Associates.

Baumeister, A. A. (1967). Problems in comparative studies of mental retardates and normals. *American Journal of Mental Deficiency, 71*, 869–875.

Baumeister, A. A. (1970). The American residential institution: Its history and character. In A. A. Baumeister & E. Butterfield (Eds.), *Residential facilities for the mentally retarded* (pp. 1–28). Chicago: Aldine.

Baumeister, A. A. (1981). Mental retardation policy and research: The unfulfilled promise. *American Journal of Mental Deficiency, 85*, 449–456.

Baumeister, A. A. (1984). Some methodological and conceptual issues in the study of cognitive processes with retarded people. In P. Brooks, R. Sperber, & C. McCauley (Eds.), *Learning and cognition in the mentally retarded* (pp. 1–38). Hillsdale, NJ: Lawrence Erlbaum Associates.

Baumeister, A. A. (1992). Policy formulation: A real world view. In F. H. Bess & J. W. Hall (Eds). *Screening children for auditory function* (pp. 111–123). Nashville, TN: Bill Wilkerson Center Press.

Baumeister, A. A. (in press). Mental retardation funding: NICHD revisited. *Monographs of the American Association on Mental Retardation.*

Baumeister, A. A., & Berkson, G. (1982). Mental retardation funding trends of the National Institute of Child Health and Human Development. *American Journal of Mental Deficiency, 87*, 119–121.

Baumeister, A. A., & Hillsinger, L. B. (1984). The role of psychologists in public institutions for the mentally retarded revisited. *Professional Psychology, 15*, 134-141.

Baumeister, A. A., & Kupstas, F. D. (1991). The new morbidity: Implications for prevention and amelioration. In A. B. D. Clarke & P. Evans (Eds.), *Combating mental handicap: A multidisciplinary approach* (pp. 46–72). London: A. B. Academic Publishers.

Baumeister, A. A., Kupstas, F. D., & Woodley-Zanthos, P. (1993). *The new morbidity: Recommendations for action and an updated guide to state planning for the prevention of mental retardation and related disabilities associated with socioeconomic conditions.* Washington, DC: U.S. Department of Health and Human Services.

Baumeister, A. A., & MacLean W. E., Jr. (1979). Brain damage and mental retardation. In N. R. Ellis (Ed.), *Handbook of mental deficiency, psychological theory and research* (pp. 197–230). Hillsdale, NJ: Lawrence Erlbaum Associates.

Baumeister, A. A., & Muma, J. R. (1975). On defining mental retardation. *The Journal of Special Education, 9*, 293–306.

Belmont, J. M. (1971). Medical–behavioral research in retardation. In N. R. Ellis (Ed.), *International review of research in mental retardation* (Vol. 5, pp. 1–81). New York: Academic Press.

Berkson, G. (1993). *Children with handicaps: A review of behavioral research.* Hillsdale, NJ: Lawrence Erlbaum Associates.

Bijou, S. W. (1966). A functional analysis of retarded behavior. In N. R. Ellis (Ed.), *International review of research in mental retardation* (Vol. 1, pp. 1–19). New York: Academic Press.

Biklen, D. (1993). *Communication unbound: How facilitated communication is challenging traditional views of autism and ability/disability.* New York: Teacher's College Press.

Bodfish, J. W., Powell, S. B., Golden, R. N., & Lewis, M. H. (1995). Blink rate as an index of dopamine function in adults with mental retardation and repetitive behavior disorders. *American Journal on Mental Retardation, 99*, 335–344.

Braddock, D. (1987). *Federal policy toward mental retardation and developmental disabilities.* Baltimore: Brookes.

Braddock, D. (1994). Presidential address 1994: New frontiers in mental retardation. *Mental Retardation, 32*, 434–443.

Bronfenbrenner, U. (1977). Toward an experimental ecology of human development. *American Psychologist, 32*, 513–531.

Brooks, P. H., & Baumeister, A. A. (1977a). A plea for ecological validity in the experimental psychology of mental retardation. *American Journal of Mental Deficiency, 81*, 407–416.

Brooks, P. H., & Baumeister, A. A. (1977b). Are we making a science of missing the point? *American Journal of Mental Deficiency, 81*, 543–546.

Brooks, P. H., Sperber, R., & McCauley (Eds.). (1984). *Learning and cognition in the mentally retarded.* Hillsdale, NJ: Lawrence Erlbaum Associates.

Brooks-Gunn, J., McCarton, C. M., Casey, P. H., McCormick, M. C., Bauer, C. R., Bernbaum, J. C., Tyson, J., Swanson, M., Bennett, F. C., Scott, D. T., Tonascia, J., & Meinert, C. L. (1994). Early intervention in low birthweight premature infants: Results through age 5 years from the Infant Health and Development Program. *Journal of the American Medical Association, 272,* 1257–1262.

Brunswick, E. (1955). Representative design and probabilistic theory in a functional psychology. *Psychological Review, 62,* 193–217.

Butterfield, E. C. (1983). To cure cognitive deficits of mentally retarded persons. In F. J. Menolascino, R. Neman, & J. A. Stark (Eds.), *Curative aspects of mental retardation: Biomedical and behavioral advances* (pp. 203–221). Baltimore: Brookes.

Campione, J. C., Brown, A. L., & Ferrara, R. A. (1982). Mental retardation and intelligence. In R. J. Sternberg (Ed.), *Handbook of human intelligence* (pp. 392–490). New York: Cambridge University Press.

Carr, E. G., Taylor, J. C., Carlson, J. I., & Robinson, S. (1991). Reinforcement and stimulus-based treatments for severe behavior problems in developmental disabilities. In *Treatment of destructive behaviors in persons with developmental disabilities* (NIH Publication No. 91-2410, pp. 173–229). Washington, DC: U.S. Department of Health and Human Services.

Cataldo, M. F. (1991). The effects of punishment and other behavior reducing procedures on the destructive behaviors of persons with developmental disabilities. In *Treatment of destructive behaviors in persons with developmental disabilities* (NIH Publication No. 91-2410, pp. 231–341). Washington, DC: U.S. Department of Human Services.

Cavalli-Sforza, L., Menozzi, P., & Piazza, A. (1994). *The history and geography of human genes.* Princeton, NJ: Princeton University Press.

Clarke, A. M., & Clarke, A. D. B. (Eds). (1958). *Mental deficiency: The changing outlook.* London: Methuen.

Clarke, A. M., & Clarke, A. D. B. (Eds). (1976). *Early experience: Myth and evidence.* New York: Free Press.

Clarke, A. M., & Clarke, A. D. B. (1989). The later cognitive effects of early intervention. *Intelligence, 13,* 289–297.

Clarke, A. M., & Clarke, A. D. B. (1992). How modifiable is the human life path? In N. W. Bray (Ed.), *International review of research in mental retardation* (Vol. 18, pp. 137–157). New York: Academic Press.

Clarke, A. M., Clarke, A. D. B., & Berg, J. M. (Eds.). (1985). *Mental deficiency: The changing outlook* (4th ed.). New York: Free Press.

Committee on Children with Disabilities. (1985). School-aged children with motor disabilities. *Pediatrics, 76,* 648–649.

Crissey, M. S. (1975). Mental retardation—past, present, and future. *American Psychologist, 30,* 800–808.

Detterman, D. K. (1986). Human intelligence is a complex system of separate processes. In R. Sternberg & D. K. Detterman (eds.), *What is intelligence? Contemporary viewpoints on its nature and definition* (pp. 57–61). Norwood, NJ: Ablex.

Detterman, D. K. (1987). Theoretical notions of intelligence and mental retardation. *American Journal of Mental Retardation, 92,* 2–11.

Detterman, D. K. (1992). Mopping up: The relation between cognitive processes and intelligence. *American Journal on Mental Retardation, 97,* 295–301.

Detterman, D. K., Mayer, J. D., Caruso, D. R., Legree, P. J., Conners, F. A., & Taylor, R. (1992). Assessment of basic cognitive abilities in relation to cognitive deficits. *American Journal on Mental Retardation, 97,* 251–286.

Doll, E. A. (1941). The essentials of an inclusive concept of mental deficiency. *American Journal of Mental Deficiency, 46,* 214–219.

Dykens, E. M., Hodapp, R. M., & Evans, D. W. (1994). Profiles and development of adaptive behavior in children with Down Syndrome. *American Journal on Mental Retardation, 98*, 580–587.

Elderton, E. M., & Pearson, K. A. (1910). A first study of the influence of parental alcoholism on the physique and ability of the offspring. *Eugenics Laboratory Memoir, 10*, 1–46.

Ellis, N. R. (Ed.). (1963). *Handbook of mental deficiency, psychological theory and research* (1st ed.). Hillsdale, NJ: Lawrence Erlbaum Associates.

Ellis, N. R. (Ed.). (1979). *Handbook of mental deficiency, psychological theory and research* (2nd ed.). Hillsdale, NJ: Lawrence Erlbaum Associates.

Evans, I. M., & Scotti, J. R. (1989). Defining meaningful outcomes for persons with profound disabilities. In F. Brown & D. Lehr (Eds.), *Persons with profound disabilities: Issues and practices* (pp. 315–350). Baltimore: Brookes.

Garbarino, J. (1991). The human ecology of human risk. In S. J. Meisels & J. P. Shonkoff (Eds.), *Handbook of early childhood intervention* (pp. 78–96). New York: Cambridge University Press.

Garmezy, N. (1991). Resiliency and vulnerability to adverse developmental outcomes associated with poverty. *American Behavioral Scientist, 34*, 416–430.

Goodman, J. F. (1990). Technical note: Problems in etiological classifications of mental retardation. *Journal of Child Psychology and Psychiatry, 31*, 465–469.

Halsey, C. L., Collin, M. F., & Anderson, C. L. (1993). Extremely LBW children and their peers: A comparison of preschool performances. *Pediatrics, 91*, 807–811.

Herrnstein, R. J., & Murray, C. (1994). *The bell curve: Intelligence and class structure in american life.* New York: Free Press.

Hodapp, R. M., & Dykens, E. M. (1991). Toward an etiology-specific strategy of early intervention for handicapped children. In K. Marfo (Ed.), *Early intervention in transition: Current perspectives on programs for handicapped children* (pp. 41–60). New York: Praeger.

Hodapp, R. M., & Dykens. E. M. (1994). Mental retardation's two cultures of behavioral research. *American Journal on Mental Retardation, 98*, 675–687.

Hoehn, T. P., & Baumeister, A. A. (1994). A critique of the application of sensory integration therapy to children with learning disabilities. *Journal of Learning Disabilities, 27*, 338–350.

House, B. J. (1977). Scientific explanation and ecological validity: A reply to Brooks and Baumeister. *American Journal of Mental Deficiency, 81*, 534–542.

Infant Health and Development Program (1990). Enhancing the outcomes of low birthweight, premature infants. *Journal of the American Medical Association, 263*, 3035–3042.

Jacobson, J. W., & Mulick, J. A. (1995). Behavior modification and technologies: Ethical dilemmas for practitioners posed by facilitated communication. *Psychology in Mental Retardation and Developmental Disabilities, 20*, 14–18.

Kahn, J. V. (1988). Review of special education: A source book. *American Journal on Mental Retardation, 92*, 550–551.

Kranzler, J. H., & Jensen, A. R. (1991). The nature of psychometric g: Unitary process or a number of independent processes? *Intelligence, 15*, 397–422.

Lachiewicz, A. M., Spiridigliozzi, G. A., Gullion, C. M., Ransford, S. N., & Rao, K. (1994). Aberrant behaviors of young boys with fragile X syndrome. *American Journal on Mental Retardation, 98*, 567–579.

Lenke, R. R., & Levy, H. L. (1980). Maternal phenylketonaria and hyperphenylalaninemia—An international study of outcome of treated and untreated pregnancies. *New England Journal of M4edicine, 303*, 1202–1208.

Lewis, M. H., & Baumeister, A. A. (1982). Stereotyped mannerisms in mentally retarded persons: Animal models and theoretical analyses. In N. R. Ellis (Ed.), *International review of research in mental retardation* (Vol. 11, pp. 124–161). New York: Academic Press.

Luckasson, R., Coulter, D. L., Polloway, E. A., Reiss, S., Schalock, R. L., Snell, M. E., Spitalnik, D. M., & Stark, J. A. (1992). *Mental retardation: Definition, classification, and systems of supports* (9th ed.). Washington, DC: American Association on Mental Retardation.

MacMillan, D. L., Gresham, F. M., & Siperstein, G. N. (1993). Conceptual and psychometric concerns about the 1992 definition of mental retardation. *American Journal on Mental Retardation, 98*, 325–335.

Magaret, A., & Thompson, C. W. (1950). Differential test responses of normal, superior, and mentally defective subjects. *Journal of Abnormal and Social Psychology, 45*, 163–167.

McGaughey, P., Starfield, B., Alexander, C., & Ensminger, M. (1991). The social environment and vulnerability of low birthweight children: A social-epidemiological perspective. *Pediatrics, 88*, 954–953.

McGee, J. J. (1992). Gentle teaching's assumptions and paradigm. *Journal of Applied Behavior Analysis, 25*, 869–872.

McPherson, M. W. (1948). A survey of experimental studies of learning in individuals who receive subnormal ratings on standardized psychometric measures. *American Journal of Mental Deficiency, 52*, 232–254.

Mental Retardation and Developmental Disabilities Branch. (1993). *Report to council.* Bethesda, MD: National Institute of Child Health and Human Development.

Mudford, O. C. (1995). Review of the gentle teaching data. *American Journal on Mental Retardation, 99*, 345–355.

Petrinovich, L. (1979). Probabilistic functionalism: A conception of research method. *American Psychologist, 34*, 373–390.

Ramey, C. T. (1993). A rejoinder to Spitz's critique of the Abecedarian experiment. *Intelligence, 17*, 25–30.

Ramey, C. T., Bryant, D. M., Wasik, B. H., Sparling, J. J., Fendt, K. H., & LaVange, L. M. (1992). Infant health and development program for low birthwight, premature infants: Program elements, family participation, and child intelligence. *Pediatrics, 89*, 454–465.

Ramey, C. T., & Ramey, S. L. (1992). Effective early intervention. *Mental Retardation, 30*, 337–345.

Ramey, S. L., & Ramey, C. T. (1992). Early educational intervention with disadvantaged children—To what effect? *Applied and Preventive Psychology, 1*, 130–140.

Rowitz, L. (1988). The homogenization of deviance. *Mental Retardation, 26*, 1–3.

Rutter, M. (1982). Prevention of children's psychosocial disorders: Myths and substance. *Pediatrics, 70*, 883–894.

Sameroff, A. J. (1983). Developmental systems: Contexts and evolution. In W. Kessen (Ed.), *Handbook of child psychology: Vol. I. History, theories, and methods* (pp. 238–294). New York: Wiley.

Sameroff, A. J., & Fiese, B. H. (1991). Transactional regulation and early intervention. In S. J. Meisels & J. P. Shonkoff (Eds.), *Handbook of early childhood intervention* (pp. 119–149). New York: Cambridge University Press.

Sameroff, A. J., Seifer, R., Barocas, B., Zax, M., & Greenspan, S. (1987). IQ scores of 4-year-old children: Social environmental risk factors. *Pediatrics, 79*, 343–350.

Schroeder, S. (1991). Ad hoc Committee on Research Advocacy. *Psychology in Mental Retardation and Developmental Disabilities, 16*, 11–12.

Scotti, J. R., Evans, I. M., Meyer, L. H., & DiBenedetto, A. (1991). Individual repertoires as behavioral systems: Implications for program design and evaluation. In B. Remington (Ed.), The challenge of severe mental handicap (pp. 139–161). New York: Wiley.

Scotti, J. R., Evans, I. M., Meyer, L. H., & Walker, P. (1991). A meta-analysis of intervention research with problem behavior: Treatment validity and standards of practice. *American Journal on Mental Retardation, 96*, 233–256.

Siperstein, G. N., Wolraich, M. L., & Reed, D. (1994). Professionals' prognoses for individuals with mental retardation: Search for consensus within interdisciplinary settings. *American Journal on Mental Retardation, 98*, 519–526.

Spitz, H. H. (1986). *The raising of intelligence: A selected history of attempts to raise retarded intelligence.* Hillsdale, NJ: Lawrence Erlbaum Associates.

Spitz, H. H. (1992). Does the Carolina Abecedarian early intervention project prevent mental prevent mental retardation? *Intelligence, 16*, 225–237.

Spitz, H. H. (1993). When prophecy fails: On Ramey's response to Spitz's critique of the Abecedarian Project. *Intelligence, 17,* 17–23.

Sternberg, R. J. (1981). Cognitive–behavioral approaches to training of intelligence in the retarded. *Journal of Special Education, 15,* 165–183.

Sternberg, R. J. (1984). Macrocomponents and microcomponents of intelligence: Some proposed loci of mental retardation. In P. H. Brooks, R. Sperber, & C. McCauley (Eds.), *Learning and cognition in the mentally retarded* (pp. 89–114). Hillsdale, NJ: Lawrence Erlbaum Associates.

Sternlicht, M. (1987). *Special education: A source book.* New York: Garland.

Sweetman, L. (1991). Organic acid analysis. In F. Hommes (Ed.), *Techniques in diagnostic human biochemical genetics* (pp. 143–176). New York: Wiley Liss.

Thompson, C. W., & Magaret, A. (1947). Differential test responses of normals and mental defectives. *Journal of Abnormal and Social Psychology, 42,* 285–293.

United States General Accounting Office. (1994, October 31). *Early childhood programs: Multiple programs and overlapping target groups* (GAO/HEHS-95-4FS). Washington, DC: U.S. Government Printing Office.

Wachs, T. D. (1992). *The nature of nurture.* Newbury Park, CA: Sage.

Weisz, J. R., & Zigler, E. (1979). Cognitive development in retarded and nonretarded persons. *Psychological Bulletin, 86,* 831–851.

Werner, E. E. (1991). Protective factors and individual resilience. In S. J. Meisels & J. P. Shonkoff (Eds.), *Handbook of early childhood intervention* (pp. 97–116). New York: Cambridge University Press.

Wilson, R. S. (1985). Risk and resilience in early development. *Developmental Psychology, 21,* 795–805.

Zigler, E. (1978). National crisis in mental retardation research. *American Journal of Mental Deficiency, 83,* 1–8.

Zigler, E. F. (1992). Early childhood intervention: a promising preventative for juvenile delinquency. *American Psychologist, 47,* 997–1006.

Zigler, E., & Hodapp, R. M. (1986). *Understanding mental retardation.* New York: Cambridge University Press.

› 2 ‹

Issues of Definition and Classification

Donald L. MacMillan
University of California at Riverside

Daniel J. Reschly
Iowa State University

Definitions of mental retardation have "extra scientific" importance given that an individual so classified qualifies for specialized services and may also be denied certain rights under the law that are guaranteed to citizens of a society. Kuhlman (1924) wrote, "Definitions of Mental Deficiency have an extra scientific interest . . . they decide the fate of thousands of human beings every year and are intimately related to social welfare in general" (p. 58). Interest in, and debate over, definitions of mental retardation appear to have elevated since the American Association on Mental Deficiency[1] published its manual on terminology and classification (Heber, 1959; revised 1961). Although this definition was not endorsed by all in the field (see Clausen, 1967; Kidd, 1964), the AAMR definition of 1961 became the most widely used and influential definition of its day—influencing the wording of state-level education codes and legislation concerned with individuals with mental retardation.

Historical accounts of the field of mental retardation (Cranefield & Federn, 1963; Kanner, 1964; Scheerenberger, 1983) recount how societies initially recognized individuals who were "different," although these primitive classification systems did not differentiate between those who were mentally ill and those with mental retardation. Nevertheless, among those people identified as "different" were some cases that would be classified as mentally retarded today. Doll (1962) noted some early attempts at defining mental retardation, or at least distinguishing it from other conditions. Fitzherbert in the *New Natura Brevium* (1534) wrote:

> And he who shall be said to be a sot (i. e., simpleton) and idiot from his birth, is such a person who cannot account or number twenty pence, nor can tell who was his father or mother, nor how old he is, etc., so as it may appear that he hath no understanding of reason what shall be

[1]This organization is now known as the American Association on Mental Retardation (AAMR), and throughout this manuscript we will refer it as AAMR, even when referring to a time period when it was formally AAMD.

> for his profit nor what for his loss. But if he hath such understanding, that he know and understand his letters, and do read by teaching or information of another man, then it seemeth he is not a sot nor a natural idiot. (Doll, 1962, p. 23)

Later, in 1690, John Locke distinguished between insanity and mental retardation as follows:

> Herein seems to lie the difference between idiots and madmen, that madmen put wrong ideas together and reason from them, but idiots make very few or no propositions and reason scarce at all. (Doll, 1962, p. 23)

Distinguishing among various types of disorders took on greater importance once services were available to those classified and efforts were made to study, and understand, the conditions being differentiated. That is, if one attempted to study individuals with mental illness and mental retardation without differentiating them, such efforts were hampered by including "apples with oranges." By the same token, if persons with mental disorders and those with mental retardation needed different treatments and/or services, the failure to differentiate between them may obscure the effectiveness of various treatment efforts. The scientific study of mental retardation and efforts to provide services to individuals with mental retardation began in the late 1800s and early 1900s, when people began seeing some serious efforts to describe or define those individuals in need of services or those to serve as subjects in research. Let us review briefly some of the efforts to define mental retardation.

Core Issues in the Mental Retardation Diagnostic Construct

Accurate classification is one of the prerequisites to scientific understanding of natural phenomena. Efforts to classify human performance phenomena typically must address five fundamental issues: purpose(s), relevant dimensions, criteria for defining cases, etiology and prognosis, and comorbidity (i.e., diagnostic overlap with other classification categories when one has two conditions at the same time). Each of these issues has been addressed in different ways over the history of classification efforts in mental retardation.

Purposes. Purposes for classification vary from meeting the need for basic communication among interested persons to establishing the group for whom expensive services are provided by law. Depending on purpose, the classification may be more or less inclusive, and persons with different perspectives (legislators who must appropriate funds vs. advocates who wish to serve all deserving persons) often attempt to promote less or more inclusive interpretations of existing diagnostic constructs.

Dimensions. The dimensions characteristic refers to the behaviors that are of interest in describing the persons who meet the criteria for a particular diagnostic construct. The dimensions of intellectual functioning and social competence have been fundamental to most definitions of mental retardation; however, the relative importance, conceptions of, and relationships between these dimensions have varied markedly in different classification schemes proposed over the years in the field of mental retardation.

Criteria. The criteria used to determine the kind and level of performance on the behavioral dimensions in order for individuals to be correctly classified are crucial to the use of the diagnostic construct. Progress in mental retardation has been hampered by use of widely varying criteria to identify cases, rendering much of the existing research difficult to interpret (MacMillan, Meyers, & Morrison, 1980) and seriously complicating efforts to provide services.

Etiology and Prognosis. The cause(s) and outcomes associated with the behavioral syndrome may or may not be included in the diagnostic construct. The historical trend in mental retardation has been to place less emphasis on specifying etiology and prognosis as essential characteristics of the diagnostic construct.

Comorbidity. The degree to which overlap with other diagnostic entities is recognized constitutes a subtle but increasingly important feature of a particular diagnostic construct. The huge fluctuations in mild mental retardation prevalence observed in recent years might be reconceptualized as a problem in comorbidity of mild mental retardation and specific learning disabilities. If the changes in detection rates are related to comorbidity, then most of the cases in recent years appear to have been classified as learning disabled rather than mentally retarded. Comorbidity issues are fundamental to the integrity of the diagnostic construct. If the behavioral dimensions and classification criteria are expanded excessively to incorporate more and more cases, perhaps as a socially acceptable means to provide services, the diagnostic constructs progressively lose meaning and usefulness. In such circumstances, changes must be made in one or both of the diagnostic constructs.

Scholars and service providers in mental retardation have struggled with these issues for over two centuries. Modern conceptions of mental retardation have not resolved these issues; however, the historical record as well as modern conceptions can be understood and evaluated in terms of how well these issues were addressed.

Historical Background

Formal emergence of the diagnostic construct now referred to as mental retardation can be found in Western Europe as the result of efforts of French physicians and educators. The pioneering efforts of Itard and Esquirol identified a human condition wherein deficient or retarded mental operations resulted in an inability to cope with everyday demands. Itard's careful description of his treatment procedures and the performance of his subjects initiated the scientific study of mental retardation (Doll, 1962, 1967). In addition, in the 1830s Esquirol provided the earliest distinction between levels of retardation in the 1830s when he identified *idiots* and *imbeciles*, distinguished on the basis of the degree of deficiency in intellectual and coping skills as well as responsiveness to intervention procedures (Doll, 1962). By the 1850s, mental retardation was distinguished from other mental diseases and was essentially regarded as a condition of arrested development as opposed to a disease entity (Reschly, 1992). The scientific study of the condition was extended dramatically by the work of Edward Seguin, who was also instrumental in the formation of the "Association of Medical Officers of American Institutions for Idiotic and Feebleminded Persons," which would become AAMR. Proceedings of the annual meetings of this organization have been published continuously since 1876 (Sloan & Stevens, 1976), and document a history of debate over terminology and classification.

It should be noted that the study of mental retardation prior to 1900 focused almost exclusively on conditions that would be considered profound, severe, or moderate mental retardation under recent guidelines. That is to say, individuals considered mentally retarded were those with probable central nervous system damage and functioning at a level that was clearly unacceptable regardless of the society in which they lived or the context in which the behavior was observed (e.g., rural or urban settings, community or school). During the very early 1900s, following compulsory attendance laws being passed, the public schools began classes for children (called "ungraded" classes) who differed substantially from those individuals previously classified as mentally retarded (Hendrick & MacMillan, 1989). Placement in these classes was based on the apparent inability of students to cope with the regular school curriculum; a phenomenon found more often among recent immigrant groups and children from low socioeconomic status homes. Such classes predated the use of intelligence tests by more than ten years and were created in response to a very practical problem—how to cope with students who displayed marked and persistent academic problems.

Overlapping with the segment of students placed in these ungraded classes was a group referred to by Goddard (1912) and others (e.g., Terman, 1917) as "feebleminded" individuals, a group of considerable interest from the early 1900s until the 1930s. Reschly (1992) noted that this period (1905–1930) was dominated by two trends: the eugenics movement and the development, dissemination, and restandardization of the Binet method of assessing intellectual functioning. The eugenics movement alleged the prolific reproductive propensities of feebleminded individuals, whose intellectual functioning was higher than that of the previously identified mentally retarded individuals yet not sufficiently high to succeed in school.

The social attitudes dominant in the early 1900s certainly played a role in shaping special education services made available to this feebleminded group of students. Most prominent of these attitudes in the minds of educated Americans were the orthodox and reform varieties of Social Darwinism. The orthodox form led its adherents to view new immigrants as hopelessly defective, and to recommend various forms of segregation. When applied to the mentally retarded, the treatments that followed were even more severe. The "eugenics scare" was fueled by publication of several investigations (Dugdale, 1877; Goddard, 1912) that purported to show that this mild form of mental retardation ran in families and was inevitably manifested in criminality, immoral behavior, and the need for public assistance. Strong position papers (e.g., Pitkin, 1928) advocated treatment policies and placements that would protect society from this perceived menace. Among the policies enacted widely to control the threat of mental retardation were segregation and sterilization (Kanner, 1964).

Subsequent developments in the field would blunt the impact of the eugenics scare, and the evidence on which it was based would be roundly criticized (see Sarason & Doris, 1969; Smith, 1985). Furthermore, many highly regarded scholars of the day were aligned with the eugenics position, and expressed concern over the menace of the mildly retarded and the need to control them. Consider the following commentary by Lewis Terman (1917):

> Feebleminded school children are present everywhere. They linger in the third, fourth, fifth, and sixth grades until well into adolescent years. They consume a disproportionate amount of the teacher's time, they drag down the standards of achievement for normal children, they tend to become incorrigible and to feed the never ending stream of juvenile court cases. . . . Not until the borderline cases have been placed in special classes, can the work of the school with normal children proceed as it ought. Feebleminded children in the regular classes not only interfere with instruction, they are also likely to be a source of moral contagion. (p. 164)

The eugenics movement, however, began prior to the IQ test developments (Reschly, 1992); nevertheless, when the Binet scales were brought to the United States and administered widely, the findings were interpreted by some to confirm the threat described by Goddard and others.

Reschly (1992) noted that the development and dissemination of the Binet method within a 10-year period was, in fact, dramatic. The subsequent influence of this method on the conceptualization of mental retardation as well as on definitional criteria and diagnostic operations was profound. From 1910 to 1940 the intellectual functioning domain dominated the conceptualization of mental retardation, and the use of IQ tests was central to criteria and diagnostic operations.

AAMR published its first official classification scheme in 1921. This scheme recognized three levels of mental retardation, defined by IQ ranges: *moron* (IQ 50–75), *imbecile* (IQ 25–50), and *idiot* (IQ less than 25). The definition and the criteria for diagnosing individuals relied almost exclusively on the IQ test, most often operationalized through application of the Stanford revision of the Binet method (Terman, 1916). Note that this approach assumes that mental retardation relies exclusively on intellectual functioning, with little attention to other dimensions such as social competence or etiology.

In sharp contrast, Edgar A. Doll (1934, 1941) advanced the notion of social competence. In 1941, Doll published a definition of mental retardation: "a state of social incompetence obtaining at maturity, or likely to obtain at maturity, resulting from developmental arrest of constitutional origin (heredity or acquired); the condition is essentially incurable through treatment and unremediable through training" (p. 215). Doll proposed six criteria for determining mental retardation: (a) social incompetence, (b) due to mental subnormality, (c) which has been developmentally arrested, (d) which obtains at maturity, (e) is of constitutional origin, and (f) is essentially incurable. Reschly (1992) observed that although Doll's definition was never officially endorsed by AAMR, his criteria were very influential throughout the 1940s and 1950s. Furthermore, the social incompetence criteria was viewed as secondary to, or caused by, the mental incompetence. Measures of intellectual functioning were readily available, whereas the measures of social competence were either nonexistent or far less precise than those for measuring intelligence. As a result, IQ continued to dominate as the major definitional criterion, and was central to any diagnostic operations.

In 1952, the American Psychiatric Association (APA) published its first *Diagnostic and Statistical Manual of Mental Disorders* (*DSM-I*), and employed a single term—"mental deficiency"—and specified three levels of severity: *mild deficiency*, *moderate deficiency*, and *severe deficiency*. The three levels were associated with IQ ranges of 70–85, 50–69, and 0–49, respectively. The IQ ranges are noteworthy, particularly because the mild category was associated with higher IQs than had been used previously. In fact, the higher IQ ranges did not correspond to cutoff scores employed by AAMR, which, at the time, was not considering someone with an IQ as high as 85 as possibly mentally retarded.

Situation in 1950s

Efforts to define mental retardation became complicated by the progressive broadening of the construct that occurred during the first half of the century (see Clausen, 1967, for a discussion). As noted previously, those individuals identified as mentally retarded initially were very low functioning, and their deficiencies were obvious across settings. Moreover, the cases invariably involved some central nervous system damage, which was frequently accompanied by physical stigmata associated with chromosomal anomalies. In short, the individuals classified as mentally retarded deviated markedly from others in the society, and decisions regarding classification as mentally retarded did not require fine-grained discriminations. However, as the feebleminded group emerged and were subsumed under the general rubric of mental retardation, the existence of "two groups" of mentally retarded individuals became evident and a number of problems emerged. First, the "deficiency" of this milder group was one of degree rather than kind. Second, their intellectual functioning could not, in most cases, be traced to central nervous system damage, per se, and they showed none of the physical stigmata found in many of the more severe cases. And third, the fact that most cases of feeblemindedness were to be found in the low social classes of society and frequently among recent immigrant groups made it difficult to distinguish between mental retardation and the effects of deprivation and/or cultural differences. Recognition of these qualitative differences has come in the form of the "two-group approach" to mental retardation (Zigler, 1967; Zigler, Balla, & Hodapp, 1984; Zigler & Hodapp, 1986).

As Clausen (1967) observed, the concept of mental deficiency expanded dramatically during the first half of the 20th century; an expansion that subsumed greater proportions of the general population, involved increasingly greater numbers of professions and disciplines, and shifted in the relative importance of different parameters defining the condition (i.e., intellectual functioning, social competence).

The stage was then set for the publication of the AAMR manual on terminology and classification (Heber, 1959; revised, 1961). Some conceptual issues faced the field as it attempted to draft a definition acceptable to a constituency representing medicine, education, psychology, social work, sociology, anthropology, and assorted other disciplines and professions with a vested interest in mental retardation. Among the issues was the relative weighting of intellectual functioning versus social competence, whether mental retardation was incurable, how to treat comorbidity and the relativity (or contextual nature) of mental retardation, and the utility of degree of retardation versus etiology in creating subgroups. These issues have proven to be vexing to the field, and although decisions have been made by various committees, these decisions have not met with universal endorsement.

GENERAL CONSIDERATIONS IN CLASSIFICATION IN MENTAL RETARDATION

Qualitative–Quantitative Distinction

Two competing models confront those attempting to define mental retardation—models that Keogh and MacMillan (in press) described as qualitative and quantitative models. In essence, the question can be posed as whether mental retardation be viewed as a separate and discrete syndrome that qualitatively differs from the norm or as an extreme on a continuum, in which case differences are quantified by degree. The qualitative–quantitative question is fundamental in the conceptualization and definition of mental retardation and influences decisions about assessment, identification, and treatment. The qualitative approach, characteristic of medical approaches, has historically been applied to the more severely mentally retarded individuals and to biologically based conditions. The quantitative perspective, characteristic of psychological approaches, has been applied to milder forms of mental retardation in which pathology cannot, or has not, been demonstrated. This approach has relied on psychometric, statistical models of definition and identification emphasizing one's position on an assumed normal curve, with cutoff points being expressed as deviations from the norm.

Mercer's (1973, 1979) conceptions of the medical and social system models of deviance are analogous to the qualitative and quantitative dimensions. According to Mercer, the distinguishing features of the medical model were biologically based behavioral deficits that were likely to be disabling regardless of social role, setting, or cultural background. In contrast, the social system model of deviance refers to deficits that exist due to discrepancies in behavior from expectations that occur within the context of particular social role(s) and setting(s). The social system forms of deviance are deeply rooted within cultural contexts and cannot be separated from that context.

The qualitative (medical model) and quantitative (social system) models gain relevance when mental retardation classification criteria are applied cross-culturally. Mental retardation based on qualitative (medical model) deficits appears to be about the same in terms of prevalence, symptomatology, etiology, and prognosis regardless of racial, ethnic, or cultural setting. In contrast, cases of mental retardation based on quantitative differences, in which there are not qualitative or biologically based indices of deviance, are markedly different in terms of prevalence as a function of racial, ethnic, and cultural factors. Whether the latter cases also vary according to symptomatology, etiology, and prognosis is the subject of debate (cf., Koegel & Edgerton, 1984; Mercer, 1973).

The qualitative–quantitative, biological–social system distinctions are related to very real differences in the number and characteristics of persons who may be diagnosed as mentally retarded. Traditional mental retardation prevalence estimates of 2% to 3% (MacMillan, 1982; Robinson & Robinson, 1976) generally assume that the mental retardation population includes both kinds of deficits. Restriction of cases of mental retardation to the qualitative differences–medical model leads to prevalence estimates that are markedly lower, by as much as a factor of 10 times lower, than the traditional estimates (Heflinger, Cook, & Thackery, 1987; Kazimour & Reschly, 1981; Reschly, 1981). Recent prevalence data suggest that some states are restricting mental retardation to medical model cases (this is discussed more fully in a later section).

Functions of Categories

Zigler and Phillips (1961) observed that the nature of categories or classes and definitional criteria vary, in part as a function of purpose. Keogh (1993) described that categories can be useful for advocacy, service provision, or research—however, she noted that nets cast for these varied purposes do not catch the same individuals. A broadly defined and nonspecific category may be desirable for advocacy or when securing services; however, such imprecision poses serious threats when employed in an effort to conduct experimental research. This point should be kept in mind as we consider controversy surrounding various definitions of mental retardation that have been proposed or adopted. Stakeholders whose primary concern is service delivery wish to identify all who need and will benefit from services, while at the same time avoiding identification of those who do not require, nor will benefit from, available services. Stakeholders whose primary concern is research attempt to identify a population with known parameters in order that samples can be drawn to represent that population and permit findings to be generalized to a known population. Some of the debate precipitated by definitions of mental retardation can be explained by different perspectives (service delivery vs. research) taken by opponents in such debates.

The classification issue is further complicated by problems of identification, that is, the process of assigning individuals to classes. Whereas classification is conceptual, identification is measurement bound (Bailey, 1973), and thus is threatened by inappropriate and/or technically inadequate measures, and by flawed applications and interpretations (Keogh & MacMillan, in press). As a consequence, assignment of individuals to classes, especially broadly defined classes, does not guarantee homogeneity of characteristics, muddying considerably the efforts of researchers to test methods and evaluate interventions.

In the following pages, we attempt to explore the issues surrounding efforts to define mental retardation, diagnose individuals as mentally retarded, and to establish a classification system. Such a treatment is timely, because AAMR has adopted a new definition (Luckasson, 1992) that has already prompted criticism (e.g., Jacobson & Mulick, 1992: MacMillan, Gresham, & Siperstein, 1993, 1995). Contemporary definitions of mental retardation have relied heavily on the AAMR definition published initially in 1959 that resulted from a committee effort, chaired by Rick Heber, to develop a consensus definition of mental retardation.

DEFINITIONS OF THE 1960s

Since publication of the Heber (1959, 1961) definition, there has been rather close agreement between the American Psychiatric Association (APA) *Diagnostic and Statistical Manual* (*DSM*) and the AAMR *Manual on Terminology and Classification* in the conceptions of mental retardation. That is, *DSM–II*, published in 1968, closely resembles the AAMR scheme published in 1959 to 1961, whereas *DSM–III* is very similar to the AAMR revisions edited by Grossman (1973, 1977, 1983).

Heber originally defined mental retardation as referring to subaverage general intellectual functioning and being associated with impairment in one or more of the following: maturation, learning, or social adjustment. However, in the 1961 revision, the definition was slightly altered to read: "mental retardation refers to subaverage general intellectual functioning which originates during the developmental period and is associated with impairment in adaptive behavior" (Heber, 1961, p. 3). It is noteworthy that this definition accomplished several goals—taking positions on certain issues that had circulated for years but had never been resolved. First, the concept of adaptive behavior was included as a classificatory principle defining mental retardation. General intellectual functioning and adaptive behavior clearly constituted the behavioral components of the conceptual basis for mental retardation (along with the age at onset). Identification procedures would entail the use of individually administered standardized tests of general ability—usually the Stanford–Binet or one of the Wechsler scales. Adaptive behavior, on the other hand, was included as a definitional parameter that was not, at the time, readily operationalized—that is, standardized scales were not available and decision rules on cutoff scores could not be established. The psychometric community would have to devise scales for assessing adaptive behavior, while clinicians and researchers awaited their development in order to identify cases that met the definition. In terms of the relative emphasis placed on these two behavioral dimensions, the 1961 definition gave primary emphasis to intellectual functioning and secondary emphasis to adaptive behavior (Reschly, 1992).

The Heber-era AAMR definition established five levels of mental retardation, each defined in terms of standard deviation units and denoted by adjectives: borderline mental retardation, mild mental retardation, moderate mental retardation, severe mental retardation, and profound mental retardation. This same classification by degree of mental retardation was adopted in the *DSM–II* scheme. Several observations seem in order, considering the effort to create more homogeneous subgroups. First, although the definition stressed *two* behavioral domains (intellectual functioning and adaptive behavior), levels of mental retardation were based exclusively on the intellectual dimension. Second, the inclusion of the borderline group would prove to be very controversial. By extending the upper IQ limit to −1 *SD*, or approximately IQ 85, the percentage of the general population eligible on the IQ dimension approached 16% as opposed to 2% to 3% eligible under the traditional cutoff scores of 70 or 75. As is discussed later, the borderline group would include disproportionately high rates of cases from certain minority group and/or low socioeconomic status families. Finally, the decision to classify by degree of mental retardation and to operationalize the definition in terms of IQ was at odds with educational practices, which employed subgrouping by degree in terms of broad-band categories such as educable mentally retarded and trainable mentally retarded, and with "the most common and basic of the differentiated conceptualizations of mental retardation" (Burack, 1990, p. 30) that distinguish among cases of mental retardation of differing etiologies.

The 1959–1961 AAMR scheme also avoided taking a position on the issues of prognosis and etiology. The scheme adopted focused exclusively on *current functioning level,* thereby acknowledging the possibility that an individual could be accurately diagnosed as mentally retarded at one time in the developmental period, but later function normally and not warrant classification. This ran counter to Doll's (1941) requirement that "the condition is essentially incurable through treatment and unremediable through training" (p. 215). Moreover, the position reflected a rejection of earlier conceptions of intelligence as fixed and was consistent with the "environmental position" advanced in the early 1960s by scholars such as J. M. Hunt (1961) and Benjamin Bloom (1964). The focus on current functioning and acceptance of the possibility of "shifting status" led to formulations on the *relativity of mental retardation* to environmental demands as individuals moved or matured. This, in turn, would result in terms such as "pseudoretardation" and the "six-hour retardate" being invoked to capture subtle nuances in the adaptation of individuals being relative to environments and sentiments concerning current functioning.

The definitions of the 1960s clearly reflected a belief that the definition should be *inclusive* in the sense that no children should be denied treatments and services available to mentally retarded children who might benefit from such services. However, establishing such a liberal upper IQ cutoff in the absence of psychometrically sound scales of adaptive behavior rendered decision making on eligibility in cases of the borderline IQ range hazardous at best. In practice, Reschly (1992) observed that for school-age children and youth, who accounted for the majority of detected cases of mental retardation, "low achievement as assessed by standardized measures of achievement along with referral for academic difficulties was sufficient to constitute a deficit in adaptive behavior" (p. 33). As a consequence, eligibility decisions in cases of borderline and mild mental retardation often proceeded as if the teacher referral of the child accompanied by reports of poor academic performance *established* the impairments in adaptive behavior. The diagnostic process then consisted of an assessment of the child on a test of intelligence to determine whether the poor academic performance that led to referral could be properly attributed to low general intellectual functioning.

Challenges to the Definitions of the 1960s

Adaptive Behavior. Including adaptive behavior as determinative of mental retardation in the AAMR and *DSM–II* schemes posed a series of problems and led to criticism by scholars in the field (Clausen, 1967, 1968, 1972; Zigler, Balla, & Hodapp, 1984; Zigler & Hodapp, 1986), particularly because it introduced error into the classification system. The essence of the criticism directed by these scholars at the 1960s definition was that adaptive behavior was elusive and that existing scales were inadequate, particularly when used in suspected cases of borderline and mild mental retardation. In the absence of adequate scales, clinicians either accepted the behavior that led to referral (e.g., poor academic performance, grade repetition) as evidence of impaired adaptive behavior *or* used clinical judgment. Clausen (1967) noted that because one determinative behavioral dimension required for diagnosis could not be assessed (i.e., adaptive behavior), one could not be certain that cases diagnosed and labeled mentally retarded in fact met the definition of mental retardation. He also observed that the rate of congruence between low IQ and impaired adaptive behavior decreased as one progressed from lower IQs, say IQ 50, toward the upper limit defining mental retardation—at the time, IQ = 85. He argued that a psychometric definition using IQ = 70 as the cutoff should be adopted because: (a) existing practices at the time used a single psychometric criterion anyway, and (b) if the upper IQ level were set at 70, most individuals scoring below that level exhibit impaired adaptive behavior by most any standard. Essentially, Clausen's contention was that cases of mental retardation were being clinically diagnosed on a single behavioral dimension despite the definition calling for two dimensions to be assessed. MacMillan (1992) characterized the situation as one in which some children who are qualified as having mental retardation would fail to meet the definition were reliable assessment of adaptation possible, whereas other children who are judged as unqualified would meet the definition were reliable measures of adaptation available.

Edward Zigler arrived at the same recommendation, although he did so via a somewhat different route. Zigler has repeatedly expressed concern over the unreliability of the classification scheme for mental retardation introduced by including adaptive behavior in the definition. The lack of reliable scales of adaptive behavior and the use of clinical judgment results in low agreement between classifiers concerning whether or not impaired adaptive behavior exists. This, in turn, leads to unreliability in classification decisions. High interrater agreement is the cornerstone of any classification system because an individual's membership in a given class is independent of the person doing the classification. Zigler and Hodapp (1986) illustrated this point employing a simple definition of social adaptation for an adult, whether or not he or she is employed. They posed the question whether a "65 IQ man who holds a job is not retarded. Yet if he is laid off, on the day his employment terminates he becomes retarded" (p. 66).

Cases near the upper limit defining mental retardation are the ones whose plight hinges on the adequacy of scales for measuring adaptive behavior or the acumen of a clinician's judgment of their adaptive status. In cases of very low IQ (e.g., < 50), impaired adaptive behavior invariably accompanies the low IQ—and does so across varying contexts (school, home, community) and developmental stages. The probability that both IQ and measured or clinically determined adaptive behavior will be low as one proceeds from IQ 50 up the intellectual continuum toward IQ 85 progressively declines. In keeping, the chance for error in classification increases as one ascends the IQ continuum toward the upper IQ cutoff.

Intellectual Dimension. Although intelligence tests have become a central issue in litigation (*Diana v. State Board of Education, Larry P. v. Riles*) on the alleged grounds that they discriminate against certain minority group children, there are other issues concerning the use of intelligence tests for defining mental retardation that, although less celebrated, warrant attention. As long as intelligence constitutes one of the behavior dimensions (or the only one) defining mental retardation and tests of intelligence are used to assess that dimension, it is essential that some awareness of psychometrics be reflected in operationalizing cutoff scores. It is obvious from a review of the literature that the setting of an upper IQ limit defining mental retardation is an arbitrary decision. Over the past 30 years, the upper IQ limit has varied considerably in the various definitions adopted by AAMR. The upper limit has been specified in standard deviation units and in absolute IQ scores—being set at –1 *SD* (Heber, 1961), –2 *SD*s (Grossman, 1973, 1977), IQ 70 (Grossman, 1983; permitting identification of cases up to IQ 75, see p. 23), to IQ 75

(Luckasson, 1992). Although these decisions are arbitrary, traditionally the upper limit has been set at either 70 or 75.

Despite the arbitrariness in setting the upper limit, one must not be misled into thinking that such decisions are insignificant or trivial. Very slight shifts in the upper limit have rather dramatic consequences in terms of the percentage of the population eligible. For example, a shift from IQ 70 and below to a criterion of IQ 75 and below results in *twice as many people being eligible.* Because of the acceleration of the curve in this portion of the normal curve, there are more cases falling in the interval of 71 to 75 (2.80%) than in the entire range scoring IQ 70 and below (2.68%). The consequences of these subtle shifts in the upper IQ defining mental retardation can be seen in Table 2.1.

Application of more or less stringent cutoff scores also influences the degree of potential overrepresentation of disadvantaged minority students. The degree of overrepresentation can be expected to be larger when higher, rather than lower, cutoff scores are employed due to the nature of the distributions of intellectual performance. As expected, Reschly and Jipson (1976) did report greater degrees of overrepresentation for African-American, Hispanic, and Native American children at the IQ cutoff score of 75 than at 70.

Another bit of mischief is introduced when tests of intelligence yield different distributions for different groups (e.g., males vs. females, or African-American vs. White). In essence, different distributions result in certain groups being at greater risk for being identified as mentally retarded. Kaufman and Doppelt (1976) analyzed the standardization data on the WISC–R and noted that the distribution of IQs for African-Americans and Whites differed in rather important ways. These data are plotted in Fig. 2.1. In this figure it is apparent that significantly different proportions of the two distributions fall below the cutoff scores of 85 (used by Heber, 1961) and 70 (used by Grossman, 1973). MacMillan (1992) discussed these data as they pertain to eligibility for services as mentally retarded and learning disabled. By subtracting the mean value for each ethnic group from the IQ cutoff score and dividing by that ethnic group's standard deviation, one obtains *z* scores that permit estimation of the percent falling above and below the arbitrary cutoff scores, which are shown in Table 2.2.

This exercise illustrates the differential eligibility of White and African-American children on the general intellectual functioning criterion. Whether the expected overrepresentation of African-American children actually occurs will depend on system-identification factors (MacMillan, Meyers, & Morrison, 1980) and the extent to which assessment of adaptive skills serves to detect "false positives" deemed eligible on the IQ criterion. Hence, the assessment of adaptive behavior becomes crucial in determining whether children meet the definition of mental retardation.

TABLE 2.1
Proportion of the Population Falling Below Certain IQ Cutoffs and Falling Within Certain IQ Intervals

IQ	*Normal Curve Percentage*
Below 70	2.28%
70 and below	2.68
Below 75	4.75
75 and below	5.48
IQ Interval	*Percentage Within Interval*
56–60	0.30%
61–65	0.69
66–70	1.52
71–75	2.80

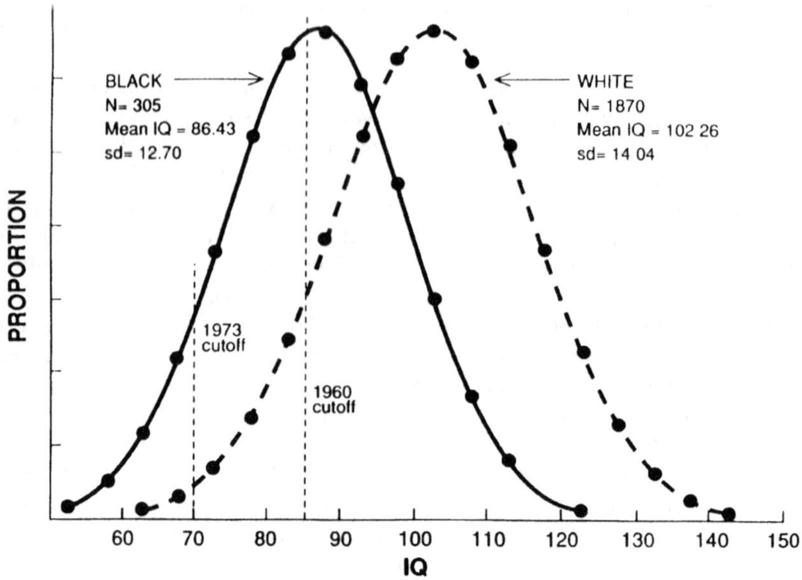

FIG. 2.1. WISC–R full-scale IQ distributions for Black and White children. (Based on Kaufman & Doppelt, 1976. Analysis of WISC–R standardization data in terms of the stratification variables. Data from Table 1.) From MacMillan (1992). Copyright © 1993, Paul H. Brookes Publishing Co. Reprinted with permission.

TABLE 2.2
Percentage of African Americans and Whites Eligible Under Three Cutting Scores on the WISC–R

	Percentage Eligible at IQ Level		
Ethnic Group	*IQ 70 and Below*	*IQ 75 and Below*	*IQ 85 and Below*
African-American	9.85%	18.4%	45.6%
White	1.07	2.62	10.9

The type of intellectual measure also influences the prevalence of mental retardation among different groups. In a study of mental retardation prevalence among four sociocultural groups, Reschly and Jipson (1976) reported markedly higher prevalence of cases eligible for the mental retardation diagnosis among Hispanic and Native American children when a verbal IQ score was used. When the nonverbal measure, Wechsler Performance IQ, was used, the overrepresentation of Hispanic and Native American children in mental retardation was virtually eliminated; however, overrepresentation of African-American children was about the same regardless of type of intellectual measure. The use of nonverbal measures, often thought to be less culturally loaded and therefore fairer, does influence prevalence for some but not all disadvantaged groups.

DEFINITIONS OF THE 1970s AND 1980s

The AAMR definitions of the next two decades (Grossman, 1973, 1977, 1983) and *DSM–III* (1980) and *DSM–III–R* (1987) remained modeled after the AAMR 1959–1961 classification with very modest, yet significant, changes in emphasis. The 1973 definition read: "Mental retardation refers to *significantly* subaverage general intellectual functioning *existing concurrently* with deficits in adaptive behavior, and manifested during the developmental period" (Grossman, 1973, p. 5). The italicized words reflect the changes in emphasis. Significantly subaverage general intellectual functioning translated into an IQ that falls two or more standard deviations below the population mean, or approximately IQ 70. In effect, the borderline category of the Heber scheme was eliminated and the upper cutoff score returned to the traditional cutoff score of IQ 70. The shift from –1 *SD* to –2 *SD*s reduced the percentage of the population psychometrically eligible for classification as mentally retarded from 16% to approximately 2% or 2.5%.

The second change consisted of the wording linking adaptive behavior to general intellectual level. The clear implication of replacing *associated* with *existing concurrently* in the phrase linking these two behavioral dimensions was the elevation of adaptive behavior to equal importance with general intellectual functioning. It is interesting to note how the Grossman committee responded to the sociopolitical forces that arose following publication of the 1959–1961 definition. They elected to eliminate the borderline group wherein the issue of overrepresentation of minority group cases was most pronounced. In so doing, they followed the recommendations of Clausen and Zigler to reduce the upper IQ limit from 85 to 70. Yet, contrary to the urging of these same critics, who denounced the inclusion of adaptive behavior, the Grossman committee actually elevated adaptive behavior in importance.

In other ways the 1973 revision was responsive to those who were critical of the adaptive behavior criterion during the school-age years. For example, Mercer (1973) reasoned that adaptation to school demands was far too limiting and argued for consideration of adaptation that went beyond the school walls to the neighborhood, family, and peer group. The revision in 1973 defined adaptive behavior as the degree to which the individual "meets that standard independence and social responsibility expected of his age and cultural group." In addressing the school-age years, the criteria were broadened (beyond academic achievement) to include "application of basic academic skills in daily life activities and application of appropriate reasoning and judgment in mastery of the environment and social skills (participation in group activities and interpersonal relationships)" (Grossman, 1973, p. 12). The committee was clear that the assessment of adaptive behavior during school years was not to be restricted to basic academic skills and their application; rather, it was to embrace coping skills in the broader environment.

One new feature of the AAMR revision in 1973 was the incorporation of the medical classification system of the International Classification of Diseases (ICD) 8th revision (World Health Organization, 1968) and the APA (1968). The AAMR scheme reflected the two-group approach (Dingman & Tarjan, 1960; Zigler, 1967); however, there was much greater differentiation of the organic etiologies. The categories were subdivided into infection and intoxication, trauma or physical agent, metabolism or nutrition, gross brain diseases, unknown diseases and conditions due to prenatal influence, chromosomal abnormality, gestational disorders, secondary to psychiatric disorder, environmental influences, and other conditions. Only environmental influences clearly addressed cases of environmental etiology, and that category was subdivided into psychosocial disadvantage and sensory deprivation. The psychosocial disadvantage etiology was believed to provide the explanation for the vast majority of mild mental retardation, which, in turn, was estimated to account for somewhere in the neighborhood of 75% of all cases of mental retardation.

Although Zigler had argued for the utility of classification by IQ and etiology, the revisions of the 1970s and 1980s did not really modify the subdivision by standard deviation units. That is, the scheme persisted in subdividing on the basis of degree of mental retardation, not by etiology. The medical classification system, incorporated in the later revisions, was merely appended to diagnostic information; however, it did not replace classification by degree of mental retardation utilizing the standard deviation units.

By the 1980s, AAMR and APA employed almost identical classification schemes. The AAMR definition read, "Mental retardation refers to significantly subaverage general intellectual functioning existing concurrently with deficits in adaptive behavior and manifested during the developmental period" (Grossman, 1983, p. 1). The *DSM–III–R* version varied from this wording only in the substitution of the phrases "accompanied by" for "existing concurrently with" and "onset before the age of 18" for "manifested during the developmental period" (*DSM–III–R*, p. 28). Reschly (1992) observed there were differences in the length and discussion of critical elements in that the AAMR manual was approximately 150 pages totally devoted to mental retardation, whereas *DSM–III–R* contained 6 pages concerning mental retardation. As a result, Reschly concluded that AAMR was the more authoritative source.

The 1983 version contained recommendations designed to reduce the "faith" in absolute IQ scores and to guard against decision rules that inflexibly ignored error of measurement inherent in IQ measurement. The general guideline for establishing the upper limit was IQ 70, however it allowed for diagnosis up to IQ 75. As shown in Table 2.1, the flexibility provided in the IQ 71–75 range doubles the percentage of the population eligible for diagnosis as mentally retarded. From a research perspective this flexibility is very troublesome, from a service delivery perspective it provided for identifying individuals needing services in various settings.

It is also noteworthy that the 1977 version "significantly subaverage general intelligence" was operationalized as performance "more than two standard deviations below the mean" (Grossman, 1977, p. 12). This accommodates the fact that different scales have different standard deviations (e.g., Stanford–Binet, *SD* = 16 points; Wechsler scales, *SD* = 15 points). The 1983 version, however adopted IQ 70:

> The IQ of 70 has been substituted for "under two standard deviations" for several reasons. The employment of two specific numbers, 67 and 69, implied a degree of precision in IQ assessment that was not intended. The use of the statement "approximately 70" avoids the implication of such precision. (Grossman, 1983, p. 23)

It is evident that such considerations were driven by clinical practices for establishing eligibility for services, rather than by research interests needing greater precision.

An even more serious problem emerges in the application of intellectual functioning to determine levels of mental retardation (mild, moderate, severe, and profound). The IQ ranges associated with levels of retardation (see Grossman, 1983, Table 1) are approximate IQ scores, not standard deviation units as had been done previously (see Grossman, 1977). In either case, recent individually administered tests of intelligence do not typically yield scores below 40. Reschly (1992) described this problem and noted that most current scales yield lowest IQ scores of between 40 and 50. In order to get lower scores, one must extrapolate extensively, "and that may be impossible at the lower age range for most tests" (Reschly, 1992, p. 41). He went on to write: "IQ scores below 55 on modern tests have a tenuous psychometric foundation. The IQs below 55 necessary to operationalize the AAMR and APA criteria for MR levels are more illusion than reality!" (p. 41).

The fact that AAMR persisted in employing a classification scheme for over three decades that differentiated levels of retardation reflects a position that *differences in retardation are primarily a matter of degree and not kind.* Later discussion in this chapter focuses on the qualitative differences that exist between the milder and more severe forms of mental retardation.

ISSUES OF DEFINITION AND CLASSIFICATION: 1960–1990

The era of the 1960s through 1990 was dominated by the AAMR definitions. The various committees and the manuals produced by these committees reached decisions on some issues, ignored others, and precipitated debate on yet others. Two behavioral dimensions, general intelligence and adaptive behavior, emerged as determinative of mental retardation in the polythetic classification AAMR embraced. Throughout this period establishment of the upper IQ level defining mental retardation proved mischievous, and the conceptualization and measurement of adaptive behavior was challenged as introducing unreliability into the classification scheme. The classification schemes also embraced a system that recognized levels of mental retardation operationalized on the exclusive basis of IQ ranges. Although more recent versions of the AAMR system *recognized* two broad classes of etiology (biologic and psychosocial), AAMR and APA never included etiology as determinative of mental retardation. Moreover, the overlap between levels of mental retardation and etiology, although acknowledged, has never been effectively resolved. As is discussed in this chapter, etiology should be at least part of the basis for distinguishing between mild and more severe forms of mental retardation.

Related to etiology is the issue of *prognosis*, which has been ignored by both AAMR and APA. The definitions were broad enough to capture the "two groups" of mentally retarded individuals; however, in so doing they included individuals for whom the prognosis was highly variable. Evidence on the mild cases of psychosocial etiology permit some optimism in prognosis, whereas the more severely retarded with biologic etiologies permit far less optimism and, in fact, appear to require some degree of protection throughout the lifespan.

Although AAMR and APA definitions and classification schemes have exerted the greatest influence on national and state legislation and Education Codes, there have been alternative definitions proposed. Let us examine briefly some of these definitions.

Zigler's Alternative Scheme

Edward Zigler went beyond mere criticism of the AAMR definition and proposed an alternative definition of mental retardation (Zigler, Balla, & Hodapp, 1984) that employed intellectual functioning and etiology as classificatory principles. Zigler's definition derives directly from the two-group approach to mentally retarded individuals. Zigler and Hodapp (1986) demonstrated that there are many more cases found with IQs less than 50 than would be predicted from theory, and went on to explain these two groups.

> There are really two separate distributions of intelligence: one for those whose intelligence is the product of some interaction between hereditary and environmental components; and the other for those whose intellectual apparatus has been physically damaged, thus altering the biological side of the formula. (p. 72)

The IQ distribution obtained for cases of organic damage is asymmetrical and beginning at IQ 0 (cases of anencephaly), peaking at about IQ 30, and then having a long tail extending to the high IQ range in order to accommodate those occasional individuals evidencing no intellectual retardation despite existing brain damage (e.g., cerebral palsy).

The classification scheme proposed (Zigler et al., 1984) defined mental retardation by an IQ of 2 *SDs* or more below the population mean and excluded adaptive behavior as determinative of mental retardation—rather treating it as a correlate instead of a classificatory principle. Once an individual was found to score –2 *SDs* or more below the mean, that individual would be classified by etiology into one of three subgroups—organic, familial, or undifferentiated. Decisions concerning assignment of cases to the three etiology classes would proceed by examining known correlates of the two classes, organic and familial, shown in Table 2.3.

It is evident that Zigler advocated this alternative approach to classification as one that would advance our understanding of mental retardation (i.e., a research perspective), which, in turn, would lead to more effective treatment (i.e., a service delivery perspective). In subsequent publications by the Zigler group (Burack, 1990; Burack, Hodapp, & Zigler, 1988; Zigler & Hodapp, 1986) this approach to classification was further refined with further differentiation within the organic and familial groups provided.

TABLE 2.3
A Three-Group Model for the Classification of Retarded Persons

	IQ		
	Organic 0–70	*Familial 50–70*	*Undifferentiated 0–70*
Classificatory Principle	Demonstrable organic etiology	No demonstrable organic etiology; parents have this same type of retardation	Cannot reliably be placed in either of the other two classes
	Found at all SES levels	More prevalent at SES levels	
	IQs most often below 50	IQs rarely below 50	
	Siblings usually of normal intelligence	Siblings often at lower levels of intelligence	
	Often accompanied by severe health problems	Health within normal range	
	Appearance often marred by physical stigmata	Normal appearance	
Correlates	Mortality rate higher (More likely to die at a younger age than the general population)	Normal mortality rate	
	Often dependent on care from others throughout life	With some support can lead an independent existence as adults	
	Unlikely to marry and often infertile	Likely to marry and produce children of low intelligence	
	Unlikely to experience neglect in their homes	More likely to experience neglect in their homes	
	High prevalence of other physical handicaps (e.g., epilepsy, cerebral palsy)	Less likely to have other physical handicaps	

Note. From Zigler and Hodapp (1986; Fig. 3.3.).

Zigler and Hodapp (1986) described several hypothesized subgroups that could be differentiated among those cases that would initially fall under the familial or undifferentiated classes:

1. Familial mental retardation, with at least one parent who also qualifies as mentally retarded.
2. "Polygenic isolates," with parents of average intelligence and a home environment considered nurturant and adequate for promoting intellectual development.
3. "Socioculturally deprived" cases, where persons qualify as mentally retarded as a result of prolonged exposure to an impoverished environment.

Considerably more empirical evidence exists to demonstrate the utility of this approach when applied to the organic group. For example, Burack et al. (1988) divided this group into several specific etiologies: chromosomal abnormalities, metabolic imbalances, neurological insults, congenital defects, and perinatal complications and infections. These authors then demonstrated differences in the stability of IQ over time for individuals with three differing etiologies: Down syndrome, fragile X syndrome, and cerebral palsy. In another study utilizing children with Down syndrome and Williams syndrome, Burack (1990) provided further evidence that the relation between etiology and certain cognitive/behavioral characteristics could be obscured if degree of retardation (and not etiology) alone is a factor in the experimental design.

Thus far, this alternative scheme with its emphasis on etiology has not been adopted by AAMR or APA; however, Burack et al. (1988) articulated a rationale for its potential to increase precision and thereby improve the science concerned with mental retardation. Certain research designs that treat etiologically formed groups as factors permit examination of additional variance explained on various behavioral outcomes. The evidence presented to date does suggest that this approach has utility for certain behavioral outcomes, and it warrants consideration in subsequent efforts in classification in mental retardation.

CURRENT DEFINITIONS OF AAMR AND APA

The most recent definitions endorsed by AAMR and the American Psychiatric Association (*DSM–IV*) have recently been published (APA, 1994; Luckasson, 1992). The 1992 AAMR definition of mental retardation reads

> *Mental retardation* refers to substantial limitations in present functioning. It is characterized by significantly subaverage intellectual functioning, existing concurrently with related limitations in two of more of the following applicable adaptive skill areas: communication, self-care, home living, social skills, community use, self-direction, health and safety, functional academics, leisure, and work. Mental retardation manifests before age 18. (Luckasson, 1992, p. 1)

At first glance, this version appears to contain all the same elements: significantly subaverage intellectual functioning, adaptive skill areas, and chronological age. However, this definition represents a substantial departure from the definitions of Heber and Grossman, and does so particularly in the lack of decision rules for the clinician and researcher in the assessment of *adaptive skill areas*.

Earlier in this chapter we noted the various purposes that categories or classes can serve. In 1992, the AAMR published a new definition of mental retardation (Luckasson, 1992) that appears designed to be useful for advocacy while providing less utility to the clinical and research communities. In fact, the early commentary on this definition from the clinical and research communities (Belmont & Borkowski, 1994; Jacobson & Mulick, 1992; MacMillan, Gresham, & Siperstein, 1993; *Region X Reporter*, 1992) has tended to be very critical of the definition as a guide to eligibility decision making.

Intellectual Dimension

In the Luckasson (1992) scheme "significantly subaverage intellectual functioning" is operationalized as "a score of approximately 70 to 75 or below" (p. 14) or, "If a valid IQ score is not possible, significantly subaverage intellectual capabilities means a level of performance that is less than that observed in the vast majority (approximately 97 percent) of persons of comparable background" (p. 14). Ignoring standard error of measurement concerns for a moment, consider the lack of precision in these guidelines in terms of the percentage of the general population eligible. As noted previously, more cases are found between IQ 70 and 75 (the loosely defined upper limit) than are found in the remainder of the distribution below IQ 70 (see Table 2.1). If one consults a table of percentile ranks for deviation IQs (e.g., Sattler, 1988, Table BC-1) for tests with a mean of 100 and *SD* of 15, one finds that 2% fall below IQ 70, 5% fall below IQ 75, and yet Luckasson suggested that 3% of those for whom a valid IQ cannot be obtained should be considered eligible! On the intellectual criterion alone then the new definition provides three different estimates of the percentage of the general population that will be eligible under the intellectual functioning dimension. Moreover, the inability to secure a valid IQ score leaves a clinician or researcher in a dilemma as to establishing that a given case performs at a level lower than 97% of what the definition terms "*persons of comparable background*" (italics added; Luckasson et al., 1992, p. 14). Comparable on the basis of what? What scales/measures permit determining this level of performance if an individually administered test of intelligence is unable to yield a valid IQ?

Specification of IQ 75 as the upper limit is justified as having "practical benefits among which are its general familiarity and acceptance by professions" (Zigler, Balla, & Hodapp, 1984). Nowhere in the article by Zigler et al. can be found a recommendation for, or acceptance of, an upper IQ limit specified in a broad range (i.e., 70–75), nor can one find any such recommendation in any of Zigler's other writings on issues of classification. Moreover, the rationale for a loose upper-level independent of standard deviations was "because such standards imply a degree of precision in measurement and construct that is not warranted" (Luckasson et al., 1992, p. 36). Why, then, the degree of precision required when describing the operationalizing of the subaverage intellectual functioning at 70–75 "on scales with a mean of 100 and standard deviation of 15" (p. 35)? If a 5-point range is defining the upper limit in order to avoid the impression of precision of IQ scores, why squabble over a score based on a scale with a 15- or 16-point standard deviation that only contributes a 2-point difference at two standard deviations below the mean?

Jacobson and Mulick (1992), in their discussion of the impact of the IQ 75 cutoff, showed that when the standard error of measurements on the Stanford–Binet and WAIS–R are taken into account, the upper boundary on the Stanford–Binet becomes 80 ($z = -1.25$), yielding 10.56% of the population scoring below that level and yielding 7.08% of the population scoring below that level on the WAIS–R. In practice, the "outdated" norms employed in using the WISC–R (established in 1974) in recent years identified far fewer than the percentage estimated to fall below a given cutoff score. That is, fewer than the normal curve percentages shown in Table 2.1 have actually scored below the various points in recent years because the norms were dated. New versions of the Wechsler scales, such as the WISC–III (Wechsler, 1992), the most frequently used instrument in assessing children "at the margin," are available with "tougher" test norms.

MacMillan et al. (1993) pointed out that the application of the 1992 definition guidelines for intellectual functioning will result in dramatically more individuals being deemed eligible for classification as mentally retarded on the basis of IQ alone. The reasons for this are the setting of the upper limit at 75 plus consideration of the standard of measurement surrounding this level effectively increases the IQ defining the upper limit. In addition, it is a well-known fact that newer editions of intelligence tests have "tougher" norms than did older editions of these same tests. That is, persons taking newer test editions have to answer more items correctly to maintain their same relative positions in a distribution than they did in taking older editions. The fact that individuals score lower on more recent editions was demonstrated by MacMillan et al. using different standardizations of the Wechsler scales. Table 2.4 shows the publication dates and renormings of the WISC, WISC–R, WISC–III, WAIS, WAIS–R, WPPSI, and WPPSI–R. Note that each restandardization of the Wechsler scales ranged from 17 to 26 years apart, and that the modal IQ difference was 8 points. The average IQ point difference per year was .314, which is strikingly close to Flynn's (1984) average difference of .332 points per year.

Persons retested with newer versions of the Wechsler scales will, on average, score between 5 to 8 points lower than on older versions. This is due, of course, because of the recalibration of norms that had become obsolete for the WISC–R. For example, suppose a child was referred in 1990 and given the WISC–R obtaining a full-scale IQ of 80. Using the 1983 criteria (Grossman, 1983), the child would not qualify for a diagnosis of mental retardation on the general intellectual functioning parameter. However, suppose this same child was referred in 1993 and was administered the WISC–III. Assuming a similar test performance (i.e., the same raw score points earned), the child's full-scale IQ on the WISC–III would be 75. On the intellectual functioning level criterion in the 1992 AAMR definition, this child would be eligible for a diagnosis of mental retardation. The net result of such likely occurrences will be to dramatically increase the proportion of the general population eligible for diagnosis as mentally retarded on the IQ criterion based solely on the obsolescence of older test norms and the subsequent "toughening" of the newer norms.

The effects of tougher test norms and the new 1992 AAMR definition will be to increase the percentage of persons qualifying for a diagnosis of mental retardation. Given

TABLE 2.4
IQ Difference in Restandardizations of the Wechsler Scales

Scale Combination	*Years Between Restandardization*	*IQ Difference*
WISC (1949)/WISC–R (1974)	25	–8 points
WISC–R (1974)/WISC–III (1992)	18	–5 points
WAIS (1955)/WAIS–R (1981)	26	–8 points
WPPSI (1967)/WPPSI–R (1991)	24	–8 points
	M = 23.25 years	M = 7.25 points

Note. WISC: Wechsler Intelligence Scale for Children (Wechsler, 1949).
WISC–R: Wechsler Intelligence Scale for Children–Revised (Wechsler, 1974).
WISC–III: Wechsler Intelligence Scale for Children–III (Wechsler, 1992).
WAIS: Wechsler Adult Intelligence Scale (Wechsler, 1955).
WAIS–R: Wechsler Adult Intelligence Scale (Wechsler, 1981).
WPPSI: Wechsler Preschool and Primary Scale of Intelligence (Wechsler, 1967).
WPPSI–R: Wechsler Preschool and Primary Scale of Intelligence–Revised (Wechsler, 1991).

a modal difference in IQ test performance of 8 points lower plus a standard error of measurement of approximately 5 points (depending on the confidence interval adopted), the 1992 AAMR definition begins to approach the 1961 AAMR intellectual criterion of 85 and below for a diagnosis of mental retardation.

Adaptive Skills Dimension

With the percentage of the population eligible on the intellectual dimension increased by the factors noted earlier, decisions of eligibility for classification will hinge on whether or not the individual qualifies as exhibiting deficits in two or more of the adaptive skill areas. It is important to note that the new definition abandoned the use of *composite* adaptive behavior and adopted 10 adaptive skill areas to be assessed. MacMillan et al. (1993) commented on this as follows:

> The rationale employed by the Committee to select 10 adaptive skill areas is unclear. In part, the Committee relied on the descriptive system developed by Ford and colleagues (Ford, Schnorr, Meyer, Davern, Black, & Dempsey 1989), but the 10 adaptive skill areas specified by Ford et al. were not empirically derived. Thus, no factor analytic studies validate the existence and independence of these 10 domains nor are there any data on the internal consistency of the skill areas. In short, there does not seem to be an empirical basis for the designation of the 10 adaptive skill areas specified by the Committee. (p. 329)

The 10 adaptive skill areas specified are: communication, self-care, home living, social skills, community use, self-direction, health and safety, functional academics, leisure, and work. Jacobson and Mulick (1992) observed that "no measures that have suitable psychometric characteristics for assessment of adaptive behavior are available for all these domains" (p. 11). MacMillan et al. (1993) noted the lack of developmental considerations in conceptualizing adaptation of individuals at different chronological ages and by degree of retardation. None of the 10 skill areas are relevant when diagnosing a newborn suspected of Down syndrome, and domains such as home living, community use, or work are not relevant when assessing a third-grade student with an IQ of 67. Because most diagnoses of mental retardation occur before CA 10, and the definition requires weaknesses in two or more areas, the result is that individuals are "differentially at risk" depending on the age at which they are being evaluated.

In a *Region X Reporter* article (1992), the lack of available instruments to measure the 10 skill areas was likened to the situation that existed in the early 1960s. "Much like in the early 60's (Heber, 1961), the AAMR will be counting on the scientific/psychometric community to play 'catch-up' with its definition and classification manual and eventually supply the clinicians and professionals with adequate assessment tools" (p. 4). Kamphaus (1987) considered psychometric issues in the measurement of adaptive behavior and noted the lack of adequate norms. Only two scales, the Vineland Adaptive Behavior Scales—Survey Form (Sparrow, Balla, & Cicchetti, 1984) and the Scales of Independent Behavior (Bruininks, Woodcock, Weatherman, & Hill, 1984) had adequate norming samples; that is, national norms. Kamphaus concluded: "The point being made here is that inadequately normed measures should not be used for making placement decisions because they introduce an unknown amount of error into the process of comparing an individual's score to the normal population. This comparison is critical as it is the crux of the process of diagnosing mental retardation" (p. 31).

MacMillan et al. (1993) discussed the poor reliability of domain scores. In Table 2.5 are shown the split-half reliabilities reported for the Vineland Adaptive Behavior Scales for domains included among the 10 adaptive skill areas specified in the new definition.

TABLE 2.5
Split-Half Reliabilities for Vineland Domain Scales Included Among the 10 Adaptive Skill Areas Specified in Luckasson (1992)

Adaptive Skill Domains	*Vineland (split-half)*
Communication	.89
Self-care	.69
Home living	.78
Social skills	.74
Community use	.78
Self-direction	—
Health and safety	—
Functional academics	—
Leisure	.71
Work	—
	Median = .75

TABLE 2.6
Adaptive Skill Cutoff Scores as a Function of Reliability and Standard Error of Measurement of Scales

Reliability	*SEM*	*95% CÎ*	*Upper AB Cutoff*	*Percentage Eligible*
.70	8.2	16	93	32%
.80	6.7	13	90	25
.90	4.7	10	87	19
.94	3.7	7	84	14

Note. .94 reliability reflects recommended level by Kelly (1927).
SEM = standard error of measurement. Calculated based on SEM = 15; SEM = 15 × square root of reliability coefficient; 95% CI = 2 × SEM.

The median reliability for the six domains is .75, well below the .94 recommended for measuring individual accomplishments (Kelly, 1927). In fact, not one of the six reached .94. Table 2.5 illustrates that the error in test scores increases as their reliability decreases. Note that the percentage of the population that would be eligible using subtests with reliabilities between .70 and .80; the level found for most adaptive behavior scores.

In an earlier draft of the 1992 definition, the 6th percentile was recommended as a cutoff. When one considers the elements of scale reliability, standard error of measurement of a scale, and adoption of a confidence level (e.g., 95%), one can readily evaluate the figures in Table 2.6. A scale, such as the self-care and leisure scales on the Vineland, with reliabilities of approximately .70 would yield a standard score as high as 93 to have a true score as low as 77, thus being eligible on a particular domain as evidencing an impaired adaptive skill. Approximately 33% of the general population would qualify on these two particular scales were the 6th percentile adopted. In the final version, Luckasson (1992) gave equal status to "professional judgment" and norm-referenced measures for assessing adaptive skills. The unreliability of professional judgment is legendary. In addition to clinical judgment having questionable reliability (Garb, 1987; Meehl, 1960), it can in some instances have important ethical, legal, and clinical ramifications (Hogarth, 1987). In mental retardation, these clinical judgments are likely to contain more error at the upper ranges of the mental retardation continuum than at the lower ranges.

In actual practice, it is likely that system factors will have a larger influence on the detection rate of mental retardation than the leniency or stringency of the AAMR classification scheme or how either adaptive skills or intellectual functioning is conceptualized and measured. A study in the late 1970s indicated that detection rates of mental retardation in school programs were not related to the leniency or stringency of the state department of education mental retardation classification criteria (Patrick & Reschly, 1982). Instead, it was related to characteristics of state populations such as literacy rate and socioeconomic status. States with higher rates of poverty had higher rates of mental retardation, a controversial relationship first identified soon after the mild level of mental retardation was recognized about 90 years ago.

According to data reported by states to the U.S. Department of Education, Office of Special Education Programs, the prevalence of mental retardation among children and youth aged 6 to 17 has declined by 39% over the last 25 years! This decline has occurred despite the AAMR classification scheme becoming more lenient in 1983 (recall that in 1983 the IQ score was permitted to be as high as 75 rather than below 70, thus doubling the potentially eligible population). The decline is even more astounding when two other factors are considered: (a) the overall proportion of children and youth identified as disabled in school settings increased dramatically during this period, and (b) monies to support special education programs and professional personnel to identify children with disabilities became available for the first time or were expanded significantly in virtually every school district in the United States in the late 1970s (*Fourteenth Annual Report to Congress*, 1992).

Some of the reduced prevalence of mental retardation in school settings may be due to more stringent state criteria for mental retardation, for example, changing the IQ criterion from 79 or 80 to 75, and to greater attention to determining deficits in adaptive behavior as well as intellectual deficits; however, in view of the Patrick and Reschly (1982) findings, these factors are highly unlikely to explain the dramatic reduction apparent in federal reports. Additional factors need to be considered.

Litigation stemming from contentions that overrepresentation of minority children and youth in the classification of mild or educable mental retardation was discriminatory undoubtedly influenced the declining prevalence. These court battles pitted minority advocates against school officials, and social scientist expert witnesses against each other, in relation to fundamental issues regarding the nature of mild mental retardation and the effects of classification and placement (Reschly, Kicklighter, & McKee, 1988). Although three of the four court opinions were in favor of the defendant school districts and state departments of education, the threat of litigation and the doubts about the equity of overrepresentation produced efforts to sharply reduce the use of the classification of mental retardation.

We might speculate that many of the students formerly classified as mentally retarded are now in special education programs under other classifications (especially specific learning disability). Research underway in southern California suggests that some children are in special education under other classifications, but many are floundering in regular education (MacMillan, Balow, Widaman, & Hemsley, 1992).

Subgroups

The Luckasson (1992) scheme discontinued the use of levels of mental retardation defined by standard deviation units. As of 1992, those following the AAMR classification scheme no longer invoked mild, moderate, severe, and profound levels as a means of differentiating subgroups. Instead of differentiating on the level of retardation, or on etiology, the new definition proposes to use "intensities of needed supports" as the basis for subgrouping within the population diagnosed as mentally retarded. The four levels of support are Intermittent, Limited, Extensive, and Pervasive. In the manual, these levels of support are to be listed in each area of intellectual functioning and adaptive skills, for psychological/emotional considerations, physical/health/etiology considerations, and environmental considerations. We can only speculate as to the length of a section in a journal article needed to describe the sample were this approach utilized. MacMillan et al. (1993) questioned whether there might be some correspondence between the earlier levels of retardation (Mild, Moderate, Severe, Profound) and the new levels of support (Intermittent, Limited, Extensive, Pervasive) given four levels in each scheme. If so, why change? Are the new levels merely proxy for the old? Regardless of the answers to these questions, the committee invoked a scheme in the absence of any instruments to evaluate levels of support. As noted for the adaptive skills areas, the new definition will require clinicians and researchers to await development of instruments and methods for reliably measuring levels of support.

CONCLUSIONS

The issues of definition and classification raised in this chapter have persisted for some time and show no signs of disappearing in the near future. As one might expect, there is agreement that general intellectual functioning is, and should be, a major behavioral dimension defining the condition. However, the issue concerning how this dimension should be assessed, particularly with individuals from sociocultural and linguistic minority groups, continues as a major controversy even after it has been debated in the professional literature and in the courts for the past two decades. Even when the fairness of tests of intelligence for use with minority individuals is put aside, however, there is disagreement over setting of the upper IQ score for defining mental retardation. This decision is an arbitrary one and the field has seen it set at various points and with varying degrees of precision over the past 30 years. Although AAMR and APA have for the past 30 years included social adaptation or adaptive behavior as a determinative aspect of mental retardation, this practice has been subjected to the greatest criticism. Primarily, that criticism has been focused on the error introduced into the diagnostic process due to the unreliability in the measures of social adaptation and adaptive behavior. We see the degree of error being compounded with the adoption of 10 adaptive skill areas, as opposed to a composite adaptive behavior measure, in the most recent AAMR definition.

It would appear that the controversy in defining mental retardation, and the failure to achieve consensus on a definition, derives from both the nature of the individuals classified as mentally retarded and the nature of professionals with a vested interest in mental retardation. Subsumed under the overarching concept of mental retardation are at least two subgroups that differ markedly from one another in terms of qualitative and quantitative features. Moreover, although these two groups both have special needs, the precise nature of the special needs varies dramatically. We question whether a single definition can adequately serve both groups equally well. The professionals involved in debates over issues of definition and classification also represent different disciplinary and professional orientations that, in turn, use different constructs and research paradigms and focus attention on different variables. In a professional organization such as AAMR one finds psychologists, physicians, educators, sociologists, social workers, anthropologists, lawyers, and the clergy. Gaining consensus from a constituency as diverse as this one presents major challenges whether working on a committee drafting the definition or in a general meeting where ratification of the committee's work is sought. These sources of diversity have perplexed efforts to design a classification system with which all will be pleased.

As noted earlier in this chapter, the most recent AAMR definition (Luckasson, 1992) represents a significant departure from previous AAMR definitions. As such, it will be interesting to follow the next years to see whether AAMR continues to exert leadership in terms of state education codes and other agencies following the general framework of AAMR. The recently published *DSM–IV* (APA, 1994) retained the IQ guidelines used in *DSM–III–R*; however, it did incorporate the 10 adaptive skill areas specified in Luckasson et al. (1992). Contrary to the AAMR scheme, *DSM–IV* retained the levels of retardation, and did not follow AAMR in employing levels of support. Currently, Division 33 of the American Psychological Association has a draft of yet another definition (see Jacobson & Mulick, 1993) providing the field with yet another definition of mental retardation from which to select. Agencies charged to serve persons with mental retardation will be free to cite any number of authorities for their definition of mental retardation, including the American Psychiatric Association's *DSM–IV*, the AAMR 1992 definition, or that resulting from the effort of Division 33 of the American Psychological Association. With the multiplicity of definitions likely to be available as models for agency criteria for who gets served, the variation from state to state in terms of who qualifies for services is likely to increase. For the research community the use of system-identified samples is likely to result in even less ability to generalize from study to study. The accumulation of knowledge about mental retardation is likely to be seriously compromised unless specification of markers characterizing samples is somehow instituted. In past years those of us working in the field of mental retardation could look on our colleagues studying learning disabilities (LD) with a sense of pity: How do they know who they are studying with the varied definitions of LD? It would appear that in the near future we will have achieved parity with our colleagues in the LD field.

ACKNOWLEDGMENTS

Preparation of this chapter was supported, in part, by grants HC023C20002, H023C80072, and H023C30103 from the U.S. Office of Education to the first author. Opinions expressed herein are those of the authors and should not be interpreted to have agency endorsement.

REFERENCES

American Psychiatric Association. (1968). *Diagnostic and statistical manual of mental disorders* (2nd ed.). Washington, DC: Author.

American Psychiatric Association. (1980). *Diagnostic and statistical manual of mental disorders* (3rd ed.). Washington, DC: Author.

American Psychiatric Association. (1987). *Diagnostic and statistical manual of mental disorders* (3rd ed.–Revised). Washington, DC: Author.

American Psychiatric Association. (1994). *Diagnostic and statistical manual of mental disorders* (4th ed.). Washington, DC: Author.

Bailey, K. (1973). Monothetic and polythetic typologies and their relation to conceptualization, measurement, and scaling. *American Sociological Review, 38*, 18–33.

Belmont, J. M., & Borkowski, J. (1994). Prudence, indeed, will dictate . . . review of *Mental retardation: Definition, classification, and systems of support* (9th ed.). *Contemporary Psychology, 39*, 495–496.

Bloom, B. (1964). *Stability and change in human characteristics.* New York: Wiley.

Bruininks, R., Woodcock, R., Weatherman, R., & Hill, B. (1984). *Scales of independent behavior.* Park Allen, TX: DLM Teaching Resources.

Burack, J. A. (1990). Differentiating mental retardation: The two-group approach and beyond. In R. M. Hodapp, J. A. Burack, & E. Zigler (Eds.), *Issues in the developmental approach to mental retardation* (pp. 27–48). New York: Cambridge University Press.

Burack, J. A., Hodapp, R. M., & Zigler, E. (1988). Issues in the classification of mental retardation: Differentiating among organic etiologies. *Journal of Child Psychology and Psychiatry, 29*, 765–779.

Clausen, J. A. (1967). Mental deficiency: Development of a concept. *American Journal of Mental Deficiency, 71*, 727–745.

Clausen, J. A. (1968). A comment on Halpern's note. *American Journal of Mental Deficiency, 72*, 950.

Clausen, J. A. (1972). Quo vadis, AAMD? *The Journal of Special Education, 6*, 51–60.

Cranefield, P. F., & Federn, W. (1963). Paracelsus on goiter and cretinism: A translation and discussion of "de struma vulgo der kropf." *Bulletin of the History of Medicine, 37*, 463–471.

Diana v. State Board of Education, Civil Action No. C-70-37 (N.D. Cal. 1970).

Dingman, H. F., & Tarjan, G. (1960). Mental retardation and the normal distribution curve. *American Journal of Mental Deficiency, 64*, 991–994.

Doll, E. A. (1934). Social adjustment of the mental subnormal. *Journal of Educational Research, 28*, 36–43.

Doll, E. A. (1941). The essentials of an inclusive concept of mental deficiency. *American Journal of Mental Deficiency, 46*, 214–219.

Doll, E. E. (1962). A historical survey of research and management of mental retardation in the United States. In E. P. Trapp & P. Himmelstein (Eds.), *Readings on the exceptional child* (pp. 21–68). New York: Appleton-Century-Crofts.

Doll, E. E. (1967). Historical review of mental retardation, 1800–1965: A symposium. *American Journal of Mental Deficiency, 72*, 165–189.

Dugdale, R. L. (1877). *The jukes.* New York: Putnam.

Flynn, J. R. (1984). Massive IQ gains in 14 nations: What IQ tests really measure. *Psychological Bulletin, 101*, 171–191.

Ford, A., Schnorr, R., Meyer, L., Davern, L, Black, J, & Dempsey, P. (1989). *The Syracuse community-referenced curriculum guide for students with moderate and severe disabilities.* Baltimore, MD: Brookes.

Fourteenth Annual Report to Congress on the Implementation of the Individuals with Disabilities Act. (1992). Washington DC: United States Department of Education, Office of Special Education Programs.

Garb, H. N. (1987). Clinical judgment, clinical training, and professional experience. *Psychological Bulletin, 105*, 387–396.

Goddard, H. H. (1912). *The Kallikak family.* Norwood, MA: Norwood.

Grossman, H. J. (Ed.). (1973). *Manual on terminology and classification in mental retardation.* Washington, DC: American Association on Mental Deficiency.

Grossman, H. J. (Ed.). (1977). *Manual on terminology and classification* (rev. ed.). Washington, DC: American Association on Mental Deficiency.

Grossman, H. J. (Ed.) (1983). *Classification in mental retardation* (3rd ed.). Washington, DC: American Association on Mental Deficiency.

Heber, R. (1959). A manual on terminology and classification in mental retardation. *American Journal of Mental Deficiency, 56*(Monograph Supplement, Rev.).

Heber, R. (1961). Modifications in the manual on terminology and classification in mental retardation. *American Journal of Mental Deficiency, 65*, 499–500.

Heflinger, C. A., Cook, V. J., & Thackrey, M. (1987). Identification of mental retardation by the System of Multicultural Pluralistic Assessment: Nondiscriminatory or nonexistent? *Journal of School Psychology, 25*, 177–183.

Hendrick, I. G., & MacMillan, D. L. (1989). Selecting children for special education in New York City: William Maxwell, Elizabeth Farrell, and the development of ungraded classes, 1900–1920. *The Journal of Special Education, 22*, 395–417.

Hogarth, R. (1987). *Judgment and choice* (2nd ed.). New York: Wiley.

Hunt, J. M. (1961). *Intelligence and experience.* New York: Ronald Press.

Jacobson, J. W., & Mulick, J. A. (1992). A new definition of mentally retarded or a new definition of practice. *Psychology in Mental Retardation and Developmental Disabilities, 18*(2), 9–14.

Jacobson, J. W., & Mulick, J. A. (1993). Walkin' the walk: APA takes a step forward in professional practice. *Psychology in Mental Retardation and Developmental Disabilities, 19*(1), 4–8.

Kamphaus, R. W. (1987). Conceptual and psychometric issues in the assessment of adaptive behavior. *The Journal of Special Education, 21*, 27–35.

Kanner, L. (1964). *A history of the care and study of the mentally retarded.* Springfield, IL: Thomas.

Kaufman, A. S , & Doppelt, J. E. (1976). Analysis of WISC–R standardization data in terms of the stratification variables. *Child Development, 47*, 165–171.

Kazimour, K., & Reschly, D. (1981). Investigation of norms and concurrent validity for the Adaptive Behavior Inventory for Children. *American Journal of Mental Deficiency, 85*, 512–520.

Kelly,. T. (1927). *Interpretation of educational measurements.* Yonkers, NY: World Book.

Keogh, B. K. (1993). Linking purpose and practice: Social, political and developmental perspectives on classification. In G. R. Lyon, D. B. Gray, J. F. Kavanagh, & N. A. Krasnegor (Eds.), *Better understanding learning disabilities* (pp. 311–324). Baltimore: Brookes.

Keogh, B. K., & MacMillan, D. L. (in press). Exceptionality. In D. Berliner & R. Calfee (Eds.), *Handbook of educational psychology.* Washington, DC: American Psychological Association.

Kidd, J. W. (1964). Toward a more precise definition of mental retardation. *Mental Retardation, 2*, 209–212.

Koegel, P., & Edgerton, R. B. (1984). Black "six hour retarded children" as young adults. In R. B. Edgerton (Ed.), *Lives in process: Mildly retarded adults in a large city* (pp. 145–171). Washington, DC: American Association on Mental Deficiency.

Kuhlman, F. (1924). Mental deficiency, feeble-mindedness, and defective delinquency. *American Association for the Study of the Feeble-minded, 29*, 58–70.

Larry P. v. Riles, 343 F. Supp. 1306 (N.D. Cal. 1972) (preliminary injunction) affirmed 502 F. 2d 963 (9th cir. 1974); 495 F. Supp. 926 (N.D. Cal. 1979) (decision on merits) affirmed (9th cir. No. 80-427), Jan. 23, 1984); order modifying judgment (C-71-2270 RFP, September 25, 1986).

Luckasson, R. (Ed.). (1992). *Mental retardation: Definition, classification, and systems of support.* Washington, DC: American Association on Mental Retardation.

MacMillan, D. (1982). *Mental retardation in school and society* (2nd ed.). Boston: Little, Brown.

MacMillan, D. L. (1992). Development of operational definitions in mental retardation: Similarities and differences with the field of learning disabilities. In G. R. Lyon, D. B. Gray, J. F. Kavanagh, & N. A. Krasnegor (Eds.), *Better understanding learning disabilities* (pp. 117–152). Baltimore: Brookes.

MacMillan, D. L., Balow, I. H., Widaman, K. F., & Hemsley, R. E. (1992). *A study of minimum competency tests and their impact: Final Report.* Riverside: University of California, Riverside.

MacMillan, D. L., Gresham, F. M., & Siperstein, G. N. (1993). Conceptual and psychometric concerns over the 1992 AAMR definition of mental retardation. *American Journal on Mental Retardation, 98*, 325–335.

MacMillan, D. L., Gresham, F. M., & Siperstein, G. N. (1995). Heightened concerns over the 1992 AAMR definition: Advocacy versus precision. *American Journal on Mental Retardation, 100*, 87–95.

MacMillan, D. L., Meyers, C. E., & Morrison, G. M. (1980). System-identification of mildly mentally retarded children: Implications for interpreting and conducting research. *American Journal of Mental Deficiency, 85*, 108–115.

Meehl, P. E. (1960). The cognitive activity of the clinician. *American Psychologist, 15*, 19–27.

Mercer, J. (1973). *Labeling the mentally retarded.* Berkeley: University of California Press.

Mercer, J. (1979). *System of multicultural pluralistic assessment technical manual.* San Antonio, TX: The Psychological Corporation.

Patrick, J., & Reschly, D. (1982). Relationship of state educational criteria and demographic variables to school-system prevalence of mental retardation. *American Journal of Mental Deficiency, 86*, 351–360.

Pitkin, W. B. (1928). *Twilight of the American mind.* New York: Simon & Schuster.

The potential impact of the new definition on the prevalence of mental retardation. *Region X Reporter, 15*(3), 4–7.

Reschly, D. J. (1981). Evaluation of the effects of SOMPA measures on classification of students as mildly mentally retarded. *American Journal of Mental Deficiency, 86*, 16– 20.

Reschly, D. J. (1992). Mental retardation: Conceptual foundation, definitional criteria, and diagnostic operations. In S. R. Hynd & R. E. Mattison (Eds.), *Assessment and diagnosis of child and adolescent psychiatric disorders: Vol. II. Developmental disorders* (pp. 23–67). Hillsdale, NJ: Lawrence Erlbaum Associates.

Reschly, D. J., & Jipson, F. J. (1976). Ethnicity, geographic locale, age, sex, and urban–rural residence as variables in the prevalence of mild retardation. *American Journal of Mental Deficiency, 81*, 154–161.

Reschly, D. J., Kicklighter, R. H., & McKee, P. (1988). Recent placement litigation Part II, Minority EMR overrepresentation: Comparison of *Larry P.* (1979, 1984, 1986) with *Marshall* (1984, 1985) and *S-1* (1986). *School Psychology Review, 17*, 20–36.

Robinson, H. B., & Robinson, N. M. (1976). *The mentally retarded child.* New York: McGraw-Hill.

Sarason, S. B., & Doris, J. (1969). *The mentally retarded child* (2nd ed.). New York: McGraw-Hill.

Sattler, J. M. (1988). *Assessment of children* (3rd ed.). San Diego, CA: Sattler.

Scheerenberger, R. C. (1983). *A history of mental retardation.* Baltimore: Brookes.

Sloan, W., & Stevens, H. A. (1976). *A century of concern: A history of the American Association on Mental Deficiency.* Washington, DC: American Association on Mental Deficiency.

Smith, J. D. (1985). *Minds made feeble: The myth and legacy of Kallikaks.* Rockville, MD: Aspen Systems Corporation.

Sparrow, S. S., Balla, D. A., & Cicchetti, D. V. (1984). *Vineland Adaptive Behavior Scales.* Circle Pines, MN: American Guidance Service.

Terman, L. M. (1916). *The measurement of intelligence.* Boston: Houghton-Mifflin.

Terman, L. M. (1917). Feeble-minded children in the public schools of California. *School and Society, 5*, 161–165.

Wechsler, D. (1949). *Wechsler intelligence scale for children.* San Antonio, TX: The Psychological Corporation.

Wechsler, D. (1955). *Wechsler adult intelligence scale.* San Antonio, TX: The Psychological Corporation.

Wechsler, D. (1967). *Wechsler preschool and primary scale.* San Antonio, TX: The Psychological Corporation.

Wechsler, D. (1974). *Wechsler intelligence scale for children–Revised.* San Antonio, TX: The Psychological Corporation.

Wechsler, D. (1981). *Wechsler adult intelligence scale–Revised.* San Antonio, TX: The Psychological Corporation.

Wechsler, D. (1991). *Wechsler preschool and primary scale of intelligence–Revised.* San Antonio, TX: The Psychological Corporation.

Wechsler, D. (1992). *Wechsler intelligence scale for children III.* San Antonio, TX: The Psychological Corporation.

World Health Organization. (1968). *International classification of diseases* (8th Rev., ICD-8). Geneva: Author.

Zigler, E. (1967). Familial mental retardation: A continuing dilemma. *Science, 155*, 292–298.

Zigler, E., Balla, D., & Hodapp, R. (1984). On the definition and classification of mental retardation. *American Journal of Mental Deficiency, 89,* 215–230.

Zigler, E., & Hodapp, R. M. (1986). *Understanding mental retardation.* New York: Cambridge University Press.

Zigler, E., & Phillips, L. (1961). Psychiatric diagnosis: A critique. *Journal of Abnormal and Social Psychology, 63,* 607–618.

› II ‹

Contemporary Psychological Perspectives on Mental Retardation

› 3 ‹

Emotion and Mental Retardation

Thomas L. Whitman
Mary O'Callaghan
Kristie Sommer
University of Notre Dame

Historically, mental retardation has been defined in terms of cognitive and behavioral deficiencies. Currently, according to the American Association on Mental Retardation (1992):

> Mental retardation refers to substantial limitations in present functioning. It is characterized by significantly subaverage intellectual functioning, existing concurrently with related limitations in two or more of the following applicable adaptive skill areas: communication, self-care, home living, social skills, community use, self-direction, health and safety, functional academics, leisure, and work. Mental retardation manifests before 18.

From an etiological perspective, theories of mental retardation have stressed the critical influences of cognitive defects in limiting adaptive skills. Considerable attention has been placed on documenting and delineating the cognitive deficiencies of the mentally retarded, the neurological bases for these cognitive deficiencies, and how cognitive functioning influences behavioral functioning.

In contrast, the role that emotional processes might play in the development of mental retardation has been virtually ignored. The effects of emotional processes on cognitive and behavioral functioning have been seldom emphasized, except for the recognition that persons with mental retardation have emotional problems (Matson & Barrett, 1982; Menolascino & Stark, 1984). However, even researchers and clinicians who have acknowledged the co-occurrence of cognitive and emotional problems in persons with mental retardation do not emphasize emotional processes as either a critical component or a potential cause of mental retardation.

Until recently, developmental psychologists have also paid little attention to the topic of emotional development. Lewis and Michalson (1983) pointed out that the study of emotion has been relatively stagnant, as indicated by the paucity of attention given to this topic in developmental textbooks. Cicchetti and Schneider-Rosen (1984) suggested that psychoanalytic, behavioral, and Piagetian theories have done little to promote the study of early emotional development. Although social–emotional functioning appears critical to a child's happiness and success, there exists a deep-seated belief that intelligence is the critical ingredient for adult success (Lewis & Michalson, 1983). This belief perseveres despite the fact that cognitive measures are poor predictors of career achievement, social functioning, and life satisfaction. When emotional responses have been examined, cognitive activities have been typically viewed not only as a necessary but also as a sufficient condition for emotional activity (Lazarus, 1982). Cognition and emotion have been fused together in such a way that cognitive evaluation has been considered crucial to the emotional response.

Within the past decade, however, developmental models have increasingly emphasized both the impact of emotion on cognition and the reciprocal influences of these processes on each other. In particular, researchers began to acknowledge the dynamic interrelationship of affective and cognitive functioning during infancy and early childhood (Cicchetti & Schneider-Rosen, 1984). Lewis and Michalson (1983) suggested that feeling and cognitive states are not really different domains of development but rather aspects of a unified developmental process.

Although a new zeitgeist has been evolving, Barrett and Campos (1987) stressed that theories of emotional development continue to be prisoners of old paradigms. They asserted that past theories of emotion have neither adequately addressed how emotions evolve nor explained why rudimentary emotions like fear are less driven by an emerging cognitive system than previously thought. Given the lack of attention to the study of emotion and emotion–cognition linkages in general developmental psychology, it is hardly surprising that emotional processes have been ignored by researchers working in the area of mental retardation.

The major thrust of this chapter is to suggest that early emotional dysfunction, whether biologically and/or environmentally produced, may inhibit cognitive development and be an important and overlooked factor in the etiology of mental retardation. This perspective is constructed with the assistance of theory and research drawn from mainstream developmental psychology. We examine emotional development and its cognitive linkages during infancy and suggest how the study of these interrelationships may facilitate our understanding of atypical cognitive development and mental retardation. The role that state as well as temperament processes, particularly those involved in reacting to and regulating environmental stimulation, play in the early development of attentional and cognitive processes are emphasized. In addition, research examining temperament and early emotional development in children with mental retardation are examined, along with the social context in which the development takes place. Based on these discussions, a future research agenda is proposed to study how early emotional dysfunction may influence the development of mental retardation. Before proceeding with this task, the meaning and measurement of emotion are discussed, along with emotion's purported relationships with cognitive processes and the social environment.

WHAT DO WE MEAN BY EMOTION?

In order to effectively evaluate the influence of emotional functioning on cognitive development, it is necessary to define the term *emotion* and to develop a working theory of how emotions develop. Ideally, for progress to occur in our understanding of emotion there should be a shared definition of what it is within the scientific community. Unfortunately, such a definition has not yet evolved. Some definitions have referred to emotion as involving the visceral and glandular systems, thalamic processes, plasmatic motion, somatic adjustment, bodily reactions, neural dispositions, and physiological changes. In contrast, other definitions of emotion have variously emphasized phenomenological, perceptual, appraisal, motor-expressive, and instrumental action components (see Plutchik, 1980, for discussion of definitional issues).

Plutchik's (1980) observation that emotions have been neither consistently defined nor always clearly defined is still relevant today. In part, these definitional problems are probably due to the fact that emotions have been basically viewed as internal, covert, and private events, less directly accessible to observation than behaviors such as motoric responses. However, the search for an adequate definition of emotion also seems to be more elusive than for other covert responses, such as cognitions. Cognitions appear to be more easily defined, for example, by a person's performance on different types of cognitive tasks or self-reported use of a specific problem-solving strategy. Moreover, a richer, more precise, and more conventional language system is available for describing cognitive than emotional processes. In contrast, emotions appear to have less explicit external indices, and to be defined in quite diverse ways, such as by a person's verbal reflection on his or her internal states, facial expressions, general motoric behaviors, and/or physiological responses. The relationship among these various defined aspects of emotion is still less than clear.

Barrett and Campos (1987), rejecting theories that attempted to define emotions in terms of a single central criterion, pointed out the modest covariation of previously proposed emotion-defining variables. Reflecting on the multiplicity of components that constitute emotion, a number of investigators have referred to emotion as a response syndrome. For example, Lewis and Michalson (1983) described the structure of emotion as a complex, involving emotional elicitors (stimulus events that trigger emotions), emotional receptors (central nervous system pathways that mediate physiological and/or cognitive states), emotional states (changes in somatic and/or neuronal activity), emotional expressions (observable changes in face, body, voice, and activity level), and emotional experiences (an individual's conscious or unconscious perception, interpretation, or evaluation of an emotional state or expression). Common to many recent definitions of emotion is a reference to a cognitive component that variously validates the existence of the emotion, evaluates its meaning, structures its expressions, and/or regulates its continuing activity.

EMOTION: THE ROLE OF COGNITIVE PROCESSES

In discussing the relationship of cognition and emotion, Lewis and Michalson (1983) suggested that no emotional experience is without some cognitive processing. Kagan (1978) similarly pointed out that affective states are linked to cognitive structures. In order for an emotion to be fully experienced, Lazarus (1982) suggested that three fused components are necessary: thoughts, action impulses, and somatic disturbances. Lazarus (1982) contended that emotions are contingent on cognitive processes, with appraisal giving rise to a particular emotion and the intensity of the emotion, depending on the person's perception of the nature of an environmental event and its relationship to the person's well-being.

In contrast, some theorists, like Zajonc (1980), assert that emotions can occur without peripheral or cognitive encoding and that emotions and cognitions are either completely or at least partially independent neurological systems. From a developmental vantage point, Lewis and Michalson (1983) suggested that during early infancy, primitive emotional responses like fear are biologically prewired and do not involve much cognitive activity other than perception of the fear-evoking event. Kagan (1978) emphasized in his discussion of emotion, however, "that there is a profound difference between the state of consciously perceived changes and the state produced by bodily changes that are not detected" (p. 28).

A quite different perspective on the nature of emotions was presented by Barrett and Campos (1987), who conceived of emotions as members of families, with emotions within families sharing in common certain intrinsic features and emotions in different families sharing some common features but also possessing unique characteristics. Included among the features that distinguish different-emotion families are: particular action tendencies, appreciations (hot cognitions), vocal and facial patterns, physiological patterns, goals, and adaptive functions. Barrett and Campos (1987) suggested that complex emotions, manifested at later stages of development, are already present at earlier stages in a rudimentary form. Early emotions are prewired, helping to ensure in fixed ways the survival of the individual. As development occurs, cognitions subsequently influence the breadth and complexity of emotionality. Barrett and Campos emphasized, however, that these cognitive processes are not always deliberate, conscious, or sophisticated, and may involve nothing more than a basic recognition that the environment has changed and possesses a certain sensory quality. Moreover, they indicated that socialization influences on emotions may be more important than cognitive influences, not only affecting how emotions look and sound but directly changing the very nature of emotionality. Barett and Campos also emphasized that emotions influence both cognitive development and the socialization process.

From our perspective, we contend that both the "weak" and "strong" cognitive positions on emotions posed by past theorists have merit; that is, emotions can operate relatively independently of the cognitive system but also can be influenced by it. Even though at first glance this position may appear inconsistent, if not paradoxical, it becomes understandable when viewed within a developmental framework. Rather than stipulating, as Lazarus did that cognition is one of the components and causally the most critical component of emotions, there are advantages to viewing emotions as evolving in complexity; specifically, in the number of critical components that comprise them.

Within this framework, more rudimentary and developmentally early emotions, such as fear, are defined exclusively or predominantly by an infant's physiological response to an environment or temperament. Such early emotions are driven by the autonomic system, which in turn is responsive to changes in both internal bodily and external environmental conditions. These emotions can become associated with situations that did not originally evoke them through the process of classical conditioning (Rovee-Collier, 1986). During early development, the cognitive system is less influential in determining emotions, both because its "cortextual" hardware is only evolving and in the process of being programmed, and because the associational links between lower and higher brain functioning are just beginning to be developed. During this stage emotions not only precede but also probably drive at or at least influence the development of the cognitive system. More is said about this issue later in the chapter.

In contrast, developmentally later occurring emotions, such as anger, are more complex and involve a reciprocally interactive relationship among the environment, autonomic responses, and the perceptual–cognitive system. During typical development, cognitive control of emotional responses increases. However, physiological responses continue to exert considerable, and sometimes during atypical development inordinate, influence on the cognitive system. Infants as well as older children and adults show considerable individual differences in these intersystem relationships and in the relative dominance of the emotional and cognitive components.

Although the assertion might be made that early autonomic responses to the environment are not true emotions, because by definition emotions are a function of the appraisal process, researchers might do well to focus less on such definitional issues. Rather, they should examine within a developmental framework the evolution of the various components of the emotional system, including the physiological, behavioral self-regulatory, and behavioral expressive and perceptual–cognitive features, and the changing relationships among these components, as well as individual differences in the way these components emerge and interrelate.

EMOTION, TEMPERAMENT, AND COGNITIVE DEVELOPMENT: THE ROLE OF THE SOCIAL ENVIRONMENT

In the last section, we suggested that emotions develop from a relatively simple, innately determined, biological response system into a more complex system, characterized by increasing cognitive activity. Insight into how this developmental process might occur was given by Als (1982). Als conceptualized early development in terms of multisystem development, intersystem interactions, and system–environment interactions. The systems focused on by Als include (in order of their development): the autonomic, motor, state-organizational, attentional/interactive, and self-regulatory. Each of the later emerging systems is dependent on the earlier emerging systems. If one of the earlier emerging systems is immature or damaged, the development of the other systems is delayed or inhibited.

As these various systems develop, they can become disorganized as a consequence of environmental stress. For example, if the young infant becomes autonomically disorganized in response to a loud noise or parental overstimulation, as indicated by respiratory pauses, startling, twitching, and spitting up, the motor system also typically shows signs of disorganization (motoric flaccidity or hypertonicity), along with the state system (rapid state oscillation and perhaps crying), the attention–interaction system (difficulty in maintaining an alert state which, in turn, inhibits the infant's ability to orient and encode information from the external environment), and the self-regulatory system (difficulty in modulating the disorganization of the other systems through motoric strategies such as sucking, tucking, and hand clasping).

When disorganization occurs the infant eventually reorganizes itself. This reorganization process can be facilitated by a sensitive social environment in which the caretaker, recognizing infant signs of becoming stressed and disorganized, responds appropriately by helping the baby through strategies, such as reducing environmental stimulation, swaddling and/or repositioning the baby, providing a pacifier, and gently stroking. As Kopp (1989) pointed out, caretakers play a crucial role in helping infants regulate their emotions. This social–environmental response to the infant, which is directed toward assisting the baby in calming himself or herself, eventually enables the baby to reengage the social environment in an alert and responsive fashion. Over time the infant acquires an increasing ability to self-regulate behavior in stressful circumstances. As these self-regulation capacities increase, the infant is able to orient and attend to the social environment for increasing periods of time, and as a consequence gains a sense of self-efficacy. As children develop, the signs of emotional disorganization change, as do the complexity of the self- and social regulatory strategies employed to control emotions, but the general effects of these state changes on the cognitive (attentional-information processing) system are similar.

The social support process just described, the objective of which is to assist the infant in emotional reorganization, is similar to the scaffolding process described by social–cognitive theorists (Day, Cordon, & Kerwin, 1989; Vygotsky, 1978). Scaffolding consists of socialization agents providing structure and assistance to children as they engage in cognitive tasks. Through the use of procedures like verbal prompting and modeling, socialization agents provide knowledge and cognitive strategies to the child. The "teacher" helps the child by reducing the child's cognitive workload, specifically by assuming responsibility for parts of the task while the child concentrates on other parts. The goal of the scaffolding process is to reduce the social supports provided to the child as the child acquires increasing cognitive competence and ability to self-regulate. We suggest that in order to facilitate emotional development, teachers (particularly the child's parents) must become adept at providing both emotional and cognitive scaffolds. If parents fail to provide either or both of these types of supports, cognitive difficulties and delays in development may well occur.

The critical point that we would like to emphasize is that more complex cognitive functioning, such as completing a math problem, or even simple cognitive tasks such as attending to the caretaker, cannot occur unless the child is emotionally organized. If the child is incapable of emotionally organizing herself or himself, for whatever reason (an immature self-regulatory system, severe environmental and/or biological stressors), the social environment needs to provide the supports and regulatory tools the child lacks in order to promote optimal functioning. Some children, such as those with "difficult" temperaments, are in particular need of emotional social supports.

Chess and Thomas (1989) emphasized that the task confronting parents of children with more "difficult" "or "slow to warm up" temperaments may be particularly challenging. The temperamentally "difficult" child is characterized by irregularity in biological functions (such as in the sleep–wake cycle, and hunger–feeding patterns), negative withdrawal reactions to new stimuli, slow adaption to change, and high-intensity affective displays. Similarly, the "slow to warm up" child, like the difficult child, also shows negative withdrawal responses to new stimuli, slow adaptability to change, and many negative mood expressions, but in contrast to the difficult child, is less intense in mood expressions and is less likely to be irregular in biological functions. More generally, children with challenging temperaments are also more active physically, more sensitive to changes in the environment, more distractible, less attentive (shorter attention span), and less able to continue an activity after interruption.

Although children with challenging temperamental traits are at greater risk for behavior as well as learning disorders, the extent to which these traits actually have a detrimental influence on development depends on the response of the familial and extrafamilial (e.g., formal educational) environments. To the extent that social environments are structured flexibly, recognize individual differences, and accommodate to children with different temperaments, development is likely to occur in a more optimal fashion. The relationship between the child's temperament and the response of the social environment is referred to by Chess and Thomas (1989) as "goodness of fit" (p. 185). According to them, the social response to the child's temperament has profound effects on the child's later personality, self-concept, and school functioning. In instances where the child's temperamental and emotional style are responded to in a sensitive fashion, the child is more likely to display positive self-esteem, a sense of self-efficacy, social competence, positive mood, persistence, adaptability, and achievement motivation.

Although there is disagreement about the precise nature of temperament, there is widespread agreement that infant temperament has genetic origins, is influenced by primary caretakers, and constitutes a foundation for early emotional style and expression as well as later personality development. We suggest further that the development of the cognitive system, both in terms of its hardware (brain) and its software (knowledge base), is influenced by the temperament and early emotional system, as mediated by the social context in which it occurs. To the extent that a child's temperament system elicits an adverse social response, emotional and social–interactional problems are more likely to occur, and cognitive development is likely to be inhibited.

In a subsequent section we emphasize that children with mental retardation often have more problematic temperaments and emotional styles, and suggest that these characteristics may inhibit the development of the cognitive system. Before we discuss the special case of mental retardation, we examine in greater detail the nature of the emotional system and emotion–cognition linkages during early infancy. Our intent in the next section is to show the importance of the emotional system during early development and how it controls cognitive functioning.

EMOTION AND COGNITION IN EARLY INFANCY

From a biological perspective, early infant functioning is basically reflexive, influenced by the environment and autonomic nervous system. The cognitive component of the emotional system is only beginning to emerge. The brain is rapidly developing, as neurological linkages between its cortical and subcortical structures are formed, neurons increase in number and size, dendritic enhancement occurs, and mylenization proceeds. We argue via a review of several diverse literatures that during early development the affective and cognitive components of the emotional system are relatively independent but in the process of becoming increasingly interdependent, and that temperament and emotional functioning are driven by the autonomic nervous system.[1] We emphasize that the primitive cognitive system emerges only after the autonomic system becomes organized. Finally, we suggest that disruptions in the autonomic system, due either to organic problems or prolonged environmental stress, are likely to result in cognitive dysfunction.

During early infancy the response systems of the newborn are primarily reflexive and subcortical in nature; cognitive processes, which are centered in the cortex and hippocampal regions, appear to be minimally involved in functioning, specifically because of their immaturity. Although newborns exhibit many seemingly complex behaviors, such as reaching and grasping, these behaviors are holistic and stereotypic in form; that is, they cannot be broken down into their component parts or combined to produce more complex behavior patterns. Under close examination, the organization of behavior patterns in early infancy bears striking resemblance to that found in species having little or no neocortex (Gibson, 1991).

Although the neural centers that mediate cognitive processing appear to be relatively immature, we know that the newborn demonstrates a variety of affective responses. Shortly after birth, infants are capable of expressing a range of emotions, including distress (Izard, Hembree, Dougherty, & Spizzirri, 1983; Izard, Hembree, & Heubner, 1987), disgust (Rosenstein & Oster, 1988), surprise (Field, 1982b), sadness (Tronick, Cohen, & Shea, 1986), and joy (Lewis, Alessandri, & Sullivan, 1990; Malatesta, Culver, Tesman, & Shepard, 1989). The varied emotional life of the young infant in the face of cortical immaturity suggests that the early affective system is operative prior to and relatively independent of cognitive processes. This depiction is in striking contrast with that presented by most nondevelopmental theories of emotions, which, as noted previously, are heavily cognitive in nature.

[1]From our perspective, during early infancy temperament and emotions are coequivalent and virtually indistinguishable processes.

LeDoux (1989) argued that one weakness of cognitive theories of emotion is their failure to account for autonomic arousal early in infancy. He pointed out that there must be a mechanism for computing the affective significance of an event prior to cognitive processing; specifically, because without this type of mechanism, all stimuli would lead to arousal. If such a mechanism can be shown to achieve functional maturity prior to higher cognitive centers and not to rely on cortical input, this would constitute evidence for an independent emotional system in the newborn period. Examination of the amygdalic region of the limbic lobe of the brain suggests this may be the mechanism (LeDoux, 1989). The amygdala is known to mature earlier than the structures involved in cognitive processing. Not only is its neurogenesis completed during the prenatal period (LeDoux, 1989), but the amygdala is partially myelinated at birth and the myelenization process is completed relatively soon thereafter (Gibson, 1991). In contrast, the cortical region is basically unmyelinated at birth (Gibson, 1991), and both neurogenesis and myelinization continue well past the neonatal period.

Although the amygdala eventually receives input from the sensory cortex and association areas, it initially receives information from the thalamus, an early maturing brainstem area that serves as a major center for the relay of sensory and motor input from the periphery to higher brain centers. This thalamic input is primitive compared to the sensory information which has been processed by the cortex. According to Le Doux (1989), the thalamo-amygdalic pathways provide, however, enough information from the environment to allow basic emotional reactions prior to cortical maturation. Indeed, classical conditioning experiments have demonstrated that when simple sensory cues are used as conditioned stimuli, the thalamo-amygdalic projections are both necessary and sufficient for the conditioning of fear responses (LeDoux, Sakaguchi, Iwata, & Reis, 1986; LeDoux, Sakaguchi, & Reis, 1984). In addition, lesions in the amygdala in monkeys have been shown to be associated with the loss of fear reactions to previously threatening stimuli and indiscriminate sexual and eating behaviors; in effect, blinding animals to the affective qualities of stimuli in their environment (Kluver & Bucy, 1937; Weiskrantz, 1956).

From a neurodevelopmental perspective, then, it appears that the emotional system is functional before the emerging cognitive system, and operates independently of it in early infancy. Although the impact of the cognitive system on early behavior of the infant is constrained by cortical immaturity, the developing emotional system has considerable impact on the organism's interactions with the environment. Moreover, it probably plays a major role in facilitating early cognitive development. In order to consider these claims, it is helpful to consider further the structures of both the early affective and cognitive systems.

As suggested previously, processing of the affective qualities of stimuli probably occurs centrally in the amygdala. Peripherally, the emotional response in infancy involves activation of the autonomic nervous system, which controls visceral, automatic functioning. Individual differences exist in the intensity of the autonomic response to environmental stimulation (Bell, Weller, & Waldrop, 1971; Clifton & Graham, 1968; Lipton, Steinschneider, & Richmond, 1961; Rothbart & Derryberry, 1981; Stratton, 1982; Yang & Halverson, 1976). The integrity of the autonomic system is reflected in infant state and state regulation. The establishment of stable, distinct states (which refers to the infant's level of arousal) and the ability to regulate states are the primary goals of the young infant. Although there are a variety of state classification systems, most researchers divide states into the following categories: fussy or crying, awake alert, nonalert waking, sleep–wake transition (e.g., drowsy, dazed), active sleep, active/quiet transition sleep, and quiet sleep (Thoman & Whitney, 1990). It is important to note that although state regulation as well as emotional reactivity reflect the integrity of the underlying nervous system, it is not solely influenced by endogenous factors, but can also be affected by the caregiving environment. Appropriate caregiving can reduce reactivity, facilitate state regulation, and increase infant attention by such behaviors as swaddling, giving a pacifier, or providing vestibular stimulation.

The autonomic nervous system influences the infant's cognitive system through its effect on infant state. Cognitive life in early infancy develops through information processing and learning (Bornstein & Lamb, 1992). In order for information processing to occur, attentional processes must be operative, which, in turn, requires state modulation. The initial steps in learning require that the infant be alert for a long enough period to perceive the cues and respond appropriately (Bornstein & Lamb, 1992). Learning appears to occur most readily when the infant is in a quiet alert state (Papousek & Bernstein, 1969).

Two information processing tasks—habituation and novelty preference—provide researchers with a window into the attentional system of the infant. The assumption underlying these tasks is that an infant develops a central representation of a repeatedly administered stimulus. As this representation develops, the infant gradually reduces attention (habituates) to that stimulus and if given the opportunity, will redirect attention to a new stimulus that is presented (i.e., show a novelty preference). Performance on these tasks is thought to be indicative of greater speed and efficiency of mental processing; specifically, greater decrements in looking times (shorter looks) in the habituation paradigm, as well as longer looks at the novel stimulus relative to the familiar stimulus in the novelty preference paradigm, are thought to index superior cognitive ability. Support for this hypothesis comes from a wide variety of research relating performance on these types of tasks to intelligence test scores in later childhood (McCall & Carriger, 1993).

The attentional processes described previously appear to be heavily influenced by the autonomic nervous system. Infant emotional reactivity and regulation influence infant state, which, in turn, influences the attentional system in several ways. Initial attention to external stimuli is largely a function of state. For example, infants are more likely to attend to quiet sounds during the quiet alert state than during sleep or crying states. Within states, the level of emotional arousal also affects attentional processing. For example, during the awake alert state, infants who are less aroused prefer more complex visual stimulation than do infants who are more aroused (Gardner & Karmel, 1983). In addition, state appears to play a critical role in the infant's ability to process and remember a stimulus once it has entered the system (Columbo & Horowitz, 1987). State and emotional reactivity are likely to have an indirect effect on early cognitive development by influencing the type and amount of stimulation that adults provide to the infant. For example, infants who spend a proportionately greater amount of time in an alert phase may elicit more talking and play behaviors from adults, whereas infants who spend a greater amount of time fussing and crying may elicit either more soothing and calming or avoidance behaviors from their caretakers.

Research on vagal tone also suggests the special importance of the autonomic system's role in infant cognition. Vagal tone is measured by a component of heart rate variability, respiratory sinus arrythmia (RSA), which is controlled by the parasympathetic branch of the autonomic nervous system (Porges, McCabe, & Yongue, 1982). Vagal tone has been found to be related to measures of attention in infancy. For example, research has shown that individual differences in RSA measures are correlated with measures of sustained visual attention (Linnemeyer & Porges, 1986). Infants with higher RSA (more variable heart rates) are less visually distractible, and show greater orienting (greater heart rate decelerations) to visual stimulation in infancy (Richards, 1985, 1987). Infants with high vagal tone (high levels of RSA) are more able to suppress irrelevant aspects of the environment and focus on relevant information.

Up to this point, the influence of the emotional system, particularly state processes, on the cognitive system in early infancy has been emphasized. It is important to point out, however, that later development is best characterized by an increasing interdependency and reciprocity between these two systems. The affective system continues to exert influence on cognitive processes. The cognitive system, however, becomes increasingly involved in the regulation of emotion. From a neurological perspective, as the cortex matures, projections from the cortex to the amygdala and other areas in the brain allow cognitive information to modulate affective processing and vice versa. With development, primitive distress reactions to events can be inhibited in favor of more complex emotional responses, such as anger (Bornstein & Lamb, 1992). In addition, increasing cognitive capacities provide infants with active resources for self-regulating and for evaluating environmental events (e.g., Thompson & Limber, 1991).

In summary, then, there is neurological evidence that during early infancy the emotional system is capable of operating independently of the cognitive system and that the emerging cognitive system is driven by the emotional system, more specifically, the autonomic nervous system. Given the importance of emotional reactivity and emotional regulatory processes for attention, learning, and the encoding and retention of information, it is likely that disruptions or deviations in the autonomic nervous system (ANS), as well as neurological structures that controls ANS processes, may have adverse affects on the developing cognitive system. Als (1986) pointed out that the emergence of the early attentional/interactional system, which likely forms the basis for the cognitive system, cannot occur until the autonomic system is organized. Gardner and Karmel (1983) expressed concern that during early infancy maladaptive arousal patterns, such as hyperarousal, may alter central nervous system (CNS) organization in permanent ways. Citing research that shows that overly aroused infants prefer less complex and informative stimuli, they suggested that such preferences may be established as functional and structural connections in the brain, and have a detrimental effect on cognitive development.

In the next section, research examining temperament processes in children with mental retardation is described. As stated in the footnote cited earlier in the chapter, temperament and emotions during early infancy are co-equivalent and virtually indistinguishable processes, both having their foundation in the ANS. During later development, temperament processes provide a critical substrate for the emergence of complex emotions.

EMOTION AND MENTAL RETARDATION

As pointed out previously, definitions of mental retardation have traditionally emphasized cognitive deficiencies and defects as both the critical defining characteristic of this disorder and as the cause of behavioral impairments. We suggest in this section that this current perspective on the nature and development of mental retardation is overly simplistic and incomplete. From both a biological and an early environmental perspective, there is reason to believe that the persons with mental retardation are not only cognitively but emotionally different and that these emotional processes may have profound effects on the development of their cognitive system. In the present section we examine what we know about the emotional processes of the mentally retarded.

Critical to any discussion of the emotional system is the consideration of individual differences. Considering infants at risk for mental retardation, several characteristics of this population may operate to make some members atypical in their early emotional functioning. First, because of genetic deficiencies, normal polygenetic variation, or post-conceptual organic problems, some infants manifest extreme temperament traits, such as very low or elevated thresholds in reacting to stimuli, hypo- or hyperactive behavior, and/or an inability to modulate (regulate) responses to stressful stimuli. Second, some infants, due to sensory (visual and hearing problems) deficiencies, differ in their ability to perceive environmental stressors and socioemotional cues. Third, due to fine and gross motor deficiencies, some infants are not able to display normative expressions of emotion or normal responses for coping with stressful stimuli. These characteristics, individually and in combination, may disrupt normal patterns of emotional response, as a consequence interfering with the infant's ability to attend to and cognitively process environmental input. These characteristics may also complicate the task of the parent-caretaker, who must interpret and react to these emotional responses in order to support and facilitate social, linguistic, and cognitive development.

One system that likely has a pronounced influence on emotional development is temperament, especially those aspects relating to the reactivity and regulation of the arousal system. Affective regulation plays a vital role in the maintenance of physiological homeostasis. The development of affective regulation is governed by constitutional and social environmental factors. Constitutional factors important to the development of affective regulation include organizational changes in the central nervous system, brain lateralization, and the development of the neurotransmitter system (Cicchetti, Ganiban, & Barrett, 1991).

At birth, the infant has a number of motoric behaviors, including hand to mouth, posturing, gaze aversion, and sucking responses, that serve to reduce arousal. These regulatory responses are, however, not always operative or successful, especially in infants who have identifiable congenital handicaps. Such infants may be in particular need of external assistance from the environment to reduce arousal associated with physiological stress. These needs are communicated to the caregiver through emotional expressions such as distress or discomfort. "The effectiveness of such expressions depends on the caregiver's ability to understand their meaning as well as the infant's ability to generate readable cues about their internal states" (Cicchetti et al., 1991; p. 18).

Cicchetti and colleagues have suggested that children with Down syndrome may have problems in the development of emotion regulation as a result of both intraorganismic vulnerabilities and exogenous factors (Cicchetti et al., 1991). During normal infant maturation, homeostatic control is decreasingly regulated by caregivers as internal regulatory processes emerge. In "the first month of life, the development of forebrain inhibition and neurotransmitter systems support self-regulation . . . through the formation of neuronal tracts that link lower hindbrain or midbrain limbic structures with cortical regions. . . . In addition, the development of interhemispheric connections enhances the infant's ability to self-regulate and inhibit their behavior during the first years of life" (Cicchetti et al., 1991, p. 23). Right brain activation has been associated with distress, whereas left brain activation and simultaneous inhibition of right brain activity occur together with the expression of positive affect. The development of interhemispheric connections is thought to facilitate an infant's ability to regulate arousal. Researchers who have examined the maturation of the brain in individuals with Down syndrome have reported that their neuronal networks appear to be less differentiated and less elaborate than in normally developing individuals (Becker, Armstrong, & Chan, 1986). This decreased maturation in turn may deter the full development of important neuronal structures that control behavioral arousal and affect expression.

Some neurological anomalies that have been associated with Down syndrome, such as delayed maturation of neuroregulatory systems and relatively low physiological reactivity, likely have implications for emotional expressivity. Babies with Down syndrome appear to be passive or disengaged during social interactions, perhaps because their affect expression is less intense and of shorter duration than those of normally developing infants (Cicchetti et al., 1991). As a consequence, there is an increased risk that caretakers will misinterpret these dampened emotional expressions as signs of disinterest; furthermore, distress cries may be seen as less urgent, thus affecting the way caregivers help infants to modulate and manage arousal and tension.

Research suggests that unique temperamental characteristics may be associated with children with developmental delays, including Down syndrome children. Marovitch, Goldberg, MacGregor, and Lojkasek (1986) used the Toddler Temperament Scale to assess temperamental characteristics of children with neurological impairments, children with Down syndrome, children with developmental delay of unknown etiology, and children without delays. Although there were differences in temperament between the groups of delayed children, the three delayed groups, when combined and compared to the normal, standardization sample, were rated as less reactive, intense, and persistent in their behavior, and as possessing a higher sensory threshold.

The temperamental characteristics of children with Down syndrome have also been compared with a standardization sample of normally developing children of the same chronological age and with normally developing children of a similar mental age by mothers using the Toddler Temperament Scale (Gunn & Andrews, 1985). When compared to their age peers, Down syndrome children were described as lower in response intensity and persistence. Compared to children at a similar developmental level, Down syndrome children were also rated as lower in response intensity. Similarly, Bridges and Cicchetti (1982) compared Down syndrome children with nondelayed children of a comparable mental age. Mothers of children with Down syndrome rated them as being less approaching and lower in their threshold for stimulation. Most importantly, 40% of the Down children were classified as temperamentally difficult, as compared to 25% of the nondelayed sample.

Research examining the development of emotional expression in children with Down syndrome has suggested that they follow the same general developmental sequence as normal infants, but that their emotional expression is delayed. For example, although infants with Down syndrome eventually smile or laugh in response to physically intense events or incongruous stimulus items, they manifest delays in these positive expressions (Cicchetti & Sroufe, 1976). Similar delays in the expression of negative emotions such as fear and distress have been reported. Cicchetti and Sroufe (1978) compared the response to looming objects of Down syndrome infants with infants who were normally developing. At 4 months of age, no difference in crying was noted between the two groups; however, by 8 and 12 months of age, nonhandicapped infants demonstrated more crying and negative affect when presented with the looming objects. Infants with Down syndrome did not show a substantial amount of distress to looming objects until 16 months of age. Furthermore, the authors noted that the propensity to cry within the group of children with Down syndrome was associated with higher scores on the Bayley Scales of Mental Development. Similar results were found when the two groups of children were introduced to the visual cliff: Fewer Down syndrome infants cried when placed on the deep side of the visual cliff. Those who did cry were again evaluated as more cognitively mature on the Bayley Scales.

Because during infancy the Bayley is basically measuring motor development, one could speculate that either delays in emotional development inhibit motor development or vice versa. Another interpretation of these studies is that the manifestation of affect relates to an individual's ability to evaluate and understand his or her world. Immature neural networks or variations in speed of information processing may produce longer latencies to smile and may result in infrequent elicitation of emotions, such as fear or surprise, that sometimes require immediate processing of complex information (Cicchetti & Schneider-Rosen, 1984).

Izard and Buechler (1982) provided a different and intriguing theoretical context for viewing these findings, proposing an interactive or feedback–feedforward relationship between emotional and perceptual–cognitive processes. Within their framework, emotions during normal development bond with cognitions and are readily triggered by perceptual–cognitive processes, including appraisal, imagery, and anticipation. In contrast, children with mental handicaps are delayed in the formation of these emotion–cognitive bonds. Thus, although retarded infants may perceive the world similarly to nonhandicapped infants, they may not display affect normally associated with such perceptions. Izard and Buechler's intepretation was compatible with Becker et al.'s research indicating that Down children have immature neuronal networks, and with Cicchetti and Ganiban's (1990) finding that there is not a strict, one-to-one correspondence between cognitive and emotional development. In this latter study, when children with developmental delay were compared with nonhandicapped children of a similar cognitive developmental level, handicapped children still showed delays in the development of emotional expression. Izard and Buechler (1982) asserted that, "Since an emotion experience can occur without prior cognitive appraisal and since there may not be cognitive prerequisites for emotion experiences, the ontogeny of emotion expression in the developmentally delayed child cannot simply be predicted to be 'slower' than normal as though the emergence of an emotion expression were a cognitive-dependent task or response" (p. 366).

Some researchers have suggested that the signals of emotion expression in the developmentally delayed infant may be qualitatively different as well as delayed in their appearance (Emde, Katz, & Thorpe, 1978). For example, the social smile, delayed in children with Down syndrome, may also be atypical. Differences in facial morphology and facial musculature may affect the actual appearance of facial expressions. Social smiles in children with Down syndrome may also be harder to read because they do not show the normal covariance with other behavioral systems, such as increased activation of the arms and legs, cooing, and brightening of the eyes.

It is important to note that infants initially influence others through their affective expression. Because facial and vocal expressions of emotion serve as the primary tool of communication during infancy, delayed development of emotions and less readable expression of affect will likely have significant consequences for the establishment of the caregiver–infant relationship. Izard and Buechler (1982) suggested that in order for sensitive and responsive parenting to occur there must be: successful communication of the emotion being expressed, knowledge of the emotion-regulation capacities of the infant, accurate appraisal of the intensity of the infant emotion being expressed, and the potential for modulating the emotion through the expression of another emotion or state. The ability of a parent to respond sensitively may be seriously compromised when a child exhibits dampened and qualitatively different affective expressions. Thus, behaviors thought commonly to elicit maternal interaction, such as crying and social smiles, may be ineffective, making it difficult for the infant's needs to be satisfied. Relatedly, because the foundations of the sense of self as a causal agent are based in the infant's understanding that his or her emotions have an impact on others, the infant must experience appropriate differentiated and contingent social responses to its emotion signals. Without such feedback, the development of social competencies and a sense of self-efficacy is likely to be delayed.

The most devastating early effects of emotional system delays and disruptions may be on the infants' ability to form secure attachments with their parents. Colin (1991) concluded that "the mother's success in responding sensitively to her baby's needs and signals is a principal determinant of the baby's attachment pattern" (p. 44). In order for the attachment bond to develop, infants must signal their needs, and mothers must accurately interpret and respond to these signals. Research by Serafica and Cicchetti (1976) suggests that infants with Down syndrome make few attempts to signal, search for, or seek the proximity of their mothers in stressful situations, such as that associated with the Strange Situation assessment developed by Ainsworth (Ainsworth, Blehar, Waters, & Wall, 1978). Borkowski et al. (1992) suggested that infants who have attachment problems may be at risk for cognitive delays to the extent that such problems inhibit the infants' ability to attend to and explore their environment.

Conversely, it seems unlikely that parents will be either as active or effective in their role as teachers of their children if a strong attachment bond between the parent and child is not present. Problems in the formation of the attachment bond are not only a function of the infant's characteristics but also the parents' perceptions of such characteristics. Research suggests that parents perceive handicapped infants more negatively (Taylor, 1982). To the extent that such perceptions engender negative emotions, such as anxiety and depression, adverse maternal interactions with their infants, including maternal inattentivity, may also occur (Bettes, 1988). Infants are less likely to engage in cognitively beneficial exploratory behavior if their mothers are not emotionally available (Bornstein & Lamb, 1992).

In summary, present conceptions of mental retardation view this disorder as consisting of cognitive and adaptive behavioral deficiencies that are produced by either biological, environmental, or more typically a combination of biological and environmental factors. The role that socioemotional system and temperament factors play in this disorder has been virtually ignored. Based on our literature review, researchers have not examined how damage to neurological structures traditionally associated with emotional expression and regulation might influence early cognitive development, including orienting, attentional, and memorial processes. Moreover, relatively little is known about the temperament of infants who manifest or are at risk for mental retardation or about how temperament in this population influences cognitive functioning. Research on temperament, which is generally viewed as genetically and constitutionally based, is important because temperament provides the foundation on which emotional development is built. Although numerous investigators have been interested in the co-occurrence of emotional psychopathology and mental retardation in older individuals, such research has been basically descriptive. In contrast, researchers have not systematically examined the emotional development of infants at risk for mental retardation, in particular the factors influencing typical and atypical emotional development, or how emotional factors facilitate and inhibit cognitive development.

DIRECTIONS FOR FUTURE RESEARCH

Based on the literature reviewed, it should be clear to the reader that there is increasing evidence from research with infants and young children that emotions early in life have a substantial influence on the development of the cognitive system. Little is known, however, about the early emotional development of infants who are at risk for or who manifest mental retardation. In fact, comparatively little is known about the emotions of older children and adults with mental retardation. There is evidence, however, that children with mental retardation appear to be temperamentally different from children who are normally developing. There is also evidence that children at risk for or with mental retardation may show both delays in their expressions of basic emotions, such as fear and pleasure, and a dampening of such expressions once they appear. Because of these delays and differences in emotional expressions, disruptions in the social interactional and attachment processes would be expected between these children and their parents. At present, the ultimate effects of these delays and differences on the cognitive development of infants at risk for mental retardation is unclear. Research with normally developing infants, however, suggests that affective factors may have a pronounced influence on attentional and information processing capabilities. Currently, a systematic program of research for studying the emotional processes of infants and children at risk for or with mental retardation is needed, not unlike that being conducted by developmental psychologists with nonhandicapped populations. In this final section we summarize and discuss some of the directions that researchers might profitably pursue. It is critical to preface this discussion with a reminder to researchers that persons with mental retardation are not a homogeneous population and that whatever questions are examined, the importance of individual difference dimensions—such as etiology, sensorimotor functioning, and intellectual level—must be acknowledged and, whenever possible, systematically evaluated.

Presently, there are many unanswered questions concerning the temperament characteristics and the basic structure of emotions in infants at risk for or displaying mental retardation. For example, do such infants differ in their thresholds and the intensity of their physiological responses to environmental stimulation, their ability to self-regulate physiological arousal, their activity level, their predominant mood, and their shyness and sociability? Second, how do these temperament characteristics influence their cognitive system; specifically their attentional processes (including their ability to focus, habituation processes, scanning behavior, and their preference for novel stimulation and information processing speed), discrimination learning capabilities, and short-term and long-term memory? Third, do these infants show different facial expressions and instrumental responses when physiologically stressed than do nonrisk infants? For example, do they show less change in facial expression or more atypical facial expressions? Are they less likely to engage in self-comforting behaviors when stressed? Are their self-comforting behaviors less effective in reducing physiological arousal? What is the developmental course of these various expressive and instrumental responses?

In addition to questions about the structure of emotions and intersystem influences, there are basic questions that need to be more extensively investigated concerning high-risk infants and their relationships with their social–caretaking environments. Specifically, what is the social impact of these infants' physiological, facial, and motor expressions of emotions on their parents? Are the parents of these infants sensitive to the communications of their babies? Do they interpret correctly their infants' emotional signals and respond in a contingent and appropriate fashion to these communications? Conversely, what are the emotional styles of the infants' parents like? Are their emotional communications more exaggerated or blunted? Are they more likely to be depressed or anxious? How do the parents' emotional communications affect their infants' emotional (behavioral/facial and motoric) responses?

Considerable attention has been given by developmental researchers to the task of identifying social processes involved in promoting emotion regulation in nonhandicapped populations. According to Malalesta (1982), a mother's facial expressions, along with her tone of voice and the infant's feeling state, comprise the major features of the mother–infant emotional interchange. Mothers appear to shape infant affect through initiation and nonverbal contingent responses; specifically, mothers initiate infant facial expressions of emotion and respond selectively to their infant affective behaviors. Beyond infancy, a parent's verbal instruction becomes increasingly important. Although mothers more often encourage positive emotions, maternal anxiety has been linked to negative affectivity in infants. Little is known, however, about how the parents of retarded and at-risk children respond to the affective behaviors of their infants. To the extent that these parents are more stressed and anxious about their child's well-being, they may be sensitized to respond to their negative affective expressions and inadvertently encourage this type of affectivity.

Research by Field (1982a) indicates that high-risk infants experience more stress in their interactions with their mothers, in part because the mothers are overstimulating. Field speculated that these infants may have more difficulty regulating their arousal and that their mothers may have more difficulty reading their infant's signals and modulating the stimulation they provide their children. Brooks-Gunn and Lewis (1982) suggested that there may be different socialization practices between mothers and infants in families with normal and handicapped children. Results of their research suggest that handicapped infants smile less often and cry more frequently. Of particular importance is their finding that mothers of handicapped infants do not seem to encourage positive affect and become increasingly less responsive to their infants' negative affective expressions.

Research is also needed to understand the broader consequences of the early emotional interactions between high-risk infants and their caretakers. Tronick and his colleagues suggested that infant (and maternal) emotionality and effectance arise out of the quality of the infant–caretaker interactions (Tronick, Cohn, & Shea, 1986). Tronick et al. proposed that the emotions generated from these interactions not only influence infants' temporary affective state but also summate to form an affective core. Most importantly, the infants' affective core influences their evaluations of new situations and interactive patterns, even before information arising from the situation has been processed. For example, an infant who is depressed or anxious as he or she encounters a particular situation is predisposed for internal reasons to evaluate that situation fearfully and, as a consequence, disengage from it. In a very real sense, the affective core, formed through social interaction, structures directly the meaning of a situation and indirectly regulates interactive behavior. Infants whose affective core is negative (e.g., anxious, depressed) are at particular risk for developmental problems because they are likely to be deprived of social experiences and support that help them understand themselves as well as the world around them.

Brazelton and Yogman (1986) provided further insight into the processes that occur during infant–caretaker interactions. Although nonverbal, the emotional displays of the infant are powerful signaling systems. Through emotional signals an infant not only indicates physical distress, but also information about his or her acceptance or rejection of an adult's response to such emotional signaling. This acceptance or rejection on the part of the infant constitutes a rudimentary form of self-regulation. In order to signal effectively, the infant must attend to and respond to the social environment. More generally, the infant must have at least partial control over his or her neuromotor and physiological systems. Brazelton and Yogman (1986) emphasized "the remarkable capacities for attention and interactive behavior of the neonate when enclosed in the envelop of an adult interactant who is sensitive to the infant's need for regulation" (p. 4). The infant's dependency is translated into competency by an appropriately nurturing environment. Infants, through employment of emotional signals, attempt to control the social environment. These signals must be read and responded to appropriately by the infants' caretakers. If such control attempts are successful, an infant experiences a positive sense of affect as well as a sense of effectance. A similar process transpires for the caretaker.

Although the general wisdom of the goodness-of-fit notion is widely acknowledged, much remains to be learned about what actually constitutes a good fit. A variety of factors that potentially influence the at-risk infant's interactional style and affective core need to be investigated through multivariate methodologies, including infant temperament; infant health; caretaker cognitive, affective, and behavioral characteristics; and social contextual factors, such as a caretaker's social support system and material resources. The at-risk infant may be specifically influenced toward a negative affective orientation by a history of health problems, physical limitations that prevent effective emotional signaling, a "difficult" temperament, negative stereotyping by caretaker, caretaker depression or anxiety, ineffective or limited social supports, and poverty. Caretakers who are either overcontrolling (intruding continuously on infant activities and persistently engaging the infant, even when the infant is looking away) or undercontrolling (being hesitant and withdrawing) probably place the child at special risk for affective and regulatory problems. Anxious or depressed infants are likely to disengage from social interactions that are aversive or nonreinforcing. As a consequence of being disengaged, the infant loses access to valuable information.

Much has been written about social referencing and social looking in infants. Through social referencing, infants initiate and control social interactions as well as gain information about the environment and the appropriateness of their actions. Clyman, Emde, Kempe, and Harmon (1986) pointed out the need to investigate "the role of the parent–child relationship as it influences the occurrence of social referencing and its developmental consequences" (p. 89). They hypothesized that an optimal level of parental emotional availability may be necessary for infant–child social referencing to occur. A discomfited child seeks out information through social referencing, and a parent sensitive to the child signals appropriately respnds through glance, gesture, or word. On one hand, a detached or emotionally unavailable parent may inhibit social referencing through nonreinforcement. On the other hand, an overprotective parent may also inhibit social referencing if a child's needs are anticipated, thus making it unnecessary for the child to pay attention to or emit social signals. From this perspective, the occurrence of infant–child social referencing may be best facilitated in an atmosphere in which uncertainty occurs. Although the role of parents in facilitating social referencing in their children is somewhat obvious, the role of the child should not be overlooked. By definition, in order to manifest social referencing the child must orient to the caretaker. Such an orientation response may be, however, diminished in at-risk children who are temperamentally difficult, stressed by health problems, and/or autonomically over- or underaroused.

Demos (1986) emphasized the central role of infant affect in development and how crying plays an essential part of empathic interchanges between infant and caregivers. She pointed out that what constitutes an optimal caretaker response to infant crying is not a simple question. On one hand, a quick caretaker response to an infant's cry may teach the infant how to elicit social support when in distress. On the other hand, a slower caretaker response may allow the infant to develop or exercise a self-regulating capability, specifically, a capacity to self-soothe. Caretakers, in deciding how to respond, must consider the function crying is serving, for example, whether crying is innately elicited or serves a more instrumental communicative function.

Demos (1986) pointed out that the ease or difficulty that a particular caretaker experiences in trying to regulate an infant negative affect state is related to both infant characteristics (e.g., vigor, threshold for stimulation, self-soothing capabilities) and caretaker characteristics (e.g., calmness, soothing skills, beliefs about infant crying). Most important, this regulation process is influenced by the affect dynamics of the caretaker. The specific affective response that crying evokes in a caretaker depends on his or her emotional state, the meaning for the caretaker of the infant's distress, the degree of responsibility the caretaker feels for having produced or moderated the infant's distress, and the caretaker's own history of personal affect regulation.

At present, research is only beginning to examine how these different infant and caretaker variables contribute to the development of an infant's affective style. In particular, we have little insight into how the infant–caretaker interactive process is affected when an infant and/or caretaker manifest atypical, non-normative characteristics, such as when an infant has congenital or postnatal medical problems, or when caretakers have distorted beliefs about their infant and their parenting role, psychiatric problems, and/or have experienced a variety of life stressors, such as poverty, abuse, drug addiction, marital conflict, single parenthood, and poor health.

Brooks-Gunn and Lewis (1982) suggested that maternal perceptions and expectations concerning their infants may have greater influence over their socialization responses than the actual behavior of their infants. They suggest that mothers of high-risk children may not only require specific instruction on how to alter their behavioral interaction patterns with their children, but also must become sensitive to how their beliefs and expectations influence these behavioral interactions. Like Field (1982a), Brooks-Gunn and Lewis (1982) emphasized that the major socialization task of mothers is to help their children manage their emotions, specifically, to facilitate positive responses and to modulate negative affect, and to assist their children in interpreting and attaching meaning to their expressed emotions.

Finally, there are also numerous questions about how the early emotional development of at-risk infants influences their later emotional and cognitive development. What is the relationship of these infants' early temperament and emotional styles and their subsequent attachment patterns to their parents? What type of emotional characteristics place infants most at risk for insecure attachment to their parents? To what extent are these infants' emotional styles consistent over situations and stable over time? How does their emotional language system (labeling and expression of feelings) develop in relationship to their nonemotional language system? Are children who display atypical emotional characteristics and disrupted and insecure attachments also more likely to display deficiencies in intellectual, academic, and social functioning?

FINAL THOUGHTS

Multiple perspectives have been offered by Cicchetti and Ganiban (1990) in an attempt to understand the relationship between the development of emotion and cognition: cognitive epiphenomenalism, in which emotions provide the context in which cognitive development occurs; emotional epiphenomenalism, wherein the emergence of new emotions is dependent on cognitive advances; parallelism, in which emotions develop along a separate pathway from cognitive advances, thereby resulting in potentially different sequences, rates, and qualitative changes within each domain; and interactionism, which proposes that emotions emerge in interaction with cognitive advances, with reciprocal influences across these two domains. We suggest that the latter framework, in which emotion and cognition function in a reciprocal and interactive fashion, is particularly useful for viewing the development of mental retardation. Izard and Buechler (1982) pointed out that "Healthy and adaptive functioning is a function of two sets of processes: normal development of separate systems (which includes the emotional and cognitive systems) and balanced harmonious interaction among systems. Dysadaptive development results from deviant or retarded development within a system and/or imbalance and dysfunction among systems" (p. 355).

Unfortunately, emotional processes in "cognitive" task situations are seldom monitored by researchers. Moss (1992) pointed out that although cognitive researchers have increasingly studied the sociocultural influences on cognitive development, they have not systematically recognized the relevance of the emotional interactional climate for cognitive endeavors. She suggested that "the progressive internalization of the affective quality of the primary attachment relationship is associated with the elaboration of cognitive executive functions—specifically, those related to socially coordinated task engagement between the mother and the child" (p. 123). From this perspective, children who have experienced affectively positive relationships with their caretakers are more likely to cognitively engage their environment in an active fashion. Future research needs to examine how this affective context is translated behaviorally to support, nurture, and energize cognitive activities. This task undoubtedly will be a challenging one.

Although developmental researchers increasingly acknowledge the dynamic reciprocity between emotional and cognitive development, appropriate measurement procedures, experimental designs, and analytic strategies for capturing these interrelationships are still evolving. Undoubtedly one of the major reasons emotions have not been studied more vigorously by the scientific community is because of the problems associated with measuring emotion, particularly in infants and young children. In order to effectively proceed, researchers will need to employ a multitude of methodologies, including physiological, observational, and self-report procedures, and recognize that most behaviors have both emotional and cognitive components. Moreover, to index the emergence of both emotional and cognitive processes, longitudinal designs need to be employed. Finally, to assess the relationship of these processes and their determinants, appropriate methodologies, including multivariate approaches, hierarchical linear modeling, and time-series analyses, need to be considered.

ACKNOWLEDGMENTS

The writing of this chapter was supported by grants from the National Institutes of Health (#HD-26456) and the Center for the Study of Children, Notre Dame, Indiana. The second and third authors also received support from a NIH Predoctoral Training Grant (#HD-07184).

REFERENCES

Ainsworth, M., Blehar, M., Waters, E. & Wall, S. (1978). *Patterns of attachment: A psychological study of the strange situation.* Hillsdale, NJ: Lawrence Erlbaum Associates.

Als, H. (1982). Toward a syntactic theory of development: Promise for the assessment and support of infant individuality. *Infant Mental Health, 3,* 229–243.

Als, H. (1986). A syntactic model of neonatal behavioral organization: Framework for the assessment of neurobehavioral development in the premature infant and for support of infants and parents in the neonatal intensive care environment. In *The high-risk neonate* (pp. 3–53). Binghampton, NY: Haworth.

American Association of Mental Retardation (1992). *Mental retardation: Definition, classification, and systems of support* (9th ed.). Washington, DC: Author.

Barrett, K., & Campos, J. J. (1987). Perspectives on emotional development: II. A functional approach to emotions. In J. D. Osofsky (Ed.), *Handbook of infant development* (2nd ed., pp. 555–578). New York: Wiley.

Becker, L., Armstrong, D., & Chan, F. (1986). Dendritic atrophy in children with Down's syndrome. *Annals of Neurology, 20,* 520–526.

Bell, R. W., Weller, G. M., & Waldrop, M. F. (1971). Newborn and preschooler: Organization of behavior and relations between periods. *Monographs of the Society for Research in Child Development, 36*(1–2).

Bettes, B. A. (1988). Maternal depression and motherese: Temporal and international features. *Child Development, 59,* 1089–1096.

Borkowski, J., Whitman, T., Wurtz Passino, A., Rellinger, E., Sommer, K., Keogh, D., & Weed, K. (1992). Unraveling the new morbidity: Adolescent parenting and developmental delays. In N.

Bray (Ed.), *International review of mental retardation* (Vol. 18, pp. 159–196). San Diego, CA: Academic Press.

Bornstein, M. H., & Lamb, M.E. (1992). *Development in infancy: An introduction.* New York: McGraw-Hill.

Brazelton, T. B., & Yogman, M. W. (1986). Introduction: Reciprocity, attachment, and effectance: Anlago in early infancy. In T. B. Brazelton & M. W. Yogman (Eds.), *Affective development in infancy* (pp. 1–10). Norwood, NJ: Ablex.

Bridges, F., & Cicchetti, D. (1982). Mothers' ratings of temperament characteristics of Down's syndrome infants. *Developmental Psychology, 18,* 238–244.

Brooks-Gunn, J., & Lewis, M. (1982). Affective exchanges between normal and handicapped infants and their mothers. In T. Field & A. F. Fogel (Eds.), *Emotion and early interaction* (pp. 161–188). Hillsdale, NJ: Lawrence Erlbaum Associates.

Chess, S., & Thomas, A. (1989). Temperamental and its functional significance. In S. I. Greenspan & G. H. Pollock (Eds.), *The course of life* (Vol. II, pp. 163–227). Madison, CT: International University Press.

Cicchetti, D., & Ganiban, J. (1990). The organization and coherence of developmental process in infants and children with Down's syndrome. In R. M. Burack & E. Zigler (Eds.), *Issues in the developmental approach to mental retardation* (pp. 169–225). Cambridge, England: Cambridge University Press.

Cicchetti, D., Ganiban, J., & Barnett, D. (1991). Contributions from the study of high-risk populations to understanding the development of emotion regulation. In J. Garber & K. A. Dodge (Eds.), *The development of emotion regulation and dysregulation* (pp. 15–48). Cambridge, England: Cambridge University Press.

Cicchetti, D., & Schneider-Rosen, K. (1984). Theoretical and empirical considerations in the investigation of the relationship between affect and cognition in atypical populations of infants: Contributions to the formulation of an integrative theory of development. In C. Izard, J. Kagan, & R. Zajonc (Eds.), *Emotions, cognition and behavior* (pp. 366–408). Cambridge, England: Cambridge University Press.

Cicchetti, D., & Sroufe, L. A. (1976). The relationship between affective and cognitive development in Down syndrome infants. *Child Development, 47,* 920–929.

Cicchetti, D., & Sroufe, L. A. (1978). An organizational view of affect: Illustrations from the study of Down's syndrome infants. In M. Lewis & L. Rosenblum (Eds.), *The development of affect* (pp. 309–350). New York: Plenum.

Clifton, R. K., & Graham, F. K. (1968). Stability of individual differences in heart rate activity during the newborn period. *Psychophysiology, 5,* 37–50.

Clyman, R. B., Emde, R. N., Kempe, J. E., & Harmon, R. J. (1986). Social referencing and social looking among twelve-month-old infants. In T. B. Brazelton & M. W. Yogman (Eds.), *Affective development in infancy* (pp. 75–94). Norwood, NJ: Ablex.

Colin, V. (1991). *Human attachment: What we know now. A report prepared under contract* (No. HHS-100-90-00 for the Office of Planning and Evaluation). Washington, DC: U.S. Department of Health and Human Services.

Columbo, J., & Horowitz, F. D. (1987). Behavioral state as a lead variable in neonatal research. *Merrill-Palmer Quarterly, 33,* 423–437.

Day, J., Cordon, L., & Kerwin, M. L. (1989). Informed instruction and development of cognitive skills: A review and critique of research. In C. B. McCormick, G. Miller, & M. Pressley (Eds.), *Cognitive strategy research: From basic research to educational applications* (pp. 83–101). New York: Springer-Verlag.

Demos, V. (1986). Crying in early infancy: An illustration of the motivational function of affect. In T. B. Brazelton & M. W. Yogman (Eds.), *Affective development in infancy* (pp. 39–74). Norwood, NJ: Ablex.

Emde, R., Katz, E., & Thorpe, J. (1978). Emotion expression in infancy: II. Early deviations in Down's syndrome. In M. Lewis & L. Rosenblum (Eds.), *The development of affect* (pp. 351–360). New York: Plenum.

Field, T. (1982a). Affective displays of high-risk infants during early interactions. In T. Field & A. F. Fogel (Eds.), *Emotion and early interaction* (pp. 101–126). Hillsdale, NJ: Lawrence Erlbaum Associates.

Field, T. M. (1982b). Individual differences in the expressivity of neonates and young infants. In R. Feldman (Ed.), *Development of nonverbal behavior in children* (pp. 279–298). New York: Springer-Verlag.

Gardner, J. M., & Karmel, B. Z. (1983). Attention and arousal in preterm and full-term neonates. In T. Field & A. Sostek (Eds.), *Infants born at risk* (pp. 69–98). New York: Grune & Stratton.

Gibson, K. R. (1991). Myelination and behavioral development: A comparative perspective on questions of neoteny, altriciality and intelligence. In K. R. Gibson & A. C. Peterson (Eds.), *Brain maturation and cognitive development* (pp. 29–63). New York: DeGruyter.

Gunn, P., & Andrews, P. (1985). The temperament of Down syndrome toddlers and their siblings. *Journal of Child Psychology and Psychiatry, 26*, 973–979.

Izard, C. E., & Buechler, S. (1982). Theoretical perspectives on emotions in developmental disabilities. In M. Lewis & L. T. Taft (Eds.), *Developmental disabilities: Theory, assessment and intervention* (pp. 353–370). New York: SP Medical & Scientific.

Izard, C. E., Hembree, E. A., Dougherty, L. M., & Spizzirri, C. C. (1983). Changes in facial expressions of 2- to 19-month-old infants following acute pain. *Developmental Psychology, 19*, 418–426.

Izard, C. E., Hembree, E. A., & Heubner, R. R. (1987). Infants' emotional expressions to acute pain: Developmental change and stability of individual differences. *Developmental Psychology, 23*, 105–113.

Kagan, J. (1978). On emotion and its development: A working paper. In M. L. Lewis & L. A. Rosenblum (Eds.), *The development of affect* (pp. 11–42). New York: Plenum.

Kluver, H., & Bucy, P. C. (1937). "Psychic blindness" and other symptoms following bilateral temporal lobectomy in rhesus monkeys. *American Journal of Physiology, 119*, 352–353.

Kopp, C. B. (1989). Regulation of distress and negative emotions: A developmental view. *Developmental Psychology, 25*, 343–354.

Lazarus, R. S. (1982). Thoughts on the relations between emotion and cognition. *American Psychologist, 37*, 1019–1024.

LeDoux, J. E. (1989). Cognitive–emotional interactions in the brain. *Cognition and Emotion, 3*, 267–289.

LeDoux, J. E., Sakaguchi, A., Iwata, J., & Reis, D. J. (1986). Interruptions of projections from the medial geniculate body to an archi-neostriatal field disrupts the classical conditioning of emotional responses to acoustic stimuli in the rat. *Neuroscience, 17*, 615–627.

LeDoux, J. E., Sakaguchi, A., & Reis, D. J. (1984). Subcortical efferent projections of the medial geniculate nucleus mediate emotional responses conditioned by acoustic stimuli. *Journal of Neuroscience, 4*, 683–698.

Lewis, M., Alessandri, S. M., & Sullivan, M. W. (1990). Violation of expectancy, loss of control, and anger expressions in young infants. *Developmental Psychology, 26*, 745–751.

Lewis, M., & Michalson, L. (1983). *Children's emotions and moods*. New York: Plenum.

Linnemeyer, S. A., & Porges, S. W. (1986). Recognition memory and cardiac vagal tone in 6 month old infants. *Infant Behavior and Development, 9*, 43–56.

Lipton, E. L., Steinschneider, A., & Richmond, J. B. (1961). Autonomic functioning in the neonate: IV. Individual differences in cardiac reactivity. *Psychosomatic Medicine, 23*, 472–484.

Malatesta, C. Z. (1982). The expression of emotion: A lifespan-perspective. In T. Field & A. Fogel (Eds.), *Emotion and early interaction* (pp. 1–24). Hillsdale, NJ: Lawrence Erlbaum Associates.

Malatesta, C. Z., Culver, C., Tesman, J. R., & Shepard, B. (1989). The development of emotional expression during the first two years of life. *Monographs of the Society for Research in Child Development, 54*(1–2).

Marovitch, S., Goldberg, S., MacGregor, D., & Lojkasek, M. (1986). Patterns of temperament variation in three groups of developmentally delayed preschool children: Mother and father ratings. *Developmental and Behavioral Pediatrics, 7*, 247–252.

Matson, J. L., & Barrett, R. P. (Eds.). (1982). *Psychopathology in the mentally retarded.* New York: Grune & Stratton.

McCall, R. B., & Carriger, M. S. (1993). A meta-analysis of infant habituation and recognition memory performance as predictors of later IQ. *Child Development, 64*, 57–79.

Menolascino, F., & Stark, J. A. (Eds.). (1984). *Handbook of mental illness in the mentally retarded.* New York: Plenum.

Moss, E. (1992). The socioaffective context of joint cognitive activity. In L. T. Winegar & J. Valsiner (Eds.), *Children's development within social context* (Vol. 2, pp. 117–154). Hillsdale, NJ: Lawrence Erlbaum Associates.

Papousek, H., & Bernstein, P. (1969). The functions of conditioning stimulation in human neonates and infants. In A. Ambrose (Ed.), *Stimulation in early infancy* (pp. 229–252). New York: Academic Press.

Plutchik, R. (1980). *Emotion: A psychoevolutionary synthesis.* New York: Harper & Row.

Porges, S. W., McCabe, P. M., & Yongue, B. G. (1982). Respiratory-heart rate interactions: Physiological implications for pathophysiology and behavior. In J. Cacioppo & R. Petty (Eds.), *Perspectives in cardiovascular psychophysiology* (pp. 223–264). New York: Guilford.

Richards, J. E. (1985). Respiratory sinus arrhythmia predicts heart rate and visual responses during visual attention in 15 and 20 week old infants. *Psychophysiology, 22*, 101–109.

Richards, J. E. (1987). Infant visual attention and respiratory sinus arrhythmia. *Child Development, 58*, 488–496.

Rosenstein, C., & Oster, H. (1988). Differential facial responses to four basic tastes in newborns. *Child Development, 59*, 1555–1568.

Rothbart, M. K., & Derryberry, D. (1981). Development of individual differences in temperament. In M. E. Lamb & A. L. Brown (Eds.), *Advances in developmental psychology* (Vol. 1, pp. 37–86). Hillsdale, NJ: Lawrence Erlbaum Associates.

Rovee-Collier, C. (1986). The rise and fall of infant classical conditioning research: Its promise for the study of early development. In L. P. Lipsitt & C. Rovee-Collier (Eds.), *Advances in infancy research* (Vol. 4, pp. 139–159). Norwood, NJ: Ablex.

Serafica, F. C., & Cicchetti, D. (1976). Down's syndrome children in a strange situation: Attachment and exploration behaviors. *Merrill-Palmer Quarterly, 22*, 137–150.

Stratton, P. (1982). Newborn individuality. In P. Stratton (Ed.), *Psychobiology of the human newborn* (pp. 57–73). New York: Wiley.

Taylor, D. C. (1982). Counseling the parents of handicapped children. *British Medical Journal, 284*, 1027–1028.

Thoman, E. B., & Whitney, M. P. (1990). Behavioral states in infants: Individual differences and individual analyses. In J. Columbo & J. Fagen (Eds.), *Individual differences in infancy: Reliability, stability, prediction* (pp. 113–136). Hillsdale, NJ: Lawrence Erlbaum Associates.

Thompson, R. A., & Limber, S. (1991). "Social anxiety" in infancy: Stranger anxiety and separation distress. In H. Leitenberg (Ed.), *Handbook of social and evaluation anxiety* (pp. 85–137). New York: Plenum.

Tronick, E. Z., Cohn, J., & Shea, E. (1986). The transfer of affect between mother and infants. In T. B. Brazelton & M. W. Yogman (Eds.), *Affective development in infancy* (pp. 11–26). Norwood, NJ: Ablex.

Vygotsky, L. S. (1978). *Mind in society: The development of higher psychological processes.* Cambridge, MA: Harvard University.

Weiskrantz, L. (1956). Behavioral changes associated with ablation of the amygdaloid complex in monkeys. *Journal of Comparative Physiology and Psychology, 49*, 381–391.

Yang, R. K., & Halverson, C. F. (1976). A study of the "inversion of intensity" between newborn and preschool-age behavior. *Child Development, 47*, 350–359.

Zajonc, R. B. (1980). Feeling and thinking: Preferences and thinking: Preferences need no inferences. *American Psychologist, 35*, 151–175.

› 4 ‹

Behavioral Genetics and the Classification of Mental Retardation

Lee Anne Thompson
Case Western Reserve University

Genetic factors play an important etiologic role for many forms of mental retardation. A recent paper detailing the gene map of mental retardation (Wahlstrom, 1990) found mental retardation to be involved in 503 diseases, for which 69 were mapped to an autosome, 73 to the X-chromosome and more than 300 were identified as having a genetic origin with unknown location. Two genetic disorders, Down syndrome and fragile X syndrome, will typically account for one third of the identified genetic cases in samples of individuals affected by mental retardation (Bregman & Hodapp, 1991).

Genetic influences on mental retardation can be studied from a variety of approaches, including chromosomal studies, pedigree analysis, and linkage analysis. This chapter does not address the entire field of genetics and mental retardation, but instead focuses on one approach that can be used to understand how genes affect intelligence—behavioral genetics. Behavioral geneticists explain the etiology of diversity in human behavior in terms of genetic and environmental influences; however, behavioral genetic studies go beyond the age old nature–nurture issue. Most scientists today see the futility of pitting one theoretical perspective against the other. Clearly, research has indicated that both nature and nurture are influential, and now the quest is to dissect and describe how they work together to create the vast array of differences in human behavior. A prominent behavioral geneticist stated, "The day has arrived when showing that some trait is under partial genetic or environmental control without accounting for, or hypothesizing about, the mechanism of that influence will simply not do" (McGue, 1989, p. 508). This statement is particularly true for the study of intellectual ability, the most widely studied human behavior in the field of behavioral genetics. Study after study has reported estimates of genetic and environmental influence on intelligence, and most scientists today agree that intelligence is at least in part inherited, with heritability accounting for approximately 50% of the variance in IQ (Plomin & Neiderheiser, 1992).

In contrast to the large volume of behavioral genetic research that has been conducted on nonretarded persons, research involving persons with mental retardation is extremely sparse. In the recent edition of the most widely used behavioral genetic textbook (Plomin, DeFries, & McClearn, 1990), approximately 25 pages are devoted to a review of studies of intelligence and cognitive abilities; less than 1 page discusses research relevant to the intellectual range associated with mental retardation. Furthermore, the only behavioral characteristic used to define mental retardation in behavioral genetic studies has been performance on IQ tests. Despite the paucity of behavioral genetic research involving individuals with mental retardation, a review of the existing studies and an overview of the relevant methodology will be a valuable tool for directing future research. Behavioral genetic approaches can provide important etiological information about mental retardation. This chapter briefly describes basic behavioral genetic methods for the study of human behavior. Then, existing behavioral genetic studies of low IQ are reviewed. Finally, recent advances in the field of behavioral genetics are discussed, with the goal of suggesting alternative ways of researching mental retardation.

OVERVIEW OF BEHAVIORAL GENETIC METHODOLOGY

Behavioral genetic research uses quantitative genetic theory to estimate genetic and environmental contributions to individual differences in behavior. Studies of human behavior have used naturally occurring family groups with different degrees of genetic relatedness (family, twin, and adoption designs) to estimate genetic influence on a variety of behaviors. Behavioral genetic methodology is also an excellent tool for studying how the environment affects behavior. Typically, two broad categories of environmental influence are studied. Shared environmental influences are those experiences that create similarity among family members. Nonshared environment is comprised of those experiences to which family members are uniquely exposed. For instance, social class, parenting style, and family traditions are all examples of shared environmental influences. In contrast, birth order, accidents and illness, and different peer groups can be classified as nonshared environmental influences.

This section provides an introduction to basic behavioral genetic research design and analysis. First the family, twin, and adoption designs are described. These three designs allow the simple estimation of heritability, shared, and nonshared environmental influences. The second part of this section introduces methods to study how genes and the environment work together. Finally, a relatively new methodological approach for the study of selected groups is described.

Family Studies. A good starting point to establish a genetic basis for a trait or a specific disorder that is measured discretely is to look for familial patterns of inheritance in pedigrees. When variation in behavior that is measured on a continuous scale is studied, then direct comparisons of the degree of similarity across family members can be made. For example, correlations and/or regression coefficients can be computed between parents and offspring, between full siblings, between half-siblings, between grandparents, and between grandchildren. If genetic factors are influencing behavior, then the magnitude of the various intrafamilial correlations should differ with respect to the genetic relatedness of the pairings. However, family members also share experiences and their home environment. Familial resemblance is necessary but not sufficient evidence for a genetic and/or a shared family environmental hypothesis. Family studies are the important first step in a program of research designed to identify genetic and environmental factors influencing behavior, but family studies are limited in that they cannot disentangle the effect of genes from family environment.

Twin Studies. Twin studies are a widely used behavior genetic design and allow the separate estimation of genetic, shared, and nonshared environmental influences. Monozygotic (MZ) or identical twins are 100% identical for additive and nonadditive genetic influences, whereas dizygotic (DZ) or fraternal twins share on average 50% of their additive genes and 25% of their dominant genes. Assuming that MZ and DZ twin pairs experience equal amounts of shared environment, genetic influences are implicated if MZ twins are significantly more similar than are DZ twins. The equal environments assumption is still a point of debate for some, but, with respect to intelligence, the assumption appears valid (Plomin et al., 1990). Intraclass correlations are calculated for each type of twin and heritability is estimated by subtracting the DZ correlation from the MZ correlation and doubling the difference. Shared environment, those environmental factors that make family members resemble each other, is estimated by subtracting the estimate of heritability from the MZ correlation. Nonshared environment, those environmental factors that make family members different from each other, is directly estimated by subtracting the MZ correlation from 1; because MZ twins are genetically identical, any differences within pairs must be due to environmental effects.

However, current published reports of twin data rarely use twin correlations in this simple manner. Structural equation model fitting approaches have become the preferred approach (Neale & Cardon, 1992). Model fitting provides greater flexibility, allows multivariate analysis, provides goodness-of-fit estimates, and allows alternative genetic models to be tested. Although model fitting may be methodologically preferable, the quantitative genetic theory supporting the approach is the same as that for the simple comparison of correlations described previously.

Adoption Studies. When individuals are adopted at a young age, they share all of the family environment with their adoptive families but do not share genes. Correlations between adoptive family members and the adoptee provide direct estimates of shared family environmental influence. Partial adoption designs, the most common type of adoption study, compare the correlation of biologically related individuals to the correlations of the adoptee with adoptive family members. For example, if the adoptive families have both an adopted child and a biological child, then higher parent–offspring resemblance for the biological child as compared to the adopted child indicates genetic influence. Related and unrelated sibling correlations can be used in the same way.

A full adoption design provides more information but can also be more difficult to conduct. This design measures both the biological and adoptive parents of adoptees. Biological parents, especially fathers, may be difficult to recruit. Heritability can be directly estimated by doubling the biological parent–adoptee correlation (a parent and child share 50% of their additive genes), and shared family environment is directly estimated via adoptive parent–adoptee resemblance.

Separated twins provide a particularly powerful version of the adoption design when twins are separated early in life and reared in uncorrelated environments. This design cleanly separates the effects of genes and the environment. In this design, the correlation between identical twins reared apart directly estimates heritability. Similarly, doubling the correlation between DZ twins reared apart also directly estimates heritability. As in the classical twin design, any differences within MZ pairs must be attributed to nonshared environmental effects.

Locating twins separated early in life is a difficult task; however, two ongoing studies have been able to recruit relatively large samples of separated twins and have made important contributions to the behavioral genetic literature (Bouchard, Lykken, McGue, Segal, & Tellegen, 1990; Pederson, Plomin, Nesselroade, & McClearn, 1992). The heritability estimates for intelligence from these studies are higher than estimates from traditional twin studies, with heritability around 80% as opposed to 50%. These studies involve adult twins and support the intriguing theory that heritability of intelligence increases across the life span. Furthermore, these studies may also imply that data collected on twins reared together underestimates genetic influence on intelligence because of twin contrast effects, where twin pairs consciously try to be different from one another in order to forge their own individual identities. Twins reared apart are not affected by these issues.

Each of the three basic behavioral genetic designs has advantages and disadvantages. For example, it is easy to recruit families for the family study approach and, if the sample is randomly selected, the results should be generalizable. However, as mentioned previously, family studies cannot disentangle genetic and environmental influences. The twin design allows genetic and environmental influences to be studied separately. Twins are relatively easy to find, 1 in every 83 births, and they are usually eager to participate in studies. However, results from twin studies may not generalize to a broader population. Twins are more at risk for perinatal problems, they have unique "twin" experiences and the equal environments assumption may not be valid for all behavioral traits under study. Adoption studies may provide the "cleanest" behavioral genetic design for the estimation of genetic and environmental parameters, but the adoption design is the most difficult to conduct. Adoptees may be difficult to locate and recruit and, once again, may not be representative of the general population. Although each approach has distinct strengths and weaknesses, research on intelligence has utilized all three approaches in combination to provide compelling evidence for both genetic and environmental influences on IQ, as is described later in this chapter.

Genetic and Environmental Coaction

Behavioral geneticists have gone beyond the simple estimation of genetic and environmental influences and have begun to study how genes and experience operate together to create behavioral variation. Clearly, genetic and environmental influences do not operate in isolation; they must affect each other. Researchers have begun to explore how genes and environments are correlated, how they interact, and how genes influence the measurement of environmental influences.

Genotype–Environment Correlation. How and why do individuals receive the environments that they experience? Some experiences are random occurrences, but most experiences are to some degree selected for the individual either by the individual themselves, by family members, or by peers and teachers. To the extent that the selection of these environments is influenced by the individual's genetic makeup, genotype–environment correlation is operating. For example, a musically talented child is likely to seek out musically oriented activities at school and at home; this is referred to as *active* genotype–environment correlation. Similarly, parents and teachers of a musically talented child are quite likely to provide the child with opportunities to play instruments, sing, and so on; this is *reactive* genotype–environment correlation. Because parents and their children share genes, parents often select experiences for their children that are compatible with their own genotypes and therefore also with their children; this is *passive* genotype–environment correlation. Detailed discussion of these categories can be found in Plomin (1986). Research on intelligence has provided evidence for substantial genotype–environment correlation; however, the topic requires additional exploration for definitive answers about how genotype–environment correlation actually operates. Research involving extreme groups, for instance gifted individuals or individuals with mental retardation, might provide additional leverage on this topic; yet little research has been conducted using extreme samples.

Genotype–Environment Interaction. The same experience or environmental influence may not affect all individuals in the same way. To the extent that the effect is mediated by the individual's genotype defines genotype–environment interaction. For instance, a gifted child would benefit a great deal from extra work at school, whereas a less capable child would be overwhelmed. To the extent that scholastic achievement is genetically influenced, this example represents genotype–environment interaction. Research on this mechanism has been disappointing. Although the animal literature provides excellent examples of genotype–environment interactions, the human literature does not. Although the concept is intuitively appealing, very little evidence has indicated that it explains a significant portion of the variation in human behavior. However, as mentioned previously, extreme groups may yield more power to study this effect, and little research has been conducted using extreme groups, especially for cognitive ability. One adoption study has failed to find any evidence of genotype–environment interaction for IQ (Capron & Duyme, 1989); this study is further discussed later in this chapter.

Genetic Mediation of Environmental Measures. Behavioral geneticists study environmental influences as much or more than genetic influences. This statement is demonstrated by a line of research assessing how well environmental indices truly measure environmental effects. Psychologists have traditionally treated measures of the home environment as "pure" measures of the environment. An article by Plomin and Bergeman (1991), however, indicates that these indices are strongly influenced by genetic factors. For example, many measures of home environment count how many books are in the home. Parents generally place the books there. If a child's IQ is correlated with this measure, the correlation is in part due to the genetic resemblance between the parent, who placed the books, and the child. It is important to realize that many indices of the home environment are "contaminated" with genetic influences. This may be particularly true when extreme groups are studied. For example, environmental deprivation that has a detrimental impact on a child's cognitive ability is more common in homes where parental cognitive ability is also low.

Genetic Analysis of Selected Groups

The research methodology described thus far addresses questions on the etiology of individual differences across the full range of behavioral variation. If a question is raised about the etiology of an extreme—mental retardation as opposed to intelligence across the continuum—then different methodologies are required. In other words, for the low end of cognitive ability, the primary question is not what distinguishes a child with an IQ of 55 from one with an IQ of 50, but rather why both children are well below average as compared to the rest of the population. The distinction becomes one of the etiology of group differences as opposed to the etiology of individual differences.

Until recently this question has been addressed through the comparison of twin concordances. Usually, a cutoff score is set to determine the diagnosis. For example, IQs below 70 could be considered as partial evidence of mental retardation. If MZ twins are more highly concordant than DZ twins for IQs below 70, then genetic influences are implicated. However, this approach requires the rather arbitrary designation of cutoff scores.

DeFries and Fulker (1985) developed a multiple regression approach that allows the estimation of genetic and environmental effects on group membership while preserving continuous data. In essence, the approach tests for significant "group" (as opposed to traditional "individual") heritability via the differential regression to the population mean of the co-twins of identical and fraternal twin probands. For instance, if the mean co-twin IQ for a group of mentally retarded probands were higher in DZ twins than in MZ twins, genetic influences are important in determining group membership. Simple *t* tests of the MZ and DZ co-twin means will provide essentially the same results; however, multiple regression provides the added advantages of flexibility in that extended models can be developed and tested (LaBuda & DeFries, 1990), and standard errors are provided for every parameter estimate.

The multiple regression approach has been used extensively with reading disability (DeFries, Fulker, & LaBuda, 1987; DeFries & Gillis, 1991) and in one study with twin data for both high and low intelligence (Thompson, Detterman, & Plomin, 1993). The results from this twin study are thoroughly discussed later in this chapter.

REVIEW OF BEHAVIORAL GENETIC STUDIES OF LOW IQ

As mentioned previously, the number of behavioral genetic studies that have included individuals with low IQ is small. In contrast, intelligence across the continuum has been the most widely studied human trait. In 1981, Bouchard and McGue published an exhaustive review of all family, twin, and adoption studies of IQ. Chipeur, Rovine, and Plomin (1990) used the summary data from the Bouchard and McGue paper and simultaneously analyzed the data with a multivariate genetic model, which provided parameter estimates for additive and nonadditive genetic effects, shared and nonshared environmental influences. The results indicated that 45% of the variance in IQ can be attributed to genetic factors, 32% additive and 13% nonadditive. The contribution of shared environment varies depending on the study design. For example, 38% of the variance in IQ was explained by shared environment in twin studies, 25% in studies of siblings, 19% in studies of parents and offspring, and 11% in studies of cousins. Family, twin, and adoption designs converge on the finding that genetics play a significant role in the determination of individual differences in IQ. This section reviews studies of low IQ using the family design, the twin design, and the adoption design.

Family Studies

Most behavioral genetic family studies of intelligence use IQ as a continuous variable and typically report correlations or regressions for family members (i.e., between parents and offspring or between siblings) to establish familial similarity. In contrast, most family studies of mental retardation do not treat IQ as a continuous variable; instead, IQ becomes a diagnostic tool to indicate the severity of retardation, and the level of retardation is measured categorically. Hence, most reports are limited to listing observed frequencies of affected relatives of probands. Furthermore, many family studies of mental retardation suffer from ascertainment bias. For instance, if an institutionalized population of probands is used as the base sample and then pedigree information is obtained, the sample is probably not representative of the entire population of mentally retarded individuals. Not surprisingly, a comparison of incidence estimates across studies shows a great deal of variability due largely to the different populations that are ascertained, although all indicate some degree of familiality for mental retardation. Table 4.1 provides a summary

TABLE 4.1
Summary of Representative Family Studies of Mental Retardation

Authors, Year	*Incidence of Retardation in Relatives*
Third Annual Report of Eugenics Society (covers all retarded in Vermont), 1929	1 MR parent—26.4% MR offspring
	2 MR parents—44.1% MR offspring
Brugger (studied relatives of retarded patients), 1930	Neither parent MR—17.8% had MR siblings
	1 MR parent—41.3% MR siblings
	2 MR parents—93.2% MR siblings
Brock (studied offspring of retarded patients), 1934	1 MR parent—25% MR offspring
Penrose (studies parents and siblings of retarded probands), 1938	1 MR parent—15% MR offspring
	9.5% MR siblings of MR proband
Akesson, 1961	1 MR parent—39.8% MR offspring
	53% MR siblings of probands with IQs between 70 and 85
Reed & Reed (studied relatives of institutionalized MR patients), 1965	28% of all first-degree relatives MR
	7.1% of all second-degree relatives MR
	3.1% of all third-degree relatives MR
	1 parent MR—12.7% offspring MR
	2 parents MR—39.4% offspring MR
Nichols (Collaborative Perinatal Project), 1984	White severe MR—0% MR siblings
	White mild MR—20.7% MR siblings
	African American severe MR—20.8% MR siblings
	African American mild MR–21.2% MR siblings

of a handful of family studies that have reported incidence figures for mental retardation among family members.

Reed and Reed (1965) conducted a family study that is frequently cited due to their careful selection, testing, and interviewing of the subjects involved. The study still stands as a landmark attempt to collect solid evidence for a genetic basis for mental retardation, and provides a great deal of detailed information about the sample involved. Their conclusions can be summarized by the following statement: "The most obvious implication of these studies is that the greatest predisposing factor for the appearance of mental retardation is the presence of retardation in one or more relatives of the person concerned" (Reed & Reed, 1965, p. 71).

In addition to analyzing the total sample, Reed and Reed also analyzed the incidence of mental retardation in relatives according to a hypothesized etiological category. Specifically, based on medical and family history, each proband was placed in one of four categories: Primarily Genetic, Probably Genetic, Environmental, and Unknown. The category of Primarily Genetic included diagnosed chromosomal anomalies and genetic syndromes, as well as consanguinity in the parents of the probands, and the incidence of one or more siblings with similar types of low-grade mental retardation. The Probably Genetic category was based on a family history of mental retardation. Evidence of disease, infection, or severe injury placed probands in the Environmental category. Many cases did not provide a clue to the cause of retardation and were placed in the Unknown group. These categories provided the following percentages of affected first-degree relatives: 33.6%, 50.7%, 21.4%, and 15.6%, for the Primarily Genetic, Probably Genetic, Environmental, and Unknown categories, respectively. Notice that the Probably Genetic group yielded the greatest number of affected relatives.

Shortly after the Reed and Reed study was published, a two-group theory of mental retardation was proposed by Zigler (1967). According to the theory, clinical retardation implies either serious brain insult or nonheritable genetic disorders and involves moderate to profound (i.e. IQ under 50). Relatives are typically not mentally retarded and the affected persons are from all levels of socioeconomic class. Cultural–familial retardation refers to mild retardation (IQ between 55 and 70), which accounts for approximately three fourths of all retarded individuals and is usually attributed to polygenic heredity combined with disadvantageous socioeconomic factors.

A reanalysis of the Reed and Reed data (Johnson, Ahern, & Johnson, 1976) provided some support for this two-group classification. Restricting the reanalysis to 242 probands with IQ scores and with at least one sibling yielded a significant effect for the frequency of retarded siblings by IQ level of the probands. In summary, lower IQ subjects have fewer mentally retarded siblings than do higher IQ subjects. Furthermore, when lower IQ individuals have a mentally retarded sibling, the sibling is likely to be lower in IQ than the mentally retarded siblings of higher IQ subjects. A reanalysis of parental information for the same sample indicated that those subjects with IQs above 40 were more likely to have one or both parents who were mentally retarded. An important distinction is made in this study. Although a significant portion of those mentally retarded individuals with severe mental retardation have a genetic basis to their disorder, mild mental retardation appears to be more heritable.

Further support for these findings is provided by Nichols (1984). A sample of children with mental retardation selected from the Collaborative Perinatal Project were studied along with their siblings. The incidence of severe retardation in the sample was 0.5% for Whites and 0.7% for African Americans. The incidence of mild retardation was 1.2% for Whites and 4.6% for African Americans. The severely mentally retarded White probands did not have any siblings who were mentally retarded, whereas 20.7% of the siblings of the mildly mentally retarded probands had mental retardation. In contrast, the African-American probands showed an equal proportion of mentally retarded siblings for both the severely and mildly retarded groups, 20.8% and 21.1%, respectively. Although these results support the two-group distinction for White samples, the same criteria may not apply to other ethnic groups.

Family studies have found support for both genetic and environmental influences on mental retardation and more important, have suggested that the etiology of mental retardation varies across the degree of severity of mental retardation. Advances in the technology used to identify genetic bases for disorders have provided new evidence that supports separate etiologies for different types of mental retardation, but also suggests that the two-group theory is too simplistic. Studies have shown that a significant portion of mildly retarded individuals may also be suffering from nonheritable genetic disorders. For example, a recent review (Bregman & Hodapp, 1991) cites two epidemiologically representative studies of children in Great Britain and Sweden (Hagberg, Hagberg, Lewerth, & Linberg, 1981; Lamont & Dennis, 1988), in which medical factors were involved in 30% to 42% of the 295 children with mild mental retardation. Around 20% of the children in the study conducted in Britain had a genetic basis for their disorder. Interestingly, for the group that indicated some form of medical cause, 39% had two parents who had received some form of special education, thus illustrating the complexity of separating polygenic and environmental etiologies in studies of this nature. In summary, although the distinction can be made between clinical and cultural–familial retardation, recent discoveries have made the definitional boundaries between the two categories less clear.

One final study is mentioned in this section. Fraser and Sadovnick (1976) asked the question of whether the IQ level of a person with mental retardation and suffering from a chromosomal abnormality is purely a function of the severity of the abnormality or whether the level is also dependent on other unaffected genes. They studied a sample of 25 people with Down syndrome reared in institutions and 23 people with Down syndrome reared at home. Their siblings and parents were also studied. Correlations among the relatives, siblings, and parent–offspring comparisons were all around .50, as expected from the literature. The correlations between Down syndrome subjects reared at home and their relatives were also around .50. The correlations between Down syndrome subjects reared in institutions and their relatives were significant for the mother–child comparison (.69) but not for the sibling–sibling or father–child, (.20 and .29, respectively). The lower familial correlations in the families with the children reared in institutions may reflect how nonshared environmental influences can decrease familial resemblance; however, the fluctuation in correlations may also be due to sampling error. Although the sample was small, this study raises an intriguing question: Can family data be used to predict the IQ level of children born with Down syndrome? It appears as if the polygenic foundation for normal variation in intelligence continues to operate in the face of a major chromosomal anomaly.

Twin Studies

As can be seen in the preceding section, relatively few family studies of mental retardation have been conducted. Several of these studies mention the incidence of retardation in a small number of twin pairs separately for identical and fraternal pairs. Table 4.2 summarizes these studies. Reed and Reed (1965) also assessed many pairs of twins in the extended kinships of their families, but did not report IQs separately by zygosity for the sample. Pooling the probandwise concordance rates across the three samples reported in Table 4.2 yields a concordance of 77% for identical twins and 35% for fraternal twins, thus suggesting a genetic basis for mental retardation.

Only one twin study has been conducted that directly addresses the etiology of low IQ—the Western Reserve Twin Project (Plomin & Thompson, 1993). The study assessed intelligence, specific cognitive abilities, and scholastic achievement in a sample of twins with average, high, and low IQ. Using a cutoff of −1.25 standard deviations below the mean, which is approximately an IQ of 85 and below, 21 fraternal twin pairs and 18 identical twin pairs yielded probandwise concordances of 69% and 76%, respectively. These concordance rates suggest the effect of shared family environment.

The search for genetic and environmental contributions to low IQ was extended through the use of the regression analyses developed by DeFries and Fulker described in the preceding methodology section. In an analysis of individual heritability, the results indicate that heritability does not change across the IQ continuum, although a trend was

TABLE 4.2
Summary of Twin Pair Data From Family Studies of Mental Retardation

	Identical		*Fraternal*	
Authors	*N*	*Concordance*	*N*	*Concordance*
Wilson & Matheny (1976)	4	100%	4	40%
Nichols (1984)				
White	1	100%	5	29%
African American	11	63%	23	36%

evident suggesting higher heritability at the high end. Shared family environment was significantly greater at the low end for a composite score of IQ and achievement combined (Thompson, Detterman, & Plomin, 1993). In other words, genetic causes of individual differences within the average, high, and low IQ groups appear to operate to the same degree, whereas shared family environment appears to be more influential in the low IQ group.

A separate paper explored the possibility that the etiology of low and high ability groups differ (Plomin & Thompson, 1993). This distinction is important, because finding a genetic contribution to individual differences within groups does not imply that average differences between groups are also genetic in origin. Group analyses indicate that the etiology for average and high IQ groups is primarily genetic, whereas the etiology for low IQ is primarily determined by shared family environmental factors. Although the results from both analytic approaches agree in direction, the second analysis essentially explored group mean differences in terms of genetic and environmental components and, therefore, had a great deal more power with the given sample size to detect significant effects.

Several other studies (Bailey & Revelle, 1991; Cherny, Cardon, Fulker, & DeFries, 1992; Reed & Rich, 1982) have attempted to explore the question of differential individual differences heritability across the IQ continuum using a variety of approaches with conflicting results. However, with the exception of the Reed and Rich (1982) study, which found evidence for greater genetic influence on low IQ, few subjects were included that actually had IQs below 70. It is clear that additional behavioral genetic studies that include a significant number of individuals with lower IQs are required before definitive answers will be found regarding differential heritability across the IQ range.

Adoption Studies

In general, fewer adoption studies of intelligence and cognitive abilities have been conducted than have twin studies. In the major adoption studies in the literature, the question of genetic influence on mental retardation has not been addressed. However, one unique and important study used a full cross-fostering design to assess the effects of socioeconomic status (SES) on IQ, a question that may be of interest to researchers of mental retardation. Capron and Duyme (1989) studied a group of 38 adoptees. Eighteen adoptees were born to high SES parents; 10 were placed in high SES adoptive homes and 8 were placed in low SES adoptive homes. Twenty adoptees were born to low SES parents; 10 were placed in high SES adoptive homes and 10 were placed in low SES adoptive homes. Mean IQs across the four groups were then compared to determine the effect of genetics (biological parents' SES) and environment (adoptive parents' SES). The mean IQs were 119.6, 107.5, 103.6 and 92.4, respectively. A significant effect for both genetic and environmental influences was found with no evidence of an interaction. With respect to this chapter, perhaps the most intriguing aspect of this study is that the group born to low SES parents (and therefore presumably lower IQ parents) being raised in a high SES environment had a mean IQ that was more than 10 points higher than the group born to low SES parents. However, these results should not be overinterpreted; the sample was small, and the low SES group had a mean IQ of 92.4.

Summary

Although the results from the handful of behavioral genetic studies that included individuals with low IQ have been interesting, perhaps the most informative aspect of this review is the glaring lack of research in this area. Given that intelligence appears to be strongly genetically influenced and that individuals with low IQ may be affected by both genetic and deleterious environmental factors, it seems that behavioral genetic methodology would be ideal for disentangling the effects of genes and environment in this population. The final section in this chapter considers several promising directions for future behavioral genetic research on the etiology of low IQ.

FUTURE DIRECTIONS

This chapter has thus far reviewed methods and studies that represent traditional, well-defined approaches to the study of behavioral genetics and intelligence. The remainder of this chapter identifies new directions under development that may hold a great deal of promise for furthering our understanding of genetic and environmental influences on intelligence and the mechanisms by which these influences are made.

Molecular Genetic Approaches

As mentioned previously, the scope and nature of behavioral genetic research is in transition. Rapid advances made in the field of molecular genetics have made possible research endeavors that just a few years ago would have been considered pure science fiction. The fields of molecular genetics and behavioral genetics that have existed separately from each other are beginning to merge, and an up-to-date review of behavioral genetic methodology would be severely lacking without at least a brief explanation of molecular genetic methods and contributions.

The use of molecular genetic techniques to identify causes of mental retardation is certainly not novel. However, most of the identified causes have been confined to major chromosomal anomalies or single-gene disorders. In general, individuals with chromosomal abnormalities that involve greater amounts of absent or excess genetic material exhibit more severe retardation, although exceptions to this rule have been found (Bregman & Hodapp, 1991). Early molecular genetic techniques (i.e., karyotyping) allowed the identification of gross chromosomal abnormalities (trisomies, monosomies, large deletions, and translocations). As techniques became more advanced, smaller abnormalities became detectable.

When restriction enzymes were first introduced in the early 1980s, the ability to identify genes responsible for single-gene disorders was realized. Restriction fragment length polymorphisms, when closely linked to a disorder within a family pedigree, have been extremely useful in mapping the location of disorders. Linkage analysis has two major limitations. First, a single gene or major gene must be causing the disorder. Second, extended family pedigrees must be used to map the gene involved. Low IQ is somewhat arbitrarily defined by imposing categorical cutoff scores onto a continuous variable. The large number of individuals with mental retardation for whom a clear etiology has been elusive are probably affected by polygenic inheritance and/or environmental insult. Linkage studies will not provide any useful information about these individuals.

The challenge is to be able to look directly at the genotypes for low IQ that are caused by multiple genes. Why is this a challenge? First, each gene in isolation has only a small effect. Second, IQ is manifested on a continuous scale rather than on a dichotomous scale. In reality, how different are two individuals when one has an IQ of 69 and the other of 71? Yet the former score would be in the mildly retarded range and the latter would not. Third, regardless of the genetic effects, the phenotype of low IQ is likely to be affected by environmental influences that can make the genetic effects harder to detect and trace.

Genes that have varying effect size and that influence quantitative traits like intelligence are called *quantitative trait loci* (QTL). A relatively new methodological approach that can be used to identify QTL is called *allelic association.*

Allelic association involves specific alleles in contrast to linkage, which involves the loci rather than the alleles. Marker alleles are either part of the gene of interest or are so close to the relevant gene that the marker allele is correlated with the trait in unrelated individuals. This approach has been used to identify a series of four gene markers that explain about 25% of the variance of serum cholesterol levels in normal populations (Sing & Boerwinkle, 1987). Some success has also been achieved for identifying marker alleles associated with alcoholism (Cloniger, 1991).

To reiterate, the major advantages that allelic association has over linkage analysis is that a sample of unrelated individuals can be used and that association analyses can be made powerful enough to study quantitative traits affected by small genetic effects. Association analyses hold a great deal of promise for the study of mental retardation.

An ongoing study is pioneering the use of allelic association to identify QTL affecting high and low cognitive ability (Plomin & Thompson, 1993; Plomin et al., 1994; Plomin et al., 1995). Blood samples were obtained from a selected group of school-age children who had participated in the Western Reserve Twin Project. Permanent cell lines have been established for low-IQ (mean IQ = 82, n = 18), middle-IQ (mean IQ = 105, n = 21), and high-IQ (mean IQ = 130, n = 24) groups. In addition, a replication sample of singleton children were recruited to form more extreme high and low IQ groups (mean IQ = 142, n = 27, and mean IQ = 59, n = 17, respectively). To date over 100 DNA markers in or near genes of neurological relevance have been screened. Two interesting results are discussed here.

The segment of the X chromosome that contains the site for fragile X mental retardation was explored in the QTL study. FMR-1, a gene at the fragile site of the X chromosome, has a repeating triplet code of cytosine (C) and two guanines (GG). This triplet code CGG sequence is polymorphic in the normal population in that the number of repetitions varies from 6 to 54 repeats with an average of about 29 (Fu et al., 1991). Individuals affected by fragile X have in excess of 200 repeats of this triplet code, CGG. The QTL study tested the hypothesis that in the general population the number of FMR-1 CGG relates to variation in IQ (Daniels et al., 1994). Specifically, the study tested the mean number of repeats across the three IQ groups: low, middle, and high. Although the sample sizes provided enough power to reliably detect an average difference of two repeats across low- and high-IQ groups, there was no evidence to support a correlation between the number of FMR-1 CGG repeats and IQ in the general population.

Another recent publication emanating from the QTL study reports that a specific restriction fragment length polymorphism (RFLP) yields significant differences between low and high IQ groups in both the original and replication QTL samples (Skuder et al., 1995). The RFLP is a brain-expressed sequence tag site, EST00083, derived from a cDNA hippocampal library. Interestingly, this RFLP is due to the absence of an Mspl restriction site (Mspl is a specific restriction enzyme) in mitochondrial DNA. Traits that are inherited via mitochondrial DNA show maternal transmission only because mitochondria are inherited from the cytoplasm of the egg. Although this finding is intriguing, the results need to be replicated before this gene is pursued more rigorously as a cause of mental retardation.

Neurophysiology

Research on the biological bases for normal variation in intelligence is a growing area (see Matarazzo, 1992). Increasing attention is being paid to the role of brain structure and function responsible for individual differences in intelligence. Recent technological advances in the area of neuroimaging have opened up new avenues for this line of research. Studies of subjects with mental retardation with positron emission tomography (PET) and functional magnetic resonance imaging (FMRI) are just beginning to emerge (Haier, Siegal, Tang, & Abel, 1992), with interesting but varied results. Given that genetic influences on mental retardation must be expressed at some level in the brain, the merging of these technologies with genetic studies will in the future provide a great deal of valuable information. At this time, however, these studies have yet to be conducted.

Electroencephalograms (EEG) monitor the amount and location of electrical activity in the brain. This technology has been available for some time. EEG can also be used to study the degree to which different brain areas function in cooperation with each other during cognitive processing. This approach is known as *EEG coherence* and is the correlation in the frequency domain that compares the degree of synchrony between two EEG signals with each signal's internal synchrony over a specific bandwidth (Thatcher et al., 1987). If coherence was measured in a system where generators were not functionally connected, the relations between such generators would be simple reflections of the distances between them. However, Nunez (1981) suggested that coherence does not follow this pattern and actually exhibits the opposite pattern with maximal values occurring at the largest distances. Therefore, significant coherence between two different brain areas may suggest that they are involved in the same information processing task.

EEG coherence has been found to be related to intelligence (Thatcher et al., 1987). In a group of 191 children, a negative relation between coherence and intelligence was found, suggesting that intelligence is related to higher brain specialization. One small twin study of EEG coherence has been conducted (Ibatoullina, Vardaris, & Thompson, 1994). The study indicates significant genetic influence on long-distance, intrahemispheric connections and environmental influences for interhemispheric connections. Again, the combined use of neurophysiological and genetic analyses could be quite important for the study of mental retardation in the future.

Differences in IQ

This chapter has thus far summarized the existing literature involving behavioral genetics and low IQ, and has also pointed out several promising avenues of research. Up until this point, only studies involving individuals with IQ below a specific criteria have been used. However, as has been pointed out several times throughout the chapter, intelligence is a continuously measured trait and any cut-off criteria is somewhat arbitrary. In this last section, it is suggested that when intelligence is lowered for any reason below a potential, interesting results may be found. For example, if a child is born with an IQ of 140 but then experiences severe environmental trauma and the resulting IQ at age 7 is 100, traditionally this child would be classified as average. Clearly, the child has been affected, given a 40-point drop in IQ. Social policy and the allocation of resources require that deficits or disabilities be defined concretely and be restricted to those that require aid; basic scientific inquiry does not.

Further examples clarify the utility of this redefinition. Identical twins share 100% of their genes; therefore, any within-pair differences must be due to environmental factors. To the extent that members of MZ twins pairs have differing IQs, the lower scoring twin may have experienced some type of environmental influence that had a lowering effect. The analysis of identical twin pairs may help to identify environmental influences that have subtle yet important detrimental effects on intelligence. Bailey and Horn (1986) used this approach across five samples of MZ twins and tentatively concluded that prenatal environmental influences unique to identical twins have a detrimental effect on intelligence.

Another related approach can be conducted with adoption data. If the biological midparent IQ is regressed onto the adopted child's IQ, then the residualized score can be used as an index of how much the child's IQ differs from his or her inherited potential. Environmental variables can then be used to predict this residualized score to suggest the nature of this difference. Studies of this type have yet to be conducted.

The family study of children with Down syndrome and their siblings indicates that Trisomy-21 has a lowering effect on IQ but that individual variation remains as it is inherited. It is possible that many genes have a small lowering effect on IQ but only result in low IQ if a significant number of them are all operating in synchrony in the same downward direction. Looking at highly discrepant sibling pairs even within the normal range with molecular genetic approaches may be useful in this respect.

CONCLUSIONS

Although behavioral geneticists have conducted a great deal of research on normal variation in intelligence, comparatively little research has been completed on low IQ. In summary, family studies support the two-group distinction between clinical and cultural–familial retardation, therefore suggesting that at least some portion of the population of individuals with mental retardation have a heritable polygenic disorder. Furthermore, a small family study of individuals with Down syndrome suggests that polygenic influences continue to influence IQ even when an individual has a major chromosomal anomaly. Preliminary results from a single twin study of low IQ suggest that shared environmental influences are more influential at the low end of the intellectual continuum as compared to the normal and high IQ groups. Little evidence was found in an adoption study for genotype–environment interaction; however, the groups were not extreme.

The etiology of low IQ is undoubtedly explained by both genetic and environmental influences. The goal is to identify specifically how genes affect IQ and to isolate deleterious environmental effects. These are lofty goals; intelligence is a complex behavior and factors that influence intelligence operate in a complex manner. Behavioral genetic studies of low IQ subjects are difficult to conduct as evidenced by the relatively few studies completed to date. However, with the new technologies available across the fields of molecular genetics, behavioral genetics, and neurology, this trend could reverse in the near future. Molecular genetics will allow the identification of specific genes and gene products that cause low IQ, advances in neuroimaging may illustrate how brain structure and function mediate the relationship between genes and complex behavior, and standard behavioral genetic studies of the environment will provide evidence for specific environmental factors that affect IQ independent of genetic etiology.

REFERENCES

Akesson, H. O. (1961). *Epidemiology and genetics of mental deficiency in a southern Swedish population.* Uppsala, Sweden: Almquist and Wiksells.

Bailey, M. J., & Horn, J. M. (1986). A source of variance in IQ unique to the lower-scoring monozygotic (MZ) cotwin. *Behavior Genetics, 16*, 509–516.

Bailey, M. J., & Revelle, W. (1991). Increased heritability for lower IQ levels? *Behavior Genetics, 21*, 397–404.

Bouchard, T. J., Jr., Lykken, D. T., McGue, M., Segal, N. L., & Tellegen, A. (1990). Sources of human psychological differences: The Minnesota study of twins reared apart. *Science, 250*, 223–228.

Bouchard, T. J., & McGue, M. (1981). Familial studies of intelligence: A review. *Science, 212*, 1055–1059.

Bregman, J. D., & Hodapp, R. M. (1991). Current developments in the understanding of mental retardation. *Journal of the American Academy of Child and Adolescent Psychiatry, 30*, 707–719.

Brock, L. G. (1934). Report of the departmental committee on sterilization. *Sessional Papers, Great Britain, 15*, 1–137.

Brugger, C. (1930). Genealogische untersuchungen an schwachsinnigen. Z. ges. *Neurologica Psychiatrica, 130*, 66–103.

Capron, C., & Duyme, M. (1989). Assessment of effects of socio-economic status on IQ in a full cross-fostering study. *Nature, 340*, 552–554.

Cherny, S. S., Cardon, L. R., Fulker, D. W., & DeFries, J. C. (1992). Differential heritability across levels of cognitive ability. *Behavior Genetics, 22*, 153–162.

Chipeur, H. M., Rovine, M., & Plomin, R. (1990). LISREL modelling: Genetic and environmental influences on IQ revisited. *Intelligence, 14*, 11–29.

Cloniger, C. R. (1991). D2 dopamine receptor gene is associated but no linked with alcoholism. *Journal of the American Medical Association, 266*, 1833–1834.

Daniels, J. K., Owen, M. J., McGuffin, P., Thompson, L., Detterman, D. K., Chorney, M., Chorney, K., Smith, D., Skuder, D., Vignetti, S., McClearn, G. E., & Plomin, R. (1994). IQ and variation in the number of fragile X CGG repeats: No association in a normal sample. *Intelligence, 19*, 45–50.

DeFries, J. C., & Fulker, D. W. (1985). Multiple regression analysis of twin data. *Behavior Genetics, 15*, 467–473.

DeFries, J. C., Fulker, D. W., & LaBuda, M. C. (1987). Evidence for a genetic aetiology in reading disability in twins. *Nature, 329*, 537–539.

DeFries, J. C., & Gillis, J. J. (1991). Etiology of reading deficits in learning disabilities: Quantitative genetic analysis. In J. E. Obrutz & G. W. Hynd (Ed.), *Neuropsychological foundations of learning disabilities: A handbook of issues, methods and practice* (pp. 29–47). New York: Academic Press.

Fraser, F. C., & Sadnovik, A. D. (1976). Correlation of IQ in subjects with Down syndrome and their parents and sibs. *Journal of Mental Deficiency Research, 20*, 179–182.

Fu, Y. H., Kuhl, D. P., Pizzuti, A., Pieretti, M., Sutcliffe, J. S., Richards, S., Verker, A. J., Holden, J. J., Fensick, R. G., Jr., Warren, S. T., et al. (1991). Variation of the CGG repeat at the fragile X site results in genetic instability: Resolution of the Sherman paradox. *Cell, 67*, 1047–1058.

Hagberg, B., Hagberg, G., Lewerth, A., & Linberg, U. (1981). Mild retardation in swedish school children. *Acta Paediatrica Scandinavia, 70*, 445–452.

Haier, R. J., Siegel, B. V., Tang, C., & Abel, L. (1992). Intelligence and changes in regional cerebral glucose metabolic rate. *Intelligence, 16*, 415–426.

Ibatoullina, A., Vardaris, R., & Thompson, L. A. (1994). Genetic and enviornmental influences on coherence of background and orienting response EEG in children. *Intelligence, 19*, 65–78.

Johnson, C. A., Ahern, F. M., & Johnson, R. C. (1976). Level of functioning of siblings and parents of probands of varying degrees of retardation. *Behavior Genetics, 6*, 473–477.

LaBuda, M. C., & DeFries, J. C. (1990). Genetics etiology of reading disability: Evidence from a twin study. In G. T. Pavlidis (Ed.), *Perspectives on dyslexia: Vol. 1. Neurology, neuropsychology and genetics* (pp. 47–76). Chichester, England: Wiley.

Lamont, M. A., & Dennis, N. R. (1988). Aetiology of mild mental retardation. *Archives of Disease in Childhood, 63*, 1032–1038.

Matarazzo, J. D. (Ed.). (1992). Biology and intelligence [Special issue]. *Intelligemnce, 16*(3–4).

McGue, M. (1989). Nature–nurture and intelligence. *Nature, 340*, 507–508.

Neale, M. C., & Cardon, L. R. (1992). *Methodology for genetic studies of twins and families*. London: Kluwer.

Nichols, P. L. (1984). Familial mental retardation. *Behavior Genetics, 14*, 161–170.

Nunez, P. (1981). *Electric fields of the brain: The neurophysics of EEG.* New York: Oxford.

Pederson, N. L., Plomin, R., Nesselroade, J. R., & McClearn, G. E. (1992). A quantitative genetic analysis of cognitive abilities during the second half of the life span. *Psychological Science, 3,* 346–353.

Penrose, L. S. (1938). *A clinical genetic study of 1,280 cases of mental defect.* (Medical Research Council, Special Report Series, No. 229). London: Medical Research Council.

Plomin, R. (1986). *Development, genetics, and psychology.* Hillsdale, NJ: Lawrence Erlbaum Associates.

Plomin, R., & Bergeman, C. S. (1991). The nature of nurture: Genetic influence on "environmental" measures. *Behavior and Brain Sciences, 14,* 373–427.

Plomin, R., DeFries, J. C., & McClearn, G. E. (1990). *Behavioral Genetics: A Primer* (2nd ed.). New York: Freeman.

Plomin, R., McClearn, G. E., Smith, D. L., Skuder, P., Vignetti, S., Chorney, M. J., Chorney, K., Kasarda, S., Thompson, L. A., Detterman, D. K., Petrill, S. A., Daniels, J., Owen, M. J., & McGuffin, P. (1995). Allelic associations between 100 DNA markers and high versus low IQ. *Intelligence, 21,* 31–48.

Plomin, R., McClearn, G. E., Smith, D. L., Vignetti, S., Chorney, M. J., Chorney, K., Venditti, C., Kasarda, S., Thompson, L. A., Detterman, D. K., Daniels, J., Owen, M. J., & McGuffin, P. (1994). DNA markers associated with high versus low IQ: The IQ quantitative trait loci (QTL) Project. *Intelligence, 19,* 107–118.

Plomin, R., & Neiderheiser, J. (1992). Quantitative genetics, molecular genetics, and intelligence. *Intelligence, 15,* 369–387.

Plomin, R., & Thompson, L. A. (1993). Genetics and high cognitive ability. In G. R. Bach & T. Ackrill (Eds.), *The origins and development of high ability* (Ciba Foundation Symposium 78, pp 67–84). Chichester, England: Wiley.

Reed, E. W., & Reed, S. C. (1965). *Mental retardation: A family study.* Philadelphia: Saunders.

Reed, S. C., & Rich, S. S. (1982). Parent–offspring correlations and regression for IQ. *Behavior Genetics, 12,* 535–542.

Sing, C. F., & Boerwinkle, E. A. (1987). Genetic architecture of inter-individual variability in apolipoprotein, lipoprotein and lipid phenotypes. In G. Bock & G. M. Collins (Eds.), *Molecular approaches to human polygenic disease* (pp. 99–127). Chichester, England: Wiley.

Skuder, P., Plomin, R., McClearn, G. E., Smith, D. L., Vignetti, S., Chorney, M. J., Chorney, K., Kasarda, S., Thompson, L. A., Detterman, D. K., Petrill, S., Daniels, J., Owen, M. J., & McGuffin, P. (1995). A polymorphism in mitochondrial DNA associated with IQ? *Intelligence, 21,* 1–12.

Thatcher, R. W., Walker, R. A., & Giudice, S. (1987). Human cerebral hemispheres develop at different rates and ages. *Science, 236,* 1110–1113.

Third Annual Report of Eugenics Society. (1929). Burlington: University of Vermont.

Thompson, L. A., Detterman, D. K., & Plomin, R. (1993). Differences in heritability across groups differing in ability, revisited. *Behavior Genetics, 23,* 331–336.

Wahlstrom, J. (1990). Gene map of mental retardation. *Journal of Mental Deficiency Research, 34,* 11–27.

Wilson, R. S., & Matheny, A. P., Jr. (1976). Retardation and twin concordance in infant mental development: A reassessment. *Behavior Genetics, 6,* 353–358.

Zigler, E. (1967). Familial mental retardation: A continuing dilemma. *Science, 155,* 292–298.

› 5 ‹

New Issues in the Developmental Approach to Mental Retardation

Robert M. Hodapp
UCLA Graduate School of Education

Edward Zigler
Yale University

Most behavioral workers in mental retardation are ambivalent about the developmental approach to mental retardation. These researchers examine specific aspects of functioning in adults with retardation and espouse defect orientations. They therefore feel that a developmental approach offers them little. Yet even so, most would acknowledge that, along with defect approaches, the developmental approach has been one of the two major approaches within the field of mental retardation (Baumeister, 1987).

Some of this ambivalence arises from a lack of attention to the changing nature of the developmental approach itself. Formally advanced by Zigler (1967, 1969) in the late 1960s, the approach features both a long history and a series of recent updates and modifications. These changes have expanded the developmental approach and applied this expanded approach to a wider range of children with retardation (Cicchetti & Beeghly, 1990; Hodapp, Burack, & Zigler, 1990). To date, however, much of this newer work has received little attention within the field of mental retardation.

DEVELOPMENTAL APPROACHES: OLD AND NEW

Developmental Forerunners

In order to understand recent issues in the developmental approach to mental retardation, it is first necessary to understand the history—even prehistory—of this approach. Throughout the 20th century, many of the most famous developmental thinkers conducted research on children with retardation, and the resulting work has continued to influence the modern developmental approach to mental retardation.

The first great developmentalist dealing with children with retardation was Heinz Werner. During the period from 1937 to 1943, Werner worked as a research psychologist at the Wayne State Training School outside of Detroit, Michigan. Along with his collaborator Alfred Strauss, Werner performed over 30 studies of children with retardation (Witkin, 1964). Although much of this research would today be considered unsophisticated methodologically, Werner initiated several influential lines of thinking. For example, Werner and Strauss (1939) were among the first developmentally oriented workers to divide subjects into those with "endogenous" versus "exogenous" forms of retardation; this division directly foreshadowed Zigler's (1967) two-group approach to mental retardation.

In other ways, too, Werner and Strauss presaged various developmental formulations. For example, Werner (1937) emphasized the importance of examining underlying mental processes as opposed to external behavior (what he called *achievement*) in studying human development; this idea of underlying mental process was later to be an important theme in all developmental formulations of mental retardation. Werner and Strauss (1939) also noted that children with endogenous retardation demonstrated mental processes that were identical to those shown by younger, nonretarded children. This sense that children with retardation developed similarly to nonretarded children set the stage for the later concepts of similar sequences and structures.

Piaget and his collaborator, Barbel Inhelder, also presented approaches and ideas that served as the background for later developmental formulations (Piaget & Inhelder, 1947). In a classic work, Inhelder (1943/1968) identified oscillations between two stages in the thinking of children with retardation at one point in time, and intrusions of lower level thought into higher level reasoning (which she termed *viscosity*). Children with retardation thus appeared more fragile or tentative in their developmental accomplishments; this more oscillating, tentative developmental pattern has recently been noted in children with Down syndrome (e.g., Dunst, 1988, 1990; Wishart & Duffy, 1990).

However, Piaget's major advance was to present developmental sequences in domains such as sensorimotor functioning, classification, seriation, length, number, and even morality. With these sequences, various developmentalists from the 1940s on examined whether children with retardation develop in the appropriate, presumably universal orderings. Abel (1941) studied moral judgment in subjects with retardation; Lovell, Healey, and Rowland (1962) examined classification, class inclusion, and geometric problems; and Woodward (1959) examined children with severe and profound levels of retardation on several sensorimotor tasks (see Woodward, 1963, 1979, for reviews). With few exceptions, children with retardation were shown to develop, in order, through Piagetian sequences in a host of areas.

The final forerunner to modern developmental approaches to mental retardation involved the work of Vygotsky. Although Vygotsky died in 1934, his ideas have only recently influenced psychologists working in the West. Briefly, Vygotsky (1962; 1978) conceptualized higher intellectual functions (including language) as developing first in collaboration with adults or more advanced peers, and only later within children themselves. Higher level development is thus "social"—beginning within interactions with others—and the adult plays a critically important role in the child's development (see Wertsch, 1985, for a review).

Two aspects of Vygotskian theory influenced developmental approaches to mental retardation. First, Vygotsky predicted that children can perform certain behaviors with adult help (the level of "potential development") at earlier ages than they can accomplish identical behaviors on their own without adult help (the level of "actual development").

He referred to the difference between levels of potential and actual development as the child's *zone of proximal development*, or ZPD. Even 50 years ago, Vygotsky recognized that the ZPD could be used to assess children with mental retardation. Although two children with retardation might have the same general level of actual development (i.e., MA), one might have a larger ZPD, thus leading to a better prognosis for later cognitive development. Vygotsky's views concerning the zone of proximal development foreshadowed the work of Campione, Brown, and Ferrara (1982; Brown & Ferrara, 1985), Budoff (1974), and others interested in the "dynamic assessment" of children with retardation.

In a larger sense, Vygotsky also foreshadowed work on adult–child interactions (Bell, 1968) within developmental psychology and developmental approaches to mental retardation. This work has recently led to closer analyses of mother–child interactions with nonretarded children and with children with mental retardation (e.g., Marfo, 1988). This focus on the ways in which mothers and other adults pull development along—in both normally developing children and in children with retardation—was foreshadowed by Vygotsky and his dialectical view of development.

Provocations From Defect Theories

In addition to strands from Werner, Piaget, and Vygotsky, modern developmental formulations toward mental retardation arose as a response to several types of defect theories. In work begun during the 1930s and 1940s, Lewin (1936) and Kounin (1941a, 1941b) found that children with retardation behaved in a more rigid fashion on a series of experimental tasks. According to the Lewin–Kounin formulation, children with mental retardation were suffering from a defect relating to a more rigid style of problem solving.

The Lewin–Kounin formulation was among the first, but not the only, defect theory in mental retardation. Throughout the 1950s and 1960s, various workers hypothesized that children with retardation suffered from one or another specific defect causing their retardation. Zeaman and House (1963) noted deficiencies in attention, Ellis (1963b) in stimulus traces, Spitz (1963) in inadequate cortical satiation, Siegel and Foshee (1960) in malfunctioning inhibitory mechanisms, and Luria (1961) in verbal mediation of thought. Although differing one from another, each defect theory proposed that the child with retardation was suffering from a particular defect compared to nonretarded children. To each theorist, the hypothesized defect of interest was the cause of mental retardation, in much the same way that workers in autism currently debate which problem—social, cognitive, linguistic, or theory of mind—is the basic underlying cause of the autistic disorder (e.g., Cohen & Donellan, 1987).

Zigler's Developmental Approach to Mental Retardation

Formulated during the mid-1960s, Zigler's developmental approach to mental retardation integrated prior developmental ideas and reacted against defect theories. Drawing from Werner and Piaget (Vygotsky was then relatively unknown in the West), Zigler too made use of ideas such as underlying processes as opposed to behavior per se, and of sequences and structures in development. At the same time, this approach arose partly to counter the many defect theories of the 1950s and 1960s.

Zigler and his colleagues first reinterpreted Lewin and Kounin's formulations by more closely examining the conditions under which children with retardation behaved more rigidly. They noted that differences between familial retarded and MA-matched nonretarded children were due to the greater degree of social deprivation experienced by children with retardation, many of whom were institutionalized (e.g., Zigler, Hodgden,

& Stevenson, 1958). These studies were among the first to show the importance of motivational-personality variables in explaining the "cognitive rigidity" of children with retardation (Zigler, 1962).

Such studies led to the examination of various aspects of motivation in children with mental retardation and to an approach that examines the whole child—as opposed to solely the child's cognitive or linguistic behaviors—when considering functioning in children with retardation (Zigler, 1971). Specifically, Zigler and his colleagues identified several different personality-motivational characteristics in persons with mental retardation (see Zigler & Burack, 1989, for a fuller treatment). These include the following.

Positive Reaction Tendency. This is the tendency of children with retardation to become overly dependent on surrounding adults. This tendency has been shown to be stronger in institutionalized versus noninstitutionalized children (Green & Zigler, 1962) and, even among institutionalized children, among those suffering from the greatest amounts of preinstitutional social deprivation (Zigler, 1961; Zigler, Balla, & Butterfield, 1968).

In focusing on the connection between social deprivation and the positive reaction tendency, Zigler and his colleagues came to realize the extent to which this overdependence on others adversely affects persons with retardation. Given some minimal intellectual level, the shift from dependence to independence may be the single most important factor enabling persons with mental retardation to become self-sustaining members of society (Zigler & Harter, 1968).

Negative Reaction Tendency. This is the tendency, even among children who highly desire contacts with surrounding adults, to be wary of such interactions, at least initially (Shallenberger & Zigler, 1961; Zigler, 1958). In some sense the opposite of the positive reaction tendency, wariness shows itself in the child's playing a simple, monotonous game with an experimenter longer in the second portion than in the first portion of the game; children come to realize that—as opposed to a doctor or another strange adult—they have nothing to fear from the game-playing experimenter (Harter & Zigler, 1968). Again, as with the overdependence described previously, the initial wariness of children with retardation lessens their effectiveness. The negative-reaction tendency motivates these children toward behaviors, such as withdrawal, that reduce the quality of their task performance.

Lowered Expectancy of Success. This is the tendency of children with retardation to "aim low" when solving unfamiliar tasks. Similar to the causes of the positive and negative reaction tendencies, a lowered expectancy of success arises from the child with retardation's history of failure experiences. As a result, these children are more likely to settle for lower levels of reinforcement in an experimental setting than are MA-matched nonretarded children (Gruen & Zigler, 1968). Such settling for lower levels of reinforcement is similar to the learned helplessness examined by Weisz and his colleagues (e.g., see Weisz, 1990, for a review).

Outerdirectedness. This is the tendency of the child with retardation to look outside one's self for solutions to intellectual problems. The two primary determinants of outerdirectedness are the child's general level of cognitive development and experiences of success and failure arising from the child's self-initiated solutions.

Increasing mental age leads to more reliance on internal solutions and less outerdirectedness in many different groups: in nonretarded children (MacMillan & Wright, 1974;

Ruble & Nakamura, 1973; Yando & Zigler, 1971; Zigler & Yando, 1972), in institutionalized children with mental retardation (Turnure, 1970a, 1970b), and in noninstitutionalized children with mild mental retardation (Balla, Styfco, & Zigler, 1971; Gordon & MacLean, 1977). For all of these groups, younger children apply outerdirected styles of problem solving instead of relying on their own poorly developed cognitive skills. Older children, in contrast, rely less on external cues and more on their own, better developed cognitive abilities.

The second important factor relates to the child's experiences of success and failure. Due to their histories of failure, children with retardation were predicted to be more outerdirected. Across several studies, children with retardation were found to be more outerdirected than were MA-matched nonretarded children (see Zigler & Burack, 1989, for a review). Such studies involve outerdirectedness tasks such as imitation (e.g., Achenbach & Zigler, 1968; Balla, Styfco, & Zigler, 1971; Yando & Zigler, 1971) and in (incorrectly) relying on an external cue provided by the experimenter in an experimental task (Sanders, Zigler, & Butterfield, 1968). Indeed, Bybee and Zigler (1992) found that, compared to nonretarded children, children with retardation relied more on all types of external cues, task-relevant as well as incidental and misleading ones.

Effectance Motivation. This is the tendency of children with retardation to take less pleasure in solving difficult problems. They rely more on tangible as opposed to intangible rewards (Zigler & deLabry, 1962; Zigler & Unell, 1962), and are much less likely to choose the difficult, the challenging, or the new when presented with tasks that vary on one or more dimensions (Harter & Zigler, 1974). In contrast to nonretarded children, then, children with retardation receive lesser amounts of intrinsic reward from attempting and solving difficult tasks.

In considering the lowered expectancy of success, greater amounts of outerdirectedness, and different effectance motivation of children with retardation, Zigler (1971) concluded that these children appear to have a different hierarchy of reinforcers. Following White's (1959) views of effectance motivation, nonretarded individuals enjoy using their cognitive resources to the maximum, as there is an intrinsic gratification to working one's hardest to attempt to solve difficult problems (hence, the popularity of crossword puzzles, brain teasers, etc.). For children with retardation, however, the effects of social deprivation and repeated failure lessen intrinsic reward in the reinforcer hierarchy. For these children, interacting with supportive adults and receiving tangible rewards seem most salient.

Self-Concept. Although not as researched in children with retardation as some of the other constructs, these children appear to differ in their self-images from nonretarded children in several ways. In line with their lower developmental levels, children with retardation have a less differentiated self-concept; that is, their abilities in one domain (e.g., athletics) are closely related to how they see themselves in other domains (e.g., friendships, academics; Silon & Harter, 1985). In addition, children with retardation are lower than nonretarded CA- and MA-matches on their ideal self-images; that is, their aspirations—how they would ideally like to be—are lower than the ideal self-images of nonretarded children (Leahy, Balla, & Zigler, 1982; Zigler, Balla, & Watson, 1972).

On each of these constructs, then, the atypical life histories of children with retardation—including more failure experiences and a greater likelihood of institutionalization (especially during the 1960s)—led Zigler to a focus on motivational-personality functioning. Research in this area has characterized the work of the Yale group for almost three decades; indeed, the emphasis on motivational-personality functioning in children with retardation has been considered "one of the richest legacies" (Weisz, 1982, p. 27) of the developmental approach to mental retardation.

The second feature of Zigler's original developmental approach was its focus on sequences and structures. Zigler proposed that children with mental retardation follow universal sequences of development, as do nonretarded children. These children thus traverse, in order, the various Piagetian stages and substages, and even the early stages of language or other areas of development. This idea, called the *similar sequence hypothesis*, remains a major tenet of the developmental approach.

The original developmental approach also hypothesized that there was a structurization of developments from one domain to another. This idea, called the *similar structure hypothesis*, involved the prediction that, if matched on overall mental age (MA), children with mental retardation would perform equally to nonretarded children on a variety of intellectual tasks. These children, therefore, did not have any particular defects over and above a slower rate of intellectual development and a lower asymptote.

A third aspect of the original developmental approach was its focus on the *two-group approach* in mental retardation. Following from Werner and Strauss (1939), Lewis (1933), Kounin (1941a), and others, Zigler noted that persons with mental retardation could be divided into two types: those who suffer from a clear organic etiology to their mental retardation, and those who show no particular etiology. Individuals in the first, or organically retarded, group present with one of 300 organic forms of mental retardation: These causes can be prenatal (e.g., genetic disorders, accidents in utero), perinatal (anoxia at birth), or postnatal (meningitis, head injury) in origin.

In contrast to mental retardation due to organic etiology, individuals with the second form show no clear cause of their mental retardation. These individuals are much more likely to have family members who are themselves mentally retarded or slow learners, and are more often from lower socioeconomic groups. This second form of mental retardation, comprising somewhat over half of all persons with retardation (Zigler & Hodapp, 1986), has been called by a variety of names: familial, cultural-familial, or sociocultural familial mental retardation; nonorganic mental retardation; retardation due to environmental deprivation; and even "garden variety" mental retardation. As the list indicates, the cause of this type of retardation remains unclear.

It was to this latter, or familial, retarded group that Zigler applied his developmental ideas, particularly the similar sequence and similar structure hypotheses. He reasoned that if this group did, in fact, simply form the lower end of the Gaussian distribution of intelligence, then all of the normal developmental processes should be operating in such individuals. These individuals should not, then, have specific defects over and above slower rates of intellectual development. They should therefore proceed in order through Piagetian and other sequences of development, just as they should show no specific areas of defect when compared to MA-matched nonretarded peers.

At the same time, Zigler was careful not to apply his original developmental approach to children with various forms of organic mental retardation. He noted that, "If the etiology of the phenotypic intelligence (as measured by an IQ) of two groups differs, it is far from logical to assert that the course of development is the same, or that even similar contents in their behaviors are mediated by exactly the same cognitive process" (Zigler, 1969, p. 533).

With its emphasis on sequences, structures, and personality-motivational characteristics, along with its application to persons with familial retardation, Zigler's developmental approach to mental retardation is widely known to workers in mental retardation. In recent years, however, several modifications and extensions of this approach have occurred, and it is to these changes and their implications that we devote the next section.

RECENT EXPANSIONS OF THE DEVELOPMENTAL APPROACH

Since the early 1980s, the developmental approach to mental retardation has been modified in three ways. These changes involve applying the approach to persons with a wider array of etiologies, using an expanded sense of development, and employing the perspective to inform more applied settings and problems.

Applying the Developmental Approach to a Wider Population

The first change applies the developmental approach to a wider range of persons with mental retardation. Beginning in the early 1980s, workers began attempting to apply developmental sequences and structures to persons with different organic retardation syndromes. Specifically, Cicchetti and his colleagues (e.g., Cicchetti & Mans-Wagener, 1987; Cicchetti & Sroufe, 1976) began examining sensorimotor sequences and structures in infants with Down syndrome. In advocating the developmental approach to examine children with this form of organic retardation, Cicchetti and Pogge-Hesse (1982) contrasted their own, more "liberal" use of the developmental approach to Zigler's more narrow, "conservative" view. Indeed, Cicchetti's use of developmental principles to conceptualize functioning in children with Down syndrome formed one component of the field of developmental psychopathology, the field that currently examines the interplay between normal development and childhood psychopathology (Cicchetti, 1990).

Since the early 1980s, developmental approaches have been used to understand children with a wide array of organic conditions. Development across various domains has been examined in children with Down syndrome (Cicchetti & Beeghly, 1990; Hodapp & Zigler, 1990), with fragile X syndrome (Dykens, Hodapp, & Leckman, 1994; Dykens & Leckman, 1990), with autism (Cohen & Donellan, 1987), and with other disorders. The wider application of the developmental approach helps one examine "development in the face of defect" (Hodapp & Zigler, 1995, p. 301), as opposed to the earlier focus on children without any obvious organicity.

Sequences and Cross-Domain Relations. This wider application has allowed for a revisitation of classic issues such as sequences and structures. As concerns sequences, it appears that virtually all children with retardation—those with familial as well as those with various organic forms—proceed in order through Piagetian and other normative developmental sequences (Weisz & Zigler, 1979). The traversing of such normative, presumably universal, sequences seems especially true across a variety of early developments (Hodapp, 1990) and for all children with retardation. With very few exceptions, then, the similar sequence hypothesis holds for all children with retardation, regardless of etiology.

But whereas sequences appear similar to nonretarded children despite the child's etiology of retardation, the similar structure hypothesis seems much more dependent on the *type* of the child's retardation. Recall that the similar structure hypothesis predicts that, when matched to nonretarded children on overall mental age, children with retardation perform equally to nonretarded children on other intellectual tasks. For children with familial mental retardation, this equivalence to MA-matched groups has held up reasonably well in regard to Piagetian tasks (Weisz & Yeates, 1981), not quite as well for information processing measures (Weiss, Weisz, & Bromfield, 1986). It remains unclear why children with familial retardation might perform worse than MA-matched nonretarded children on selected information processing tasks but not on Piagetian tasks; Weisz (1990) argued for the lack of ecological validity (leading to boredom and inattention) of many of these tasks, whereas Mundy and Kasari (1990) hypothesized that children with familial mental retardation may indeed have a deficit in the more molecular information processing tasks that does not show itself in the more molar Piagetian measures.

But the nature of cross-domain relations is most interesting in regard to children with different forms of organic mental retardation. Many different etiological groups show particular, etiology-specific profiles of abilities (Burack, Hodapp, & Zigler, 1988; Hodapp & Dykens, 1994). To take one example, boys with fragile X syndrome are particularly deficient in tasks assessing sequential (i.e., serial, bit-by-bit) processing, compared to simultaneous (i.e., holistic) processing abilities (Dykens, Hodapp, & Leckman, 1987; Kemper, Hagerman, & Altshul-Stark, 1988). Such deficits in sequential processing are not found in children with Down syndrome (Hodapp et al., 1992; Pueschel, Gallagher, Zartler, & Pezzullo, 1987).

These findings of strengths and weaknesses in different etiological groups have occurred as developmental psychologists have reexamined the entire issue of cross-domain relations for individual nonretarded children. During the 1960s, most workers assumed that development was horizontally organized, that there was a *structure d'ensemble* by which developments in different areas went together (this view is also compatible with a *g* or general factor of intelligence; Humphries & Parsons, 1979). The child, say, in sensorimotor Stage IV object permanence (i.e., uncovering a desired object under a cloth) would also show Stage IV means–ends abilities (i.e., using a blanket as a support) or imitation skills, or skills in other sensorimotor domains.

However, as Flavell (1982) noted, even for individual nonretarded children, sequences within specific domains have worked much better than has horizontal organization across domains. The presence of such variable patterns from one domain to another has even led researchers to speak of the "modularity" of development (Fodor, 1983), or the idea that humans may possess several "multiple intelligences" (Gardner, 1983) that have little relationship one to another. To these researchers, children's abilities in one area (e.g., language) are virtually unrelated to that same child's abilities in other areas (e.g., social skills, cognition).

In mental retardation, too, there has been a movement from *structures d'ensemble* to different types of cross-domain relations. The first of these ideas involves local homologies of shared origin (Bates, Benigni, Bretherton, Camaioni, & Volterra, 1979). Local homologies involve two or more behavioral manifestations of a single underlying scheme or concept. For example, infant abilities in means–ends abilities with objects (e.g., using a stick to retrieve an object) seem related to early communicative pointing and vocalizations (Bates, Camaioni, & Volterra, 1975). In both cases, the infant understands the means-ends relationship, the use of a means (a rake, a point) to obtain a desired end (object, adult attention, or adult's retrieval of an object). This particular developmental connection has now been shown in nonretarded infants, in children with several different etiological conditions of retardation (Mundy, Seibert, & Hogan, 1984), and in children with autism (Curcio, 1978). Other cross-domain connections—for example, the connection between levels of symbolic play and early language—have also been shown for nonretarded children (McCune-Nicholich & Bruskin, 1982), and for children with autism (Mundy, Sigman, Ungerer, & Sherman, 1987), and for children with Down syndrome (Beeghly & Cicchetti, 1987).

Local homologies might be considered as smaller cross-domain organizations, of an organizational structure that consists of numerous small behavioral units. But there may also be a limit to how far advanced one small packet of behaviors can be from another. Consider the fact that children with Down syndrome are often advanced in social skills relative to overall mental age. Cornwell and Birch (1969) found that social skills can only be advanced beyond overall mental abilities to a certain, limited extent. This limit of social abilities over MA arises because many higher level social behaviors require high-level cognitive or linguistic abilities; weaknesses in cognition and language thus "rein in" the development of social skills for children with Down syndrome.

Even as homologies and limits are present in some syndromes, other syndromes demonstrate widely divergent functioning across two or more domains. The best example here is Williams syndrome, a rare genetic disorder in which children show much higher communicative-linguistic skills than would be predicted by their overall mental ages (Bellugi, Marks, Bihrle, & Sabo, 1988; Reilly, Klima, & Bellugi, 1991). Compare the following two storytelling narratives, one for a child with Down syndrome, the other for a child of the same MA, CA, and IQ with Williams syndrome. Both children are describing a picture-book story about a boy and dog's pet frog and how, during the night, the frog escapes from its bowl.

Down syndrome child:

"He looks in the bowl. He . . . sleep. Then the frog got away. He looked in the bowl . . . and it empty.

Willams syndrome child:

"Once upon a time there was this boy who had a dog and a frog. And there was a . . . bowl. And the boy and the dog looked in the . . . looked in the bowl. Then, it was nighttime and time for the boy to go to bed. But, as the boy and the dog were sleeping the frog climbed out. And, when it was morning [whispers] 'The frog was gone.'" (Reilly et al., 1991, p. 377)

Even given the problems that children with Down syndrome show in grammar (Fowler, 1990), the linguistic skills of children with Williams syndrome are striking. As shown in the previous quote, they use long and complicated sentences, as well as time clauses ("Once upon a time"; "Then . . . ') and vocal strategies (whispering, sound effects) that heighten interest in the story. These children also demonstrate abilities in receptive vocabulary that are 3 or more years above the child's mental age; for example, a Williams syndrome child of MA 5½ years functioned at the 9-year level on the PPVT–R, correctly identifying words such as *peninsula, slumbering, solemn, dissecting,* and *hoisting* (Bellugi et al., 1988). Other children with Williams syndrome show a similar dissociation between linguistic and nonlinguistic functioning.

The conceptualization of cross-domain relations, then, has changed greatly over the past 20 years. Although children with familial retardation perform equal to MA-matched nonretarded children (at least for Piagetian tasks), other etiological groups show various homologies, limits, and dis-synchronies from one domain to another. Many of these strengths or weaknesses also appear specific to the child's etiology of mental retardation.

Regressions and Rates. In addition to sequences and cross-domain relations, other developmental topics have received sustained attention in recent years. Several of these topics—including regressions and rates—have always characterized developmental formulations. Recall Inhelder's (1943/1968) sense of the oscillating, tentative nature of development in children with retardation; such work directly foreshadows recent work on regressions in development. In the same way, Bayley (1955) first examined individual variations in developmental rate with age, and such intersubject variations in rate were used by McCall, Eichorn, and Hogarty (1977) to denote qualitative shifts in development.

Both regressions and changing rates are, then, venerable developmental topics, now examined in either new ways or with new populations.

Like cross-domain relations, patterns of regression have been shown in specific etiological groups. In examining the sensorimotor development of children with Down syndrome, Dunst (1988, 1990) found that these children often display regressions from one month to the next. To some extent, this pattern of "two steps forward, one backward" is also seen in nonretarded infants (Kopp, Sigman, & Parmelee, 1974; Uzgiris, 1987). For infants with Down syndrome, however, regressions from one session to the next occur about 2.5 times more often than regressions occur with nonretarded infants (Dunst, 1990).

Changes in developmental rate are also seen in children with specific types of mental retardation. In males with fragile X syndrome, age-related developmental plateaus seem to begin at or near the pubertal years. This plateau can be seen in the development of both intelligence (Dykens et al., 1989; Hodapp et al., 1990) and adaptive behaviors (Dykens, Hodapp, Ort, & Leckman, 1993). In contrast to boys with fragile X syndrome, children with Down syndrome alternately develop and plateau at various ages throughout the childhood years. This alternating pattern of spurts and lags reoccurs several times throughout childhood, and seems to occur in linguistic grammar (Fowler, 1988), in intelligence (Gibson, 1966), and, possibly, in adaptive behavior (Dykens, Hodapp, & Evans, 1994). In the cases of both fragile X and Down syndromes, then, etiology-specific (but as yet unspecified) brain changes may be causing these age-related changes in developmental rate.

Just as there are slowings in development due to age-related changes, so too are there task-related slowings during development for certain etiological groups. Dunst (1988) found that children with Down syndrome show particular delays in making the transition from one to another Piagetian sensorimotor stage (especially from sensorimotor stages 3 to 4 and 4 to 5). At later ages, Fowler (1988) showed that children with Down syndrome have particular problems in attaining certain levels of grammatical development (Brown's Stage III grammar). Again, such task-related problems appear related to the etiological group under consideration.

Lessons From a Wider Application of the Developmental Approach. In considering studies of sequences, cross-domain relations, regressions, and changing rates of development, three themes emerge. The first of these themes involves the need to examine separately different etiological groups (Burack, Hodapp, & Zigler, 1988, 1990). Even though we currently have few sophisticated studies of development in most etiological groups, behavioral differences are already emerging. Many different etiological groups are showing specific strengths and weaknesses, regressions, and variations in rates of development, and many of these characteristics seem specific to a particular etiological group.

At the same time, however, not every aspect of development will differ in every group. Hodapp and Dykens (1991, 1994) noted that there will be both differences and similarities when examining development from one etiological group to another. As noted previously, for instance, sequential development seems to be a general phenomenon: all children with retardation, regardless of etiology, traverse Piagetian and other developmental stages in the hypothesized order. Yet cross-domain relations, regressions, rate changes, and even specific types of maladaptive behavior are often specific to the child's cause of mental retardation (Hodapp & Dykens, 1994). In short, there are both general and specific aspects of development, with some characteristics that are common to all children with retardation, others that are etiology-specific.

A third theme—the use of children with retardation as an experiment of nature—arises from the general and specific aspects of development in mental retardation. Among developmental workers interested in different organic forms of mental retardation (e.g., Cicchetti & Pogge-Hesse, 1982), there has often been a desire to examine persons with retardation as "experiments of nature." That is, developmentally oriented researchers would like to use data from diverse retarded groups to shed light on various aspects of normal development. Given the presence of certain, etiology-specific characteristics, however, we need to move beyond merely examining "individuals with retardation" to focus instead on specific types of mental retardation.

As Hodapp and Burack (1990) noted, the movement from examining mental retardation as a single entity to many separate entities can be useful in the experiment of nature approach. Indeed, the analogy could be considered as one of a "signal-to-noise" ratio, of a true developmental signal coming through despite a great deal of etiological noise. That is, if a particular connection, or sequence, or other characteristic shows itself even in the face of so many etiology-specific aspects of development, then the developmental nature of that characteristic would seem even more supported.

Take the example of local homologies. Children with Down syndrome, fragile X syndrome, Williams syndrome, and other disorders vary widely in their intellectual strengths and weaknesses. But if certain connections continue to obtain, even given such etiology-specific differences, this finding indicates that the connection may indeed necessarily occur in development. As noted earlier, to date such cross-domain connections appear between levels of symbolic play and early language, and between certain sensorimotor skills and the earliest communicative abilities. Although this list is at present very small, the many different types of retardation should eventually tell us much about nonretarded development.

A Wider Sense of Development

In applying the developmental approach to a wider population of persons with mental retardation, the issues of sequences, cross-domain relations, regressions, and rates have been reexamined to inform us about both retarded and nonretarded development. But at the same time as the approach has been more widely applied, so too has the very meaning of the word *development* expanded for developmental psychologists. This larger, more expanded sense of development is rapidly being applied to conceptualize children with mental retardation.

The main emphasis of the expanded developmental perspective involves the environment in which children develop. Both the nature and breadth of the environment currently interest developmental psychologists and developmentalists working with children with retardation.

The first issue pertains to the nature of the environment itself. Traditional developmental thinkers generally described the environment as relatively static and object oriented. To Piaget (1977), the environment was composed of objects that the child manipulates or people about whom the child learns. He noted that the environment is *aliment* or food to the child's developing schemes. Similarly, Werner (1948) discussed the environment as *Umwelt*; that is, the environment as seen from the perspective of the child. Even so, the *Umwelt* was relatively static, changing only in response to changes in the developing child (e.g., parental input language becomes part of the child's environment only as that child begins developing language). Despite both Piaget's and Werner's interest in the environment, however, both wrote little on its nature or effects.

In contrast to Piaget and Werner, Vygotsky did present a more contextualized, interactive sense of child development. To Vygotsky, the environment is both more human and more active. It features adult interactors who tailor their level of interaction just slightly above the child's present abilities. The very idea of a zone of proximal development presupposes an adult interactor who can assess the child's level, provide input that is slightly above that level, and raise the demands and expectations as the child's abilities grow.

Although Vygotsky presented the background to a more interactive sense of the child's development, movements within Western developmental psychology itself more directly propelled the movement from child-alone to child-in-context developmental perspectives. Thus, the socialization (Zigler, Lamb, & Child, 1982), interactional (Bell, 1968), and transactional (Sameroff & Chandler, 1974) perspectives have all directly influenced developmental analyses. These theoretical additions, in turn, have directly affected the conceptualization of development for all children, those with and without mental retardation.

As a result of these changes, many studies have now examined mother–child interaction with children who have mental retardation and other disabilities. Although a review of these studies is beyond the scope of this chapter (cf. Marfo, 1988), the major finding seems to be that, compared to interactions with nonretarded children at identical levels of functioning, mothers perform both "the same and differently" in interactions with their children with mental retardation. They act the same in that they shorten their sentences (Rondal, 1977), repeat key words, talk in a higher pitched voice, and in other ways provide the simpler interactive input that may help children to develop. Yet at the same time, mothers of children with disabilities appear more didactic, intrusive, and "pushy" in their styles of interaction. They more often teach the child, clash with the child (i.e., speak at the same time as the child speaks), and have trouble following the child's lead or allowing the child to initiate interactions (Cardoso-Martins & Mervis, 1985; Jones, 1977).

Why such stylistic differences emerge is another matter. Some researchers (Mahoney, 1988) argue that maternal emotional reactions and needs force them to become more intrusive with their children. But certain children with disabilities may also require a more intrusive maternal style (e.g., the most hypotonic—and most impaired—infants with Down syndrome studied by Cicchetti and Sroufe, 1976). Although the presence of differences in maternal interactive styles seems well established, we really do not know why such differences occur, or what the effect of such differences might be on the child's development.

A second major shift has been to examine the many environments in which children develop. Begun by Bronfenbrenner (1979) and others, the ecological perspective has led to much work on families, schools, neighborhoods, and other social systems in which children develop. In mental retardation, this more ecological perspective has directly influenced work on family functioning (Krauss, Simeonsson, & Ramey, 1989), changes in family adaptation over time (Minnes, 1989), and issues of transitions among various social systems (e.g., school to work, family changes with age, etc.). Many of these issues are detailed in other chapters of this *Handbook* (e.g. Stoneman, chap. 15, this volume).

We are left, then, with a wider application of a developmental perspective that is itself more expanded, more elaborated, more contextual. As in the expansion of topics about the child's own development, this more contextual perspective is leading to new and exciting developmental findings about children with retardation and their families.

Applications to Applied Settings and Problems

Ever since the identification of sequences and various cross-domain relations, developmental ideas have been used to inform applied settings and problems. Woodward's (1959) use of Piagetian sequences and structures to examine severely and profoundly retarded children was an early attempt in this regard, and others have followed.

At present, developmental formulations are ubiquitous in intervention programs, especially during the earliest years and in attempts to train sensorimotor or preoperational abilities. For example, Dunst (1980) adapted Uzgiris and Hunt's (1975) Ordinal Scales of Infant Development for use with young children with disabilities. Dunst's adaptation is very much in the developmental tradition. In order to assess the child's underlying schemes (as opposed to behaviors per se), he added items that are motorically easier but that nevertheless tap skills of particular levels of each sensorimotor domain. In addition, as many developments either co-occur or are prerequisite to later important developments (e.g., language), the interventionist can often "teach to the test" in an effort to promote the child's development.

Just as such developmental ideas are used in assessment, so too have developmentally oriented workers incorporated sequences and prerequisite skills into the interventions themselves. Most explicit in this regard have been interventions in language and communication. A host of intervention programs developed during the 1970s and early 1980s have included sequences in pragmatics (or the uses of language), semantics, and grammar (e.g., McLean & Snyder-McLean, 1978). In addition to the developmental content of these programs, several also teach language "in context" (MacDonald, 1985); such contextual views of how development occurs reflect the focus on development in context seen within developmental psychology proper.

In addition to the use of sequences and structures, several aspects of personality-motivational functioning are now being applied to children with retardation. For example, Bybee and Zigler (1992) discovered relatively simple manipulations to decrease the child with retardation's degree of outerdirectedness, or the practice of looking outside oneself for the solution to difficult problems. Specifically, those children who received easier tasks of outerdirectedness on initial trials were much less likely to imitate on subsequent, harder tasks. In contrast, children who initially received difficult tasks continued to imitate and to look to others for help, even when the later tasks were easier. Moreover, the experimental manipulation of personality-motivational variables may not be limited to outerdirectedness: Kreitler, Zigler, and Kreitler (1990) showed that rigidity too may be "manipulable" by the nature and ordering of experimental tasks. Such findings would seem directly relevant to teaching and learning in children with mental retardation.

Other, seemingly less direct, developmental applications are also being attempted with individuals with retardation. Most recent in this regard involves the use of Zigler and Glick's (1986) developmental approach to adult psychopathology to address issues in dually diagnosed persons—that is, persons with retardation who show additional psychiatric impairments. In adapting this work to dually diagnosed populations, Glick and Zigler (1995) first employed the idea that persons with retardation are at lower developmental levels (Werner, 1948). As such, dually diagnosed persons were predicted to predominantly show symptoms that involve "turning against others" (e.g., assaultive, hostile, threatens assault) as opposed to symptoms involving "turning against the self" (depressed, insomnia, suicidal ideas or attempts). In addition, action-oriented symptoms were predicted to predominate over thought-oriented symptoms.

In performing such fine-grained analyses, Glick and Zigler (1995) matched adults with and without retardation on chronological age, gender, diagnostic category, specific state hospital to which the patient had been admitted, and number of previous hospitalizations. The patients with retardation, all of whom were mildly retarded, did indeed show differences in their psychiatric symptoms, even when of the same diagnosis as nonretarded patients. Compared to nonretarded patients, patients with mild mental retardation showed more symptoms reflecting turning against others, and fewer symptoms of turning against the self. More action and fewer thought symptoms were also found in the group with retardation.

Even within the single category of schizophrenia, several interesting developmental results were found. Specifically, the developmentally lower level symptom of hallucinations alone (Zigler & Levine, 1983), involving "false perceptions" (and no delusional thinking), occurred in 50% of the schizophrenic patients with retardation, whereas only 23% of nonretarded schizophrenics showed hallucinations only. Conversely, delusions alone (without hallucinations) were found in only 7% of psychiatric inpatients with retardation, whereas 31% of nonretarded schizophrenics were reported to have only delusions. Even granting any possible problems with sampling, symptom reporting, or diagnostic overshadowing, these findings strongly suggest that persons with retardation show different symptomatology from nonretarded persons, and that the developmental approach is a fruitful way to conceptualize such psychopathology.

FUTURE DIRECTIONS

From the early forerunners to Zigler's original formulation to the expanded populations, definition, and use to which the perspective has been addressed, the developmental approach to mental retardation continues to guide research and practice. Four trends (a discussion of which follows) would seem to characterize this approach in the years to come.

Closer Ties to Genetics and Biomedical Fields

As they study a host of issues in children with mental retardation, developmental workers are coming to realize that it is not enough to divide persons with mental retardation by their degree of intellectual impairment. All children who are mildly retarded, or who are either moderately, severely, or profoundly retarded, are not identical one to another, and at least some of the variation is attributable to the child's type of mental retardation.

On realizing the importance of etiology, however, it becomes apparent that we know little about behavioral development in most of the 300 etiologies of mental retardation. The only exception is Down syndrome, a disorder that enjoys a long tradition of sophisticated developmental work (e.g., Cicchetti & Beeghly, 1990; Fowler, 1990; Gibson, 1978). In contrast, other disorders have few if any behavioral studies. Over the period from 1985 to 1990, for example, the main journal in mental retardation, the *American Journal on Mental Retardation*, featured 35 studies on Down syndrome, 6 on fragile X syndrome, 0 on Prader–Willi syndrome, and only 6 on all other genetic disorders (Hodapp & Dykens, 1994). Nor do many behavioral research articles on specific etiological groups appear in journals such as *Mental Retardation, Research in Developmental Disabilities*, and the British *Journal of Mental Deficiency Research* (now called the *Journal of Intellectual Disability Research*).

A second realization is that, for many disorders, the majority of behavioral articles that do exist are found in journals of child psychiatry, clinical genetics, and other biomedical professions. However, as a result of their authors' biomedical orientation, many of these articles are relatively unsophisticated in their measurement of psychological functioning, providing only IQ scores and vague (or nonexistent) descriptions of language, adaptive behavior, social skills, family characteristics, or other aspects of functioning of either the child or the child's environment.

What is needed, then, is a joining of these two "cultures" of behavioral research in mental retardation (Hodapp & Dykens, 1994). All psychologists studying functioning in populations with retardation—be their interests in developmental, clinical, information processing, behaviorist, or other aspects of psychological functioning—will need to join with workers in other areas (Dykens, 1995). Granted, such collaborations across disciplines will not be easy, but they are increasingly necessary to understand those aspects of development that are common to all persons with retardation versus those that are specific to one or another etiological group.

Greater Use of Mental Retardation as an Experiment of Nature

As developmentalists begin discovering the different behavioral characteristics of different mental retardation disorders, they can begin to answer a variety of developmental questions, even for nonretarded populations (Hodapp & Burack, 1990). This technique of using retardation as an experiment of nature is beginning to tell us much about the necessity of particular orderings and structures in development.

Take the recent work on Williams syndrome as an example. For many years, developmentalists have argued as to whether levels of development are the same from one domain or another, or whether diverse areas lack interconnections. With the work of Bellugi and her colleagues, developmentalists are coming to appreciate the extent to which linguistic and nonlinguistic cognitive abilities can vary. Although the details remain to be filled in, different etiologies of mental retardation provide a powerful experiment of nature concerning cross-domain relations.

In the process of using different types of retardation as experiments of nature, developmentally oriented workers are increasingly connecting their approaches with analogous approaches in other branches of developmental psychopathology. Glick and Zigler's (1995) study is a good example in this regard: An approach originally designed to conceptualize adult psychopathology has now been used to understand psychopathology in individuals with retardation. In this sense, the developmental approach is a worldview that is applicable to many different phenomena: to children, to individuals with retardation, to children and adults with psychopathology, and, in some sense, to any living system (Werner, 1948). Like all approaches that emphasize developmental psychopathology, Glick and Zigler also tied together the normal and the abnormal. Their approach follows Cicchetti's (1984) dictum that we "can learn more about the normal functioning of an organism by studying its pathology, more about its pathology by studying its normal condition" (p. 1).

More Applied Focus of Findings

At the same time as the developmental approach is becoming theoretically richer and more tied to developmental psychopathology, so too is it becoming more applied. Personality-motivational constructs are rapidly being translated into schools and other settings, just as developmental approaches to dual diagnosis will eventually allow for better understandings and treatments of persons with various psychiatric disorders.

In the same way, the differences in development between etiological groups are increasingly guiding intervention efforts. For example, Gibson (1991) noted that young children with Down syndrome might require etiology-specific programs of early intervention, just as the hyperactivity and problems in social relatedness of males with fragile X syndrome might require specific types of clinical interventions (Dykens et al., 1994). In short, as we come to know more about the development and psychopathology of children with different types of mental retardation, we are increasingly able to tailor the program of intervention to the child's specific developmental needs.

Increasingly Sopisticated Views of the Environments in Which Children With Retardation Develop

A final, and related, issue concerns the environment. Beginning with Zigler's (1971) focus on the whole child who is influenced by institutionalization and repeated failure experiences, developmentalists have attempted to understand how environments work and what their effects might be. Explanations of the environment have expanded with the transactional and ecological perspectives of the 1970s and 1980s, such that we now have reasonable understandings of the many environments in which children develop.

With each passing year, researchers develop clearer ideas about the nature and processes of children's environments. Some of this work—for example, Bronfenbrenner's ecological view—has been directly transported into examinations of the interconnected environments of children with retardation. Other ecological formulations—for example, the double ABCX model (Minnes, 1989)—derive more from work on disabled populations per se. In either case, we are increasingly understanding the environments in which children with retardation develop. Closely linked to this understanding are the therapeutic and counseling approaches that allow the families of these children to continually meet the challenge of raising a child with mental retardation.

CONCLUSION

We began this chapter by noting that many workers in mental retardation were ambivalent about the developmental approach to mental retardation. Much of this ambivalence stems from the field's inattention to the many changes that the approach has undergone over the years, and to the need of developmentally oriented workers to put into context this more expanded and elaborated developmental approach.

Until recently, such evolving concepts of the developmental approach have yet to reach the field of mental retardation research. If this *Handbook* can be used as a guide, one sees only inconsistent or incomplete attention to developmental approaches. In the original edition (Ellis, 1963a), Woodward (1963) described the early Piagetian studies to American workers who were only beginning to be exposed to Piaget's writings and thinking. In 1979, Woodward expanded on this work, with little mention of Zigler's developmental formulation or two-group approach; nor did other chapters explicitly elaborate on other developmental issues. Yet this state of affairs may be changing, at least as demonstrated by this current edition. In addition to our own chapter, the present edition of the *Handbook* includes chapters on language development (Warren & Yoder, chap. 14), behavioral genetics (and its focus on gene-environment interactions; Thompson, chap. 4), family adaptation (Stoneman, chap. 15), and motivation (Switzsky, chap. 13). All are common topics in modern developmental thinking; all are topics that we expect to see more of in future years.

From our perspective, then, the developmental approach is a vibrant enterprise that continues to influence the field of mental retardation. Although it has changed and evolved over the years, the approach retains its basic focus on the child with retardation's development and the environment in which that child develops. We can only hope that the developmental approach continues to inform thinking, research, and intervention efforts concerning children with retardation in the years to come.

REFERENCES

Abel, T. M. (1941). Moral judgments among subnormals. *Journal of Abnormal and Social Psychology, 36*, 378–392.

Achenbach, T., & Zigler, E. (1968). Cue-learning and problem-solving strategies in normal and retarded children. *Child Development, 39*, 827–848.

Balla, D., Styfco, S., & Zigler, E. (1971). Use of the opposition concept and outerdirectedness in intellectually average, familial retarded, and organically retarded children. *American Journal of Mental Deficiency, 75*, 863–880.

Bates, E., Benigni, L., Bretherton, I., Camaioni, I., & Volterra, V. (1979). *The emergence of symbols: Cognition and communication in infancy.* New York: Academic Press.

Bates, E., Camaioni, L., & Volterra, V. (1975). The acquisition of performatives prior to speech. *Merrill-Palmer Quarterly, 21*, 205–226.

Baumeister, A. (1987). Mental retardation: Some concepts and dilemmas. *American Psychologist, 42*, 796–800.

Bayley, N. (1955). On the growth of intelligence. *American Psychologist, 10*, 805–818.

Beeghly, M., & Cicchetti, D. (1987). An organizational approach to symbolic development in children with Down syndrome. In D. Cicchetti & M. Beeghly (Eds.), *Symbolic development in atypical children. New directions for child development* (No. 36, pp. 5–29). San Francisco: Jossey-Bass.

Bell, R. Q. (1968). A reinterpretation of the direction of effects in studies of socialization. *Psychological Review, 75*, 81–95.

Bellugi, U., Marks, S., Bihrle, A. M., & Sabo, H. (1988). Dissociation between language and cognitive functions in Williams Syndrome. In D. Bishop & K. Mogford (Eds.), *Language development in exceptional circumstances* (pp. 177–189). London: Churchill Livingstone.

Bronfenbrenner, U. (1979). *The ecology of human development.* Cambridge, MA: Harvard University Press.

Brown, A., & Ferrara, R. (1985). Diagnosing zones of proximal development. In J. V. Wertsch (Ed.), *Culture, communication and cognition: Vygotskian perspectives* (pp. 273–305). New York: Cambridge University Press.

Budoff, M. (1974). *Learning potentional and educability among the educable mentally retarded.* Cambridge, MA: Research Institute for Eductional Problems.

Burack, J. A., Hodapp, R. M., & Zigler, E. (1988). Issues in the classification of mental retardation: The two-group approach and beyond. *Journal of Child Psychology and Psychiatry, 29*, 765–779.

Burack, J. A., Hodapp, R. M., & Zigler, E. (1990). Technical note: Toward a more precise understanding of mental retardation. *Journal of Child Psychology and Psychiatry, 31*, 471–475.

Bybee, J. A., & Zigler, E. (1992). Is outerdirectedness employed in a harmful or beneficial manner by students with and without mental retardation? *American Journal on Mental Retardation, 96*, 512–521.

Campione, J. C., Brown, A. L., & Ferrara, R. A. (1982). Mental retardation and intelligence. In R. Sternberg (Ed.), *Handbook of human intelligence* (pp. 392–490). New York: Cambridge University Press.

Cardoso-Martins, C., & Mervis, C. (1985). Maternal speech to prelinguistic children with Down Syndrome. *American Journal of Mental Deficiency, 89*, 451–458.

Cicchetti, D. (1984). The emergence of developmental psychopathology. *Child Development, 55*, 1–7.

Cicchetti, D. (1990). An historical perspective on the discipline of developmental psychopathology. In J. Rolf, A. Masten, D. Cicchetti, K. Neuchterlein, & S. Weintraub (Eds.), *Risk and protective factors in the development of psychopathology* (pp. 2–28). New York: Cambridge University Press.

Cicchetti, D., & Beeghly, M. (Eds.). (1990). *Children with Down Syndrome: A developmental perspective.* New York: Cambridge University Press.

Cicchetti, D., & Mans-Wagener, L. (1987). Sequences, stages, and structures in the organization of cognitive development in infants with Down Syndrome. In I. Uzgiris & J. McV. Hunt (Eds.), *Infant performance and experience: New findings with the Ordinal Scales* (pp. 281–310). Urbana: University of Illinois Press.

Cicchetti, D., & Pogge-Hesse, P. (1982). Possible contributions of the study of organically retarded persons to developmental theory. In E. Zigler & D. Balla (Eds.), *Mental retardation: The developmental-difference controversy* (pp. 277–318). Hillsdale, NJ: Lawrence Erlbaum Associates.

Cicchetti, D., & Sroufe, L. A. (1976). The relationship between affective and cognitive development in Down Syndrome infants. *Child Development, 47*, 920–929.

Cohen, D., & Donellan, A. (Eds.). (1987). *Handbook of autism and pervasive developmental disorders*. New York: Wiley.

Cornwell, A., & Birch, H. (1969). Psychological and social development in home-reared children with Down's Syndrome (mongolism). *American Journal of Mental Deficiency, 74*, 341–350.

Curcio, F. (1978). Sensorimotor functioning and communication in mute autistic children. *Journal of Autism and Childhood Schizophrenia, 12*, 264–287.

Dunst, C. J. (1980). *A clinical and educational model for use with the Uzgiris–Hunt Scales for Infant Development*. Baltimore: University Park Press.

Dunst, C. J. (1988). Stage transitioning in the sensorimotor development of Down's syndrome infants. *Journal of Mental Deficiency Research, 32*, 405–410.

Dunst, C. J. (1990). Sensorimotor development of infants with Down Syndrome. In D. Cicchetti & M. Beeghly (Eds.), *Children with Down Syndrome: A developmental perspective* (pp. 180–230). New York: Cambridge University Press.

Dykens, E. M. (1995). Measuring behavioral phenotypes: Provocations from the "New Genetics." *American Journal on Mental Retardation, 99*, 522–532.

Dykens, E. M., Hodapp, R. M., & Evans, D. W. (1994). Profiles and development of adaptive behavior in children with Down Syndrome. *American Journal on Mental Retardation, 98*, 580–587.

Dykens, E. M., Hodapp, R. M., & Leckman, J. F. (1987). Strengths and weaknesses in the intellectual functioning of males with fragile X syndrome. *American Journal of Mental Deficiency, 92*, 234–236.

Dykens, E. M., Hodapp, R. M., & Leckman, J. F. (1994). *Development and psychopathology in fragile X syndrome*. Newbury Park, CA: Sage.

Dykens, E. M., Hodapp, R. M., Ort, S. I., Finucane, B., Shapiro, L., & Leckman, J. F. (1989). The trajectory of cognitive development in males with fragile X syndrome. *Journal of the American Academy of Child and Adolescent Psychiatry, 28*, 422–428.

Dykens, E. M., Hodapp, R. M., Ort, S. I., & Leckman, J. F. (1993). Trajectory of adaptive behavior in males with fragile X syndrome. *Journal of Autism and Developmental Disorders, 23*, 135–145.

Dykens, E. M., & Leckman, J. F. (1990). Developmental issues in fragile X syndrome. In R. M. Hodapp, J. A. Burack, & E. Zigler (Eds.), *Issues in the developmental approach to mental retardation* (pp. 226–245). New York: Cambridge University Press.

Ellis, N. R. (Ed.). (1963a). *Handbook of mental deficiency, psychological theory and research*. New York: McGraw-Hill.

Ellis, N. R. (1963b). The stimulus trace and behavioral inadequacy. In N. R. Ellis (Ed.), *Handbook of mental deficiency, psychological theory and research* (pp. 134–158). New York: McGraw-Hill.

Flavell, J. (1982). Structures, stages, and sequences of cognitive development. In W. A. Collins (Ed.), *The concept of development: The Minnesota symposia on child psychology* (Vol. 15, pp. 1–27). Hillsdale, NJ: Lawrence Erlbaum Associates.

Fodor, J. A. (1983). *The modularity of mind*. Cambridge, MA: MIT Press.

Fowler, A. (1988). Determinants of rate of language growth in children with Down syndrome. In L. Nadel (Ed.), *The psychobiology of Down Syndrome* (pp. 217–245). Cambridge, MA: MIT Press.

Fowler, A. (1990). The development of language structure in children with Down Syndrome. In D. Cicchetti & M. Beeghly (Eds.), *Children with Down Syndrome: A developmental perspective* (pp. 302–328). New York: Cambridge University Press.

Gardner, H. (1983). *Frames of mind: The theory of multiple intelligences*. New York: Basic Books.

Gibson, D. (1966). Early developmental staging as a prophesy index in Down's Syndrome. *American Journal of Mental Deficiency, 70*, 825–828.

Gibson, D. (1978). *Down's Syndrome: The psychology of mongolism*. Cambridge, England: Cambridge University Press.

Gibson, D. (1991). Down syndrome and cognitive enhancement: Not like the others. In K. Marfo (Ed.), *Early intervention in transition: Current perspectives on programs for handicapped children* (pp. 61–90). New York: Praeger.

Glick, M., & Zigler, E. (1995). Developmental differences in the symptomatology of mildly retarded and nonretarded psychiatric inpatients. *American Journal on Mental Retardation, 99*, 407–417.

Gordon, D. A., & MacLean, W. E. (1977). Developmental analysis of outerdirectedness in institutionalized EMR children. *American Journal of Mental Deficiency, 81*, 508–511.

Green, C., & Zigler, E. (1962). Social deprivation and the performance of retarded and normal children on a satiation type task. *Child Development, 33*, 499–508.

Gruen, G., & Zigler, E. (1968). Expectancy of success and the probability learning of middle-class, lower-class, and retarded children. *Journal of Abnormal Psychology, 73*, 343–352.

Harter, S., & Zigler, E. (1968). The effectiveness of adult and peer reinforcement on the performance of institutionalized and noninstitutionalized retardates. *Journal of Abnormal Psychology, 73*, 144–149.

Harter, S., & Zigler, E. (1974). The assessment of effectance motivation in normal and retarded children. *Developmental Psychology, 10*, 169–180.

Hodapp, R. M. (1990). One road or many? Issues in the similar sequence hypothesis. In R. M. Hodapp, J. A. Burack, & E. Zigler (Eds.), *Issues in the developmental approach to mental retardation* (pp. 49–70). New York: Cambridge University Press.

Hodapp, R. M., & Burack, J. A. (1990). What mental retardation tells us about typical development: The examples of sequences, rates, and cross-domain relations. *Development and Psychopathology, 2*, 213–226.

Hodapp, R. M., Burack, J. A., & Zigler, E. (Eds.). (1990). *Issues in the developmental approach to mental retardation.* New York: Cambridge University Press.

Hodapp, R. M., & Dykens, E. M. (1991). Toward an etiology-specific strategy of early intervention with handicapped children. In K. Marfo (Ed.), *Early intervention in transition: Current perspectives on programs of handicapped children* (pp. 41–60). New York: Praeger.

Hodapp, R. M., & Dykens, E. M. (1994). Mental retardation's two cultures of behavioral research. *American Journal on Mental Retardation, 98*, 675–687.

Hodapp, R. M., Dykens, E. M., Hagerman, R., Schreiner, R., Lachiewicz, A., & Leckman, J. (1990). Developmental implications of changing trajectories of IQ in males with fragile X syndrome. *Journal of the American Academy of Child and Adolescent Psychiatry, 29*, 214–219.

Hodapp, R. M., Leckman, J. F., Dykens, E. M., Sparrow, S., Zelinsky, D., & Ort, S. I. (1992). K-ABC profiles in children with fragile X syndrome, Down Syndrome, and nonspecific mental retardation. *American Journal of Mental Retardation, 97*, 39–46.

Hodapp, R. M., & Zigler, E. (1990). Applying the developmental perspective to individuals with Down syndrome. In D. Cicchetti & M. Beeghly (Eds.), *Children with Down syndrome: A developmental perspective* (pp. 1–28). New York: Cambridge University Press.

Hodapp, R. M., & Zigler, E. (1995). Past, present, and future issues in the developmental approach to mental retardation and developmental disabilities. In D. Cicchetti & D. Cohen (Eds.), *Manual of developmental psychopathology* (Vol. 2, pp. 299–331). New York: Wiley.

Humphries, L., & Parsons, C. (1979). Piagetian tasks measure intelligence and intelligence tests measure cognitive development: A reanalysis. *Intelligence, 3*, 369–381.

Inhelder, B. (1943/1968). *The diagnosis of reasoning in the mentally retarded.* New York: The John Day Company. (Original work published 1943)

Jones, O. (1977). Mother–child communication with prelinguistic Down's Syndrome and normal infants. In H. R. Schaffer (Ed.), *Studies in mother–infant interaction* (pp. 379–401). New York: Academic Press.

Kemper, M., Hagerman, R., & Altshul-Stark, D. (1988). Cognitive profiles of males with fragile X syndrome. *American Journal of Medical Genetics, 30*, 191–200.

Kopp, C., Sigman, M., & Parmelee, A. (1974). Longitudinal study of sensorimotor development. *Developmental Psychology, 10*, 687–695.

Kounin, J. (1941a). Experimental studies of rigidity: I. The measurement of rigidity in normal and feebleminded persons. *Character and Personality, 9*, 251–272.

Kounin, J. (1941b). Experimental studies of rigidity: II. The explanatory power of the concept of rigidity as applied to retarded persons. *Character and Personality, 9*, 273–282.

Krauss, M. W., Simeonsson, R., & Ramey, S. L. (Eds.). (1989). Special issue on research on families. *American Journal on Mental Retardation, 94*(Whole No. 3).

Kreitler, S., Zigler, E., & Kreitler, H. (1990). Rigidity in mentally retarded and nonretarded children. *American Journal on Mental Retardation, 94*, 550–562.

Leahy, R., Balla, D., & Zigler, E. (1982). Role taking, self-image, and imitation in retarded and nonretarded individuals. *American Journal of Mental Deficiency, 86*, 372–379.

Lewin, K. (1936). *A dynamic theory of personality.* New York: McGraw-Hill.

Lewis, E. O. (1933). Types of mental deficiency and their social significance. *Journal of Mental Science, 79*, 347–364.

Lovell, K., Healey, D., & Rowland, A. (1962). Growth of some geometric concepts. *Child Development, 33*, 751–767.

Luria, A. (1961). *The role of speech in the regulation of normal and abnormal behavior.* New York: Pergamon.

MacDonald, J. D. (1985). Language through conversation: A model of intervention with language delayed persons. In S. F. Warren & A. K. Rogers-Warren (Eds.), *Teaching functional language: Generalization and maintenance of language* (pp. 89–122). Austin, TX: Pro-Ed Press.

MacMillan, D., & Wright, D. (1974). Outerdirectedness in children of three ages as a function of experimentally induced success and failure. *Journal of Educational Psychology, 68*, 919–925.

Mahoney, J. (1988). Enhancing the developmental competence of handicapped infants. In K. Marfo (Ed.), *Parent–child interactions and developmental disabilities: Theory, research, and intervention* (pp. 203–219). New York: Praeger.

Marfo, K. (Ed.). (1988). *Parent-child interactions and developmental disabilities: Theory, research, and intervention.* New York: Praeger.

McCall, R., Eichorn, D., & Hogarty, P. (1977). Transitions in early mental development. *Monographs of the Society for Research in Child Development, 42.*

McCune-Nicholich, L., & Bruskin, C. (1982). Combinatorial competency in symbolic play and language. In D. Pepler & K. Rubin (Eds.), *The play of children* (pp. 30–45). New York: Karger.

McLean, J., & Snyder-McLean, L. K. (1978). *A transactional approach to early language training.* Columbus, OH: Bobbs-Merrill.

Minnes, P. M. (1989). Family stress associated with a developmentally handicapped child. *International Review of Research in Child Development, 15*, 195–226.

Mundy, P., & Kasari, C. (1990). The similar structure hypothesis and differential rate of development in mental retardation. In R. M. Hodapp, J. A. Burack, & E. Zigler (Eds.), *Issues in the developmental approach to mental retardation* (pp. 71–92). New York: Cambridge University Press.

Mundy, P., Seibert, J., & Hogan, A. (1984). Relationship between sensorimotor and early communication abilities in developmentally delayed children. *Merrill-Palmer Quarterly, 30*, 33–48.

Mundy, P., Sigman, M., Ungerer, J., & Sherman, T. (1987). Nonverbal communication and play correlates of language development in autistic children. *Journal of Autism and Developmental Disorders, 17*, 349–364.

Piaget, J. (1977). Problems of equilibration. In M. S. Appel & L. S. Goldberg (Eds.), *Topics in cognitive development* (Vol. 1, pp. 3–13). New York: Plenum.

Piaget, J., & Inhelder, B. (1947). Diagnosis of mental operations and theory of intelligence. *American Journal of Mental Deficiency, 51*, 401–406.

Pueschel, S., Gallagher, P., Zartler, A., & Pezzullo, J. (1987). Cognitive and learning processes in children with Down Syndrome. *Research in Developmental Disabilities, 8*, 21–37.

Reilly, M., Klima, E., & Bellugi, U. (1991). Once more with feeling: Affect and language in atypical populations. *Development and Psychopathology, 2*, 367–391.

Rondal, J. (1977). Maternal speech in normal and Down's syndrome children. In P. Mittler (Ed.), *Research to practice in mental retardation* (Vol. 2, pp. 239–243). Baltimore: University Park Press.

Ruble, D., & Nakamura, C. (1973). Outerdirectedness as a problem solving approach in relation to developmental level and selected task variables. *Child Development, 44*, 519–528.

Sameroff, A., & Chandler, M. (1974). Reproductive risk and the continuum of caretaking casualty. In F. D. Horowitz, M. Hetherington, S. Scarr-Salapatek, & G. Siegel (Eds.), *Review of child development research* (Vol. 4, 187–244). Chicago: University of Chicago Press.

Sanders, B., Zigler, E., & Butterfield, E. (1968). Outer-directedness in the discrimination learning of normal and mentally retarded children. *Journal of Abnormal Psychology, 73*, 368–375.

Shallenberger, P., & Zigler, E. (1961). Negative reaction tendencies and cosatiation effects in normal and feebleminded children. *Journal of Abnormal and Social Psychology, 63*, 20–26.

Siegel, P., & Foshee, J. (1960). Molar variability in the mental defective. *Journal of Abnormal and Social Psychology, 61*, 901–907.

Silon, E., & Harter, S. (1985). Assessment of perceived competence, motivational orientation, and anxiety in segregated and mainstreamed educable mentally retarded children. *Journal of Educational Psychology, 77*, 217–230.

Spitz, H. (1963). Field theory in mental deficiency. In N. R. Ellis (Ed.), *Handbook of mental deficiency* (pp. 11–40). New York: McGraw-Hill.

Turnure, J. (1970a). Children's reactions to distractors in a learning situation. *Developmental Psychology, 2*, 115–122.

Turnure, J. (1970b). Reactions to physical and social distractors by moderately retarded, institutionalized children. *Journal of Special Education, 4*, 283–294.

Uzgiris, I. (1987). The study of sequential order in cognitive development. In I. Uzgiris & J. McV. Hunt (Eds.), *Infant performance and experience: New findings with the Ordinal Scales* (pp. 131–167). Urbana: University of Illinois Press.

Uzgiris, I., & Hunt, J. McV. (1975). *Assessment in infancy: Ordinal scales of psychological development*. Urbana: University of Illinois Press.

Vygotsky, L. S. (1962). *Thought and language*. Cambridge, MA: MIT Press.

Vygotsky, L. S. (1978). *Mind in society*. Cambridge, MA: MIT Press.

Weiss, B., Weisz, J. R., & Bromfield, R. (1986). Performance of retarded and nonretarded persons on information-processing tasks: Further tests of the similar structure hypothesis. *Psychological Bulletin, 100*, 157–175.

Weisz, J. R. (1982) Learned helplessness and the retarded child. In E. Zigler & D. Balla (Eds.), *Mental retardation: The developmental-difference controversy* (pp. 27–40). Hillsdale, NJ: Lawrence Erlbaum Associates.

Weisz, J. R. (1990). Cultural-familial mental retardation: A developmental perspective on cognitive performance and "helpless" behavior. In R. M. Hodapp, J. A. Burack, & E. Zigler (Eds.), *Issues in the developmental approach to mental retardation* (pp. 137–168). New York: Cambridge University Press.

Weisz, J. R., & Yeates, K. (1981). Cognitive development in retarded and nonretarded persons: Piagetian tasks of the similar structure hypothesis. *Psychological Bulletin, 90*, 153–178.

Weisz, J., & Zigler, E. (1979). Cognitive development in retarded and nonretarded persons: Piagetian tests of the similar sequence hypothesis. *Psychological Bulletin, 86*, 831–851.

Werner, H. (1937). Process and achievement: A basic problem of education and developmental psychology. *Harvard Educational Review, 7*, 353–368.

Werner, H. (1948). *Comparative psychology of human development* (Rev. ed.). New York: Follett.

Werner, H., & Strauss, A. (1939). Problems and methods of functional analysis in mentally deficient children. *Journal of Abnormal and Social Psychology, 34*, 37–62.

Wertsch, J. (1985). *Vygotsky and the social formation of mind*. Cambridge, MA: Harvard University Press.

White, R. (1959). Motivation reconsidered: The concept of competence. *Psychological Review, 66*, 297–333.

Wishart, J. G., & Duffy, L. (1990). Instability of performance of cognitive tests in infants and young children with Down's Syndrome. *British Journal of Educational Psychology, 60,* 10–22.

Witkin, H. (1964). Heinz Werner: 1890–1964. *Child Development, 30,* 307–328.

Woodward, M. (1959). The behavior of idiots interpreted by Piaget's theory of sensorimotor development. *British Journal of Educational Psychology, 29,* 60–71.

Woodward, M. (1963). The application of Piaget's theory to research in mental deficiency. In N. Ellis (Ed.), *Handbook of mental deficiency* (pp. 297–324). New York: McGraw-Hill.

Woodward, M. (1979). Piaget's theory and the study of mental retardation. In N. Ellis (Ed.), *Handbook of mental deficiency: Psychological theory and research* (2nd ed., pp. 169–195). Hillsdale, NJ: Lawrence Erlbaum Associates.

Yando, R., & Zigler, E. (1971). Outerdirectedness in the problem-solving of institutionalized and noninstitutionalized normal and retarded children. *Developmental Psychology, 5,* 290–299.

Zeaman, D., & House, B. (1963). The role of attention in retardate discriminant learning. In N. R. Ellis (Ed.), *Handbook of mental deficiency, psychological theory and research* (pp. 159–223). New York: McGraw-Hill.

Zigler, E. (1958). *The effect of preinstitutional social deprivation on the performance of feebleminded children.* Unpublished doctoral dissertation, University of Texas, Austin.

Zigler, E. (1961). Social deprivation and rigidity in the performance of feebleminded children. *Journal of Abnormal and Social Psychology, 62,* 413–421.

Zigler, E. (1962). Rigidity in the feebleminded. In E. P. Trapp & P. Himelstein (Eds.), *Readings on the exceptional child* (pp. 141–162). New York: Appleton-Century-Crofts.

Zigler, E. (1967). Familial mental retardation: A continuing dilemma. *Science, 155,* 292–298.

Zigler, E. (1969). Developmental versus difference theories of mental retardation and the problem of motivation. *American Journal of Mental Deficiency, 73,* 536–556.

Zigler, E. (1971). The retarded child as a whole person. In H. E. Adams & W. K. Boardman (Eds.), *Advances in experimental clinical psychology* (pp. 47–121). Oxford, England: Pergamon.

Zigler, E., Balla, D., & Butterfield, E. (1968). A longitudinal investigation of the relationship between preinstitutional social deprivation and social motivation in institutionalized retardates. *Journal of Personality and Social Psychology, 10,* 437–445.

Zigler, E., Balla, D., & Watson, N. (1972). Developmental and experiential determinants of self-image disparity in institutionalized and noninstitutionalized retarded and normal children. *Journal of Personality and Social Psychology, 23,* 81–87.

Zigler, E., & Burack, J. (1989). Personality development and the dually diagnosed person. *Research in Developmental Disabilities, 10,* 225–240.

Zigler, E., & deLabry, J. (1962). Concept switching in middle-class, lower-class, and retarded children. *Journal of Abnormal and Social Psychology, 65,* 267–273.

Zigler, E., & Glick, M. (1986). *A developmental approach to adult psychopathology.* New York: Wiley.

Zigler, E., & Harter, S. (1968). The effectiveness of adult and peer reinforcement on the performance of institutionalized and noninstitutionalized retardates. *Journal of Abnormal Psychology, 73,* 368–375.

Zigler, E., & Hodapp, R. M. (1986). *Understanding mental retardation.* New York: Cambridge University Press.

Zigler, E., Hodgden, L., & Stevenson, H. (1958). The effect of support on the performance of normal and feebleminded children. *Journal of Personality, 26,* 106–122.

Zigler, E., Lamb, M., & Child, I. (1982). *Socialization and personality development* (2nd ed.). New York: Oxford University Press.

Zigler, E., & Levine, J. (1983). Hallucinations versus delusions: A developmental approach. *Journal of Nervous and Mental Disease, 171,* 141–146.

Zigler, E., & Unell, E. (1962). Concept switching in normal and feebleminded children as a function of reinforcement. *American Journal of Mental Deficiency, 66,* 651–657.

Zigler, E., & Yando, R. (1972). Outerdirectedness and imitative behavior of institutionalized and noninstitutionalized younger and older children. *Child Development, 43,* 413–425.

› 6 ‹

Prevention and Early Intervention During Early Childhood: Theoretical and Empirical Bases for Practice

Samuel L. Odom
Ann P. Kaiser
John F. Kennedy Center for Research on Human Development
Vanderbilt University

Prevention of disability and early intervention for children with identifiable disabilities is a theme for this decade and the 21st century. Strong theoretical and empirical foundations now serve as a base upon which to build social policies and intervention programs that may reduce the threat of disability, or lessen the effects of existing disabilities, for individuals, families, and society. Clearly, this is a movement whose time has come. In fact, the appearance of this chapter in this text on research related to mental deficiency and disability indicates the academic community's increased interest in prevention and early intervention. Neither of the first two editions contained such a chapter.

Events occurring in the United States also reflect an interest in prevention and early intervention. Federal task forces (Baumeister, Kupstas, Zanthos, & Klindworth, 1993), professional organizations (Institute of Medicine, 1985), and key government agencies (Adams & Hollowell, 1992) have brought prevention of disabilities in children to the forefront of their professional agendas. Federal laws (PL 99-457, amended by PL 102-119) have created incentives for early intervention/early childhood special education for preschool children with disabilities and provided support for development of programs for infants and toddlers and their families (Smith & McKenna, 1994). Head Start, perhaps the largest social program with a prevention and early intervention emphasis, is expanding greatly to move closer to the goal of providing services to all children in need. Pre- and postnatal care programs, such as WIC, are offered in many health departments across the country, with the goal of reducing the damaging effects of undernutrition (Lozoff, 1989). Prevention and early intervention is not solely a U.S. phenomena; similar programs exist in industrialized and developing countries throughout the world (Chen & Simeonsson, 1991; Serpell & Nabuzoka, 1991; Simeonsson, 1991a; Sturmey et al., 1992).

Although prevention of disability and early intervention for children with disabilities tend to have similar goals (e.g., to reduce the prevalence of disability or reduce the severity of the disability), the nature of prevention and intervention programs vary according to their theoretical bases, characteristics of the populations for which programs are developed, and the research on effective practice supporting the content and form of the programs.

The purpose of this chapter is to provide an overview of prevention and early intervention from a theoretical and practical perspective. We begin by examining the concepts of disability and risk and reviewing definitions of prevention and early intervention. Next, we examine the prominent theoretical perspectives that underlie prevention and early intervention practice and current research that reflects state-of-the-art trends. We address questions related to the efficacy of prevention and early intervention programs and conclude with a discussion of directions for the future.

NATURE OF DISABILITY AND RISK

Disability

Essential to any discussion of prevention and early intervention are the concepts of disability and risk. Disability is the anchoring construct around which risk is defined. The common notion of disability refers to an individual's inability to function effectively in society without specialized interventions, protheses, or modifications of the environment (Brown, 1991). Examples of disabilities that occur with infants and young children are physical impairments such as cerebral palsy, various degrees of mental retardation, visual and hearing impairments, autism, communication disorders, behavior disorders, and learning disabilities (usually identified after children enter public school). In an effort to avoid early misidentification and inappropriate stigmatization, Smith and Schakel (1986) and others (Shonkoff & Meisels, 1991) recommended that young children be identified by a more generic classification of developmental delay during the early childhood years.

The concepts of disability and handicap are tied inextricably to cultural norms (Gartner, Lipsky, & Turnbull, 1991). Culture defines the standards for acceptable performance in society, and such standards vary across cultures. For example, Brown (1991) noted that the normative performance of individuals in some developing countries would be considered a disability in other developed countries. Cultural norms also determine the tolerance of variance from accepted standards. In one country, behaviors associated with disabilities such as autism or severe mental retardation might prevent an individual from participating in life in his or her community, whereas in another country such behaviors are not the basis for exclusion. The implication of such cultural differences for prevention and early intervention programs are discussed later in this chapter.

Risk

Whereas disability refers to an existing condition, risk refers to the probability that an individual will develop a disability (Dunst, 1993). Different types of factors may put a child at risk for developing disabilities. *Biological* risk factors are conditions that directly affect the physical organism (Shonkoff & Marshall, 1990). These factors could be genetic conditions such as Trisomy 21 or fragile X syndrome, metabolic factors such as phenylketonuria, exposure to toxins (lead, alcohol, cocaine) in utero, or early physiological insults such as prematurity or low birthweight. *Environmental* risk factors (Kopp & Kaler, 1989) represent a second set of conditions existing within children's social environments; Sameroff and Chandler (1975) identified these conditions as representing a "caretaking" continuum for children. These risk factors might include maternal education level, socioeconomic status, and access to a stimulating physical and communicative environment. Table 6.1 shows risk factors identified by Dunst (1993) that are related to disability

TABLE 6.1
A Proposed List of Risk and Opportunity Factors Influencing Human Development and Functioning

Variables	*Risk Factors*	*Opportunity Factors*
Mother's age	Younger or older than normal childbearing years	Within optimal childbearing years
Parent education	Low educational attainment	High educational attainment
Income	Inadequate income	Adequate income
Occupation status	Low occupation status of head of household	High occupation status for head of household
Socioeconomic status (SES)	Low SES	High SES
Job stability	Repeated job changes or unemployment	Stable job
Pregnancy	Unplanned	Planned
Number of siblings	More than four children	One or two children
Residential stability	Repeated relocations	None or few relocations
Marital status	Absence of spouse or partner	Supportive spouse or partner present
Marital relationship	Conflictive	Harmonious
Marital stability	Repeated changes in a conjugal relationship	Stable conjugal relationship
Child temperament	Avoidant, difficult	Warm, responsive
Infant separation	Prolonged separation in first year	Limited separation in first year
Parental health	Poor physical health	Excellent physical health
Parental mental health	Repeated occurrences of mental health related problem	Stable emotional well-being
Parental self-esteem	Low self-esteem	High self-esteem
Parental locus of control	External	Internal
Parental social skills	Poor	Good
Coping strategies	Reactive	Proactive
Quality of primary caregiver/child interaction	Controlling and emotionally unavailable	Stimulating and warm
Parenting style	Authoritarian/directive	Responsive/facilitative
Toxic substances	High exposure	No exposure
Nutritional intake	Inadequate	Adequate
Accidents	Frequent	Infrequent
Infections/illnesses	Frequent	Infrequent
Alternative caregivers	None	One or more
Presence of extended family	None or few available	Many and supportive
Extrafamily support	Poor/unsupportive	Good/supportive
Life events	Negative life events	Positive life events

Note. From "Implications of risk and opportunity factors in assessment and intervention practice" by C. J. Dunst, 1993, *Topics in Early Childhood Special Education, 13*(2), 143–153. Copyright by PRO-ED, Inc. Reprinted by permission.

and have appeared in the literature. Following Garbarino's (1982) risk-opportunity framework, Dunst identified conditions associated with these factors that could lead to heightened risk status or, conversely, opportunity for positive child development.

NATURE OF PREVENTION AND EARLY INTERVENTION

Prevention and early intervention programs may be viewed as part of a continuum that reflects the needs of related but slightly different populations. A risk–disability continuum is found in Fig. 6.1. At the left end of the continuum would be children or individuals (e.g., parents or potential parents) with established risk but without clearly established disabilities. These might be teenage women who are likely to become mothers, infants and young children living in poverty whose mothers have a low education level, or infants and young children whose parents are mentally retarded. In the middle of the continuum are children who have identifiable disabilities that are amenable to intervention. Examples might be children with communication disorders, children with some types of behavior disorders, and some children with autism (although most of these children would be at the right of the continuum, indicating the severity of their disability). To the far right of the continuum would be children with established disabilities that would not be eliminated through intervention. These disabilities, noted earlier, could be moderate and severe mental retardation, substantial physical disabilities, or sensory impairments.

The risk–disability continuum relates directly to current conceptualizations of primary prevention and early intervention. Simeonsson (1991b) used the three-level concept of prevention, originally proposed by Caplan and Grunebaum (1967) for preventive psychiatry, to provide a conceptual framework for early intervention. *Primary prevention* represents programs that are designed to prevent a disabling condition from occurring. From an epidemiological perspective, these programs are designed to reduce the incidence of disability (i.e., appearance of new cases). *Secondary prevention* are programs designed to treat individuals with established disabling conditions in order to remediate the disability. These programs attempt to reduce the prevalence of a disability (i.e., percentage of

	Risk ————	————	Disability
Nature	Established risk	Established disability amendable to reduction (in prevalence) through treatment	Established disability not amenable to reduction (in prevalence) through treatment
Type of program	Primary prevention	Secondary prevention (early intervention)	Tertiary prevention (early intervention)
Purpose	Prevent disability from occurring (reduce incidence and prevalence)	Remediate disability through treatment (reduce incidence)	Reduce effects associated with disability; maximize normalized participation in community and home
Example of program	Programs for prenatal care	Programs to remediate communication or behavioral disorder	Programs to provide early intervention in a community-based context for children with cerebral palsy.

FIG. 6.1. Risk–Disability continuum.

population experiencing the disability). *Tertiary prevention* represents programs that ameliorate the disability, reduce secondary disabilities that might develop, and maximize the normalized participation of children in the community and home. For this discussion, both secondary and tertiary prevention will be characterized as "early intervention."

Prevention

Primary prevention of disabilities has emerged from the fields of public health and mental health. Early on, Goldston (1977) identified primary prevention as "activities directed toward specifically identified vulnerable groups within the community who have not been labeled . . . and for whom measures can be undertaken to avoid the onset of emotional disturbances and/or enhance their level of positive mental health" (p. 20). In utilizing this concept of prevention for developmental disabilities, researchers and policymakers have attempted to identify programs that are likely to reduce the incidence or prevalence of disability. For example, Wouk (1990) stated that one goal of Healthy People 2000 is to reduce the incidence of serious mental retardation from 2.7 to 2.0 per 1,000, and described primary prevention strategies related to four conditions (maternal alcoholism, environmental deprivation, Down syndrome, and other specific genetic syndromes). In a comprehensive review, Crocker (1992) identified 43 data collection and service indicators that could be used in primary prevention of mental retardation. Prevention programs in the states of New Jersey (Cohen, 1992) and Virginia (Whitley, 1992) have used these indicators successfully in providing primary prevention services.

Critical to the primary prevention of disability are the concepts of "sensitivity" and "specificity." Sensitivity relates to the correct identification of children who will benefit from prevention services; specificity refers to the degree to which children who do not need the services are identified (Baumeister, Kupstas, Zanthos, & Klindworth, 1993). The precise identification of such children is important because general risk indicators may identify a large number of children who would not benefit from the prevention services and divert resources needed for basic health care (Wise & Lowe, 1992).

Early Intervention

In contrast to prevention, the bases for early intervention may be found in the disciplines of early childhood education, maternal and child health, special education, and child psychology (Shonkoff & Meisels, 1990). Meisels (1989) defined early intervention as "multidisciplinary programs from birth to three years . . . intended to enhance development, minimize potential developmental delay, remediate existing problems, prevent deterioration or secondary handicap, and/or improve family functioning" (p. 452). In his definition of early intervention, Odom (1989) reflected the same theme of development promotion, although he proposed that early intervention also included programs for children up to the "time when children normally enter elementary school classes, which ranges from 5 to 7 years of age . . ." (p. 3).

Like prevention, early intervention is a generic term for many different types of programs that provide services to infants and young children with different types of characteristics and their families (Guralnick, 1991). Eayrs and Jones (1992) noted that there is little formal consensus on standard "best" practices that underlie early intervention, possibly because the characteristics of the population necessitate different types of practices. However, in the United States, professionals have based their work on several operating assumptions. Meisels (1989) proposed that early intervention is based on the assumptions that effective practice requires contributions from different disciplines, and that families are the center of the program for any child.

In their effort to identify exemplary practices in early intervention/early childhood special education, the Division for Early Childhood of the Council for Exceptional Children used five operating assumptions that guide early intervention (Odom, McLean, Johnson, & LaMontagne, 1995). Importantly, two of these assumptions (involvement of multiple disciplines and family-centeredness) are identical to the ones described previously, providing some convergence across literatures. A third assumption is that early intervention practices be empirically based, and in the absence of empirical evidence to support practices (e.g., family-center programming, cultural relevance of practices), practices should be based on a consensus of values in the field. A fourth operating assumption is that early intervention should be conducted in normalized settings and follow normalized procedures, to the extent possible (Bailey & McWilliam, 1990). The fifth assumption is that early intervention practices will be compatible with the culture in which the infant or child and family reside (Hanson & Lynch 1992; Roberts, 1990).

CONCEPTUAL AND THEORETICAL FRAMEWORKS

Primary Prevention

Programs for primary prevention of disability are based on conceptualizations of the relationship between risk factors and childhood disability. Investigators have proposed different models for explaining this relationship. In a *main effects* model, single risk factors may be seen as creating a vulnerability within a child that has a high probability of leading to a disabling condition (Luthar, 1993). For example, Trisomy 21 is a genetic risk factor that may be influenced somewhat by other factors (e.g., SES, maternal education), but other factors are not likely to exert a great effect on the probability that mental retardation will eventually occur.

An *interactive* model of risk is more likely to explain the appearance or lack of appearance of disability for many children. In this model, a single risk factor may not account for the appearance of disability, but when risk factors occur in combination with other factors, an interactive effect may produce poor outcomes for children. Sameroff and Chandler (1975) were among the first to propose such an interactive model. In their study of low-birthweight infants in Hawaii, they proposed that the early biological insults created a risk condition, but such risk factors were most often related to poor outcomes when they occurred in families with low SES. In this situation the biological risk factor (called the *reproductive risk*) interacted with environmental risk (described as *caretaking casualty*) to produce poor outcome. Since their landmark study, other investigators have noted similar interactive risk factors that may lead to negative developmental outcomes for infants and young children (Carta et al., 1994; Coie et al., 1993; Ramey & Ramey, 1992).

In some instances, risk factors may have an *additive* as well as interactive effect; that is, as the child or family experiences a larger number of risk factors, likelihood of positive outcomes decreases. In their investigation of the relationship of IQ scores and socioeconomic status, Sameroff, Seifer, Barocas, Zax, and Greenspan (1987) examined 10 environmental variables related to SES that could contribute to negative developmental outcomes for children. They found an inverse relationship between the number of environmental risk variables experienced by the family and children's IQ score. Figure 6.2 depicts this relationship. In a somewhat similar study, Goldberg, McLaughlin, Grossi, Tytum, and Blum (1992) used assignment to special education as the criterion variable in their examination of risk variables. They found that three variables (gender, low SES, and medical complication) in combination were most likely to predict placement. With infants who had high prenatal exposure to cocaine, alcohol, and/or harmful substances, Carta et

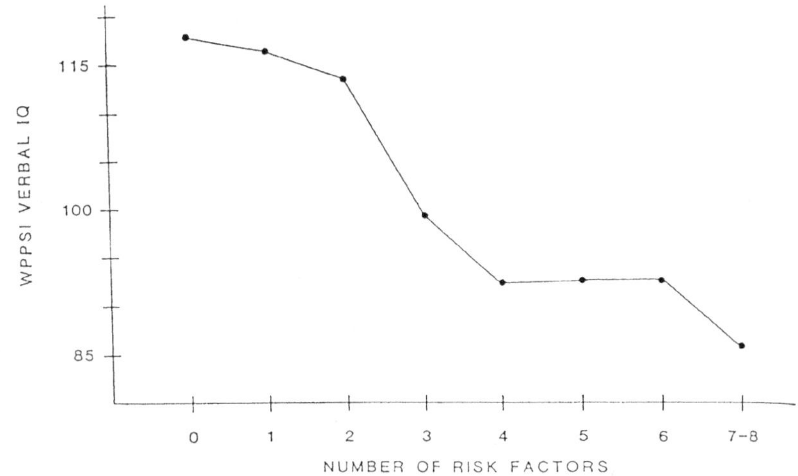

FIG. 6.2. Effects of multiple risk scores on preschool intelligence (from Sameroff et al., 1987). Reproduced by permission of PEDIATRICS, Vol. 79, p. 343. Copyright © 1987.

al. (1994) examined the relationship between the number of risk factors and developmental outcomes. Substantial decreases in positive developmental outcomes occurred when two or more risk factors were present for the infants and families.

For children who are at high risk for disability, there is little agreement on which factors best identify children for prevention or intervention programs. In a large-scale prevention program planned by the Centers for Disease Control, maternal education level has been proposed as the single environmental risk variable for qualifying children (Centers for Disease Control, 1993). More typically, researchers recommend using multiple indicators. Harbin, Gallagher, and Terry (1991) reviewed state guidelines for identifying children who were environmentally at risk and recommended an additive strategy in which children would qualify if they experienced three or more risk variables. Similarly, Meisels (1991) noted that early identification of children who may develop disabilities should involve a multiple risk index.

A Note on Resilience in Children and Risk. A particularly compelling and active research literature relates to risk and resilience in children. Despite experiencing multiple variables that place most children at great risk for disabilities (i.e., create a vulnerability), some children do not experience such negative outcomes (Garmezy, 1974). With such "resilient" children, there may well be biological and environmental protective factors that provide a buffer against environmental risk (Garmezy, 1985; Rutter, 1985). For example, in the Kauai Longitudinal Study, Werner and Smith (1982) found that about one third of the children who had been exposed to multiple risk factors experienced developmental or behavioral problems. However, about 10% of the high-risk sample (all of whom had experienced at least four or more risk factors) developed into competent adults. In her review of this and other projects studying resilience in children (e.g., Murphy, 1987), Werner (1990) proposed that three general classes of protective characteristics appear to exist. First, resilient children tend to have dispositional attributes that allow them to recruit positive responses from their environment (i.e., physical robustness, easy temperament). Second, these children are more likely to have an affectional tie to at least one caregiver and/or a family that encourages trust and initiative. Third, resilient children often have external social supports (e.g., friends, teacher) who provide positive models and encourage competence.

The New Morbidity: A Model for Risk and Disability. Baumeister, Kupstas, and Klindworth (1990) developed a theoretical model of the relationship among risk factors and both health and developmental outcomes. Building on a concept originated by Haggerty, Roghmann, and Pless (1975) in their investigation of children's health, Baumeister et al. proposed that poor developmental outcomes (i.e., "new morbidity") may be related to either single factors or an interaction of a range of intrafamilial and sociological factors. The new morbidity model appears in Fig. 6.3. In this model, both prenatal (i.e., prenatal care) and perinatal problems (e.g., low birthweight) are identified as proximal variables and are related directly to morbidity (which could be defined in terms of poor developmental or health outcomes). In this model, predisposing variables consist of demographic (e.g., race, maternal education), behavioral (e.g., drug or alcohol use by mother during pregnancy, cultural beliefs), and genetic or biological (e.g., fragile X syndrome, pediatric AIDS) factors. The latter set of variables is related directly to poverty, which Baumeister et al. (1993) proposed as the catalytic variable within this model; that is, poverty is the link between predisposing and resource variables and acts to "initiate or limit the operation of other variables" (p. 36). Resource variables, which may well stem the effects of morbidity, include services designed to "enhance the health and well-being of individuals through education, nutrition, and medical services" (p. 36). Such variables are similar to the protective factors that Werner (1990) identified.

Early Intervention

The conceptual and theoretical models that underlie primary prevention may also relate to some aspects of early intervention. However, the theoretical bases noted in the

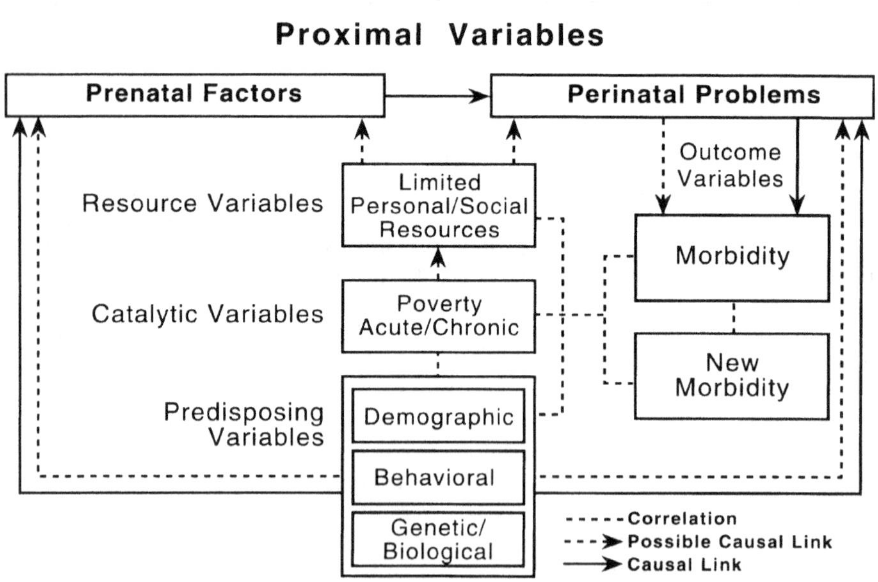

FIG. 6.3. Generalized model of the new morbidity (from Baumeister, Kupstas, Zanthos, & Klindworth, 1993). Reprinted with permission.

following discussion seem to exert a more direct and stronger influence over early intervention.

Bronfenbrenner's Ecological Systems Approach. By applying an ecological systems analysis to the conceptualization of human development, Bronfenbrenner (1979) shaped the theoretical constructs that underlie contemporary early intervention. Bronfenbrenner postulated that four levels of overlapping systems (micro-, meso-, exo-, and macrosystem) operate in concert to directly and indirectly affect the child's emergent development. For example, the developmental outcomes for preschool children with identified disabilities are influenced by the children themselves (e.g., skills, abilities, areas of disability, standing patterns of behavior), by interactions with children's families, by classroom peers and teachers, by the community in which they all reside, and by the larger cultural and political systems. Bronfenbrenner's focus on multiple systems and the transactional influences among these systems has been the basis for identifying the spectrum of behavioral, environmental, cultural, and political factors that affect child health, social–emotional, and behavioral outcomes.

By moving the view of developmental influences beyond the child and into the family system, Bronfenbrenner's theoretical framework promoted the definition of early intervention as family and community focused rather than exclusively child focused. In this model, the relationship between child and parent is a core factor in the child's development; however, the support provided to the family is also seen as a critical influence on both the family and the child. The ecological systems model addresses the functional, social, political, and cultural supports that families of children with disabilities may require to fulfill their roles as family members and care for a young child with a disability. In turn, both the child and family are viewed in the context of the supports and barriers the existing community and cultural context may present.

The ecological system proposed by Bronfenbrenner (1979) is dynamic rather than static, and the processes influencing development are continuous and interactive. The influence of a single factor within any system at any given point can be predicted only by viewing the child in context of the broader ecological system. The multivariate, multisystem, and dynamic characteristics of this model are useful in accounting for the complex influences that shape development. The complexity of the model, however, does not specify the exact mechanisms by which multiple factors interactively influence development. Thus, although the model provides a general framework for intervention, specification of ecological interventions that address all levels of the interactive systems has proved challenging.

Sameroff and Chandler: A Transactional Theory of Development. Sameroff and Chandler's (1975) description of reproductive risk, the continuum of causality, and the dynamic, transactional processes that occur between child and caregiver is central to early intervention. Sameroff and Chandler provided a synthesis of studies demonstrating that behavioral deviations in children were not related to reproductive risk in a strictly linear fashion; rather, the effects of birth complications on later development were mediated by the attitudes of children's caretakers. Further, they posited that children influence their own development. As they interact with their caregivers, children alter their environment and in turn are altered by their changed world. Sameroff and Chandler proposed a dynamic theory of development in which there is a continual and progressive interplay between the organism and its environment. The environment is "plastic" and amenable to change; children are active participants in their own growth. Deviant development occurs when insults to children's integrative mechanisms prevent the functioning of their self-righting ability or when environmental forces present throughout development are so severe that they prevent the normal process of integration that would occur in a more typical environment. The range of developmental outcomes are presumed to be the result of children and their caring environments mutually altering each other.

Sameroff and Chandler's theoretical model has influenced the conceptualization of early intervention for 20 years. Most clearly, their model provided support for intervening to teach parents interactive strategies to promote their child's development (cf. Mahoney & Powell, 1988; Seitz & Provence, 1990; Tannock & Girolametto, 1992). Rather than identifying parents as being solely responsible for patterns of interaction that might be less than optimal in supporting development, Sameroff and Chandler's model provided a conceptual basis for viewing parent behavior as arising, at least in part, from the child's behavior. For example, parents of children with disabilities have frequently been observed to be more directive in parent–child interactions than have parents of children without disabilities (cf. Brookes-Gunn & Lewis, 1984; Mahoney & Robenalt, 1985; Maurer & Sherrod, 1987). From a transactional perspective, this difference in parental directiveness might be the adaptive result of the child's less responsive style rather than the cause of it (Dunst, 1983). Recognizing that both parent and child contribute to the present pattern of interaction, this model suggests that interventions facilitate change in both partners' behavior with the goal of establishing new, developmentally supportive patterns. Sameroff and Chandler's model, with its emphasis on the potentially positive mediating effects of caregiver–child interaction, was among the first conceptual models to clearly articulate a social interactionist perspective. Research on the interactions of caregivers with typically developing children, with preterm infants, and with children with disabilities has supported this general framework (cf. Powell, 1988). Several widely used parent–child communication programs have derived from this perspective (Tannock & Girolametto, 1992; MacDonald, 1989; Weiss, 1981).

Behaviorism. The operant behaviorism of B. F. Skinner (1953) influenced the field of special education perhaps more than any other theoretical perspective. Its impact on early intervention through early childhood special education is still felt today. The fundamental conceptualization of the operant approach to intervention and instruction (stated very simply here) is that children's performance is determined by stimuli and reinforcement contingencies within their environment. Stimuli within the environment provide cues or setting events that signal that reinforcement will follow if a certain response occurs. Child development occurs as a result of continued and repeated participation in more complex environmental-response contingencies (Bijou, 1993). The implication for intervention and instruction is that, by arranging these contingencies, children may be taught skills necessary for mature functioning and successful participation in normative settings (Strain et al., 1992).

The application of behaviorism to early intervention has changed over the years. Initially, applied behavior analysis models of intervention placed great emphasis on teacher presentation of content or directions and use of teacher-administered reinforcers for teaching academically related skills (Bereiter & Englemann, 1966; Bushell, 1970), positive behavior (Allen, Turner, & Everett, 1970), and functional skills (Fredericks et al., 1975). Models for group instruction and sophisticated methods for reducing prompts (Wolery, Doyle, Gast, Ault, & Simpson, 1993) continue to be used today. However, there has also been a shift to less didactic applications of operant models of intervention. Naturalistic approaches to language intervention (Camarata, 1993; Hart & Risley, 1968; Kaiser, Yoder, & Keetz, 1992; Koegel, O'Dell, & Koegel, 1987) and activity-based intervention (Bricker & Cripe, 1991) base their procedures on analysis of events in the environment, child initiation of an activity, and arrangement of "natural" reinforcers within the environment.

Similarly, within the field of applied behavior analysis, some investigators have adopted a contextualistic perspective (Hayes & Hayes, 1992; Morris, 1992). Its application to early intervention suggests that intervention procedures must be based on immediate variables operating in a child's natural environment as well as more distally related cultural, familial, and societal variables (Odom & Haring, 1994). For example, Vincent, Salisbury, Strain, McCormick, and Tessier (1990) suggested that the operant behavioral approach be embedded within the ecological systems (particularly the family ecology) noted previously.

Constructivism. Constructivist views of child development derive largely from the theories of Piaget (1952, 1970) and Vygotsky (1934/1986). Piaget included in his complex model of child psychology a central tenet that the child is an active learner who constructs his or her experiences of reality through interaction with the environment. Maturing children generalize from one action situation to another, in part because they develop schemes or internal representations of patterns of actions. Although Piaget gave considerable credit to biological basis for capacity to structure information, he emphasized that knowledge depends on children's interactions with the physical world and their active engagement to construct increasingly complex schemas (Piaget, 1970).

Vygotsky centered his theories of child development on three central premises: experience is essential to development; external social experiences are transformed into internalized cognitions (i.e., experience is the basis for thought); and adults support the organization of children's unfocused knowledge through mediation in activity contexts (Kozulin, 1990). Like Piaget, Vygotsky saw children as active learners whose development benefits from their interactions with others and with aspects of the material environment. Unlike Piaget, Vygotsky did not see learning as bounded by stages shaped by the biology of the individual. For Vygotsky, development was dynamic and transformational; adults in the child's environment played a critical mediating role in promoting development. His "zone of proximal development" concept suggested that children determine the parameters in which adult mediation is effective in promoting rapid learning of new concepts (Vygotsky, 1978).

Constructivist views have influenced early intervention in several important ways. These views have counterbalanced the behaviorally based direct instruction approach to learning by suggesting that children cannot be taught critical concepts; concepts are acquired when the child has the prerequisite knowledge for constructing the concept. The stage-based description of conceptual development and the emphasis on core concepts rather than specific skills support a model of development in which instruction supports rather than leads children's advancement. Intervention models that rely on child-directed learning (such as the High Scope curriculum; Hohmann & Weikart, 1995) embody this constructivist principle. Constructivists have produced a shift toward viewing children as active participants in their own development. Although the quality of the environment is important to the extent that it supports exploration and engagement, the child is seen as initiating and controlling the unfolding processes of learning. Learning is viewed as a socially situated activity that is enhanced in functional, meaningful, and authentic contexts (Palincsar & Klenk, 1993); thus, the intervention approach is potentially more holistic and less fragmented. The constructivist perspective on child development has placed greater emphasis on cognitive development and use of cognitively based strategies (Meltzer & Reid, 1994). For example, in the area of language development, Piagetian views have led to a clearer articulation of how sequential levels of cognitive development are necessary for the development of increasingly complex language structures (Bricker & Bricker, 1974; McLean & Snyder-McLean, 1978). The importance of early sensorimotor activity to the development of later more complex cognitive skills has influenced curriculum development in early intervention (DeVries & Kohlberg, 1990).

PREVENTION AND EARLY INTERVENTION PROGRAMS

An exhaustive review of all prevention and early intervention programs is beyond the scope of this chapter. Rather, in this section we provide a conceptual organization of types of prevention and early intervention programs, examples of such programs, and research (when available) that has been conducted with such programs.

Primary Prevention Programs

Primary preventions are designed to reduce the incidence of new cases of a particular disabling condition or health impairment. Simeonsson (1994) identified seven steps in developing effective and efficient primary prevention initiatives: operationalize the target conditions and risk factors; generate risk models and causal, sequential, or risk chains; define the nature of risk in child-by-environment transactions; differentiate the characteristics of universal, selected, and indicated primary prevention; propose temporal frames for primary prevention; prioritize the form and nature of primary prevention efforts; and monitor and evaluate the outcomes of the prevention effort.

Simeonsson's procedural model captures the key elements of effective preventions; however, relatively few prevention efforts have been systematically directed by such a clear framework. Largely, prevention efforts have arisen from an informal combination of experimental research, epidemiological studies, and emergent public policy in response to advocacy efforts. Prevention efforts have been driven more by a deficit model than by one of health promotion (Bronfenbrenner & Weiss, 1983).

Primary prevention can occur at several points in children's development: before birth, immediately after birth, and throughout early childhood. Such prevention services can be continuous as well as discrete. For example, ongoing nutritional supplements, early education programs, and family support and training are continuous primary preventions; immunizations and specific treatments in the NICU are discrete interventions. The range of primary preventions is necessarily broad and driven by the specific risk conditions presented in child-by-environment transactions. As new risks emerge (e.g., use of specific drugs, identification of previously unknown environmental toxins), new prevention efforts are required. For primary prevention to be effective and efficient, it must be targeted to the specific population most at risk and therefore most likely to benefit from the intervention. Although some interventions, such as immunizations and primary health care during pregnancy, have universal applicability, targeted provision of these services is required only for those populations that are significantly less likely to access them.

Prenatal Prevention. Four broad classes of prenatal prevention efforts are well established as positively benefiting infant health and development: (a) screening for chromosomal and developmental abnormalities (including inborn errors of metabolism, neural tube defects, and blood type incompatibilities), (b) prevention and treatment of maternal and fetal infections, (c) maternal nutrition, and (d) prevention of prenatal exposure to toxins (including drugs, alcohol, smoking, and environmental toxins). In general, provision of prenatal health care, including screening and treatment as required in these four areas, could significantly prevent the occurrence of mental retardation and many health-related disabilities (Baumeister, Kupstas, Zanthos, & Klindworth, 1993).

There are several examples of successful prenatal prevention efforts. Neural tube defects, a primary cause of anencephalus and spina bifida, have declined significantly in the United States because of improved prenatal diagnosis, improved maternal nutrition, and provision of folic acid supplements to women at high risk for giving birth to children with neural tube defects (Centers for Disease Control, 1991). The provision of health care to young pregnant women living in poverty is a powerful approach to increasing birthweight and decreasing perinatal complications and poor health and developmental outcomes for mothers and children. There are numerous examples of local and state programs that have been effective in this area of prevention (cf. Hardy, King, & Repke, 1986; Unger & Wandersman, 1985). Currently, the Healthy Start initiative targets 15 communities with extremely high infant mortality rates to develop new models for ensuring that the needs of high-risk pregnant women and their infants are met (Strickland & McPherson, 1994). Often these programs provide more than primary health care for the mother during her pregnancy; they also provide access to nutritional supplement programs such as WIC, and they provide parenting information and supportive counseling to the young mother.

Reducing smoking, alcohol consumption, and drug use during pregnancy, in both the general population and in young mothers, are important ongoing primary prevention efforts (Edmondson, 1994). Concurrent efforts to reduce the incidence of teenage pregnancy and exposure to sexually transmitted diseases continue. In each of these areas, the risks for poor health and developmental outcomes for exposed infants are extremely high, as are the costs of subsequent health care for these children. Estimates of the success of such prevention efforts are difficult to ascertain, but given the increasing incidence of babies with fetal alcohol syndrome, prenatal drug exposure, and AIDS/HIV complex, these areas are priorities for continuing prenatal prevention efforts (Simeonsson, 1994).

Perinatal Prevention. Perinatal prevention addresses the needs of the infant at birth and in the first few months of life. Provision of adequate health care during and immediately after birth, together with ensuring adequate social stimulation, supporting bonding and formation of a solid primary relationship with the caregiver and providing adequate nutrition are the core of perinatal prevention activities.

Access to medical care for families who are poor in the United States is not ensured. Even when care is available, it may not be of the same quality that is available to families with more resources. The mortality rates for infants in the United States remains among the highest of developed countries, about 9.2 deaths per 1,000 live births. The availability of health care interventions prenatally and perinatally is strongly associated with infant mortality rates (Baumeister et al., 1993). Babies born to mothers in poverty are about twice as likely to die in the first year of life as are babies born in more advantaged circumstances (Chamberlin, 1994).

Low birthweight is a marker variable signaling both poor prenatal outcomes and increased perinatal risk. Relative risk for poor developmental outcome generally increases with declining birthweight. Thus, although most babies under 2,000 grams are considered to be at risk, smaller babies (e.g., under 1,000 grams) have an increased probability of significant disabilities (Hack et al., 1994; Nickel, Bennett, & Lamson, 1982). Three factors appear to interact with low birthweight to place the infant at further risk: the presence of specific medical conditions (e.g., severe periventricular-intraventricular hemorrhage, bronchopulmonary dysplasia, intrauterine growth retardation, or perinatal asphyxia); the absence of high-quality, appropriately timed medical care; and limited parenting and relationship support skills of the child's primary caregiver.

The first tier of perinatal preventions is the provision of adequate health care prenatally (i.e., prevention of perinatal risk through prenatal preventative intervention with the mother or her child); the second is health care during delivery and immediately after birth. This care should include monitoring, diagnosis, and timely treatment of medical conditions that place the infant at risk for poor health or adverse developmental outcomes. The third tier focuses on providing a supportive developmental environment for the child with perinatal risks. This tier overlaps with postnatal early intervention efforts described later in this section.

A primary example of perinatal prevention programs for premature, low-birthweight infants involves provision of family-focused, individualized developmental care in neonatal intensive care units (NICUs). Als and her colleagues (Als et al., 1986; Als et al., 1994) developed a model for initially assessing the behavioral characteristics of premature, high-risk infants; they used this information to modify the reactive dimensions of the environment and determine the nature of care provided. Such care appears to result in significant reductions in morbidity, and length of hospital stay, as well as improved electrophysiological and neurological functioning (Als, 1994; Als et al., 1994; Buehler, Als, Duffy, McAnulty, & Liederman, in press). In another program operating in an NICU setting and with premature, low-birthweight infants, neonatal nurses from the Mother–Infant Transaction Project have taught mothers to be aware of their infants' behavioral characteristics and respond appropriately to their behavioral cues (Nurcombe et al., 1984). In this program there was also follow-up visits to the mothers in the home. This relatively minimal intervention produced small initial (but important) effects on development (Nurcombe et al., 1984), which have actually become more pronounced across time (Achenbach, Phares, Hovel, Rauh, & Nurcombe, 1990; Rauh, Achenbach, Nurcombe, Howell, & Teti, 1988).

Postnatal Interventions. The goal of postnatal interventions is to promote the health of the child by ensuring supportive developmental contexts and, thus, systematically preventing developmental deficits associated with poor health outcomes. Postnatal interventions span the ecological system and necessarily include support for the health and functioning of the family unit, the child's physical environment, the education system, and the community (Simeonsson & Covington, 1994).

Child health, particularly in young children, depends on the presence and involvement of supportive caregivers. Caregivers provide the critical social context for development and mediate the child's access to those aspects of the environment that may support or impede healthy development. Interventions that teach parenting skills (cf. Forehand, 1993; Weinman, Schreiber, & Robinson, 1992), assist young parents in meeting their children's nutritional needs (e.g., WIC), provide continuing health and developmental monitoring, and provide support to families who are isolated by poverty, age, or location (cf. Olds, 1982; Provence & Naylor, 1983) alter the critical contexts of development by changing the behavior and/or the resources available to caregivers. Throughout children's lives, interventions that promote appropriate parenting skills and monitoring of child behavior across behavior settings may improve children's mental health and social development (Patterson & Bank, 1989). Interventions that teach positive parent–child interactions and child management skills may also have the preventative benefit of reducing child abuse and neglect (Huntington, Lima, & Zipper, 1994; Lutzker & Campbell, 1994). Early interventions with some specific risk populations, such as low-birthweight infants, consistently have been shown to improve child health and developmental outcomes (Resnick, Eyler, Nelson, Eitzman, & Bucciarelli, 1987).

The provision of appropriate health care including specific preventative care such as well-baby checks and immunizations constitutes the second large class of postnatal preventative interventions. The developmental effects of serious diseases, particularly for children living in poverty and receiving less-than-standard medical treatment, can be devastating (White, Koplan, & Orenstein, 1985). Provision of health care services can be combined with family support and teaching appropriate parenting skills. For example, the

Hawaii Early Start program provides home visits, developmental assessment, and a liaison to preventative health care services. The positive outcomes of this health-oriented intervention include fewer serious illnesses, fewer instances of abuse and neglect, and better child developmental outcomes at age 3 (Huntington et al., 1994).

Provision of child-care and preschool services is the most widely known strategy for preventing poor developmental outcomes. The long-term cognitive and social effects of participation in the Head Start program and its conceptual predecessors, the Perry Preschool Project (Weber, Foster, & Weikart, 1978), The Early Training Project (Gray, Ramsey, & Klaus, 1983), and Harlem IDS project (Deutsch, Deutsch, Jordan, & Grallo, 1983) have been systematically evaluated. For most children studied, positive and enduring benefits of participation were evident, even though the large gains on IQ scores and other cognitive measures declined over time (Lazar & Darlington, 1982).

Federally funded Head Start programs now serve more than 500,000 children, and the program is slated for expansion to serve more children in the near future. Head Start programs vary widely in philosophy, curriculum, and capacity to provide the array of health and supplemental services to children and families envisioned in the original legislation (Piotrowski, Collins, Knitzer, & Robinson, 1994; Schnorr, 1989). Evaluation of individual programs suggests positive health outcomes (Hale, Seitz, & Zigler, 1990) and social support for mothers (Parker, Piotrowski, & Peay, 1987) are important secondary effects of this prevention effort.

Findings from three related projects—the Abecedarian Project (Martin, Ramey, & Ramey, 1990), Project Care (Wasik, Ramey, Bryant, & Sparling, 1990), and the Infant Health and Development Program (IHDP, 1990; Ramey et al., 1992)—corroborate the value of intensive early intervention focused on children at risk due to poverty (Ramey & Ramey, 1994). In each of these studies, children who participated in comprehensive early intervention programs, including center-based day cares, supplemented by home visits, showed much higher intellectual performance than did children in a home-based-only treatment group or the control group. Children in the IHDP study (Ramey et al., 1992) included infants born both prematurely and with a low birthweight and children from a wider range of socioeconomic groups than the two previous studies. Ramey and Ramey (1994) noted four important findings of this study: the most positive outcomes were associated with the most intensive treatment; the most positive child outcomes were associated with high levels of parent participation; in the IHDP study, heavier (2,000–2,500 grams) infants made much greater gains than did lighter infants (less than 2,000 grams); and mother IQ was significantly associated with child IQ across age in both the treatment and control groups (children of mothers with relatively higher IQs performed better in both groups, with an increasing advantage noted at 36 months). These findings have implications for both the targeting and design of effective interventions (e.g., provide intense intervention, support and encourage level of family involvement).

Postnatal interventions are not limited to educational interventions. Childhood injury is a leading cause of death and developmental disabilities in children. Motor vehicle-related injuries, homicide and suicide, pedestrian injuries, bicycle-related injuries, and burns are the most common. Injury prevention efforts have focused on caregivers, children, and environmental modifications with varying levels of success. A multicomponent intervention to increase the use of child safety seats in Cincinnati (cited in Zins, Gracia, Tuchfarber, Clark, & Laurence, 1994) is an example of a program that targeted specific high-risk populations (parents of infants and preschoolers) with several different educational approaches. Substantial increases in the use of safety restraints and marked decreases in severe injuries to children were observed within a single year.

Finally, the effects of prevention efforts in each of the areas discussed are not limited to the preschool years. Targeting interventions for children and families at highest risk may have the important effect of preventing health and developmental problems in the next generation of parents and children. For example, programs designed to support high-risk children academically and keep them in school may have the secondary effect of reducing violent crime, teenage pregnancies, and unemployment. Early intervention efforts may have the added effect of changing family attitudes toward education and parenting, as observed in the 20-year follow-up study of children participating in the DARCEE project (Gray et al., 1983).

Early Intervention

As noted earlier, early intervention services are designed to remediate the delays that occur in children's development or to reduce the impact of disabilities (i.e., Simeonsson's conceptualization of secondary and tertiary prevention). Within the United States, the provision of early intervention services has been mandated by federal and state laws. Public Law (PL) 99-457 (reauthorized as PL 102-119) has created strong incentives for states to provide services to children with disabilities as young as the age of 3. Virtually all states now provide such services (Smith & McKenna, 1994). The public laws have also created incentives for states to provide early intervention services to infants and toddlers with disabilities and their families, and most states have established some services (Gallagher, Harbin, Eckland, & Clifford, 1994). As noted earlier, early intervention services also occur in other countries and are seen as a part of an international "vision of excellence" for children with disabilities (Mittler, 1992).

Early intervention programs for children with disabilities and their families vary in the purposes for which they are designed and the nature of service delivery. The individualized nature of the programs, differing needs of children with disabilities and families, and differing demographics of geographic locations all contribute to the varied purposes and forms of early intervention.

Purposes of Early Intervention. Early intervention programs can be broadly characterized as focusing on promoting the development of children, promoting social interactions that might occur between children and parents, or addressing the needs of the families in order to support the development of the child. Each of these approaches is examined next.

The purpose of *child-focused* programs is to enhance the development of children with disabilities. In such programs, the specific needs of children are identified through a multidisciplinary evaluation (Neisworth & Bagnato, 1996) and a plan for addressing those needs through instruction in the home or a center is established. Differing approaches to instruction reflect the differing theoretical bases mentioned previously. Direct teaching or didactic approaches often follow a behavioral orientation and include a range of specific strategies for teaching skills (Wolery & Sainato, 1996). This range extends from direct prompting and reinforcement (Wolery, 1994) to such naturalistic intervention as activity-based instruction (Bricker & Cripe, 1991) and incidental teaching (Kaiser et al., 1992). Developmentally Appropriate Practice (Bredekamp, 1987; Bredekamp & Rosegrant, 1992), as defined by the National Association for the Education of Young Children (NAEYC), represents a more constructivist orientation. Both the NAEYC materials and curricula based on the work of Piaget, Vygotsky, and Feurerstein (Haywood, Brooks, & Burns, 1992; Hohmann & Weikart, 1995) represent this form of early intervention. The choice of curricular/intervention approach and its application for young children with disabilities is a hotly debated issue (Carta, Schwartz, Atwater, & McConnell, 1991; Johnson & Johnson, 1992; Mallory & New, 1994), and professionals are making efforts to establish the two approaches as complementary rather than antithetical (Wolery & Bredekamp, 1995).

In *family-focused* programs, emphasis is placed on responding to families' concerns and priorities about the child as well as assessing the families' resources (Bailey & Henderson, 1993; Bailey et al., 1986; Winton, 1993). An underlying assumption is that the family is the central supporting context for a child's life, and the basic needs of the family must be addressed in order to support the development of the child (Beckman, Robinson, Rosenberg, & Filler, 1994). Family participation is also seen as a legal right in that family members may be viewed as equal members of an early intervention team and may participate in all aspects of their child's care and decision making about their child (Vincent & Beckett, 1993). Although family-focused approaches have been associated with the birth to age 3 population in the past (Mahoney, O'Sullivan, & Dennebaum, 1990), a range of programs representing the broader population has shifted to a more family-focused view of intervention (Duwa, Wells, & Lalinde, 1993). For example, in a recent examination of recommended early intervention practices for children between birth and 6 years of age, McLean and Odom (1993) found practices related to family involvement present across most service areas. The challenge currently faced by professionals in early intervention is how to balance a family-centered approach without undercutting the child-focused emphasis that has served as the foundation of the field in the past.

A third type of early intervention program, which actually straddles the child-focused and family-focused intervention purposes, supports the development of positive and competent *adult–child interactions*. The focus of these intervention approaches is to develop the skills of the parent and/or the infant for engaging in positive and enjoyable social interactions with one another (McCollum & Bair, 1994). The rationale is that through successful interactions with their children, parents may provide a "scaffold" to more complex social experiences that positively affect important communication and social skills. To promote such positive interactions, intervention programs have followed different approaches. In a historic study, Fraiberg (1971) taught mothers of infants who were blind to recognize and respond to the social cues of their infants. Working with parents of children with a broader range of disabilities, Bromwich (1981) established a continuum of caregiver behaviors that began with the parents simply finding time or activities that were mutually enjoyable for the infant and themselves, and moving to other activities that related more directly to providing developmentally appropriate activities for their infant.

Another strategy has been to teach parents to be responsive to infants. Mahoney and Powell (1988) conducted a program that taught parents a responsive form of interaction and noted changes in both the types of interactions occurring for both parents and infants as well as positive changes in the children's development. Later research has incorporated the dual notions of parents serving in both a directive and responsive role during interaction with their children with disabilities, shifting such roles with the demand of the social context (Marfo, 1991; McCollum, 1991). For example, Girolametto, Verbey, and Tannock (1994) taught parents to use interaction prompting, language modeling, and child-oriented strategies (e.g., following the child's lead, responding to the child's communication), and noted increases in parents' and infants' joint engagement in playful social interactions. Parent–child intervention approaches are often embedded within child- and family-focused programs but represent an intervention strategy that is based more directly on social transactions between parents and children than either of the other approaches.

Forms of Service Delivery. Early intervention programs for children with disabilities and their families take different forms. Intervention services may be provided in the home or in a center-based classroom program.

Home-based models of early intervention are characterized by the delivery of services by a home visitor to family members in the home. The rationales for providing such services in the home may be that the child is very young (an infant) and the home is the most natural environment, the child may not be able to leave the home because of health-related issues (e.g., may be technology dependent), or the family and child live in a sparsely populated area in which there are too few children to form a center-based program. Home visits often occur on a weekly or biweekly basis and last for 1 to 2 hours (Roberts & Wasik, 1990; Stayton & Karnes, 1994). The elements of a home visit might include establishing a rapport with child and family members, reviewing progress made by the child and family since the last visit, and/or planning intervention activities that will occur before the next visit (Wasik, Bryant, & Lyons, 1990).

Home-based intervention programs may be child-focused in nature. The Portage Project (Shearer & Shearer, 1976) was one of the earliest programs to provide such child-focused services in the home. In this model, the home visitors established targeted skills for the child to learn at home, and the parent served in a teacher role. The Portage Project, although at times criticized for its didactic nature (Sturmey et al., 1992), has been replicated internationally (Mittler, 1992). Project SKI*HI (Strong, Clark, Barringer, Walden, & Williams, 1992) is a child-focused, home-based program for infants and young children with hearing impairments. It is designed to teach parents how to use and maintain hearing aids for their children as well as promote their children's language development. Results from evaluations of SKI*HI as well as other similar programs have shown increases in children's language skills (Robinshaw, 1994).

Home-based programs for infants and toddlers with disabilities have taken on a more family-focused approach in recent years. For example, in a home-based program for new mothers of children who were likely to develop disabilities, Dawson, Robinson, Butterfield, van Doorninck, Gaensbaur, and Harmon (1991) reported that home visitors made weekly home visits to provide emotional support and help with specific problems, opportunities for extending the mothers' social networks, and suggestions about infant care. This type of family support resulted in positive changes in parent–infant interactions as well as a tendency for infants to develop more secure parental attachments.

A second general type of early intervention program occurs in classrooms located in public school, service agency, or community child-care or preschool buildings. *Center-based* models of early intervention occur for infants, toddlers, and preschool children. Classes are of variable size and are usually led by a teacher with training in early intervention. Two advantages of center-based programs are that children with disabilities have access to a peer group and that ancillary services (e.g., speech therapy, physical therapy) may be provided more efficiently because children in need of such services are located in the same building. The Model Preschool Program for Children with Down Syndrome and other Developmental Delays is one of the earliest and most well-known center-based programs for young children (Hayden & Haring, 1976). This program focused on promoting the development of children with Down syndrome through specific programming, involving parents in children's instruction, and replication of the program in different sites. Fewell and Oelwein (1990) reported the significant positive impact that the program has on accelerating development of program participants across a range of developmental areas.

Another center-based program developed in the early years of the early intervention movement is Project PEECH. Begun in 1970, this program combined both child- and teacher-initiated approaches within a classroom setting (Karnes, Kokotovic, & Shwedel, 1982). Central components in this program include the close linkage between assessment of the child and programming, involvement of the family, and transdisciplinary collaboration. Project PEECH has been replicated in more than 71 sites nationally. Research on performance of children in the original site and replication sites indicates significant effects on language and social development (Karnes, Beauchamp, & Pfaus, 1993) as well as enduring effects after children transition into public school classes (Karnes, Shwedel, Lewis, Ratts, & Esry, 1981).

EFFICACY OF PREVENTION AND EARLY INTERVENTION

Prevention and early intervention, as noted previously, have emerged from different disciplines. Although linked in their common purpose of eliminating, reducing, or ameliorating the effects of disability, issues related to measurement of efficacy differ substantially.

Efficacy of Prevention Efforts

The key to effective prevention efforts is targeting high-risk populations with appropriate interventions at a developmentally appropriate point in time. Simeonsson and Covington (1994) suggested that the three primary foci for prevention should be universal preventions targeted to all children without selection or screening, selected preventions for children identified on the basis of group identity associated with increased risk and increased need, and indicated prevention efforts for children identified on the basis of individual characteristics associated with high risk and high need. Following their framework, adequate health care might be considered universally preventative for all children, whereas the provision of clinic-based health care in neighborhood day-care centers might be provided for only those children living in impoverished areas and for whom risk of poor health is established. Continued monitoring of child health through home visiting nurses might be implemented for low-birthweight children born to very young mothers in these same neighborhoods.

Identifying factors dependably associated with increased risk allow systematic targeting of interventions of differing intensity for specific groups. Prevention efforts become cost efficient only when they are accurately targeted to provide the level of support or intervention needed without over- or underestimating need or the parameters of risk. The same basic service (e.g., adequate health care) may be needed universally, but the probability that such care will be accessed by a specific group determines the form of targeted prevention effort (e.g., providing health care in day-care centers vs. individual home visiting, and health monitoring). A number of health interventions can be provided universally with efficiency (e.g., immunizations against childhood diseases, screening for prenatal and perinatal infections, screening for genetically caused diseases). Other preventative measures may have both universal targets and selected targets. For example, efforts to promote child safety and reduction of alcohol and drug use during pregnancy should be widespread, with focused prevention targeting younger and at-risk mothers. Selected educational, nutritional, and prenatal care preventative programs should be made accessible for all families in reduced economic circumstance, with particular targeting again occurring for mothers who are young or themselves at risk.

Poverty is primary among the factors that place children at risk, although the majority of children who manifest developmental disabilities resulting from identifiable risk factors are not poor (Baumeister et al., 1993). Thus, targeting the poorest children for health and developmental interventions may be necessary but not sufficient to decrease markedly the incidence of developmental disabilities. For example, particular populations at increased risk for inheritable diseases such as PKU would not be addressed if only poor children were targeted. Similarly, among any population of children at risk, some children will fare better than others because they differ in significant, apparently protective ways. In most instances, risk is multiply determined and increases with the number of factors indicative of risk. To efficiently target intervention efforts, systematic assessment of risk is necessary.

Efficacy and Studies of Prevention. The assessment of the efficacy of interventions designed to reduce risk depends on conceptualization of a model of risk, identification and measurement of variables associated with elevated risk, and measurement of outcomes at sufficient appropriate intervals to detect changes in outcome. Within a conceptual framework, parameters for population selection can be determined. Most risks are multiply determined, meaning the degree of risk increases with the number of risk factors present and, in the case of continuous variables, with the intensity of these factors (e.g., decreased birthweight, increased exposure to environmental toxins). Thus, a conceptual model will specify parameters for population selection and the relationship between levels of risk and the predicted severity of outcomes. Although IQ scores or global measures of child health status have been used as outcome measures in many prevention studies, well-conceived risk studies specify outcomes more precisely and, ideally, describe and measure the processes that link specific risk factors to particular outcomes (Simeonsson, 1994).

Although epidemiological data can provide a gauge for measuring the efficacy of prevention efforts, randomized treatment designs are the standard preferred design in studying prevention of disability. Construction of treatment and control groups through random assignment of high-risk individuals, used in combination with appropriate population selection procedures and valid measurement, ensures that the primary threats to the internal validity of the study will be controlled sufficiently. However, random assignment is not sufficient to ensure that the population selected will manifest the risk behavior or that the population will be sensitive to the intervention. Prevention studies utilize a general epidemiological approach (reduction of risk from a known base rate) when risk factors are well established, the risk level in the general population is relatively high and known, the intervention can be made available to large numbers of at-risk individuals, and variation in treatment can be tolerated. Randomized treatment design comparing outcomes for treatment and control groups are used to test conceptual models of risk and with smaller, specifically selected participant populations to test treatments that require concurrent measures of treatment fidelity.

Early Intervention

Efficacy of early intervention has been an important issue for more than a decade. Its importance initially stemmed from the expansion of publicly funded early intervention services to a wider range and larger number of infants, young children, and families, and the need for policymakers to understand that such services actually were having positive effects. With the passage of laws that mandated early intervention services, studies of efficacy have shifted to address more defined questions related to the nature of services provided and the types of child and family outcomes produced, given specific family and child characteristics (Guralnick, 1988).

Efficacy as a Global Question. In early efficacy research that Guralnick (1993) called "first generation," the primary research question was "Is early intervention effective?" In retrospect, this question was too simplistic because early intervention is actually not a uniform treatment administered to all children. Initial attempts to answer this question consisted of reviews of the literature that examined child outcomes and/or research methodology (Dunst & Rheingrover, 1981; Odom & Fewell, 1983; Simeonsson, Cooper, & Scheiner, 1982; White & Casto, 1984). These reviews, although mostly positive about the efficacy of early intervention, were all critical of the research methodology employed to address the question.

To synthesize efficacy data in a more systematic fashion, researchers have employed meta-analysis (Glass, McGaw, & Smith, 1981). This secondary analysis allows one to examine child outcomes across studies that have used different dependent variables and that have different program features. In a comprehensive study that sparked this trend, Casto and Mastropieri (1986) found a medium average effect size (.68) for early intervention in general, and increasing effect sizes as number of service hours increased (reflecting the relationship between intensity and outcomes). They also found limited evidence for more powerful effects occurring for programs in which children who began earlier rather than later (i.e., infant vs. preschool programs) and programs in which there is more (contrasted with less) family involvement. This particular meta-analysis was criticized on methodological grounds (Dunst & Synder, 1986; Strain & Smith, 1986). A subsequent reanalysis of a subset of these data revealed substantial outcome effect sizes for children with disabilities below the age of 3, although the effect sizes were smaller for children with severe disabilities in comparison with children having mild and moderate disabilities (Shonkoff & Hauser-Cram, 1987).

More Defined Efficacy Questions. Perhaps in response to individuals questioning whether global efficacy questions related to early intervention are even relevant (Anastasiow, 1986; Meisels, 1985), research has tended to address more defined questions related to the effectiveness of program features for specific populations. Guralnick (1993) termed this type of research "second-generation" efficacy research, because it addresses more specific efficacy questions. He proposed that questions related to efficacy might be organized conceptually as a three-dimensional matrix, with child and family characteristics, program features, and program outcomes representing the dimensions of the matrix. In this framework, each cell represents a well-defined research question.

Several examples of this type of second generation work exist. To compare the effects of a direct instructional approach and a child-oriented, cognitive education approach to teaching language skills, Cole, Dale, and Mills (1991) assigned children with communication disorders and other mild developmental delays to the two different treatments. They found significant differences between treatments, with each treatment generating stronger effects on the dependent measures theoretically consistent with the goals of that treatment. Also, generally, they found that children with greater delays benefited more from child-directed treatment, and children with lesser developmental delays did better in the direct instruction program; this trend was also detected in a subsequent follow-up of these children (Mills, Dale, Cole, & Jenkins, 1995). This research illustrates the specificity of questions addressed in the second generation efficacy research (e.g., What are the specific outcomes of specific types of intervention for children with a specific type of disability?).

A series of studies conducted by the Early Intervention Research Institute on Efficacy (EIRI) illustrates the difficulty in conducting efficacy research, especially with a longitudinal focus. This institute conducted specific studies on the intensity of interventions (Behl, White, & Escobar, 1993; Goetze et al., 1993; Taylor, White, & Kusmierek, 1993), age at start of intervention (Boyce, Smith, Immel, Casto, & Escobar, 1993), and parent involvement (Boyce, White, & Kerr, 1993; Innocenti, Hollinger, Escobar, & White, 1993). The researchers attempted to follow high standards in using randomized group design methodology, naive data collectors, and treatment verification (White, 1993). With some exceptions, these researchers found essentially no differences between treatments for *all* of their studies, replicating this lack of treatment effects across years. Criticisms of this series of studies have addressed issues related to the analysis of dependent measures (Telzrow, 1993), the confounding of independent variables (Guralnick, 1993), and the methodology used for measuring treatment integrity (Telzrow, 1993)—with White et al. (1994) responding to each criticism. However, both Guralnick (1993) and Telzrow (1993) noted that the early intervention field has moved to a family-centered, ecological approach to treatment that was not represented by the interventions examined in the carefully executed series of efficacy studies. The problem is that the conceptualization of "best practice" in early intervention shifts over time (McLean & Odom, 1996; Peters & Heron, 1993), making longitudinal efficacy research a bit like shooting at a moving target. If major conceptual shifts in the field result in substantial changes in practice, one may find that longitudinal research is being conducted on interventions that no longer reflect current thinking about acceptable practices in the field.

FUTURE DIRECTIONS IN PREVENTION AND EARLY INTERVENTION RESEARCH

Prevention

Prevention research related to disability is multidisciplinary, based in the biological sciences and medicine, psychology and human development, education and special education, developmental therapies (e.g., occupational therapy, physical therapy), and social services. Advancing knowledge about the causes of disability, procedures for detection of elevated risk, and newly developed interventions to reduce risk set the content agenda for future prevention research. Within the framework set by disciplinary content and contemporary knowledge of risk factors, guidelines can be offered for advancing prevention research as a scientific endeavor. These principles are adapted from those suggested by Coie et al. (1993) for studying the prevention of human dysfunction.

Causal Processes. Prevention research must examine fundamental causal processes. Theories of prevention must be offered that specify the developmental processes that lead to the onset or the maintenance of disabilities. Such theories will depend on the development of complex models that specify predictor variables, outcomes, and mediating variables, and that describe the dynamic developmental processes that link these variables (e.g., Baumeister et al., 1993). Prevention research then begins to serve the dual purpose of testing the model and providing information about the efficacy of the intervention to reduce risks within that model.

Early Identification of Factors. Research should be designed so that risk factors are addressed as early as possible, before these factors have stabilized in their role as predictors of dysfunction or disability. Prevention efforts should occur before the onset of dysfunction. Extended exposure to risk factors, whether they are environmental or social, tends to increase the associated poor developmental outcomes.

Target Individuals at Highest Risk. Prevention research should target individuals who are at highest risk, particularly those who have intense exposure to multiple risk factors. It is often the case that the highest-risk individuals are among the most difficult to enroll in research studies (e.g., children living in poverty who do not attend day care or Head Start are potentially at higher risk than children whose families have enrolled in such programs). Innovative strategies for the recruitment of highest risk populations will be needed for prevention research to reach its potential.

Target Multiple Domains. Because risk is multiply determined, interventions must target multiple domains and systems. Ecological or systems frameworks for understanding and intervening to reduce risk continue to be timely conceptual guides for prevention research. The specification of transactions within levels of the system, identification of keystone behaviors and social supports, and the overall evaluation of ecological models is needed. Large-scale interventions will require collaboration across the systems mapped in these ecological models; coordination of implementation across health education and human services will be needed in comprehensive interventions.

Follow Developmental Research Principles. Prevention research should be guided by developmental research principles. These principles include attention to the patterns of development over time, attention to person by environment adaptive processes, selection and timing of measures so that both development and adaptation can be monitored, and a cycle of testing theory and reformulating theory on the basis of empirical data.

Research to Practice. In addition to theory-based research to specify risk and its amelioration, there is a pressing need for research on ensuring high-quality implementation of large-scale interventions. This type of translative research (Odom, 1988) will be essential in moving the knowledge base into actual prevention of disability. Similarly, public policy analysis and research are needed to target the processes that support large-scale implementations of interventions in the public interest. The ethics of prevention research, especially the public identification of individuals at risk and the appropriate use of experimental designs when risk outcomes are well established, must be a part of the future agenda.

Early Intervention

Substantial changes have occurred in the field of early intervention over the past decade and may reflect well the trends that will carry the field through this decade and into the next century. These trends are related to inclusion of children with disabilities in community-based programs for children without disabilities, responsiveness of programs to cultural diversity existing within their programs and society, and transition of children from early intervention to elementary school programs. In addition, there has been a conceptual shift in the relevance of questions addressed and range of research methodologies needed to address these questions.

Inclusion. Inclusion (also termed *mainstreaming* and *integration*) has been an important theme in early intervention for many years (Allen, Benning, & Drummond, 1972; Bricker & Bricker, 1971; Guralnick, 1976). However, more than any time in the past, professional organizations and parents are now advocating inclusive service models for young children with disabilities (DEC, 1993; TASH, 1991). Research generally has indicated that the developmental effects for children with disabilities in inclusive programs are strong and positive and are not significantly different from effects for children in noninclusive special education programs (Buysee & Bailey, 1993; Lamorey & Bricker, 1993; Odom & McEvoy, 1988). In some specific developmental skill areas, such as social competence and play skills, there is some evidence that inclusive programs may have positive effects relative to noninclusive settings (Guralnick & Groom, 1988; Jenkins, Odom, & Speltz, 1989).

To date, research on inclusion has examined primarily the effects on children's development (e.g., Jenkins et al., 1989), social participation in classroom activities (Guralnick & Groom, 1988), and family's attitudes and perspectives (Winton, 1993). A research theme representing a clear trend for the future is the examination of factors affecting the implementation of inclusion in community-based programs (Peck, Odom, & Bricker, 1993). Such a research direction will undoubtedly examine inclusion from an ecological perspective (Peck, 1993), which will entail determining factors operating at the classroom, family, community, social policy, and cultural dimensions of the social ecology. The challenge for this research will be to determine the linkages that exist across systems variables, their mutual and reciprocal influences, and their meaning for inclusion of children with disabilities (Odom et al., in press).

Cultural Relevance of Programs. As the demographics of the U.S. population have shifted to create a very diverse society in the 1990s, the needs of young children and families have changed also. Programs designed for the middle-class, White population may have limited relevance or may be difficult to implement for children and families from nonmainstreamed cultural groups. Currently, and even more so in the future, programs will be designed to fit the cultural perspective of the family. Lynch (1992) noted that "cultural competence" is an essential attribute for professionals providing early intervention services and for service programs. Such competence requires that service providers be sensitive to cultural values and perspectives when working with families in the home (Wayman, Lynch, & Hanson, 1990), respond to cultural factors when collecting assessment information (Hanson, Lynch, & Wayman, 1990), develop a self-awareness of their own cultural values (Harry, 1992), and understand the development of children within a cultural context (Bowman & Stott, 1994). Early intervention programs are being developed for children and families from specific cultural groups (e.g., Bruder, Anderson, Schutz, & Caldera, 1991), and this trend will undoubtedly continue into the future. Generally absent from this literature on program development is research documenting that specialized programs and programs that are culturally competent achieve the goals established for children and families, although this database will undoubtedly emerge in the next decade.

Transition. Systematic plans for moving children and families across programs is an important component of early intervention programs. During the early intervention years, such transitions may occur for some children and families when an infant leaves an NICU and goes home (Odom & Chandler, 1990), when an infant and family enter an early intervention program (Rice & O'Brien, 1990), when an infant and family move from a birth-to-3 program to a preschool program (Rosenkoetter, Hains, & Fowler, 1994), and when a child moves from a preschool program into kindergarten or the first grade (Conn-Powers, Ross-Allen, & Holburn, 1990). Although each transition is qualitatively different, research indicates that certain factors may be essential for a successful transition to occur (Bruder & Chandler, in press). These factors include collaboration and communication across agencies, establishing a partnership and preparing families for the transition, and preparing the child for the transition (Bruder & Chandler,1996). An emerging database exists that describes characteristics of various programs, teacher expectations, and strategies for accomplishing successful transitions (Rosenkoetter et al., 1994). We foresee an elaboration and extension of this research base for practice in the future.

Research Questions and Methodologies. As early intervention has begun to embrace an ecological conceptual base, the research questions have become more complex. Moreover, the recognition that research questions have different purposes (e.g., technical, practical, emancipatory purposes identified by Habermas, 1984) has led some researchers to propose that particular methodologies may be directly linked with particular purposes (Ewert, 1991). The complexity and purpose of research questions has challenged researchers to search beyond traditional research methodologies for ways of answering important and relevant questions. Efficacy research serves as a good example of the need for using a fuller range of methodologies for addressing such questions.

Randomized group designs have been held as the "gold standard" for efficacy research (White & Pezzino, 1986), with research utilizing other designs being vaguely described as "pseudo-science" (White, 1993). However, researchers have pointed out that early intervention programs are just one variable that affects the development of children with disabilities (Marfo & Dinero, 1991; Shonkoff, Hauser-Cram, Krauss, & Upshur, 1992). A useful model for understanding the relative effects of early intervention in the context of other ecological variables might follow a multiple regression approach (Dunst, 1986; Marfo & Dinero, 1991). In addition, for understanding more fully the processes underlying implementation of treatments and how those treatments affect individual children and families, researchers have proposed using qualitative, naturalistic, or interpretist methodologies (Odom & Shuster, 1986; Peck & Furman, 1992). Other researchers have proposed that employing mixed methodology (i.e., both qualitative and quantitative methods) may be useful for some questions, and in some contexts the methodological approaches may provide complementary information (Greene, Caracelli, & Graham, 1989). Certainly, in the future the range of methods used to examine the effects of early intervention, as well as for addressing other questions in the field, will continue to broaden. The key to the successful elaboration of such methodologies will be for the procedures to adhere to the standards of each specific methodological approach.

CONCLUSION

More than 30 years of behavioral and biomedical research have provided a fundamental understanding of many of the factors contributing to poor developmental outcomes and disabilities. In many cases, the benefits of preventative health care, education, and social services are well documented. Perhaps the most pressing current problem is one of delivering established prevention and early intervention services to those children and families in greatest need. Implementation is a challenge to be shared by researchers and policymakers. Expert design, analysis, and evaluation of service delivery systems, and informed public policy to garner support for effective prevention and early intervention services are needed in equal parts. No area of applied research or public policy is likely to have a greater impact on the lives of children and families.

REFERENCES

Achenbach, T. M., Phares, V., Howell, C. T., Rauh, V. A., & Nurcombe, B. (1990). Seven-year outcome of the Vermont Intervention Program for low birthweight infants. *Child Development, 61*, 1672–1681.

Adams, M. J., & Hollowell, J. G. (1992). Community-based projects for the prevention of developmental disabilities. *Mental Retardation, 30*, 331–336.

Allen, K. E., Benning, P. M., & Drummond, W. T. (1972). Integration of normal and handicapped children in a behavior modification preschool: A case study. In G. Semb (Ed.), *Behavior analysis and education* (pp. 127–141). Lawrence: University of Kansas.

Allen, K. E., Turner, K. I., & Everett, P. M. (1970). A behavior modification classroom for Head Start children with problem behaviors. *Exceptional Children, 37,* 119–127.

Als, H. (1994, December). *Effectiveness of implementing developmental care in newborn-intensive care units.* Paper presented at the Project Directors Conference of the Early Education Programs for Children with Disabilities, Washington, DC.

Als, H., Lawhon, G., Brown, E., Gibes, R., Duffy, F. H., McAnulty, G., & Blickman, J. G. (1986). Individualized behavioral and environmental care for the very low birth weight preterm infant at high risk for bronchopulmonary dysplasia: Neonatal intensive care unit and developmental outcome. *Pediatric, 78,* 1123–1132.

Als, H., Lawhon, G., Gibes, R., Duffy, R. H., McAnulty, G., & Blickman, J. G. (1994). Individualized developmental care for the very low birthweight preterm infant at high risk for chronic lung disease and intraventricular hemorrhage: Medical and neurofunctional effects. *Journal of the American Medical Association, 272,* 853–858.

Anastasiow, N. J. (1986). The research base for early intervention. *Journal of the Division for Early Childhood, 10,* 99–117.

Bailey, D. B., & Henderson, L. W. (1993). Traditions in family assessment: Toward an inquiry-oriented, reflective model. In D. Bryant & M. Graham (Eds.), *Implementing early intervention: From research to effective practice* (pp. 124–146). New York: Guilford.

Bailey, D. B., & McWilliam, R. (1990). Normalizing early intervention. *Topics in Early Childhood Special Education, 10*(3), 33–47.

Bailey, D. B., Simeonsson, R. J., Winton, P. J., Huntington, G. S., Comfort, T. M., Isbell, P., O'Donnell, K. J., & Helms, J. (1986). Family-focused intervention: A functional model for planing, implementing, and evaluating individualized family services in early intervention. *Journal of the Division for Early Childhood, 10,* 156–171.

Baumeister, A. A., Kupstas, F. D., & Klindworth, L. M. (1990). New morbidity: Implications for prevention of children's disabilities. *Exceptionality, 1,* 1–16.

Baumeister, A. A., Kupstas, F. D., Zanthos, P. W., & Klindworth, L. M. (1993). *Guide to planning for the prevention of mental retardation and related disabilities associated with socioeconomic conditions.* Washington, DC: President's Commission on Mental Retardation.

Beckman, P. J., Robinson, C. C., Rosenberg, S., & Filler, J. (1994). Family involvement in early intervention. In L. Johnson, R. Gallagher, M. LaMontagne, J. Jordan, J. Gallagher, P. Hutinger, & M. Karnes (Eds.), *Meeting early intervention challenges* (pp. 13–31). Baltimore: Brookes.

Behl, D., White, K. R., & Escobar, C. M. (1993). New Orleans early intervention study of children with visual impairment. *Early Education and Development, 4,* 256–273.

Bereiter, C., & Engelmann, S. (1966). *Teaching disadvantaged children in the preschool.* Englewood Cliffs, NJ: Prentice-Hall.

Bijou, S. W. (1993). *Behavior analysis of child development* (2nd rev.). Reno, NV: Context Press.

Bowman, B. T., & Stott, F. M. (1994). Understanding development in a cultural context: The challenges for teachers. In B. Mallory & R. New (Eds.), *Diversity and developmentally appropriate practices* (pp. 119–134). New York: Teachers College Press.

Boyce, G. C., Smith, T. B., Immel, N., Casto, G., & Escobar, C. (1993). Early intervention with medically fragile infants: Investigating the age-at-start questions. *Early Education and Development, 4,* 290–305.

Boyce, G. C., White, K. R., & Kerr, B. (1993). The effectiveness of adding a parent involvement component to an existing center-based program for children with disabilities and their families. *Early Education and Development, 4,* 327–345.

Bredekamp, S. (1987). *Developmentally appropriate practice in early childhood programs serving children from birth through age 8.* Washington, DC: National Association for the Education of Young Children.

Bredekamp, S., & Rosegrant, S. (1992). *Reaching potentials: Appropriate curriculum and assessment for young children.* Washington, DC: National Association for the Education of Young Children.

Bricker, D., & Bricker, W. (1971). Toddler Research and Intervention Project Report—Year I. *IMRID Behavioral Science Monograph No. 20*. Nashville, TN: Institute on Mental Retardation and Intellectual Development.

Bricker, D., & Cripe, J. (1991). *An activity-based approach to early intervention*. Baltimore: Brookes.

Bricker, W. A., & Bricker, D. D. (1974). An early language training strategy. In R. L. Schiefelbusch & L. L. Lloyd (Eds.), *Language perspectives: Acquisition, retardation, and intervention* (pp. 431–468). Baltimore: University Park Press.

Bromwich, R. (1981). *Working with parents and infants: An interactional approach*. Austin, TX: PRO-ED.

Bronfenbrenner, U. (1979). *The ecology of human development: Experiments by nature and design*. Cambridge, MA: Harvard University Press.

Bronfenbrenner, U., & Weiss, H. (1983). Beyond policies without people: An ecological perspective on child and family policy. In E. Zigler, S. Lynn-Kagan, & E. Klugman (Eds.), *Children families, and government* (pp. 393–414). New York: Cambridge University Press.

Brookes-Gunn, J., & Lewis, M. (1984). Maternal responsiveness in interactions with handicapped infants. *Child Development, 55*, 782–793.

Brown, R. (1991). Changing concept of disability in developed and developing countries. In D. Mitchell & R. Brown (Eds.), *Early intervention studies for young children with special needs* (pp. 1–18). New York: Chapman & Hall.

Bruder, M. B., Anderson, R., Schutz, G., & Caldera, M. (1991). Project Profile: Ninos Especiales Program, a culturally senstive early intervention model. *Journal of Early Intervention, 15*, 268–277.

Bruder, M. B, & Chandler, L. (1996). Recommended practices in transition. In S. Odom & M. McLean (Eds.), *Early intervention/early childhood special education: Recommended practices* (pp. 287–308). Austin, TX: PRO-ED.

Buehler, D., Als, H., Duffy, F. H., McAnulty, G. B., & Liederman, J. (in press). Effectiveness of individualized developmental care for low risk preterm infants: Behavioral and electrophysiological evidence. *Pediatrics*.

Bushell, D. (1970). *The behavior analysis classroom*. Lawrence: University of Kansas, Department of Human Development.

Buysee, V., & Bailey, D. B. (1993). Behavioral and developmental outcomes in young children with disabilities in integrated and segregated settings: A review of comparative studies. *Journal of Special Education, 26*, 434–461.

Camaratta, S. (1993). The application of naturalistic conversation training to speech production in children with speech disabilities. *Journal of Applied Behavior Analysis, 26*, 173–182.

Caplan, G., & Grunebaum, H. (1967). Perspectives on primary prevention. *Archives of General Psychiatry, 17*, 331–346.

Carta, J. J., Atwater, J., Greenwood, C., McEvoy, M. A., McConnell, S. R., & Williams, R. (1994, December). *Longitudinal study of young children prenatally exposed to drugs and/or alcohol*. Paper presented at Project Directors Conference of the Early Education Program for Children with Disabilities, Washington, DC.

Carta, J. J., Schwartz, I., Atwater, J. B., & McConnell, S. R. (1991). Developmentally appropriate practice: Appraising its usefulness for young children with disabilities. *Topics in Early Childhood Special Education, 11*(1), 1–20.

Casto, G., & Mastropieri, M. A. (1986). The efficacy of early intervention programs: A meta-analysis. *Exceptional Children, 52*, 425–435.

Centers for Disease Control and Prevention. (1991). Use of folic acid for prevention of spina bifida and other neural tube defects: 1983–1991. *Morbidity and Mortality Weekly Report, 40*, 513–516.

Centers for Disease Control and Prevention. (1993). *Project BEGIN: Bringing early growth (and development) into neighborhoods*. Atlanta, GA: Author.

Chamberlin, R. W. (1994). Primary prevention: The missing piece in child development legislation. In R. Simeonsson (Ed.), *Risk, resilience & prevention: Promoting the well being of all children* (pp. 33–52). Baltimore: Brookes.

Chen, J., & Simeonsson, R. J. (1991). Prevention of disability in the People's Republic of China. *Child: Care, Health, and Development, 19*(2), 71–88.

Cohen, D. E. (1992). Utilization of the fateful forty-three in New Jersey. *Mental Retardation, 30,* 319.

Coie, J. D., Watt, N. F., West, S. G., Hawkins, J. D., Asarnow, J. R., Markman, H. J., Ramey, S. L., Shure, M. B., & Long, B. (1993). The science of prevention: A conceptual framework and some directions for a national research program. *American Psychologist, 48*(10), 1013–1022.

Cole, K., Dale, P., & Mills, P. (1991). Individual differences in language delayed children's responses to direct and interactive preschool instruction. *Topics in Early Childhood Special Education, 11*(1), 91–105.

Conn-Powers, M. C., Ross-Allen, J., & Holburn, S. (1990). Transition of young children into the elementary education mainstream. *Topics in Early Childhood Special Education, 9*(4), 91–105.

Crocker, A. C. (1992). Data collection for the evaluation of mental retardation prevention activities: The fateful forty-three. *Mental Retardation, 30,* 303–318.

Dawson, P. M., Robinson, J. L., Butterfield, P. M., van Doorninck, W. J., Gaensbauer, T. J., & Harmon, R. J. (1991). Supporting new parents through home visits: Effects on mother–infant interaction. *Topics in Early Childhood Special Education, 10*(4), 29–45.

Division for Early Childhood. (1993). DEC position statement on inclusion. *DEC Communicator, 19*(4), 4.

Deutsch, M., Deutsch, C. P., Jordan, T. J., & Grallo, R. (1983). The IDS program: An experiment in early and sustained enrichment. In *Consortium for Longitudinal Studies, As the twig is bent . . . Lasting effects of preschool programs* (pp. 377–410). Hillsdale, NJ: Lawrence Erlbaum Associates.

DeVries, R., & Kohlberg, L. (1990). *Constructivist early education: Overview and comparison with other programs.* Washington, DC: National Association for the Education of Young Children.

Dunst, C. J. (1983). Communicative competence and deficits: Effects on early social interactions. In E. McDonald & D. Gallagher (Eds.), *Facilitating social–emotional development in the young multiply handicapped child* (pp. 198–223). Philadelphia: Home of Merciful Saviour Press.

Dunst, C. J. (1986). Overview of the efficacy of early intervention. In L. Bickman & D. Weatherford (Eds.), *Evaluating early intervention programs for severely handicapped children and their families* (pp. 79–148). Austin, TX: PRO-ED.

Dunst, C. J. (1993). Implications of risk and opportunity factors for assessment and intervention practices. *Topics in Early Childhood Special Education, 13,* 143–153.

Dunst, C. J., & Rheingrover, R. (1981). An analysis of the efficacy of infant intervention programs with organically handicapped children. *Evaluation and Program Planning, 4,* 287–323.

Dunst, C. J., & Synder, S. W. (1986). A critique of the Utah State University early intervention meta-analysis research. *Exceptional Children, 53,* 269–276.

Duwa, S. M., Wells, C., & Lalinde, P. (1993). Creating family-centered programs and policies. In D. Bryant & M. Graham (Eds.), *Implementing early intervention: From research to effective practice* (pp. 92–123). New York: Guilford.

Eayrs, C. B., & Jones, R. S. (1992). Methodological issues and future directions in the evaluation of early intervention programmes. *Child: Care, Health, and Development, 18,* 15–28.

Edmondson, R. (1994). Drug use and pregnancy. In R. Simeonsson (Ed.), *Risk, resilience, & prevention: Promoting the well-being of all children* (pp. 151–169). Baltimore: Brookes.

Ewert, G. D. (1991). Habermas and education: A comprehensive overview of the influence of Habermas in educational literature. *Review of Educational Research, 61,* 345–378.

Fewell, R. F., & Oelwein, P. L. (1990). The relationship between time in integrated environments and developmental gains in young children with special needs. *Topics in Early Childhood Special Education, 10*(2), 104–116.

Forehand, R. (1993). Twenty years of research on parenting: Does it have practical implications for clinicians working with parents and children? *The Clinical Psychologist, 46*(4), 169–176.

Fraiberg, S. (1971). Intervention in infancy: A program for blind infants. *Journal of the American Academy of Child Psychiatry, 10,* 315–335.

Fredericks, H. D., Jordan, V., Gage, M. A., Levak, L., Alrick, G., & Wadlow, M. (1975). *A data-based classroom for moderately and severely handicapped.* Monmouth, OR: Teaching-Research.

Gallagher, J. J., Harbin, G., Eckland, J., & Clifford, R. (1994). State diversity and policy implementation: Infants and Toddlers. In L. Johnson, R. Gallagher, M. LaMontagne, J. Jordan, J. Gallagher, P. Hutinger, & M. Karnes (Eds.), *Meeting early intervention challenges: Issues from birth to three* (pp. 235–251). Baltimore: Brookes.

Garbarino, J. (1982). *Children and families in the social environment.* New York: Aldine.

Garmezy, N. (1974). The study of competence in children at risk for severe psychopathology. In E. Anthony & C. Koupernik (Eds.), *The child in his family* (Vol. 3, pp. 77–98). New York: Wiley.

Garmezy, N. (1985). Stress-resistant children: The search for protective factors. In J. Stevenson (Ed.), *Journal of Child Psychology and Psychiatry, Book Supplement No. 4* (pp. 213–233). Oxford, England: Pergamon.

Gartner, A., Lipsky, D. K., & Turnbull, A. P. (1991). *Supporting families with a child with a disability: An international outlook.* Baltimore: Brookes.

Girolametto, L., Verbey, M., & Tannock, R. (1994). Improving joint engagement in parent-child interaction: An intervention study. *Journal of Early Intervention, 18,* 155–167.

Glass, G. V., McGaw, B., & Smith, M. L. (1981). *Meta-analysis in social research.* Beverly Hills, CA: Sage.

Goetze, L. D., Immel, N., Escobar, C. M., Gillette, Y., Coury, D., & Hansen, N. (1993). Does more intensive neonatal intensive care unit follow-up service result in better outcomes? A cost-effectiveness analysis. *Early Education and Development, 4,* 327–345.

Goldberg, D., McLaughlin, M., Grossi, M., Tytum, A., & Blum, S. (1992). Which newborns in New York City are at risk for special education placement? *American Journal of Public Health, 82,* 438–440.

Goldston, S. E. (1977). Defining primary prevention. In G. Albee & J. Joffe (Eds.), *Primary prevention in psychotherapy* (Vol. 1, pp. 18–23). Burlington, VT: University Press of New England.

Gray, S. W., Ramsey, B. K., & Klaus, R. A. (1983). The Early Training Project 1962–1980. In *Consortium for Longitudinal Studies, As the twig is bent . . . Lasting effects of preschool programs* (pp. 33–69). Hillsdale, NJ: Lawrence Erlbaum Associates.

Greene, J. C., Caracelli, V. J., & Graham, W. F. (1989). Toward a conceptual framework for mixed-method evaluation design. *Educational Evaluation and Policy Analysis, 11,* 255–274.

Guralnick, M. J. (1976). The value of integrating handicapped and nonhandicapped preschool children. *American Journal of Orthopsychiatry, 46,* 236–245.

Guralnick, M. J. (1988). Efficacy research in early childhood intervention programs. In S. Odom & M. Karnes (Eds.), *Early intervention for infants and children with handicaps* (pp. 75–88). Baltimore: Brookes.

Guralnick, M. J. (1991). The next decade of research on effectiveness of early intervention. *Exceptional Children, 58,* 174–183.

Guralnick, M. J. (1993). Second generation research on the effectiveness of early intervention. *Early Education and Development, 4,* 366–378.

Guralnick, M. J., & Groom, J. M. (1988). Friendships of preschool children in mainstream playgroups. *Developmental Psychology, 24,* 595–604.

Habermas, J. (1984). *The theory of communicative action: Vol. 1. Reason and the rationalization of society.* Boston: Beacon Press.

Hack, M., Taylor, H. G., Klein, N., Eiben, R., Schatschneider, C., & Mercuri-Minich, N. (1994). School age outcomes in children with birthweight under 750 g. *New England Journal of Medicine, 331*(12), 753–759.

Haggerty, R. J., Roghmann, K. J., & Pless, I. B. (1975). *Child health and the community.* New York: Wiley.

Hale, B. A., Seitz, V., & Zigler, E. (1990). Health services and Head Start: A forgotten formula. *Journal of Applied Developmental Psychology, 11,* 447–458.

Hanson, M. J., & Lynch, E. W. (1992). Family diversity: Implications for policy and practice. *Topics in Early Childhood Special Education, 12*(3), 283–306.

Hanson, M. J., Lynch, E. W., & Wayman, K. I. (1990). Honoring the cultural diversity of families when gathering data. *Topics in Early Childhood Special Education, 10*(1), 112–131.

Harbin, G., Gallagher, J. J., & Terry, D. V. (1991). Defining the eligible population: Policy issues and challenges. *Journal of Early Intervention, 15*, 13–20.

Hardy, J. B., King, T. M., & Repke, J. T. (1986). *The Johns Hopkins Adolescent Pregnancy Program.* Unpublished report from the Department of Pediatrics and Gynecology and Obstetrics, the Johns Hopkins University School of Medicine, and the Johns Hopkins University Hospital, Baltimore, MD.

Harry, B. (1992). *Cultural diversity, families and the special education system: Communication and empowerment.* New York: Teachers College Press.

Hart, B. M., & Risley, T. R. (1968). Establishing the use of descriptive adjectives in the spontaneous speech of disadvantaged preschool children. *Journal of Applied Behavior Analysis, 1*, 109–120.

Hayden, A. H., & Haring, N. G. (1976). Early intervention for high risk infants and young children: Programs for Down's syndrome children. In T. Tjossem (Ed.), *Intervention strategies for high risk infants and young children* (pp. 573–608). Baltimore: University Park Press.

Hayes, S. C., & Hayes, L. J. (1992). Some clinical implications of contextualistic behaviorism: The example of cognition. *Behavior Therapy, 23*, 225–249.

Haywood, H. C., Brooks, P., & Burns, S. (1992). *Bright start: Cognitive curriculum for young children.* Watertown, MA: Charlesbridge.

Hohmann, M., & Weikart, D. P. (1995). *Educating young children.* Ypsilanti, MI: High/Scope Foundation.

Huntington, G. S., Lima, L., & Zipper, I. N. (1994). Child abuse: A prevention agenda. In R. J. Simeonsson (Ed.), *Risk, resilience, & prevention: Promoting the well-being of all children* (pp. 169–182). Baltimore: Brookes.

Infant Health and Development Program. (1990). Enhancing the outcomes of low-birth-weight, premature infants: A multisite, randomized trial. *Journal of the American Medical Association, 263*(22), 3035–3042.

Innocenti, M. S., Hollinger, P. D., Escobar, C., & White, K. R. (1993). The cost-effectiveness of adding one type of parent involvement to an early intervention program. *Early Education and Development, 4*, 306–315.

Institute of Medicine. (1985). *Preventing low birthweight.* Washington, DC: National Academy Press.

Jenkins, J. R., Odom, S. L., & Speltz, M. L. (1989). Effects of integration and structured play on the development of handicapped children. *Exceptional Children, 55*, 420–428.

Johnson, J. E., & Johnson, K. M (1992). Clarifying the developmental approach in response to Carta, Schwartz, Atwater, and McConnell. *Topics in Early Childhood Special Education, 12*(4), 439–457.

Kaiser, A. P., Yoder, P. J., & Keetz, A. (1992). Evaluating milieu teaching. In S. Warren & J. Reichle, *Causes and effects in communication and language intervention* (pp. 9–47). Baltimore: Brookes.

Karnes, M. B., Beauchamp, K. D., & Pfaus, D. B. (1993). PEECH: A nationally validated early childhood special education model. *Topics in Early Childhood Special Education, 13*, 120–135.

Karnes, M. B., Kokotovic, A. M., & Shwedel, A. M. (1982). Transporting a model program for young handicapped children: Issues, problems, and efficacy. *Journal of the Division for Early Childhood, 6*, 42–51.

Karnes, M. B., Shwedel, A. M., Lewis, G. F., Ratts, D. A., & Esry, D. R. (1981). Impact of early programming for the handicapped: A follow-up study into the elementary school. *Journal of the Division for Early Childhood, 4*, 62–69.

Koegel, R., O'Dell, M., & Koegel, L. (1987). A natural language paradigm for teaching nonverbal autistic children. *Journal of Autism and Developmental Disorders, 17*, 187–199.

Kopp, C. B., & Kaler, S. R. (1989). Risk in infancy: Origins and implications. *American Psychologist, 44*, 224–230.

Kozulin, A. (1990). *Vygotsky's psychology: A biography of ideas.* Cambridge, MA: Harvard University Press.

Lamorey, S., & Bricker, D. D. (1993). Integrated programs: Effects on young children and their parents. In C. Peck, S. Odom, & D. Bricker (Eds.), *Integrating young children with disabilities into community-based programs: From research to implementation* (pp. 249–269). Baltimore: Brookes.

Lazar, I., & Darlington, R. (1982). Lasting effects of early education: A report from the Consortium for Longitudinal Studies. *Monographs of the Society for Research in Child Development, 47*(2–3, Serial No. 195).

Lozoff, B. (1989). Nutrition and behavior. *American Psychologist, 44,* 231–236.

Luthar, S. S. (1993). Methodological and conceptual issues in research on childhood resilience. *Journal of Child Psychology and Psychiatry, 34,* 441–453.

Lutzker, J. R., & Campbell, R. (1994). *Ecobehavioral family intervention in developmental disabilities.* Pacific Grove, CA: Brooks/Cole.

Lynch, E. W. (1992). Developing cultural competence. In M. Hanson & E. Lynch (Eds.), *Developing cross-cultural competence* (pp. 35–62). Baltimore: Brookes.

MacDonald, J. (1989). *Becoming partners with children: From play to conversation.* San Antonio, TX: Special Press.

Mahoney, G., O'Sullivan, P., & Dennebaum, J. (1990). Maternal perception of early intervention services: A scale for assessing family-focused intervention. *Topics in Early Childhood Special Education, 10*(1), 1–15.

Mahoney, G., & Powell, A. (1988). Modifying parent–child interaction: Enhancing the development of handicapped children. *Journal of Special Education, 22,* 82–96.

Mahoney, G., & Robenalt, K. (1985). A comparison of conversation patterns between mothers and their Down syndrome and normal infants. *Journal of the Division of Early Childhood, 10,* 172–180.

Mallory, B. L., & New, R. S. (Eds.). (1994). *Diversity and developmentally appropriate practices.* New York: Teachers College Press.

Marfo, K. (1991). The maternal directiveness theme in mother–child interaction research: Implications for early intervention. In K. Marfo (Ed.), *Early intervention in transition: Current perspectives on programs for handicapped infants* (pp. 177–203). New York: Praeger.

Marfo, K., & Dinero, T. E. (1991). Assessing early intervention outcomes: Beyond program variables. *International Journal of Disability, Development, and Education, 38,* 289–303.

Martin, S. L., Ramey, C. T., & Ramey, S. L. (1990). The prevention of intellectual impairment in children of impoverished families: Findings of a randomized trial of educational daycare. *American Journal of Public Health, 80,* 844–847.

Maurer, H., & Sherrod, K. B. (1987). Context of directives given to young children with Down syndrome and nonretarded children: Development over two years. *American Journal of Mental Deficiency, 91,* 579–590.

McCollum, J. A. (1991). At a crossroads: Reviewing and rethinking interaction coaching. In K. Marfo (Ed.), *Early intervention in transition: Current perspectives on programs for handicapped infants* (pp. 137–176). New York: Praeger.

McCollum, J. A., & Bair, H. (1994). Research in parent-child interaction: Guidance to developmentally appropriate practice for young children with disabilities. In B. Mallory & R. New (Eds.), *Diversity and developmentally appropriate practices* (pp. 84–106). New York: Teachers College Press.

McLean, J. E., & Snyder-McLean, L. K. (1978). *A transactional approach to early language training.* Columbus, OH: Merrill.

McLean, M. E., & Odom, S. L. (1993). Practices for young children with and without disabilities: A comparison of DEC and NAEYC identified practices. *Topics in Early Childhood Special Education, 13,* 274–293.

McLean, M. E., & Odom, S. L. (1996). Establishing recommended practices in early intervention/early childhood special education. In S. Odom & M. McLean (Eds.), *Early intervention/early childhood special education: Recommended practices* (pp. 1–22). Austin, TX: PRO-ED.

Meisels, S. J. (1985). The efficacy of early intervention: Why are we still asking this question? *Topics in Early Childhood Special Education, 5*, 1–11.

Meisels, S. J. (1989). Meeting the mandate of Public Law 99–457: Early childhood intervention in the nineties. *American Journal of Orthopsychiatry, 59*, 451–460.

Meisels, S. J. (1991). Dimensions of early identification. *Journal of Early Intervention, 15*, 26–35.

Meltzer, L., & Reid, D. K. (1994). New directions in the assessment of students with special needs: The shift toward a constructivist perspective. *Journal of Special Education, 28*, 338–355.

Mills, P. E., Dale, P. S., Cole, K. N., & Jenkins, J. R. (1995). Follow-up of children form academic and cognitive preschool curricula at age 9. *Exceptional Children, 61*, 378–393.

Mittler, P. (1992). International visions of excellence for children with disabilities. *International Journal of Disability, Development, and Education, 39*, 115–126.

Morris, E. K. (1992). The aim, progress, and evolution of behavior analysis. *Behavior Analyst, 15*, 3–29.

Murphy, L. B. (1987). Further reflections on resilience. In E. Anthony & B. Cohler (Eds.), *The invulnerable child* (pp. 84–105). New York: Guilford.

Neisworth, J. T., & Bagnato, S. J. (1996). Assessment for early intervention: Emerging themes and practices. In S. Odom & M. McLean (Eds.), *Early intervention/early childhood special education: Recommended practices* (pp. 23–58). Austin, TX: PRO-ED.

Nickel, R. E., Bennett, F. C., & Lamson, F. N. (1982). School performance of infants with birthweights of 1000 grams or less. *American Journal of Diseases of Children, 136*, 105–110.

Nurcombe, B., Howell, D. C., Rauh, V. A., Titi, D. M., Ruoff, D., & Brennan, J. (1984). An intervention program for mothers of low birthweight infants: Preliminary results. *Journal of the American Academy of Child Psychiatry, 23*, 319–325.

Odom, S. L. (1988). Research in early childhood special education: Methodologies and paradigms. In S. Odom & M. Karnes (Eds.), *Early intervention for infants and children with handicaps: An empirical base* (pp. 1-22). Baltimore: Brookes.

Odom, S. L. (1989). Editorial. *Journal of Early Intervention, 13*, 3–5.

Odom, S. L., & Chandler, L. (1990). Transition to parenthood for parents of technology-assisted infants. *Topics in Early Childhood Special Education, 9*(4), 43–55.

Odom, S. L., & Fewell, R. F. (1983). Program evaluation in early childhood special education: A meta-evaluation. *Educational Evaluation and Policy Analysis, 5*, 445-460.

Odom, S. L., & Haring, T. G. (1994). Contextualism and applied behavior analysis: Implications for early childhood special education: In R. Gardner, D. Sainato, W. Heward, J. Cooper, & T. Herron (Eds.), *Behavior analysis in education* (pp. 87–99). San Francisco: Brooks/Cole.

Odom, S. L., & McEvoy, M. A. (1988). Integration of young children with handicaps and normally developing children. In S. Odom & M. Karnes (Eds.), *Early intervention for infants and children with handicaps: An empirical base* (pp. 241–268). Baltimore: Brookes.

Odom, S. L., McLean, M. E., Johnson, L., & LaMontagne, M. (1995). Recommended practices in Early Childhood Special Education: Validation and current use. *Journal of Early Intervention, 19*, 1–17.

Odom, S. L., Peck, C. A., Hanson, M., Beckman, P., Lieber, J., Kaiser, A., Schwartz, I., Horn, E., & Brown, W. H. (in press). Inclusion at the preschool level: An ecological systems analysis. *Social Policy Report: Society for Research in Child Development.*

Odom, S. L., & Shuster, S. K. (1986). Naturalistic inquiry and the assessment of young handicapped children and their families. *Topics in Early Childhood Special Education, 6*(2), 68–82.

Olds, D. L. (1982). Improving formal services for mothers and children. In J. Garbarino & S. H. Stocking (Eds.), *Protecting children from abuse and neglect* (pp. 173–197). San Francisco: Jossey-Bass.

Palincsar, A. S., & Klenk, L. (1993). Broader visions encompassing literacy, learners, and contexts. *Remedial and Special Education, 14*(10), 19–25.

Parker, F. L., Piotrowski, C. S., & Peay, L. (1987). Head Start as a social support for mothers: The psychological benefits of involvement. *American Journal of Orthopsychiatry, 57,* 220–233.

Patterson, G. R., & Bank, C. L. (1989). Some amplifying mechanisms for pathologic processes in families. In M. Gunnar & E. Thelen (Eds.), *Systems and development: Symposia on child psychology* (pp. 167–210). Hillsdale, NJ: Lawrence Erlbaum Associates.

Peck, C. A. (1993). Ecological perspectives on the implementation of integrated early childhood programs. In C. Peck, S. Odom, & D. Bricker (Eds.), *Integrating young children with disabilities into community programs* (pp. 3–16). Baltimore: Brookes.

Peck, C. A., & Furman, G. C. (1992). Qualitative research in special education: An evaluative review. In R. Gaylord-Ross (Ed.), *Research issues in special education* (pp. 1–42). San Diego, CA: College Hill Press.

Peck, C. A., Odom, S. L., & Bricker, D. D. (Eds.). (1993). *Integrating young children with disabilities into community programs.* Baltimore: Brookes.

Peters, M. T., & Heron, T. E. (1993). When is best not good enough: An examination of best practice. *Journal of Special Education, 26,* 371–385.

Piaget, J. (1952). *The origins of intelligence in children.* New York: International Universities Press.

Piaget, J. (1970). *Structuralism.* New York: Harper & Row.

Piotrowski, C. S., Collins, R. C., Knitzer, J., & Robinson, R. (1994). Strengthening mental health services in Head Start: A challenge for the 1990s. *American Psychologist, 49*(2), 133–139.

Powell, D. (Ed.). (1988). *Parent education as early childhood intervention: Emerging directions in theory, research, and practice* (pp. 209–227). Norwood, NJ: Ablex.

Provence, S., & Naylor, A. (1983). *Working with disadvantaged parents and their children.* New Haven, CT: Yale University Press.

Ramey, C. T., Bryant, D. M., Wasik, B. H., Sparling, J. J., Fendt, K. H., & LaVange, L. M. (1992). The Infant Health and Development Program for low birthweight, premature infants: Program elements, family participation, and child intelligence. *Pediatrics, 89,* 454–465.

Ramey, C. T., & Ramey, S. L. (1992). Effective early intervention. *Mental Retardation, 30,* 337–345.

Ramey, C. T., & Ramey, S. L. (1994, October). *Longitudinal studies of early intervention.* Paper presented at the Sante Fe Institute, Sante Fe, MN.

Rauh, V. A., Achenbach, T. M., Nurcombe, B., Howell, C. T., & Teti, D. M. (1988). Minimizing adverse effects of low birthweight: Four year results of an intervention program. *Child Development, 59,* 544–553.

Resnick, M. B., Eyler, F., Nelson, R., Eitzman, D., & Bucciarelli, R. (1987). Developmental intervention for low birth weight infants: Improved early development outcomes. *Pediatrics, 80*(1), 68–74.

Rice, M. L., & O'Brien, M. (1990). Transitions: Times of change and accommodation. *Topics in Early Childhood Special Education, 9*(4), 1–14.

Roberts, R. N. (1990). *Developing culturally competent programs for families of children with special needs* (2nd ed.). Washington, DC: National Center for Networking Community-Based Services, Georgetown University.

Roberts, R. N., & Wasik, B. H. (1990). Home visiting for families with children birth to three: Results of a national survey. *Journal of Early Intervention, 14,* 274–284.

Robinshaw, H. M. (1994). Deaf infants, early intervention, and language acquisition. *Early Child Development and Care, 99,* 1–22.

Rosenkoetter, S. E., Hains, A. H., & Fowler, S. A. (1994). *Bridging early services for children with special needs and their families.* Baltimore: Brookes.

Rutter, M. (1985). Resilience in the face of adversity: Protective factors and resistance to psychiatric disorder. *British Journal of Psychiatry, 147,* 598–611.

Sameroff, A. J., & Chandler, M. J. (1975). Reproductive risk and the continuum of caretaking casualty. In F. Horowitz, M. Hetherington, S. Scarr-Salapatek, & G. Siegel (Eds.), *Review of child development* (Vol. 4, pp. 187–244). Chicago: University of Chicago Press.

Sameroff, A. J., Seifer, R., Barocas, B., Zax, M., & Greenspan, S. (1987). IQ scores of 4-year-old children: Social-environmental risk factors. *Pediatrics, 79,* 343–350.

Schnorr, R. E. (1989). "Peter? He comes and goes . . .": First graders' perspectives on a part-time mainstream student. *Journal of the Association for Persons With Severe Handicaps, 15*(4), 231–240.

Seitz, V., & Provence, S. (1990). Caregiver-focused models of early intervention. In S. J. Meisels & J. P. Shonkoff (Eds.), *Handbook of early childhood intervention* (pp. 400–427). Cambridge, England: Cambridge University Press.

Serpell, R., & Nabuzoka, D. (1991). Early intervention in third world countries. In D. Mitchell & R. Brown (Eds.), *Early intervention studies for young children with special needs* (pp. 93–126). New York: Chapman & Hall.

Shearer, D. E., & Shearer, M. S. (1976). The Portage Project: A model for early childhood intervention. In T. Tjossem (Ed.), *Intervention strategies for high risk infants and young children* (pp. 335–350). Baltimore: University Park Press.

Shonkoff, J., & Hauser-Cram, P. (1987). Early intervention for disabled infants and their families: A quantitative analysis. *Pediatrics, 80*, 650–658.

Shonkoff, J., P., Hauser-Cram, P., Krauss, M. W., & Upshur, C. C. (1992). Development of infants with disabilities and their families. *Monographs of the Society for Research in Child Development, 57*(6, Serial No. 230).

Shonkoff, J. P., & Marshall, P. C. (1990). Biological bases of developmental dysfunction. In S. Meisels & J. Shonkoff (Eds.), *Handbook of early childhood intervention* (pp. 35–52). New York: Cambridge University Press.

Shonkoff, J. P., & Meisels, S. J. (1990). Early childhood intervention: The evolution of a concept. In S. Meisels & J. Shonkoff (Eds.), *Handbook of early childhood intervention* (pp. 2–32). New York: Cambridge University Press.

Shonkoff, J., & Meisels, S. J. (1991). Defining eligibility for services under PL 99-457. *Journal of Early Intervention, 15*, 21–25.

Simeonsson, R. J. (1991a). Early prevention of childhood disability in developing countries. *International Journal of Rehabilitation Research, 14*, 1–12.

Simeonsson, R. J. (1991b). Primary, secondary, and tertiary prevention in early intervention. *Journal of Early Intervention, 15*, 124–134.

Simeonsson, R. J. (1994). Toward an epidemiology of developmental, educational, and social problems of childhood. In R. J. Simeonsson (Ed.), *Risk, resilience, & prevention: Promoting the well-being of all children* (pp. 13–31). Baltimore: Brookes.

Simeonsson, R. J., Cooper, D., & Scheiner, A. (1982). A review and analysis of the effectiveness of early intervention programs. *Pediatrics, 69*, 635–641.

Simeonsson, R. J., & Covington, M. (1994). Policy and practice: Implications of a primary prevention agenda. In R. J. Simeonsson (Ed.), *Risk, resilience, & prevention: Promoting the well-being of all children* (pp. 299–320). Baltimore, MD: Brookes.

Skinner, B. F. (1953). *Science and human behavior.* New York: Macmillan.

Smith, B. J., & McKenna, P. (1994). Early intervention public policy: Past, present, and future. In L. Johnson & M. LaMontagne (Eds.), *Meeting early intervention challenges: Issue from birth to three* (pp. 251–264). Baltimore: Brookes.

Smith, B. J., & Schakel, J. A. (1986). Noncategorical identification of preschool handicapped children: Policy issues and options. *Journal of the Division for Early Childhood, 11*, 78–86.

Stayton, V. D., & Karnes, M. B. (1994). Model programs for infants and toddlers with disabilities and their families. In L. Johnson, R. Gallagher, M. LaMontagne, J. Jordan, J. Gallagher, P. Hutinger, & M. Karnes (Eds.), *Meeting early intervention challenges* (pp. 33–58), Baltimore: Brookes.

Strain, P. S., McConnell, S. R., Carta, J. J., Fowler, S. A., Neisworth, J. T., & Wolery, M. (1992). Behaviorism in early intervention. *Topics in Early Childhood Special Education, 12*, 121–141.

Strain, P. S., & Smith, B. J. (1986). A counter-interpretation of early intervention effects: A response to Casto and Mastropieri. *Exceptional Children, 53*, 260–268.

Strickland, B., & McPherson, M. (1994). Maternal and child health: A collaborative agenda for prevention. In R. J. Simeonsson (Ed.), *Risk, resilience, & prevention: Promoting the well-being of all children* (pp. 53–73). Baltimore: Brookes.

Strong, C. J., Clark, T. C., Barringer, D. G., Walden, B. E., & Williams, S. A. (1992). *SKI*HI home-based programming for children with hearing impairments: Demographics, child identification, and program effectiveness*. Unpublished research report, SKI*HI Institute, Utah State University, Logan.

Sturmey, P., Thorburn, M. J., Brown, J. M., Reed, J., Kaur, J., & King, G. (1992). Portage guide to early intervention: Cross cultural aspects and intra-cultural variability. *Child: Care, Health, and Development, 18*, 377–394.

Tannock, R. & Girolametto, L. (1992). Reassessing parent-focused language intervention programs. In S. Warren & J. Riechle (Eds.), *Causes and effects in communication and language intervention* (pp. 49–80). Baltimore: Brookes.

TASH (The Association for Persons with Severe Handicaps). (1991). Supported education resolution. In L. Meyer, C. Peck, & L. Brown (Eds.), *Critical issues in the lives of people with severe disabilities* (p. 244). Baltimore: Brookes.

Taylor, M. J., White, K. R., & Kusmierek, A. (1993). The cost effectiveness of increasing hours per week of early intervention services for young children with disabilities. *Early Education and Development, 4*, 238–255.

Telzrow, C. F. (1993). Commentary on comparative evaluation of early intervention alternatives. *Early Education and Development, 4*, 359–365.

Unger, D. G., & Wandersman, L. P. (1985). Social support and adolescent mothers: Action research contributions to theory and application. *Journal of Social Issues, 41*(1), 29–45.

Vincent, L. J., & Beckett, J. A. (1993). Family participation. In DEC Recommended Practices Task Force (Eds.), *DEC recommended practices: Indicators of quality in programs for infants and young children with special needs and their families* (pp. 19–29). Reston, VA: Council for Exceptional Children.

Vincent, L. J., Salisbury, C. L., Strain, P. S., McCormick, C., & Tessier, A. (1990). A behavioral–ecological approach to early intervention: Focus on cultural diversity. In S. Meisels & J. Shonkoff (Eds.), *Handbook of early childhood intervention* (pp. 173–195). New York: Cambridge University Press.

Vygotsky, L. S. (1986). *Thought and language*. Cambridge, MA: MIT Press. (Original work published 1934)

Vygotsky, L. S. (1978). *Mind in society: The development of psychological processes*. Cambridge, MA: Harvard University Press.

Wasik, B. H., Bryant, D., & Lyons, C. (1990). *Home visiting: Procedures for helping families*. Newbury Park, CA: Sage.

Wasik, B. H., Ramey, C. T., Bryant, D. M., & Sparling, J. J. (1990). A longitudinal study of two early intervention strategies: Project CARE. *Child Development, 61*, 1682–1692.

Wayman, K. I., Lynch, E. W., & Hanson, M. J. (1990). Home-based early childhood services: Cultural sensitivity in a family systems approach. *Topics in Early Childhood Special Education, 10*(4), 56–75.

Weber, C. U., Foster, P. W., & Weikart, D. P. (1978). *An economic analysis of the Ypsilanti Perry Preschool Project*. Monographs of the High/Scope Educational Research Foundation, No. 5. Ypsilanti, MI: High/Score Educational Research Foundation.

Weinman, M. L., Schreiber, N. B., & Robinson, M. (1992). Adolescent mothers: Were there any gains in a parent education program? *Family and Community Health, 15*(3), 1–10.

Weiss, R. (1981). INREAL intervention for language handicapped and bilingual children. *Journal of the Division for Early Childhood, 4*, 24–27.

Werner, E. E. (1990). Protective factors and individual resilience. In S. Meisels & J. Shonkoff (Eds.), *Handbook of early childhood intervention* (pp. 97–116). New York: Cambridge University Press.

Werner, E. E., & Smith, R. S. (1982). *Vulnerable but invincible: A longitudinal study of resilient children and youth*. New York: McGraw-Hill.

White, C. C., Koplan, J. P., & Orenstein, W. A. (1985). Benefits, risks, and costs of immunizations for measles, mumps, and rubella. *American Journal of Public Health, 75*, 739–744.

White, K. R. (1993). Using research to improve the cost-effectiveness of early intervention programs. *Early Education and Development, 4*, 346–358.

White, K. R., Boyce, G. C., Casto, G., Innocenti, M. S., Taylor, M. J., Goetze, L., & Behl, D. (1994). Comparative evaluations of early intervention alternatives: A response to Guralnick and Telzrow. *Early Education and Development, 5*, 56–68.

White, K. R., & Casto, G. (1984). An integrative review of early intervention efficacy studies with at-risk children: Implications for the handicapped. *Analysis and Intervention in Developmental Disabilities, 5*, 7–31.

White, K. R., & Pezzino, J. (1986). Ethical, practical, and scientific considerations of randomized experiments in early childhood special education. *Topics in Early Childhood Special Education, 6*(3), 100–116.

Whitley, E. B. (1992). Reflection on the use of the fateful forty-three in Virginia. *Mental Retardation, 30*, 320–322.

Winton, P. J. (1993). Providing family support in integrated settings: Research and recommendations. In C. Peck, S. Odom, & D. Bricker (Eds.), *Integrating young children with disabilities into community programs* (pp. 65–80). Baltimore: Brookes.

Wise, P. H., & Lowe, J. A. (1992). Noise or fugue: Seeking logic of child health indicators. *Mental Retardation, 30*, 323–330.

Wolery, M. (1994). Instructional strategies for teaching young children with special needs. In M. Wolery & J. Wilbers (Eds.), *Including children with special needs in early childhood programs* (pp. 119–150). Washington, DC: National Association for the Education of Young Children.

Wolery, M., & Bredekamp, S. (1995). Developmentally appropriate practices and young children with special needs: Contextual issues and a framework for convergence. *Journal of Early Intervention, 18*, 331–341.

Wolery, M., Doyle, P. M., Gast, D. L., Ault, M. J., & Simpson, S. L. (1993). Comparison of progressive time delay and transition-based teaching with preschoolers who have developmental delays. *Journal of Early Intervention, 17*, 160–176.

Wolery, M., & Sainato, D. M. (1996). General curriculum and intervention strategies. In S. Odom & M. McLean (Eds.), *Early intervention/early childhood special education: Recommended practices* (pp. 125–158). Austin, TX: PRO-ED.

Wouk, V. H. (1990, May). *The year 2000 objective for mental retardation.* Paper presented at the annual meeting of the American Association on Mental Retardation, Atlanta, GA. (ERIC Reproduction Document No. ED324875)

Zins, J. E., Garcia, V. F., Tuchfarber, B. S., Clark, K. M., & Laurence, S. C. (1994). Preventing injury in children and adolescents. In R. J. Simeonsson (Ed.), *Risk, resilience, & prevention: Promoting the well-being of all children* (pp. 183–201). Baltimore: Brooks.

› III ‹

Psychological and Psychomotor Processes

> 7 <

Rigidity in the Behavior of Mentally Retarded Persons

Cynthia L. Dulaney
Xavier University

Norman R. Ellis
University of Alabama

The idea that mentally retarded persons are inherently more rigid in their behavior than are nonretarded persons has prevailed since the early 1900s. Rigid behavior is stereotyped, perseverative, inflexible, repetitive, and unchanging. Rigid behavior is detrimental to the survival of organisms who need flexible, adaptive behaviors to meet the changing demands of their daily environment. It is this type of behavior that may lead to the inability of mentally retarded persons to function adequately in a normal environment. Various explanations for the causes underlying rigid behavior in mentally retarded persons have been put forth. The initial research on this issue was conducted by Lewin (1935) and Kounin (1941). Although their early work provided the impetus for studying rigidity, it also has been the source of a great deal of confusion and controversy. Much of the later research on rigidity in mentally retarded persons was in reaction to this initial work.

In this chapter, we provide a historical review of theories of rigidity as they relate to mentally retarded persons. This is followed by a discussion of the most recent approach to the study of rigidity proposed by Ellis and his associates (Ellis & Dulaney, 1991; Ellis, Woodley-Zanthos, Dulaney, & Palmer, 1989). Because this more recent approach arose from research in the area of automatic and effortful processing, a brief review of research and theory relating to this area is presented. Next, a discussion of the Stroop (1935) paradigm, used in some of our research, is discussed. Finally, a discussion of rigidity emerging from our research on automatic processing is presented.

EARLY THEORIES OF RIGIDITY IN MENTALLY RETARDED PERSONS

Kounin–Lewin Theory

Lewin (1935) advanced a structural explanation for cognitive rigidity in mentally retarded persons based on a Gestalt perspective. According to Lewin, each person has a psychological "life space" made up of inner-personal regions that influence behavior. These regions are a product of life experiences and compose the behavioral repertoire of an individual. It was hypothesized that mentally retarded persons possess fewer of these regions than do nonretarded persons; that is, mentally retarded persons are less differentiated cognitively. However, the primary cause of rigidity in mentally retarded persons is due to a greater "stiffness" or impermeability between these regions, and this produces decreased communication between regions.

To assess his theory, Lewin (1935) compared the performance of mentally retarded and nonretarded children on a satiation task. Subjects were instructed to draw as many "moon faces" as they wished. A longer satiation time (i.e., persistence in drawing faces) by 10- and 11-year-old mentally retarded children as compared with 10- and 11-year-old nonretarded children was taken as evidence for greater cognitive rigidity in the mentally retarded. However, there were no differences between satiation times of 9- and 10-year-old retarded and nonretarded subjects, and for 8- and 9-year-olds the nonretarded had longer satiation times than did the retarded. Therefore, according to Lewin's own index of rigidity, mentally retarded persons were more rigid in only one of the age groups tested.

In addition to this inconsistent finding, another problem in Lewin's (1935) experiment was that group comparisons were made on individuals differing in degree of differentiation as measured by mental age (MA), a factor that Lewin pointed out may influence rigidity. Therefore, the longer satiation times of the 10- and 11-year-old retarded as compared with the 10- and 11-year-old nonretarded children cannot be unequivocally accounted for by differences in permeability between regions. The obtained differences could be due to greater differentiation in nonretarded persons than in mentally retarded persons, greater permeability of life-space regions in nonretarded persons than in mentally retarded persons, or some combination of both factors.

Kounin (1941) expanded Lewin's (1935) theory and advanced the idea that cognitive rigidity is a function of chronological age (CA). As individuals mature, their life space becomes more differentiated, but, at the same time, the boundaries between regions of their life space become more impermeable. Thus, if a comparison were made between two individuals having the same degree of differentiation, the older individual would possess greater cognitive rigidity.

To further assess the theory of cognitive rigidity, Kounin (1941) conducted several experiments. All of his experiments employed individuals who were MA-matched and either old retarded (*M* CA = 42 years), young retarded (*M* CA = 15 years), or young nonretarded subjects (*M* CA = 7 years). The MA matching was employed to equate the subjects on degree of differentiation, a factor that had not been controlled in Lewin's (1935) study.

In one experiment, Kounin instructed subjects to draw as many cats as they wished until satiated, followed by bugs, turtles, and rabbits. A cosatiation score was calculated by subtracting the time spent on the second task (or third or fourth task) from the time spent on the first task divided by the time spent on the first task. This cosatiation score was used as an index of rigidity. Kounin predicted that a more rigid individual would spend about the same amount of time on each task because the rigid boundaries would prevent one region from cosatiating a neighboring region. If so, that individual would show a small cosatiation score. A less rigid individual would spend more time on the first task compared to the other tasks, because time spent on the first task would partially cosatiate other neighboring regions. Thus, the less rigid individual would show a large cosatiation effect. Results revealed that old retarded subjects exhibited the least amount of cosatiation, followed by young retarded subjects, with nonretarded subjects exhibiting the greatest amount of cosatiation. That is, the drawing of one animal affected the drawing of another animal least in old retarded individuals due to greater impermeability among different "animal-drawing" regions.

In another experiment, Kounin (1941) instructed subjects to release marbles from an apparatus by depressing a lever for 90 trials, and then instructed subjects to raise the lever for 60 trials. Because retarded persons were purported to have more impermeable boundaries, the two tasks were not expected to affect each other. That is, for mentally retarded persons the two tasks would not overlap because the boundaries between the regions involved in completing each task are less permeable; for nonretarded persons the two tasks would overlap because these boundaries are more permeable. Greater rigidity in mentally retarded persons would be indicated by the mentally retarded making fewer errors than the nonretarded. In fact, mentally retarded persons did make fewer errors than nonretarded persons in changing from lever depressing to lever raising. This finding supported Kounin's hypothesis that nonretarded individuals were more likely than were mentally retarded individuals to be in an overlapping situation, due to nonretarded persons' possessing greater communication between regions of their life space.

Kounin (1941) also used a card-sorting task to assess rigidity. Subjects were instructed to sort a deck of cards that could be sorted by either color or form. After sorting on one dimension, subjects were instructed to sort the cards in a different way. Kounin hypothesized that mentally retarded persons and older persons would have greater difficulty changing from one sorting task to another than would nonretarded or younger individuals. As predicted by Kounin, old mentally retarded subjects had the most difficulty shifting from one sorting principle to another, followed by young mentally retarded persons, with nonretarded persons exhibiting the least difficulty.

Generalizing from Kounin's theory, Plenderleith (1956) predicted that mentally retarded persons would have difficulty on discrimination reversal tasks because they have more rigid boundaries between regions of their life space, which would lead to difficulty shifting from one region to another. Mentally retarded and MA-matched nonretarded subjects were presented with a pair of pictures. One member of the pair was reinforced, and then the correct solution was reversed to the previously incorrect member of the pair. No differences were found between mentally retarded and nonretarded persons in ability to shift. Thus, these results were not supportive of Kounin's position.

Plenderleith's (1956) generalization about discrimination reversal performance by retarded and nonretarded individuals from Kounin's (1941) theory provides a good example of the lack of clarity in parts of Kounin's theory. Plenderleith predicted that mentally retarded individuals would have greater difficulty performing a discrimination reversal task than would nonretarded individuals due to the greater rigidity in the mentally retarded, but no differences in performance were found. Although this is not in line with the prediction made by Plenderleith based on the Kounin–Lewin theory, Kounin (1948) previously had pointed out that his theory does not make any predictions about "ability to shift." However, in discussing the results of his card-sorting task, Kounin stated that "the old feeble-minded were least able to change from one to the other method of classification, and the normal subjects were most able to change from one classification to the other" (p. 270). This is clearly a statement about ability to shift; thus, Plenderleith's interpretation of Kounin's theory seems appropriate.

The basis for determining when a task would involve switching to a new life-space region or involve overlapping regions is not clear in Kounin's (1941) studies. In the satiation task, Kounin suggested that drawings of one animal are in a different region from drawings of another animal. However, it may be that the shift from drawing of one animal to a different animal does not involve psychological movement to a new region. Subjects may not see the drawing of different animals as several different tasks but as one general drawing task. Thus, mentally retarded persons may perseverate at a general drawing task whereas nonretarded persons simply become bored or satiated, thus discontinuing the drawing task sooner. A similar argument can be made for the card-sorting task. That is, mentally retarded individuals may be capable of changing from one sorting principle to another once a perseverative tendency is stopped. Nonretarded persons are able to change from one sorting principle to another, and they do not have a perseverative tendency hindering such switching.

In the lever-pressing task, Kounin stated that lever pressing and lever raising composed two different regions. Because the nonretarded have more permeable boundaries than do the mentally retarded, Kounin hypothesized that these regions are more likely to overlap and, therefore, nonretarded persons are likely to make more errors due to an inadequate separation of the two tasks. There should be a clearer psychological separation between the two tasks for mentally retarded persons because they have more rigid boundaries resulting in fewer errors. However, in the card-sorting and the satiation tasks, Kounin predicted that less rigidity in nonretarded individuals would lead to an easier transfer from one task to another than in the more rigid mentally retarded individuals. That is, greater rigidity is detrimental to performance in the card-sorting task and the satiation task but is advantageous to performance in the lever task. Although the prediction of when the rigidity of mentally retarded persons will be an advantage rather a disadvantage in a task is an asset to Kounin's theory, his determination of task types in which this will and will not occur is not well defined.

Goldstein's Theory

Although Kounin (1941) applied his theory only to mental retardation of the familial type, Goldstein (1942) treated mental retardation as a homogeneous group with all members having some organic pathology. He also made a distinction between primary and secondary rigidity. The former occurs when a pathological condition leads to a defect in the *Einstellung* or set mechanism. A defective *Einstellung* mechanism would leave an individual unable to shift voluntarily from one task to another when the shift required a change in set. *Secondary rigidity* refers to a defect in higher mental processes wherein individuals possess less abstraction ability and less adaptability, and exhibit more concrete behavior, when coping with their environment. Individuals affected by secondary rigidity also have abnormal levels of distractibility that lead them either to be distracted easily and unable to fixate on a specific event or to be so fixated on one event that it is difficult to divert their attention to another. This type of rigidity occurs only when an individual is in a situation beyond his or her capabilities due to a lack of differentiation of mental functions. Thus, Goldstein placed degree of differentiation at the center of secondary rigidity.

Goldstein (1942) alternated between discussing rigidity due to structural limitations and rigidity due to behavioral limitations. Thus, it is unclear as to which type of rigidity his theory applies. Goldstein emphasized degree of differentiation as the primary cause of secondary rigidity. Kounin (1941) equated subjects on degree of differentiation, however, and still found retarded–nonretarded differences. Goldstein's theory cannot account for Kounin's data. Furthermore, Goldstein offered no data to support his theory other than casual observations.

Werner's Theory

Werner (Strauss & Werner, 1942; Werner, 1946, 1948) argued that rigidity in mentally retarded persons was not a uniform trait and would differ as a function of the cause of mental retardation. He distinguished between abnormal and subnormal rigidity as occurring in brain-injured and familial types of retardation, respectively. According to Werner, persons with familial retardation are integrated organisms who lack the ability to differentiate mental functions. This lack of differentiation results in familial mentally retarded persons failing to distinguish between situations, and therefore behaving in stereotyped, invariable ways. Werner also commented that familial retarded persons behave either too globally or too specifically in their approach to situations in the environment. In contrast, the brain-injured mentally retarded persons are not integrated organisms. While performing a behavior, these retarded individuals become so fixated that they are unable to change even when the behavior is no longer adaptive. Werner discussed brain-injured mentally retarded persons as approaching situations in an erratic and incoherent manner.

Three experiments comparing behaviors of brain-injured and familial mentally retarded persons were conducted to examine abnormal and subnormal rigidity (Werner, 1946). Subjects were matched on MA and IQ. All of the tasks required some form of reproduction of presented materials. One experiment required subjects to reproduce sound patterns. A second experiment required subjects to quickly identify pictures presented in series that were similar visually (e.g., moon, baseball, walnut, bowl, basket). Each picture was presented for one fifth of a second. In both experiments, the brain-injured mentally retarded and the familial mentally retarded had an equal number of single repetitions of an immediately preceding stimulus (simple perseverations). However, the brain-injured mentally retarded repeated previous stimuli more than once (repetitive perseverations), and they more frequently repeated stimuli that had been presented two or more trials earlier in a series (delayed perseverations). Werner (1946) interpreted these findings as supportive of a distinction between abnormal and subnormal rigidity. That is, there are two qualitatively different types of rigidity in mentally retarded persons with lack of differentiation resulting in subnormal rigidity in the familial mentally retarded and functional isolation resulting in abnormal rigidity in brain-injured mentally retarded persons.

A third experiment further examined the notion of two types of rigidity (Werner, 1946). Based on the idea that familial mentally retarded individuals, but not brain-injured mentally retarded individuals, were more rigid due to poor discrimination abilities, the performance of these two groups on highly discriminable and highly similar stimuli was compared. Werner hypothesized that the highly discriminable stimuli would eliminate rigidity in the familial mentally retarded, but the brain-injured mentally retarded would continue to exhibit rigidity due to factors other than discrimination ability. Subjects were presented a dot pattern for one tenth of a second, and then were instructed to reproduce the pattern. Two dot-pattern series were presented. In the similar series, all of the dot patterns were similar in configuration. In the nonsimilar series, all dot patterns were dissimilar.

Werner (1946) hypothesized that familial mentally retarded persons would commit simple perseverations only in the similar series due to their inability to differentiate the dot patterns. On the other hand, he maintained that brain-injured mentally retarded persons would exhibit simple, repetitive, and delayed perseverations for both the similar and nonsimilar series due to a lack of functional integration of their behavior. The results supported Werner's hypothesis with familial mentally retarded persons exhibiting simple perseverations for the highly similar stimuli, but not for the highly discriminable stimuli. Brain-injured mentally retarded persons produced simple, delayed, and repetitive perseverations for both stimulus types.

Although the results obtained by Werner (1946) appear to support his predictions, there were several design problems in these experiments that complicated his interpretation. The exposure to stimuli was very brief, and no effort was made to ensure that all subjects encoded the stimuli equally well. Therefore, in reproducing the similar series, familial retarded subjects may have been producing their best estimate of each stimulus, and because all stimuli were highly similar they would be more likely to produce the same pattern repeatedly. Also, subjects were required to hold encoded items in memory until the time of item reproduction. The obtained group differences in reproduction performance could have been due to memory differences and, therefore, cannot be unequivocally attributed to discrimination ability or to functional isolation of mental operations.

Siegel–Foshee Theory

Siegel and Foshee (1960) defined *rigidity* as decreased response variability in individuals. The ability to vary responses is essential for individuals who must adapt to an ever-changing environment, and Kounin (1948) mentioned that an increase in degree of differentiation leads to an increase in behavioral variability. Siegel and Foshee (1960) designed a task to compare the response variability of mentally retarded and nonretarded persons. Subjects were required to use any one of four switches to turn off a light. The response patterns of mentally retarded and nonretarded subjects revealed that the mentally retarded subjects' responses were less variable (i.e., they tended to use fewer switches). Siegel and Foshee interpreted the reduced variability as due to disinhibition. They assumed that emitting a response temporarily inhibits making the same response. Greater distractibility in mentally retarded persons would cause a just-completed response to be disinhibited and, hence, repeated soon after. This would lead to the appearance of rigid behavior in mentally retarded persons.

Several experiments conducted by Smith (1984) examined the disinhibition theory, and only partial support for the theory was obtained. A review of response variability research by Smith and Siegel (1986) also revealed mixed results regarding the response variability hypothesis.

Zigler's Theory

According to Kounin (1941), motivational factors such as fear of failure and insecurity toward approaching new situations are possible secondary factors influencing rigidity in retarded persons. In contrast, Zigler (1962) hypothesized that motivational factors constituted the primary cause of rigidity in mentally retarded persons. Zigler proposed that the cognitive development of mentally retarded persons progresses more slowly than does the cognitive development of nonretarded persons, but both proceed through a similar sequence. Therefore, mentally retarded and nonretarded individuals matched on MA should perform the same on a cognitive task if all other noncognitive variables are controlled. Zigler (e.g., see Zigler & Balla, 1982) argued that most studies making comparisons between mentally retarded and nonretarded persons have not controlled for motivational factors. For example, in the examination of rigidity, mentally retarded and nonretarded individuals' persistence at a task has often been examined. Zigler hypothesized that because mentally retarded persons are typically more socially deprived than are nonretarded persons, the mentally retarded are more likely to persist at a task longer than are the nonretarded in order to prolong social contact with an adult experimenter.

Zigler's (1962) motivational hypothesis followed a study conducted by Stevenson and Zigler (1957) in which they examined the Kounin–Lewin theory of rigidity. Stevenson and Zigler predicted that in a discrimination reversal task, mentally retarded persons would have more difficulty reversing than would nonretarded persons because the reversal problem requires movement from one life-space region to another, and mentally retarded persons have more rigid boundaries separating those regions.

Two experiments were conducted employing MA-matched young mentally retarded (*M* CA = 11 years), old mentally retarded (*M* CA = 27 years), and young nonretarded (*M* CA = 5 years) individuals. In the first experiment, subjects were taught a size discrimination, and then the solution to the problem was reversed (an intradimensional shift). Subjects were given no indication that the correct solution had changed other than that the previously correct response was no longer reinforced. The second experiment used a more difficult discrimination task requiring an extradimensional shift. Subjects learned a discrimination based on the size dimension of the stimuli, and then the correct solution was changed to a discrimination based on position. Perseveration errors (i.e., responses made to the previously correct stimulus) were used as a measure of rigidity. In both experiments there were no performance differences among young mentally retarded, old mentally retarded, and MA-matched nonretarded subjects. These findings were viewed as evidence against Kounin's (1941) prediction that the mentally retarded are more rigid than are the nonretarded, and that rigidity increases with CA.

Stevenson and Zigler (1957) offered a motivational explanation for the differences between their results and those of Kounin (1941). In Kounin's tasks, subjects were not required to learn a response, only to comply with the experimenter's instructions. Stevenson and Zigler pointed out that in Kounin's lever-pressing task, mentally retarded persons may have shown superior performance to nonretarded persons more because of a greater desire to please the experimenter than because of greater rigidity. On the other hand, in the Stevenson and Zigler study, the experimenter had minimal interaction with the subjects, which suggests that mentally retarded individuals were not influenced by an increased desire to please the experimenter.

In order to formally test this hypothesis, Zigler, Hodgden, and Stevenson (1958) employed a satiation task similar to that used by Kounin (1941), but with one exception. There were two reinforcement conditions: a social support condition in which the experimenter reinforced the subject's performance, and a nonsupport condition in which there was minimal subject–experimenter interaction. As in Kounin's study, mentally retarded subjects performed longer than did MA-matched nonretarded subjects in both conditions. Mentally retarded persons also performed longer in the support condition than in the nonsupport condition. Nonretarded persons were unaffected by amount of support. This result confirmed Zigler et al.'s prediction that mentally retarded persons are more affected by motivational factors when performing tasks than are nonretarded persons.

Following these initial studies, Zigler and his associates (Balla & Zigler, 1964; Green & Zigler, 1962; Shallenberger & Zigler, 1961; Shepps & Zigler, 1962; Zigler, 1961, 1962, 1963; Zigler & Butterfield, 1966; Zigler & DeLabry, 1962; Zigler & Unell, 1962) examined the influence of such motivational factors as positive and negative reaction tendencies, social deprivation, and type of reinforcement on the expression of rigid behavior in mentally retarded persons. On the face, numerous studies show considerable support for the motivational theory. However, there are several problems with interpreting some predictions based on this theory. For example, Zigler (Zigler & Balla, 1982) stated that mentally retarded persons persist on a satiation task in order to prolong social contact with the experimenter; that is, they are more rigid due to the increased social support provided by the presence of the experimenter. However, Zigler et al. (1958) also stated that minimal interaction or nonsupport from the experimenter will lead to rigid behavior in mentally retarded persons because, without the social interaction of the experimenter, they are unmotivated to comply with the task instructions. That is, decreased social support leads to rigidity in mentally retarded persons. Although both of these predictions are related to motivational factors, they seem somewhat contradictory.

Another example of ambiguity in the motivational theory involves subject characteristics. Zigler (1963) hypothesized that high socially deprived subjects would persist on a task, and thus exhibit more rigid behavior. However, Shepps and Zigler (1962) argued that more socially deprived mentally retarded individuals and mentally retarded individuals from a restrictive environment would perform less rigidly on a task in a supportive task environment. On the face, these statements seem contradictory. Zigler (1962) also stated that mentally retarded persons will persist (i.e., perform more rigidly) at a task in order to prolong social contact with the experimenter. On the other hand, Zigler and Butterfield (1966) said that mentally retarded persons will decline more frequently to participate or continue in a task due to an increased wariness of the experimenter and a desire to avoid situations in which they might experience failure. So, due to motivational reasons, do mentally retarded persons persist at a task or decline to do a task? Zigler predicted both of these outcomes, but he did not clarify when one or the other would occur.

The empirical research conducted by Zigler and his colleagues also has produced mixed conclusions regarding rigidity in mentally retarded persons. For example, Zigler (1961) reported that mentally retarded subjects who were more socially deprived exhibited greater rigidity than those who were less deprived. However, Zigler and Butterfield (1966) reported that subjects from a restrictive institutional environment (i.e., more socially deprived subjects) exhibited less rigidity due to their increased motivation to please the experimenter. Stevenson and Zigler (1957) had argued previously that Kounin obtained results indicating greater rigidity in mentally retarded persons than in nonretarded persons because Kounin had selected the most motivated individuals. Thus, in one instance Zigler argued that mentally retarded persons exhibited less rigidity when properly motivated in the task situation. In another instance, he seemed to argue that mentally retarded persons exhibited greater rigidity when properly motivated in the task situation.

Although the studies mentioned in this section were designed to test Zigler's motivational theory, some of these studies have shown partial support for the Kounin (1941) rigidity hypothesis. Several studies designed to test the motivational theory (Kreitler, Zigler, & Kreitler, 1990; Zigler & Butterfield, 1966; Zigler et al., 1958) could also be interpreted as providing evidence that mentally retarded persons were more rigid than were nonretarded persons in agreement with Kounin's hypothesis of retarded–nonretarded differences in cognitive rigidity. Two studies (Butterfield & McIntyre, 1969; Zigler, 1963) showed that rigidity decreased as MA or CA increased in mentally retarded and nonretarded children, which was supportive of Kounin's theory of cognitive rigidity.

Additional Studies of Rigidity

Thus far, we have cited studies that directly related to the concept of rigidity. A number of studies have used some type of discrimination reversal paradigm, for example, concept-switching tasks (Kounin, 1941; Kreitler et al., 1990; Zigler & Butterfield, 1966; Zigler & DeLabry, 1962) and various discrimination reversal tasks (Balla & Zigler, 1964; Stevenson & Zigler, 1957), which may also provide a measure of rigidity. The discrimination reversal paradigm usually requires subjects to respond to one aspect of a pair of stimuli (e.g., color) for a certain number of trials until a particular criterion is met. Then a reversal phase is instigated in which a new stimulus (e.g., form) is reinforced. The critical measure is the number of trials required by subjects to change their responding to the new correct solution of the reversal problem. Subjects who are slow to change are considered to be more rigid than are subjects who are quick to change. Because the rigidity theories of Goldstein (1942), Werner (1946, 1948), and Siegel and Foshee (1960) do not make predictions about the performance of mentally retarded and nonretarded persons in discrimination reversal tasks, the following review discusses these studies only in relation to the rigidity theories of Kounin (1941) and Zigler (1961).

Results obtained from discrimination reversal studies are generally supportive of Kounin's (1941) predictions relating MA and CA to cognitive rigidity. Halpin (1958) and O'Malley, Dunn, and Rudnick (1975) produced evidence supportive of the Kounin (1941) hypothesis that rigidity decreases with increases in MA and CA in mentally retarded and nonretarded children. Shanab and McClure (1983) showed a decline in ability to shift in elderly nonretarded individuals, which is supportive of Kounin's prediction that rigidity increases as CA increases beyond the developmental years.

Discrimination reversal studies have revealed mixed findings in relation to retarded–nonretarded differences in rigidity. Some of these studies provided no evidence for retarded–nonretarded differences in rigidity (Budoff & Pagell, 1968; Rondal & Lambert, 1975; Sanders, Ross, & Heal, 1965). These studies do not support Kounin's (1941) cognitive rigidity theory. However, even though no differences were obtained between mentally retarded and nonretarded persons in rigidity, these studies do not necessarily support Zigler's (1962) motivational theory. Only one discrimination reversal study examined motivational factors (Budoff & Pagell, 1968), and mixed results were obtained as far as Zigler's position is concerned. Two studies (O'Connor & Hermelin, 1959; Sanders et al., 1965) found that mentally retarded persons behaved less rigidly than did nonretarded persons. However, the results obtained by O'Connor and Hermelin were not replicated (Rondal & Lambert, 1975). Other studies (Heal, 1966; Heal, Ross, & Sanders, 1966; Iwahara & Sugimura, 1962; Lobb & Stogdill, 1974; Penney, Croskery, & Allen, 1962; Richman, Adams, Nida, & Richman, 1978; Umetani, Kitao, & Katada, 1985) showed that mentally retarded persons were more rigid than were nonretarded persons on discrimination reversal tasks, which supports Kounin's theory of cognitive rigidity. Overall, the majority of studies support Kounin's theory of cognitive rigidity.

Summary of Early Theories and Research on Rigidity

Past theories of rigidity and related empirical evidence have been reviewed. There is little evidence to support the rigidity theories posited by Goldstein (1942) and Werner (1946, 1948; Strauss & Werner, 1942). Their theories are vague and have instigated little or no research to determine the validity of the theories. Research examining the Siegel–Foshee (1960) disinhibition hypothesis has produced mixed findings (Smith, 1984).

Most of the empirical evidence examining rigidity has been related to either the Kounin–Lewin (Kounin, 1941; Lewin, 1935) or the Zigler (1962) theories of rigidity. It appears that both positions have some merit. Both cognitive and motivational factors appear to play a role in the expression of rigid behavior. Also, evidence has generally been supportive of the idea that rigidity decreases as MA and intelligence increase, and rigidity increases as CA increases beyond the developmental years. These findings are supportive of the Kounin–Lewin (Kounin, 1941; Lewin, 1935) theory. More recently, Ellis and his associates (Ellis & Dulaney, 1991; Ellis et al., 1989) studied rigidity using the interplay of automatized and controlled processing as an explanation of the phenomenon. The following is a discussion of this approach.

AUTOMATICITY APPROACH TO RIGIDITY

Rigid behavior deriving from the automatization of responses has been examined by Dulaney and Ellis (1994), Ellis et al. (1989), and Ellis and Dulaney (1991). Prior to a discussion of this approach, we briefly describe automatic processing. The Stroop paradigm (Stroop, 1935) also is described because the Stroop effect has been used to study automatic and effortful (controlled) processing, and because it is the paradigm used by Ellis and his associates to demonstrate automaticity-related rigidity.

Automaticity and the Stroop Paradigm

According to some cognitive theorists, there are two ways to process information. Some information processing requires control, effort, strategy use, and attentional resources. Other information processing is carried out automatically and does not require effort or strategy use (Hasher & Zacks, 1979; Posner & Snyder, 1975; Schneider & Shiffrin, 1977; Shiffrin & Schneider, 1977). The modal view of attention (e.g., Kahneman, 1973) holds that individuals process information within a single-capacity attention mechanism. This limited capacity system constrains how much information can be processed at a given time. If the information currently being processed requires much attention and effort, then little or no attentional capacity will remain for processing other information. However, if certain information is processed automatically then little or no attentional capacity will be used, which leaves the attentional system relatively free for other processing.

Automatic information processing capabilities are usually obtained by virtue of extended practice, but once they become automatized they are effortless and obligatory. An example of an acquired automatic process is reading. For beginning readers, word meaning is obtained by attending to each letter of a word, and effortful processing is required. With extended practice, however, a letter-by-letter analysis of a word is no longer necessary, and word meaning is accessed automatically (LaBerge & Samuels, 1974). Once access to word meaning is automatized, more attentional capacity is available to process other information, such as processing the meaning of entire sentences and paragraphs.

Automatizing a behavior is usually considered advantageous because it frees up attentional capacity for additional processing. However, automaticity can be detrimental to performance as evidenced by the Stroop effect. Stroop (1935; Experiment 2) conducted an experiment in which college students were instructed to name colors of color patches as fast as possible. The students also named colors of color words printed in incongruent colors (e.g., RED printed in blue ink; hereafter referred to as *Stroop words*). He found that students were much slower in color naming the Stroop words than the color patches. This finding is commonly referred to as the *Stroop interference effect.* Stroop attributed this finding to the relative strength of the association between the reading response and color words compared with the weaker association between the color-naming response and the color stimuli. Because the reading/word association was stronger than was the color naming/color association, the former response interfered with the production of the latter response.

Since Stroop's (1935) original research, numerous studies have replicated the Stroop effect (see MacLeod, 1991, for a review). Two theories have been used frequently to explain the Stroop effect: the "horse race" model and the automaticity theory. The race or relative speed of processing model (Dyer, 1973; Morton & Chambers, 1973; Posner & Snyder, 1975) is based on the finding that word reading is faster than color naming. When attention is directed to Stroop words, a color-naming and a word-reading response are activated. Both responses race for an output mechanism, and the faster response wins. Thus, if reading is faster than color naming, the reading response reaches the output mechanism first and must be suppressed in order for the color-naming response to be made.

Although the relative speed hypothesis fared well for a number of years (see Dyer, 1973, for a review), more recent research (Dunbar & MacLeod, 1984) has demonstrated the ineffectiveness of the speed of processing model to explain the Stroop effect. The speed of processing model predicts that the faster response will always win the race to the output mechanism. Therefore, if the reading response is sufficiently slowed by some experimental manipulation, then a reversed Stroop effect should occur. Dunbar and MacLeod had subjects read transformed words (e.g., printed backwards and upside down). This transformation hindered subjects' reading rate such that it was slower than color naming. However, when colors and transformed words were combined in a manner similar to the standard Stroop test, there was not a reversed Stroop effect even when the reading response was slower than the color-naming response. This finding was inconsistent with the speed of processing hypothesis because the slower response interfered with the faster response.

An explanation for the Stroop effect that has fared better than the speed of processing model is based on the theory of automaticity (Hasher & Zacks, 1979; Posner & Snyder, 1975; Schneider & Shiffrin, 1977; Shiffrin & Schneider, 1977). In the terms of automaticity theory, reading is a more automatic process than is color naming. Thus, reading requires less attentional capacity than does color naming. Reading occurs automatically, whereas color naming requires some attentional capacity. When Stroop words are presented, subjects automatically read the words, and they must suppress the automatic reading response in order to name the color of the Stroop word. The automaticity theory does not require that the automatic response be faster than the opposing response in order to produce interference.

Using a Stroop-like paradigm, MacLeod and Dunbar (1988) examined the automaticity theory as an explanation of the Stroop effect. First, color-naming latencies of color control items were obtained for college students. Next, they were taught color names to abstract shapes. After learning the shape names, subjects practiced naming the shapes that were presented in white on a black background. Students' response times were obtained for color naming and shape naming of control items, congruent items (e.g., the learned shape name and the color in which the shape was printed were the same), and incongruent items (the learned shape name and the color in which the shape was printed were different).

With a small amount of shape-naming practice, incongruent colors interfered with shape naming, and congruent colors facilitated shape naming. That is, there was strong asymmetry with color affecting shape naming, but shape naming did not affect color naming. The more automatic color-naming response interfered with the newly learned shape-naming response. As amount of shape-naming practice increased, subjects began showing interference when trying to name colors that were presented on incongruent shapes. There was also interference when subjects named shapes that were presented in incongruent colors. That is, there was a symmetrical effect with the two dimensions interfering with and facilitating each other.

After extensive shape-naming practice, subjects named shapes and colors at the same rate in the control conditions. However, there was an asymmetrical interference effect. Shape naming was not slowed when the shapes were printed in incongruent colors. However, color naming was slowed when colors were printed on incongruent shapes (i.e., a Stroop-like interference effect). This finding was inconsistent with the relative speed hypothesis, which would predict equal interference because color naming and shape naming were processed at the same rate. The automaticity view, however, can account for these data. Shape naming becomes more automatic with extended practice and, therefore, interferes with the less automatic color-naming response. Thus, MacLeod and Dunbar linked Stroop-like interference to the amount of practice of a response, or, in theoretical terms, with the amount of automaticity of a response.[1]

[1]The parallel distributed processing model of Stroop interference offered by Cohen, Dunbar, and McClelland (1990) gives a similar account for these data. Their model discusses Stroop interference in terms of attentional modulation and the strength of color-naming and word-reading pathways.

Relation Among MA, CA, IQ, and Stroop Interference

MacLeod (1991) reviewed numerous studies examining the magnitude of the Stroop effect in nonretarded individuals across their life span. Of course, Stroop interference is nonexistent in first-grade children who have not yet learned to read. Stroop interference is greatest in second and third graders, whose reading abilities are most vulnerable (e.g., Schiller, 1966). Thereafter, Stroop interference declines until about 60 years of age when the amount of Stroop interference begins to increase again (Comalli, Wapner, & Werner, 1962).

Das (1969) examined Stroop interference in CA-matched mentally retarded and nonretarded individuals (CA = 13 years) and in nonretarded individuals ranging in CA from 10 to 15 years on the Stroop task. The Stroop interference exhibited by nonretarded persons decreased as CA increased. Mentally retarded persons exhibited greater Stroop interference than did the CA-matched nonretarded persons. However, because the MAs of the subjects were not reported, it is unclear whether the performance differences were affected by differential reading abilities of the words.

In a subsequent study, Das (1970) matched mentally retarded and nonretarded individuals on MA (MA = approximately 6 years, 6 months) and also included mentally retarded individuals varying in MA from 6 years, 8 months to 12 years. Stroop interference increased in mentally retarded persons as MA increased. However, the MA measure may not have adequately evaluated mentally retarded subjects' reading skill, and reading skills are necessary for Stroop interference to occur. Therefore, Stroop interference may have increased in the mentally retarded group due to their slower attainment of sufficient reading skills. There was no difference in Stroop interference between young MA-matched mentally retarded and nonretarded individuals. However, Das noted that his nonretarded subjects were approximately 4 months younger in MA than were the mentally retarded subjects; therefore, there may have been no Stroop interference differences obtained due to MA differences in the subjects. Also, at 6 years of age the reading ability of the nonretarded children may not have been developed sufficiently to cause Stroop interference, which is dependent on the possession of reading abilities by the subject.

Das (1970) also compared the Stroop interference data of mentally retarded persons with MAs of 10, 11, and 12 years with the Stroop interference data of the nonretarded subjects of the same MAs in his earlier study (Das, 1969). The same experimental procedure was used in both studies. The Stroop interference effect in mentally retarded persons having MAs of 10 and 12 years was greater than that of nonretarded persons of the same MA.

Bergen and Mosley (1994) examined performance on the Stroop task in mentally retarded individuals (CA = 30 years, MA = 11 years) with the performance of nonretarded individuals of similar CA (CA = 24 years) and MA-matched nonretarded individuals (MA = 11 years). Mentally retarded persons had greater difficulty naming the colors of Stroop words than did nonretarded persons of similar CA. There was no difference in latency to name the color of Stroop words for MA-matched mentally retarded and nonretarded persons. However, the MA-matched nonretarded individuals showed no Stroop interference effect whatsoever. The similarity in latencies to color name Stroop words is, therefore, not necessarily due to similarities in the ability to inhibit word reading.

Cognitive Inertia in Mentally Retarded Persons

Although different degrees of Stroop interference could be due solely to differences in the strength of the reading response, the reported differences in Stroop interference could be due to cognitive control differences rather than reading differences (Ellis et al., 1989). A cognitive control deficit in mentally retarded persons is a frequently cited finding (e.g., see Belmont, 1978; Bray, 1979; Brown, 1974, 1975; Butterfield & Belmont, 1977; Ellis, 1978). On the assumption that mentally retarded persons have greater control deficits than do nonretarded persons, Ellis et al. (1989) predicted that mentally retarded persons would exhibit greater Stroop interference. Color naming Stroop words requires the effortful suppression of an automatic reading response; therefore, those persons with greater effortful or control capacities would exhibit less Stroop interference than would persons with less cognitive control. In line with previous research (Das, 1969), Ellis et al. (1989; Experiment 1) showed that mentally retarded persons exhibited greater Stroop interference than did nonretarded persons of similar CA.

Before attributing the retarded–nonretarded differences in Stroop interference to lack of cognitive control, possible differences in degree of automatization had to be eliminated as a potential confounding factor. Using a variation of the Stroop paradigm, Ellis et al. (1989; Experiment 2) examined rates of automatization by mentally retarded and nonretarded individuals. Retarded and nonretarded subjects were given pretests on color naming colored Xs (color-naming control), reading color words printed in white on a black background (reading control), and reading Stroop words. Subjects then practiced color naming Stroop words for 3 days. Such practice required subjects to learn to suppress an automatic reading response in order to name the colors of Stroop words.

An analysis of the practice data indicated that mentally retarded and nonretarded persons had similar rates of improvement in color naming Stroop words. This finding was taken as evidence for similar rates of automatization of a reading suppression response by mentally retarded and nonretarded persons. Posttest measures assessing the effects of practice also were administered. The pre- and posttest data are presented in Fig. 7.1. Reading control words was unaffected by practice in both experiments. Color naming

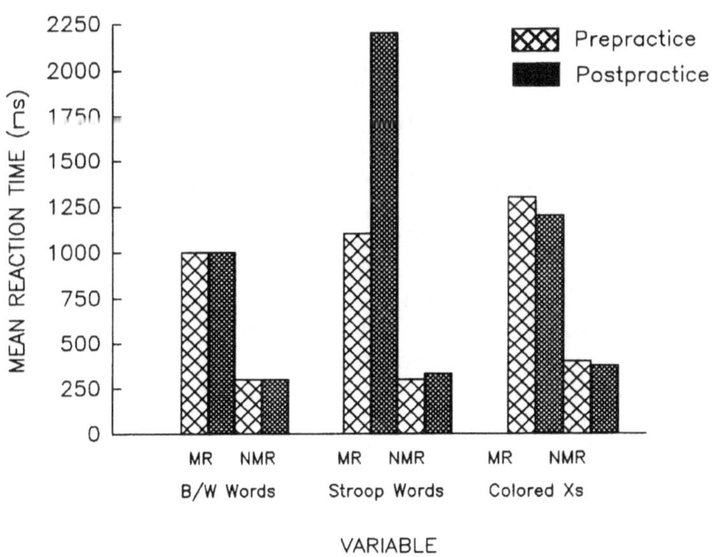

FIG. 7.1. Pre- and postpractice means (item response times) for reading black/white words (B/W) and Stroop words and color naming (Experiment 2; Ellis, Woodley-Zanthos, Dulaney, & Palmer, 1989). Reprinted by permission of the American Association on Mental Retardation.

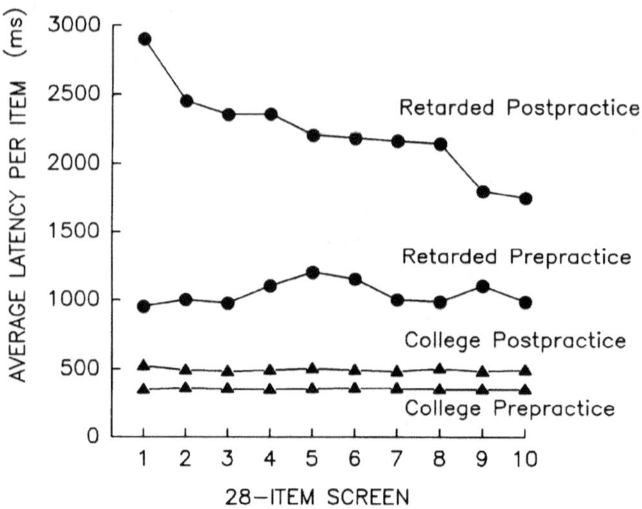

FIG. 7.2. Pre- and postpractice reading rates on Stroop words across ten 28-item screens (Experiment 2; Ellis, Woodley-Zanthos, Dulaney, & Palmer, 1989). Reprinted by permission of the American Association on Mental Retardation.

control items was slightly faster following practice. Reading rate of Stroop words was significantly slower as a result of color-naming practice, and this effect was much more pronounced in mentally retarded individuals. Although the difference between pre- and posttest reading performance was smaller in nonretarded persons than in mentally retarded persons, it was persistent for both groups (Fig. 7.2).

Ellis et al. (1989; Experiment 3) also found that the decline in reading rate was a function of a learned reading suppression response rather than an increased attentional response to color. Some mentally retarded and nonretarded subjects practiced color naming control items, whereas other mentally retarded and nonretarded subjects practiced color naming Stroop words. If an attentional response to color rather than a reading suppression response to the word was being learned, then color-naming practice of control items should also slow the reading of Stroop words at posttest. However, if a reading suppression response was learned, then subjects practicing color naming of control items should not have a slower reading rate of Stroop words at posttest. The results indicated that subjects who practiced color naming control items did not show a decline in reading rate at the posttest. Subjects who practiced color naming Stroop words showed a significant decline in reading rate at the posttest. Therefore, the hypothesis that subjects learned a reading suppression response was supported.

In light of these data, Ellis et al. (1989) offered an explanation based on the automaticity of the reading suppression response. With practice of color naming Stroop words, an automatic reading suppression response was developed. This was evidenced by the slower reading of Stroop words following color-naming practice of Stroop words, and the lack of slower reading of Stroop words following color-naming practice of control items. To return to the reading of Stroop words following color-naming practice of Stroop words, the newly acquired reading suppression response must be inhibited. If the color naming of Stroop words was a strategic process, then subjects should have shifted easily from color naming to reading; they did not. Therefore, the slowed reading effect was not due to a strategic process, but, instead, was due to the persistence of an automatic process. The slowed reading rate following practice was attributed to *cognitive inertia* of the automatized reading suppression response. The cognitive inertia exhibited by mentally retarded persons was much more pronounced than that in nonretarded persons.

Cognitive inertia was viewed as being similar to the Kounin (1941) notion of cognitive rigidity. This concept is not new. Spearman (1927) proposed a "law of inertia," which referred to a lag in a mental process after that process apparently is no longer needed. Cattell and Winder (1952) mentioned a type of rigidity that is the "mere temporal continuation, as by a momentum, of the immediate conscious or behavioral process" (p. 23).

A seldom-cited experiment by Stroop (1935; Experiment 3) also demonstrated an effect similar to that demonstrated by Ellis et al. (1989). Pre- and postpractice response times of college students were obtained for reading of Stroop words and naming colors of colored squares. A practice phase consisted of 8 days of practice color naming Stroop words (1,600 words). Although there was a slight increase in speed of color naming following practice, there was a considerable decrease in reading speed (i.e., cognitive inertia of the reading suppression response).

To assess further the pronounced cognitive inertia effect in mentally retarded individuals, Ellis and Dulaney (1991) varied the amount of color-naming practice of Stroop words completed by subjects. Mentally retarded and nonretarded individuals were given pretests on reading control words and Stroop words. Subjects then practiced color naming Stroop words for 20, 40, 80, or 160 trials (each trial contained 28 stimuli).

Slower reading following color-naming practice was assessed by comparing the difference between pre- and posttest reading latencies. These data are depicted in Fig. 7.3. Reading rates of control words slowed slightly following color-naming practice for mentally retarded and nonretarded persons. This finding was attributed to stimulus generalization of the reading suppression response. Reading rate of Stroop words slowed significantly for both mentally retarded and nonretarded persons following color-naming practice. Postpractice reading rates of Stroop words slowed as amount of color-naming practice increased from 20 to 80 trials, and became asymptotic after 80 trials. The increase in the amount of interference as practice increased was much more pronounced in

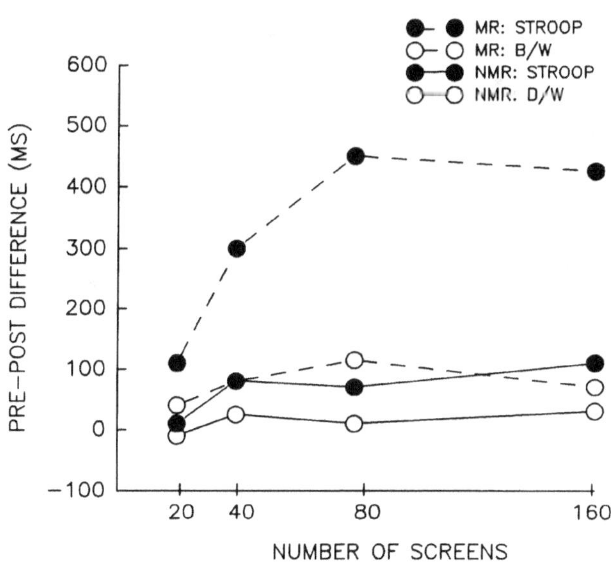

FIG. 7.3. Mean pre–post difference scores for reading rate of Stroop words and black/white (B/W) words for each practice condition (Experiment 1; Ellis & Dulaney, 1991). Reprinted by permission of the American Association on Mental Retardation.

mentally retarded persons than in nonretarded persons. That is, mentally retarded persons exhibited pronounced cognitive inertia. Because the degree of cognitive inertia exhibited was directly related to degree of practice, Ellis and Dulaney concluded that degree of automatization affected cognitive inertia. The greater cognitive inertia in mentally retarded persons as compared with nonretarded persons was attributed to the greater inability of mentally retarded persons to effortfully suppress an automatic response.

A second experiment (Ellis & Dulaney, 1991) compared the persistence of cognitive inertia in mentally retarded and nonretarded persons. All subjects practiced color naming Stroop words for 80 trials. Mentally retarded persons exhibited a more pronounced cognitive inertia than did nonretarded persons, as indicated by their greater slowing of Stroop word reading from pre- to posttest. The persistence of the reading suppression response was also examined 1 month and 3 months later (Fig. 7.4). After one month, the nonretarded subjects had returned to their original reading rates. That is, their cognitive inertia had dissipated. However, mentally retarded persons were not yet reading at their pretest rate. At 3 months, the mentally retarded group still had not returned to their pretest reading rate. Thus, cognitive inertia persisted in mentally retarded persons much longer than in nonretarded persons. These findings further support the concept of a pronounced cognitive inertia of automatic responding in mentally retarded persons.

A Stroop paradigm was employed by Dulaney and Ellis (1994) to compare the constructs of cognitive rigidity and cognitive inertia. If cognitive rigidity and cognitive inertia are the same phenomenon, the results obtained using the cognitive inertia paradigm should be similar to those obtained using the cognitive rigidity paradigm. Therefore, in line with Kounin's (1941) hypotheses, cognitive inertia should vary as a function of CA, MA, and mental retardation.

As in the previous studies of cognitive inertia, all subjects practiced color naming Stroop words, and pre- and posttest measures of reading rates of Stroop and control words was assessed. First, the relation between cognitive inertia and intelligence was examined.

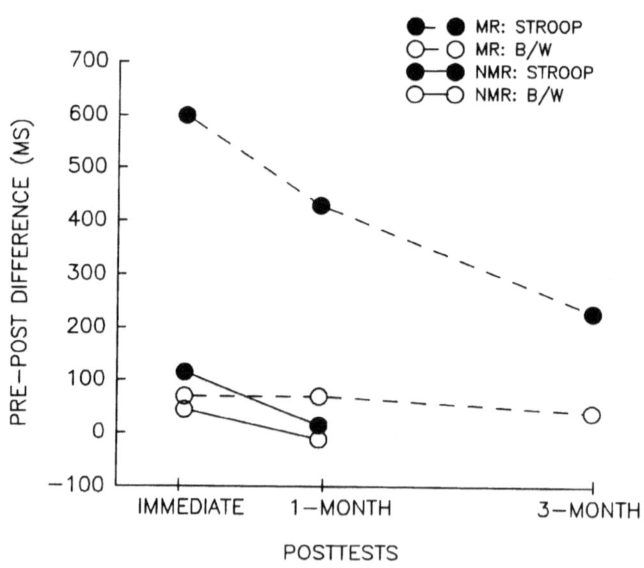

FIG. 7.4. Mean pre–post difference scores for reading rate of Stroop words and black/white (B/W) words at immediate, one-month, and three-month posttests (Experiment 2; Ellis & Dulaney, 1991). Reprinted by permission of the American Association on Mental Retardation.

Cognitive inertia in mentally retarded persons was compared to cognitive inertia in MA-matched and CA-matched nonretarded persons. Mentally retarded persons exhibited less cognitive inertia than did MA-matched nonretarded persons. This finding was contrary to the prediction that mentally retarded persons would have greater cognitive inertia than would MA-matched nonretarded persons. However, this finding might be attributed to the reading skills and amount of cognitive control possessed by the MA-matched nonretarded individuals (i.e., third graders). Schiller (1966) demonstrated that the Stroop effect is greatest in third-grade children who are beginning readers. As third graders were practicing color naming Stroop words (Dulaney & Ellis, 1994), they were having to deal with a weak reading habit as well as the color-naming response. When they returned to reading following color-naming practice, not only were they dealing with a newly learned reading suppression response but they were dealing with a weak reading habit as well. Therefore, greater cognitive inertia in MA-matched nonretarded persons was likely due to weaker cognitive control of the reading habit.

A comparison of mentally retarded and CA-matched nonretarded persons replicated earlier research by Ellis and his colleagues (Ellis & Dulaney, 1991; Ellis et al., 1989). Mentally retarded persons exhibited greater cognitive inertia than did CA-matched nonretarded persons.

Another study conducted by Dulaney and Ellis (1994) compared rigidity in young and old mentally retarded persons. Old mentally retarded persons exhibited greater rigidity than did young mentally retarded persons. This finding was consistent with the relation between rigidity and CA demonstrated by Kounin (1941).

The studies conducted by Ellis and Dulaney (Dulaney & Ellis, 1994; Ellis & Dulaney, 1991; Ellis et al., 1989) have demonstrated a type of rigidity (i.e., cognitive inertia) that can be manipulated experimentally. These studies demonstrated that rigidity could be a product of automatic processing components of a task (i.e., cognitive inertia), and that cognitive inertia was related to degree of mental retardation and to CA in mentally retarded persons.

Based on this review of studies examining rigidity in mentally retarded persons, it appears that there may be several causes of rigid behaviors. Kounin (1941) hypothesized that rigidity was due to structural limitations in communication among regions in an individual's life space. Cognitive inertia is caused by the automatization of a behavior and a deficit in effortful processing resulting in a failure to control the automatized behavior. The amount of cognitive inertia can be manipulated experimentally by varying the amount of practice, as shown in the research by Ellis and Dulaney (1991). This is a distinct advantage over the explanations of rigidity offered by Kounin and Lewin (Kounin, 1941; Lewin, 1935), and Zigler (1962).

Moreover, motivational factors cannot explain cognitive inertia (Dulaney & Ellis, 1994; Ellis & Dulaney, 1991; Ellis et al., 1989). First, subjects read Stroop words in the posttest rather than named the color of Stroop words as in the practice task. Therefore, mentally retarded and nonretarded persons are changing their responses as instructed by the experimenter. Zigler's motivational theory might predict that mentally retarded persons would persist at the old task (i.e., continue to color name rather than read Stroop words) in order to prolong social contact with the experimenter. The motivational theory might also predict that mentally retarded persons would easily comply with the experimenter's instructions in order to gain social approval. Therefore, they would read as fast at the Stroop posttest as they did at the Stroop pretest. Either finding might be taken as evidence that mentally retarded persons are more rigid than nonretarded persons due to motivational factors. However, mentally retarded persons did not show a pattern of behavior based on either prediction. Furthermore, nonretarded persons also exhibited behaviors similar to mentally retarded persons, although not to the same degree as mentally retarded persons.

Finally, the slowed rate of responding was substantial for reading of Stroop words but not for the reading of control words or color naming of control items. Therefore, cognitive inertia was not due to a general behavioral mechanism such as motivation. Motivational factors may sometimes lead to rigid behaviors but they cannot account for rigidity, as demonstrated in the studies by Ellis and Dulaney.

The studies by Ellis and Dulaney (Dulaney & Ellis, 1994; Ellis & Dulaney, 1991; Ellis et al., 1989) indicated that rigid behaviors can be due to factors related to automatic information processing, and such factors can cause greater rigidity in mentally retarded persons than in nonretarded persons. However, there may be more than one cause of rigidity. First, rigidity can be a consequence of automatic processing of a behavior (Ellis & Dulaney, 1991; Ellis et al., 1989). Second, rigidity can be a function of effortful or strategic processing components of a task. For example, some effortful tasks are affected by motivational factors causing mentally retarded persons to behave more rigidly than do nonretarded persons (e.g., Shallenberger & Zigler, 1961; Zigler & Unell, 1962). Discrimination reversal tasks require effort on the part of the subject in order to learn a new discrimination, and mentally retarded persons usually appear more rigid in the reversal phase of such tasks (e.g., Penney et al., 1962). Kounin's (1941) category sorting was such a task, and when performing it mentally retarded persons behaved more rigidly than did nonretarded persons.

The findings of Kounin (1941), Zigler and his colleagues (see Zigler & Balla, 1982, for a review), and Ellis and Dulaney (Dulaney & Ellis, 1994; Ellis & Dulaney, 1991; Ellis et al., 1989) that indicate greater rigidity in mentally retarded persons than in nonretarded persons may derive from different causes. Both effortful and automatic processes are likely to be involved in any instance of rigid behavior. Performance on cognitive tasks such as those used by Kounin and Zigler are likely to require effortful processing, and this may be affected by a number of factors including motivation and disinhibition. Therefore, although some rigid behaviors may be due mainly to motivational factors, other rigid behaviors seem to result from automatic responding that is uncontrolled by higher mental processes.

Rigidity related to automatic and effortful processing may be an important aspect of cognition and behavior in mentally retarded persons as well as in nonretarded persons. Rigidity such as that demonstrated in our research may account for many of the stereotyped, perseverative behaviors so often reported for mentally retarded persons. Frequently, classroom instruction requires rote rehearsal of learning information and skills. If the research findings related to cognitive inertia withstand experimental scrutiny, the implication of the cognitive inertia phenomenon is that mentally retarded persons would benefit more from instructions that foster flexibility rather than rigidity. This may be true even if the acquisition of a skill is slower.

ACKNOWLEDGMENTS

Preparation of this chapter was supported by Grant No. 15558 from the National Institute of Child Health and Human Development awarded to Norman Ellis at the University of Alabama, and a Center of Excellence Grant from the State of Tennessee to the Department of Psychology at the University of Memphis.

REFERENCES

Balla, D., & Zigler, E. (1964). Discrimination and switching learning in normal, familial retarded, and organic retarded children. *Journal of Abnormal and Social Psychology, 69*, 664–669.

Belmont, J. M. (1978). Individual differences in memory: The case of normal and retarded development. In M. M. Gruneberg & P. Morris (Eds.), *Aspects of memory* (pp. 152–185). London: Metheun.

Bergen, A. E., & Mosley, J. L. (1994). Attention and attentional shift in individuals with and without mental retardation. *American Journal on Mental Retardation, 98*, 688–743.

Bray, N. W. (1979). Strategy production in the retarded. In N. R. Ellis (Ed.), *Handbook of mental deficiency* (2nd ed., pp. 569–617). Hillsdale, NJ: Lawrence Erlbaum Associates.

Brown, A. L. (1974). The role of strategic behavior in retardate memory. In N. R. Ellis (Ed.) *International review of research in mental retardation* (Vol. 7., pp. 55–111). New York: Academic Press.

Brown, A. L. (1975). The development of memory: Knowing, knowing about knowing, and knowing how to know. In H. W. Reese (Ed.), *Advances in child development and behavior* (Vol. 10, pp. 103–152). New York: Academic Press.

Budoff, M., & Pagell, W. (1968). Learning potential and rigidity in the adolescent mentally retarded. *Journal of Abnormal Psychology, 73*, 479–486.

Butterfield, E. C., & Belmont, J. M. (1977). Assessing and improving the executive control functions of mentally retarded people. In I. Bailer & M. Sternlicht (Eds.), *Psychological issues in mental retardation: Issues and approaches* (pp. 277–318). New York: Academic Press.

Butterfield, E. C., & McIntyre, A. (1969). Cognitive and motivational factors in concept switching among the retarded. *American Journal of Mental Deficiency, 74*, 235–241.

Cattell, R. B., & Winder, A. E. (1952). Structural rigidity in relation to learning theory and clinical psychology. *Psychological Review, 59*, 23–39.

Cohen, J. D., Dunbar, K., & McClelland, J. L. (1990). On the control of automatic processes: A parallel distributed processing account of the Stroop effect. *Psychological Review, 97*, 332–361.

Comalli, P. E., Wapner, S., & Werner, H. (1962). Interference effects in childhood, adulthood, and aging. *The Journal of Genetic Psychology, 100*, 47–53.

Das, J. P. (1969). Development of verbal abilities in retarded and normal children as measured by Stroop test. *British Journal of Social and Clinical Psychology, 8*, 59–66.

Das, J. P. (1970). Changes in Stroop-test responses as a function of mental age. *British Journal of Social and Clinical Psychology, 9*, 68–73.

Dulaney, C. L., & Ellis, N. R. (1994). Automatized responding and cognitive inertia in persons with mental retardation. *American Journal on Mental Retardation, 99*, 8–18.

Dunbar, K., & MacLeod, C. M. (1984). A horse race of a different color: Stroop interference patterns with transformed words. *Journal of Experimental Psychology: Human Perception and Performance, 10*, 622–639.

Dyer, F. N. (1973). The Stroop phenomenon and its use in the study of perceptual, cognitive, and response processes. *Memory and Cognition, 1*, 106–120.

Ellis, N. R. (1978). Do the mentally retarded have poor memory? *Intelligence, 2*, 41–54.

Ellis, N. R., & Dulaney, C. L. (1991). Further evidence for cognitive inertia in persons with mental retardation. *American Journal on Mental Retardation, 95*, 613–621.

Ellis, N. R., Woodley-Zanthos, P., Dulaney, C. L., & Palmer, R. L. (1989). Automatic–effortful processing and cognitive inertia in mentally retarded persons. *American Journal on Mental Retardation, 93*, 412–423.

Goldstein, K. (1942). Concerning rigidity. *Character and Personality, 11*, 209–226.

Green, C., & Zigler, E. (1962). Social deprivation and the performance of retarded and normal children on a satiation type task. *Child Development, 33*, 499–508.

Halpin, V. G. (1958). The performance of mentally retarded children on the Weigl–Goldstein–Scheerer color form sorting test. *American Journal of Mental Deficiency, 62*, 916–919.

Hasher, L., & Zacks, R. T. (1979). Automatic and effortful processes in memory. *Journal of Experimental Psychology: General, 108*, 356–388.

Heal, L. W. (1966). The role of cue value, cue novelty, and overtraining in the discrimination shift performance of retardates and normal children of comparable discrimination ability. *Journal of Experimental Child Psychology, 4*, 126–142.

Heal, L. W., Ross, L. E., & Sanders, B. (1966). Reversal and partial reversal in mental defectives and normal children of a comparable mental age. *American Journal of Mental Deficiency, 71*, 411–416.

Iwahara, S., & Sugimura, T. (1962). The effect of different amounts of training upon shifted discrimination learning as a function of intellectual level. *Psychologia, 5*, 93–98.

Kahneman, D. (1973). *Attention and effort.* Englewood Cliffs, NJ: Prentice-Hall.

Kounin, J. S. (1941). Experimental studies of rigidity: I. The measurement of rigidity in normal and feeble-minded persons. *Character and Personality, 9*, 251–272.

Kounin, J. S. (1948). The meaning of rigidity: A reply to Heinz Werner. *Psychological Review, 55*, 157–166.

Kreitler, S., Zigler, E., & Kreitler, H. (1990). Rigidity in mentally retarded and nonretarded children. *American Journal on Mental Retardation, 94*, 550–562.

LaBerge, D., & Samuels, S. J. (1974). Toward a theory of automatic information processing in reading. *Cognitive Psychology, 6*, 293–323.

Lewin, K. (1935). *A dynamic theory of personality.* New York: McGraw-Hill.

Lobb, H., & Stogdill, D. (1974). Low-IQ deficit in intradimensional discrimination shift despite overtraining and verbal feedback. *American Journal of Mental Deficiency, 79*, 455–461.

MacLeod, C. M. (1991). Half a century of research on the Stroop effect: An integrative review. *Psychological Bulletin, 109*, 163–203.

MacLeod, C. M., & Dunbar, K. (1988). Training and Stroop-like interference: Evidence for a continuum of automaticity. *Journal of Experimental Psychology: Learning, Memory, and Cognition, 14*, 126–135.

Morton, J., & Chambers, S. M. (1973). Selective attention to words and colours. *Quarterly Journal of Experimental Psychology, 25*, 387–397.

O'Connor, N., & Hermelin, B. (1959). Discrimination reversal learning in imbeciles. *Journal of Abnormal and Social Psychology, 59*, 409–413.

O'Malley, J. J., Dunn, D., & Rudnick, P. (1975). Amount of training, age of subject, and perseveration in reversal learning. *The Journal of Genetic Psychology, 93*, 261–268.

Penney, R. K., Croskery, J., & Allen, G. (1962). Effect of training schedules on rigidity as manifested by normal and mentally retarded children. *Psychological Reports, 10*, 243–249.

Plenderleith, M. (1956). Discrimination learning and discrimination reversal learning in normal and feebleminded children. *The Journal of Genetic Psychology, 88*, 107–112.

Posner, M. I., & Snyder, C. R. (1975). Attention and cognitive control. In R. L. Solso (Ed.), *Information processing and cognition: The Loyola symposium* (pp. 55–85). Hillsdale, NJ: Lawrence Erlbaum Associates.

Richman, C. L., Adams, K. A., Nida, S. A., & Richman, J. (1978). Performance of MA-matched nonretarded and retarded children on discrimination learning and transfer-shift tasks. *American Journal of Mental Deficiency, 83*, 262–269.

Rondal, J. A., & Lambert, J. (1975). A twofold failure to replicate the results of O'Connor and Hermelin in discrimination learning with reversal in the case of mentally retarded children. *The Journal of Genetic Psychology, 126*, 157–158.

Sanders, B., Ross, L. E., & Heal, L. W. (1965). Reversal and nonreversal shift learning in normal children and retardates of comparable mental age. *Journal of Experimental Psychology, 69*, 84–88.

Schiller, P. H. (1966). Developmental study of color- word interference. *Journal of Experimental Psychology, 72*, 105–108.

Schneider, W., & Shiffrin, R. M. (1977). Controlled and automatic human information processing. I. Detection, search, and attention. *Psychological Review, 84*, 1–55.

Shallenberger, P., & Zigler, E. (1961). Rigidity, negative reaction tendencies, and cosatiation effects in normal and feebleminded children. *Journal of Abnormal and Social Psychology, 63*, 20–26.

Shanab, M. E., & McClure, F. H. (1983). Age and sex differences in discrimination learning. *Bulletin of the Psychonomic Society, 21*, 387–390.

Shepps, R., & Zigler, E. (1962). Social deprivation and rigidity in the performance of organic and familial retardates. *American Journal of Mental Deficiency, 67*, 262–268.

Shiffrin, R. M., & Schneider, W. (1977). Controlled and automatic human information processing. II. Perceptual learning, automatic attending, and a general theory. *Psychological Review, 84,* 127–189.

Siegel, P. S., & Foshee, J. G. (1960). Molar variability in the mentally defective. *Journal of Abnormal and Social Psychology, 61,* 141–143.

Smith, S. A. (1984). *The effect of disinhibition on the molar response variability of the mentally retarded.* Unpublished doctoral dissertation, University of Alabama, Tuscaloosa.

Smith, S. A., & Siegel, P. S. (1986). Molar variability and the mentally retarded. In N. R. Ellis (Ed.), *International review of research in mental retardation* (Vol. 14, pp. 73–104). New York: Academic Press.

Spearman, C. (1927). *The abilities of man.* New York: MacMillan.

Stevenson, H. W., & Zigler, E. (1957). Discrimination learning and rigidity in normal and feebleminded individuals. *Journal of Personality, 25,* 699–711.

Strauss, A. A., & Werner, H. (1942). Experimental analysis of the clinical symptom "perseveration" in mentally retarded children. *American Journal of Mental Deficiency, 47,* 185–188.

Stroop, J. R. (1935). Studies of interference in serial and verbal reactions. *Journal of Experimental Psychology, 18,* 643–662.

Umetani, T., Kitao, S., & Katada, A. (1985). Discrimination shift learning and response inhibition of moderately and severely mentally retarded and non-retarded children. *Journal of Mental Deficiency Research, 29,* 219–224.

Werner, H. (1946). Abnormal and subnormal rigidity. *Journal of Abnormal and Social Psychology, 41,* 15–24.

Werner, H. (1948). The concept of rigidity: A critical evaluation. *Psychological Review, 53,* 43–53.

Zigler, E. (1961). Social deprivation and rigidity in the performance of feebleminded children. *Journal of Abnormal and Social Psychology, 62,* 413–421.

Zigler, E. (1962). Rigidity in the feebleminded. In E. Trapp & P. Himmelstein (Eds.), *Readings on the exceptional child* (pp. 141–162). New York: Appleton Century-Crofts.

Zigler, E. (1963). Rigidity and social reinforcement effects in the performance of institutionalized and noninstitutionalized normal and retarded children. *Journal of Personality, 31,* 258–269.

Zigler, E., & Balla, D. (1982). Rigidity—A resilient concept. In E. Zigler & D. Balla (Eds.), *Mental retardation: The developmental-difference controversy* (pp. 61–82). Hillsdale, NJ: Lawrence Erlbaum Associates.

Zigler, E., & Butterfield, E. C. (1966). Rigidity in the retarded: A further test of the Lewin–Kounin formulation. *Journal of Abnormal Psychology, 71,* 224–231.

Zigler, E., & DeLabry, J. (1962). Concept-switching in middle class, lower class, and retarded children. *Journal of Abnormal and Social Psychology, 65,* 267–273.

Zigler, E., Hodgden, L., & Stevenson, H. (1958). The effect of support on the performance of normal and feebleminded children. *Journal of Personality, 26,* 106–122.

Zigler, E., & Unell, E. (1962). Concept-switching in normal and feebleminded children as a function of reinforcement. *American Journal of Mental Deficiency, 66,* 651–657.

› 8 ‹

Cognitive Competencies and Strategy Use in Individuals With Mental Retardation

Norman W. Bray
Kathryn L. Fletcher
University of Alabama at Birmingham

Lisa A. Turner
University of South Alabama

One important goal for research on mental retardation is the development of a theory of the cognitive nature of mental retardation. Although a comprehensive theory has not yet been developed, most theoretical discussions of this topic include deficits in memory abilities as an important aspect of the cognitive limitations of these individuals (e.g., Belmont & Mitchell, 1987; Bray & Turner, 1986, 1987, Detterman, 1987; Ellis, 1978; Ferretti & Cavalier, 1991; Spitz, 1979). Therefore, a substantial treatment of the role of memory deficits will be a precursor to theory development. The purpose of this chapter is to review and discuss the current state of research on the memory abilities and limitations of individuals with mild mental retardation.

Memory deficits could refer to many things, so we must delimit their domain. Ericsson (1988) noted that a person without a memory would have no identity. Not being able to remember the past would result in no continuity with the present, and learning would not occur. It is clear that the memory deficits of individuals with mental retardation are not this profound (Turnure, 1991); they do function within a context of the past and present. So, first, it is important to note that the "memory deficits" in individuals with mental retardation are less severe than the exceptional memory deficits due to traumatic brain injury.

In comparison to understanding severe amnesia, understanding less severe memory deficits may seem relatively simple. This, however, is not the case; it is not the severity of the deficit that gives this problem its complexity. Because the deficits are subtle, great care must be taken in defining adequately the nature and extent of these deficiencies. But how would we know if the nature and extent of memory deficiencies have been adequately defined? This could never be known in any absolute sense, of course, but it seems possible to define the broad limits for pursuing these questions. These limits may help us determine if we are making progress toward an adequate definition of memory deficiencies in individuals with mental retardation.

We could imagine two general approaches and two outcomes for each. The ideal approach would be that a large number of different tasks representing a wide range of experiences and functions in daily life would have been studied, and memory abilities would have been assessed in each. In the more limited approach at the other extreme, a relatively narrow range of tasks would have been used to study memory abilities. Possible outcomes with either of these approaches could be that deficits would be observed with all tasks or only with a subset of the tasks.

Bray and Turner (1986, 1987) noted that memory abilities of individuals with mental retardation have been studied within a limited range of laboratory tasks adapted, largely, from studies of adult verbal learning and memory. Within this narrow range of tasks, however, memory deficits have not always been observed (Bray, Saarnio, Borges, & Hawk, 1994; Bray & Turner, 1986, 1987). Based on the current literature, the extent of the deficiencies can only be characterized as narrow, because only a limited range of tasks have been used to study memory deficits and deficits are not always found, even in the limited range of tasks that have been studied. It may be that memory deficits in individuals with mental retardation would be evident in a wide range of situations but, for now, the research literature cannot legitimately make such a claim because of the narrow sampling of tasks and the fact that deficiencies have not always been observed. Overgeneralization of memory deficits may have led to a neglect of evidence for strategy competencies.

In this chapter we elaborate on the notion introduced by Bray and Turner (1986) that individuals with mental retardation have a number of important cognitive competencies. We believe that additional competencies would be discovered if more investigators looked for similarities rather than differences. It is important to recognize, however, that focusing exclusively on cognitive competencies would result in an incomplete picture of cognition, just as would an exclusive focus of cognitive deficits. It is the relations between competencies and deficits that will provide a more complete depiction of cognition in individuals with mental retardation.

We begin with an overview of the deficit approach to mental retardation and contrast this with the cognitive competency positions beginning to emerge in developmental psychology. We then provide an overview of some competencies that have been observed in laboratory research with individuals with mental retardation, first discussing competencies in nonstrategic information processing. This includes research on automatic processing, spread of activation, short-term retention rate, use of stimulus organization, organization of semantic memory, and long-term retention. We then consider the nature and extent of strategy competencies in individuals with mental retardation. Research is reviewed that focuses on developmental changes in strategy competency, including both cross-sectional and longitudinal studies. Task variables that influence strategy use and the implications of these studies for strategy competency are then presented. These include studies of the importance of task comprehension, the effects of information processing demands, and the use of external memory strategies that do not require the use of verbal processing. We then discuss the general issue of how limitations of working memory may limit competency in strategy use. The final section sketches a direction for further research on strategy competency and deficiency as a central component of a general theory of mental retardation.

THE STATUS OF THE DEFICIT APPROACH IN MENTAL RETARDATION

It seems safe to say that most psychological theories of mental retardation have focused on limitations rather than competencies. Vernon (1976) offered a very reasonable explanation for the historical focus on deficits. Before the late 1950s and early 1960s, psychological theories of mental retardation were very global, simply stating that individuals with mental retardation failed to learn because they had low intelligence. This view resulted in a circular explanation, however, because intelligence tests were originally devised to identify children having learning problems in school. To say that individuals with mental retardation have difficulty learning because they have low intelligence adds nothing to the understanding of the nature of mental retardation.

In order to break the circularity of this global approach, more specific theories of mental retardation began to evolve in the late 1950s and early 1960s. For instance, Zeaman and House (1963) developed an attention-deficit theory of mental retardation that localized the learning problem in attention. Ellis (1963) identified the deficit in learning as a faulty short-term memory trace. Later, Ellis (1970) and Belmont and Butterfield (1971) attributed the locus of the learning deficit to inadequate use of rehearsal strategies.

All of these approaches attempted to break the circularity of the low-intelligence explanation of learning deficits in individuals with mental retardation. If low intelligence is seen as the result of a deficit in a relatively localized area of function such as inadequate attention, inadequate stimulus traces, or inadequate rehearsal strategies, then the circularity of the low intelligence explanation would be broken. The deficit approach, however, has resulted in a focus on limitations of individuals with mental retardation. The nearly exclusive focus on identifying deficits overlooks the larger goal of describing the relations between deficits and competencies. The description of these relations is needed to determine how the cognitive system of individuals with mental retardation functions.

Part of our argument for more research and increased theoretical attention to the cognitive competencies of individuals with mental retardation is based on the process of theory development. In a theoretical vacuum created by ignoring the possibilities of cognitive competencies, new deficits may be hypothesized without any cumulative consideration of the cognitive nature of individuals with mental retardation. For instance, since the early 1970s, research has focused on a variety of deficiencies, including deficits in rehearsal, verbal elaboration, organization, imagery, metamemory, levels of processing, encoding, semantic memory, and automatic processing, among others. In each case a new paradigm, a new theoretical advance, or new emphases in adult cognition gave birth to possible deficits without balanced consideration of the cognitive competencies of individuals with mental retardation. This is not to say that ideas should not be borrowed from research in adult cognition, but rather that research has gone through cycles driven more by developments in adult cognition than by cumulative efforts to develop a theory of the nature of cognition in individuals with mental retardation. Cumulative theory development will require a more balanced treatment of competencies and deficiencies.

Raising the issue of the nature and extent of the cognitive competencies of individuals with mental retardation would seem to require a close examination of what is meant by "cognitive abilities." It seems clear that "abilities" has obtained a traitlike status in psychological research in mental retardation. In fact, the strong influence of differential psychology (with its emphasis on measures that are stable over time) has led to a view of relatively static abilities that can characterize an individual for a long period of time (if not the person's entire lifetime). Possibly because deficits have been treated as traits, developmental changes in specific cognitive abilities of individuals with mental retardation have received very little attention. The desire for stable cognitive structures that would be related to individual differences in intelligence may have its roots in differential psychology and the concept of *g*. Zeaman (1978) noted that a theory of mental retardation must deal with what is stable across time. Although this view resonates well with the methods and philosophy of differential psychology, Sternberg (1990) noted that this static view of abilities neglects the considerable body of literature that demonstrates that specific abilities develop and change across the life span.

What developmental theorizing there has been in the cognition of mental retardation has been at a relatively molar level (e.g., Zigler, 1969; Zigler & Balla, 1982). As noted by Detterman (1987), the long dispute between the deficit theorist and the developmental theorist has been due, in large part, to a difference in the level of analysis. The developmental approach of Zigler is concerned with molar aspects of development, whereas the deficit approach of Ellis and others is more molecular, focusing on specific abilities (e.g., rehearsal). Unfortunately, the area of information processing in individuals with mental retardation has relied most heavily on deficit theories to the exclusion of a very large and vigorous body of research on the development of cognition.

STATUS OF THE COGNITIVE COMPETENCE ISSUE IN DEVELOPMENTAL PSYCHOLOGY

In developmental psychology, there has been considerable discussion concerning the age at which a child "has" an ability or "understands" a concept. Siegler (1991) noted that at one end of the continuum, Braine (1959) argued that this should be the earliest age at which a child can successfully perform on tasks requiring a particular ability or concept, whereas Brown (1976) argued that it should be the age of mastery, when the ability or concept can be used under a variety of conditions. Siegler pointed out problems with both ends of this continuum. The early development approach implies that growth occurs after the concept or ability develops, and the late development approach clearly neglects important emerging competencies of the child. Siegler (1991) wrote:

> One alternative to stating an age at which children acquire a cognitive capability is to produce more-encompassing models of whatever knowledge they have at different ages that is relevant to that capability. These models would not only specify how children of a particular age perform on various tasks associated with a concept, they also would indicate the conditions under which children applied various types of knowledge that they had. (p. 351)

In the area of mental retardation, the concern with identification of deficits without reference to competencies is analogous to the focus in developmental psychology on the age at which a child "has" an ability. Deficits attributed to individuals with mental retardation have typically been inferred from findings in which a CA or MA comparison group performs at a higher level than does a group of individuals with mental retardation. If differences are found, a deficit is inferred without an exploration of the emerging competencies of the individuals with mental retardation. This seems to be most analogous to the late development criterion used by Brown (1976), but, in this case, mastery is equated with performance equivalent to individuals without mental retardation. Following the alternative approach described by Siegler (1991), a more active concern with emerging cognitive competencies would counterbalance the nearly exclusive focus on deficits.

In developmental psychology, until recently, most research on the cognition of pre-school children focused on their deficits relative to older children (Flavell, 1992). Little attention was paid to the emergence of competencies during this period of development. The relative neglect of emerging competencies in developmental psychology may be understood in light of the influence of Piaget. Piaget (1954) described *development* as progressing through a sequence of stages marked by qualitative changes in concept formation and understanding. Piaget's stage theory of development greatly influenced research on cognitive development. Piaget provided extensive empirical data and theoretical treatments of the patterns of children's thinking at different ages, and contended that, during a particular stage, these patterns were similar across a variety of task situations. Thus, children in a particular stage were characterized by early stage theorists as having certain abilities or deficiencies.

Although Piaget argued that these patterns of thinking were similar across a variety of task situations, evidence for these patterns was based on only a few task situations. More recent research on cognitive abilities from a neo-Piagetian point of view has been conducted with a wider range of tasks and has demonstrated that younger children possess considerably more cognitive competence than presumed by Piaget (Flavell, 1992; Siegler, 1991).

For example, Piaget (1954) contended that 12-month-old infants did not understand *object permanence*, the concept that an object continues to exist when it is subjected to a transformation involving movement. This description, however, was based on a task that required the child to use a motor response to attempt to retrieve a hidden object. In a task merely requiring a looking response, Baillargeon and DeVos (1991) found that infants as young as 3.5 to 4.5 months showed evidence that they realized that objects continued to exist when they were hidden. Because Piaget used only one type of task situation to describe object permanence concept, infants' emerging abilities were overlooked.

Other studies have also reported competencies at earlier ages than did Piaget, following slight modifications in his procedures. For instance, in studies of class inclusion concepts, Inhelder and Piaget (1964) contended that preschool children only focus on one dimension in classification even if more than one dimension was relevant. Markman and Seibert (1976) showed kindergarten and first-grade children class inclusion problems with four big frogs and two small frogs and asked various types of class inclusion questions. The standard question type (patterned after those used by Piaget) was "Who would have more pets, someone who owned the baby frogs or someone who owned the frogs?" Questions using collection nouns were also asked such as "Who would have more pets, someone who owned the baby frogs or someone who owned the family? The children had difficulty with the standard question but frequently answered questions using collection nouns such as *family* and *bunch* correctly.

Much of the recent neo-Piagetian research has shown that when a greater variety of tasks and methods is used than those used by Piaget, emerging abilities can be demonstrated. The cumulative effects of such demonstrations in many different areas of cognitive development led Siegler (1991) to state that infants and preschool children have considerably more cognitive competence than previously supposed. In this chapter, we present evidence to support the assertion that the same holds for the cognitive competence of individuals with mental retardation.

COMPETENCIES IN NONSTRATEGIC INFORMATION PROCESSING IN INDIVIDUALS WITH MENTAL RETARDATION

Brown (1974) noted that not all aspects of information processing were deficient in individuals with mental retardation. She observed that nonstrategic processes such as visual recognition memory were equivalent in groups with and without mental retardation, whereas deficiencies were consistently observed in tasks requiring the use of strategies. Partly due to Brown's position, research on information processing began to focus on "metamemory" (the presumed locus of strategy deficiencies) and on strategy training in the hope that strategy deficiencies could be reduced or eliminated.

Although it was not recognized at the time, Brown's conclusion concerning the lack of deficiencies in nonstrategic processing were based on only one type of task, recognition memory. There have, however, been a number of studies of nonstrategic information processing that greatly extend the range of situations in which no deficiencies have been found. Several of these are now described briefly.

Automatic Processing

Research on automatic processing in individuals with mental retardation has been motivated by the work of Hasher and Zacks (1979), who made a distinction between automatic and effortful processes. Automatic processes are those that do not require attention, such as the use of the rhythm of speech to understand sentences, the incidental memory for spatial location, remembering how frequently an event has occurred, or remembering the presentation mode (auditory or visual) of a sentence. These are processes that contrast with effortful processes that require attention such as solving a math problem, reconstructing from memory what you were doing 4 years ago, or remembering a sequence of digits.

There have been a number of studies showing essentially identical performance for groups with and without mental retardation of the same chronological age on tasks involving automatic processing. For instance, Dann (1984) showed that individuals with and without mental retardation were equally dependent on the rhythm of speech for comprehension of simple sentences. In two separate studies he presented simple sentences that either did or did not describe a picture (e.g., "The green shoe is above the gold ring"). Some sentences were presented with normal prosody and others were presented with the same prosody shifted by one syllable. Dann found that the interruption of the rhythm of a sentence interfered with comprehension for both groups, and that the degree of interference was identical for both.

Ellis, Katz, and Williams (1987), who set out to find deficits in automatic processing, actually found little or no difference in automatic processing between individuals with and without mental retardation. For instance, there were no differences between adolescents with mental retardation and college students in the ability to remember spatial location of pictures of common objects on the page of a book. Ellis and his colleagues showed subjects sequences of pictures, each located in one of four quadrants on a page. At the end of the book, the subjects were shown each picture once more and asked to identify the quadrant in which the picture had appeared. Some of the subjects were forewarned about the test for spatial location of the pictures and others were not. Regardless of whether the subjects were forewarned, ability to recall the quadrant in which a picture was placed was excellent for both adolescents with mental retardation and for college students. Similar results were found in several other studies (Dulaney & Ellis, 1991; Ellis, Woodley-Zanthos, & Dulaney, 1989; Nigro & Roak, 1987).

Ellis, Palmer, and Reeves (1988) found similar results in two studies of memory for frequency of occurrence. The participants were shown a large number of simple words, one at a time. Some of the words occurred only once but others were repeated as often as four times. At the end of the sequence a participant was shown each of the words again and asked to estimate the number of times the word had occurred in the sequence. At the beginning of the sequence some were told about the upcoming test and others were not. Memory for frequency was high in both the informed and uninformed conditions, and there were no differences between adolescents with mental retardation and college students. These experiments provide strong support for the contention that automatic processing of spatial and frequency information is equivalent in individuals with and without mental retardation.

Spread of Activation

There are certain basic processes involved in memory that seem to be intact in individuals with mental retardation. One of these is a process called *spreading activation*. This process is usually studied using a priming procedure in which one stimulus speeds the processing of the next. For instance, if a person hears the word *animal* immediately before seeing a picture of a dog, the person can name the picture faster than if the same picture was preceded by the word *plant*. Thus, the word *animal* primes the retrieval of the word *dog*. This priming effect is thought to occur because the representation of animal and dog are closer in memory than the representation of plant and dog. Semantic priming studies by Sperber, Ragain, and McCauley (1976) found that priming effects in adolescents and adults with and without mental retardation are equivalent, leading to the conclusion that spreading activation is a competency of individuals with and without mental retardation.

Use of Stimulus Organization

Spitz and Webreck (1972) found that with relatively short sequences of digits, adolescents with and without mental retardation performed at the same level on a task requiring the use of stimulus organization. Sequences of digits with redundancy (e.g., 175175) were remembered better than were sequences without redundancy by both groups. With long sequences, however, the subjects with mental retardation did not use the redundancy, whereas subjects without mental retardation did. Although Spitz and Webreck emphasized the poor performance on the longer sequences, the shorter sequences were supraspan. The equivalent performance of the two groups indicates that adolescents with mental retardation are able to use stimulus organization, although they do not if the task is extremely difficult. This limitation, however, does not negate the observation of this cognitive competency.

Short-Term Retention Rate

The rate of loss of information from short-term memory would seem like a basic structural feature of the information processing system. Ellis (1963) proposed the possibility that individuals with mental retardation have a deficit in the short-term memory trace, hypothesizing that information is lost more quickly in individuals with mental retardation. This hypothesis, however, has not been supported (Detterman, 1987). There are a number of studies that have shown that information is lost from short-term memory at the same rate in both populations (e.g. Ellis, 1978; Ellis, McCartney, Ferretti, & Cavalier, 1977; Ellis, Meador, & Bodfish, 1985; Ferretti, 1979; Spitz, 1973).

Interference Effects in Short-Term Memory

Winters (1982, 1985) conducted a series of experiments on possible differences in the buildup of proactive interference in the short-term memory of individuals with and without mental retardation. Using the release from proactive inhibition paradigm developed by Wickens (1970), subjects were given a series of trials with triads of words, each triad from the same category. Accuracy decreased across trials because of the buildup of within-category proactive interference. After several trials a new category was introduced, and accuracy increased because of the release from proactive interference. Although there were different levels of accuracy in recall, the rate of buildup of proactive interference (indexed by a negative slope across trials) and the release from proactive interference was the same in both groups. This pattern of results indicates that taxonomic categories are equally accessible in this situation for both intelligence groups.

Long-Term Retention

Properly controlled studies of long-term retention (24 hours or more) have consistently found either small differences or no differences in rate of loss of information from long-term memory for subjects with and without mental retardation (cf. Turnure, 1991). For instance, McCartney (1987) reported a carefully controlled study that equated adolescents with mental retardation and college students on initial level of memory performance. The subjects were shown a sequence of over 100 pictures of faces. A retention test on a subset of the pictures was given immediately after the presentation, after 1 day, after 1 week, and after 6 months. There was no difference between intelligence groups in rate of forgetting across these retention intervals. Turnure (1991) provided a recent review of the research on long-term memory in individuals with mental retardation and concluded that:

> Evidence is accumulating that the LTM capacity of young mildly handicapped individuals is intact and functions within the normal range on an array of tasks. . . . Mildly retarded individuals appear to have both implicit and explicit memory systems that have sufficient capacity or potential for retaining quite extensive amounts of learned information and skills. (p. 212)

Organization of Semantic Memory

One method for studying the organization of semantic memory is to ask subjects to name as many instances of a taxonomic category as possible within a specified time (Battig & Montague, 1969). Using this methodology, Winters (1985) found that the organization of semantic memory of individuals with and without mental retardation is strikingly similar. He found some deviations that might be attributed to different schooling experience, but the similarities of the category responses of the two groups were much more similar than different.

Whereas Brown (1974) relied heavily on recognition memory studies to develop her hypothesis of no deficiencies in nonstrategic processing of individuals with mental retardation, the recent studies on automatic processing, spread of activation, short-term retention rate, use of stimulus organization, long-term retention, and organization of semantic memory greatly extend the base for this hypothesis. Collectively, these studies make a strong case for the position that many structural features of memory in individuals with mental retardation are equivalent to those found in individuals without mental retardation.

COMPETENCIES IN STRATEGY USE IN INDIVIDUALS WITH MENTAL RETARDATION

Strategy competency refers to the skills and knowledge that underlie the use of strategies. In this section, we deal with two interrelated issues concerning strategy competency in individuals with mental retardation. These include the developmental course of strategy competency and its comparison to the developmental course in individuals without mental retardation, and the conditions that influence strategy use and therefore demonstrate the nature of the underlying strategy competency.

Developmental Changes in Strategy Competency

There have been surprisingly few cross-sectional and longitudinal studies of memory strategies focusing on individuals with mental retardation. One of the first cross-sectional studies for memory strategies in this area was conducted by Brown and Barclay (1976). Groups of children and adolescents with mental retardation (with mean ages of 10 and 12) were trained to use either a rehearsal or an anticipation strategy in a recall readiness task in which they were allowed to study a series of pictures as long as they wished. In a prompted posttest 1 day following training, both the younger and older children used the trained strategies. On unprompted posttests 1 day and 2 weeks later, however, only the older children with mental retardation maintained the strategy. In a follow-up study with the same subjects 1 year later, Brown, Campione, and Barclay (1979) found that the older children who learned the anticipation and rehearsal strategies (which require self-checking) also generalized strategy training on the list learning task to a reading task. Thus, older children with mental retardation showed evidence of strategy maintenance and generalization.

Turner and Bray (1985) tested children and adolescents (10, 12, and 14 years old) with mental retardation on a recall readiness task similar to that used by Brown and Barclay (1976). The participants were allowed to study the sequences as many times as they wished. The number of repetitions for the three age groups were 3.8, 4.3, and 6.2, respectively, showing a developmental increase in the likelihood that a repetition strategy would be used. In this study, 97% of the participants showed evidence of rehearsal as indicated by studying the items more than once.

Turner and Bray (1993) also used a recall readiness task with 11-and 15-year-old children and adolescents with and without mental retardation. When the self-paced study-time patterns were classified by strategy type, the participants with mental retardation used labeling strategies more often than did the participants without mental retardation, but labeling decreased with age for both intelligence groups. Participants without mental retardation used more "peaked" strategies in which they paused within the presentation of a sequence (as in "chunking" strategies), but individuals with mental retardation used such strategies on 36% of the trials. The use of peaked strategies increased for both groups across age groups.

Bray, Turner, and Hersh (1985) studied rehearsal strategies in 11-, 15-, and 18-year-olds with mental retardation in a self-paced sequential memory task. They found that the proportion of subjects using rehearsal increased from 19% to 31% across this age range, indicating that there are developmental changes in strategy competency in adolescents with mental retardation. In a similar study, however, subjects without mental retardation in the same age range showed an increase in the proportion using a selective rehearsal strategy from 25% to 75%, indicating that the rate of change in strategy use is greater in adolescents without mental retardation (Bray, Hersh, & Turner, 1985).

In addition to these cross-sectional studies of strategy development, there has been one longitudinal study of children with mental retardation. Turner, Hale, and Borkowski (1996) tested a group of 10-year-old students with and without mental retardation each year for 3 years on several memory tasks. Developmental changes were consistent across the two intelligence groups. In the recall readiness task (described previously), both intelligence groups increased in the number of times items were studied and in the number of items recalled across the 3-year period. Similarly, in a semantic organization task, recall and categorical organization of items recalled increased across time for both intelligence groups, indicating developmental improvements.

Although the number of cross-sectional studies is very small and there is only one longitudinal study, the results of these provide consistent evidence for developmental change in the strategy competency of children and adolescents with mental retardation. There were developmental progressions from little strategy use to more. The rate of progress for individuals without mental retardation was faster, but there was consistent evidence of development in the individuals with mental retardation. There is, however, much to be learned about the factors that impact the relatively slow rate of strategy development in individuals with mental retardation. Resolving these issues would be facilitated by incorporating research and theory from the area of cognitive development (e.g., Flavell, 1992). A more active focus on developmental changes in strategy use in children and younger adolescents with mental retardation would likely provide a broader and potentially richer avenue of investigation and theory development than would be provided by continuing a nearly exclusive focus on strategy defects in older adolescents and adults with mental retardation.

Factors Affecting the Demonstration of Strategy Competency

Research on strategy competency with children and adolescents with mental retardation has identified three general factors that influence the demonstration of underlying strategy competency, including the degree of task comprehension, information processing constraints (such as memory load), and the degree to which a task allows the possibility of external representation. Research on each of these topics is now reviewed briefly.

The Role of Task Comprehension

Bray (1979) described a program of research on selective remembering in children and adolescents with mental retardation that demonstrated the importance of comprehension of task demands for effective strategy use. In a selective remembering task, the participants were asked to remember a sequence of items (e.g., picture names, digits, or words). Occasionally during the sequence the color background of the items would change, indicating that the prior items in the sequence were to be forgotten and only subsequent items would be tested.

Although there was no strategy training in any of these experiments, both intelligence groups adopted effective strategies, although there appeared to be qualitative differences in the types of strategies typically adopted by individuals with and without mental retardation (Bray, Goodman, & Justice, 1982; Bray & Palmer, 1993). Individuals without mental retardation used a selective rehearsal strategy in which items were rehearsed until a forget cue was given. Following the cue, only the subsequent to-be-remembered items were rehearsed. Some adolescents with mental retardation used this selective rehearsal strategy, but others used a qualitatively different strategy (Bray, Turner, & Hersh, 1985). In the "selective retrieval" strategy, the to-be-forgotten and to-be-remembered items were apparently differentiated on the basis of spatial–temporal cues, and the subjects selectively retrieved the most recent items. Both the selective rehearsal and selective retrieval strategies facilitated recall relative to trials with the same number of items and no forget cue. Both strategies were effective in eliminating interference from the to-be-forgotten items.

When the significance of the forget cue was not explained, neither group used a selective rehearsal or selective retrieval strategy (Bray, Justice, & Simon, 1978). Adolescents without mental retardation required a brief explanation of the forget cue before they would use a selective rehearsal strategy. Adolescents with mental retardation, however, required a very careful explanation of the task demands before they began to use a selective rehearsal or selective retrieval strategy (Bray, Goodman, & Justice, 1982;

Bray et al., 1978). Thus, the use of a selective remembering strategy by individuals with and without mental retardation requires comprehension of the specific task demands (the forget cue in this case), and adolescents with mental retardation require a more extensive explanation of these task demands but do not require strategy training.

This pattern of results is apparently not specific to the selective remembering task. Belmont, Ferretti, and Mitchell (1982) found that adolescents with mental retardation used a rehearsal strategy in a circular recall task, whereas in many prior studies subjects had not. The main difference between the Belmont et al. study and others using circular recall was that the participants were given a very careful explanation of the task requirements. As was true in the selective remembering studies, there was no strategy training. When the adolescents with mental retardation understood the task demands, many were able to devise an appropriate strategy.

In an effort to assess task comprehension among students with and without mental retardation, Turner, Matherne, and Heller (1994) presented a sequential memory task either with or without performance feedback. A small number of students with mental retardation described the task as one of looking at or naming pictures, and others described it as a task requiring remembering. The students describing the task as a looking or a naming task recalled less than those who described it as a memory task. A failure to comprehend the nature of the task seems to have negatively influenced performance. Feedback was expected to increase comprehension and strategy use, but for the students with mental retardation it did not. The limited number of trials and/or the restriction of number of times the items could be studied may have contributed to the failure of feedback to influence task comprehension.

Information Processing Demands

Bray and Turner (1986) noted that several information processing demands influence strategy use in individuals with mental retardation. These include (a) the number of to-be-remembered items, (b) whether a retention interval is filled with a distracting activity or not, (c) the presentation rate, (d) the number of presentations, and (e) the amount of practice. Studies investigating the influence of each of these variables on strategy use in individuals with mental retardation were reviewed in detail by Bray and Turner (1986) and are mentioned only briefly here.

Number of To-Be-Remembered Items. Borys and Spitz (1976) found evidence for rehearsal with two, three, and four items per trial, but not for five items. They noted:

> When no distracting activity was interposed there was no forgetting for up to 4 pictures relative to the amount of material acquired at 0 sec delay. This suggests that retarded Ss, as do nonretarded Ss, adopt a rehearsal strategy to maintain information in short-term store, thereby resisting . . . simple decay. With 5 pictures, however, forgetting occurred . . . probably because five objects exceed the rehearsal set size of retarded individuals. (p. 214)

As noted previously, Spitz and Webreck (1972) found that adolescents with mental retardation could use repetition redundancy within supraspan digit strings when the "chunk size" was relatively short (e.g., 153153) but did not with longer sequences. More recently, Fletcher and Bray (1995) found that children and adolescents with mental retardation were more likely to report using a verbally based strategy when the number of to-be-remembered items was three or fewer than when the number was greater than three.

Perhaps the most extensive program of research on the influence of amount of to-be-remembered information on strategy use was reported by Spitz (1979). In several investigations of the Tower of Hanoi problem (which requires that stacked rings be moved from one pile to another without placing a larger ring atop a smaller ring), individuals with mental retardation were able to solve such problems as long as the number of steps "ahead" was relatively small. When conditions required that more than two steps be held in memory, individuals with mental retardation were very likely to fail. The Tower of Hanoi research and the other studies that have explicitly manipulated memory load indicate that limitations on the functional capacity of working memory influence strategy use in individuals with mental retardation. The same is likely to be true for individuals without mental retardation, although research on the effects of much higher memory loads on strategy use is yet to be conducted. The important point here seems to be that individuals with mental retardation demonstrate strategy competency with relatively low memory loads, suggesting that there are information processing limits that may mask the underlying strategic competency. Under some conditions (e.g., Borys & Spitz, 1976), individuals with mental retardation appear to be as strategic as individuals without mental retardation.

Filled Versus Unfilled Retention Intervals. A number of studies have been conducted with the assumption that a neutral but effortful activity such as counting backward or counting circles in a display would prevent rehearsal, whereas unfilled retention intervals would allow rehearsal (Bray & Turner, 1986). All of the studies that have included individuals with mental retardation have shown that they perform better with unfilled than with filled retention intervals (Anders, 1971; Belmont, 1972; Borys & Spitz, 1976; Fagan, 1968; Winters & Semchuk, 1982). These studies suggest that without distracting activity and with the requirement of maintaining a relatively small amount of information over a short period of time (up to 3 minutes), individuals with mental retardation use a rehearsal strategy.

Presentation Rate. Several studies of rehearsal strategies with individuals with mental retardation have varied presentation rate with the expectation that, if rehearsal is used, recall should increase as the rate of presentation becomes slower. Studies that varied the rate of presentation between .5 and 2.0 seconds have found better recall for adults without mental retardation but no effect for adults with mental retardation (Ellis, 1970, Experiments 1 and 2). However, studies that have included presentations rates slower than 2 seconds per item have found that longer presentations times result in increased recall for individuals with mental retardation (Detterman, 1974, Experiments 1 & 2; Dugas, 1975; Haynes, 1970). These studies imply that individuals with mental retardation may not use effective strategies with presentation rates equal to or less than 2 seconds per item, but may use rehearsal at rates slower than 2 seconds per item.

Number of Presentations. There have been two studies with children and adolescents with mental retardation that have allowed the subjects to determine the number of self-paced presentations before being tested for recall. Turner and Bray (1985) used a recall readiness task with children and adolescents with mental retardation, and found that 97% of the participants used a rehearsal strategy. On nearly every sequence of items, the subjects opted to view the items more than once and the older subjects viewed the sequence an average of six times. The self-initiated repetitions indicated that, when given the option, individuals with mental retardation will use a repetition strategy.

Similar results were obtained by Turner and Bray (1993). When children and adolescents were given the standard sequential memory task with one presentation per sequence, their self-paced study time patterns indicated little rehearsal. The groups given versions of the recall readiness tasks with self-initiated repetitions of the sequence showed marked evidence of the use of rehearsal, replicating the results of Turner and Bray (1985). For groups of children and adolescents without mental retardation, there were marked developmental increases in the use of rehearsal in both presentation conditions. The results of these two studies indicate that individuals with mental retardation are particularly sensitive to task demands constraining the number of presentations. When allowed to initiate multiple presentation, they usually do so, indicating that single-presentation tasks mask part of their strategy competency.

Amount of Practice. Several studies with adolescents and adults with mental retardation have found that indices of strategy use increase when practice is extended across multiple sessions. Ellis (1970, Experiment 2) tested subjects on a sequential memory task during 12 sessions with 36 trials per session. Primacy effects, usually taken as an index of the use of rehearsal, increased across sessions. Turnbull (1974) used a similar task with 14 sessions with seven trials each and also found that primacy increased across sessions. Bray (1973) conducted four experiments with 4 to 20 sessions each and found an increase in primacy across session in each experiment. In contrast, some of the most frequently cited studies of strategy abilities have used a single session and have found no evidence of primacy in individuals with mental retardation (e.g., Belmont & Butterfield, 1971). Thus, it appears that, with practice, primacy increases for individuals with mental retardation.

The studies on information processing demands such as memory load, filled versus unfilled retention intervals, presentation rate, number of self-initiated presentations, and amount of practice support the conclusion that there is considerable evidence for strategy competency in individuals with mental retardation. As noted by Bray and Turner (1986), this competency appears to be more fragile than the competency of individuals without mental retardation, but we have yet to understand the nature and extent of this competency. For instance, Bray, Saarnio, Borges, and Hawk (1994) noted that virtually all the studies of information processing demands and strategy use in individuals with mental retardation have used tasks that require verbal processing, and suggested that tasks that allow strategies that are not verbally based may demonstrate additional strategy competence. Studies on this issue are described next.

Tasks Allowing External Representation

It has been demonstrated that toddlers without mental retardation use external orientation strategies (e.g., touching, pointing) when required to remember the location of objects (Wellman, 1988). For instance, DeLoache, Cassidy, and Brown (1985) found that children 18 to 24 months of age will look at the hiding place, point to it, stand near it, and even peek at it during a delay interval. Wellman, Ritter, and Flavell (1975) demonstrated that 3-year-old children will visually fixate on a target, point to it, or touch it as a means of remembering the location of a hidden object. Preschool children will also manipulate to-be-remembered objects, and this manipulation may increase recall accuracy (Baker-Ward, Ornstein, & Holden, 1984; Fletcher, 1993), although not all attempts to use external strategies are successful (Ornstein, Baker-Ward, & Naus, 1988). These and other similar studies suggest that before children without mental retardation enter school they are capable of using external memory strategies in remembering objects or object locations.

Bray, Saarnio, Borges, and Hawk (1994) investigated external memory strategies in 11-year-old children with mental retardation and 7- and 11-year-old children without mental retardation. The task allowed the use of both internal (e.g., verbal) and external memory strategies (e.g, pointing at, orienting toward, and manipulating objects). The participants were shown movable objects and fixed targets and asked to follow sequences of instructions such as "Put the eraser on the chair; put the pencil on the table."

In a baseline condition, the children with mental retardation and the 7-year-olds were *more* likely to use an object-oriented (pointing to or holding the movable objects) than were the 11-year-olds. Although these strategies were not as beneficial as target-oriented strategies (holding and moving objects toward the targets), it is clear that children with mental retardation were actively attempting to remember the instructions. It is also important to note that when object-oriented strategies were used, all three groups used the same tactics. Thus, the groups differed in the likelihood that an object-oriented strategy would be used, but the similarities in the choice of tactics used suggest commonalities in the cognitive abilities that underlies this choice.

In a minimal prompt condition, the participants were told that it was okay to pick up the objects and move them, but they were not given any instructions concerning where to move the objects. This minimal prompt was sufficient to result in a substantial shift in the type of strategy used. In contrast to baseline, in which few participants used a target-oriented strategy, 90% of the participants used these strategies following the minimal prompt. Nearly every instance of this type of strategy in all three groups involved placing the object in front of the target. Bray et al. noted: "A relatively minimal prompt resulted in very active strategy use that was anything but random and which included tactics that went beyond the information given in the prompt; participants in all three age/intelligence groups moved the objects so that they were oriented to the target, not placed haphazardly" (p. 29).

This pattern of results suggests that when children with mental retardation are given very minimal prompts, they are able to devise more efficient and beneficial strategies that incorporate the same tactics as do children without mental retardation. There appears to be a great deal of commonality in the cognitive competencies that underlie the selection of strategies and tactics when children with and without mental retardation are given minimal prompts. In contrast to a substantial literature showing deficiencies in the use of verbally based strategies (e.g., see Bray & Turner, 1986), this study indicated areas of overlap in strategy competency in children with and without mental retardation in a task that allows external representation as a memory strategy.

Similar results were obtained by Fletcher and Bray (1995) in a somewhat more complex task that allowed both verbal and external strategies. The memory task was embedded in a tape-recorded story in which the participant was guided through a haunted house by a friendly ghost. As the participant entered each imaginary room, he or she was given from one to seven instructions such as "The broom is above the ghost" and "The lamp is on the blue side of the broom," where the "blue side" was the right-hand side and "pink side" was the left-hand side. At the end of the sequence the experimenter opened a plexiglass door and the participant placed the miniature objects (e.g., broom, lamp) on a computer screen with a small plastic ghost at the center. The screen represented the imaginary room. The participants were 11- and 18-year old children and adolescents with mental retardation, and 7-, 9-, 11-, and 18-year-old children and adolescents without mental retardation.

As in Bray, Saarnio, Borges, and Hawk (1994), all groups in the Fletcher and Bray (1995) study used a variety of external memory strategies, including pointing to the objects and holding and/or moving them on the table in front of them. In addition, many participants arranged the objects either in their hands or on the table. The arrangement strategies were the most interesting and most effective. With these strategies the participants arranged the objects around a central point either in their hand or on the table. When asked, some reported that the central point represented the ghost on the screen. The objects were arranged relative to the central point (e.g., for "The broom is above the ghost; the lamp is on the blue side of the broom," the broom was placed above the central point and the lamp to the right of the broom).

For all groups, the proportion of trials on which an arrangement strategy was used increased as the number of to-be-remembered instructions increased. Although the adolescents without mental retardation used arrangement strategies most frequently, adolescents with mental retardation used these elaborate and very effective strategies on more than 20% of the trials. Also, the use of pointing and holding the objects (the least effective strategies) decreased as memory load increased for the children and adolescents with mental retardation. The participants with mental retardation used pointing and holding less frequently than did the younger children without mental retardation and with the same frequency as their chronological age peers.

Although there was considerable similarity in the pattern of performance on the arrangement strategy and virtual overlap in performance on pointing and holding strategies between the two intelligence groups, there was no overlap on a task that allowed no external strategies. In this task, the participants were given similar verbal instructions (with different objects and different prepositions) but were asked to recall the instructions verbatim. As has been observed in many studies using verbally based tasks, the participants with mental retardation performed very poorly and showed very little evidence of strategy use. This pattern of results indicated that individuals with mental retardation have strategy capabilities that are underestimated by the use of verbally based tasks. In tasks that allow external representation, children and adolescents with mental retardation demonstrate considerably more strategy competency than they do on verbally based tasks.

One particularly important finding in the Fletcher and Bray (1995) study was that when the frequency of all observed external strategies and verbal strategies was combined on trials with three or less sentences, there were no differences between the children with and without mental retardation. This indicates that at the lower memory loads (without a ceiling effect), the children with mental retardation were as likely to use a memory strategy as were children of the same chronological age. These results provide a clear demonstration that children with mental retardation do not have production deficiencies as has been previously assumed.

Although the results of Fletcher and Bray (1995) indicate that external memory tasks may offer more support than do verbal memory tasks, additional supports such as verbal or physical cues may also increase external strategy use in children with and without mental retardation. A study by Bray, Fletcher, Huffman, Hawk, and Ward (1994) described the use of external strategies in conditions that varied in the degree of situational support for strategy use.

The participants were 264 children: 7-, 9-, 11-, and 17-year-old typical students, and 11- and 17-year-old students with mental retardation. The participants were given the instruction following (haunted house) task of Fletcher and Bray (1995). There were four between-subjects conditions. In the model/prompt condition, a model of the computer screen was available during sentence presentation. During the first day the participants were given a verbal prompt of "You can do anything that you think will help yourself remember." During the second day, the participants were given the verbal prompt of "I want you to move the objects in a way that will help you to remember where the objects are." In the no-model/no-prompt condition the participants were tested without the model and were given no verbal prompt. The other two conditions were no model/prompt and model/no-prompt.

For the 7-year-old children, the physical cues but not the verbal cues facilitated use of external arrangement strategies. For the 9- and 11-year olds, both the verbal cues and physical cues facilitated the use of arrangement strategies, whereas only the verbal cues did in the 17-year-old group. The arrangement strategy facilitated recall. For the 11-year-old children with mental retardation, neither the verbal nor the physical cues were sufficient to increase the use of arrangement strategies, but for the 17-year-old children with mental retardation, the combination of physical and verbal cues resulted in a level of strategy use equivalent to that of their chronological age peers.

These results demonstrate that the strategy competency of children with mental retardation may be accessed and activated to the same level of children without mental retardation without direct instruction. It appears that strategy competency in children with and without mental retardation is similar, but the cognitive potential of children with mental retardation requires more situational support before strategies are adopted (but direct strategy training is not always necessary). It now seems that the issue of strategy training and strategy generalization should be reassessed; generalization of strategies that children discover without direct strategy training may be broader than generalization following direct strategy training. Given that individuals with mental retardation typically fail to generalize strategy training (e.g., Belmont & Mitchell, 1987), the possibility of increased breadth of generalizing following strategy discovery without direct strategy training is a important issue for further research.

We would like to note that the external memory task was derived from observation of the performance of young children without mental retardation. In fact, Wellman (1988) suggested that external orientation strategies may be precursors of verbally based strategies. External representation and other types of strategies that develop in young children (e.g., counting, early addition, searching, route planning) may be rich areas for future investigation of strategy competency in individuals with mental retardation. If we look to developmental psychology as a source of tasks and phenomena to investigate, rather than relying exclusively on adaptations of tasks used with adults (college students), we may obtain a more comprehensive and less pessimistic picture of the abilities of individuals with mental retardation.

CONCLUSION: STRATEGY COMPETENCIES AND DEFICITS IN WORKING MEMORY

We have presented evidence for competencies in nonstrategic aspects of memory functioning and strategy competency for individuals with mental retardation. The research on nonstrategic aspects of information processing indicated that much of the "machinery" necessary for cognition appears to be intact in individuals with mental retardation. This includes many aspects of information processing that would seem to be a part of the basis for cognition, including the use of rhythm for comprehension of speech, spread of activation, use of stimulus organization, short-term retention rate, long- term retention, and organization of semantic memory. These cognitive competencies can now be used to constrain the development of hypotheses concerning the nature of other cognitive competencies and deficiencies.

We think the collective impact of the studies on strategy competencies is even more dramatic. In cross-sectional and longitudinal studies, there are developmental increases in memory performance and strategy use in individuals with mental retardation. On sequential memory tasks, many individuals with mental retardation use rehearsal strategies if they comprehend the task demands (e.g., Belmont et al., 1982; Bray, Turner, & Hersh, 1985). They also use maintenance strategies during an unfilled retention interval of up to 3 minutes if the number of to-be-remembered items is fewer than five. They use increased exposure time to increase their recall as long as the presentation time is greater than 2 seconds. They show increases in the amount of primacy if given several sessions on a sequential memory task (Bray, 1973; Ellis, 1970, Experiment 2; Turnbull, 1974). They use repetition strategies in tasks that allow them to re-present the items as often as they would like (Turner & Bray, 1985, 1993). They move objects in order to construct an external representation of the location of information to be remembered or arrange objects in a spatial array in external memory tasks (Bray, Fletcher, Huffman, Hawk, & Ward, 1994; Bray, Saarnio, Borges, & Hawk, 1994; Fletcher & Bray, 1995).

We think that this pattern of results obtained from a variety of tasks and situations is sufficient to conclude that individuals with mental retardation have considerable strategy competency. In this pattern of results we see evidence that individuals with mental retardation have cognitive structures that allow them to devise strategies in a variety of situations. There is strategy competency that is drawn on when individuals with mental retardation attempt to cope with the information processing demands of diverse situations.

Although we have come to understand something important about the strategy competency of individuals with mental retardation, the observation of Bray and Turner (1986) that these competencies are fragile remains valid. This strategy competency is not as broad or as robust as that found in individuals without mental retardation, but we think the nature of this competency is the same in both intelligence groups. We think that the strategy competency of individuals with mental retardation is modulated by a deficit in working memory. In particular, the evidence seems to suggest that there are functional limitations in the capacity of working memory and that these limits appear to be more severe in individuals with mental retardation than in individuals without mental retardation (Spitz, 1979). We hypothesize that these limitations play a central role in the slower developmental change in strategy use in individuals with mental retardation, in the restrictions on the number of items that can be maintained during a blank retention interval, in the amount of explanation of task demands required before a strategy is used, in restrictions on the presentation rate that can be used to show a facilitation in recall, in the requirement of an option for self-initiated re-presentation of sequences for clear evidence of a repetition strategy, in the requirement of multiple sessions for the emergence of primacy effects, and for the use of external objects (and their accompanying reduction on memory demands) before sophisticated external representation strategies are used.

This pattern of constraints on the strategy competency is consistent with the conclusion that the performance of individuals with mental retardation may be restricted by the functional capacity of working memory (Spitz, 1979). What we have added is that within the constraints imposed by the more limited capacity of working memory in individuals with mental retardation, the strategy competency, per se, appears to be similar regardless of intelligence level. This conclusion is radically different than that reached by the majority of investigators of memory processes in individuals with mental retardation, but we think it is warranted based on the nature and range of situations in which strategy competency has been observed.

Much work remains to be done before this hypothesis can be either confirmed more directly or disconfirmed. One important step will be to tie the observation of strategy competencies and strategy deficiencies to measures of the functional capacity of working memory and to describe these relationships across a wide variety of tasks. Another important step will be to continue widening the range of situations studied in which strategy use functionally reduces the load on working memory. For this issue, it is likely that situations allowing external representation will prove to be very fruitful. These would include those allowing counting on one's fingers to solve simple addition and subtraction or calculating the number of months between specific dates within a year. Also, planning routes on simple maps is likely to be an area in which individuals with mental retardation have competence because of the external representation possible in this situation. Search tasks may also be fruitful for the same reason. These tasks may represent familiar problems encountered in daily life in which memory load can be reduced by the use of external aids such as maps, tools, orientation of objects, or simple bodily orientation. In all these situations, competence should be evident as long as the task is within the functional working memory capacity of the individual with mental retardation, and deficits should become evident when the demands of the task exceed these limits. We would also expect to see important developmental changes in the functional limitations of working memory and accompanying increases in strategy competency. In a similar way, within a particular age group, we would expect individual differences in strategy use to be related to the relationship between the demands of the task and the functional limitations on the capacity of working memory.

The investigation and theoretical discussion of competencies along with deficits may result in the discovery and appropriate attention to a continuum of strategic behaviors and a clearer understanding of the factors that influence the discovery and use of strategies. We agree with Gelman (1979), who noted that "many of the best insights will come from understanding exactly what conditions interfere with the use and accessibility of those capacities the child does possess" (p. 904). We believe that such an approach to strategy competencies will make important contributions to a general theory of the cognitive nature of mental retardation.

REFERENCES

Anders, T. R. (1971). Short-term memory for serially presented supraspan information in non-retarded and mentally retarded individuals. *American Journal of Mental Deficiency, 75*, 571–578.

Baillargeon, R., & DeVos, J. (1991). Object permanence in young infants: Further evidence. *Child Development, 62*, 1227–1246.

Baker-Ward, L., Ornstein, P. A., & Holden, D. J. (1984). The expression of memorization in early childhood. *Journal of Experimental Child Psychology, 37*, 555–575.

Battig, W. F., & Montague, W. E. (1969). Category norms for verbal items in 56 categories: A replication and extension of the Connecticut category norms. *Journal of Experimental Psychology Monograph, 80*, 1–46.

Belmont, J. M. (1972). Relations of age and intelligence to short-term color memory. *Child Development, 43*, 19–29.

Belmont, J. M., & Butterfield, E. C. (1971). Learning strategies as determinants of memory deficiencies. *Cognitive Psychology, 2*, 411–420.

Belmont, J. M., Ferretti, R. P., & Mitchell, D. W. (1982). Memorizing: A test of untrained retarded children's problem solving. *American Journal of Mental Deficiency, 87*, 197–210.

Belmont, J. M., & Mitchell, D. W. (1987). The general strategies hypothesis as applied to cognitive theory in mental retardation. *Intelligence, 11*, 91–105.

Borys, S. V., & Spitz, H. H. (1976). Short-term retention in retarded adolescents as a function of load, delay, and interpolated activity. *Journal of Psychology, 94*, 207–216.

Braine, M. D. S. (1959). The ontogeny of certain logical operations: Piaget's formulation examined by nonverbal methods. *Psychological Monographs, 73* (Whole No. 475).

Bray, N. W. (1973). Controlled forgetting in the retarded. *Cognitive Psychology, 5*, 288–309.

Bray, N. W. (1979). Strategy production in the retarded. In N. R. Ellis (Ed.), *Handbook of mental deficiency, psychological theory and research* (2nd ed., pp. 699–726). Hillsdale, NJ: Lawrence Erlbaum Associates.

Bray, N. W., Fletcher, K. L., Huffman, L. F., Hawk, T. M., & Ward, J. L. (1994, April). *Developmental differences in the use of models and verbal prompts in support of external strategies*. Poster presented at the Conference on Human Development, Pittsburgh, PA.

Bray, N. W., Goodman, M. A., & Justice, E. M. (1982). Task instructions and strategy transfer in the directed forgetting performance of mentally retarded adolescents. *Intelligence, 6*, 187–200.

Bray, N. W., Hersh, R. E., & Turner, L. A. (1985). Selective remembering during adolescence. *Developmental Psychology, 21*, 290–294.

Bray, N. W., Justice, E. M., & Simon, D. L. (1978). The sufficient conditions for directed forgetting in normal and educable mentally retarded adolescents. *Intelligence, 2*, 153–167.

Bray, N. W., & Palmer, R. L. (1993). *Mechanisms of selective remembering in young children.* Unpublished manuscript.

Bray, N. W., Saarnio, D. A., Borges, L. M., & Hawk, L. W. (1994). Intellectual and developmental differences in external memory strategies. *American Journal on Mental Retardation, 99*, 19–31.

Bray, N. W., & Turner, L. A. (1986). The rehearsal deficit hypothesis. In N. R. Ellis & N. W. Bray (Eds.), *International review of research in mental retardation* (Vol. 14, pp. 47–71). New York: Academic Press.

Bray, N. W., & Turner, L. A. (1987). Production anomalies (not strategic deficiencies) in mentally retarded individuals. *Intelligence, 11*, 49–60.

Bray, N. W., Turner, L. A., & Hersh, R. E. (1985). Developmental progressions and regressions in the selective remembering strategies of EMR individuals. *American Journal of Mental Deficiency, 90*, 198–205.

Brown, A. L. (1974). The role of strategic behavior in retardate memory. In N. R. Ellis (Ed.), *International review of research in mental retardation* (Vol. 7, pp. 55–111). New York: Academic Press.

Brown, A. L. (1976). Semantic integration in children's reconstruction of narrative sequences. *Cognitive Psychology, 8*, 247–262.

Brown, A. L., & Barclay, C. R. (1976). The effects of training specific mnemonics on the metamnemonic efficiency of retarded children. *Child Development, 47*, 71–80.

Brown, A. L., Campione, J. C., & Barclay, C. R. (1979). Training self-checking routines for estimating test readiness: Generalization from list learning to prose recall. *Cognitive Development, 50*, 501–512.

Dann, L. E. (1984). *Effects of rhythmic cues in speech and sentence information load on comprehension in educable mentally retarded and nonretarded children.* Unpublished doctoral dissertation, University of Alabama, Tuscaloosa.

DeLoache, J. S., Cassidy, D. J., & Brown, A. L. (1985). Precursors of mnemonic strategies in very young children's memory. *Child Development, 56*, 125–137.

Detterman, D. K. (1974). Primacy effects in short-term memory with the mentally retarded. *Child Development, 45*, 1077–1082.

Detterman, D. K. (1987). Theoretical notions of intelligence and mental retardation. *American Journal of Mental Deficiency, 92*, 2–11.

Dugas, J. (1975). Effects of stimulus familiarity on the rehearsal transfer mechanism in retarded and nonretarded individuals. *American Journal of Mental Deficiency, 80*, 349–356.

Dulaney, C. L., & Ellis, N. R. (1991). Long-term recognition memory for items and attributes by retarded and nonretarded persons. *Intelligence, 15*, 105–115.

Ellis, N. R. (1963). The stimulus trace and behavioral inadequacy. In N. R. Ellis (Ed.), *Handbook of mental deficiency* (pp. 134–158). New York: McGraw-Hill.

Ellis, N. R. (1970). Memory processes in retardates and normals. In N. R. Ellis (Ed.), *International review of research in mental retardation* (Vol. 4, pp. 1–32). New York: Academic Press.

Ellis, N. R. (1978). Do the mentally retarded have poor memory? *Intelligence, 2*, 41–54.

Ellis, N. R., Katz, E., & Williams, J. E. (1987). Developmental aspects of memory for spatial location. *Journal of Experimental Child Psychology, 44*, 401–412.

Ellis, N. R., McCartney, J. R., Ferretti, R. P., & Cavalier, A. R. (1977). Recognition memory in mentally retarded persons. *Intelligence, 1*, 310–317.

Ellis, N. R., Meador, D. M., & Bodfish, J. W. (1985). Differences in intelligence and automatic memory processes. *Intelligence, 9*, 265–273.

Ellis, N. R., Palmer, R. L., & Reeves, C. L. (1988). Developmental and intellectual differences in frequency processing. *Developmental Psychology, 24*, 38–45.

Ellis, N. R., Woodley-Zanthos, P., & Dulaney, C. L. (1989). Memory for spatial location in children, adults, and mentally retarded persons. *American Journal on Mental Retardation, 93*, 521–527.

Ericsson, K. A. (1988). Analysis of memory performance in terms of memory skills. In R. J. Sternberg (Ed.), *Advances in the psychology of human intelligence* (Vol. 4, pp. 137–179). Hillsdale, NJ: Lawrence Erlbaum Associates.

Fagan, J. F. (1968). Short-term memory processes in normal and retarded children. *Journal of Experimental Child Psychology, 6*, 279–296.

Ferretti, R. P. (1979). *An analysis of passive memory in normal and mentally retarded persons.* Unpublished doctoral dissertation, University of Alabama, Tuscaloosa.

Ferretti, R. P., & Cavalier, A. R. (1991). Constraints on the problem solving of persons with mental retardation. In N. W. Bray (Ed.), *International review of research in mental retardation* (Vol. 17, pp. 153–192). San Diego, CA: Academic Press.

Flavell, J. H. (1992). Cognitive development: Past, present, and future. *Developmental Psychology, 28*, 998–1005.

Fletcher, K. L. (1993). *External orientation and memory strategy use in preschool children.* Unpublished master's thesis, University of Alabama, Birmingham.

Fletcher, K. L. (1995). *Instructional and contextual effects on external strategy use in preschool children.* Unpublished doctoral dissertation, University of Alabama, Birmingham.

Fletcher, K. L., & Bray, N. W. (1995). External and verbal strategies in children with and without mild mental retardation. *American Journal on Mental Retardation, 99*, 363–375.

Gelman, R. (1979). Preschool thought. *American Psychologist, 34*, 900–905.

Hasher, L., & Zacks, R. T. (1979). Automatic and effortful processes in memory. *Journal of Experimental Psychology: General, 108*, 356–388.

Haynes, J. R. (1970). Effects of white noise and presentation rate on serial learning in mentally retarded individuals. *American Journal of Mental Deficiency, 74*, 574–577.

Inhelder, B., & Piaget, J. (1964). *The early growth of logic in the child: Classification and seriation.* London: Routledge.

Markman, E. M., & Seibert, J. (1976). Classes and collections: Internal organization and resulting holistic properties. *Cognitive Psychology, 8*, 561–577.

McCartney, J. R. (1987). Mentally retarded and nonretarded subjects' long-term recognition memory. *American Journal of Mental Retardation, 92*, 312–317.

Nigro, G. N., & Roak, R. M. (1987). Mentally retarded and nonretarded adults' memory for spatial location. *American Journal of Mental Deficiency, 91*, 392–397.

Ornstein, P. A., Baker-Ward, L., & Naus, M. J. (1988). The development of mnemonic skill. In F. E. Weinert & M. Perlmutter (Eds.), *Memory development: Universal changes and individual differences* (pp. 31–50). Hillsdale, NJ: Lawrence Erlbaum Associates.

Piaget, J. (1954). *The construction of reality in the child.* New York: Basic Books.

Siegler, R. S. (1991). *Children's thinking.* Englewood Cliffs, NJ: Prentice-Hall.

Sperber, R. D., Ragain, R. D., & McCauley, C. (1976). Reassessment of category knowledge in retarded individuals. *American Journal of Mental Deficiency, 81*, 227–234.

Spitz, H. H. (1973). The channel capacity of educable mental retardates. In D. K. Routh (Ed.), *The experimental psychology of mental retardation* (pp. 133–156). Chicago: Aldine.

Spitz, H. H. (1979). Beyond field theory in the study of mental deficiency. In N. R. Ellis (Ed.), *Handbook of mental deficiency, psychological theory and research* (2nd ed., pp. 121–141). Hillsdale, NJ: Lawrence Erlbaum Associates.

Spitz, H. H., & Webreck, C. A. (1972). Effects of spontaneous vs. externally-cued learning on the permanent storage of a schema by retardates. *American Journal of Mental Deficiency, 77*, 163–168.

Turnbull, A. P. (1974). Teaching retarded persons to rehearse through cumulative overt labeling. *American Journal of Mental Deficiency, 79*, 331–337.

Turner, L. A., & Bray, N. W. (1985). Spontaneous rehearsal in mildly mentally retarded children and adolescents. *American Journal of Mental Deficiency, 90*, 57–63.

Turner, L. A., & Bray, N. W. (1993). *The role of tasks and measures in developmental change in strategy use.* Unpublished manuscript.

Turner, L. A., Hale, C., & Borkowski, J. G. (1996). Influence of intelligence on memory development. *American Journal on Mental Retardation, 100*, 468–480.

Turner, L. A., Matherne, J. L., & Heller, S. S. (1994). The effects of performance feedback on memory strategy use and recall accuracy in students with and without mild mental retardation. *Journal of Experimental Education, 62*, 303–315.

Turnure, J. E. (1991). Long-term memory and mental retardation. In N. W. Bray (Ed.), *International review of research in mental retardation* (Vol. 17, pp. 193–217). San Diego, CA: Academic Press.

Vernon, P. E. (1976). Development of intelligence. In V. Hamilton & M. D. Vernon (Eds.), *The development of cognitive processes* (pp. 507–547). London: Academic Press.

Wellman, H. M. (1988). The early development of memory strategies. In F. E. Weinert & M. Perlmutter (Eds.), *Memory development: Universal changes and individual differences* (pp. 3–29). Hillsdale, NJ: Lawrence Erlbaum Associates.

Wellman, H. M., Ritter, K., & Flavell, J. H. (1975). Deliberate memory behavior in the delayed reactions of very young children. *Developmental Psychology, 11*, 780–787.

Wickens, D. D. (1970). Encoding categories of words: An empirical approach to meaning. *Psychological Review, 77*, 1–15.

Winters, J. J., Jr. (1982). Proactive inhibition in retarded persons: Factors influencing accumulation and release. In K. D. Gadow & I. Bialer (Eds.), *Advances in learning and behavioral disabilities: An annual compilation of theory and research* (Vol. 1, pp. 151–190). Greenwich, CT: JAI.

Winters, J. J., Jr. (1985). Proactive inhibition in retarded persons: Some clues to short-term memory processing. In N. R. Ellis & N. W. Bray (Eds.), *International review of research in mental retardation* (Vol. 13, pp. 279–300). Orlando, FL: Academic Press.

Winters, J. J., Jr., & Semchuk, M. T. (1982). Proactive inhibition by mentally retarded persons: Effects of distractor vocalization. *American Journal of Mental Deficiency, 87*, 231–233.

Zeaman, D. (1978). Some relations of general intelligence and selective attention. *Intelligence, 2*, 55–73.

Zeaman, D., & House, B. J. (1963). The role of attention in retardate discrimination learning. In N. R. Ellis (Ed.), *Handbook of mental deficiency* (pp. 159–223). New York: McGraw-Hill.

Zigler, E. (1969). Developmental vs. difference theories of mental retardation and the problem of motivation. *American Journal of Mental Deficiency, 73*, 536–556.

Zigler, E., & Balla, D. (1982). Introduction: The developmental approach to mental retardation. In E. Zigler & D. Balla (Eds.), *Mental retardation: The developmental-difference controversy* (pp. 3–8). Hillsdale, NJ: Lawrence Erlbaum Associates.

› 9 ‹

Attention in Mentally Retarded Persons

Phillip D. Tomporowski
University of Florida

Veronica Tinsley
Brescia College

The construct of attention has played a central role in the study of mental retardation. Practitioners and academicans alike have invoked attentional processes to explain many of the behaviors of mentally retarded persons. Several general theories of attention have guided research in the field. The following review provides a summary of several approaches to the study of attention within the framework of information processing theory, as well as a selective overview of research on attention in mentally retarded persons.

VARIETIES OF ATTENTION

Attention is a multifaceted construct that is manifested in a variety of ways. Although a number of schemes have been proposed to classify attention, most identify three types: focused attention, which involves selective processing of information; divided attention, which involves processing two or more sources of information; and sustained attention, which involves vigilance (Davies & Parasuraman, 1982; Parasuraman & Davies, 1984; Treisman, 1969). Numerous theoretical views have been proposed over the past three decades to both describe and explain attention. Current theories of attention can be viewed as descendants of the classical information processing models of cognition developed in the 1950s and 1960s. Models of cognitive processing developed by Broadbent (1958), Miller, Galanter, and Pribram (1960), and Atkinson and Shiffrin (1968), for example, attempted to explain how cognitive processes intervene between the detection of stimuli and the execution of responses. Common to these models is the assumption that cognitive processes are involved in the selection, organization, and utilization of information provided by the environment to determine behavior.

Many current theories of attention can be linked to common ancestors; however, their evolution over the past 30 years has resulted in considerable diversity. Broadbent's (1982) historical review of theories of attention led him to conclude that a variety of theoretical approaches to attention exist, because different academic traditions provided fertile ground for growth and development. Current theories of attention tend to reflect such diverse areas of study as psychophysics, learning, mathematical psychology, human factors, artificial intelligence, and higher mental processes. Broadbent further concluded that research and theory development tended to be restricted within the various academic traditions with relatively little communication occuring across traditions.

Despite the diversity of the approaches that have been taken to study attentional processes and the lack of a comprehensive theory of attention, a body of knowledge has gradually accumulated that provides insights into the functions of attentional processes. Next we describe four theoretical approaches to the conceptualization of attention that have had an impact on the study of mentally retarded persons.

1. Attention Viewed as a Filter. It has long been suggested that we live in "noisy" environments; that is, our sensory systems are continuously bombarded with stimulation. Broadbent (1958) provided an early conceptualization of the manner in which information is analyzed and selected for further processing. In his theory, stimuli from a variety of sensory channels converge on a single attentional processor that functions much like a switchboard, in that it can analyze input from only one sensory channel at a time. The attentional processor can switch rapidly from one input channel to the next, but the architecture of the system limits the amount of information that enters memory systems. The notion that attention worked like a filtering mechanism prompted considerable research to evaluate the characteristics and locus of the attentional "bottleneck" (Deutsch & Deutsch, 1963; Kahneman & Treisman, 1984; Keele, 1973; Treisman, 1969, 1988; Treisman & Gelade, 1980). More recently, Broadbent (1982) suggested that the selection of information is governed by three strategies: a fast-acting filtering strategy that selects information on the basis of shared physical properties, a slow-acting categorization strategy that selects information on the basis of class membership, and a pigeonholing strategy that selects information on the basis of a bias that develops toward certain categories. The selection of information for processing is believed to occur soon after the registration of environmental events in the sensory system. The assumption that attentional processing takes place during the early phases of information processing has prompted considerable research on processes that underlie stimulus detection, pattern recognition, and perceptual organization.

2. Attention Viewed as Capacity. Moray (1969) suggested that cognitive systems function somewhat like computer systems. The ability of a system to process information is limited by its architecture and available computational space. It was hypothesized that, as the amount or the complexity of data to be processed increases, there is a corresponding increase in demand for processing space. When processing demands exceed available computational space, performance will deteriorate unless the space that is available is differentially allocated to the various processing tasks. In a sense, attention can be viewed as fuel that provides the energy necessary for information processing systems to function. The cognitive systems involved in the detection and selection of stimuli, the maintenance of information in memory, and the retrieval of information from memory draw on a limited pool of attentional capacity.

The notion that attention is a capacity that can be allocated to different cognitive processes is central to an influential theory proposed by Kahneman (1973). He suggested that one could choose to allocate available attention to various concurrent cognitive processes. One's allocation policy is affected by such factors as current level of arousal, momentary intentions, enduring dispositions, and previous experience. Kahneman's theory (1973) and others that have emphasized the capacity model (Navon & Gopher, 1979; Norman & Bobrow, 1975; Wickens, 1984, 1987) provide the bases for a great deal of research on factors that underlie divided attention and shifts in the allocation of attentional resources.

3. Attention Viewed as Automatic or Effortful Processing. Attention is often linked to such phenomenological states as awareness or consciousness. Traditionally, tests of attention focus on conditions under which stimuli are detected, classified, and become part of memory systems. Tests of these types demand effortful processing in the sense that changes in performance are related to the availablity of attentional resources. Since the late 1970s, however, there has been an interest in attentional processes that do not impinge on consciousness; that is, information processing without awareness. Several theorists have dichotomized attention as automatic and effortful. Attention of the former type is characterized as rapid, not under voluntary control, and unaffected by memory processing (Schneider & Shiffrin, 1977; Shiffrin & Schneider, 1977). Other theorists tend to view attention in terms of the mixture of effortful and automatic processing (Kahneman & Treisman, 1984), or in terms of a continuum in which some cognitive processes are highly automatic and others are highly effortful (Hasher & Zacks, 1979).

A considerable literature exists on the nature of automatic and effortful processing and its relation to the allocation of attention (see Kahneman & Treisman, 1984; Logan, 1988; Schneider, Dumais, & Shiffrin, 1984). Automatic processing has been linked to inherent biological systems and to learning experiences (Hasher & Zacks, 1979; Posner, 1978; Shiffrin & Schneider, 1977). It also plays a role in directing attention, because prior experience with specific types of stimulus information prepares, or primes, responding without awareness (Marcel, 1983; Posner, 1978, 1980; Posner, Nisser, & Ogden, 1978). Automatic processing is thought to enhance the efficiency of cognitive processing as it allows some aspects of behavior to take place without conscious attention and without the need to draw on attentional resources (Carr, 1984). Reading, for example, is more efficient when an entire word is processed than it is when one attends to each letter of the word.

4. Attention Viewed as a Part of Working Memory. Theorists have also incorporated attentional processes into larger conceptual frameworks. Baddeley (1986) suggested that research undertaken to study attention in isolation of other underlying cognitive processes will not be very profitable. Baddeley and Hitch (1974) introduced a model that integrated the functions of memory structures with the processes that control those structures, and Baddeley (1986, 1990) provides considerable empirical support for the system. The central activity of working memory is to make decisions concerning the storage and manipulation of information. Efficient processing involves trade-offs between processing functions and storage functions. The system has a central executive processor that attends to and integrates information from a variety of sources and selects strategies that are necessary for efficient functioning. The central processor combines the functions of attention and metacognition to orchestrate the activities of the working memory system.

These four approaches to the study of attention emphasize different aspects of attention; however, they adhere to a common framework—the information processing model. Recent theories of attention in mentally retarded individuals have drawn greatly from this model. A general hypothesis derived from the model is that the cognitive performance of retarded individuals will be more adversely affected than that of nonretarded individuals as increased demands are placed on attentional processes. Earlier theories of attention in mentally retarded persons were typically couched in terms of general learning theory. Intelligence-related differences in discrimination learning were usually explained as examples of mentally retarded individuals' failure to attend to relevant stimulus dimensions associated with task demands (Denny, 1964, 1966; Luria, 1963; O'Connor & Hermelin, 1963; Zeaman & House, 1963, 1979) or to distractibility (Crosby & Blatt, 1968). Although theories of attention in retarded persons tend to reflect the zeitgeist, the main topics of interest have remained the same. In the next section, we provide an overview of one information processing approach to the study of attention.

MENTAL RETARDATION, INFORMATION PROCESSING, AND ATTENTION

Information processing theories of attention emphasize interactions between structure and control processes. Mosley (1980) provided an example of such a model as it relates to the study of mental retardation. The proposed relation between structural components and control processes is depicted in Fig. 9.1. The structural components of the system include the sensory registers, a short-term memory store, and a long-term memory store. Information that flows through the system is stored within these structures. The manner in which information is evaluated and transferred among storage structures is directed by control processes; they are involved in stimulus detection and selection, and in the manipulation of information in short- and long-term memory stores. Attention is viewed in Mosley's model as central to the activities of control processes. The case is made that retarded and nonretarded individuals differ in the way they allocate attentional resources.

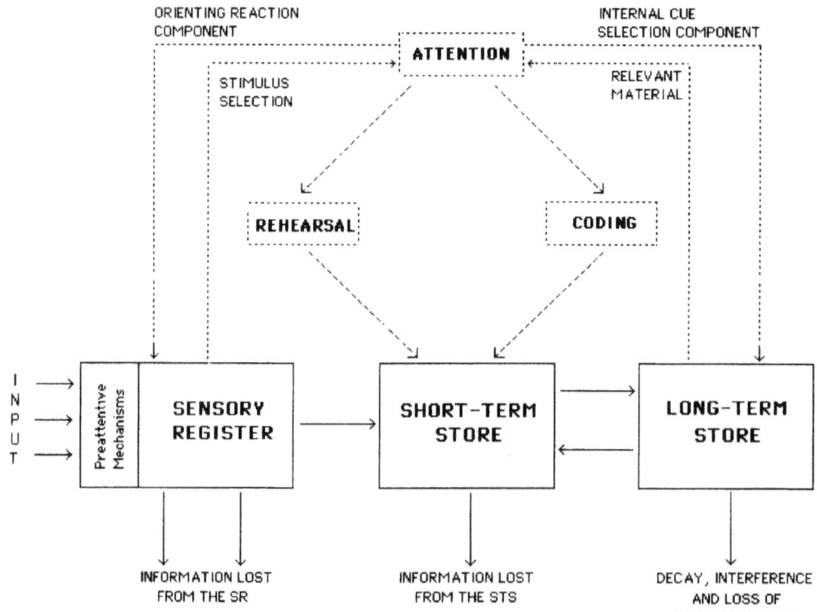

FIG. 9.1. A multistore model of attention that shows the relation between structural features of the memory system (solid lines) and control processes (broken lines). (From Mosley, 1980). Reprinted by permission of the American Association on Mental Retardation.

As a result, IQ-related differences in performance are predicted at each stage of the information processing system. Mentally retarded individuals are believed either to possess fewer attentional resources than do nonretarded individuals, or they elect not to allocate their available resources to process information (see Merrill, 1990; Sperber & McCauley, 1984, for reviews).

Researchers over the past 2 decades have accumulated considerable information concerning IQ-related differences in cognition. Sophisticated methodological techniques have been developed to isolate factors that underlie differences between the performance of mentally retarded and nonretarded persons. The use of interaction-type experimental designs, in which the performance of groups of subjects who differ with regard to level of intelligence is assessed under several levels of task conditions, has provided the basis for specific explanations of IQ-related differences in cognition (Stanovich, 1978). Despite an increase in the sophistication of the research methods used, studies that assess differences between the performance of retarded and nonretarded individuals have certain methodological difficulties. For instance, problems arise in the interpretation of research findings obtained with tasks that have been modified to equate their level of difficulty across level of intelligence. Furthermore, laboratory tests that measure basic cognitive processes often place subjects in environments that can be intimidating and perhaps anxiety provoking. Such variables as subjects' test-taking experience, level of motivation, and practice history are known to affect performance. (See Baumeister, 1984, and Merrill, 1990, for discussions of design issues.)

The research selected for the following review bears on relations between attention and the function of basic information processing structures and the extent to which attention can be called on to explain individual differences in the cognitive performance. The model proposed by Mosley (1980) guided our review. We examined how focused and selective attention play a role in processing at the sensory-registration stage, the role of divided attention during stimulus encoding and central processing, and how sustained attention is related to vigilance.

Sensory Registration

Information input begins with sensory registers (e.g., auditory, visual, and haptic structures). Stimulus information remains active within the registers for only brief periods of time and then decays rapidly. Considerable preattentive and selective processing occurs during this brief period, however.

Preattentive Processing

Information processing within sensory registers is thought to be manipulated by preattentive mechanisms that are not under conscious control. Considerable research has examined how preattentive processing may underlie differences in cognitive performance in both retarded and nonretarded persons.

A strong case for the existence of basic physiological differences in the manner in which retarded and nonretarded persons register and organize stimuli at the preattentional level is provided by work conducted by Fox and Oross (1988, 1990, 1992). Employing random element stereogram tasks that require subjects to detect information embedded in visual arrays, retarded adults were consistently found to perform more poorly on detection tasks than nonretarded persons matched on either mental age (MA) and chronological age (CA). Fox and Oross suggested that the difference between the performance of retarded and nonretarded persons is substantial and cannot be explained in terms of visual anomalies, low motivation, or inattention. Additional support for the view that retarded individuals have basic perceptual deficits at the preattentive level comes from research using classical tests of psychophysical threshold (Dugas & Baumeister, 1968; Thor & Thor, 1970), iconic memory (Pennington & Luszcz, 1975), and stimulus masking procedures (Spitz & Thor, 1968; Welsandt & Meyer, 1974).

The case is made that retarded persons have perceptual deficits that may underlie later information processing difficulties; however, it can also be argued that IQ-related differences in performance on laboratory tasks such as these may reflect other variables that affect subjects' performance. For example, retarded individuals exhibit greater off-task behavior, such as glancing away from the task at hand, than do nonretarded individuals (Krupski, 1977). Thus, IQ-related differences in the perception of stimuli may be related to both cognitive and noncognitive factors.

Selection Processes

Following preattentive processing, stimuli in the sensory register elicit an orienting response that, in turn, leads to selection of information for additional processing. The manner in which individuals come to attend to and select information for processing underscores much of the published research on attention in retarded individuals. Numerous tests have been developed to assess the manner in which information is evaluated, manipulated, and selected for processing. In general, these tasks measure how individuals orient to stimuli, focus attention to stimuli, and organize stimulus patterns.

Orienting to Stimuli. Early physiological studies conducted by Luria (1963) and Sokolov (1963) provided the basis for an enduring explanation for differences in the cognitive performance of retarded and nonretarded persons. Their work suggested that retarded individuals have poorly functioning central nervous systems that render their orienting responses to environmental stimuli inefficient.

On the basis of Luria's and Sokolov's work, a general theory of mental retardation was proposed by Furby (1974) in which retarded persons are characterized as possessing a weak orienting response that habituates more slowly than does that of nonretarded persons. Furby suggested that the magnitude of an individual's orienting response to stimuli is critical to later cognitive processing. The orienting response determines subsequent attentional activation, which in turn determines the individual's integration of the information provided by the stimulus into a schema. A retarded person's orienting response is weak and it habituates slowly; the individual's attention becomes focused on characteristics of stimuli that may not be related to solving problems in either the same fashion or as efficiently as does a nonretarded person. Unfortunately, Luria's initial observations of weaker orienting responses in retarded persons received only limited empirical support (Ball, Barber, & Kohler, 1975; Bower & Das, 1972; Elliott & Johnson, 1971; Powazek & Johnson, 1973), thus weakening theories of attention that are based on the habituation of the orienting response.

Another approach that has been used to study IQ-related differences in orienting to stimuli focuses on retarded and nonretarded persons' ability to take advantage of warning signals during simple reaction time tests. Subjects are instructed to respond as quickly as possible to the presentation of a target signal; on some trials a warning signal precedes the target signal. Subjects' response times are typically faster when warning signals are presented than when no warning is provided. Furthermore, measures of physiological functioning, such as heart rate and galvanic skin response, change in a systematic fashion prior to and following target onset. These findings have led researchers to assume that the interval between the warning and target signals provides individuals with an opportunity to make attentional adjustments that maximize their readiness to respond (Baumeister &

Kellas, 1968; Krupski, 1977; Nettelbeck, 1982). Results of several studies have shown differences between retarded and nonretarded persons in terms of their physiological response to target stimuli (Krupski, 1975; Runcie & O'Bannon, 1975), suggesting IQ-related differences in the ability to prepare to respond to the onset of stimuli.

The manner in which warning cues affect the performance of retarded and nonretarded individuals has been found to be related to the level of processing demanded by the task. Powazek and Johnson (1973) found differences between retarded and nonretarded persons' physiological responses during a simple reaction time test only when subjects associated target stimuli with reward. There were no IQ-related differences in heart rate responses when novel target stimuli were presented. Likewise, Merrill and McCauley (1988) contrasted retarded and nonretarded persons' ability to mobilize attentional resources following the presentation of a warning signal. The warning cue in their study preceded presentation of stimulus pairs to be compared. Subjects compared stimuli on the basis of their physical characteristics under one condition; in another condition comparisons were based on the semantic properties of the stimuli. The duration between the warning cue and the onset of the first stimulus of a stimulus pair was manipulated. The warning cue interval had no effect on subjects' ability to make comparisons on the basis of physical identity. However, retarded persons were hindered more by a short warning cue interval than were nonretarded persons under the semantic condition. Merrill and McCauley suggested that retarded individuals mobilize their attentional resources less efficiently than did nonretarded persons under cognitively demanding task conditions. Retarded and nonretarded persons performed similarily under the physical identity condition, reflecting the possibility that stimuli are unaffected by attentional resources under some conditions.

Focused Attention. Stimuli held in the sensory register undergo some analysis. Focused attention is believed to determine which stimuli receive additional processing and which stimuli do not. Several approaches have been taken to assess differences between retarded and nonretarded individuals' abilities to focus attention.

Zeaman and House (1963, 1979) and Fisher and Zeaman (1973) proposed theories of attention that hypothesized that retarded and nonretarded persons differ in the ability to select relevant dimensions of a stimulus complex. They found in their research that the rate at which retarded and nonretarded individuals learned a discrimination task depended on how they selected elements from a complex stimulus display. Retarded individuals required considerably more training trials to identify the task-appropriate stimulus dimension; however, once the correct stimulus dimension was identified, the rate at which retarded individuals learned the discrimination task was similar to that of nonretarded individuals. For example, a study conducted by Fisher, Martin, McBane, and Zeaman (1969; described by Fisher & Zeaman, 1973) used a demonstration trial procedure to assess the number of stimulus dimensions that could be attended to by retarded and nonretarded individuals (i.e., their breadth of attention). Subjects were first presented with a complex target stimulus (e.g., a blue square) and then pairs of complex stimuli (e.g., blue or red square). The subject was asked to select the stimulus of the pair that was like the target. It was found that low-MA subjects were unable to attend to both dimensions of the target stimulus. These results were taken to suggest that the poor performance of retarded individuals during discrimination tests could be explained as a lack of effective attention to appropriate elements of the stimulus complex. Zeaman (1978) argued that the number of stimulus dimensions that could be attended to by the individual was a relatively stable and unalterable capacity that was related to level of intelligence.

Theories proposed by Zeaman and House (1963, 1979) and Fisher and Zeaman (1973) provided the impetus for a number of studies of attention in retarded persons. Evidence in support of their models of attention is mixed, however. Mackie and Mackay (1982) assessed retarded and nonretarded individuals' discrimination with the demonstration trial method and found that breath of attention was similar for both IQ groups. They suggested that IQ-related performance differences were due to subjects' memory abilities and not attention, per se. More recently, Whiteley, Zaparniuk, and Asmundson (1987) elected to assess the breadth of attention of retarded and nonretarded persons with a matching-to-sample task. The retarded individuals' poorer performance was not found to be related to memory or rehearsal processes; rather, it was suggested that retarded persons are capable of attending to multiple stimulus dimensions, but they attend to fewer dimensions than do children with similar mental ages.

Studies of visual spatial attention have provided considerable information concerning the manner in which stimuli are selected for processing. The assumption that underlies much of the research on visual spatial attention is that the environment provides individuals with a complex array of stimuli from which a subset of stimuli may be selected for processing. Focused attention implies that attention is directed toward some stimuli and away from other stimuli. Several researchers suggest that attention can be focused like a spotlight (LaBerge, 1983) or a zoom lens (Eriksen & St. James, 1986; Eriksen & Yeh, 1985). The attentional spotlight can be directed to specific areas of the visual field and the area under focus can be varied in size.

The width of the spotlight has been shown to change as a function of processing requirements (Egeth, 1977; LaBerge, 1983; LaBerge, Brown, Carter, Bash, & Hartley, 1991). The ability to narrow attention to those stimuli that are relevant to the performance of a given task and direct attention away from nonrelevant stimuli is considered to be a characteristic of optimal information processing. An enduring view of retarded individuals is that they are assumed to focus their attention inefficiently, and that they are more affected by irrelevant stimuli or distractors than are nonretarded individuals (Crosby & Blatt, 1968). The study of distractibity in retarded individuals has a long history. Some educators have suggested that mentally retarded individuals' distractibility is one of the greatest impediments to their learning. The study of the overt behavior of retarded children in classroom settings supports the general observations made by educators—retarded children display more inattentive behaviors than do nonretarded children (Krupski, 1979).

Laboratory studies of the effects of distractors on the performance of retarded persons have provided conflicting results, however. Distractors interfere with performance under some conditions (Follini, Sitkowski, & Stayton, 1969; Wolitzky, Hofer, & Shapiro, 1972), whereas they have no effect under other conditions (Brown, 1966; Cromwell & Foshee, 1960; Crosby, 1972; Ellis, Hawkins, Pryer, & Jones, 1963; Girardeau & Ellis, 1964) or even enhance performance (Baumeister & Ellis, 1963; Belmont & Ellis, 1968). These laboratory studies of the effects of distractors on performance often measured the influence of some form of extraneous stimulation on subjects' rate of learning. The stimuli selected as distractors varied considerable among studies; types of stimuli ranged from the repetition of words (Brown, 1966), subjects' reflections in a mirror (Ellis et al., 1963), to changes in patterns of lights generated by a display designed to advertise a brand of beer (N. R. Ellis, personal communication, 1993). The learning tasks selected to assess the effects of distractors also vary considerably among these early studies. The lack of agreement regarding the results of these experiments may be accounted for by differences in procedural variables and methods of testing.

A series of theory-based studies was conducted to assess retarded persons' abilities to focus attention and to deal with the effects of distractor stimuli (Cha & Merrill, 1992,

1994). This research was based on the view that stimulus selection requires the allocation of attentional resources, not only to facilitate the extraction of relevant stimuli, but also to suppress irrelevant stimuli (Neill, 1977; Tipper, 1985; Tipper & Cranston, 1985). In one study, Cha (1992) measured the ability of retarded and nonretarded persons to focus attention during a visual selective attention task in which a central target stimulus letter was presented between two flanker stimuli. The type of flanker stimulus and the distance between flankers and target stimuli was varied systematically. Response time was slowed when flankers were letters that had previously served as target stimuli. Subjects' slower response time was viewed as the result of response competition between flanker and target stimuli (Egeth, 1977; Eriksen & Eriksen, 1974; Eriksen & Hoffman, 1972; Flowers & Wilcox, 1982). A comparison of retarded and nonretarded individuals' performance revealed that retarded individuals were unable to restrict the size of their attentional spotlight and that their performance was more influenced by the distracting effects of flankers than was the performance of nonretarded individuals.

In a second study, Cha (1992) evaluated the degree to which retarded individuals are able to overcome the effects of the onset of distractors. They employed a response-competition task in which flanker stimuli were presented 0, 100, 250, or 500 ms prior to the onset of the target stimulus. Flanker stimuli were found to increase subjects' response times, suggesting that they were distracting. The magnitude of the distractor effect differed between IQ groups. Whereas nonretarded individuals were able to suppress the effects of distractors when the interval between flanker and target stimuli was greater than 250 ms, retarded individuals' performance was affected at all delay intervals. These results led Merrill and Cha to conclude that irrelevant stimuli are more powerful attractors of attention for retarded individuals than they are for nonretarded individuals.

The view that retarded individuals are unable to suppress the effects of irrelevant stimuli is supported by the results of several studies that assessed learning in retarded individuals. Hagen and Huntsman (1971) employed a central-incidential learning task in which subjects were shown cards with a relevant and an irrelevant picture. Institutionalized retarded adults were less able to select target pictures and more likely to recall incidential pictures than were nonretarded subjects matched on mental age. Likewise, Nugent and Mosley (1987) evaluated subjects' ability to listen to stimuli presented aurally in both ears and to detect target words presented in a designated ear and not to respond to stimuli presented in the nondesignated ear. They found that retarded adults were less able than were nonretarded adults to detect targets from the designated channel, and they were more likely to respond to stimuli presented in the nondesignated channel.

Stimulus Organization

Stimuli that are attended to and selected for further processing appear to be grouped together prior to being encoded into short-term memory. The manner in which stimuli become organized has been discussed in great detail. Treisman and her colleagues (Treisman, 1969, 1988; Treisman & Gelade, 1980; Treisman & Gormican, 1988; Treisman & Paterson, 1984; Treisman & Souther, 1985) suggested that stimuli within the same central focus of attention are integrated into unitary objects. Her theoretical position implies that there is a "top down" component to information processing; an individual's past experience and the contextual information present at any given moment affect the manner in which stimuli are transformed into objects.

Retarded individuals have been hypothesized to have lower sensitivity to relational material than do nonretarded individuals (Brown, 1970; Caruso & Detterman, 1983; Hall, 1971; Soraci, Alpher, Deckner, & Blanton, 1983; Soraci & Carlin, 1992; Soraci, Deckner, Baumeister, & Carlin, 1990; Spitz, 1963, 1966). Soraci and his colleagues (Soraci & Carlin,

1992; Soraci et al., 1983; Soraci et al., 1990) employed an oddity test paradigm to assess intelligence- and developmental-related differences in stimulus organization and relational learning. The oddity task requires subjects to choose between stimulus arrays on the basis of the arrangement of characteristics or properties of components within stimulus arrays. Subjects' ability to recognize relationships that may exist among stimulus arrays is believed to be dependent on attentional processes. Soraci et al. (1990) employed a two-choice matching-to-sample task in which the symmetry and disparity of stimuli within stimulus arrays were manipulated. There were no IQ-related differences in stimulus encoding; however, retarded individuals exhibited a lower sensitivity to available relational information when arrays were presented at a moderate level of stimulus disparity.

Summary

The studies reviewed in this section provide evidence that retarded and nonretarded individuals differ in the manner in which they process information within the sensory register. Retarded individuals are less able than are nonretarded individuals to perceive, orient toward, select, and group stimuli. Intelligence-related differences in the ability to perceive stimuli appear to be explained best in terms of physiological factors, and differences between retarded and nonretarded individuals' abilities to orient toward, select, and group stimuli are best explained in terms of attentional processes. This generalization is based on the findings of several studies that contrasted the performance of retarded and nonretarded individuals under test conditions in which the level of processing demanded of participants was varied. Interactions were observed in which retarded individuals' performance declined more than did the performance of nonretarded individuals as the level of processing demand was increased. Given the assumption that processing demands draw on individuals' attentional resources, it would be expected that retarded individuals would be more adversely affected than nonretarded individuals. Also, the observation that IQ-level by processing demand interactions were found in a variety of tasks that measured different aspects of stimulus detection and selection suggests that individuals' performance was controlled by a unitary factor, such as attention.

Encoding and Central Processing

Information selected from sensory registers for further processing is encoded into memory. The process of encoding involves a dynamic interaction among short-term memory, long-term memory, and attentional processes. Short-term memory is typically conceived of as a limited-capacity information storage structure. In Mosley's (1980) model, the contents of short-term memory are maintained by rehearsal and coding strategies that are controlled by attention. The manner in which information enters short-term memory and is processed centrally has provided the basis for numerous approaches to the study of divided attention. Tasks that require individuals to process more information than can be held in short-term memory increase competition for attentional resources, and trade-offs occur between the processing and the storage of information. Carr (1984) described three types of situations under which trade-offs occur: work/storage trade-offs occur when attention is allocated to the processing of information at the expense of its storage (or, conversely, when the storage of information occurs at the expense of processing); speed/accuracy trade-offs occur when attention is allocated to rate of processing at the expense of an increase in errors; and task/task trade-offs occur when priority is given to the performance of one of two or more tasks that compete for attentional resources. A number of methods have been developed to assess stimulus encoding and central processing. Several of these methods have been used to contrast retarded and nonretarded individuals' ability to process information.

The Inspection-Time Method

Nettelbeck and his colleagues (Lally & Nettelbeck, 1977, 1980; Nettelbeck, 1982, 1985, 1987; Nettelbeck, Hirons, & Wilson, 1984; Nettelbeck & Lally, 1976; Nettelbeck & McLean, 1984) proposed a two-stage model of information processing with an encoding component and a central processing component. They incorporated the inspection time paradigm developed by Vickers (1970, 1979) to assess information processing. The experimental procedure used to assess inspection time involves measuring subjects' ability to discriminate between two stimuli under conditions in which the duration that stimuli are visually presented is varied systematically. The duration of the presentation of stimuli is directly related to subjects' discrimination performance. When performing the inspection time task, subjects are believed to gather a threshold amount of information from the sensory register before a response is made. Subjects are hypothesized to take a series of discrete samples from the sensory register until threshold levels are attained.

Numerous studies have used the inspection time paradigm to assess IQ-related differences in performance (see Kranzler & Jensen, 1989, for a review). When retarded and nonretarded individuals' inspection times are compared, it is typically the case that retarded persons require roughly twice the time that nonretarded persons do to accumulate sufficient information before making a response. Nettelbeck and McLean (1984) proposed that the capacity to inspect information in the sensory register reflects a basic information proccessing ability that limits the rate at which stimuli are encoded into memory. Retarded individuals' slower inspection times are thought to reflect structural deficits within their information processing system that are not under voluntary control (Nettelbeck et al., 1984). Retarded individuals are also hypothesized to have deficits in central mechanisms that direct attention to information processing structures (Nettelbeck & Brewer, 1981). The poorer functioning of attentional systems is thought to be due to the inability of retarded individuals to select processing strategies that involve trade-offs between speed and accuracy of responding (Lally & Nettlebeck, 1980), or to suppress intrusive information (Nettelbeck et al., 1984). Intelligence-related differences in neural activity have also been suggested as an explanation for differences between the performance of retarded and nonretarded individuals on inspection time tasks (Nettelbeck et al., 1984).

The Encoding-Function Method

Encoding time differences between retarded and nonretarded individuals have also been evaluated with tasks that assess subjects' abilities to make rapid comparisons between visually presented stimuli. Posner (1978) developed a method to estimate the time required to encode stimulus information. Subjects decide if two sequentially presented stimuli are the same or different in the standard encoding function task. The interval between stimuli is varied systematically. The logic of the task is that optimal matching performance can be attained only when the first stimulus of the pair has been adequately encoded. Thus, the shortest interval at which optimal performance is demonstrated corresponds to the time needed to encode the first stimulus of the pair. Merrill et al. (1987) employed a modified Posner stimulus-matching task in which the interval between stimulus pairs and the types of stimuli were manipulated. Stimulus pairs were compared on the basis of physical identity, name identity, or superordinate identity. Retarded persons' encoding speeds were found to be approximately 100 ms slower than were nonretarded persons' under all three stimulus-pair conditions. Similar results were obtained by Merrill and McCauley (1988) and Merrill (1992) using similar test methods. The consistently longer encoding times of retarded individuals in these studies led Merrill (1990, 1992) to conclude that they allocate less attention to basic processes of information transmission than do nonretarded individuals.

The Additive-Factors Method

Sternberg (1966, 1969) introduced a method for analyzing information processing components that underlie speeded choice responses. He suggested that these responses are determined by the manner in which information is encoded, compared, leads to a decision, and sets the conditions for the selection of a response. Reaction time can be affected by any one or a combination of underlying processes. The procedure involves having subjects first memorize a list of items (e.g., digits) that are then referred to as members of the "positive set." Once learned, subjects are presented a series of probe items and asked to indicate whether the probe is a member of the positive set by saying "yes" if it is and "no" if it is not. Positive set size is manipulated and subjects' performance is typically evaluated by plotting mean RT to positive and/or negative probes as a function of the number of items in the positive set. The relation between reaction time and set size is usually linear. Reaction times are typically found to lengthen as set size increases; this change in reaction time is taken as an index of subjects' rate of memory retrieval and scanning.

Maisto and Baumeister (1984) provided a review of research that used the additive factor model to assess the differences between retarded and nonretarded individuals' reaction time. In general, studies using the additive factors method have indicated that retarded individuals perform poorer at encoding information (Silverman, 1974) and on memory scanning (Dugas & Kellas, 1974; Harris & Fleer, 1974; Merrill, 1985; Mosley, 1985; Owings, Baumeister, Laine, & Lewis, 1980) than do nonretarded individuals. There is little difference between retarded and nonretarded persons with respect to the function of the decision (Dugas & Kellas, 1974) and response organization stages (Baumeister & Kellas, 1968).

Several studies provide evidence to suggest that attentional allocation is involved in subjects' performance of speeded choice tasks. Maisto and Jerome (1977), for example, assessed encoding and memory scanning in retarded and nonretarded individuals under conditions in which stimulus quality and set size were manipulated. The degradation of stimulus quality resulted in larger intercept differences for retarded individuals. Furthermore, retarded individuals' longer encoding times were associated with a decreased rate of memory scanning. The IQ-related differences in performance were attributed to retarded individuals' slower encoding and the use of different information processing strategies; that is, retarded subjects chose to allocate more processing time to one stage than to another. Additional evidence for differences between retarded and nonretarded individuals' allocation of processing time to specific stages was provided by Owings et al. (1980). They observed that retarded individuals encoded compound stimuli more rapidly than nonretarded individuals, suggesting that, under specific conditions, retarded individuals elect to decrease encoding time in order to increase memory scanning time. Subjects' ability to select and switch modes of information processing may be related to their allocation of attentional resources.

Merrill (1985, 1990) suggested that the attentional processes that mediate speeded responding increase as tasks become difficult. He contrasted the performance of retarded and nonretarded persons with a modified Sternberg task in which information processing demands were manipulated (Merrill, 1985). Under one condition, items of the positive memory set and probe stimuli were basic objects. Under a second condition, items of the positive memory set were superordinate category labels (e.g., *animals*, *furniture*) and probes were object names (e.g., *dog*, *table*). Merrill hypothesized that the two tasks tapped short-term and long- term memory processes, respectively. Response times for retarded persons were 1.9 times longer than they were for nonretarded persons under the short-term memory condition, and 2.2 times longer under the long-term memory condition. These results were taken as evidence for less efficient allocation of attentional resources by retarded individuals.

The Semantic-Priming Method

Sperber and McCauley (1984) pointed out that subjects are required to memorize items prior to probe tasks in the standard Sternberg paradigm. Given the IQ-related differences in learning and memory, this places retarded persons at a disadvantage and makes inferences concerning information processing abilities problematic (see also Silverman, 1974; Silverman & Harris, 1982; Stanovich, 1978). On the basis of a methodology introduced by Posner and Snyder (1975), Sperber and McCauley developed semantic processing priming tasks that permit the assessment of retarded and nonretarded persons' ability to retrieve and evaluate permanently stored knowledge about objects and relationships that exist among objects. The semantic priming task involves the sequential presentation of two stimuli, such as pictures of objects, to subjects who are asked simply to name the objects as quickly as possible. On some trials, object pairs are members of the same category; on other trials, object pairs are unrelated. Analysis of subjects' naming times typically shows faster response times to pairs of objects that are related than to those that are unrelated. The first stimulus is hypothesized to serve to prime an automatic activation process that operates without the subjects' conscious awareness in the related-pair condition. The priming stimulus initiates subjects' retrieval of information from memory more rapidly under the related-pair condition than under the unrelated-pair condition.

A series of studies revealed IQ-related differences in semantic priming. Although the response times of retarded and nonretarded individuals did not differ under testing conditions in which subjects were required to name pictures of common objects, retarded persons' response times were significantly slower than were nonretarded persons' under testing conditions where subjects were required to verify the categorial relationships between object pairs (Davies, Sperber, & McCauley, 1981; Sperber, Davies, Merrill, & McCauley, 1982; Sperber, Ragain, & McCauley, 1976). It is assumed that, unlike simple object naming, the verification of the class membership of two objects requires subjects to activate attentional resources in order to make semantic decisions. Retarded persons' slower response times were viewed as evidence for IQ-related processing limitations (Merrill, 1990; Sperber & McCauley, 1984).

The Dual-Task Method

Another approach to the study of IQ-related differences in attention has been to examine the manner in which individuals perform under competing task conditions. The dual-task method involves having subjects perform two cognitive tasks simultaneously. In most cases, subjects come to view one of the tasks as primary and the other task as secondary. The distinction between tasks comes about either explicitly through instructions or implicitly by manipulating payoff schedules. The logic of the dual-task method is that both tasks draw attention from the individual's limited pool of attentional resources. The extent to which the subject's performance decreases on the secondary task as the difficulty of the primary task increases is taken to reflect a task/task trade-off and the degree to which the subject elects to allocate attentional resources to the primary task.

Few studies have contrasted the performance of retarded and nonretarded individuals under competing task conditions. The first of two dual-task experiments conducted by Merrill (1992) examined retarded and nonretarded individuals' rate of stimulus encoding while retaining information in memory. The primary task required subjects to maintain either full- or half-digit spans in memory. The secondary task was a modified Posner encoding function task (Posner, 1978) in which subjects matched stimulus pairs on the basis of either physical or name identity. Retarded individuals' encoding and decision-making times were slowed by the memory load conditions more than those of nonretarded individuals, suggesting greater attentional allocation to these processes on the part of nonretarded persons. In the second study, the primary task was the semantic matching task used in the first study, whereas the secondary task required subjects to detect auditory probes. As in the first experiment, retarded individuals' response times were slowed more by the demands of the primary task than were those of nonretarded individuals.

Similar results were obtained by Merrill and Peacock (1994). In their study, the primary task required subjects to perform a category decision task that differed in level of difficulty, whereas the secondary task required the detection of an auditory probe. There were no IQ-related differences in subjects' response times to probe stimuli when the competing task required basic level identity classification; however, retarded individuals' response times were slowed more than those of nonretarded individuals when superordinate identity classification was required. Again, differences in performance were explained in terms of attentional allocation.

Methods of Assessing Automatic and Effortful Processing

The ability to encode information in an automatic manner has been viewed as adaptive. Given that attentional capacity is limited, it would benefit individuals not to expend their limited resources on processing all stimuli. The reduction of the attentional allocation to some processes would leave the individual more attention to allocate to other processes (Kahneman & Treisman, 1984). This view has prompted several lines of research that have compared automatic and effortful processing in retarded and nonretarded persons.

Hasher and Zacks (1979) proposed that there are two types of automatic processing: one that is biologically based and one that is learned. The biologically based form of automatic processing was thought to be invariant across age and level of intelligence. Ellis and his colleagues conducted several studies that support this contention. They found that specific types of environmental information, such as frequency of occurrence (Ellis & Allison, 1988; Ellis, Palmer, & Reeves, 1988) and spatial location of objects (Ellis, Katz, & Williams, 1987; Ellis, Woodley-Zanthos, & Dulaney, 1989) are encoded in a similar fashion by both retarded and nonretarded individuals. Further, Meador and Ellis (1987) employed a Posner-type (Posner & Snyder, 1975) stimulus-priming procedure to evaluate automatic and effortful attentional processing in retarded and nonretarded persons. Subjects in this study were required to judge whether two letters presented simultaneously were the same or different. Letter pairs were preceded by one of three types of warning cues: a letter identical to the target pair, a letter different from the target pair, or a nonletter symbol. The interval between warning cue and letter pairs ranged between 0 and 2,000 ms. Facilitation effects were found to be similar for retarded and nonretarded persons under short-warning cue conditions; however, facilitation and inhibition effects developed more slowly in retarded persons than in nonretarded persons when the warning-cue interval was long. These findings were taken to suggest that automatic—but not effortful—information processing mechanisms function in a similar fashion in retarded and nonretarded persons.

The processing of some components of cognitive tasks are believed to become "automatic" through repeated experience with specific stimulus and response relations (Ackerman & Schneider, 1985; Logan, 1979; Shiffrin & Schneider, 1977). Several studies provide evidence to suggest that, unlike biologically based automatic attentional processes, retarded and nonretarded persons differ in their ability to utilize learned automatic responses to stimuli. Ellis, Meador, and Bodfish (1985) evaluated automatic and effortful encoding of stimulus information into memory. They contrasted retarded and nonretarded persons' ability to recall semantic and nonsemantic information during a continuous recognition memory test. Retarded individuals were consistently poorer at encoding stimulus information under both conditions of the recognition memory test than were nonretarded individuals. Similar results were obtained on a delayed matching-to-sample task (Ellis & Meador, 1985).

The manner in which individuals come to process stimuli in an automatic fashion has been studied extensively. As a result, considerable information has been gathered regarding the conditions under which responses to stimuli become automatic in nature. A recent study by Merrill, Goodwyn, and Gooding (in press) contrasted the rate at which retarded and nonretarded individuals develop automatic processing. They employed a visual search task in which the consistency of stimulus mapping was manipulated. Nonretarded persons were found to develop the ability to process stimuli automatically about twice as fast as retarded persons.

Retarded individuals also appear to exert less control over their learned automatic behavior than do nonretarded individuals. Ellis and his colleagues (Ellis & Dulaney, 1991; Ellis et al., 1989) conducted several studies that employed the Stroop paradigm (Stroop, 1935) to examine the degree to which the development of an automatic reading suppression response could be controlled by retarded and nonretarded individuals. In these studies, both IQ groups learned to suppress responding in a similar fashion; however, retarded individuals lacked the ability or the capacity to overcome the learned suppression response following changes in test conditions (see Dulaney & Ellis, chap. 7, this volume).

Summary

Several generalizations can be drawn from the studies reviewed in this section. It is the case that IQ-related differences in stimulus encoding are task dependent. Retarded and nonretarded individuals encode information similarily during tasks that elicit some forms of automatic attentional processing; for example, identity priming tasks and tasks that involve memory for frequency of events or the spatial location of stimuli. Retarded individuals' stimulus encoding is less efficient than that of nonretarded individuals on tasks that demand effortful attentional processing; for example, semantic priming tasks and tasks that require memory search or retrieval. Furthermore, the differences between the encoding abilities of retarded and nonretarded persons become more apparent as processing demands of tasks are increased. Another generalization that can be drawn from these studies is that retarded individuals consistently perform less efficiently than do nonretarded individuals when required to perform tasks that involve trade-offs between processing and storage of information.

Sustained Attention

There is general agreement among researchers that the capacity to sustain attention to environmental conditions over a period of time plays an important role in adaptive behavior (Davies, Jones, & Taylor, 1984; Davies & Parasuraman, 1982; Warm, 1984). Factors that contribute to changes in the sustained attention of nonretarded individuals have been studied extensively, and several theories of sustained attention have been proposed (see Davies & Parasuraman, 1982; Loeb & Alluisi, 1984; Parasuraman, 1986, for in-depth reviews). A recent review of research that examined the sustained attention of retarded individuals concluded that IQ-related differences in performance, when found, could be explained in terms of information processing limitations (Tomporowski & Hager, 1992). Evidence supporting this view comes from several lines of research employing different methods of assessing sustained attention.

Brief-Duration Methods

Rosvold, Mirsky, Sarason, Bransome, and Beck (1956) introduced the Continuous Performance Test (CPT) in a study designed to differentiate between brain-damaged and non-brain-damaged individuals. The original version of the CPT consisted of two parts, each 10 minutes in duration. In the first part, subjects were instructed to view individual letters of the alphabet and to respond to all occurrences of the letter X; in the second part, subjects were instructed to respond to the letter X only if it was immediately preceded by the letter A. There was a 2-minute rest period between the two parts of the test. Target letters occurred on 25% of stimulus presentations in Part 1 and 19% of stimulus presentations in Part 2 of the test. The dependent measure was the average number of targets detected under each of the two test conditions. Rosvold et al. hypothesized that the A–X task would be the more difficult of the two test conditions because performance would be more susceptible to subjects' lapses of attention. The CPT and variations of it have become a widely used method for assessing the development of attention in children (Gale & Lynn, 1972) and the clinical assessment of children with Attention Deficit-Hyperactivity Disorder (ADHD) and learning disablities (see Krafft & Dietrich, 1985).

The few studies that have been conducted with the CPT to assess retarded individuals' vigilance provide evidence to suggest that they are less attentive than nonretarded individuals. Rosvold et al. (1956) contrasted the performance of brain-damaged and non-brain-damaged retarded adults, nonretarded adults, and children. Both groups of retarded individuals performed more poorly than nonretarded adults and children. Similarily, Crosby (1972) found that brain-damaged and non-brain-damaged institutionalized adolescents performed more poorly on a CPT than did non-brain-damaged, noninstitutionalized mentally retarded adolescents, MA-matched children, and CA-matched adolescents.

The traditional CPT has weaknesses as a measure of subjects' vigilance, however. It does not provide an index of the change in subjects' performance over time, nor are subjects' false alarm rates taken into account. Research conducted by Nuechterlein and his colleagues (Nuechterlein, 1983; Nuechterlein, Parasuraman, & Jiang, 1983) addressed these methodological weaknesses by developing a method in which visual stimuli are presented rapidly and in a degraded fashion. Subjects' target detection and false alarms are assessed jointly using techniques from signal detection theory (Green & Swets, 1974). In these studies, subjects' detection performance was found to decline rapidly, presumably because of the demands placed on attentional processes. As of yet, comparisons between retarded and nonretarded individuals' sustained attention using this methodological approach have not been made. This method would appear to be particularly useful in assessing attentional and cognitive processing during the sensory registration and stimulus encoding stages of information processing.

Posner, Nissen, and Ogden (1978) provided another method of studying sustained attention during the early stages of information processing that would appear to be particularly useful to assess IQ-related differences. They developed a visual–spatial detection task that measures subjects' ability to disengage, move, and reengage attention to stimuli presented at various locations within the visual field. A stimulus priming manipulation provides an index of the degree to which performance is related to either automatic (covert) or effortful (overt) attentional processes. This method was used recently by Swanson et al. (1991) to contrast the performance of ADHD and non-ADHD children. Group differences in detection performance occurred under effortful processing conditions; the poorer performance of ADHD children was viewed as a failure to sustain focused attention to the location of targets. Similar differences between retarded and nonretarded persons' ability to sustain attention to stimuli presented briefly are predicted on the basis of research that has examined IQ-related differences in focused attention and distractibility. Research that contrasts retarded and nonretarded individuals' ability to sustain focused attention is warranted.

Long-Duration Methods

Interest in applied human performance issues such as watchkeeping and job productivity led to the assessment of individuals' ability to sustain attention for long periods of time. Mackworth (1948) developed the first laboratory test of this type, requiring subjects to view the movements of a pointer along the circumference of a blank face clock for 2 hours. The pointer moved slightly every second; however, the pointer would make infrequent double movements. The double movement was the target event. Subjects' detection performance was found to decrease throughout the observation period. The decline in detection performance over time is typically referred to as the *vigilance decrement*.

Several studies have assessed IQ-related differences in sustained attention. Typically, subjects in these studies are required to make comparisons between target and nontarget stimuli on the basis of slight differences between their physical properties (e.g., shape, size, intensity). Research of this type has determined that retarded children display a more rapid decline in vigilance than do nonretarded children of similar chronological age (Kirby, Nettelbeck, & Thomas, 1979; Semmel, 1965; Thomas, 1989); however, retarded and nonretarded adults display similar declines in vigilance (Kirby, Nettelbeck, & Bullock, 1978; Simpson, 1993; Tomporowski & Allison, 1988; Ware, Baker, & Sipowicz, 1962). These results suggest that the ability of retarded individuals to sustain attention develops at a slower pace than does that of nonretarded individuals (Kirby et al., 1979; Thomas, 1989).

A series of studies by Tomporowski and his colleagues (Tomporowski & Allison, 1988; Tomporowski, Hayden, & Applegate, 1990; Tomporowski & Simpson, 1990; Tomporowski & Tinsley, 1992) investigated IQ-related differences during vigilance tests that place demands on subjects' working-memory processes. Tomporowski and Simpson (1990) developed a 60-minute digit-matching task in which memory demands were equated for retarded and nonretarded adults. The detection performance of both groups was similar during the initial 30 minutes of the task; however, the retarded individuals' performance declined more rapidly than that of nonretarded individuals for the remainder of the vigil. Similar results were obtained by Tomporowski and Tinsley (1994) in two studies that evaluated the vigilance of retarded and nonretarded adults during 60-minute missing-digit detection tasks in which the probability of targets was manipulated. In the first study, retarded adults were found to detect fewer targets than nonretarded adults did as the vigil progressed. Retarded individuals also displayed a more conservative criterion for responding than nonretarded adults. The results of a second study suggested that retarded adults' vigilance is affected to a greater degree than that of nonretarded adults when memory demands are increased. Retarded adults detected fewer targets and evidenced a more rapid decline in vigilance under high memory-demanding conditions than did nonretarded adults. Similarly, Das (1970) observed that severely mentally retarded persons became less able to sustain attention to words and numbers than mildly mentally retarded persons were as task difficulty increased.

Summary

The results of these studies of sustained attention suggest that vigilance develops more slowly in retarded children and that the ability of both retarded and nonretarded adults to maintain attention is task dependent. Retarded and nonretarded adults demonstrate similar sustained attention under test conditions that place limited demands on encoding and memory processes; however, when detection tasks place greater demands on information processing components, retarded adults evidence a more rapid vigilance decrement than do nonretarded adults.

CONCLUDING COMMENTS

An information processing model of cognition was used as a heuristic to examine attention in mentally retarded persons. On the basis of our review, we conclude that the construct of attention has considerable explanatory power when it is viewed as a control process that influences the function of elementary cognitive structures. Consistent differences have been observed between retarded and nonretarded individuals' performance on tasks that assessed various information processing functions. Furthermore, the magnitudes of the differences in performance between IQ groups were in line with the general prediction that retarded individuals are more affected by increases in processing demands than are nonretarded individuals. Retarded and nonretarded individuals perform similarly when effortful processing demands are absent or minimized; however, retarded individuals' performance is more affected than that of nonretarded individuals as processing demands increase.

There are, however, several issues yet to be addressed that are central to understanding how control processes are related to performance. It has been suggested that retarded individuals possess less attentional capacity and, as a result, are less able than nonretarded individuals to control the processing of information (Hasher & Zacks, 1979). There are, however, alternative explanations for IQ-related differences in the allocation of attention. The observed differences in performance could be due to retarded individuals' inability to comprehend how the allocation of attention is related to efficient task performance (Stankov, 1989). It may be the case that retarded individuals have less metacognitive knowledge than do nonretarded individuals (Borkowski & Cavanaugh, 1979; Borkowski, Reid, & Kurtz, 1984; Justice, 1985) or inefficient executive processing systems (Detterman, 1987; Detterman et al., 1992) and, as a result, they are inefficient in developing and modifying problem-solving skills. Alternatively, retarded individuals may perform more poorly than do nonretarded individuals on cognitively demanding tasks because they lack sufficient motivation to allocate the attention necessary to maintain performance (see Zigler & Balla, 1982).

It will be important for researchers to determine the validity of various constructs that are hypothesized to control information processing. It is vital that studies be conducted that provide empirical data that link specific cognitive control processes to observed behavior. Currently, the boundaries that separate such constructs as attention, metacognition, executive processing, and motivation are not well defined. It is known that the development of mental constructs that lack empirical support can lead to tautological explanations of behavior that impede understanding and theory development (Underwood, 1957). The study of attention has a long history, and the conundrums that can develop when explanatory concepts are accepted on the basis of limited empirical evidence have been discussed (see Johnson & Dark, 1986).

Historically, the term *attention* has been used in a variety of ways. Educators, for example, often describe children as having short attention spans, having lapses of attention, and being easily distracted. An area of research that has received only limited attention is the extent to which tests developed on the basis of information processing theories can identify individual differences in classroom behavior (Krupski, 1979; Siegel, Crawford, & Evelsizer, 1985). It is often assumed that the analysis of basic information processing abilities at a molecular level can be related meaningfully to the analysis of behavior at more global levels. Cognitive-based tests of attention, such as the Continuous Performance Test, have been used with some success to assist in the prediction of classroom attentiveness (Kupietz & Richardson, 1978; Murphy-Bergman & Wright, 1987). The extent to which the results of laboratory-based tests of attention predict retarded individuals' behavior in educational and training settings remains to be determined, however.

A better understanding of IQ-related differences in the development of attention is also warranted. Few studies have compared the performance of retarded individuals who differ in age to that of CA- and MA-matched nonretarded individuals. Whether retarded individuals are delayed in the onset of attentional processes or have permanent deficits in attention is not known. Findings that shed light on this issue will be of considerable importance to both theoretical and applied psychologists.

REFERENCES

Ackerman, P. L., & Schneider, W. (1985). Individual differences in automatic and controlled information processing. In R. F. Dillon (Ed.), *Individual differences in cognition* (Vol. 2, pp. 35–66). New York: Academic Press.

Atkinson, R. C., & Shiffrin, R. M. (1968). Human memory: A proposed system and its control processes. In K. W. Spence & J. T. Spence (Eds.), *The psychology of learning and motivation* (Vol. 2, pp. 89–195). New York: Academic Press.

Baddeley, A. (1986). *Working memory.* Oxford, England: Clarendon Press.

Baddeley, A. D. (1990). *Human memory: Theory and practice.* London: Lawrence Erlbaum Associates.

Baddeley, A. D., & Hitch, G. J. (1974). Working memory. In G. Bower (Ed.), *Recent advances in learning and motivation* (Vol. 8, pp. 47–90). New York: Academic Press.

Ball, T. S., Barber, J., & Kohler, H. (1975). Galvanic skin response orienting response as a measure of tactile discrimination in retarded children. *American Journal of Mental Deficiency, 79,* 559–564.

Baumeister, A. A. (1984). Some methodological and conceptual issues in the study of cognitive processes with retarded people. In P. H. Brooks, R. Sperber, & C. McCauley (Eds.), *Learning and cognition in the mentally retarded* (pp. 1–38). Hillsdale, NJ: Lawrence Erlbaum Associates.

Baumeister, A. A., & Ellis, N. R. (1963). Delayed response performance of retardates. *American Journal of Mental Deficiency, 67,* 714–722.

Baumeister, A. A., & Kellas, G. (1968). Reaction time and mental retardation. In N. R. Ellis (Ed.), *International review of research in mental retardation* (Vol. 3, pp. 163 -193). New York: Academic Press.

Belmont, J. M., & Ellis, N. R. (1968). Effects of extraneous stimulation upon discrimination learning in normals and retardates. *American Journal of Mental Deficiency, 72,* 525– 532.

Borkowski, J. G., & Cavanaugh, J. C. (1979). Maintenance and generalization of skills and strategies by the retarded. In N. R. Ellis (Ed.), *Handbook of mental deficiency* (2nd ed., pp. 569–617). Hillsdale, NJ: Lawrence Erlbaum Associates.

Borkowski, J. G., Reid, M. K., & Kurtz, B. E. (1984). Metacognition and retardation: Paradigmatic, theoretical, and applied perspectives. In P. H. Brooks, R. Sperber, & C. McCauley (Eds.), *Learning and cognition in the mentally retarded* (pp. 55–75). Hillsale, NJ: Lawrence Erlbaum Associates.

Bower, A. C., & Das, J. P. (1972). Acquisition and reversal of orienting responses to word signals. *British Journal of Psychology, 63*, 195–203.

Broadbent, D. E. (1958). *Perception and communication*. London: Pergamon.

Broadbent, D. E. (1982). Task combination and selective intake of information. *Acta Psychologica, 50*, 253–290.

Brown, A. L. (1970). Subject and experimental variables in the oddity learning of normal and retarded children. *American Journal of Mental Deficiency, 75*, 142–151.

Brown, R. I. (1966). The effects of extraneous auditory stimulation on learning and performance. *American Journal of Mental Deficiency, 71*, 283–290.

Carr, T. H. (1984). Attention, skill, and intelligence: Some speculations on extreme individual differences in human performance. In P. H. Brooks, R. Sperber, & C. McCauley (Eds.), *Learning and cognition in the mentally retarded* (pp. 189–215). Hillsdale, NJ: Lawrence Erlbaum Associates.

Caruso, D. R., & Detterman, D. K. (1983). Stimulus encoding by mentally retarded and nonretarded adults. *American Journal on Mental Deficiency, 87*, 649–655.

Cha, K.-H. (1992). The effect of flanking context and its time course in focused attention processes of mentally retarded and nonretarded persons. *Dissertation Abstracts International, 53*, 2087.

Cha, K.-H., & Merrill, E. C. (1994). Facilitation and inhibition in visual selective attention processes of individuals with and without mental retardation. *American Journal on Mental Retardation, 98*, 594–600.

Cromwell, R. L., & Foshee, J. G. (1960). Studies in activity level: IV. Effects of visual stimulation during task performance in mental defectives. *American Journal of Mental Deficiency, 65*, 248–251.

Crosby, K. G. (1972). Attention and distractibility in mentally retarded and intellectually average children. *American Journal of Mental Deficiency, 77*, 46–53.

Crosby, K. G., & Blatt, B. (1968). Attention and mental retardation. *Journal of Education, 150*, 67–81.

Das, J. P. (1970). Vigilance and verbal conditioning in the mildly and severely retarded. *American Journal of Mental Deficiency, 75*, 253–259.

Davies, D. R., Jones, D. M., & Taylor, A. (1984). Selective- and sustained-attention tasks: Individual and group differences. In R. Parasuraman & D. R. Davies (Eds.), *Varieties of attention* (pp. 395–447). New York: Academic Press.

Davies, D. R., & Parasuraman, R. (1982). *The psychology of vigilance*. New York: Academic Press.

Davies, D., Sperber, R. D., & McCauley, C. (1981). Intelligence-related differences in semantic processing speed. *Journal of Experimental Child Psychology, 31*, 307–402.

Denny, M. R. (1964). Learning and performance. In H. A. Stevens & R. Heber (Eds.), *Mental retardation: A review of research* (pp. 100–142). Chicago: University of Chicago Press.

Denny, M. R. (1966). A theoretical analysis and its application to training the retarded. In N. R. Ellis (Ed.), *International review of research in mental retardation* (Vol. 2, pp. 1–27). New York: Academic Press.

Detterman, D. K. (1987). Theoretical notions of intelligence and mental retardation. *American Journal of Mental Deficiency, 92*, 2–11.

Detterman, D. K., Mayer, J. D., Caruso, D. R., Legree, P. J., Conners, F. A., & Taylor, R. (1992). Assessment of basic cognitive abilities in relation to cognitive deficits. *American Journal on Mental Retardation, 97*, 251–286.

Deutsch, J. A., & Deutsch, D. (1963). Attention: Some theoretical considerations. *Psychological Review, 70*, 80–90.

Dugas, J. L., & Baumeister, A. A. (1968). A comparison of intra-subject variability in auditory difference limens of normals and retardates. *American Journal of Mental Deficiency, 73*, 500–504.

Dugas, J. L., & Kellas, G. (1974). Encoding and retrieval processes in normal children and retarded adolescents. *Journal of Experimental Child Psychology, 17*, 177–185.

Egeth, H. (1977). Attention and preattention. In G. Bower (Ed.), *The psychology of learning and motivation* (Vol. 2, pp. 277–320). New York: Academic Press.

Elliott, L. S., Jr., & Johnson, J. T. (1971). The orienting reflex in intellectually average and retarded children to a relevant and an irrelevant stimulus. *American Journal of Mental Deficiency, 76*, 332–336.

Ellis, N. R., & Allison, P. (1988). Memory for frequency of occurence in retarded and nonretarded persons. *Intelligence, 12*, 61–75.

Ellis, N. R., & Dulaney, C. L. (1991). Further evidence of cognitive inertia of persons with mental retardation. *American Journal on Mental Retardation, 95*, 613–622.

Ellis, N. R., Hawkins, W. F., Pryer, M. W., & Jones, R. W. (1963). Distraction effects in oddity learning by normal and mentally defective humans. *American Journal of Mental Deficiency, 67*, 576–583.

Ellis, N. R., Katz, E., & Williams, J. E. (1987). Developmental aspects of memory for spatial location. *Journal of Experimental Child Psychology, 44*, 401–412.

Ellis, N. R., & Meador, D. M. (1985). Forgetting in retarded and nonretarded persons under conditions of minimal strategy use. *Intelligence, 9*, 87–96.

Ellis, N. R., Meador, D. M., & Bodfish, J. W. (1985). Differences in intelligence and automatic memory processes. *Intelligence, 9*, 265–273.

Ellis, N. R., Palmer, R. L., & Reeves, C. L. (1988). Developmental and intellectual differences in frequency processing. *Developmental Psychology, 24*, 38–45.

Ellis, N. R., Woodley-Zanthos, P., & Dulaney, C. L. (1989). Memory for spatial location in children, adults, and mentally retarded persons. *American Journal of Mental Retardation, 93*, 521–527.

Eriksen, B. A., & Eriksen, C. W. (1974). Effects of noise letters upon the identification of a target letter in a nonsearch task. *Perception & Psychophysics, 16*, 143–149.

Eriksen, C. W., & Hoffman, J. E. (1972). Temporal and spatial characteristics of selective encoding from visual displays. *Perception & Psychophysics, 12*, 201–204.

Eriksen, C. W., & St. James, J. D. (1986). Visual attention within and around the field of focal attention: a zoom lens model. *Perception & Psychophysics, 40*, 225–240.

Eriksen, C. W., & Yeh, Y. (1985). Allocation of attention in the visual field. *Journal of Experimental Psychology: Human Perception & Performance, 11*, 583–597.

Fisher, M. A., & Zeaman, D. (1973). An attention-retention theory of retardate discrimination learning. In N. R. Ellis (Ed.), *International review of research in mental retardation* (Vol. 6, pp. 169–256). New York: Academic Press.

Flowers, J. H., & Wilcox, N. (1982). The effect of flanking context on visual classification: The joint contribution of interactions at different processing levels. *Perception & Psychophysics, 32*, 581–591.

Follini, P., Sitkowski, C. A., & Stayton, S. E. (1969). The attention of retardates and normals in distraction and non-distraction conditions. *American Journal of Mental Deficiency, 74*, 200–205.

Fox, R., & Oross, S., III. (1988). Deficits in stereoscopic depth perception by mildly mentally retarded adults. *American Journal on Mental Retardation, 93*, 232–244.

Fox, R., & Oross, S., III. (1990). Mental retardation and perception of global motion. *Perception & Psychophysics, 48*, 252–258.

Fox, R., & Oross, S., III. (1992). Perceptual deficits in mildly mentally retarded adults. In N. W. Bray (Ed.), *International review of research in mental retardation* (Vol. 18, pp. 1–27). New York: Academic Press.

Furby, L. (1974). Attentional habituation and mental retardation. *Human Development, 17*, 118–138.

Gale, A., & Lynn, R. (1972). A developmental study of attention. *British Journal of Educational Psychology, 42*, 260–266.

Girardeau, F. L., & Ellis, N. R. (1964). Rote verbal learning by normal and mentally retarded children. *American Journal of Mental Deficiency, 68*, 525–532.

Green, D. M., & Swets, J. A. (1974). *Signal detection theory and psychophysics.* New York: Wiley.

Hagen, J. W., & Huntsman, N. (1971). Selective attention in mental retardation. *Developmental Psychology, 5*, 151–160.

Hall, J. E. (1971). Effect of response bias of mental retardates upon oddity learning. *American Journal of Mental Deficiency, 75*, 579–585.

Harris, G. J., & Fleer, R. E. (1974). High speed memory scanning in mental retardates: Evidence for a central processing deficit. *Journal of Experimental Child Psychology, 17*, 452–459.

Hasher, L., & Zacks, R. T. (1979). Automatic and effortful processing in memory. *Journal of Experimental Psychology: General, 108*, 356–388.

Johnson, W. A., & Dark, V. J. (1986). Selective attention. *Annual Review of Psychology, 37*, 43–75.

Justice, E. M. (1985). Metamemory: An aspect of metacognition in the mentally retarded. In N. R. Ellis & N. W. Bray (Eds.), *International review of research in mental retardation* (Vol. 13, pp. 79–107). New York: Academic Press.

Kahneman, D. (1973). *Attention and effort.* Englewood Cliffs, NJ: Prentice-Hall.

Kahneman, D., & Treisman, A. M. (1984). Changing views of attention and automaticity. In R. Parasuraman & R. Davies (Eds.), *Varieties of attention* (pp. 29–61). New York: Academic Press.

Keele, S. W. (1973). *Attention and human performance.* Pacific Palisades, CA: Goodyear.

Kirby, N. H., Nettelbeck, T., & Bullock, J. (1978). Vigilance performance of mildly mentally retarded adults. *American Journal of Mental Deficiency, 28*, 394–397.

Kirby, N. H., Nettelbeck, T., & Thomas, P. (1979). Vigilance performance of mildly mentally retarded children. *American Journal of Mental Deficiency, 84*, 184–187.

Krafft, K. M., & Dietrich, K. N. (1985). Methodological considerations in the assessment of vigilance in children. In R. E. Eberts & C. G. Eberts (Eds.), *Trends in ergonomics/human factors II* (pp. 169–179). Amsterdam: Elsevier.

Kranzler, J. H., & Jensen, A. R. (1989). Inspection time and intelligence: A meta-analysis. *Intelligence, 13*, 329–347.

Krupski, A. (1975). Heart rate changes during a fixed reaction time task in normal and retarded adult males. *Psychophysiology, 12*, 262–267.

Krupski, A. (1977). Role of attention in the reaction-time performance of mentally retarded adolescents. *American Journal of Mental Deficiency, 82*, 79–83.

Krupski, A. (1979). Are retarded children more distractible? Observational analysis of retarded and nonretarded children's classroom behavior. *American Journal of Mental Deficiency, 84*, 1–10.

Kupietz, S. S., & Richardson, E. (1978). Children's vigilance and inattentiveness in the classroom. *Journal of Child Psychology and Psychiatry, 19*, 145–154.

LaBerge, D. L. (1983). Spatial extent of attention to letters and words. *Journal of Experimental Psychology: Human Perception and Performance, 9*, 371–379.

LaBerge, D. L., Brown, V., Carter, M., Bash, D., & Hartley, A. (1991). Reducing the effects of adjacent distractors by narrowing attention. *Journal of Experimental Psychology: Human Perception and Performance, 17*, 65–76.

Lally, M., & Nettelbeck, T. (1977). Intelligence, reaction time, and inspection time. *American Journal of Mental Deficiency, 82*, 273–281.

Lally, M., & Nettelbeck, T. (1980). Inspection time, intelligence, and response strategy. *American Journal of Mental Deficiency, 84*, 553–560.

Loeb, M., & Alluisi, E. A. (1984). Theories of vigilance. In J. S. Warm (Ed.), *Sustained attention in human performance* (pp. 179–205). New York: Wiley.

Logan, G. D. (1979). On the use of concurrent memory load to measure attention and automaticity. *Journal of Experimental Psychology: Human Perception and Performance, 5*, 189–207.

Logan, G. D. (1988). Toward an instance theory of automatization. *Psychological Review, 95*, 492–527.

Luria, A. (1963). *The mentally retarded child.* New York: Pergamon.

Mackie, R., & Mackay, C. K. (1982). Attention vs. retention in discrimination learning of low-MA retarded adults and MA-matched nonretarded children. *American Journal on Mental Deficiency, 87*, 543–547.

Mackworth, N. H. (1948). The breakdown of vigilance during prolonged visual search. *Quarterly Journal of Experimental Psychology, 1*, 6–21.

Maisto, A. A., & Baumeister, A. A. (1984). Dissection of component processes in rapid information processing tasks: Comparison of retarded and nonretarded people. In P. H. Brooks, R. Sperber, & C. McCauley (Eds.), *Learning and cognition in the mentally retarded* (pp. 165–188). Hillsdale, NJ: Lawrence Erlbaum Associates.

Maisto, A. A., & Jerome, M. A. (1977). Encoding and high speed memory scanning of retarded adolescents. *American Journal of Mental Deficiency, 82*, 282–286.

Marcel, A. J. (1983). Conscious and unconscious perception: Experiments on visual masking and word recognition. *Cognitive Psychology, 15*, 197–237.

Meador, D. M., & Ellis, N. R. (1987). Automatic and effortful processing by mentally retarded and nonretarded persons. *American Journal of Mental Deficiency, 91*, 613–619.

Merrill, E. C. (1985). Differences in semantic processing speed of mentally retarded and nonretarded persons. *American Journal of Mental Deficiency, 90*, 71–80.

Merrill, E. C. (1990). Attentional resource allocation and mental retardation. In N. W. Bray (Ed.), *International review of research in mental retardation* (Vol. 16, pp. 51 -88). New York: Academic Press.

Merrill, E. C. (1992). Attentional resource demands of stimulus encoding for persons with and without mental retardation. *American Journal on Mental Retardation, 97*, 87 -98.

Merrill, E. C., Goodwyn, E. H., & Gooding, H. L. (in press). Mental retardation and the acquisition of automaticity. *American Journal on Mental Retardation.*

Merrill, E. C., & McCauley, C. (1988). Phasic alertness and differences in encoding speed. *American Journal on Mental Retardation, 93*, 245–249.

Merrill, E. C., & Peacock, M. P. (1994). Allocation of attention and task difficulty. *American Journal on Mental Retardation, 98*, 588–593.

Merrill, E. C., Sperber, R. D., McCauley, C., Littlefield, J., Rider, E. A., & Shapiro, D. (1987). Picture encoding speed and mental retardation. *Intelligence, 11*, 169–191.

Miller, G. A., Galanter, E., & Pribram, K. (1960). *Plans and the structure of behavior.* New York: Holt.

Moray, N. (1969). *Attention: Selective processes in vision and hearing.* New York: Academic Press.

Mosley, J. L. (1980). Selective attention of mildly mentally retarded and nonretarded individuals. *American Journal of Mental Deficiency, 84*, 568–576.

Mosley, J. L. (1985). High-speed memory scanning task performance of mildly mentally retarded and nonretarded individuals. *American Journal of Mental Deficiency, 90*, 81–89.

Murphy-Bergman, V., & Wright, G. (1987). Measures of attention. *Perceptual and Motor Skills, 64*, 1139–1143.

Navon, D., & Gopher, D. (1979). On the economy of the human processing system. *Psychological Review, 86*, 214–255.

Neill, W. T. (1977). Inhibitory and facilitatory processes in selective attention. *Journal of Experimental Psychology: Human Percpetion and Performance, 3*, 444–450.

Nettelbeck, T. (1982). Inspection time: An index for intelligence? *Quarterly Journal of Experimental Psychology, 34*, 299–312.

Nettelbeck, T. (1985). Inspection time and mild mental retardation. In N. R. Ellis & N. W. Bray (Eds.), *International review of research in mental retardation* (Vol. 13, pp. 109–141). New York: Academic Press.

Nettelbeck, T. (1987). Inspection time and intelligence. In P. A. Vernon (Ed.), *Speed of information processing and intelligence* (pp. 295–346). Norwood, NJ: Ablex.

Nettelbeck, T., & Brewer, N. (1981). Studies of mild mental retardation and timed performance. In N. R. Ellis (Ed.), *International review of research in mental retardation* (Vol. 10, pp. 62–106). New York: Academic Press.

Nettelbeck, T., Hirons, A., & Wilson, C. (1984). Mental retardation, inspection time and central attentional impairment. *American Journal of Mental Deficiency, 89*, 91–98.

Nettelbeck, T., & Lally, M. (1976). Inspection time and measured intelligence. *British Journal of Psychology, 67*, 17 -22.

Nettelbeck, T., & McLean, J. (1984). Mental retardation and inspection time: A two-stage model for sensory registration and central processing. *American Journal of Mental Deficiency, 89*, 83–90.

Norman, D., & Bobrow, D. (1975). On data limited and resource limited processing. *Journal of Cognitive Psychology, 7*, 44–60.

Nuechterlein, K. H. (1983). Signal detection in vigilance tests and behavioral attributes among offspring of schizophrenic mothers and among hyperactive children. *Journal of Abnormal Psychology, 92*, 4–28.

Nuechterlein, K. H., Parasuraman, R., & Jiang, Q. (1983). Visual sustained attention: Image degradation produces rapid sensitivity decrement over time. *Science, 220*, 327–329.

Nugent, P. M., & Mosley, J. L. (1987). Mentally retarded and nonretarded individuals' attention allocation and capacity. *American Journal of Mental Deficiency, 91*, 598–605.

O'Connor, N., & Hermelin, B. (1963). *Speech and thought in severe subnormality.* New York: Pergamon.

Owings, R. A., Baumeister, A. A., Laine, R. A., & Lewis, M. H. (1980). Memory scanning of shades, colors, and compounds: A comparison of retarded and nonretarded adults. *Intelligence, 4*, 243–254.

Parasuraman, R. (1986). Vigilance, monitoring, and search. In K. R. Boff, L. Kaufman, & J. P. Thomas (Eds.), *Handbook of perception and human performance: Vol. II. Cognitive processes and performance* (pp. 43-1–43-39). New York: Wiley.

Parasuraman, R., & Davies, D. R. (Eds.). (1984). *Varieties of attention.* New York: Academic Press.

Pennington, F. M., & Luszcz, M. A. (1975). Some functional properties of iconic storage in retarded and nonretarded subjects. *Memory & Cognition, 3*, 295–301.

Posner, M. I. (1978). *Chronometric explorations of mind.* Hillsdale, NJ: Lawrence Erlbaum Associates.

Posner, M. I. (1980). Orienting of attention. *Quarterly Journal of Experimental Psychology, 32*, 3–25.

Posner, M. I., Nissen, M. J., & Ogden, W. C. (1978). Attended and unattended processing modes: The role of set for spatial location. In H. L. Pick & I. J. Saltzman (Eds.), *Modes of perceiving and processing information* (pp. 137–157). Hillsdale, NJ: Lawrence Erlbaum Associates.

Posner, M. I., & Snyder, C. R. (1975). Facilitation and inhibition in the processing of signals. In P. M. A. Rabbitt & S. Dornic (Eds.), *Attention and performance* (Vol. 5, pp. 669–682). New York: Academic Press.

Powazek, M., & Johnson, J. T., Jr. (1973). Heart rate response to novel and signal stimuli in nonretarded and retarded subjects. *American Journal of Mental Deficiency, 78*, 286–291.

Rosvold, H. E., Mirsky, A. F., Sarason, I., Bransome, E. D., & Beck, L. N. (1956). A continuous performance test of brain damage. *Journal of Consulting Psychology, 20*, 343–350.

Runcie, D., & O'Bannon, R. M. (1975). Relationship of reaction time to deceleration and variability of heart rate in nonretarded and retarded persons. *American Journal of Mental Deficiency, 79*, 553–558.

Schneider, W., Dumais, S. T., & Shiffrin, R. M. (1984). Automatic and control processing and attention. In R. Parasuraman & D. R. Davies (Eds.), *Varieties of attention* (pp. 1–27). New York: Academic Press.

Schneider, W., & Shiffrin, R. M. (1977). Controlled and automatic human information processing: I. Detection, search, and attention. *Psychological Review, 84*, 1–66.

Semmel, M. I. (1965). Arousal theory and vigilance behavior of educable mentally retarded and nonretarded children. *American Journal of Mental Deficiency, 79*, 44–51.

Shiffrin, R. M., & Schneider, W. (1977). Controlled and automatic human information processing: II. Perceptual learning, automatic attending, and a general theory. *Psychological Review, 84*, 127–190.

Siegel, P. S., Crawford, K. A., & Evelsizer, Z. (1985). Attention in discrimination learning in relation to certain teacher-rated behavior anomalies. *American Journal of Mental Deficiency, 89*, 389–392.

Silverman, W. P. (1974). High speed scanning of nonalphanumeric symbols in culture-familially retarded and nonretarded children. *American Journal of Mental Deficiency, 79*, 44–51.

Silverman, W., & Harris, G. (1982). Reaction time and mild mental retardation: High speed scanning reexamined. *American Journal of Mental Deficiency, 87*, 96–102.

Simpson, R. (1993). [Response criterion change of mentally retarded and nonretarded individuals during tests of sustained attention]. Unpublished raw data.

Sokolov, E. N. (1963). *Perception and the conditioned reflex.* New York: Macmillan.

Soraci, S. A., Jr., Alpher, V. S., Deckner, C. W., & Blanton, R. L. (1983). Oddity performance and the perception of relational information. *Psychologia, 26*, 175–184.

Soraci, S. A., Jr., & Carlin, M. T. (1992). Stimulus organization and relational learning. In N. W. Bray (Ed.), *International review of research in mental retardation* (Vol. 18, pp. 29–53). New York: Academic Press.

Soraci, S. A., Jr., Deckner, C. W., Baumeister, A. A., & Carlin, M. T. (1990). Attentional functioning and relational learning. *American Journal on Mental Retardation, 95*, 304 -315.

Sperber, R. D., Davies, D., Merrill, E. C., & McCauley, C. (1982). Cross-category differences in the processing of subordinate-superordinate relationships. *Child Development, 53*, 1249–1253.

Sperber, R., & McCauley, C. (1984). Semantic processing efficiency in the mentally retarded. In P. H. Brooks, R. Sperber, & C. McCauley (Eds.), *Learning and cognition in the mentally retarded* (pp. 141–163). Hillsdale, NJ: Lawrence Erlbaum Associates.

Sperber, R. D., Ragain, R. D., & McCauley, C. (1976). Reassessment of category knowledge in retarded individuals. *American Journal of Mental Deficiency, 81*, 227–234.

Spitz, H. H. (1963). Field theory in mental deficiency. In N. R. Ellis (Ed.), *Handbook of mental deficiency: Psychological theory and research* (pp. 11–40). New York: McGraw-Hill.

Spitz, H. H. (1966). The role of input organization in the learning and memory of mental retardates. In N. R. Ellis (Ed.), *International review of research in mental retardation* (Vol. 2, pp. 29–56). New York: Academic Press.

Spitz, H. H., & Thor, D. H. (1968). Visual backward masking in retardates and normals. *Perception & Psychophysics, 4*, 245 -246.

Stankov, L. (1989). Attentional resources and intelligence: A disappearing link. *Personality and Individual Differences, 10*, 957–968.

Stanovich, K. E. (1978). Information processing in mentally retarded individuals. In N. R. Ellis (Ed.), *International review of research in mental retardation* (Vol. 9, pp. 29 -60). New York: Academic Press.

Sternberg, S. (1966). High-speed scanning in human memory. *Science, 153*, 652–654.

Sternberg, S. (1969). The discovery of processing stages: Extensions of Donders' method. *Acta Psychologia, 30*, 276 -315.

Stroop, J. R. (1935). Studies in interference in serial verbal reactions. *Journal of Experimental Psychology, 18*, 643–661.

Swanson, J. M., Posner, M., Potkin, S., Bonforte, S., Youpa, D., Fiore, C., Cantwell, D., & Crinella, F. (1991). Activating tasks for the study of visual–spatial attention in ADHD children: A cognitive anatomical approach. *Journal of Child Neurology, 6*, 119–127.

Thomas, P. G. (1989). *Vigilance performance of mildly mentally retarded children and adults.* Unpublished doctoral dissertation, University of Adelaide, Australia.

Thor, D. H., & Thor, C. J. (1970). Dark interval threshold and intelligence. *Journal of Experimental Psychology, 85*, 270– 274.

Tipper, S. P. (1985). The negative priming effect: Inhibitory effects of ignored primes. *Quarterly Journal of Experimental Psychology, 37*, 571–590.

Tipper, S. P., & Cranston, M. (1985). Selective attention and priming: Inhibitory and facilitatory effects of ignored primes. *Quarterly Journal of Experimental Psychology, 37*, 591–611.

Tomporowski, P. D., & Allison, P. (1988). Sustained attention of adults with mental retardation. *American Journal on Mental Retardation, 92*, 525–530.

Tomporowski, P. D., & Hager, L. D. (1992). Sustained attention in mentally retarded individuals. In N. W. Bray (Ed.), *International review of research on mental retardation* (Vol. 18, pp. 111–136). New York: Academic Press.
Tomporowski, P. D., Hayden, A. M., & Applegate, B. (1990). The effects of background event rate on the sustained attention of mentally retarded adults during cognitive vigilance tests. *American Journal on Mental Retardation, 94*, 499–508.
Tomporowski, P. D., & Simpson, R. G. (1990). Sustained attention and intelligence. *Intelligence, 14*, 27–38.
Tomporowski, P. D., & Tinsley, V. (1994). Effects of target probability and memory demands on the vigilance of adults with and without mental retardation. *American Journal on Mental Retardation, 98*, 688–703.
Treisman, A. M. (1969). Strategies and models of selective attention. *Psychological Review, 76*, 282–299.
Treisman, A. M. (1988). Features and objects: The fourteenth Bartlett memorial lecture. *The Quarterly Journal of Experimental Psychology, 40*, 201–237.
Treisman, A. M., & Gelade, G. (1980). A feature-integration theory of attention. *Cognitive Psychology, 12*, 97–136.
Treisman, A., & Gormican, S. (1988). Feature analysis in early vision: Evidence from search asymmetries. *Psychological Review, 95*, 15–48.
Treisman, A., & Paterson, R. (1984). Emergent features, attention, and object perception. *Journal of Experimental Psychology: Human Perception and Performance, 10*, 12–31.
Treisman, A., & Souther, J. (1985). Search asymmetry: A diagnostic for preattentive processing of separable features. *Journal of Experimental Psychology: General, 114*, 285–310.
Underwood, B. J. (1957). *Psychological research.* New York: Appleton Century Crofts.
Vickers, D. (1970). Evidence for an accumulator model of psychophysical discrimination. *Ergonomics, 13*, 37–58.
Vickers, D. (1979). *Decision process in visual perception.* London: Academic Press.
Ware, J. R., Baker, R. A., & Sipowicz, R. R. (1962). Performance of mental deficients on a simple vigilance task. *American Journal of Mental Deficiency, 66*, 647–650.
Warm, J. S. (Ed.). (1984). *Sustained attention in human performance.* New York: Wiley.
Welsandt, R. F., & Meyer, P. A. (1974). Visual masking, mental age, and retardation. *Journal of Experimental Child Psychology, 18*, 512–519.
Whiteley, J. H., Zaparniuk, J., & Asmundson, G. J. G. (1987). Mentally retarded adolescents' breadth of attention and short-term memory processes during matching-to-sample discriminations. *American Journal of Mental Deficiency, 92*, 207–212.
Wickens, C. D. (1984). Processing resources in attention. In R. Parasuraman & D. Davies (Eds.), *Varieties of attention* (pp. 63–102). New York: Academic Press.
Wickens, C. D. (1987). Attention. In P. A. Hancock (Ed.), *Human factors psychology* (pp. 29–79). New York: North-Holland.
Wolitzky, D. L., Hofer, R., & Shapiro, R. (1972). Cognitive controls and mental retardation. *Journal of Abnormal Psychology, 79*, 296–302.
Zeaman, D. (1978). Some relations of general intelligence and selective attention. *Intelligence, 2*, 55–73.
Zeaman, D., & House, B. J. (1963). The role of attention in retardate discrimination learning. In N. R. Ellis (Ed.), *Handbook of mental deficiency* (pp. 159–223). Hillsdale, NJ: Lawrence Erlbaum Associates.
Zeaman, D., & House, B. J. (1979). A review of attention theory. In N. R. Ellis (Ed.), *Handbook of mental deficiency: Psychological theory and research* (2nd ed., pp. 63–129). Hillsdale, NJ: Lawrence Erlbaum Associates.
Zigler, E., & Balla, D. (Eds.). (1982). *Mental retardation: The developmental-difference controversy.* Hillsdale, NJ: Lawrence Erlbaum Associates.

› 10 ‹

Speed of Information Processing and Cognition

Ted Nettelbeck
Carlene Wilson
University of Adelaide

The study of human information processing is concerned essentially with hypothetical capacities and mechanisms within the brain whereby external events registered by the sense organs are manipulated by the brain and give rise to observable behavior. The cognitive processes intervening between external stimulation and the response that follows can only be inferred, on the basis of theoretical assumptions about how the information processing system is organized. Because the time from the onset of a signal to the initiation of a response can be measured with high precision in a laboratory situation, a number of measures derived from reaction time (RT), together with similar "real-time" measures of mental events, have emerged as the most widely used dependent variables for investigating information processing. These measures have been central to the attempt over the past 3 decades to formulate theories of individual differences in intellectual abilities. The interested reader is referred to Welford (1980) and Jensen (1982) for accounts of these developments.

A fundamental conceptual assumption underpinning most research directed toward understanding human cognition is that information processing can, in principle, be described in terms of a sequence of discrete stages. Of course, various versions of this basic model exist and there is by no means consensus about specific details. However, virtually all versions include the following four stages: initial sensory storage of brief duration; perceptual encoding of registered information into a more stable form; central processing, involving comparison with previously stored information and leading to decision making; and response selection and execution. A second assumption is that overall RT represents the sum of all processes within these stages. Given these two assumptions, a third is that by appropriate experimental manipulation it is possible to isolate separate stages or processes.

As applied to the investigation of group characteristics or individual differences in information processing, the use of RT also usually rests on the assumption that experimental conditions are equivalent for all subjects. It is certainly the case that most measures of this kind are derived from relatively uncomplicated procedures that apparently require little by way of specific knowledge requirements. Nonetheless, particularly now that moderately strong correlations between IQ and various measures of speed of information processing derived from RT have been confirmed within nonretarded ranges of IQ (Jensen, 1982, 1987), this is an issue that should be treated cautiously. There is strong evidence that RT is not simply a pure measure of the biological efficiency of the brain, as is sometimes assumed, and that more besides is involved. Most important, the speed of a reaction and the accuracy with which it is made are not independent parameters of performance. Interdependence is found in two quite different ways. First, considered across subjects representing a wide range of IQ, speed and accuracy tend to be positively correlated and both correlate positively with IQ. Thus, higher IQ persons tend to be speedier and more accurate, an outcome compatible with the view that RT is tapping basic processing efficiency. However, it is also the case that each subject has direct control over both covariates and typically will tend to trade off speed against accuracy, so that high accuracy is associated with instances of slower RT and faster RTs are only accomplished by sacrificing accuracy to some extent. Furthermore, when performance is in the vicinity of optimally fast and errorless RT, relatively small improvements in speed are accompanied by relatively large increases in the number of errors made; whereas markedly slowing RTs can only produce little effect on accuracy (Pachella, 1974). This speed–accuracy trade-off therefore strongly suggests that individual differences in RT in part reflect differences in strategies that may be learned, and that will confound any differences in basic neural activities that may exist.

A distinction between basic neurophysiology and learned strategies is central to the study of mental retardation and has generated a great deal of debate. Physical *structural* characteristics of the information processing system are envisaged as permanent and not subject to modification by training. *Functional* aspects of processing, on the other hand, are those responsible for the control of processing within the structure and include plans and strategies applied in search, selection, and the transformation and organization of information within the system (Atkinson & Shiffrin, 1968). It is commonly assumed that control functions can be changed by appropriate intervention. An important conceptual issue arising from this distinction concerns whether the nature of those cognitive differences observed between retarded and nonretarded persons is the consequence of structure or function. Although there are considerable difficulties in maintaining this distinction (Nettelbeck & Brewer, 1981), it has served to emphasize the many methodological inadequacies of much research into the cognitive aspects of mental retardation that has tended to ignore the relevance of complex strategies to an understanding of retarded performance. Baumeister (1984) provided a thorough, informative discussion of these issues, and it would be redundant to address them further here. However, problems associated with group comparisons that Baumeister described, and that essentially reflect failure to ensure functional comparability across groups in terms of experimental demands and motivational requirements, are clearly critical to an evaluation of research considered here. Moreover, Baumeister's (1984) account of the debate about whether the nature of retarded–nonretarded differences in cognition is better described in terms of some fundamental defect or as a difference reflecting normal variation in rate and ultimate extent of development is highly recommended. The issues discussed by Baumeister are directly relevant to questions of research design and to the central purpose of recent research into the RTs of mentally retarded persons—namely, whether slower response speed reflects "quantitative" (i.e., functional) or "qualitative" (i.e., structural) differences.

The investigation of information processing among persons with mental retardation now has a considerable history, with previous reviews by Baumeister and Kellas (1968), Stanovich (1978), Nettelbeck and Brewer (1981), and Maisto and Baumeister (1984) describing what has been accomplished. In this chapter, therefore, we have not attempted to review earlier research comprehensively and have instead focused on work during the past decade, although it has sometimes been necessary to reconsider earlier studies in the light of more recent research. Following a brief summary of conclusions drawn from previous RT research, our review is organized around the application of five methodologies that have formed the basis of more recent work.

REACTION TIME (RT)

As Baumeister and Kellas (1968) first established, the RT performance of mentally retarded persons is significantly slower, more variable, and more positively skewed by exceptionally slow responses than that of nonretarded CA controls. Slowing generally covaries with IQ if the range of IQ scores is not too restricted, particularly when more complex choice (CRT) tasks are involved. Within-subject mean RT and variance are correlated. Between-subject variance is also higher, so that retarded samples show greater heterogeneity than do nonretarded samples. Baumeister and Kellas (1968) emphasized that variance of RT seemed to identify an attribute of mental retardation of potential theoretical importance. Consistent with this conclusion, Aufderheide (1984; cited by Zelaznik & Aufderheide, 1986) confirmed that the fastest RTs of retarded and nonretarded adults were not significantly different.

Several studies following Baumeister and Kellas' lead were designed to measure the effects of manipulating various temporal and intensity parameters of simple RT (see Nettelbeck & Brewer, 1981, for a review). Results were not always clear cut, but taken together with investigations of physiological indices of orientation and attention, they were broadly consistent with the proposition that retarded persons are less efficient at formulating and maintaining appropriate expectancy. This conclusion therefore linked cognitive deficiencies to less effective strategies for making use of information. Although it was acknowledged that autonomic functioning associated with arousal and stimulus registration might also be deficient to some extent, particularly at lower levels of retardation, these activities were not considered to be the major determinant of cognitive deficiencies, at least for the majority of participants in these studies. Nettelbeck and Brewer (1981) also observed that there appeared to be considerable similarities among the patterns of RTs obtained from retarded samples, normal elderly samples, and those of groups representing various forms of mental disorders and brain damage. They argued that, because wider differences in the nature of impairment could be assumed to underlie these very diverse conditions, it was unlikely that an explanation for poorer RT performance could be found in terms of some single structural deficiency.

Nettelbeck and Brewer's (1981) review included a large number of investigations of information processing by retarded persons, conducted within the conceptual framework of a stage model (as described earlier in this chapter), with the general aim of attempting to locate specific deficient processes or stages. These authors concluded that some evidence could be found to support deficiencies associated with mental retardation in all distinguishable stages, but that different research outcomes were the consequence of the methodologies involved. Thus, the manipulation of temporal and contextual factors appeared to implicate attention and expectancy; backward masking threshold procedures limiting exposure duration suggested poorer encoding; complex discriminations in association with predominantly simple ballistic movements highlighted central stimulus–response translation; and tasks involving movements under feedback control reflected poor response organization. In short, limitations appeared according to the emphasis given relative processing requirements within the different experimental situations.

In principle, it is conceivable that this outcome was the consequence of a specific deficit at one stage but that impairment at one influences processing at all others. If so, it would be, at the very least, very difficult to isolate the deficit by applying an independent stage model for information processing. (An attempt to do this is described later in this chapter, however, when providing an account of the Responding Time measure.) Alternatively, this outcome was the consequence of a deficit in some global mechanism within the processing system. A recent meta-analysis by Kail (1992) of archival data from comparisons between mildly retarded and nonretarded adults is consistent with this possibility, finding that slower processing among the former reflects a general component. Kail included a wide variety of speeded tasks from 45 studies involving 515 pairs of mean response times from both groups. Plotting retarded response times against those of nonretarded subjects resulted in a highly reliable linear function, the slope coefficient for which suggested that retarded persons process more slowly than CA controls by a factor of about 2. Kail's preferred explanation in terms of a slower cycle time avoids the connotation of executive control inherent in other explanations to be considered here. However, insofar as this hypothesis predicts error-free performance under conditions without time constraints, it encounters difficulties with evidence from Brewer and Smith (1990; discussed later in the chapter) that residual error is characteristic of the performance of retarded persons, even when responses are extremely slow.

A somewhat different emphasis is found in suggestions that, in order to account for information processing, some general regulatory control component is required. Sanders (1977) concluded that it was necessary to invoke an "immediate arousal" factor that operated executively to influence all stages of processing. Similarly, Sternberg (1977) proposed that intelligent behavior could not be accounted for satisfactorily without supposing that executive "metacomponents" were available to direct and control the strategies and plans for action by which problem solving advanced. Consistent with these suggestions, Nettelbeck and Brewer (1981) concluded that the more variable and, therefore, generally slower average RT of retarded persons was the consequence of a general impairment to central executive functions that govern all aspects of information processing.

Although this conclusion may have seemed inevitable, the problem with it is that it does not shift the level of explanation for mental retardation beyond that provided by a single attribute like IQ, used to categorize an individual in the first place. The term *executive function* in this sense becomes another metaphor for *intelligence*—like MA or *g* or homunculus. Nettelbeck and Brewer (1981) recognized this difficulty but argued, nonetheless, that it may be possible to clarify the nature of control processes by inducing change in strategies that determine performance. Specifically, they suggested two possible means for achieving this. First, whereas most CRT studies with retarded subjects had largely ignored comparative differences in error rates across different ability groups, Nettelbeck and Brewer (1981) proposed that a systematic examination of the speed–accuracy trade-off adopted by retarded and nonretarded subjects might reveal important strategy differences between groups. Second, systematic training might be applied to test the limits of improvement. Nettelbeck and Brewer (1981) suggested that, to the extent that special strategic intervention proved essential, this would help to define a basic structural limitation as a characteristic of mental retardation. Research in response to these proposals is included in the next two sections.

TRIAL-BY-TRIAL ANALYSIS OF CRT

Rabbitt (1981) emphasized that the speed–accuracy trade-off that characterizes CRT performance is the consequence of regulatory cognitive processes whereby subjects monitor the accuracy of their responses so as to avoid errors, and monitor and adjust speed of responding, consistent with task instructions to be as fast but as accurate as possible. In this way subjects are able to "track" in (i.e., stay within) narrow, fast "bands" (i.e., ranges) of CRT near their optimal level of performance. Consistent with this proposal, Rabbitt's trial-by-trial analyses revealed that CRT typically becomes shorter across a sequence of trials until an error is made, whereupon CRT slows to a level just above the average for correct responses for a trial or two before the downward trend begins again. For young nonretarded adults, the opportunity afforded by early practice is sufficient for them to learn quickly how to operate efficiently, with very high accuracy, within a relatively narrow band of CRTs just above those levels where the likelihood of error increases markedly. Longer practice does continue to produce improvement, essentially by narrowing the "safe" operating band within which subjects confine their responses, but the major impact of practice is found during earlier, rather than later, trials.

Brewer and Smith (1984) applied this model in a detailed investigation of the relative efficiency of the executive processes of young adults with moderate to mild mental retardation when compared to CA controls. Initial experiments demonstrated convincingly that retarded subjects completing a four-choice RT task were able to discriminate as reliably as nonretarded subjects between correct responses and errors, so that CRT differences in speed or accuracy were not attributable to accuracy monitoring.

The main study involved 2,000 trials, permitting analyses of trial-by-trial CRT and accuracy. By comparing group *conditional error functions*, which described the number of errors associated with different levels of CRT, and supporting this with analyses of trial-by-trial variations in CRT preceding and following those trials on which an error was made, Brewer and Smith were able to show that:

1. Retarded subjects produced a markedly wider range of CRTs than did CA controls, with a small number of CRTs actually being shorter than any made by CA controls; but with several much longer and some extending into several seconds.
2. Relatively rare, very fast CRTs by retarded subjects were associated with very high probabilities of error around chance levels of accuracy.
3. Slower CRTs by retarded subjects were also associated with increasing probabilities of error that, although much higher than usual, never approached chance levels.
4. Error rates among retarded subjects were always higher than those for controls; and whereas slower CRTs among the latter were entirely error-free, retarded subjects did not achieve 100% accuracy within any range of CRT.
5. Most retarded subjects required about 10 times more training trials than nonretarded controls to ensure familiarity with task requirements (200 vs. 20). Following this, the appreciable degree of practice afforded by 2,000 trials still did not reduce group differences in CRT. In fact, nonretarded subjects continued to show a slight but consistent reduction throughout, but retarded subjects' CRTs were asymptotic after 1,200 trials, so that the two groups were actually tending to draw apart.
6. Retarded subjects were much less efficient than were controls at constraining CRTs within relatively narrow fast bands just above a level where errors would occur. Although retarded and nonretarded groups both responded in broadly the same way, insofar as they tracked progressively shorter CRTs until an error was made, with immediate posterror slowing, there were a number of important differences between the groups. Thus, retarded subjects were generally much slower overall, they much more frequently produced sequences of trials for which successive errors occurred, and adjustments to CRT were relatively coarse, involving many instances of inappropriate under- and overadjustments. Retarded subjects did produce long sequences of error-free responding but, typically, these involved much slower than average CRTs.

As Brewer and Smith (1984) acknowledged, some aspects of this general pattern are plausibly attributed to lapses in attention. However, these authors also concluded that more than this was involved. Their theory was that retarded CRT performance is characterized by an inadequate regulatory mechanism that mediates the speed and accuracy of CRTs. Whereas fast, accurate tracking within a narrow band is the consequence of fine adjustments that are guided by learning derived from relevant information accumulated across a wide range of trials, retarded subjects are guided much more by immediate past experiences; that is, by circumstances within the immediately preceding trial or trials. The outcome of this is higher rates of error, greater variability and positive skewing to the distribution of CRTs, and therefore longer average CRT.

In a follow-up experiment, Brewer and Smith (1990) investigated the effects of constraining the influence of hypothetical regulatory mechanisms by requiring both retarded and nonretarded young adult subjects to respond within a specified time. This "deadline" procedure therefore equated available processing time for both groups so that CRTs should be the same. By varying the duration of the deadline and measuring the consequential changing relationship between speed and accuracy, it was possible to test whether patterns of errors across groups were similar or not. Essentially, the argument was that if, having removed or at least severely constrained opportunities for subjects to apply strategies, patterns were similar, then this would confirm that retarded–nonretarded differences in processing speed under normal self-paced condition are predominantly the consequence of regulatory mechanisms. If, however, retarded subjects made more errors, then this would be taken as implicating structural capacity limitations on processing.

The outcome was consistent with the latter interpretation. Retarded subjects failed to meet deadline restrictions on over 50% more trials than nonretarded controls; and for responses that did conform (so that responding times were approximately equivalent), error rates were markedly higher. In both groups error rate increased with increasing constraint on CRT, but at a rate among retarded subjects that was twice that for CA controls. Moreover, regression analysis suggested that comparative error rates would never be the same, predicting a residual 13% error among retarded subjects after nonretarded subjects had achieved error-free performance.

A second study by Brewer and Smith (1990) was designed to determine whether training under a deadline procedure would improve the processing of retarded persons. The rationale was that by learning to control regulatory processes within relatively short time constraints subjects should reduce the range of adjustments, thereby reducing variance and hence average CRT. Three mildly retarded adults had extensive training involving 5,000 deadline trials (350 ms) within a multiple-baseline across-subjects design that involved an additional 5,000 normal self-paced trials. Deadline training was effective in that subjects learned to respond within the time constraint and postdeadline mean CRTs were substantially shortened because of reduced variability, irrespective of whether training was introduced early or late in practice. This improvement was unrelated to relative error rates, which were essentially the same during predeadline and postdeadline trials, but did represent a significant shift in the pattern of errors, those at relatively long CRTs (cf. Brewer & Smith, 1984) being substantially reduced. However, although Brewer and Smith (1990) found strong support for their conclusion that training under time constraints had assisted retarded subjects to track CRTs within much narrower bands, they also observed that, even after 5,000 trials within the deadline phase, subjects' accuracy did not improve from initial levels, so that error rates were always appreciably higher than those registered by CA controls after only 400 trials with a more stringent deadline (300 ms).

Further comment on this very promising research approach is warranted. Brewer and Smith (1989) also applied trial-by-trial analysis to the investigation of improvements in speed of information processing during childhood. In effect, they followed Brewer and Smith's (1984) procedures to examine speed–accuracy trade-off functions in children aged 5, 7, 9, 11, 13, and 15 years, and compared these with the adult group from the 1984 study. It is therefore possible in broad terms to compare the performance of their 1984 retarded subjects with that of their 1989 children.[1] On the basis of the IQ scores of the retarded subjects, a plausible estimate for average MA is between 9 and 10 years. Assuming this, comparisons between the retarded subjects and the children suggest that performance among the former represents an MA lag of 1 to 2 years in terms of overall median CRT. Following Spitz (1982), we interpret this to mean that the differences in strategies revealed by this research are attributable to defective rather than delayed development. This conclusion appears to be supported by examinations of the conditional error functions relating CRT to the probability of error, and by the trial-by-trial analyses of pre- and posterror CRTs and error-to-error sequences of different lengths.

Conclusions

The trial-by-trial approach adopted by Brewer and Smith has yet to be taken up by other researchers. Undoubtedly it is a very demanding procedure in terms of what is required by way of investment of effort from both researchers and participants. We believe, however, that it has considerable potential for explicating individual and group differences in both the quantity and quality of information processing. It provides a powerful comparative method for analyzing IQ-related differences in information processing because it directly addresses the operation of regulatory mechanisms mediating important differences in trial-to-trial changes in speed and accuracy of performance. Brewer and Smith (1984, 1990) convincingly demonstrated that the poorer information processing of retarded persons can be improved by specific training that focuses on regulating responding within time constraints, to levels better than 30% above those achieved by substantial but nondirected practice. Given the extent to which less efficient information processing limits the general functioning of retarded individuals, this outcome is extremely promising. Moreover, it emphasizes the point made by Wade, Hoover, and Newell (1984) that studies reporting slower information processing among the retarded may actually be reporting a group difference in learning rates.

Further research should attempt to delineate more precisely the nature of those changes that occur as a consequence of training that results in improved information processing. Brewer and Smith (1989) obtained some indication that developmental trends might be distinguishable in terms of different relative rates of change in the regulation of speed of responding and in control over monitoring accuracy, with the latter emerging at a later ontological stage. Thus, one direction for the future would be to investigate similarities and differences between retarded performance and that of children at different developmental levels.

Further research should also focus on whether gains in processing efficiency are maintained over time—and to what extent they can be made to generalize across different situations. The last question is particularly important because we believe that Brewer and Smith (1990) also provided strong evidence for structural limitations to the capacity of retarded persons to process information efficiently. Consistent with this, we observed that the significantly improved levels of CRT achieved by retarded subjects after the extended training provided by Brewer and Smith (1990) appeared still to be slower than the median CRT recorded by these authors (1989) for 9-year-olds from only one fifth as many trials. In a similar vein, Wade et al. (1984) acknowledged that, even after 600 trials of practice and directed training, RT and associated movement in a simple movement task among

[1]These authors have not yet examined these comparisons but we have encouraged them to do so (N. Brewer, personal communication, February 1993).

retarded subjects remained significantly slower than levels readily achieved by nonretarded subjects without specific training. In this regard, on the basis of our reading of this literature, we make the following predictions:

1. Compared to appropriate MA controls, conditional error functions accounting for speed and accuracy of CRTs among adults with mild mental retardation will show a significant MA lag of 2 years or more.
2. Autocorrelation functions relating strength of correlation between two trials either adjoining or separated by an increasing number of intermediate trials will confirm trends consistent with the previous prediction. (This form of analysis is described by Brewer & Smith, 1989, who compared children and adult groups in this way).
3. Particularly among persons with mental retardation, the extent to which the likelihood of error increases with shortening CRT will be predicted by general intelligence. An obvious tests of this prediction would involve correlating IQ with the regression coefficient best fitting the individual's conditional error function derived from the Vincentizing procedure described by Brewer and Smith (1990).

STERNBERG'S MEMORY-SCANNING PROCEDURE

Theories of information processing have emphasized that short-term memory functioning involves a complex combination of several processes and structures. Consistent with this approach, research into some aspects of the short-term memory of persons with mental retardation has utilized an experimental procedure developed by Sternberg (1966) to make inferences about processes assumed to underlie choice reaction time (CRT) in recognition-memory tasks. Sternberg's *additive factors* method is so called because it was conceived as providing a means for identifying hypothetical separate stages of processing, by testing whether experimental manipulations within factorial designs produce additive or nonadditive effects on CRT (see Sternberg, 1975, for a review). Essentially, if the experimental manipulation of one variable produces constant change across all levels in other variables, this is interpreted as an additive effect, which helps to define a separate stage. Significant statistical interaction between variables, on the other hand, would be interpreted as reflecting the operation of a common factor.

A detailed description of the method is available from several sources, including Phillips and Nettelbeck (1985). Essentially, the subject first memorizes a short list of items (the "positive set") and must decide as quickly and as accurately as possible whether or not a test stimulus presented subsequently was a member of the positive set. The positive set can be changed for each trial (varied set procedure) or the same for every trial (fixed set procedure). When the number of items in the positive set increases, CRT for positive responses and also for negative responses generally increases linearly and at the same rate. This finding of parallel linear "item recognition functions" led Sternberg to conclude that memory scanning involves the *serial and exhaustive* comparison of the encoded test probe with every item in the positive set.

Sternberg and others identified four separate, sequential stages: encoding the test probe into a stable form; a comparison stage involving the serial, exhaustive scan through the items stored in memory; a binary (yes–no) decision; and translation of the decision into a response and the organization and execution of that response. The rate of memory scanning at the second stage is defined by the angle of the slope of the item recognition regression function. The zero intercept of this function is held to represent the time required for the other three operations combined. Because the memory scanning stage is held to be independent from the other stages on the basis of additivity, Sternberg argued that the slopes and intercepts of item recognition functions obtained from individuals should not be correlated, unless some subject variable not under experimental control was influencing the duration of both scanning rate and some other stage or stages (Sternberg, 1969). However, beyond considerations of this kind, it is not necessarily the case that high negative correlation between slope and intercept implies dependence between stages. This is because both parameters are derived from the same set of CRTs and they therefore share variance that is negatively correlated in the two parameters (Valentine, Wilding, & Mohindra, 1984). Thus, negative covariation in slope and intercept parameters is predictable on purely statistical grounds, but without challenging the discrete identity of processing stages. Todman and Gibb (1985) concluded that this eventuality provides a likely explanation for the negative correlations found in their study between slope and intercept for all IQ groups. (This is an issue to which we return later.) Another hypothesis suggested by Maisto and Baumeister (1984) is that some subjects achieve faster scanning by encoding more slowly, and vice versa. A similar proposal in relation to analogical problem solving is discussed in the section that follows. The idea should certainly be explored further, because the extent to which encoding depends on effective strategic behavior is clearly an issue with implications for an improved understanding of retarded performance.

Despite criticisms (Pachella, 1974; Stanovich & Pachella, 1977; Sternberg, 1979; Theios, Smith, Haviland, Traupmann, & Moy, 1973), the additive factors method generated a great deal of research during the 2 decades following Sternberg's (1966) initial publication.

Twelve published studies have investigated memory scanning processes in relation to mental retardation (Detterman et al., 1992; Dugas & Kellas, 1974; Harris & Fleer, 1974; Maisto & Jerome, 1977; Maisto & Sipe, 1980; Merrill, 1985; Mosley, 1985; Owings, Baumeister, Lane, & Lewis, 1980; Phillips & Nettelbeck, 1984a, 1984b; Silverman, 1974; Todman & Gibb, 1985). All have involved adults or adolescents who were mildly retarded; none has included retarded children or persons with moderate to severe levels of retardation.

Slope Parameter

Results have generally suggested serial, exhaustive scanning, but with rates much more variable across studies than are typically found with nonretarded adults. Among earlier studies, higher slopes for item recognition functions consistent with slower scanning rates were found for retarded groups compared to nonretarded mental age (MA) and chronological age (CA) controls, using digits (Dugas & Kellas, 1974; Harris & Fleer, 1974) and random shapes as items (Maisto & Jerome, 1977), although Silverman (1974) did not find any intelligence-related difference using continuously displayed random shapes, a procedure that probably resulted in visual scanning rather than memory scanning.

More recently, Merrill (1985) and Mosley (1985) reported retarded–nonretarded group differences in rate of memory scanning. Merrill's study is unusual because, in addition to examining speed of working memory scanning, he included a procedure for also examining speed of processing permanently stored semantic information. This was accomplished by including a condition in which memory sets were composed of labels to common superordinate categories (e.g., "furniture"), whereas probes were basic-level names for common objects (e.g., "table"). For this condition, then, the slope parameter to the item recognition function was interpreted as reflecting memory scanning, together with additional category decision time (i.e., whether a probe name was an exemplar of one of the categories in the memory set). Because the experiment also included a control condition that provided an independent estimate of memory scanning with identical stimuli (category labels), category decision time could be isolated by subtractive methodology. The results suggested that both memory scanning and category decision time for retarded subjects were only about 50% as efficient as among CA controls. Because this outcome was equivalent across both domains, Merrill concluded that it was the consequence of a central processing mechanism.

However, Todman and Gibb (1985) found no reliable slope difference between retarded adolescents and below-average to above-average IQ controls, and Owings et al. (1980) also found no evidence for slower memory scanning among retarded subjects compared with CA controls, except when the positive set consisted of compounds of different attributes (shape and color) with in-built redundancy. Retarded and nonretarded groups were both able to scan compounds more quickly than items with single defining attributes, but persons with retardation scanned compounds more slowly than did nonretarded persons. Maisto and Baumeister (1984) subsequently observed that the Owings et al. results could be regarded as reconciling the differences between earlier investigations. Consistent with Silverman (1974) and Todman and Gibb (1985), Owings et al. demonstrated that retarded and nonretarded persons could scan at the same rate under some circumstances, but findings of slower scanning by retarded subjects with stimuli comprising digits and random shapes might reflect redundant characteristics within such stimuli. Maisto and Baumeister (1984) also considered the possibility that relatively slower scanning among retarded persons when stimuli include redundant information reflects higher susceptibility to associative interference in short-term memory between the different attributes of the compound items. Maisto and Baumeister included an account of a series of unpublished studies by Baumeister that appear to support this hypothesis. By manipulating the associative interference contained in compound items constituting the negative set, Baumeister was able to demonstrate increasingly relatively slower scanning among retarded subjects (compared with nonretarded subjects), with increasing degree of interference. This potentially interesting outcome could usefully be followed up. It is also possible, however, that slope differences have reflected motivational considerations emphasized by Zigler (1969). As Stanovich (1978) pointed out, participants in early studies were recruited from residential institutions and were therefore more likely to be disadvantaged motivationally.

Sample sizes in the studies reviewed have all been small, so that failure to find a difference in slopes from different ability groups might be attributable to Type II error. However, this is probably not the case. Two investigations by Phillips and Nettelbeck (1984a, 1984b) appear to have resolved to some extent the issue of how the slope parameter of the item recognition function is influenced by intellectual ability. Phillips and Nettelbeck (1984a) compared the performance of mildly retarded adults with that of CA and MA nonretarded controls, under fixed and varied set procedures and with memory sets comprising one to six digits. Results for the retarded group were markedly different than those of either CA or MA controls, suggesting that retarded subjects had adopted different processing strategies under the two procedures. Whereas slopes from nonretarded subjects were always predictably linear, irrespective of the procedure followed, for retarded subjects the slopes for positive responses under both procedures and for negative responses to the fixed set were significantly steeper than among nonretarded subjects; but negative responses to the varied set were not linear across set size. Such disparate slopes to positive and negative functions indicated that, unlike for nonretarded subjects, memory search by retarded subjects was not always exhaustive. Moreover, the retarded group found the varied set procedure to be more difficult, as indicated by much higher error rates. A follow-up study with different retarded participants and an upper limit of four items in the memory set replicated these results, demonstrating that they were not the consequence of limitations in memory span.

Phillips and Nettelbeck (1984b) went on to investigate practice effects in a group of mildly retarded adults compared with CA and MA controls, initially under both fixed and varied set procedures. Consistent with previous research, seven practice sessions produced little change to slopes for nonretarded adults, which were near asymptotic from the outset. Practice reduced slopes for nonretarded children to adult levels. Slopes for retarded subjects became consistently linear under both procedures, although correlations between slopes and intercepts were negative and moderately high throughout. Slopes for retarded subjects always remained steeper than for the other groups, but were significantly reduced by practice. Because slopes in the retarded group did not appear to be asymptotic after seven sessions whereas those for both control groups were, practice in the retarded group was extended for an additional 18 sessions, limited to a varied set procedure. Although practice markedly reduced variance in CRT overall, slopes never became stable, continuing to fluctuate considerably across sessions and averaging (52 ms/item)—significantly above CA (33 ms/item) and MA (34 ms/item) levels. However, when within-subject variability was reduced by excluding 6% of excessively long CRTs, slope levels comparable with nonretarded performance were achieved. Phillips and Nettelbeck (1984b) therefore concluded that specific structures supporting memory scanning processes are not deficient among persons with mild mental retardation and that, where steeper item recognition functions have been found, this is interpretable as reflecting inconsistent performance characterized by marked lapses in concentration. This conclusion was supported by the observation that, although practice reduced errors by retarded subjects, error rate never improved below 2% to 3%, whereas nonretarded adults were below 2% from the outset.

Merrill's (1985) finding of less efficient memory scanning and category decision processing to an equivalent extent among his retarded subjects is plausibly attributed to deficient central executive functioning. Phillips and Nettelbeck (1985) speculated on the nature of this deficiency, demonstrating that the pattern of CRTs from retarded persons early during practice is consistent with these subjects adopting two mutually exclusive response strategies. One is serial search but the other is a very slow deadline response, made in trials when attention to critical events is poor. The probability of the latter may increase with increasing task demands as the size of the memory set increases.

Taking Phillips and Nettelbeck's (1984b) eventual outcome for scanning by retarded subjects together with their result of equivalent scanning rates following practice among nonretarded children and adults, and Seymour and Moir's (1980) finding that a wide IQ range from 70 to 130 had no significant effect on slope values, a reasonable conclusion is that structural capacity for memory scanning is essentially constant, at least across a very wide range of mental maturity. However, slower scanning performance by retarded persons is not attributable simply to developmental delay. As Phillips and Nettelbeck (1984b) found, their retarded subjects required vastly more practice to approach levels achieved relatively quickly by MA controls; and to the extent that CRTs in about 6% of trials were excessively long, consistent with problems of concentration and production, these subjects always demonstrated an MA lag, plausibly the consequence of structural deficiency relating to executive control rather than to structures specifically supporting memory scanning.

Intercept Parameter

Studies have also failed to establish consistent results from comparisons between the zero intercepts from item recognition functions estimated for retarded and nonretarded groups. Thus, Harris and Fleer (1974), Silverman (1974), and Maisto and Jerome (1977) all found near-equal intercepts across groups, whereas Dugas and Kellas (1974), Merrill (1985), Mosley (1985), and Todman and Gibb (1985) reported higher intercepts in their retarded samples. Moreover, in a condition within which quality of the test probe was degraded, Maisto and Jerome (1977) found that the intercept for retarded subjects was markedly more raised than was the case for nonretarded CA controls. This outcome was therefore consistent with less efficient encoding processes among retarded subjects, a conclusion that Maisto and Sipe (1980) subsequently confirmed by independently manipulating test probe quality and probability of occurrence. In effect, retarded performance was profoundly influenced by probe degradation, and retarded subjects were unable to take advantage of information about test probe probability.

Phillips and Nettelbeck's (1984b) results following extensive practice do not resolve these discrepancies, but they do add weight to the proposition that a higher intercept to the item recognition function than is found among nonretarded adults is characteristic of the performance of mentally retarded adults. Much higher intercepts from initial sessions compared to those for MA and CA controls were lowered appreciably by practice, with this reduction accounting substantially for the overall reduction in mean CRT. Intercepts for both positive and negative responses were asymptotic after about 15 sessions. Intercepts thereafter across the final 10 sessions were remarkably stable, unlike slope parameters, which, as described previously, showed considerable variation as a consequence of the presence of occasional very slow CRTs, consistent with poor attention to task events. However, intercepts in the retarded group always remained significantly higher than those for CA controls, never approaching the levels reached in that group after only seven sessions (480 ms vs. 350 ms, positive and negative responses combined). Compared with MA controls, intercepts in the retarded group were much higher initially but improved rapidly to outperform children beyond the fifth trial. Extrapolating from the children's performance across seven sessions, the zero intercept for children after a further 18 sessions would not have improved below about 660 ms.

Conclusions

It is clear that extensive practice improves both the slope and zero intercept of the item recognition function for mildly retarded adults, to an extent that in absolute terms far exceeds levels of improvement among MA or CA controls. This is important, because such may not be the case with children compared to adults. Although the critical experiments comparing practice effects on the memory scanning performance of children and adults have not yet been done, Kail (1991) demonstrated for RT in mental rotation tasks that the considerable impact of practice does not differ qualitatively for children and adults. Children always lag behind adults by a constant value that is age related but declines with age as a decreasing exponential function, so that performance beyond adolescence is very close to adult level. Thus, a reasonable interpretation at this stage is that initial performance by retarded persons includes a component that reflects poorer understanding of task demands. Practice-related improvement incorporates slower learning, whereby strategies are modified to better accommodate domain-specific requirements. However, differences between retarded and nonretarded persons reflect more than the slower learning of more effective strategies.

Residual steeper slope after practice among retarded subjects appears attributable to poorer attentional and production control, instances of which are greatly reduced by practice but never eradicated. Thus, rate of memory scanning appears to be correlated with intelligence because lower IQ is characterized by inconsistent responding. It is only when this effect is partialled out artificially that the scanning performance of retarded subjects becomes comparable to that of nonretarded children and adults. Nonetheless, doing this demonstrates that scanning performance is independent of maturational capacity, at least beyond about 9 years, the age of children in the Phillips and Nettelbeck (1984b) study. For the zero intercept, however, despite enhanced consistency, retarded subjects display limitations relative to CA that are resistant to practice, although retarded adults overcome an initial MA lag to outperform MA controls. Because the zero intercept among retarded subjects appears to be relatively unaffected by the poor attentional control that influences slope, the slower speed of perceptual encoding and/or response selection and execution indicated by the higher intercept for retarded subjects may be inferred to reflect some additional deficiency. Although this presumably reflects in some way the quantity of information processing resources available, it seems improbable that the difference between retarded and nonretarded adults is equivalent to the general maturational factor hypothesized by Kail (1991) to be responsible for normal age differences in processing speed, because normal children do eventually develop into normal adults. However, this issue can only be ultimately determined by experiments that not only equate practice for children and adults, but also include retarded and nonretarded children and adults in appropriate cross-sequential comparisons.

Even following prolonged practice, Phillips and Nettelbeck (1984b) reported continuing to find significant negative correlations between slope and intercept parameters to the item recognition function for retarded adults. They took this to indicate that hypothesized stages of processing are not independent, possibly as a consequence of the subsequent dependence of decision processes on initial encoding, as suggested by Maisto and Baumeister (1984), and raised this as a methodological problem confronting further investigations. However, this conclusion may have been premature. As the only researchers to have evaluated such correlations after taking between-subjects variance into account, Todman and Gibb (1985) showed that their observed negative correlations, although substantial, were entirely predictable on statistical grounds, so that slope and intercept from the item recognition function could be interpreted as reflecting discrete independent processing stages. None of the other relevant publications provided details necessary to permit a thorough check on this possibility, although Valentine et al. (1984) did reanalyze data cited by Maisto (1978) but without being able to take account of variance between subjects or linear relation between mean and slope. They found no reliable evidence permitting rejection of independence between processes reflected in slope and intercept. The same equation, applied to Phillips and Nettelbeck's (1984b) correlations (available from Phillips, 1981), confirmed this conclusion. Clearly, it is desirable that future researchers follow Todman and Gibb's example in checking the extent to which negative correlations between slope and intercept are statistically predictable. It is important to note, however, that relatively large samples would be required to test reliably whether observed correlations between slope and intercept diverged from predictable levels—not a light undertaking. Moreover, even predictable negative correlations negate the possibility of the strong claim of stage independence, which relies on an absence of correlation.

From our review of the literature, it seems that although Detterman et al. (1992) included the memory scanning procedure in their battery, it has fallen from favor since 1985 as a means for explicating information processing differences between retarded and nonretarded persons. In part this may be because, as our discussion has emphasized, the work required to address the issues raised would be demanding of subjects and researchers alike. However, despite limitations discussed here, we believe that the procedure continues to provide a useful method for comparing relative effects on stage durations of experimental manipulations across different ability groups. Besides the directions for future research already pointed out in this section, there is a need to follow up the limitation identified by the relatively higher intercept to the item recognition function of retarded adults. The procedure has served to demonstrate that, at least among persons with mild retardation, the nature of this limitation appears different to the occasional lapses in attention influencing the slope parameter, although it would obviously be of interest to test the limits of this conclusion. In addition, what is now required is an analysis aimed at manipulating encoding and decision stages independently, along the lines of the experiment made by Maisto and Sipe (1980).

POSNER'S ENCODING FUNCTION TASK

Posner (1978) developed a procedure that integrated two-choice RT to make same–different judgments within a threshold method, to measure encoding time required for different levels of abstraction. For example, matching two stimuli on the basis of name identity (NI) should require additional time beyond physical identification (PI) because the former is assumed to involve access to semantic knowledge. The procedure involves presenting two stimuli sequentially, separated by a variable interstimulus interval (ISI) between onsets. The rationale is that extending ISI beyond very brief durations facilitates encoding the first stimulus up to a point by which sufficient time has been allowed. Thus, the ISI at which the CRT function becomes asymptotic is taken as the time required to encode the first item in the stimulus pair.

Merrill et al. (1987) compared mildly retarded adults with CA and MA controls on a modified version of this task. Across three experiments involving different but comparable participants, pictures of common objects were matched, either on the basis of PI, NI, or superordinate identity (e.g., SI "animal" when the first stimulus was "dog"). For retarded subjects, ISI was significantly delayed in all three conditions, compared to both CA and MA controls, leading to the conclusion that slower encoding was related to lower IQ, not MA. Moreover, because essentially the same outcome was found, irrespective of the kind of semantic knowledge involved, Merrill et al. suggested that a constant, relatively permanent difference was responsible. A follow-up study by Merrill and McCauley (1988) strongly supported this suggestion, finding highly significant correlations between encoding speeds for PI and NI conditions examined within subject, for retarded and MA samples separately. This study also tested whether group encoding differences were attributable to relative differences to which subjects were prepared for stimulus onset, but no evidence was found for this.

Merrill and Mar (1987) extended this analysis to the comprehension of speech. Essentially, they predicted that slower fundamental encoding would limit higher level cognitive activities. They found broad support for this hypothesis; comprehension among retarded adolescents compared to MA controls declined more markedly as the presentation rate of short prose passages was increased. Speed of verbal coding was then devolved into two components: phonological analysis and semantic analysis. The former was tested by a memory-scanning technique whereby a sentence was first presented, followed by a probe involving either a word from the sentence or a rhyming, grammatically appropriate replacement. Sentences were presented at varying ISIs, the dependent variable being correct responses. Decline in comprehension with increasing time constraint was virtually identical among retarded subjects and MA controls, with performance in both groups reaching asymptote at the same ISI. Finally, semantic analysis was examined, using a modified version of the Posner task in which the initial stimulus was a sentence and the paired probe was a drawing that either depicted sentence events and actions or not. Retarded subjects demonstrated a significant ISI lag, indicating slower semantic analysis compared to MA controls, and were much slower overall. Merrill and Mar observed that if quality of semantic analysis depends on rapid processing to achieve deeper comprehension, then slower overall performance may indicate poorer quality of semantic representation. They recognized that this could, in turn, be the consequence of different processing strategies.

Recently, Merrill (1992) attempted to address the issue of possible group differences in strategies, focusing in two experiments on how attentional resources are allocated by retarded subjects and CA controls. His procedures combined his version of the encoding function task with secondary concurrent tasks designed to stress ongoing encoding. This permitted an examination of interference effects, interpreted as reflecting the reallocation of attentional resources. The reliability of results from the first experiment was checked by modifying procedures in the second, the main change being that the concurrent task manipulating equivalent memory load in the first study was replaced in the second by an auditory probe in different locations that were equivalent across groups.

These experiments clearly demonstrated that encoding operations involve active rather than automatic cognitive processes. Results generally replicated those from the earlier studies but found, additionally, that mentally retarded subjects allocated fewer attentional resources to encoding than did CA controls.

Conclusions

The line of research followed by Merrill and his coworkers seems to have been guided by questions about the extent to which higher cognitive activities are circumscribed by the operation of lower level processes. Taking as a starting point his convincing demonstration that retarded persons are significantly slower than MA controls when encoding simple visual stimuli, he showed that this is related to the effectiveness of more complex activities, such as language comprehension. It is by no means clear, however, that the direction of this relationship reflects bottom-up processing, with output passed from sensory analysis up to the highest levels of analysis, as opposed to top-down, with early analysis facilitated by higher level information. Merrill appears to have begun on the assumption that the former applied but found evidence to the contrary, suggesting that encoding requires active cognitive effort. The procedures applied have the advantage of operationalizing the extent to which this is so. However, an explanation for why retarded persons allocate fewer attentional resources when encoding is still required. One possibility is that they are more confused and less certain about what to do in these experimental tasks, which are clearly quite demanding.

STERNBERG'S COMPONENTIAL METHOD

Sternberg (1977) was essentially concerned with developing a procedure that would operationally define Spearman's "principles of cognition"–"the apprehension of experience," "the eduction of relations," and "the eduction of correlates." The "componential method" is based on CRT when solving analogies of the form A:B as C:D, where the relationship between C and D is identical to that between A and B. In the procedure considered here, D involves a choice between two alternatives offered as solutions, one of which is correct. Performance is quantified as the CRT to reach a solution. By "precuing" different terms of the analogy, it is possible to separate overall CRT into durations representing different "components"—that is, elementary processes underlying performance in the composite task. Essentially, component times are estimated by mathematical modeling following the application of a subtractive technique that involves various combinations of precued analogical terms followed by the full analogical problem. This permits each component to be isolated in turn, assuming that preprocessing of analogical terms during the precuing period reduces the amount of processing required subsequently to reach a solution. Thus, like Donders' original subtractive method, Sternberg's procedure is based on the assumption that the various component times are additive and that deleting components from overall CRT by precuing does not change the nature of the remaining constituent operations in any way. Although this assumption has always attracted criticism (Pachella, 1974), Sternberg (1977) did find broad support that components were additive.

Sternberg proposed that analogical reasoning requires five components: *encoding* (i.e., transforming) each term in the analogy into an internal concept on which further transformations could be performed (Spearman's first principle); inferring relationships between terms A and B (Spearman's second principle); *mapping* these to a higher relationship—as when, having determined the relationship between A and C, the relationship between all four terms is extracted; the *application* of the principle derived to produce a solution (Spearman's third principle); and *preparation–response*, which includes all remaining processes, such as preparing, executing, and monitoring a response. He also described four mathematical models that differed according to whether each component of processing is *exhaustive* (i.e., all aspects of each term in the analogy are fully processed) or *self-terminating* (i.e., processing only continues for as long as is required to extract sufficient aspects to reach a correct solution). To the extent that the strategy adopted involves more exhaustive processing, it is assumed that this increases demands on short-term memory, because larger amounts of information have to be stored.

McConaghy (1988) and McConaghy and Kirby (1987a, 1987b) reported a series of experiments that, together with an unpublished doctoral dissertation (Smith, 1981; cited by McConaghy, 1988), are the only investigations of analogical reasoning procedures in persons with significantly below-average IQ. All studies used a version of Sternberg's (1977) People–Piece analogies task involving cartoon representations of human figures characterized in terms of four two-dimensional elements. These were height (tall–short), girth (fat–thin), gender (male–female), and shaded (filled–not filled). The aim was to identify qualitative as well as quantitative differences between the cognitive processes of persons having markedly different levels of IQ. Specifically, McConaghy and Kirby predicted that young adults with lower IQ would spend *less* time encoding than would higher IQ subjects, with associated slower subsequent componential processing and slower overall CRTs. This followed a similar finding by Sternberg and Rifkin (1979) in relation to normal childhood development. These authors also reported evidence of more reliance among younger children on simpler self-terminating strategies, so that McConaghy and Kirby predicted a similar outcome in relation to IQ. In addition to Sternberg and Rifkin's results, Sternberg (1977) found that, among young adults with above-average general abilities, those with high reasoning abilities produced longer encoding times in People–Piece and verbal analogies than did those with less high reasoning abilities, with this slower encoding being coupled with more rapid processing of subsequent components and overall.

The componential method, therefore, appeared to be sensitive to qualitative differences between subjects at different developmental levels and with different levels of ability. It seemed likely then that qualitative differences additional to the quantitative differences generally found between disparate IQ adult groups could be identified—and regarding encoding, moreover, of providing an instance where low-IQ subjects perform more quickly than do high-IQ subjects. If confirmed, this finding would not of itself improve understanding of mental retardation, because it was precisely this distinction that led Sternberg (1977) to conclude that executive "metacomponents" were determining the kinds of strategies adopted. As clarified in the section on reaction time, earlier in this chapter, an account of mental retardation in terms of low "executive functioning" is tautological, because this term is really a metaphor for intelligence. However, if it proved possible to support this finding by distinguishing between different strategies in qualitative terms, then some advance would have been made.

In their first three experiments, McConaghy and Kirby (1987a) encountered considerable difficulties that were not overcome by longer preliminary training and various procedural modifications, not withstanding that their low-IQ subjects were relatively high functioning, with only a third or less of their samples drawn from the mild retardation range. Above-average- and low-IQ groups, but particularly the latter, encountered problems with the precuing procedure. Results, although generally consistent with the predictions presented earlier, suggested low levels of reliability, with poor fits to all four models tested. McConaghy and Kirby did succeed in reducing the complexity of the precuing procedure by presenting just two cue conditions (A:B precued vs. the full analogy), with precued terms removed following presentation, thereby forcing subjects to memorize these in order to solve the problem. These changes increased reliability appreciably in both groups, and to acceptable levels in the above-average group, results from these subjects now being consistent with previous research (Sternberg, 1977). However, the two predictions concerning qualitatively different results from low-IQ subjects were not upheld. Compared to above-average subjects, the low-IQ group spent more time encoding, although this did not result in faster subsequent processing. Outcomes for all four models were not reliably distinguishable, particularly for the low-IQ group. If anything, there appeared to be a weak trend toward exhaustive processing among these subjects (i.e., opposite to the prediction), but this was associated with very slow overall CRT and a very high error rate. In short, the performance of low-IQ subjects suggested that the task was too complex, placing too high a load on short-term memory, to be used reliably with persons with even borderline to mild levels of mental retardation.

Two further experiments (McConaghy & Kirby, 1987b) tested whether the difficulties that low-IQ subjects encountered with the analogical reasoning task would be overcome by training. Subjects were similar to those in the previous studies, with IQs in the borderline to mild retardation range. Training was designed to teach subjects how to identify and describe the changes and nonchanges occurring between the A and B terms in the analogy, and to compare these to the pattern of changes and nonchanges between the C and D terms, so as to decide whether the analogy was true or false. Controls at the same average IQ level had the same opportunities for practice but received no instructions during the training phase, other than the usual ones to try to identify the A:B relationship and check whether this matched that between C and D.

McConaghy and Kirby (1987b) found that training was successful, in that variability and error rates were reduced substantially, so that mathematical models provided better fits to data, although not to the extent commonly found for nonretarded adults. However, the initial predictions in terms of specific qualitative differences were not supported, the results generally confirming the previous findings. Thus, no evidence was found that subjects with low IQ tended to adopt self-terminating processing strategies. As in the previous studies, all four models provided similar fits to the data, with models that reflected as much exhaustive as self-terminating processing showing a marginal advantage. This outcome was therefore not discernibly different from results from nonretarded adults (McConaghy & Kirby, 1987a; Sternberg, 1977). Manipulating precuing in conjunction with training, by either presenting precued terms throughout the trial or removing these following presentation, found longer encoding times under the latter procedure, which arguably resulted in marginally more efficient subsequent processing. However, encoding times for low-IQ groups were always longer than those for nonretarded subjects, and there was no reliable evidence that the encoding times of low-IQ subjects were disproportionately shorter within the overall response duration than the encoding times of above-average subjects.

Conclusion

In light of the previous findings, McConaghy and Kirby (1987b) concluded that there are problems inherent in the componential method that severely limit its useful application to the study of mental retardation. As is clear from the foregoing account, the major difficulty encountered was that even subjects with above-average intelligence did not voluntarily make adequate use of precued terms under the original procedure described by Sternberg (1977). Moreover, although modifying the method by withdrawing precued terms before proceeding with the trial was successful with persons with above-average IQ, this change rendered the task too difficult for subjects with low IQs. Even when the complexity of the task was reduced, the altered procedure for precuing terms remained more difficult for these subjects, as shown by much higher error rates and markedly lower reliability when fitting mathematical models. In the event, no reliable evidence was found to support specific predictions of qualitative differences in processing associated with levels of intelligence, although the poorer fit to the models tested does raise the possibility that low-IQ subjects were using processes different to those assumed by these models. In what sense, however, is not clear. That low-IQ subjects were able to solve analogies at well above chance level suggests that they had understood what was required and responded along broadly the same lines as nonretarded subjects. Also, presumably whatever strategies were used by low-IQ subjects were applied more erratically, because of distractibility and uncertainty. However, it is not known to what extent this might have resulted in *incomplete* encoding—an aspect to processing not considered under the mathematical models tested. But if encoding was incomplete, then this raises the question as to whether a different type of model to those tested by McConaghy and Kirby might be developed, which incorporated this aspect along with considerations like exhaustive and self-terminating processing.

From hindsight, it seems a pity that McConaghy and Kirby (1987a) did not include MA controls. Sternberg and Rifkin's (1979) report of qualitative differences between normal children and adults in preferred processing strategies was based on relatively marginal differences in amounts of variances accounted for by the various models tested, and it would have been useful to have reexamined this issue under circumstances permitting comparisons with low-IQ adults matched for MA. Because the youngest children in Sternberg and Rifkin's study who coped adequately with the componential method were 8 years of age, this comparison may have helped to clarify the nature of the difficulties encountered by McConaghy and Kirby's (1987a) low-IQ subjects. That aside, however, our review of this literature generally confirms McConaghy and Kirby's (1987b) conclusions and we share their opinion that the componential method involves tasks that are too difficult for mentally retarded persons, so that it is not likely to prove useful for examining limitations to the information processing of such individuals. McConaghy (1988) drew attention to alternative less complex models developed by Mulholland and others for examining analogical reasoning, but at this time none has been used to investigate the performance of mentally retarded persons.

INSPECTION TIME (IT)

Inspection time (IT) is essentially a measure of threshold accuracy made by using a backward masking procedure to limit the exposure duration of stimulus material. As such, it is one of a range of masking procedures assumed to isolate rate of input processing from other components in the information processing sequence. The theoretical background and development of IT has been comprehensively documented elsewhere (Nettelbeck, 1987; Vickers, Nettelbeck, & Willson, 1972; Vickers & Smith, 1986) and is not discussed here. By the mid-1980s IT had gained considerable interest as a means for investigating defining characteristics of information processing in retarded persons (Nettelbeck, 1985), as well as individual differences within the normal population and how these related to IQ. With regards to the latter area of interest, significant correlations (median corrected value about –.5) have been confirmed by a number of researchers (Kranzler & Jensen, 1989; Nettelbeck, 1987).

Research based on masking procedures is noteworthy for the extent to which procedural variations complicate interpretation of the data. In part this reflects lack of uniformity in the stimuli and procedures used. By contrast, the vast majority of IT studies have followed essentially the same procedure. There are, moreover, other advantages associated with IT. Discrimination and responding difficulty is minimized, in the sense that the discrimination involves large relative differences in line length (a form of discrimination that Piagetian work indicates is acquired very early in development), rather than letter or number recognition. IT has proved relatively trouble free with diverse groups—elderly persons, children, and retarded and nonretarded adults—without ceiling or floor effects. IT remains fairly stable across measures, although occasional large fluctuations occur. Generally, however, individuals retain relative position within a group despite considerable practice effects. Test–retest reliabilities are comparably high for retarded adults (M = .71), nonretarded adults (.65), children (.72), and elderly persons (.70; Nettelbeck, 1985; Nettelbeck & Rabbitt, 1992). Furthermore, experimental work has been directed to validating, for these different populations, IT as a measure of speed of input processing that is located centrally rather than peripherally (Nettelbeck, Hirons, & Wilson, 1984; Nettelbeck & Wilson, 1985).

Despite procedural inconsistencies, reviews of masking research have concluded that mental retardation is characterized by slower central processing (Nettelbeck, 1985; Ross & Ward, 1978). Between-subjects variance and positive skewing in IT distributions are higher for retarded groups, increasing mean differences, but these remain substantial following transformation of data to reduce variance. Although attempts to localize the source of the group difference within an MA or IQ factor have produced ambiguous results (Wilson, Nettelbeck, Turnbull, & Young, 1992), in general speed of input processing as indexed by IT improves with MA, at least until early adolescence (Nettelbeck & Wilson, 1985), consistent with what has been found for CRT (Kail, 1991). The source of developmental improvement in processing has also been debated, with some contending that differential performance reflects age-determined differences in the strategies used and others seeking an explanation in terms of structural changes held to support perceptual encoding.

Several studies have attempted to establish an explanation for the longer ITs among retarded persons in procedural variables that disadvantage this group in relation to nonretarded persons. Because stimulus duration is constrained with the intention of constantly testing the limits of discrimination, IT is clearly dependent on focusing attention at a critical time and maintaining concerted concentration throughout a period of time lasting perhaps 10 minutes and involving 100 or more trials. Attempts to address inattentiveness have suggested that part of the group difference in IT is attributable to less effective scanning strategies by retarded subjects, resulting in less effective stimulus registration (Nettelbeck, 1985). Nettelbeck, Robson, Walwyn, Downing, and Jones (1986) further refined this conclusion in a sequence of five experiments designed to examine the relationship between scanning patterns and IT. Essentially, these experiments confirmed that although retarded subjects made many more off-target glances, they utilized task cues appropriately so that orientation at critical times was not less efficient. Nettelbeck et al. (1986) therefore concluded that lower discriminative accuracy could not simply be accounted for in terms of off-target glances and was predominantly the consequence of some nonvoluntary dysfunction within central processing.

Another procedural variable considered has been the extent to which some subjects are able to use subtle postmasking cues (e.g., apparent movement or brightness variation) to define the location of critical aspects with the target figure (Evans & Nettelbeck, 1993; Knibb, 1992; Nettelbeck, 1987). Essentially, using such strategies changes the nature of the discrimination because the backward mask is evaded. A possibility, therefore, is that retarded–nonretarded group differences in IT simply reflect differences in the proportions of subjects in each group using such cues, although no association between IQ and cue use has yet been found among nonretarded subjects (Mackenzie & Cumming, 1986). Moreover, although nonuse of such cues significantly increases IT in normals, these performance levels are still much faster than ITs typically measured among retarded subjects.

Recent attempts using IT to clarify the nature of deficient general processing have not advanced understanding significantly, although these studies have strengthened the proposition that IT does successfully index general intelligence among retarded and nonretarded groups (Nettelbeck, 1987), as well as cognitive development during childhood (Nettelbeck & Vita, 1992) and age-related cognitive decline in the normal elderly population (Nettelbeck & Rabbitt, 1992). Moreover, IT is certainly sensitive to the less efficient information processing characterizing mental retardation; MA comparisons have found a lag of at least 4 years and, by mapping mean IT across a wide range of IQ, a considerable discontinuity in the resulting function has been demonstrated to occur at IQ scores below 80 (Nettelbeck, 1985).

Wilson et al. (1992) attempted to test the proposition that increasingly faster processing during normal childhood development, as indexed by IT, may be a necessary but not a sufficient condition for average and above-average IQ. It is possible, for example, that IT correlates with MA up to some point defining asymptotic speed (e.g., MA 12–15), but beyond that the factor is a less important determinant of intellectual functioning. Five testable predictions follow from this hypothesis:

1. IT should correlate with CA among normally developing children up until ages 12 to 15 but not beyond. There is evidence that supports this prediction (Nettelbeck & Wilson, 1985; Wilson & Nettelbeck, 1986).

2. Among children representing a normal range of IQ, IT should correlate more with MA than with CA. Evidence for this is problematical; Wilson et al. (1992) obtained a result in the direction required (–.46 vs. –.39) from a sample of 155 children aged about 6 to 12, but the difference was not statistically significant. Clearly, with correlations of this order, a very large sample would be necessary to test this prediction adequately.

3. Among adults with mental retardation, IT should correlate with IQ because this provides an index of intellectual development. This prediction has strong support (Kranzler & Jensen, 1989; Nettelbeck, 1985, 1987).

4. Among high-IQ adults, IT will correlate only weakly with IQ because speed is not critical to intelligence beyond an adolescent MA level. There is not direct evidence available on this issue. Indirect support comes from suggestions in Nettelbeck and Kirby's (1983) data that higher-IQ subjects contributed little to the IT–IQ correlation overall, and from lower IT–IQ correlations among nonretarded groups compared with retarded groups (Nettelbeck, 1987), although Kranzler and Jensen's (1989) meta-analysis casts doubt on the earlier conclusion.

5. No nonretarded subject should have a long IT, although some retarded persons may have short ITs. These cases, if not deficient in processes indexed by IT, must therefore be expected, on the basis of IQ, to demonstrate specific deficits in other areas, possibly with uneven profiles of abilities. In our view, this is a prediction that could most usefully be pursued. Unsurprisingly, a small number of nonretarded subjects do register abnormally long ITs, but these are plausibly attributable to unreliability in the measure and it should not be difficult to confirm this. Wilson et al. (1992) did identify a number of retarded subjects with short ITs, a finding subsequently confirmed by Frank (1992). However, Frank's study did not support the prediction, finding no differences between the Weschler IQ or memory profiles for short and long IT retarded subjects; but because of procedural shortcomings it also failed to test adequately an alternative hypothesis that IT differences between the two retarded samples reflected use of postmasking cues. The issue is therefore unresolved.

Conclusions

Within the normal population, IT as a single measure correlates with IQ to an extent only achievable with CRT if multiple regression is used to accumulate the effects of several parameters (Jensen, 1987). As a single measure sensitive to a general processing deficiency, IT could prove useful in a number of ways as outlined previously, and also, for example, to future attempts to relate processing limitations to electrophysiological measures such as average evoked potential (Jensen, Schafer, & Crinella, 1981). Moreover, a cross-sequential study like that of Nettelbeck and Wilson's (1985) but directed to the ontogeny of IT among retarded children would provide a useful comparison with existing data on normal development.

However, its convenience as a single measure notwithstanding, there must be considerable uncertainty as to whether IT is restricted predominantly to speed of input processing, particularly for retarded persons, among whom opportunities for contamination from noncognitive environmental and motivational variables are high. In the longer term, progress in addressing this difficulty will depend on how successful future research is in further explicating the nature of processes indexed by IT (Levy, 1992; White, 1994). For example, an assumption underpinning this procedure is that processing involved is precategorical, so that outcome should not be influenced by individual differences in acquired knowledge. Clearly, it would be desirable to test this assumption, especially because Hornstein and Mosley's (1987) findings that recognition threshold for both retarded and nonretarded subjects was advantaged by stimulus familiarity would seem to cast doubt on it.

Responding Time

Kirby and McConaghy (1986) attempted to develop a response equivalent to IT, to distinguish response aspects of information processing from input processing. Responding time (RsT) was conceived as measuring the time required for stimulus–response translation together with response execution, independent from input processing speed, because this latter factor was first equated for each subject. The rationale was to measure first an individual's IT so as to estimate the duration required to make the discrimination involved with very high accuracy. RsT—defined as "the minimum time required to make a correct response, assuming correct identification of the stimulus" (Kirby & McConaghy, 1986, p. 688)—could then be compared for retarded and nonretarded groups, to discern the relative influence of differences in the speed of IT and RsT on documented group differences in RT. This approach therefore represents the theoretical perspective, referred to in the earlier discussion of reaction time, wherein it might be possible to isolate a specific deficiency, assumed on the basis of IT research to be located within input processing. Under this arrangement impaired input processing should not influence processing in subsequent stages. To measure RsT, target duration was always set equal to the individual's IT. The time between target offset and onset of the next trial (i.e., the next target) was systematically varied across trials. Response accuracy at each intertrial interval was recorded, with RsT defined operationally as the critical intertrial interval at which high accuracy was achieved.

Low nonsignificant correlations between RsT and IT among both undergraduates and a low-IQ group (range of PIQ 51 to 107; $M = 78$) were accepted as confirming the independence of these variables, although small samples ($n = 12$) favored this conclusion. Over and above significant group differences in IT, low-IQ participants had significantly longer RsT. Kirby and McConaghy therefore concluded that group RT differences could not be explained in terms of input processing differences alone. Because total response time (the sum of IT and RsT) correlated –.63 with PIQ, Kirby and McConaghy also concluded that general intelligence might set a limit on the efficiency of all stages in the information processing sequence, although the operation of stages could still be independent.

In a later study, Kirby and Thomas (1989) investigated the nature of group differences in 2-, 4-, and 8-choice IT, RsT, and RT. They argued that manipulating choice within RsT and IT tasks would test whether more marked CRT slowing with increasing choice among retarded subjects, compared to CA controls, was due to input processing rather than to response organization factors or vice versa. Results essentially confirmed those from Kirby and McConaghy (1985), with stages again appearing to be relatively independent, although samples were again small ($n = 12$). The test for the relative influence of input or response processing rested on whether the group IQ difference interacted with slowing IT, RsT, and CRT as choice increased. This interaction was confirmed for CRT and IT but not for RsT. However, a conclusion that input processing was relatively more deficient than response organization was not warranted because regression analyses on which these comparisons were based suggested unreliability in RsT estimates.

Conclusions

Estimates of CRT were much shorter than the corresponding sums of IT and RsT for each level of choice, suggesting that the RsT task was significantly more difficult for both retarded and nonretarded subjects, requiring additional resources to those required in the CRT task. The procedure provides only limited opportunity for a subject to recover between trials (cf. Baumeister & Kellas, 1968) and the extent to which this introduces confounding by vigilance or by a refractory factor has not been determined. Moreover, with the benefit of hindsight it is arguable that this task has demonstrated what Nettelbeck and Brewer (1981) concluded—namely, that if slower CRT among retarded persons is the consequence of impaired control functions, then processing limitations will appear to be consistent with processing requirements encapsulated by the experimental procedure. The idea from which the measure was developed was a good one and had the outcome from the studies previously discussed here discounted this prediction then an attempt to refine the RsT index would have been warranted. However, the prediction appears to have been upheld and, because of the procedural difficulties outlined previously, we are doubtful about the future usefulness of this technique.

MULTIPLE COGNITIVE TASKS AND MENTAL RETARDATION

Detterman et al. (1992) tested a "modal" model of information processing designed to elucidate individual and group differences in IQ. Performance on nine tasks commonly used to study basic cognitive abilities (learning, relearning, reaction time [RT], probe recall, Sternberg search, self-paced probe, stimulus discrimination, tachistoscopic full report, and tachistoscopic partial report) was compared between 20 predominantly mildly retarded adults and 20 college students. Thirty-one dependent measures were operationalized in these tasks to provide estimates of the functioning of various hypothetical stores (very short-term memory, primary memory, secondary memory, and tertiary memory), and mechanisms (stimulus coding, retrieval, output, and executive functioning [including rehearsal]), as well as an index of general efficiency. These components of the model were conceived as together constituting a complex interrelated system capable of accounting for general intellectual functioning.

The results reiterate the research findings described in this chapter. Variance in all tasks was higher among those with mental retardation. In addition, performance correlated more highly with intelligence in this group than among the CA subjects (.40 vs. .15). Group differences could not be explained parsimoniously in terms of impairment localized to one store or mechanism. Instead, virtually every basic cognitive parameter measured demonstrated a significant difference between groups, the direction of this difference confirming the slower speed and higher error rates reported for retarded subjects in other research. Beyond this, however, the results of Detterman et al. (1992) do extend our understanding of the nature of information processing in both retarded and nonretarded persons. They illustrate that each component of the model (with the exception of rehearsal and secondary memory, which in later analyses were grouped with executive functioning and tertiary memory, respectively) accounted for a unique source of variance not accounted for by other parts of the model; together, all variables accounted for 86% of variance in IQ across the combined groups.

A number of other results are worth summarizing here. Nine of the 10 variables that showed the largest between-group differences were measures of accuracy of responding rather than of latency, suggesting that speed of performance may be less paramount than some theories have proposed (Jensen, 1982). Consistent with this is the finding that efficiency, measured by variables like decision time in the RT task, accounted for only 19% of variance. Also, more basic processes (e.g., memory, encoding, and retrieval) accounted for more variance than more global processes (e.g., efficiency, rehearsal, executive functioning), thereby emphasizing the relative utility of bottom-up compared to top-down processing models. Finally, principal components analysis of the 31 variables indicated that the unrotated principal components accounted for 19%, 36%, and 48% of variance in the nonretarded, retarded, and both groups combined. These results therefore support Detterman et al.'s proposition that relatively independent elements within a system may be as important or more so than a general factor.

Conclusions

Results from Detterman et al. (1992) suggest important new leads for future research. Performance differences both between and within groups may be explained in terms of a number of independent components that, together, combine to describe general intelligence as indexed by IQ. This would seem to be particularly the case among those with retardation, where substantially more variance was accounted for by the proposed model.

The results of the study attest to the utility of a multifactor approach as a means for investigating group differences, particularly where results are used to construct profiles of cognitive abilities that differentiate between retarded and nonretarded persons (Detterman, 1992).

GENERAL DISCUSSION

Early hopes that the information processing approach to the investigation of group differences in cognition would identify the source of poor performance have largely been unfulfilled. The reason for this rests primarily with difficulty in distinguishing a structural from a functional explanation. The dependent measures operationalized under the various paradigms considered here have primarily served to attest to the ubiquity of group differences. Such differences can plausibly be attributed to structural limitations that affect all stages of processing but can with equal plausibility be interpreted as the consequence of the selection or exercise of less efficient strategies for the task at hand. The second interpretation is not, of course, incompatible with a very general structural deficiency that influences the entire range of functioning, a point that we believe Detterman et al. (1992) took an important step toward elucidating.

A number of procedural shortcomings evident in the studies in the 1970s have persisted in the past decade, resulting in severe limitations to interpretation. For example, Stanovich (1978) and Baumeister (1984) both noted that research into the information processing of mentally retarded persons had been restricted to adolescents and adults whose IQ scores fell in the mild category and beyond, so that on the basis of IQ many research participants were technically not retarded. The majority of studies reviewed by these authors had excluded cases with defined etiologies, so that most participants had been categorized as without organic impairment. Moreover, as Baumeister (1984) noted, very few studies had addressed developmental issues of information processing among retarded children. We can only confirm that this situation has not changed during the past decade, and support the earlier contentions that theoretical development requires that research be directed toward a wider age range, including older adults as well as children, wider etiological classification, and a less restricted range of mental retardation—with, we would add, larger samples where possible. Baumeister's (1984) point that little is currently known about how different environments define competence is well made; future research should attempt to avoid relying solely on IQ as a basis for selecting research subjects and consider relationship between cognitive processes and indices of adaptive behavior, and interpersonal competencies also.

Another procedural issue that was identified a decade ago (Nettelbeck & Brewer, 1981) but that has received only limited research attention is that of similarities and differences in the performance of samples from various pathological conditions, like schizophrenia, autism, brain damage, and even normal and abnormal aging (e.g., Alzheimer's disease). Finding that a group of people with mental retardation function more slowly than do those without retardation does not further our understanding about the defining characteristics of the retarded group, except in that it tells us that they are less efficient in the specific task. The lack of utility of this finding is further highlighted by the observation that most exceptional groups (e.g., those distinguished by psychiatric, intellectual, or extreme age factors) are similarly divergent from the norm. However, if future research is able to establish differences in the manner in which representatives of different exceptional populations arrive at this end point, then there is an opportunity for better defining the cognitive characteristics of retarded persons. The multifactor approach advocated by Detterman (1992) would seem to have promise here.

The procedural difficulties that have continued to exist in research during the past decade aside, it is nonetheless true that closer examination of the precise nature of performance revealed in the various paradigms has provided some insight into group differences. Three results have consistently been found in all tasks. First, within-subject variance is almost invariably higher among the retarded. In other words, mentally retarded persons are either unwilling or unable to constrain their performance in line with the demands of the task (or the instructions of the experimenter). Second, error rates of retarded persons are higher. Whether these higher error rates are attributable to an inability to cope with task demands or an inability to maintain commitment and thereby concentration is as yet undetermined. The fact that errors are observed in very easy as well as difficult trials suggests that the latter, rather than the former, is at least part of the explanation. Third, between-subjects variance indicates differences between the homogeneity of retarded and nonretarded groups. The wider range of individual differences in performance in retarded samples may indicate qualitative differences within existing samples that confound between-group effects. In other words, although nonretarded subjects constitute a relatively homogenous group for these simple tasks because individuals learn task requirements easily and perform comfortably within the limits of their abilities, a retarded sample is likely to consist of some individuals who will struggle for a variety of cognitive and noncognitive experiential factors to meet the basic task requirements—and frequently also will initially include some cases excluded subsequently because they could not meet acceptance criteria. The end result of a comparison, between a sample operating within its performance limits, with a subsample made up of some individuals who are struggling to conform to task expectations but from which others have been excluded, is an invalid test of between-group differences.

Future research can address this concern by two routes. First, studies of group differences should practice performance to asymptote in both groups. On the basis of this review, we would anticipate that this would minimize both within- and between-subjects variability. Alternatively, for those paradigms where it is feasible, nonoptimal trials should be removed from analyses. To the extent that these modifications failed to eliminate group differences, a structural explanation is implicated.

Second, future studies should examine the strategies used by individuals within both groups, in order to discern whether group differences reflect differences in routes by which individual subjects reach a solution in the task at hand. Where possible, investigation should rely on more than introspection (as used thus far, e.g., to discern influence from the apparent movement strategy in the IT task), and should instead involve analysis of actual performance—like the trial-by-trial analysis of Brewer and Smith (1984, 1990). We strongly commend Brewer and Smith's results as following both routes described previously and thereby providing the most accurate record to date of the nature of control processes characterizing group differences.

The information processing approach to understanding the cognitive structures and processes that define group membership has generally foundered when researchers have attempted to implicate causal factors that are distinct from a general intelligence factor. The researcher is inevitably faced with the conundrum of whether the operation of individual processes or structures defines the limits of intelligence, or whether intelligence defines the functional limits of processing efficiency. Proponents of the former view are commonly resistant to suggestions that the defect is general or structural, as implied in the latter position. Detterman et al. (1992) provided an exception, because they integrated both defect and developmental perspectives in a manner reminiscent of the Hebbian distinction between Intelligence A and Intelligence B. They argued that essentially structural impairment within a range of basic cognitive components will inevitably limit the ways in which higher order cognitive functions become organized. Many developmentalists, however, regard the idea of structural limitation as suggesting that remediation designed to decrease group differences could not succeed. We wish to emphasize our view, therefore, that a defect position is not irreconcilable with intervention aimed at reducing performance differences between groups with different abilities to levels of practical nonsignificance.

We suggest that few, if any, individuals, operate even occasionally at the limits of their capacities. Furthermore, those persons with retardation would usually operate both below their limit and below the benchmark of average performance. Those without retardation also operate within their capacity limits but, by definition, at or above the benchmark. There is scope, therefore, to at least reduce group differences by undertaking specific training of retarded persons, as described in a number of articles reviewed in this chapter. Such intervention could enable those with retardation to reduce the underutilization of capacities, thereby miminizing group differences and approaching the normality benchmark. This is the challenge for the information processing approach to the investigation of cognition among mentally retarded persons.

Summary

Research in the past decade examining the cognition of persons with mental retardation has made most progress in explicating the extent to which performance differences, in a variety of information processing tasks, are mitigated by strategies. Brewer and Smith's (1984) trial-by-trial analysis of RT has provided the first detailed account of how individual differences in operating a speed–accuracy trade-off across trials impact on average group differences. Furthermore, these results showed that, although practice alone reduced group differences, specific training to use a deadline procedure improved performance to a far greater extent. The beneficial effects of practice on the performance of persons with retardation was also highlighted by Phillips and Nettelbeck (1984b). Improvement among retarded subjects to both the slope and the zero intercept of the item recognition function far exceeded levels of improvement among MA and CA controls. Thus, it is arguable that some part of the group differences observed in S. Sternberg's memory scanning procedure and conventional CRT is attributable to poor task knowledge that can readily be remediated by increasing exposure to task demands.

However, training apparently does not eliminate all group differences, even when accompanied by specific instruction on the task requirements. Brewer and Smith (1984) reported a median CRT among subjects with retardation that was significantly longer than that reported for 9-year-olds after far fewer trials. This outcome was consistent with results from Phillips and Nettelbeck (1984a) who found that even after extended practice for retarded subjects, group differences in scanning rate could only be eliminated by discounting occasional very slow trials suggestive of poor concentration. These results suggest that although the slower RTs of persons with retardation in a variety of information processing tasks may be partially explained by poor task-specific knowledge that may be remediated by practice, an overall performance difference remains that is attributable to structural impairment.

Analyses of group differences in CRT using Sternberg's (1977) componential approach and Kirby's responding time model (Kirby & McConaghy, 1986) have served to highlight problems with comparative research utilizing more difficult cognitive tasks. In these circumstances, comparisons of group differences are invalidated by the sheer difficulty of the task demands and consequent concern about the reliability and validity of the indices across populations. Thus, McConaghy and Kirby (1987a, 1987b) reported extreme difficulty in getting their participants with retardation to make use of precued terms in the componential procedure, thereby making group comparison impossible. Similarly, the duration of RsTs obtained from both retarded and nonretarded participants, by comparison to CRT estimates, suggested that the RsT task was significantly more difficult. Unless future research is able to demonstrate that subjects with retardation are not disadvantaged by the complexity of task demands, reliability and validity can be challenged and task utility in the explication of group differences will be severely curtailed.

Although the IT paradigm has attracted significant attention in the last decade, its usefulness for explicating group differences has been limited. IT, like the other processing measures described, is penetrable by strategies, despite initial optimism that such was not the case, so that although a moderately strong IT–IQ correlation may reflect a significant *g* loading for IT, the task reveals little about the nature of underlying processes. To the present time it has relied predominantly on face validity as an index of input processing, a matter requiring urgent attention.

Research during the past decade has improved our understanding from that summarized by Nettelbeck and Brewer (1981). We now have a greater awareness of the extent to which speed differences are observed in virtually all comparisons involving persons with and without retardation and the extent to which these differences are generally mitigated by a strategy factor. However, recent work by Detterman et al. (1992) underscored the possibility that strategy limitations are the consequence of widespread deficiencies in basic cognitive structures, and demonstrated the importance of future research aimed at defining relative levels of performance across tasks indexing different basic cognitive components. The detailed nature of the mechanism by which strategies develop and the extent to which their production can be modified remains to be revealed.

REFERENCES

Atkinson, R. C., & Shiffrin, R. M. (1968). Human memory: A proposed system and its control processes. In K. W. Spence & J. T. Spence (Eds.), *The psychology of learning and motivation* (Vol. 2, pp. 87–195). New York: Academic Press.

Baumeister, A. A. (1984). Some methodological and conceptual issues in the study of cognitive processes in retarded people. In P. H. Brooks, R. Sperber, & C. McCauley (Eds.), *Learning and cognition in the mentally retarded* (pp. 1–38). Hillsdale, NJ: Lawrence Erlbaum Associates.

Baumeister, A. A., & Kellas, G. (1968). Reaction time and mental retardation. In N. R. Ellis (Ed.), *International review of research in mental retardation* (Vol. 3, pp. 163–193). New York: Academic Press.

Brewer, N., & Smith, G. A. (1984). How normal and retarded individuals monitor and regulate speed and accuracy of responding in serial choice tasks. *Journal of Experimental Psychology: General, 113*, 71–93.

Brewer, N., & Smith, G. A. (1989). Developmental changes in processing speed: Influence of speed–accuracy regulation. *Journal of Experimental Psychology: General, 118*, 298–310.

Brewer, N., & Smith, G. A. (1990). Processing speed and mental retardation: Deadline procedures indicate fixed and adjustable limitations. *Memory & Cognition, 18*, 443–450.

Detterman, D. K. (1992). Mopping up: The relationship between cognitive processes and intelligence. *American Journal on Mental Retardation, 97*, 295–301.

Detterman, D. K., Mayer, J. D., Caruso, D. R., Legree, P. J., Conners, F. A., & Taylor, R. (1992). Assessment of basic cognitive abilities in relation to cognitive deficits. *American Journal on Mental Retardation, 97*, 251–286.

Dugas, J. L., & Kellas, G. (1974). Encoding and retrieval processes in normal children and retarded adolescents. *Journal of Experimental Child Psychology, 17*, 177–185.

Evans, G., & Nettelbeck, T. (1993). Inspection time: A flash mask to reduce apparent movement effects. *Personality and Individual Differences, 15*, 91–94.

Frank, N. K. (1992). *Post-masking cues as an explanation for short inspection times with low IQ?* Unpublished honours thesis, University of Adelaide, South Australia.

Harris, G. J., & Fleer, R. E. (1974). High speed memory scanning in mental retardates: Evidence for a central processing deficit. *Journal of Experimental Child Psychology, 17*, 452–459.

Hornstein, H. A., & Mosley, J. L. (1987). Iconic memory deficit of mildly mentally retarded individuals. *American Journal of Mental Deficiency, 91*, 415–421.

Jensen, A. R. (1982). Reaction time and psychometric g. In H. J. Eysenck (Ed.), *A model for intelligence* (pp. 93–132). New York: Springer-Verlag.

Jensen, A. R. (1987). Individual differences in the Hick paradigm. In P. A. Vernon (Ed.), *Speed of information-processing and intelligence* (pp. 101–175). Norwood, NJ: Ablex.

Jensen, A. R., Schafer, E. W. P., & Crinella, F. M. (1981). Reaction time, evoked brain potentials, and psychometric g in the severely retarded. *Intelligence, 5*, 179–197.

Kail, R. (1991). Developmental change in speed of processing during childhood and adolescence. *Psychological Bulletin, 109*, 490–501.

Kail, R. (1992). General slowing of information-processing by persons with mental retardation. *American Journal on Mental Retardation, 97*, 333–341.

Kirby, N. H., & McConaghy, J. (1986). Responding time: A response equivalent to inspection time. *Personality and Individual Differences, 7*, 687–694.

Kirby, N. H., & Thomas, P. D. (1989). Choice inspection time and responding time. *Personality and Individual Differences, 10*, 1301–1310.

Knibb, K. (1992). A dynamic mask for inspection time. *Personality and Individual Differences, 13*, 237–248.

Kranzler, J. H., & Jensen, A. R. (1989). Inspection time and intelligence: A meta-analysis. *Intelligence, 13*, 329–347.

Levy, P. (1992). Inspection time and its relation to intelligence: Issues of measurement and meaning. *Personality and Individual Differences, 13*, 987–1002.

Mackenzie, B., & Cumming, S. (1986). How fragile is the relationship between inspection time and intelligence: The effects of apparent-motion cues and previous experience. *Personality and Individual Differences, 7*, 721–729.

Maisto, A. A. (1978). Comments on the use of the additive factor method with mentally retarded persons: A reply to Silverman. *American Journal of Mental Deficiency, 83*, 191–193.

Maisto, A. A., & Baumeister, A. A. (1984). Dissection of component processes in rapid information processing tasks: Comparison of retarded and nonretarded people. In P. H. Brooks, R. Sperber, & C. McCauley (Eds.), *Learning and cognition in the mentally retarded* (pp. 165–188). Hillsdale, NJ: Lawrence Erlbaum Associates.

Maisto, A. A., & Jerome, M. A. (1977). Encoding and high-speed memory scanning of retarded and nonretarded adolescents. *American Journal of Mental Deficiency, 82*, 282–286.

Maisto, A. A., & Sipe, S. (1980). An examination of encoding and retrieval processes in reading disabled children. *Journal of Experimental Child Psychology, 30*, 223–230.

McConaghy,J. (1988). Mental retardation, analogical reasoning, and the componential method. In N. W. Bray (Ed.), *International review of research in mental retardation* (Vol. 15, pp. 125–154). New York: Academic Press.

McConaghy, J., & Kirby, N. H. (1987a). Analogical reasoning and ability level: An examination of R. J. Sternberg's componential method. *Intelligence, 11*, 137–159.

McConaghy, J., & Kirby, N. H. (1987b). Using the componential method to train mentally retarded individuals to solve analogies. *American Journal of Mental Deficiency, 92*, 12–23.

Merrill, E. C. (1985). Differences in semantic processing speed of mentally retarded and nonretarded persons. *American Journal of Mental Deficiency, 90*, 71–80.

Merrill, E. C. (1992). Attentional resource demands of stimulus encoding for persons with and without mental retardation. *American Journal on Mental Retardation, 97*, 87–98.

Merrill, E. C., & Mar, H. H. (1987). Differences between mentally retarded and nonretarded persons' efficiency of auditory sentence processing. *American Journal of Mental Deficiency, 91*, 406–414.

Merrill, E. C., & McCauley, C. (1988). Phasic alertness and differences in picture encoding speed. *American Journal on Mental Retardation, 93*, 245–249.

Merrill, E. C., Sperber, R., McCauley, C., Littlefield, J., Rider, E. A., & Shapiro, D. (1987). Picture encoding speed and mental retardation. *Intelligence, 11*, 169–191.

Mosley, J. L. (1985). High-speed memory-scanning task performance of mildly retarded and nonretarded individuals. *American Journal of Mental Deficiency, 90*, 81–89.

Nettelbeck, T. (1985). Inspection time and mild mental retardation. In N. R. Ellis & N. W. Bray (Eds.), *International review of research in mental retardation* (Vol. 13, pp. 104–141). New York: Academic Press.

Nettelbeck, T. (1987). Inspection time and intelligence. In P. A. Vernon (Ed.), *Speed of information-processing and intelligence* (pp. 295–356). Norwood, NJ: Ablex.

Nettelbeck, T., & Brewer, N. (1981). Studies of mild mental retardation and timed performance. In N. R. Ellis (Ed.), *International review of research in mental retardation* (Vol. 10, pp. 61–106). New York: Academic Press.

Nettelbeck, T., Hirons, A., & Wilson, C. (1984). Mental retardation, inspection time, and central attentional impairment. *American Journal of Mental Deficiency, 89*, 91–98.

Nettelbeck, T., & Kirby, N. H. (1983). Measures of timed performance and intelligence. *Intelligence, 7*, 39–52.

Nettelbeck, T., & Rabbitt, P. M. A. (1992). Aging, cognitive performance, and mental speed. *Intelligence, 16*, 189–205.

Nettelbeck, T., Robson, L., Walwyn, T., Downing, A., & Jones, N. (1986). Inspection time as mental speed in mildly retarded adults: Analysis of eye gaze, eye movement, and orientation. *American Journal of Mental Deficiency, 91*, 78–91.

Nettelbeck, T., & Vita, P. (1992). Inspection time in two childhood age cohorts: A constant or a developmental function? *British Journal of Developmental Psychology, 10*, 189–197.

Nettelbeck, T., & Wilson, C. (1985). A cross-sequential analysis of developmental differences in speed of visual information processing. *Journal of Experimental Child Psychology, 40*, 1–22.

Owings, R. A., Baumeister, A. A., Lane, R. A., & Lewis, M. H. (1980). Memory scanning of shapes, colors, and compounds: A comparison of retarded and nonretarded adults. *Intelligence, 4*, 243–254.

Pachella, R. G. (1974). The interpretation of reaction time in information processing research. In B. H. Kantowitz (Ed.), *Human information processing: Tutorials in performance and cognition* (pp. 41–82). Hillsdale, NJ: Lawrence Erlbaum Associates.

Phillips, C. J. (1981). *Mental retardation and the development of recognition memory.* Unpublished doctoral dissertation, University of Adelaide, South Australia.

Phillips, C. J., & Nettelbeck, T. (1984a). Effects of procedure on memory scanning of mildly mentally retarded adults. *American Journal of Mental Deficiency, 88*, 668–677.

Phillips, C. J., & Nettelbeck, T. (1984b). Effects of practice on recognition memory of mildly retarded adults. *American Journal of Mental Deficiency, 88*, 678–687.

Phillips, C. J., & Nettelbeck, T. (1985). Mild mental retardation and memory scanning. In N. R. Ellis & N. W. Bray (Eds.), *International review of research in mental retardation* (Vol. 13, pp. 143–179). New York: Academic Press.

Posner, M. I. (1978). *Chronometric explorations of mind.* Hillsdale, NJ: Lawrence Erlbaum Associates.

Rabbitt, P. M. A. (1981). Sequential reactions. In D. H. Holding (Ed.), *Human skills* (pp. 153–175). London: Wiley.

Ross, L. E., & Ward, T. B. (1978). The processing of information from the short-term visual store: Developmental and intellectual level differences. In N. R. Ellis (Ed.), *International review of research in mental retardation* (Vol. 9, pp. 1–27). New York: Academic Press.

Sanders, A. F. (1977). Structural and functional aspects of the reaction process. In S. Dornic (Ed.), *Attention and performance VI* (pp. 3–25). Hillsdale, NJ: Lawrence Erlbaum Associates.
Seymour, P. H. K., & Moir, W. L. N. (1980). Intelligence and semantic judgement time. *British Journal of Psychology, 71*, 53–61.
Silverman, W. P. (1974). High speed scanning of nonalphanumeric symbols in cultural–familially retarded and nonretarded children. *American Journal of Mental Deficiency, 79*, 44–51.
Spitz, H. H. (1982). Intellectual extremes, mental age, and the nature of human intelligence. *Merrill-Palmer Quarterly, 28*, 167–192.
Stanovich, K. E. (1978). Information processing in mentally retarded individuals. In N. R. Ellis (Ed.), *International review of research in mental retardation* (Vol. 9, pp. 29–60). New York: Academic Press.
Stanovich, K. E., & Pachella, R. G. (1977). Encoding, S-R compatibility, and stages of processing. *Journal of Experimental Psychology: Human Perception and Performance, 3*, 411–421.
Sternberg, R. J. (1977). *Intelligence information processing and analogical reasoning: The componential analysis of human abilities.* Hillsdale, NJ: Lawrence Erlbaum Associates.
Sternberg, R. J. (1979). Intelligence research at the interface between differential and cognitive psychology: Prospects and proposals. In R. J. Sternberg & D. K. Detterman (Eds.), *Human Intelligence: Perspectives on its theory and measurement* (pp. 33–60). Norwood, NJ: Ablex.
Sternberg, R. J., & Rifkin, B. (1979). The development of analogical reasoning processes. *Journal of Experimental Child Psychology, 27*, 195–232.
Sternberg, S. (1966). High speed scanning in human memory. *Science, 153*, 652–654.
Sternberg, S. (1969). Memory scanning: Mental processes revealed by reaction-time experiments. *American Scientist, 57*, 421–457.
Sternberg, S. (1975). Memory-scanning: New findings and current controversies. *Quarterly Journal of Experimental Psychology, 27*, 1–32.
Theios, J., Smith, P., Haviland, S., Traupmann, J., & Moy, M. (1973). Memory scanning as a serial self-terminating process. *Journal of Experimental Psychology, 97*, 323–336.
Todman, J., & Gibb, C. M. (1985). High speed memory scanning in retarded and nonretarded adolescents. *British Journal of Psychology, 76*, 49–57.
Valentine, J., Wilding, J., & Mohindra, N. (1984). Independence of slope and intercept in Sternberg's memory-scanning paradigm. *British Journal of Mathematical and Statistical Psychology, 37*, 122–127.
Vickers, D., Nettelbeck, T., & Willson, R. J. (1972). Perceptual indices of performance: The measurement of "inspection time" and "noise" in the visual system. *Perception, 1*, 263–295.
Vickers, D., & Smith, P. (1986). The rationale for the inspection time index. *Personality and Individual Differences, 7*, 609–623.
Wade, M. G., Hoover, J. H., & Newell, K. M. (1984). Training reaction and movement times of moderately and severely mentally retarded persons in aiming movements. *American Journal of Mental Deficiency, 89*, 174–179.
Welford, A. T. (1980). *Reaction times.* New York: Academic Press.
White, M. (1994). The inspection time rationale fails to demonstrate that inspection time is a measure of the speed of post-sensory processing. *Personality and Individual Differences, 15*, 185–198.
Wilson, C., & Nettelbeck, T. (1986). Inspection time and the mental age deviation hypothesis. *Personality and Individual Differences, 7*, 669–675.
Wilson, C., Nettelbeck, T., Turnbull, C., & Young, R. (1992). IT, IQ and age: A comparison of developmental functions. British *Journal of Developmental Psychology, 10*, 179–188.
Zelaznik, H. N., & Aufderheide, S. K. (1986). Attentional and reaction time analysis of performance: Implications for research with mentally handicapped individuals. In M. G. Wade (Ed.), *Motor skill acquisition of the mentally handicapped: Issues in research and training* (pp. 131–153). Amsterdam: North-Holland.
Zigler, E. (1969). Developmental versus difference theories of mental retardation and the problem of motivation. *American Journal of Mental Deficiency, 73*, 536–556.

› 11 ‹

Motor Skills and Mental Retardation

Karl M. Newell
The Pennsylvania State University

Mental retardation is a social concept that is usually measured in terms of deficits in cognitive skills as reflected, for example, in IQ and adaptive behavior tests. However, individuals with mental retardation also tend to exhibit various performance deficiencies in motor skills when compared to chronologically age-matched individuals of average or above intelligence. For example, it is common to find individuals with mental retardation exhibiting slowness of movement, clumsiness, stereotypic behavior, low levels of motor performance, slow rates of motor skill acquisition, and the failure to generalize motor skills across changes in context and task constraints. These abnormal movement phenomena and performance deficiencies associated with mental retardation have stimulated considerable research (cf. Anwar, 1981; Berkson, 1967; Bruininks, 1974; Henderson, 1986; Nettelbeck, 1979; Newell, 1985a; Wade, Hoover, & Newell, 1983), although there has never been, and there is not today, a unifying or even predominating theoretical approach to the study of motor skills and mental retardation.

Examination of the linkage between cognition and abnormal motor behavior is, in part, bound by the inherent difficulty of separating the component processes of human action and the subsequent selection of tasks to reflect, and hence measure, a particular process. An additional difficulty is that movement is a necessary but not sufficient condition for action. The degree and type of movement sequence exhibited in action varies according to the task demands. Actions that have a substantive movement component are often called physical activities or motor skills, to contrast them from other activities such as mental, perceptual, and communication skills. It is not that these latter activity categories do not involve movement; rather, there is generally more *emphasis* on the movement component in activities designated as motor skills or physical activities. Given the inherent difficulty of separating the processes that support performance in the fundamental categories of behavior, it should be recognized a priori that there are both artifactual and conceptually viable reasons why there has been an observed link between cognitive and motor deficiencies.

Over the years the theoretical influences on the study of motor skills and mental retardation have tended to follow the particular contemporary zeitgeist of psychology. These theoretical frameworks have included individual differences, behavioral analysis, information processing, cognitive psychology, and the ecological approach to perception and action. There has also been a linkage between the motor control and skill learning literatures, and the physical fitness domain. All of these different theoretical orientations have given varying degrees of emphasis to the role of genetic and environmental influences and their interaction in relation to mental retardation and the development of motor skills. There have also been various applied considerations to the nature of the research conducted that have generally been stimulated by the attempt to ameliorate the movement problems listed previously, and the desire to improve, in a variety of contexts, the motor skills of people with mental retardation (e.g., Rarick, 1973; Wade & Gold, 1978).

Traditionally, research on motor skills and mental retardation has examined the movement problems without recognizing the influence that movement dynamics and task constraints impose on the individual engaged in action. In this established viewpoint an action is in essence an action, and any movement skill can be used to study particular aspects of motor behavior and mental retardation. Scholars of mental retardation have historically selected experimental motor tasks either for convenience or for their practical importance, rather than on a principled understanding of the nature of movement dynamics and the influence of task constraints (Newell, 1985b). Over the last 20 years or so, however, there has been increasing attention to this area by scholars with an interest in the study of movement per se. These movement scientists have examined movement phenomena associated with mental retardation primarily to test aspects of motor control theory. Contrasting orientations to the role of movement per se to the study of motor skills and mental retardation can be complementary, but they can also be either neutral or antagonistic to each other. The diverse theoretical influences on the study of motor skills and mental retardation have inevitably led to eclecticism in theoretical position and, as a consequence, the empirical work is thinly spread over a broad range of movement phenomena and theoretical issues.

There are many ways in which a review of mental retardation and motor skills could be organized. To structure this review I have limited the range of topics to those concerning key movement *problems* evident in people with mental retardation. The movement problems selected for review include delays in the development of phylogenetic and ontogenetic activities, stereotypic behavior, hypotonia, and slowness of movement. The overarching theoretical issue is how, and in what way, the level or etiology of mental retardation may relate to these abnormal movement phenomena and performance deficits. For example, the motor performance of individuals with Down syndrome has been a particular focus of empirical inquiry over the last decade or so (cf. Anwar, 1981; Henderson, 1986).

The chapter emphasizes the theoretical issues and empirical findings that have been of most interest in motor skills and mental retardation since about 1980. A major action emphasis is how mental retardation influences the learning and performance of phylogenetic and ontogenetic physical activities. The phylogenetic activities are those that are seen to be indigenous to the species with all members of the population exhibiting the activity, and include posture, locomotion, and prehension. Ontogenetic activities are those activities that are presumed not to be indigenous to the species, but rather develop over time due to the shorter term time demands of family, society, and culture. One of the larger extant literatures is that dealing with information processing and mental retardation, but this theme is omitted from the current review in light of the chapter by Nettlebeck and Wilson (chap. 10) in this volume. This chapter also does not consider formal attempts to overcome particular movement problems of mentally retarded individuals through specialized movement training procedures and sensorimotor training programs (see Wade, Hoover, & Newell, 1983), even though training has both practical and theoretical relevance to the study of motor skills and mental retardation.

THE DEVELOPMENT OF PHYLOGENETIC ACTIVITIES

The concept of *development* is central to the general study of mental retardation. Early development is characterized to a large degree by the progressive change in motor behavior, a feature that has given motor development a significant role in the study of infancy. Thus, the motor performance of infants, as reflected at the onset of the fundamental phylogenetic activities, has been used to provide a window into the status of the developing child and the possible degree and nature of mental retardation. A number of the motor problems evident in adults with mental retardation may have direct links to problems apparent in the development of the phylogenetic activities during infancy. This linkage reflects the general and important influence of development in mental retardation and motor skills, and subsequent deprivation of movement opportunities and motor skill training.

A consistent finding in examinations of the motor ability of infants diagnosed as mentally retarded is that the development of the phylogenetic activities is delayed in contrast to that of their chronologically age-matched nonretarded counterparts. The most established literature detailing this relation is that focusing on infants with Down syndrome (cf. Anwar, 1981; Henderson, 1986). Down syndrome is a congenital syndrome due most frequently to an extra number 21 chromosome (trisomy 21; Patterson, 1987). The facility provided by a genetic categorization is appealing, not the least of reasons being that it affords the opportunity to reduce the natural variance associated with the broad mental retardation classification. Although there is no behavioral characteristic unique to Down syndrome (Shapiro, 1983), there are certain structural (e.g., eye shape, short height, flexible joints, stubby fingers, reduced brain weight) and functional (e.g., hypotonia, poor balance, movement slowness) tendencies that are prevalent. There do not appear to have been any experimental attempts to determine the way in which the structural characteristics of Down syndrome may influence functional problems of movement behavior (and vice versa).

There are many factors, however, that can delay the development of the fundamental posture, locomotion, prehension, and communication skills. The theoretical implications of the relation between cognitive deficits and motor delays is not, however, as straightforward as it might first appear. The general approach to the observation of infant motor development in mentally retarded individuals has tended to follow the literature on motor development in nonretarded infants. The received experimental strategy has been to use a motor ability test that charts performance on some aspect of the development of infant movement behavior at particular chronological ages (Carr, 1970, 1975; Cowie, 1970; Cunningham, 1979; Fishler, Share, & Koch, 1964; Hogg & Moss, 1983). Standard tests such as the Gesell and Amatruda (1941) or Bayley (1969) scales have most commonly been used; at other times, tests with less well-established or even nonexistent psychometric properties have been employed. It is difficult to compare the findings from different motor ability tests with any degree of confidence because only an intuitive basis (face validity) is available for estimating or comparing construct validity. However, to provide a general perspective of the infant motor delays in mentally retarded individuals I have reproduced in Table 11.1 a synthesis from Henderson (1986) of the developmental motor milestones for Down syndrome children from birth to 4 years of age.

The table shows that at all ages from birth to 4 years, Down syndrome children tend to perform less well at the phylogenetic movement skills than do their nonretarded chronologically age-matched counterparts. In addition, the performance difference between the groups increases over this age span, although Down syndrome children do show progressions in their ability to execute a broader range of fundamental movement skills. The onset of particular movement tasks not only occurs at a more advanced chronological

TABLE 11.1.
Developmental Milestones for Children With Down Syndrome

	Children With Down Syndrome		*Normal Children*	
	Average	*Range*	*Average*	*Range*
Gross Motor Activities				
Holds head steady and balanced	5	3–9	3	1–4
Rolls over	8	4–12	5	2–10
Sits without support for 1 minute or more	9	6–16	7	5–9
Pulls to stand using furniture	15	8–26	8	7–12
Walks with support	16	6–30	10	7–12
Stands alone	18	12–38	11	9–16
Walks alone	19	13–48	12	9–17
Walks up stairs with help	30	20–48	17	12–24
Walks down stairs with help	36	24–60+	17	13–24
Fine Motor Activities				
Follows objects with eyes, in circle	3	1.5–6	1.5	1–3
Grasps dangling ring	6	4–11	4	2–6
Passes objects from hand to hand	8	6–12	5.5	4–8
Pulls string to attain toy	11.5	7–17	7	5–10
Finds objects hidden under cloth	13	9–21	8	6–12
Puts 3 or more objects into cup or box	19	12–34	12	9–18
Builds a tower of 2-inch cubes	20	14–32	14	10–19
Completes a simple three-shape jigsaw	33	20–48	22	16–30+
Copies a circle	48	36–60+	30	24–40
Personal/Social/Self-Help Activities				
Smiles when touched and talked to	2	1.5–4	1	1–2
Smiles spontaneously	3	2–6	2	1.5–5
Takes solids well	8	5–18	7	4–12
Feeds self with biscuit	10	6–14	5	4–10
Plays pat-a-cake, peek-a-boo games	11	9–16	8	5–13
Drinks from cup	20	12–30	12	9–17
Uses spoon or fork	20	12–36	13	8–20
Undresses	38	24–60+	30	20–40
Feeds self fully	30	20–48	24	18–36

Note. All ages in months. Adapted from Henderson (1986). Adapted by permission of Kluwer Academic Publishers.

age when compared to a nonretarded group, but the pattern of the performance onset and duration of the progressions within particular movement tasks is different over the developmental time span. Henderson's (1986) assessment of motor development in infancy of Down syndrome children suggests that it is both *delayed* and *qualitatively* distinct from that of normal children.

This analysis of infant and early childhood motor development in Down syndrome is, like its counterparts in the broader child development literature, essentially descriptive with an implicit and sometimes explicit backdrop to a maturational theoretical frame of reference (Gesell, 1929; McGraw, 1943). The use of the motor milestone tests tends to imply a maturational viewpoint, even if not expressed explicitly. Nevertheless, these descriptions of motor performance deficits in Down syndrome children reveal an important category of performance limitation in this population, and the mentally retarded population in general. A key question, however, is what are the theoretical implications of these observations for understanding the development of motor skills of Down syndrome children? The theoretical significance of these findings is difficult to articulate beyond a general recognition that maturational and developmental processes are *somehow* involved in these population differences.

Some studies have examined certain motor control aspects of Down syndrome infant motor development and have been driven by a narrower theoretical perspective with particular developmental hypotheses. A central purpose of these studies is to examine essential functional components of the motor system that may be contributing factors to the developmental trends of motor ability as observed in the motor milestone tests. Rast and Harris (1985) investigated specific postural reactions in Down syndrome infants and a companion nonretarded control group using a neuromotor assessment tool developed for use in screening low-birthweight infants—the Movement Assessment of Infants Inventory (Chandler, Andrews, & Swanson, 1980). The postural reactions included head righting (lateral, flexion, and extension) and active use of the hips. The infants were aged 3½ to 4½ months and the Down syndrome subjects had been enrolled in an early intervention program for 9½ weeks prior to testing. The results showed that Down syndrome subjects showed less righting reaction responses than did their age-matched peers. For example, the Down syndrome infants had more difficulties adjusting their heads in space against the pull of gravity and showed less antigravity control of their lower extremities. The motor performance differences obtained between Down syndrome and normal infants appear strikingly clear cut in this study. Rast and Harris (1985) suggested that the righting reaction tests are more sensitive to developmental differences than are the traditional motor milestone tests. This lack of sensitivity to developmental change of certain motor ability tests may contribute to the ambiguity present in the literature as to whether the delays in the motor development of infants with Down syndrome are present in the first 6 months of life. Haley (1987) suggested that both the delay and the dissimilar sequence of postural reactions should be considered in evaluations of the motor development of children with Down syndrome.

A challenge to the implicit if not explicit assumption that the delay in the onset of the fundamental motor skills in infants diagnosed as mentally retarded and/or Down syndrome is due to neural deficits has recently been provided by Ulrich, Ulrich, and their colleagues (Ulrich, Ulrich, & Collier, 1992; Ulrich, Ulrich, Collier, & Cole, 1995). These authors used a treadmill technique (Thelen, 1986) to provide stimulation to 11-month-old infants with Down syndrome that typically induces alternating stepping movements in normal infants of the same chronological age. Six out of seven Down syndrome infants exhibited stepping behavior, and there was a modest rank-order correlation between degree of stepping behavior and the eventual age at which the same infants began to walk independently. On the basis of these findings, Ulrich and Ulrich concluded that the neural substrate necessary for independent locomotion was available to the Down syndrome infant group long before the actual onset of independent walking. If future research was to substantiate this hypothesis, then theoretical concepts other than neural deficits would need to be pursued to explain the delay in the onset of the fundamental motor skills in infants with Down syndrome.

The contribution of information to the delayed development of motor skills in the mentally retarded population has also received some theoretical and empirical attention.

Butterworth and Cicchetti (1982) had previously shown that discrepant visual feedback was more disruptive of standing than sitting balance in a group of Down syndrome infants. MacLean and Baumeister (1982) examined whether vestibular stimulation in the form of rotational experience (Clark, Kreutzberg, & Chee, 1977) would facilitate the motor development of four developmentally delayed children. The findings suggested that the intervention of the rotational experience facilitated muscular tonicity and the development of fine and gross motor skills. It is interesting that this passive vestibular manipulation should have this positive effect on motor development, given the general benefits of active over passive manipulations in the movement domain. This is a line of enquiry that needs further work, because the theoretical implications of this manipulation are considerable, and the practical implications for activities, such as parental handling techniques, are equally significant.

A large-scale prospective study of the motor performance of Finnish infants (n = 12,058) was undertaken by von Wendt, Makinen, and Rantakallio (1984). The results showed that mental retardation is associated with subnormal motor development in the first year of life, and that this finding is evident even when children with cerebral palsy were not considered. Children who could neither walk nor speak at 12 months were shown to be a high-risk group for mental retardation, the risk being 14-fold higher in this group than among other children. This study also revealed that the motor development of a small group of children who were eventually diagnosed as mentally retarded was in the normal range during the first year of life. This later finding highlights the important point that the motor performance of retarded and nonretarded children tends to overlap, rather than being two distinct population groups.

There have also been studies of phylogenetic activities of mentally retarded children during the early childhood period. For example, kinematic analyses of the gait pattern of children with Down syndrome (trisomy 21) have been conducted (Parker & Bronks, 1980; Parker, Bronks, & Snyder, 1986). The children with Down syndrome showed greater variability on almost all the biomechanical variables analyzed. The authors concluded that the continuum of locomotor development may be a function of the degree of impairment of associated neuromuscular mechanisms. Thus, the kinematic analysis failed to provide any new insights into the development of gait patterns characteristic of Down syndrome. A similar kinematic analysis was made of the jumping coordination patterns of mildly mentally retarded 4- to 7-year-old children (DiRocco, Clark, & Phillips, 1987). The qualitative properties of the jumping pattern were similar between the retarded and nonretarded groups, suggesting that the performance decrement of the mentally retarded group (less distance jumped) is a function of the control processes producing the coordination pattern.

Burton (1990) examined the performance of developmentally disabled preschoolers and nonhandicapped kindergarteners and fourth graders on a gross motor task that would also allow measurement of the perceptual sensitivity of the children to their personal constraints and those present in the environment. Subjects were required to move over a sequence of barriers that varied in height as well as in a baseline condition that required passage through this pathway without the barriers. The different barrier heights afforded different jumping, walking, and running activities through the pathway. The findings revealed that some of the problems in the fundmental movement actions exhibited by the developmentally disabled preschoolers were due to perceptual difficulties of fitting their actions to the constraints imposed. This study nicely demonstrates the significance in action of the subject's perception of their movement constraints relative to the environment, and that difficulties by children with mental retardation in the phylogenetic activities can be due to a range of performance influences.

In summary, the recent examinations of the fundamental skills in infants diagnosed with mental retardation have generally confirmed the observation that there is a delay in the onset of the phylogenetic activities. Our understanding of the reasons for this delay has, however, not apparently advanced during the same period. It is generally accepted that there is not a single reason for the delay in onset of the fundamental activities. This position is consistent with the prevailing perspective that there are wide variations in the manifestations and etiology of mental retardation (Clarke & Clarke, 1985; Richardson & Koller, 1985). However, it is unlikely that this general and broad conclusion will be challenged and refined without systematic examinations of particular hypotheses that may relate to the phenomenon at hand. Observing and describing motor delays as a function of age and population subgroup is one thing, but an experimental unpacking of the delayed movement phenomena within a coherent theoretical perspective is quite another.

Over the years, several hypotheses for the delay in onset of the phylogenetic activities in children diagnosed as mentally retarded have been suggested. These include delayed neural development, difficulties in monitoring feedback information, lack of strength, poor stiffness regulation, and lack of relevant experience in interacting with the environment. These hypotheses are generally consistent with either a maturational or environmental account of motor development. At this point in time, however, none of these hypotheses can be ruled out as contributors to the observed delays in the development of the phylogenetic activities. A major limitation of this area of study is that there has not been a sufficient critical mass of studies focused on any of the candidate hypotheses for fundamental movement skill delays in infants with mental retardation. There has also been a less than adequate manipulation of the severity or etiology of mental retardation in the subject pool examined. Systematic operational examinations of the candidate hypotheses are required to move forward our understanding of the delays in the development of the phylogenetic activities in children with mental retardation.

THE DEVELOPMENT OF ONTOGENETIC ACTIVITIES

The phylogenetic activities of posture, locomotion, and prehension form the essential movement organization elements of all physical activities, although many of the ontogenetic activities in the contexts of sport, dance, work, and the activities of daily living reveal certain properties in the movement dynamics that are unique. The acquisition and performance of these ontogenetic activities has received some attention in the area of motor skills and mental retardation, although it has often been peripheral to (merely an example of) the cognitive information processing issue (see reviews by Anwar, 1981, 1983; Sugden & Keogh, 1990) rather than a reflection of a direct examination of the learning and performance of ontogenetic activities by people with mental retardation. This is a subtle conceptual distinction, but one that can influence the operational manipulations carried out in the experimental setting and the theoretical perspectives.

The general finding from studies of individuals with mental retardation is that the delay in acquisition and the lower level of performance shown in phylogenetic activities is also evident in ontogenetic activities. These parallel trends have been observed in manual control tasks; for example, Fitts' stylus aiming (Sugden, 1980; Sugden & Gray, 1981; Wade, Newell, & Wallace, 1978); bimanual control (Elliott, 1985); tracking (Henderson, Morris, & Frith, 1981; Holden & Corrigan, 1980; Horgan, 1982; Kerr & Blais, 1985); coincidence timing (Wade, 1980); and bicycle brake assembly (Gold, 1977; Wade & Gold, 1978). There are also clear performance deficits in physical capacity tasks involving strength, flexibility, and endurance (Dobbins, Garron, & Rarick, 1981; Molnar & Alexander, 1983).

The empirical examination of the learning and performance of ontogenetic activities by individuals with mental retardation has been more diverse and shallow than in the phylogenetic activities because of the many tasks and age groups (chronological and developmental) that have been examined on only a single experimental occasion. Nevertheless, the data are generally consistent in showing that people with mental retardation perform at a lower level and show greater variability of motor performance in ontogenetic activities. The findings from the studies mentioned previously also provide some clues as to the nature of the performance deficit in people with mental retardation, even if no prevailing theoretical hypothesis has emerged.

In the motor development and learning literatures on nonretarded individuals there has traditionally been a separation between the study of phylogenetic and ontogenetic activities. The theoretical and operational (age and task) perspectives driving the empirical work in these respective domains has been unrelated. The study of phylogenetic activities in people with mental retardation is consonant with the work of motor development and the study of ontogenetic activities in people with mental retardation is consonant with the work of motor learning and control. Whether different theoretical perspectives are required for the study of development and learning has been challenged by inferences drawn from the ecological approach to perception and action (Newell, Kugler, van Emmerik, & McDonald, 1989), but a unified approach to action in the mental retardation domain has not been pursued.

Given that the theorizing in motor skill and mental retardation is very eclectic, it follows that there has been a range of issues examined using either an ontogenetic activity or a motor skill. As a consequence of this diverse orientation to the study of the learning and performance of ontogenetic activities, there have been very few, if any, substantive insights or theoretical developments about mental retardation and ontogenetic activities per se. Rather, the empirical work has merely provided some preliminary clues about the nature of the motor performance deficits associated with mental retardation. A good example of this orientation is the study of timing in movement control, a factor that is seen intuitively as linked to the commonly observed problem of clumsiness in mental retardation.

It is axiomatic that the human movement that is generated in support of action takes place in space and time. Actions invariably have space–time constraints, with different emphases on the dimensions of space and time according to the particular task conditions. There has been an increasing recognition that examination of the movement dynamics, in addition to the movement outcome, provides a window on the organization of movement coordination and control. A representative study with this orientation is that of Henderson et al. (1981), who examined sinusoidal tracking, accelerating tracking, track continuation, and drawing from memory performance, in three groups of subjects—nonretarded, Down syndrome, and a group of non-Down syndrome mentally retarded children (CA > 7 years, IQ > 40). Figure 11.1 shows some sample sinusoidal tracking time-series from both mentally retarded and nonretarded children.

There are striking differences in the space–time tracking profile between the nonretarded subjects and those of the children with mental retardation. In addition, although not shown in Fig. 11.1, the Down syndrome children performed more poorly on the tracking task than did the comparison group with mental retardation. The major performance difference between the nonretarded and retarded subjects was in the temporal rather than the spatial aspects of the task, and this difference was magnified when the model to be tracked was absent from the display. These findings led Henderson et al. (1981) to suggest that timing was a key component in which motor performance deficits occurred in people with mental retardation, particularly in children with Down syndrome. Timing has been

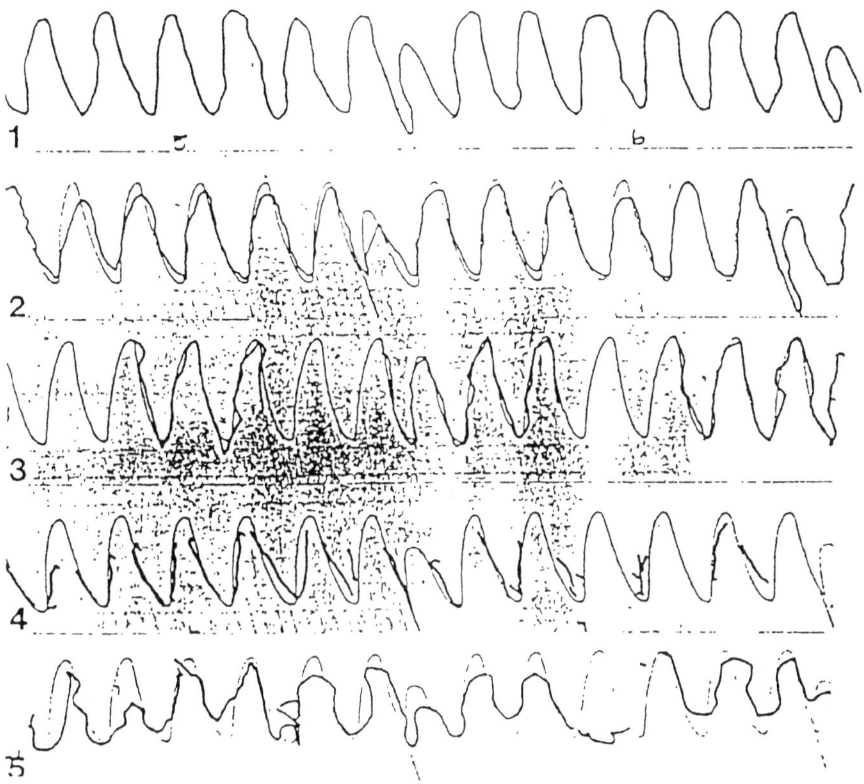

FIG. 11.1. Sinusoidal tracking trials from normal (trace 1) and mentally retarded (traces 2–5) children (adapted from Henderson et al., 1981). Reprinted with permission from the Association for Child Psychology and Psychiatry.

examined in other tasks (e.g., coincident timing—Wade, 1980), but further systematic examinations of these particular movement phenomena have not been forthcoming.

The timing data of Henderson et al. (1981) are consistent with the pervasive notion in the popular literature that Down syndrome children are more clumsy than their non-Down syndrome mentally retarded counterparts (Burns & Gunn, 1993; Selikowitz, 1990). Clumsiness is a construct that is prevalent in the literature on Down syndrome, but its conceptual and operational definitions are usually so vague that it is not particularly helpful to invoke in a scientific sense, even if (perhaps because) it is a term that is common in everyday language. Timing in movement sequences will undoubtedly be part of attempts to unravel the concept of clumsiness in Down syndrome and mental retardation, but the mental age differences reported here on timing are only a preliminary step to the development of a relevant theoretical perspective. This reservation on the degree of significance of the proposed link between data and theory is reflective of similar limitations in other areas of study about mental retardation and ontogenetic activities.

In summary, the findings on the delays and performance decrements in ontogenetic activities of children and adults with mental retardation hold similar limitations to those outlined previously with phylogenetic activities. The list of candidate hypotheses for the delays in phylogenetic activities are also relevant to the performance decrements in ontogenetic activities. Many motor performance differences have been reported between nonretarded and retarded children in ontogenetic activities, but again there has been insufficient examination of these differences in regard to particular theoretical hypotheses. Thus, our understanding of these performance decrements in children with mental retardation has not moved forward in the last decade or so and it is unlikely to do so in the future without systematic empirical work of a given theoretical view.

STEREOTYPIC BEHAVIOR

Stereotypic behaviors are common among people with mental retardation (Baumeister & Forehand, 1973; Berkson, 1967). Indeed, Berkson, McQuiston, Jacobson, Eyman, and Borthwick (1985) suggested that some 50% to 70% of mentally retarded individuals living in institutional settings exhibit stereotypic behaviors. The definition of stereotypy varies somewhat from domain to domain (see Schroeder, 1970), but *stereotypic behaviors* are generally viewed as superfluous movement sequences that appear unrelated to an action goal, involuntary, low in movement variability (invariant), and inappropriate for the context at hand (Berkson, 1983; Cooper & Dourish, 1990).

The term *stereotypy* has been applied to many classes of behavior that include normal animal behaviors, pacing, and other repetitive behaviors of caged animals; repetitive behaviors of normally developing infants; self-injurious behavior; consequences of injecting high doses of stimulant drugs; dyskinesia following psychotropic drug administration or neurological diseases; common unusual behaviors of socially deprived higher primates; and autistic behaviors of children and adults with developmental disabilities (Berkson, in press). Berkson also suggested that the concept of stereotypy may be applied to many other behaviors of people with mental retardation that include abnormal focused affections, obsessions and compulsions, clothes and food fetishes, and rigidities of childhood. Thus, the term *stereotypy* has come to capture a very broad behavior base (cf. Mason, 1991; Schroeder, 1970)—a move that has both enhanced and detracted from our understanding of stereotypies.

There are two particular types of stereotypies evident in people with mental retardation that I focus on here. This classification approach has been adopted in part because these two general categories have received the most theoretical and empirical attention. One category is comprised of non-drug-induced stereotypy, and is usually interpreted as arising from prolonged periods of social isolation and deprivation of environmental stimulation (Berkson, 1983). The second category of stereotypy is that involved in tardive dyskinesia and arises as a side effect from prolonged regimens of neuroleptic medication that are given often for behavior modification in residential settings (Kalachnik, 1984; Sprague & Newell, 1987). Thus, there are drug-and non-drug-induced stereotypies observed in people with mental retardation. Surprisingly, these types of stereotypies have not been systematically contrasted to determine what different conditions lead to differences in type, prevalence, or organization of the respective stereotypy. Accordingly, we consider these two types of stereotypy in distinct categories before considering their possible similarities and differences.

The exhibition of stereotypic behavior in adults has been typically viewed as a reflection of a problem or a set of problems with the sensorimotor system. Thus, stereotypies provide interesting movement sequences to study in their own right in regard to issues in motor control, irrespective of their behavioral or social consequences. However, it is the case, particularly in the neuroleptically induced stereotypies, that they have the potential to interfere with the conduct of everyday motor skills. Such practical concerns provide an additional rationale for the study of stereotypies in persons with mental retardation.

Non-Drug-Induced Stereotypies

The presence of stereotyped behaviors in individuals who are mentally retarded is well established (Baumeister & Forehand, 1973; Berkson, 1967). In this chapter I do not consider the self-injurious stereotypic behaviors (Guess & Carr, 1991; MacLean, Stone, & Brown, 1994; Schroeder, 1991), although there are a number of ways in which these actions are complementary to what are often called the *self-stimulating stereotypies*. The issues to be addressed here include the clinical prevalence of stereotypies, individual differences in stereotypies, the movement form of stereotypies, and the antecedents of stereotypic behavior.

The display of stereotypies in people with mental retardation is typically viewed as abnormal behavior. Mason (1991), in an insightful review of the stereotypy concept, raised the challenge as to whether the abnormal designation is always appropriate, and, furthermore, what the nature of the abnormality is. One intuitive interpretation of abnormal simply means away from the norm for the respective population group. On these grounds, given the prevalence of stereotyped behavior among people with severe to profound mental retardation, self-stimulating stereotypies could be seen to be the norm rather than the exception and, therefore, should not be considered abnormal. A second view of abnormal interprets it as lacking in function or that which is maladaptive. Although self-injurious behaviors may clearly be viewed as maladaptive (Guess & Carr, 1991), it is not clear that the majority of self-stimulating behaviors are necessarily maladaptive. Indeed, the very notion of producing stereotypic behaviors for stimulation or control reasons is arguably a clear instance of adaptive behavior (Berkson & Gallagher, 1986). Thus, the prefix of *abnormal* to the label *stereotypic* needs to be interpreted cautiously, not only in the infant age group where the evidence of stereotypies is viewed as reflective of normal developmental transitions (Thelen, 1979, in press; Wolff, 1968), but also in all aspects of adult human stereotypies, including those of people with mental retardation.

The significance of the fine line between normal and abnormal motor behavior was highlighted in a study by MacLean, Ellis, Galbreath, Halpern, and Baumeister (1991), who examined rhythmic motor behavior in normal infant motor development, Down syndrome infants, and children with profound motor impairment. It is generally assumed that developmental level predicts the form and degree of rhythmical motor behavior in infant motor development (Thelen, 1979, in press; Wolff, 1979). MacLean and colleagues carried out a longitudinal study whereby they examined rhythmical motor behavior over 12 biweekly sessions between the 9- and 14-month age range. The motor-impaired subjects in general displayed less rhythmic motor behavior than did the Down syndrome and the nondisabled groups. The group differences varied, however, when the prevelance and type of stereotypy were analyzed as a function of the particular effector system, head, torso, mouth, arm, and leg. Thus, the failure to produce sufficient rhythmical behavior or stereotypies at the critical age periods in infancy is viewed as abnormal or a departure from normal motor development.

Further definitional ambiguities relate to the movement criteria essential to the description and characterization of stereotypies. For example, Newell, van Emmerik, and Sprague (1993) recently drew contrasts in the variability of the movement dynamics between stereotypic and skilled behaviors. The central stereotypic criterion of invariant action pattern or low movement variability is also a hallmark characteristic of skilled behavior. Typically, the more skilled the individual in a given activity, the less variability is evident in the outcome of the act and in certain properties of the movement dynamics. There are, however, exceptions to this pattern of organization in movement sequences requiring the coordination of many biomechanical degrees of freedom, where sometimes there is greater variability in the joint motion of skilled performers (cf. Newell & Corcos,

1993). Thus, an interesting theoretical question arises: Where on a movement variability dimension does one draw the line between stereotypic and skilled behavior? Newell et al. (1993) suggested that the movement invariance criterion is not sufficient to draw any such activity category conclusions, leaving adaptability and relevance of the action to the contextual demands as more useful criteria for defining stereotypy (see also Touwen, 1978). In spite of these conceptual and operational ambiguities there has been considerable theoretical and empirical study of stereotypies in the mentally retarded population over the last decade or so. The following sections discuss some of the major issues arising from this work.

Clinical Prevalence. It is generally accepted that stereotypies are prevalent in mentally retarded individuals, particularly those with severe–profound mental retardation living in institutional settings (Baumeister & Forehand, 1973; Lewis & Baumeister, 1982), but a detailed survey of the nature and degree of stereotypy as a function of the level of mental retardation is not available. It is also the case that estimates of the prevalence and the nature of stereotypy in different residential settings and contexts are influenced by the type of survey instrument employed, the skill of the observer in categorizing stereotypies, and the context (e.g., work vs. free time) in which it is observed. Accurate demographic data for individuals being observed are also required to provide unambiguous classifications of stereotypies. For example, without knowing the drug history of an individual, tardive dyskinesia and non-drug-induced stereotypies could probably not be determined reliably on the basis of the behavior alone.

A number of stereotypic actions are common to groups of people with mental retardation, but there is also a broad array of unique stereotypic movement sequences produced. Body rocking, head banging, hand waving, lip smacking, tongue protrusions, and eye blinking are some of the common stereotypies reported across the age and mental retardation dimensions (Baumeister & Forehand, 1973). Some stereotypies appear to be unique to a given individual and involve intricate movement sequences requiring the coordination and control of many biomechanical degrees of freedom. These idiosyncratic movement sequences are typically undefined. Thus, descriptions of stereotypies are limited to either a general relationship to mental retardation or an anecdotal set of individual observations.

The characterization of stereotypies is usually effected operationally by natural observation, sometimes with the aid of a categorical rating scale and sometimes employing a second observer to ensure the reliability of the observations. The determination by sight of a particular movement pattern may be difficult, depending on the intricacy of the movement pattern. This is particularly the case when the number of biomechanical degrees of freedom employed in the action is large and the duration of the movement sequence is long. The current widespread availability of computerized movement recording and analysis systems opens the door to direct measurement of the movement dynamics of stereotypic actions. This approach has been sparsely used to date and primarily limited to single degree of freedom movements (Newell et al., 1993).

Movement notation has also been used as a tool to describe the stereotypic movement sequences of animal stereotypies (Golani, 1976). There are a number of languages of movement notation, each with their own advantages and disadvantages (cf. Kleinman, 1975). Movement notation could be particularly useful in providing qualitative assessments of long duration stereotypic movement sequences in which the standard biomechanical analysis may prove either difficult or expensive to conduct. Teitelbaum, Pellis, and DeVietti (1990) applied the Esckol-Wachmann movement notation scheme to the analysis of movement disorders in rats and indirectly demonstrated the power of this technique for studying movement disorders in humans.

There is some evidence that the occurrence of stereotypies is influenced both by the level of mental retardation and the age of the individual (Berkson, McQuiston, Jacobson, Eyman, & Borthwick, 1985; Jacobson, 1982). The general finding is that stereotyped behaviors increase with age from 1 year up to the teenage period, with a decrease over the remainder of the life span. Figure 11.2 shows the relationship among age, level of mental retardation, and stereotypic behavior as revealed from a 1978 survey from Lanterman State Hospital in California (Berkson et al., 1985). It appears that some 50% to 70% of persons in institutional settings exhibit stereotypies. The percentage of stereotyped behaviors is directly related to level of mental retardation with people who are profoundly mentally retarded exhibiting the highest level of stereotypy. This study also revealed the increase in the prevalence of stereotypies through the childhood years to continue over a longer time period as the severity of mental retardation increased.

These trends on the prevalence of stereotypies in individuals with mental retardation need to be interpreted cautiously, because the criteria for defining stereotypy and the skill level of the observer varies from survey to survey. One might anticipate, however, that these possible confounding factors of survey design would most likely influence the absolute estimates of the stereotypic behaviors, rather than the qualitative pattern of the relative data over age and level of mental retardation. On the other hand, the current makeup of the population of mentally retarded people living in residential facilities is very different to what it was even 10 years ago. The residential population is smaller than it was and proportionally has a more severe level of mental retardation. More complete and recent survey data of stereotypies and mental retardation would be useful to unambiguously determine the influence of environmental conditions, age, gender, severity, and etiology of mental retardation, together with their interactions, on the nature and prevalence of stereotypic behavior. The generation of appropriate longitudinal data showing the stability and change of stereotypies within an individual over time is also long overdue.

Movement Form. An issue central to the description and understanding of stereotypic behavior is a formal assessment of the *form* of the movement sequence. Berkson and Gallagher (1986) were the first to appreciate the importance of the concept of movement form in the study of stereotyped behaviors associated with mental retardation. Stereotypic

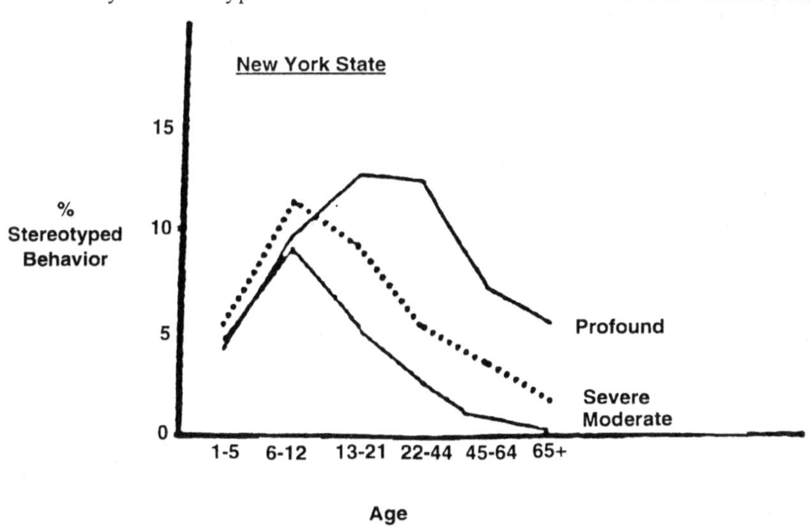

FIG. 11.2. The relation between age and stereotyped behavior (adapted from Berkson et al., 1985). Reprinted by permission of the American Association on Mental Retardation.

behaviors have traditionally been assessed by clinical observation, occasionally with the aid of observer checklists or rating scales. The concept of *movement form* has been usually implicit in the assessment of stereotypies, although where it has been explicit the methods used to analyze the form have not been sufficient to accommodate the concept.

An early study reporting a movement analysis of stereotypic behaviors in persons with mental retardation was that of Lewis et al. (1984). These authors examined the dynamics of body rocking and its relation to cardiac activity in persons with severe mental retardation and autism. A single dimension accelerometer was used to measure the anterior-posterior back or shoulder motion of the subject in the body rocking action. Data collection sessions were conducted with each subject over several days. The findings confirmed the rhythmical nature of stereotypic behavior and, furthermore, showed an entrained relation between heart rate and the rhythm of the body rocking. This study by Lewis and colleagues (1984) demonstrates the potential value of a direct recording of aspects of the movement dynamics to an understanding of the nature of the stereotypic behavior. Unfortunately, this approach to the study of non-drug-induced stereotypies has not been followed up in any systematic way either in body rocking or other common stereotypies of people with mental retardation.

MacLean et al. (1985) examined the frequency of eyeblinks in mentally retarded individuals as a function of the percentage of time that each person engaged in stereotypic behavior. Blink rate was used as an indirect measure of dopamine involvement in the nigrostriatol pathway in the role of regulating behavior. The authors found that the spontaneous rate of eyeblink was inversely related to the level of stereotypic behavior. Furthermore, the male stereotypic subjects exhibited a lower rate of blinking than did same-gender control subjects. The simple frequency analysis of blink rate that was used in this study reveals again the power of observing directly the movement kinematics of stereotypies, although further work is required to fully understand the role of dopamine receptor sensitivity in the mediation of blink rate or other stereotypic activities.

Berkson and Gallagher (1986) suggested that the simplest way to analyze and contrast stereotypies was on the basis of their movement form. These authors provided no definition of movement form but proposed that a topographical analysis of stereotypies would provide the necessary information. Furthermore, the notion of a topographical analysis of stereotypies was not developed, but applying the term *topographical* to the movement domain would suggest that such an analysis of movement provides a detailed spatial (configuration) analysis of the relevant body parts at a given point in time. In many ways a topographical analysis would parallel a detailed geography map that charts the spatial layout of a given location.

Movement sequences, however, whether in stereotypic or nonstereotypic actions, take place in space–time. This suggests that the time evolution of the configuration of the body parts in stereotypies is also required in order to analyze movement form (Newell, 1985a, 1985b). Stereotypic motions, like other movement sequences, also tend to be produced or repeated over multiple trials or behavioral occurrences. It is well established that there is always some intraindividual variability in the absolute motion properties of the movement dynamics from trial to trial, even in highly skilled performers (Bernstein, 1967). The expectation is that this principle holds for stereotypic motions, although no formal tests of this assumption have been made to date (Newell et al., 1993).

Given these time-varying properties of the movement dynamics, it would be useful to analyze stereotypic movement sequences by considering their absolute, common, and relative motion properties (Cutting & Proffitt, 1982). It is anticipated that the relative motion properties define the form of a given stereotypic movement sequence. Indeed, it has been proposed that movement sequences, or the movement form, may be qualitatively defined by a unique set of relative motion properties in the movement dynamics (Newell, 1985b). In this movement framework some topological kinematic properties will be preserved in the face of transformations of the absolute scale of certain movement properties, due to either intrinsic variability or external task demands (e.g., the similar constraining circumstances of chairs used in the case of body rocking). Thus, the movement form of stereotypies can be assessed by the topological properties of the time-varying movement dynamics (McGinnis & Newell, 1982).

This approach to the assessment of movement form could be used to formally distinguish types of stereotypies and the nature of individual differences in stereotypic behavior. Another way of expressing this conclusion is that this approach provides a vehicle to formally determine what properties of stereotypies remain invariant from behavioral occurrence to occurrence. Indeed, the postulation is that the standard definitional claim that stereotypies lack variability or are low in variability is no more than saying that the individual is producing the same set of topological properties in the movement kinematics from behavior to behavior (Newell, in press; Newell et al., 1993). The absolute motion properties of stereotypies (e.g., amplitude, frequency) may be as or more variable than are similar normal voluntary movement sequences.

In this movement analysis framework it is assumed that the relative motion properties provide the dynamic basis on which observations of the qualitative properties of the movement sequence are determined. Experimental work from the visual perception literature suggests that individual observers are adept at picking up the relative motion properties in movement sequences (Cutting & Proffitt, 1982; Johansson, von Hofsten, & Jansson, 1980). What is now needed is the examination of the direct formal link between the relative motion properties of movement sequences and the clinical observations of the qualitative dynamic properties of stereotypies. This would help verify the categorical judgments of the standard clinical assessment protocols and provide the beginnings of a dynamical analysis to the movement sequences of stereotypic behavior.

Drug-Induced Stereotypies

The prolonged intake of neuroleptic medication can lead to emergent movement disorder side-effects—a syndrome known as *tardive dyskinesia*. This movement disorder syndrome was first identified some 35 years ago (Schonecker, 1957). Subsequently, a considerable body of research on this movement disorder has accumulated (cf. American Psychiatric Association, 1979, 1992; Haag, Ruther, & Hippius, 1992; Jeste & Wyatt, 1982), much of which has focused on individuals diagnosed as schizophrenic. Tardive dyskinesia is characterized by involuntary jerky and sometimes rhythmical motions of the peripheral effector systems, and is particularly manifest in the facial and oral areas (eye, lip, and tongue movements), fingers, toes, upper and lower limbs, and even head movements. Paulson, Rizvi, and Crane (1975) were apparently the first to reveal similar emergent movement disorders in an institutionalized developmentally disabled population. Over the last 2 decades there has been considerable interest in tardive dyskinesia and mental retardation because of both the prevalence of tardive dyskinesia following neuroleptic medication and the widespread application of neuroleptics in institutional settings (Kalachnik, 1984; Sprague & Newell, 1987).

The use of the term *stereotypy* to describe both non-drug-induced and drug-induced involuntary rhythmical movement has added to the confusion about its meaning and whether stereotypies are or are not present in tardive dyskinesia. This is because a number of scholars in the mental retardation domain prefer to reserve the term *stereotypy* for non-drug-induced superfluous motions. However, if one adopts the definition of stereotypy outlined earlier, it needs to be recognized that it is based on the behavioral characteristics of the action without respect to other levels of analysis. Similar problems of definition have arisen in relation to the term *tremor* (cf. Findley & Capildeo, 1984), which, interestingly by definition, reflects many of the same movement properties of actions defined as stereotypic. Thus, from a behavioral standpoint, superfluous involuntary rhythmical motions exist in both tardive dyskinesia and non-drug-induced repetitive behavior, reflecting again the broad use of the term *stereotypy*.

Clinical Prevalence. The prevalence of tardive dyskinesia among populations with mental retardation is not well established. However, some estimates of particular population segments suggest that its clinical prevalence is widespread in this population, particularly in institutional settings (Kalachnik et al., 1984). This trend appears consistent with the fact that institutions tend to include a greater proportion of the profoundly and severely mentally retarded population and that the prevalence of behavioral problems in institutions is higher than in noninstitutional settings.

Estimates of the prevalence of tardive dyskinesia vary considerably both in mentally retarded and nonmentally retarded individuals (Cunningham Owens & Johnstone, 1982; Kane & Smith, 1982). The reasons for this variability in the estimates of the prevalence of tardive dyskinesia are likely to be similar to the rationale provided earlier for the variable estimates of non-drug-induced stereotypies; namely, inconsistency in the observation protocol and the varying skill level of the observer from study to study. There have been two large studies of the prevalence of tardive dyskinesia in individuals diagnosed as mentally retarded.

Stone, May, Alvarez, and Ellman (1989), on the basis of a large developmentally disabled population (n = 1,227), found that dyskinesia was evident in 48% of the population, and its prevalence was greater among females and increased with age (demographic risk factors that are generally established with tardive dyskinesia; Haag et al., 1992). This study also reported that 29% of this population had dystonia, 13% had akathisia, 3% had parkinsonism, and 4% had paroxysms. In total, 72% of the population had one or more of these movement disorder syndromes.

Kalachnik et al. (1984) provided the only study to have randomly assigned developmentally disabled subjects to neuroleptic and nonneuroleptic reduction conditions. The results showed that withdrawal produced an initial increase in the diagnosis of tardive dyskinesia that exceeded 80% of the subjects originally on neuroleptic medication over a 9-month withdrawal period. The Stone et al. (1989) and Kalachnik et al. (1984) studies confirm that tardive dyskinesia is very prevalent among people with mental retardation who are taking neuroleptic medication.

As suggested previously, the prevalence of tardive dyskinesia can be masked by the continued application of the neuroleptic medication. Neuroleptics have a dual and opposing influence in that the prolonged regimen of the medication leads to the onset of the movement disorder but the behavioral manifestation of the disorder is suppressed to some degree by the continued presence of the drug itself. Withdrawing the medication usually leads to enhanced abnormal movements and can even reveal the presence of tardive dyskinesia in cases where it was not apparent during the presence of the medication regimen. There has been considerable debate about whether tardive dyskinesia is reversible with continued withholding of neuroleptic medication, but the data are equivocal due in large part to the failure of studies to continue with observations over a sufficient duration of the drug-withdrawal period.

The side effects arising from neuroleptic medication have also created a behavioral and ethical dilemma with respect to the management of drug regimens. This dilemma is particularly acute in mental retardation residential facilities, because the continued application of the neuroleptic drug is a major factor in the reduction or even minimization of behavioral disorders. Thus, there is a fine line between considerations of the emergent side effects from the medication that detrimentally influence the individual and the individual and social needs in relation to behavioral management in residential settings. In the last decade or so, there has been increased litigation over the prescription of neuroleptics to people with mental retardation (Slaw & Kalachnik, 1985; Sprague, 1982).

The work of Sprague and colleagues to refine techniques of observation and classification of tardive dyskinesia in mental retardation may help substantiate the prevelance of tardive dyskinesia in mental retadation (Sprague, et al., 1984; Sprague, Kalachnik, & Shaw, 1989). The shortened and revised DISCUS test (Dyskinesia Identification System Coldwater User Scale) has been constructed with strict adherence to psychometric test construction principles, and Sprague and colleagues also constructed training programs to minimize the variance in assessment practices. For example, Kalachnik, Sprague, and Shaw (1988) showed that, with a modicum of training, allied health personnel such as nurses can detect and classify tardive dyskinesia as validly and reliably as can medical doctors. These kinds of training procedures are very important in reducing the variance in assessment practices, and Sprague has developed them specifically with respect to the classification of tardive dyskinesia among people with mental retardation.

The use of rating scales or clinical observations of movement disorders rely on natural observation by a human observer. This approach can be quite valid and reliable for the detection of certain movement properties, but less so for others, due to the limitations of perceptual thresholds of the observer (Newell & Sprague, 1990). This limitation, which exists in the observation of all stereotypies, suggests the possibility of not detecting some important movement properties of a population group or action category. As in the case of non-drug-induced stereotypies that were reviewed earlier, the observation of tardive dyskinesia can be enhanced by direct recording of the movement dynamics that reflect the movement form of the stereotypy. Consistent with this theme, May (1987) advocated that measurement of tremor may be a good indicator of tardive dyskinesia.

A central question that underlies much of the direction of studies of the movement form of tardive dyskinesia is whether there is a unique dynamical signature to this movement disorder. In other words, does tardive dyskinesia produce unique spatial–temporal properties in the movement dynamics? Furthermore, one can ask whether there is a unique dynamical signature to tardive dyskinesia in individuals diagnosed with mental retardation. Such a possibility holds interesting theoretical implications with regard to the nature and evaluation of the movement disorder. This movement dynamics approach to stereotypy also holds important practical applications, particularly with respect to the early detection of tardive dyskinesia and subsequent informed modulation of the drug protocol.

Newell and Sprague have been conducting a movement dynamics analysis of the stereotypic movements associated with tardive dyskinesia in people with mental retardation to directly assess whether there is a unique signature to the movement dynamics of tardive dyskinesia in this population, and the direct measures of the movement dynamics are more sensitive than clinical observation and rating scale techniques to the measurement of the movement disorder (Newell, in press; Newell et al., 1993; Newell & Sprague, 1990; Sprague & Newell, 1987). This project has emphasized the analysis of postural activities due to their common place in everyday contexts, and also the possibility that these activities may be very sensitive to the detection of tardive dyskinesia. There has also been a focus on distinguishing the contribution of the neuroleptic medication from that of the mental retardation to the change in movement dynamics. Although much work remains to be done to provide unambiguous statements with respect to these proposed relations, the work conducted to date suggests that there may be some general and distinct trends to the movement dynamics of tardive dyskinesia in people with mental retardation (Ko, van Emmerik, Sprague, & Newell, 1992; Newell, van Emmerik, Lee, & Sprague, 1993; van Emmerik, Sprague, & Newell, 1993a, 1993b, 1993c). Here I amplify on two examples from this work.

In the maintenance of upright bipedal posture, subjects with tardive dyskinesia produce greater variability in the motion of the center of pressure, which in effect is the location of the collective ground reaction force that is being used to regulate the position and sway of the body (Ko et al., 1991). Of more interest is that the subjects with mental retardation and tardive dyskinesia showed a different postural strategy than did nonretarded subjects with tardive dyskinesia, and a normal healthy matched control group of subjects in regard to the pattern of the center of pressure (see also van Emmerik et al., 1993b). In extreme instances the pattern of the center of pressure was very rhythmical, as reflected in one of the examples shown in Fig. 11.3. Indeed, some 38% of the trials of the subjects with severe and profound mental retardation and tardive dyskinesia exhibited rhythmical behavior (Ko et al., 1991). A nonlinear dynamic analysis revealed that the dimensionality of the center of pressure time series was lower in the group with tardive dyskinesia than in the normal group, suggesting that fewer degrees of freedom are regulated in the group with tardive dyskinesia (Newell et al., 1993). The analysis also showed that the dimen-

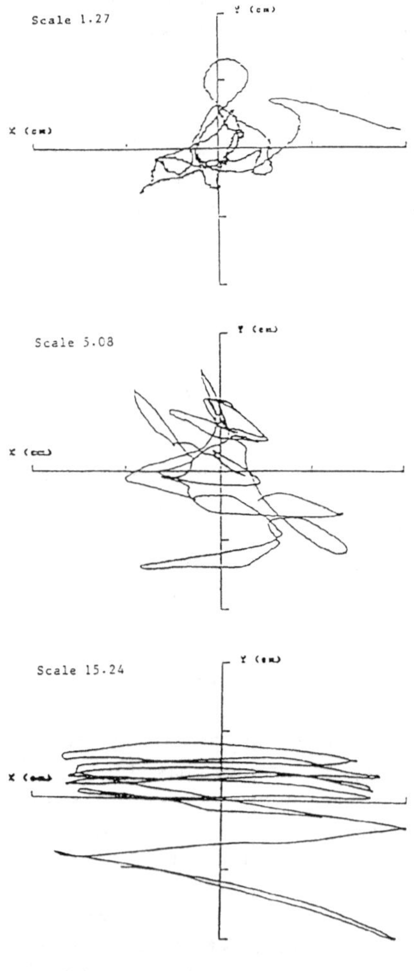

FIG. 11.3. Examples of center of pressure time-series in: normal subject; nonrythmical tardive dyskinetic subject; and rhythmical tardive dyskinetic subject (adapted from Newell et al., 1993). Adapted by permission of the publishers, Butterworth-Heinemann Ltd.

sionality measure differentiated between the postural profiles of subjects differing in severity of tardive dyskinesia when analysis by eye of the observer failed to detect group differences. The findings from this series of postural studies indicate that the neuroleptic medication overconstrains the organization of the motor system, which in turn leads to greater variability as reflected in traditional movement outcome scores.

An analysis of arm tremor in tardive dyskinetic subjects shows the dual and opposing influence of medication on motor performance (van Emmerik et al., 1993a). In this study, subjects with tardive dyskinesia produced lower variability in the motion of the arms as they were held outstretched parallel to the ground than did the subjects with mental retardation without tardive dyskinesia. This performance effect shows that the drug regimen can modify behavior in a fashion consistent with the task goals and social expectations. However, the analysis of physiological tremor revealed that the group with tardive dyskinesia shifted their modal tremor to a lower and more broadband frequency than did the normal subjects and those with mental retardation without tardive dyskinesia. Thus, there were movement organization changes to this behavioral modification revealing a dual influence of the medication regimen. The behavior appears appropriately or sufficiently modulated with help of the medication, but the more microscopic changes in sensorimotor system organization reflect changes of state on the system. Similar findings have been obtained in an analysis of finger tremor in subjects with mental retardation and tardive dyskinesia (van Emmerik et al., 1993c).

These detrimental effects of neuroleptic medication on the sensorimotor system were only revealed through the more direct and sensitive analysis of the movement dynamics. There has been an increasing trend in this direction in the study of tardive dyskinesia in general, both in human (Alpert, Diamond, & Friedhoff, 1976; Caligiuri & Lohr, 1990; Hansen, Glazer, & Moore, 1986; Tyron & Pologe, 1987) and animal models (Alpert, Diamond, Weisenfreund, Taleporos, & Friedhoff, 1978; Ellison & See, 1991; Ellison, See, Levin, & Kinney, 1987). These developments promise a formal basis to unambiguously answer the question of whether there is a unique signature to the dynamics of tardive dyskinesia in either mentally retarded or nonretarded populations.

In spite of the increased focus on tardive dyskinesia in people with mental retardation, there is no evidence in the rating scale or movement dynamic data sets that the prevalence, severity, or type of tardive dyskinetic disorder is different in mentally retarded as opposed to nonretarded subjects. Furthermore, there is no evidence available as to whether the type of neuroleptic drug differentially interacts with level of mental retardation. The appropriately designed studies have not been conducted to determine this possible interaction of mental retardation with neuroleptic medication, and, furthermore, they will be difficult to execute due to the inherent difficulty of obtaining accurate medication records of people with mental retardation, particularly those living in residential facilities. Thus, significant work remains to be done to tease out population and individual difference effects in non-drug-induced stereotypic and tardive dyskinetic behavior.

Antecedents of Stereotypic Behavior

Stereotypies reflect a very broad class of behaviors. In the preceding sections the focus has been on two classes of stereotypies common to, although not peculiar to, mental retardation. The environmental factors associated with non-drug-induced and tardive dyskinetic stereotypies are, by definition, clearly very different. However, in spite of this difference, there could still be common mediating factors to these classes of stereotypies. In closing this section on stereotypies and mental retardation I briefly explore the issue of the antecedents and etiology of non-drug-induced and tardive dyskinetic stereotypies in individuals diagnosed with mental retardation (cf. Cooper & Dourish, 1990).

The currently received view on non-drug-induced stereotypies is that they are manifest due to the need for self-stimulation on the part of the individual (Berkson & Gallagher, 1986). The lack of stimulation that arises from an impoverished environment motivates the individual to seek stimulation through repetitive movement sequences. Berkson and Gallagher (1986) suggested that it is not merely the stimulation that arises from the movement sequence that initiates and maintains stereotypies, but importantly the control of that stimulation by the self-imposed regulation of the stereotypic activity. Thus, for example, passive movement would not realize the same control for the individual as would active movement, even if the stimulation arising from the feedback was of the same order. There has been little direct empirical examination of the self-stimulation hypothesis, but it has sufficient intuitive appeal to warrant further study. Non-drug-induced stereotypies are usually analyzed at only a behavior level and, therefore, it is difficult to evaluate the self-stimulation hypothesis directly on the same levels of analysis as the hypotheses offered in regard to the stereotypies of tardive dyskinesia.

Tardive dyskinesia is, by definition, the movement disorder syndrome that arises from prolonged intake of neuroleptic medication. The cause of tardive dyskinesia is clear-cut by definition, although how the neuroleptic drug interacts with other environmental or organismic constraints is less well established. A number of risk factors for tardive dyskinesia have been isolated, including age, gender, and schizophrenia, and other subject factors are suspected of influencing the prevalence of tardive dyskinesia. The received view of tardive dyskinesia is that the medication blocks the central postsynaptic dopamine receptors of the basal ganglia, which, in turn, mediates the normal regulation of posture and movement (Khot, Egan, Hyde, & Wyatt, 1992; Klawans, 1973). There are several specific models of basal ganglia functioning in tardive dyskinesia, but the pathophysiology and psychopharmacology of tardive dyskinesia are beyond the scope of the current chapter. However, it is important to note that there is no evidence from neurochemistry as to if or how mental retardation may interact with the challenge of drug intake to the central nervous system. This neural level of analysis of the stereotypies associated with tardive dyskinesia is very different from that typically available in the cases of non-drug-induced stereotypies, particularly in the study of humans.

Lewis, Gluck, Bodfish, Beauchamp, and Mailman (in press) recently proposed that impaired dopamine function, involving decreased synaptic concentrations of dopamine with subsequent increased sensitivity of dopamine receptors, is a common feature that mediates the drug-induced stereotypies in rodents and non-drug-induced stereotypies in humans. The inference is that the dopamine hypothesis can be extended to the categories of drug-induced and non-drug-induced stereotypies in humans that are being discussed here. A key experimental finding in support of this hypothesis was that social deprivation of infant rhesus monkeys alters the chemoarchitecture of the peptidergic and dopaminergic systems within the basal ganglia (Lewis, Gluck, Beauchamp, Keresztury, & Mailman, 1990; Martin, Spicer, Lewis, Gluck, & Cork, 1991) in a manner that holds similarities to that evident in tardive dyskinesia. Dopamine is also seen as a mediator of the observed relation between blink rate and stereotyped behavior in adult humans (MacLean et al., 1985). Thus, although considerably more work is required to fully map out the etiology to the classes of drug and non-drug-induced stereotypies, these studies do point to the possibility of a common neuropsychopharmacological mechanism mediating stereotypies.

HYPOTONIA AND MOVEMENT SKILL

Hypotonia is a commonly identified motor deficit in individuals with mental retardation, particularly those with Down syndrome. The typical definition of *hypotonia* in the movement context is that of less than normal muscle tone or tension. Other labels have been used in the literature as synonyms for hypotonia and these include muscle flaccidity and stiffness (or the lack thereof). The use of the term *hypotonia* has been usually directed solely toward the muscle but, as we see in this section, a broader system definition of stiffness can be useful in a motor control sense. The muscle, after all, is only one component of the movement system.

There have been a number of methods used to measure hypotonia in people with mental retardation. These methods range from natural observation through clinical assessment to experimental approaches based on neuromuscular concepts of limb control. The range of methods employed has contributed to rather diverse perspectives about the role of muscle tone in movement control of mentally retarded individuals. A particularly contentious issue is whether, and in what way, people with mental retardation may be disadvantaged in movement skill due to hypotonia.

The observation of hypotonia is common in children with Down syndrome, although the degree of muscle flaccidity often reduces through the childhood period (Gunn, 1993). Experimental neuromuscular tests of hypotonia have not been conducted in neonates and young infants where the observation of hypotonia appears more apparent and prevalent. There are also differences in the meaning of the term *hypotonia* as interpreted across the medical, motor control, and special population literatures. This ambiguity could contribute to the apparent discrepancy between the clinical observations through the life span and the experimental findings that are subsequently reviewed from a number of different protocols.

An early empirical study on hypotonia and mental retardation was reported by Morris, Vaughan, and Vaccaro (1982), who examined the neuromuscular tone and strength of children with and without Down syndrome aged 4 to 17 years. The tone measures included both a clinical assessment on a hypotonicity to hypertonicity muscle palpation scale by a trained evaluator, and a patellar knee reflex test. Strength was measured using a hand dynamometer. The results showed that the children with Down syndrome had a slower and more irregular patellar reflex response than did the comparison group. Furthermore, the older children in both the Down syndrome and comparison group had stronger reflex responses than did the younger children. The clinical muscle evaluations revealed that the muscle tone and grip strength measures of children with Down syndrome were also lower than in the comparison group, although strength increased with advance in age in both groups. These data provide a direct empirical confirmation of the general observation regarding lower muscle tone in children with Down syndrome, but suggest that improvements in stiffness are made through the 4- to 17-years age range.

Shumway-Cook and Woollacott (1985) provided an indirect test of hypotonia in 1- to 3- and 4- to 6-year-old children with and without Down syndrome. They studied the neural control processes supporting upright bipedal posture using perturbations to a platform that provided the surface of support. A key finding for the issue being addressed here was that the presence of the monosynaptic reflex in children with Down syndrome was at comparable latencies to those of the age matched children without Down syndrome. This experimental outcome suggests that hypotonia is not a contributor to balance problems in young children with Down syndrome, but rather that the often reported balance problem in this population is a reflection of defects in higher level postural mechanisms (see also Woollacott & Shumway-Cook, 1986). These findings are counter to those of Morris et al. (1982) that were reported previously, but it should be noted that the age groups studied were not the same, the tasks were different, and there were probably other undocumented differences in the experimental protocols.

The first direct experimental examination of the stiffness regulation by subjects with Down syndrome was undertaken by Davis and Kelso (1982). They employed an experimental protocol introduced by Asatryan and Feldman (1965) to assess the length-tension dynamics of a human muscle-joint system. In this protocol, subjects are required to maintain arm joint angles under different initial limb loadings and subsequent torque perturbations (loading and unloading) of the arm. The subject is asked voluntarily "not to intervene" to the perturbation leaving the change in the position of the limb due to the perturbation and a consequence of the initial conditions and the changing limb dynamics. The length-tension recordings provide a direct measure of system stiffness, which is defined by the ratio of the change in position to the change in torque. In essence, the muscle-joint complex is modeled after a mass-spring system with the control arising from the shifts in particular invariant dynamic properties of the system.

Davis and Kelso (1982) tested seven adults diagnosed with Down syndrome and six comparison subjects without Down syndrome over a set of unloading and initial joint angle conditions. The resulting length-tension curves for the two groups are shown in Fig. 11.4a. Stiffness is reflected in the slope of the length-tension functions. The identical slopes of length-tension curves for the two groups suggest that the system stiffness is similar in normal and Down syndrome subjects. Davis and Kelso also asked subjects to increase the system stiffness by co-contracting the muscles while holding each of the initial joint angles for a similar set of torque perturbations. The resulting length-tension curves are shown in Fig. 11.4b. The combined data from these experimental protocols demonstrate that the subjects with Down syndrome can regulate the stiffness of the muscle-joint system, although their range of stiffness change was smaller than that for the control subjects.

The Davis and Kelso (1982) paper presented a very important experiment because the data challenge the commonly held beliefs about hypotonia in Down syndrome. The experimental protocol provides a direct measure of stiffness (and its complement compliance) and shows that within normal ranges of length-tension operation there appears to be no difference in stiffness properties associated with Down syndrome. Furthermore, subjects with Down syndrome could voluntarily regulate stiffness although they could not produce extreme stiffness levels comparable to the levels of the normal comparison subjects. These findings suggest that there is a deficiency in the production of high-force levels in individuals with Down syndrome, but that the muscle-joint control system is operating qualitatively the same in regard to stiffness regulation. Davis and Sinning (1985) showed similar findings in a study that also included a mentally retarded non-Down syndrome group.

A different but related approach to the muscle stiffness and mental retardation issue was taken by Latash and Corcos (1991). They examined the kinematic and electromyographic characteristics of single-joint movements of people with Down syndrome. In one experimental protocol, the subjects made arm movements as fast as possible over different distances in part to examine the speed-sensitive and speed-insensitive strategies of subjects with Down syndrome for the control of single-joint motions (Gottlieb, Corcos, & Agarwal, 1989). In another protocol, the subjects held a limb position against a resisting torque that subsequently changed (increased or decreased) and to which subjects were instructed to "let go" or "react" as fast as possible. On the basis of the collective findings that resulted from these two experimental protocols, the authors concluded, as had Davis and Kelso (1982) previously, that there were no qualitative deficits in the stiffness regulation of people with Down syndrome. It was proposed that the problem in Down syndrome was in the modulation of the motor commands that produced the operational phenomena of slowness of movement and latency to respond to perturbations.

In summary, the experimental findings on stiffness regulation in the motor control of people with mental retardation tend to run counter to the clinical observations reported on this phenomenon. Clinical observations of people with mental retardation suggest that hypotonia is a significant problem in this population, particularly in young children with Down syndrome. The experimental data, however, show that the stiffness of adult

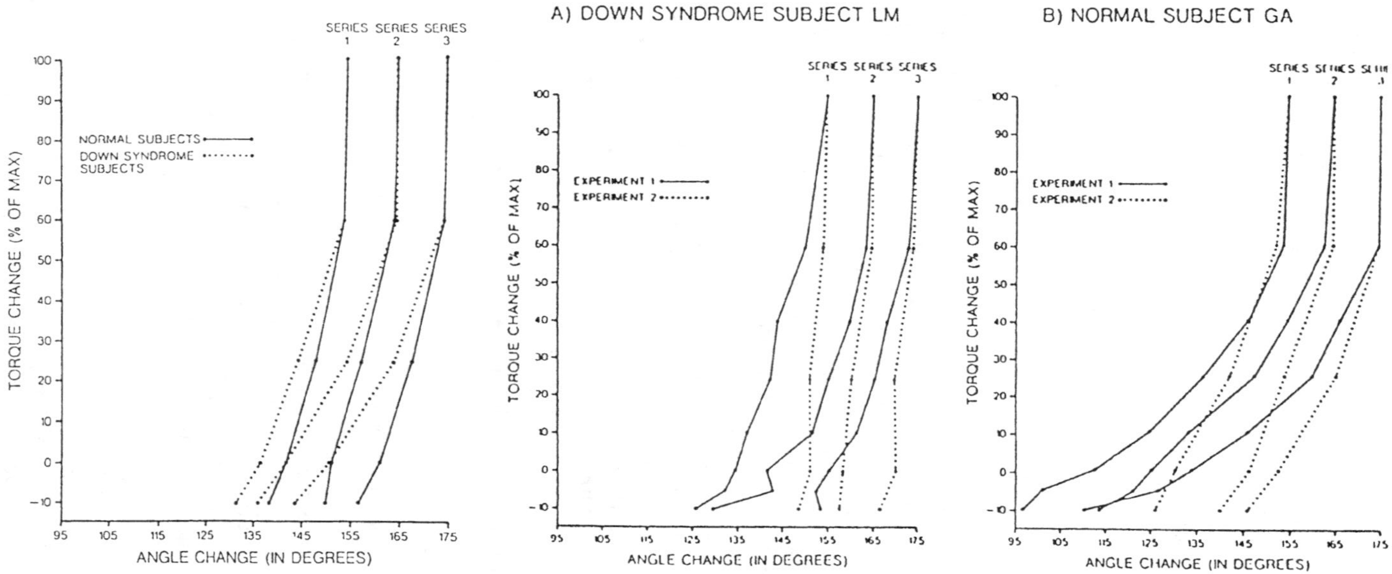

FIG. 11.4. Joint angle and torque change as a function of Down syndrome (A) and instruction and Down syndrome (B). Adapted from Journal of Motor Behavior, 14, 194–212, 1982. Adapted with permission of the Helen Dwight Reid Educational Foundation. Published by Heldref Publications, 1319 Eighteenth St. N.W., Washington, DC 20036-1802. Copyright © 1982.

subjects with Down syndrome, at least as it is defined operationally in the previously mentioned experimental protocols, is qualitatively the same as age-matched counterparts without Down syndrome. People with Down syndrome can also regulate stiffness on instructional demand, although they may not be able to manipulate stiffness through the range exhibited by people without Down syndrome. These findings open the question as to whether the clinical observation of stiffness in Down syndrome is operationally focusing on the same sensorimotor property as that measured in the experimental studies. Furthermore, where the quantitative differences between people with Down syndrome and comparison groups exist in stiffness regulation, they seem to be accommodated by possible differences in the understanding of the instructional constraints, or the apparent preferred mode of people with mental retardation to operate at lower energy output level (Latash, 1993). This difference in operating levels is best reflected in the well-known observation of movement slowness—a phenomenon that is reviewed later in this chapter.

The observation of exaggerated compliance in the movement system of infants with Down syndrome children is a well-recorded phenomenon (Burns & Gunn, 1993), as is the decrease of this trend over the childhood years. The cause of this compliance is not understood, nor is the possible role of this compliance in the delay in the development of the fundamental phylogenetic motor skills. Compliance is often implicated in this developmental process, but there is no experimental evidence or indeed even a test of this potential movement control link. Stiffness regulation is currently viewed as a central property of motor control (Feldman, 1986; Latash, 1993) and one that in principle could contribute to the differences in the qualitative and quantitative properties of movement coordination in people with and without mental retardation.

There is no body of evidence that directly addresses the question of whether there are influences of level of mental retardation on stiffness regulation. The observation of hypotonia is more prevalent in Down syndrome individuals, and the single study on level of mental retardation suggests that this does not differentially effect stiffness regulation (Davis & Sinning, 1985). Clearly, more experimental work is required to unravel the many influences on muscle-joint compliance that appears to be a hallmark characteristic of mental retardation, and particularly of Down syndrome. Furthermore, the developmental aspects of this phenomenon do not appear to be as clear cut as is sometimes implied from the applied literature when one considers the findings from the experimental studies collectively.

SLOWNESS OF MOVEMENT

One of the most commonly observed deficits in the motor control of people with mental retardation is the tendency for the speed of movement to be much slower than that of age-matched nonretarded subjects. This penchant to move slowly seems to occur in all action contexts and is widespread across all subgroups of the mentally retarded population. Part of this slowness of response arises from longer latencies in reaction and decision making situations (see Nettelbeck & Wilson, chap. 10, this volume). In this section I focus predominantly on the movement time component of the slowness of movement speed phenomenon, particularly as evident in manual control.

Movement speed is often equated with movement time where fast and slow movement speeds are associated with short and long movement times, respectively. The relation between movement time and average movement velocity is reciprocal when the movement amplitude is constant. Thus, with practice at a given manual task on a fixed set of task constraints, movement time often reduces and average velocity increases. However, changing movement amplitude conditions can decouple this link between movement speed and time so that subjects can move slowly with a short duration movement and rapidly with a long duration movement.

A representative example of the response speed deficits of people with mental retardation is shown in Fig. 11.5 and is adapted from Wade, Newell, and Wallace (1978). In this study, adults with moderate and severe mental retardation performed a discrete Fitts aiming task (Fitts & Peterson, 1964) over a range of target amplitude-width conditions. The movement time and reaction time data of the mentally retarded group was significantly longer than that of the respective times of the nonretarded group. Of more significance to the issue here is that the rate of gain of the movement time with increments of the movement index of difficulty was more rapid in the mentally retarded group than in the nonretarded group.

Similar movement speed and index of difficulty results have been found in the comparison of nonretarded and mentally retarded boys (Sugden, 1980; Sugden & Gray, 1981). That is, the increment of movement time over gains in movement difficulty were greater in the group with mental retardation than in the nonretarded group. There have been attempts to determine the influence of movement difficulty on movement time in children with Down syndrome (Clausen, 1968; Frith & Frith, 1974; Seyfort & Spreen, 1979), but distinguishing trends for this Down syndrome group from those reported previously for mental retardation groups are not apparent.

The effect of enhanced index of difficulty in producing increments of movement time have generally been interpreted within an information processing theoretical framework, consistent with the original Fitts formulation. That is, more difficult movements require more bits of information to be processed per unit time, and this is why individuals with mental retardation have greater gains than age-matched nonretarded subjects in move-

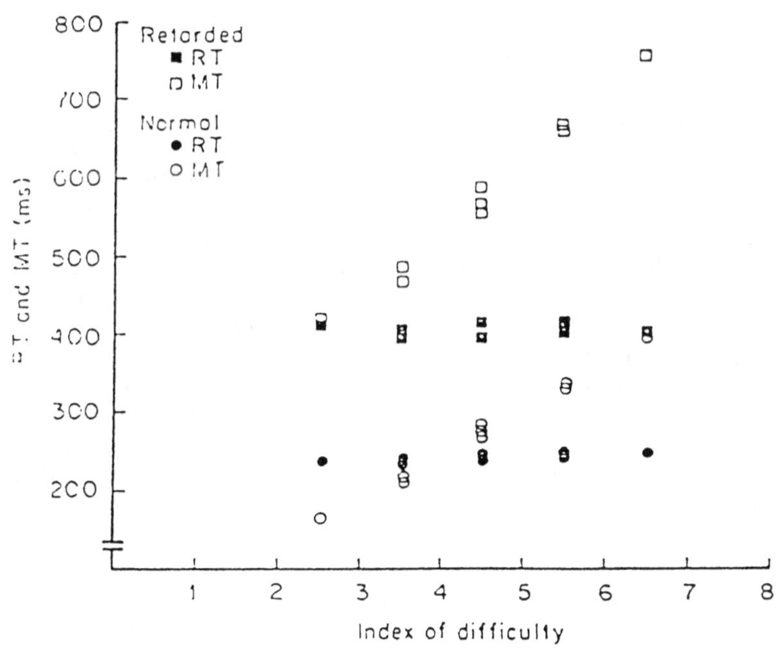

FIG. 11.5. Reaction time and movement time for mentally retarded and normal adult groups as a function of index of difficulty (adapted from Wade et al., 1978). Reprinted by permission of the American Association on Mental Retardation.

ment time per given increment of the index of difficulty. This hypothesis is consistent with the general mental retardation and decision-making literature (see Nettelbeck & Wilson, chap. 10, this volume), but other hypotheses are available. For example, Latash (1993) suggested that the slower movement speed may be a consequence of reluctance to expend energy, a hypothesis that is consistent with the reluctance of subjects with mental retardation to exercise. It is also the case that people with mental retardation seem to prefer to operate at a different speed–accuracy criterion than that of nonretarded subjects. There is a trend for people with mental retardation to be less susceptible to engaging error to improve movement speed (Wade et al., 1983).

The postulate that people with mental retardation may operate with different speed–accuracy ratios than do nonretarded people is given further support by the finding that training protocols can reduce the movement time and movement speed quite considerably (Hoover, Wade, & Newell, 1981; Wade, Hoover, & Newell, 1984). The reduction of movement time occurs simultaneously with an increase in movement speed up to approximately the speed–accuracy ratio of people without mental retardation on a given task. Thus, movement time can be reduced by practice through changing the conservative speed–accuracy criterion that people with mental retardation naturally adopt. The success of training protocols in improving movement speed also leaves open the possibility that further gains in performance could be available with further practice sessions, or even structured training protocols (Wade & Gold, 1978).

We are a long way from understanding the limits of motor performance and training effects on movement speed in people with mental retardation. The relation between hypotonia and slowness of movement speed has not been sufficiently explored experimentally, in spite of its intuitive theoretical link. The examination of training or long-term practice studies would also be useful to help unravel the sources of constraint on movement speed in people with mental retardation.

CLOSING REMARKS

This review has focused on the movement problems most commonly associated with mental retardation. As I indicated in the introduction to the chapter, the research in this area tends to be theoretically diverse and operationally uneven in both quality and quantity. Nevertheless, some progress has been made in the last decade or so in understanding the nature of the movement deficits apparent in people with mental retardation. A general theme emerging is that although there is often a motor performance decrement evident in people with mental retardation, as reflected in the outcome measure of the particular task, the qualitative properties of the movement organization hold many parallels to those evident in age-matched nonretarded subjects.

Reflection on the research on mental retardation and motor skills previously reviewed suggests that there are a number of general issues that could be given consideration in future research in this area and that would help further to reveal the particular problems in the motor skill development of people with mental retardation. The issues that I briefly mention in closing are distinct from the general need for systematic and sustained research in this area.

Population Differentiation. Much of the motor skills research has focused on an isolated segment of the population with mental retardation without attempting to understand the influence of the degree of severity or etiology of the mental retardation. A very small proportion of the motor skills studies reviewed have included more than one group with mental retardation. For example, the research involving people with Down syndrome typically has not included the appropriate controls to distinguish etiology or level of mental retardation, in spite of the evidence for the need to do so (see Davis, Sparrow, & Ward, 1991; Henderson et al., 1981). Thus, it is difficult to know whether the movement deficits are peculiar to individuals with Down syndrome or simply the level of mental retardation. Subgroup manipulations within the mental retardation population are sometimes difficult to realize operationally due to the limited subject availability, but they reflect one important experimental focus that is required to unpack the influence of etiology and severity of mental retardation on motor learning and performance, and make more direct conceptual and experimental contact with the mental retardation literature of other behavioral domains.

Developmental Approach. A common criticism of the inferences drawn from motor deficits evident in people with mental retardation is that they may only reflect the lack of understanding of the subjects with respect to the imposed task constraints. One way to finesse this concern is to observe performance over longer periods of time. This experimental strategy would also increase the probability of revealing the stable as opposed to only the transient movement differences or decrements in people with mental retardation. An extension of this approach is that it would also lead to a richer appreciation of intraindividual trends in performance over time—a factor that appears to be almost completely absent from the movement and mental retardation literature. This operational approach would in essence provide a stronger developmental emphasis to the theoretical study of motor skills in mental retardation—an emphasis that has languished in much of the contemporary work (although see MacLean, Stone, & Brown, 1994, in the context of the psychopathology of destructive behavior). Mental retardation is such a global concept that the study of individual differences over time would provide another valuable complement to the study of the links between motor skills and mental retardation.

Knowing and Doing. In spite of the intuitive and explicit link between the cognitive and motor aspects of movement deficits in people with mental retardation, there has been little empirical study of their conjoint relations (although see Macpherson & Butterworth, 1988). This is a very difficult problem to approach both theoretically and operationally, and there has been little emphasis on this issue in either the general motor skills or cognitive literatures. The relation between knowing how and knowing that (Ryle, 1949), or declarative and procedural knowledge (Anderson, 1976), would seem to be of particular relevance to considering the movement deficits associated with mental retardation. Such an approach would also help to unpack the particular contributions of mental retardation to the development of action over the life span to enrich our understanding of the well-established movement deficits that have been identified and discussed here.

ACKNOWLEDGMENTS

The preparation of this chapter was supported in part by NIH Grant RO1 HD21212. Thanks are due to Jim Bodfish, Walter Davis, Mark Lewis, Bill MacLean, Tony Sparrow, and Robert Sprague for helpful comments on an earlier version of the chapter.

REFERENCES

Alpert, M., Diamond, F., & Friedhoff, A. J. (1976). Tremorgraphic studies in tardive dyskinesia. *Psychopharmacology Bulletin, 12*, 5–7.

Alpert, M., Diamond, F., Weisenfreund, J., Taleporos, E., & Friedhoff, A. J. (1978). The neuroleptic hypothesis: Study of the covariation of extraphyramidal and therapeutic drug effects. *British Journal of Psychiatry, 133,* 169–175.

American Psychiatric Association. (1979). *Tardive dyskinesia.* Washington, DC: Author.

American Psychiatric Association Task Force on Tardive Dyskinesia. (1992). *Tardive dyskinesia: A task force report of the American Psychiatric Association.* Washington, DC: American Psychiatric Association.

Anderson, J. R. (1976). *Language, memory, and thought.* Hillsdale, NJ: Lawrence Erlbaum Associates.

Anwar, F. (1981). Motor function in Down's Syndrome. *International Review of Research in Mental Retardation, 10,* 107–138.

Anwar, F. (1983). Vision and kinesthesis in motor movement. In J. Hogg & P. Mittler (Eds.), *Advances in mental handicap research* (Vol. 2). Chichester, England: Wiley.

Asatryan, D. G., & Feldman, A. G. (1965). Functional tuning of the nervous system with control of movements or maintenance of a steady posture. I. Mechanographic analysis of the work of the limb on execution of a postural task. *Biophysics, 10,* 925–935.

Baumeister, A. A., & Forehand, R. (1973). Stereotyped acts. In N. R. Ellis (Ed.), *International review of research in mental retardation* (Vol. 6, pp. 55–96). New York: Academic Press.

Bayley, N. (1969). *Manual for the Bayley scales of infant development.* New York: Psychological Corporation.

Berkson, G. (1967). Abnormal stereotyped motor acts. In J. Zubin & H. F. Hunt (Eds.), *Comparative psychopathology—animal and human* (pp. 76–94). New York: Grune & Stratton.

Berkson, G. (1983). Repetitive stereotyped behaviors. *American Journal of Mental Deficiency, 88,* 239–246.

Berkson, G. (in press). Development of abnormal focused affections and other stereotyped behaviors. In R. L.Sprague & K. M. Newell (Eds.), *Stereotypies: Brain-behavior relationships.* Washington, DC: American Psychological Association.

Berkson, G. S., & Gallagher., R. J. (1986). Control of feedback from abnormal stereotyped behaviors I. In M. G. Wade (Ed.), *The development of coordination, control and skill in the mentally handicapped* (pp. 7–24). Amsterdam: North-Holland.

Berkson, G., McQuiston, S., Jacobson, J. W., Eyman, R., & Borthwick, S. (1985). The relationship between age and stereotyped behaviors. *Mental Retardation, 23,* 31–33.

Bernstein, N. (1967). *The coordination and regulation of movements.* New York: Pergamon.

Bruininks, R. H. (1974). Physical and motor development of retarded persons. In N. R. Ellis (Ed.), *International review of research in mental retardation* (Vol. 7, pp. 209–261). New York: Academic Press.

Burns, Y., & Gunn, P. (Eds.). (1993). *Down syndrome: Moving through life.* London: Chapman & Hall.

Burton, A. W. (1990). Assessing the perceptual-motor interaction in developmentally disabled and nonhandicapped children. *Adapted Physical Activity Quarterly, 7,* 325–337.

Butterworth, G., & Cicchetti, D. (1982). Visual calibration of posture in normal and motor retarded Down's syndrome infants. *Perception, 7,* 513–525.

Caligiuri, M., & Lohr, J. B. (1990). Fine force instability: A quantitative measure of neuroleptic-induced dyskinesia in the hand. *Journal of Neuropsychiatry, 2,* 395–398.

Carr, J. (1970). Mental and motor development in young mongol children. *Journal of Mental Deficiency Research, 14,* 205–220.

Carr, J. (1975). *Young children with Down's syndrome.* London: Butterworth.

Chandler, L. S., Andrews, M. S., & Swanson, M. W. (1980). *Movement assessment of infants: A manual.* Rolling Bay, WA: Authors.

Clark, D. L., Kreutzberg, J. R., & Chee, F. K. W. (1977). Vestibular stimulation influence on motor development in infants. *Science, 196,* 1228–1229.

Clarke, A. M., Clarke, A. D. B. (1985). Criteria and classification. In A. M. Clarke, A. D. B. Clarke, & J. M. Berg (Eds.), *Mental deficiency: The changing outlook* (4th ed., pp. 27–52). New York: The Free Press.

Clausen, J. (1968). Behavioral characteristics of Down syndrome subjects. *American Journal of Mental Deficiency, 73*, 118–126.

Cooper, S. J., & Dourish, C. T. (Eds.). (1990). *Neurobiology of stereotyped behavior.* Oxford, England: Clarendon Press.

Cowie, V. A. (1970). *A study of the early development of Mongols.* Oxford, England: Pergamon.

Cunningham, C. C. (1979). *Aspects of early development in Down's syndrome infants.* Unpublished doctoral dissertation. University of Manchester, England.

Cunningham Owens, D. S., & Johnstone, E. C. (1982). Spontaneous involuntary disorders of movement: Their prevalence, severity, and distribution in chronic schizophrenics with and without treatment with neuroleptics. *Archives of General Psychiatry, 39*, 452–461.

Cutting, J. E., & Proffitt, D. R. (1982). The minimum principle and the perception of absolute, common and relative motions. *Cognitive Psychology, 14*, 211–246.

Davis, W. E., & Kelso, J. A. S. (1982). Analysis of "invariant characteristics" in motor control of Down's syndrome and normal subjects. *Journal of Motor Behavior, 14*, 194–212.

Davis, W. E., & Sinning, W. E. (1985). Muscle stiffness in Down syndrome and other mentally handicapped subjects: A research note. *Journal of Motor Behavior, 19*, 130–144.

Davis, W. E., Sparrow, W. A., & Ward, T. (1991). Fractionated reaction times and movement times of Down syndrome and other adults with mental retardation. *Adapted Physical Activity Quarterly, 8*, 221–233.

DiRocco, P. J., Clark, J. E., & Phillips, S. J. (1987). Jumping coordination patterns of mildy mentally retarded children. *Adapted Physical Activity Quarterly, 4*, 178–191.

Dobbins, D. A., Garron, R., & Rarick, G. L. (1981). The motor performance of educable mentally retarded and intellectually normal boys after covariate control for differences in body size. *Research Quarterly for Exercise and Sport, 52*, 1–8.

Elliott, D. (1985). Manual asymmetries in the performance of sequential movement by adolescents and adults with Down syndrome. *American Journal of Mental Deficiency, 90*, 90–97.

Ellison, G., & See, R. E. (1991). A computerized methodology for the study of neuroleptic-induced oral dyskinesias. In A. Boulton, G. Baker, & M. Martin-Inverson (Eds.), *Neuromethods, Vol. 18: Animal Methods in Psychiatry I* (pp. 363–397). Totowa, NJ: Humana Press.

Ellison, G., See, R., Levin, E., & Kinney, J. (1987). Tremorous mouth movements in rats administered chronic neuroleptics. *Psychopharmacology, 92*, 122–126.

Feldman, A. G. (1986). Once more on the equilibrium-point hypothesis (& model) for motor control. *Journal of Motor Behavior, 18*, 17–54.

Findley, L. J., & Capildeo, R. (Eds.). (1984). *Movement disorders: Tremor.* New York: Oxford University Press.

Fishler, K., Share, J., & Koch, R. (1964). Adaptation of Gesell development scales for evaluation of development in children with Down's syndrome (Mongolism). *American Journal of Mental Deficiency, 68*, 642–646.

Fitts, P. M., & Peterson, J. R. (1964). Information capacity of discrete motor responses. *Journal of Experimental Psychology, 67*, 103–112.

Frith, U., & Frith, C. D. (1974). Specific motor disabilities in Down's syndrome. *Journal of Child Psychology and Psychiatry, 15*, 293–301.

Gesell, A. (1929). Maturation and infant behavior pattern. *Psychological Review, 36*, 307–319.

Gesell, A., & Amatruda, C. S. (1941). *Developmental diagnosis.* New York: Harper.

Golani, L. (1976). Homeostatic motor processes in mammalian interaction: A choreography of display. In P. T. G. Bateson & P. H. Klopher (Eds.), *Perspectives in ethology* (pp. 69–134). New York: Plenum.

Gottlieb, G. L., Corcos, D. M., & Agarwal, G. C. (1989). Strategies for the control of voluntary movements with one mechanical degree of freedom. *Behavioral and Brain Sciences, 12*, 189–250.

Guess, D., & Carr, E. (1991). Emergence and maintenance of stereotypy and self-injury. *American Journal on Mental Retardation, 96,* 299–319.

Gunn, P. (1993). Characteristics of Down syndrome. In Y. Burns & P. Gunn (Eds.), *Down syndrome: Moving through life* (pp. 1–17). London: Chapman & Hall.

Haag, H., Ruther, E., & Hippius, H. (1992). *Tardive dyskinesia.* Seattle, WA: Hogrefe & Huber.

Haley, S. M. (1987). Sequence of development of postural reactions by infants with Down syndrome. *Developmental Medicine and Child Neurology, 29,* 674–679.

Hansen, T. E., Glazer, W. M., & Moore, D. C. (1986). Tremor and tardive dyskinesia. *Journal of Clinical Psychiatry, 47,* 461–464.

Henderson, S. E. (1985). Motor skill development. In D. Lane & B. Stratford (Eds.), *Current approaches to Down's syndrome* (pp. 187–218). London: Holt, Rinehart & Winston.

Henderson, S. E. (1986). Some aspects of the development of motor control in Down's syndrome. In H. T. A. Whiting & M. G. Wade (Eds.), *Themes in motor development* (pp. 69–92). Dordrecht, The Netherlands: Martinus Nijhoff.

Henderson, S. E., Morris, J., & Frith, U. (1981). The motor deficit of Down's syndrome children: A problem of timing? *Journal of Child Psychology and Psychiatry, 22,* 233–245.

Hogg, J., & Moss, S. C. (1983). Prehensile development in Down's syndrome and nonhandicapped preschool children. *British Journal of Developmental Psychology, 1,* 189–204.

Holden, E. A., Jr., & Corrigan, J. G. (1980). Self-paced vs. externally paced motor tracking by retarded and nonretarded persons. *American Journal of Mental Deficiency, 84,* 387–392.

Hoover, J. H., Wade, M. G., & Newell, K. M. (1981). Training moderately and severely mentally retarded adults to improve reaction and movement times. *American Journal of Mental Deficiency, 85,* 389–395.

Horgan, J. S. (1982). Comparison of mildly mentally retarded and nonretarded children on a rotary pursuit task under optimal task conditions. *American Journal of Mental Deficiency, 87,* 316–324.

Jacobson, J. W. (1982). Problem behavior and psychiatric impairment within a developmentally disabled population I: Behavior frequency. *Applied Research in Mental Retardation, 3,* 121–139.

Jeste, J. V., & Wyatt, R. J. (1982). *Understanding and treating tardive dyskinesia.* New York: Guilford.

Johansson, G., von Hofsten, C., & Jansson, G. (1980). Event perception. *Annual Review of Psychology, 31,* 27–63.

Kalachnik, J. E. (1984). Tardive dyskinesia and the mentally retarded: A review. In S. E. Bruening (Ed.), *Advances in mental retardation and developmental disabilities* (Vol. 2, pp. 329–356). Greenwich, CT: JAI.

Kalachnik, J. E., Harder, S. R., Kidd-Nielson, P., Errickson, E., Doebler, M., & Sprague, R. L. (1984). Persistent tardive dyskinesia in randomly assigned neuroleptic reduction, neuroleptic nonreduction, and no-neuroleptic history groups: Preliminary results. *Psychopharmacology Bulletin, 20,* 27–32.

Kalachnik, J. E., Sprague, R. L., & Shaw, K. M. (1988). Training clinical personnel to assess for tardive dyskinesia. *Progress in Neuro-Psychopharmacology, Biology, and Psychiatry, 12,* 749–762.

Kane, J. M., & Smith, J. M. (1982). Tardive dyskinesia. *Archives of General Psychiatry, 39,* 473–481.

Kerr, R., & Blais, C. (1985). Motor skill acquisition by individuals with Down syndrome. *American Journal of Mental Deficiency, 90,* 313–318.

Khot, V., Egan, M. F., Hyde, T. M., & Wyatt, R. J. (1992). Neuroleptics and classic tardive dyskinesia. In A. E. Lang & W. J. Weiner (Eds.), *Drug-induced movement disorders* (pp. 121–166). Mt. Kisco, NY: Futura.

Klawans, H. L. (1973). The pharmacology of tardive dyskinesia. *American Journal of Psychiatry, 130,* 82–86.

Kleinman, S. (1975). Movement notation systems: An introduction. *Quest, 23,* 33–56.

Ko, Y. G., van Emmerik, R. E. A., Sprague, R. L., & Newell, K. M. (1992). Postural stability, tardive dyskinesia and developmental disability. *Journal of Intellectual Disability Research, 36,* 309–323.

Latash, M. L. (1993). *Control of human movement.* Champaign, IL: Human Kinetics.

Latash, M. L., & Corcos, D. M. (1991). Kinematic and electromyographic characteristics of single-joint movements in Down syndrome. *American Journal of Mental Retardation, 96*, 189–201.

Lewis, M., MacLean, W. E., Jr., Bryson-Brockmann, W., Arendt, R., Beck, B., Fidler, P. S., & Baumeister, A. A. (1984). Time-series analysis of stereotyped movements: Relationship of body-rocking to cardiac activity. *American Journal of Mental Deficiency, 89*, 287–294.

Lewis, M. H., & Baumeister, A. A. (1982). Stereotyped mannerisms in mentally retarded persons: Animal models and theoretical analyses. In N. R. Ellis (Ed.), *International review of research in mental retardation* (Vol. 11, pp. 123–161). New York: Academic Press.

Lewis, M. H., Gluck, J. P., Beauchamp, A. J., Keresztury, M. F., & Mailman, R. B. (1990). Long-term effects of early social isolation in *Macaca mulatta*: Changes in dopamine receptor function following apomorphine challenge. *Brain Research, 513*, 67–73.

Lewis, M. H., Gluck, J. P., Bodfish, J. W., Beauchamp, A. J., Mailman, R. B. (in press). Neurobiological basis of stereotyped movement disorder. In R. L. Sprague & K. M. Newell (Eds.), *Stereotypies: Brain-behavior relationships*. Washington, DC: American Psychological Association.

MacLean, W. E., Jr., & Baumeister, A. A. (1982). Effects of vestibular stimulation on motor development and stereotyped behavior of developmentally delayed children. *Journal of Abnormal Child Psychology, 10*, 229–245.

MacLean, W. E., Jr., Ellis, D. N., Galbreath, H. N., Halpern, L. F., & Baumeister, A. A. (1991). Rhythmic motor behavior of preamblatory motor impaired, Down syndrome and nondisabled children: A comparative analaysis. *Journal of Abnormal Child Psychology, 19*, 319–330.

MacLean, W. E., Jr., Lewis, M. H., Bryson-Brockmann, W. A., Ellis, D. N., Arendt, R. E., & Baumeister, A. A. (1985). Blink rate and stereotyped behavior: Evidence for dopamine involvement? *Biological Psychiatry, 20*, 1321–1325.

MacLean, W. E., Jr., Stone, W., & Brown, W. H. (1994). Developmental psychopathology of destructive behavior. In T. Thompson & D. B. Gray (Eds.), *Destructive behavior in developmental disabilities* (pp. 68–79). Thousand Oaks, CA: Sage.

Macpherson, F., & Butterwoth, G. (1988). Sensorimotor intelligence in severely mentally handicapped children. *Journal of Mental Deficiency Research, 32*, 465–478.

Martin, L. J., Spicer, D. M., Lewis, M. H., Gluck, J. P., & Cork, L. C. (1991). Social deprivation of the infant rhesus monkeys alters the chemoarchitecture of the brain: I. Subcortical regions. *The Journal of Neuroscience, 11*, 3344–3358.

Mason, G. J. (1991). Stereotypies: A critical review. *Animal Behavior, 41*, 1015–1037.

May, P. R. A. (1987). Measurement of extrapyramidal symptoms and involuntary movement by electronic instruments. *Psychopharmacology Bulletin, 23*, 187–188.

McGinnis, P. M., & Newell, K. M. (1982). Topological dynamics: A framework for describing movement and its constraints. *Human Movement Science, 1*, 289–305.

McGraw, M. B. (1943). *The neuromuscular maturation of the human infant*. New York: Columbia University Press.

Molnar, G. E., & Alexander, J. (1983). Strength development in retarded children: A comparative study on the effect of intervention. In J. Hogg & P. J. Mittler (Eds.), *Advances in mental handicap research* (Vol. 2, pp. 285–307). New York: Wiley.

Morris, A. F., Vaughan, S. E., & Vaccaro, P. (1982). Measurements of neuromuscular tone and strength in Down's syndrome children. *Journal of Mental Deficiency Research, 26*, 41–46.

Nettlebeck, T. (1979). Skill and mental retardation. In W. T. Singleton (Ed.), *The study of real skills: Vol 2. Compliance and excellence* (pp. 63–81). Baltimore, MD: University Park Press.

Newell, K. M. (1985a). Coordination, control and skill. In D. Goodman, I. Franks, & R. Wilberg (Eds.), *Differing perspectives in motor control* (pp. 295–318). Amsterdam: North Holland.

Newell, K. M. (1985b). Motor skill acquisition and mental retardation: Overview of traditional and current orientations. In J. E. Clark & J. H. Humphrey (Eds.), *Motor development* (Vol. 1, pp. 183–192). Princeton, NJ: Princeton Book Company.

Newell, K. M. (in press). The dynamics of stereotypic behaviors. In R. L. Sprague & K. M. Newell (Eds.), *Stereotypies: Brain–behavior relationships*. Washington, DC: American Psychological Association.

Newell, K. M., & Corcos, D. M. (Eds.). (1993). *Variability and motor control*. Champaign, IL: Human Kinetics.

Newell, K. M., Kugler, P. N., van Emmerik, R. E. A., & McDonald, P. V. (1989). Search strategiesand the acquisition of coordination. In S. A. Wallace (Ed.), *Perspectives on coordination of movement* (pp. 85–122). Amsterdam: North-Holland.

Newell, K. M., & Sprague, R. L. (1990). Early diagnosis of tardive dyskinesia. In A. Vermeer (Ed.), *Motor development, adapted physical activity and mental retardation* (pp. 30–46). Amsterdam: North-Holland.

Newell, K. M., van Emmerik, R. E. A., Lee, D., & Sprague, R. L. (1993). On postural stability and variability. *Gait & Posture, 4*, 225–230.

Newell, K. M., van Emmerik, R. E. A., & Sprague, R. L. (1993). Stereotypy and variability. In K. M. Newell & D. M. Corcos (Eds.), *Variability and motor control* (pp. 475–496). Champaign, IL: Human Kinetics.

Parker, A. W., & Bronks, R. (1980). Gait of children with Down Syndrome. Archives of *Physical Medicine and Rehabilitation, 61*, 345–351.

Parker, A. W., Bronks, R., & Snyder, J. (1986). Walking patterns in Down's syndrome. *Journal of Mental Deficiency Research, 30*, 317–330.

Patterson, D. (1987). The causes of Down syndrome. *Scientific American, 257*, 42–48.

Paulson, G. W., Rizvi, C. A., & Crane, G. E. (1975). Tardive dyskinesia as a possible sequence of long-term therapy with phenothiazines. *Clinical Pediatrics, 14*, 953–955.

Rarick, G. L. (1973). Motor performance of mentally retarded children. In G. L. Rarick (Ed.), *Physical activity: Human growth and development* (pp. 227–256). New York: Academic Press.

Rast, M. M., & Harris, S. R. (1985). Motor control in infants with Down syndrome. *Developmental Medicine & Child Neurology, 27*, 675–685.

Richardson, S. A., & Koller, H. (1985). Epidemiology. In A. D. B. Clarke & J. M. Berg (Eds.), *Mental deficiency: The changing outlook* (4th ed., pp. 356–400). New York: The Free Press.

Ryle, G. (1949). *The concept of mind*. Chicago: The University of Chicago Press.

Schonecker, M. (1957). Ein eigentumliches Syndrom im oralen Bereich bei Megaphenapplikation [A particular syndrome in the oral region after application of metaphor]. *Nervenarzt, 28*, 35–36.

Schroeder, S. R. (1970). Usage of stereotypy as a descriptive term. *The Psychological Record, 20*, 337–342.

Schroeder, S. R. (1991). Self-injury and stereotypy. In J. L. Matson & J. A. Mulick (Eds.), *Handbook of mental retardation* (2nd ed., pp. 382–396). New York: Pergamon.

Selikowitz, M. (1990). *Down syndrome: The facts*. Oxford, England: Oxford University Press.

Seyfort, B., & Spreen, O. (1979). Two-plated tapping performance by Down's syndrome and non-Down's syndrome retardates. *Journal of Child Psychology and Psychiatry, 20*, 351–355.

Shapiro, B. L. (1983). Down Syndrome—A disruption of homeostasis. *American Journal of Medical Genetics, 14*, 241–269.

Shumway-Cook, A., & Woollacott, M. H. (1985). Dynamics of postural control in the child with Down syndrome. *Physical Therapy, 65*, 1315–1322.

Slaw, K. M., & Kalachnik, J. E. (1985). Tardive dyskinesia: Facts the mental health administrator may not know. *Journal of Mental Health Administration, 12*, 22–27.

Sprague, R. L. (1982). Litigation, legislation, and regulations. In S. E. Breuing & A. D. Poling (Eds.), *Drugs and mental retardation* (pp. 377–414). Springfield, IL: Thomas.

Sprague, R. L., Kalachnik, J. E., & Slaw, K. M. (1989). Psychometric properties of the Dyskinesia Identification System: Condensed User Scale (DISCUS). *Mental Retardation, 27*, 141–148.

Sprague, R. L., Kalachnik, J. E., Bruening, S. E., Davis, V. J., Ullmann, R. K., Cullari, S., Davidson, N. A., Ferguson, D. G., & Hoffner, B. A. (1984). The Dyskinesia Identification System—Coldwater (DIS-Co): A tardive dyskinesia rating scale for the developmentally disabled. *Psychopharmacology Bulletin, 20*, 328–338.

Sprague, R. L., & Newell, K. M. (1987). Toward a movement control perspective of tardive dyskinesia. In H. Y. Meltzer (Ed.), *Psychopharmacology: The third generation of progress* (pp. 1233–1238). New York: Raven.

Stone, R. K., May, J. E., Alvarez, W. F., & Ellman, G. (1989). Prevalence of dyskinesia and related movement disorders in a developmentally disabled population. *Journal of Mental Deficiency Research, 33,* 41–53.

Sugden, D. A. (1980). Movement speed in children. *Journal of Motor Behavior, 12,* 125–132.

Sugden, D. A., & Gray, S. M. (1981). Capacity and strategies of educationally subnormal boys on serial and discrete tasks involving movement speed. *British Journal of Educational Psychology, 51,* 77–82.

Sugden, D. A., & Keogh, J. F. (1990). *Problems in movement skill development.* Columbia: University of South Carolina Press.

Teitelbaum, P., Pellis, S. M., & DeVietti, T. L. (1990). Disintegration into stereotypy induced by drugs or brain damage: A microdescriptive behavioral analysis. In S. J. Cooper & C. T. Dourish (Eds.), *Neurobiology of stereotyped behavior* (pp. 200–231). Oxford, England: Clarendon.

Thelen, E. (1979). Rhythmical behavior in infancy: An ethological perspective. *Developmental Psychology, 17,* 237–257.

Thelen, E. (1986). Treadmill-elicited stepping in seven-month-old infants. *Child Development, 57,* 1498–1506.

Thelen, E. (in press). Normal infant stereotypies: A dynamic systems approach. In R. L. Sprague & K. M. Newell (Eds.), *Stereotypies: Brain–behavior relationships.* Washington, DC: American Psychological Association.

Touwen, B. (1978). Variability and stereotypy in normal and deviant development. In J. Apley (Ed.), *Care of the handicapped child: Clinics in developmental medicine* (No. 67, pp. 99–110). Philadelphia: Lippincott.

Tyron, W. W., & Pologe, B. (1987). Accelerometric assessment of tardive dyskinesia. *American Journal of Psychiatry, 144,* 1584–1587.

Ulrich, B. D., Ulrich, D. A., & Collier, D. H. (1992). Alternating stepping patterns: Hidden abilities of 11-month-old infants with Down syndrome. *Developmental Medicine & Child Neurology, 34,* 233–239.

Ulrich, B. D., Ulrich, D. A., Collier, D. H., & Cole, E. L. (1995). Developmental shifts in the ability of infants with Down syndrome to produce treadmill steps. *Physical Therapy, 75,* 20–29.

van Emmerik, R. E. A., Sprague, R. L., & Newell, K. M. (1993a). Arm tremor, tardive dyskinesia, and developmental disability. *American Journal of Mental Retardation, 98,* 74–83.

van Emmerik, R. E. A., Sprague, R. L., & Newell, K. M. (1993b). Assessment of postural dynamics in tardive dyskinesia and developmental disability: Sway profile orientation and stereotypy. *Movement Disorders, 8,* 305–314.

van Emmerik, R. E. A., Sprague, R. L., & Newell, K. M. (1993c). Finger tremor and tardive dyskinesia. *Experimental and Clinical Psychopharmacology, 1,* 259–268.

von Wendt, L., Makinen, H., & Rantakallio, P. (1984). Psychomotor development in the first year and mental retardation—a prospective study. *Journal of Mental Deficiency Research, 28,* 219–225.

Wade, M. G. (1980). Coincidence anticipation of young normal and handicapped children. *Journal of Motor Behavior, 12,* 103–112.

Wade, M. G., & Gold, M. W. (1978). Removing some of the limitations of mentally retarded workers by improving job design. *Human Factors, 20,* 339–348.

Wade, M. G., Hoover, J. H., & Newell, K. M. (1983). Training and trainability in motor skills performance of mentally retarded persons. In J. Hogg & P. J. Mittler (Eds.), *Advances in mental handicap research* (Vol. 2., pp. 175–201). New York: Wiley.

Wade, M. G., Hoover, J. H., & Newell, K. M. (1984). Training reaction and movement times of moderately and severely retarded persons in aiming movements. *American Journal of Mental Deficiency, 89,* 174–179.

Wade, M. G., Newell, K. M., & Wallace, S. A. (1978). Decision time and movement time as a function of response complexity in retarded persons. *American Journal of Mental Deficiency, 83*, 135–144.

Wolff, P. H. (1968). Stereotypic behavior and development. *Canadian Psychologist, 9*, 474–484.

Woollacott, M. H., & Shumway-Cook, A. (1986). The development of the postural and voluntary motor control systems in Down's syndrome children. In M. G. Wade (Ed.), *Motor skill acquisition of the mentally handicapped: Issues in research and training* (pp. 45–71). Amsterdam: North-Holland.

› IV ‹

Social, Communicative, and Adaptive Processes

› 12 ‹

Social Intelligence and Developmental Disorder: Mental Retardation, Learning Disabilities, and Autism

Stephen Greenspan
Peter F. Love
University of Connecticut

The term *social intelligence* (SI) refers to "the ability to act wisely in human relations" (Taylor & Cadet, 1989, p. 424). Specifically, it refers to one's ability to understand interpersonal situations and transactions and to use that understanding to assist one in achieving desired interpersonal outcomes. In short, SI may be considered the cognitive underpinning of social competence and is an important contributor to success in social activities such as work and personal relationships. SI has obvious relevance to the field of disabilities, because children and adults with a variety of handicapping conditions are less likely to demonstrate skill in interpersonal relationships and the attendant success that comes with such skill (Greenspan, 1981b).

There has been a significant increase in scholarly writing about SI, both in psychology generally and in the disability field specifically, in the 15 years since the earlier version of this chapter (Greenspan, 1979) was written. Our purpose in the current chapter is to provide a bibliographic update on important literature on SI appearing since 1978, emphasizing work pertaining to mental retardation (MR) and related disorders. In contrast to the earlier chapter, the construct of SI is addressed here on a relatively molar level; that is, we discuss mainly the overall construct rather than specific components, such as "person perception" or "emotional insight." This reflects limitations of space as well as belief that establishing the still-disputed utility of the construct should precede a focus on specific subconstructs. Another way in which the current chapter differs from its 1979 precursor is that we do not limit our focus only to MR, but also look at autism and learning disabilities (LD). Such a broader approach reflects the fact that much of the most interesting recent work on SI has been done in these two other areas, and also reflects the current move toward a cross-categorical approach.

There are three substantitive sections in this chapter. In the first section, we review some recent normative literature on SI. Our purpose in this section is to give some indication of the growth of interest in SI as an aspect of intelligence and personality, an aspect that makes an important contribution to success in everyday life for people in general, not just people with disabilities. In the second section, we review some of the recent research on SI deficits in children and adults with MR, LD, and autism. This literature suggests that: (a) SI deficits are typically found along with deficits in other areas of intelligence in people with MR; (b) are often, but not necesarily, found in people with LD; and (c) are always found in people with autism, sometimes without deficits in other areas of intelligence. Implications of the SI construct for successful outcomes for people with developmental disorders are also discussed in this section. In the third section, we discuss relevance of the SI construct to current controversies surrounding efforts to redefine all three categories of disability and to develop new classification schemes in the human services.

RECENT NORMATIVE LITERATURE ON SOCIAL INTELLIGENCE

Although in this chapter we emphasize work on SI relating to people with MR, autism, and LD, it is necessary to briefly note some of the writing on SI in the broader psychology literature. As indicated in several papers by Greenspan (1979, 1981a, 1981b), earlier writing about SI (e.g., Thorndike, 1920; Weschler, 1974) was motivated in large part by concern over the content validity of measures of "intelligence." Wechsler (1974), in particular, protested the tendency to substitute measures of educational achievement for measures of IQ, in the mistaken belief that the former were more comprehensive in scope or less culturally biased. In fact, as many psychometricians (e.g., Anastasi, 1976) have pointed out, both measure essentially the same thing. This is not surprising, considering that the original Binet–Simon instrument, after which most subsequent measures have been modeled, was developed primarily to identify students at risk of eduational failure (Binet & Simon, 1976/1905).

Wechsler (1974), alluding to a tripartite model proposed by Thorndike (1920), suggested that what is needed is not throwing out IQ, which he saw as a good measure of Thorndike's category of "abstract," or what Greenspan (1979) termed *conceptual intelligence*, but rather the development of instruments that measure two other aspects of intelligence identified by Thorndike, namely mechanical (or practical) and social intelligence (SI). This content model of intelligence is highly similar to the content plane of Guilford's (1967) "cube" model of ability, with "figural ability" substituting for practical intelligence and "behavioral ability" substituting for SI. The equivalence of behavioral ability and SI was highlighted by Guilford when he developed an instrument to measure behavioral ability, which he labeled a test of "social intelligence" (O'Sullivan, Guilford, & deMille, 1965).

Recent interest in the multivariate nature of intelligence has been stimulated primarily by the widespread popularity of a book by Howard Gardner (1983), in which he described what he called "multiple intelligences." In that book, Gardner argued that there are at least seven varieties of intelligence, each as important as the two varieties—"linguistic and logical-mathematical" (corresponding to Guilford's semantic and symbolic abilities)—tapped by measures of IQ. Gardner's belief in the existence of multiple intelligences stemmed, as pointed out by Brody (1992), from two influences: (a) findings in brain-injured persons of highly specific areas of deficit associated with specific lesions, co-existing with areas of average or above-average functioning, and (b) an interest in the phenomenon of precocity in specific areas of talent, in persons who otherwise have average or (in the case of "savants") below-average IQ. For Gardner, the notion of multiple intelligences was useful in getting educators, and the general public, to adopt a broader approach to defining and nurturing talent. Thus, the primary implications of Gardner's model, at least as pointed out by him, are for the treatment of children identified as "gifted" rather than of children with developmental disorders.

SI is incorporated, in Gardner's theory, into what he termed the "personal intelligences," a category that includes (in contrast to writings of most other scholars) both interpersonal ability (understanding of others) and intrapersonal ability (understanding of self). In the initial discussion of personal intelligences, Gardner (1983) largely emphasized intrapersonal (self-oriented) aspects of personal intelligences, although in the one sentence devoted to personal intelligences in his recent book on applying the theory, Gardner (1993, p. 37) appeared to be placing more emphasis on its interpersonal aspects.

Unlike other theorists in the area of multiple intelligence, Gardner did not seek to base or validate his typology on empirical studies by himself or others. This opens his typology up to the criticism of being either under- or overinclusive. Gardner (1993) noted that this model emerged out of what he called a "subjective factor analysis," which is reflected in his failure to cite much, if any, of the substantial amount of previous writing on the topic of multiple intelligences. Such an approach may work in areas such as musical and artistic ability, about which Gardner had previously written and is obviously knowledgeable, but it is apparent that social intelligence as it is typically defined does not occupy a central place in Gardner's model or interests.

SI does, however, occupy a central role in the writings of another major intelligence theorist, Robert Sternberg. In his triarchic theory of intelligence, Sternberg (1988) emphasized three loci of intelligence: that which is inside the individual, that which is in the environment, and that which emerges from the interaction between the individual and his or her environment. As nicely summarized in Sternberg (1986), the within-individual locus has four levels: a "biological" level; a "molar" level, including both cognition (meta-cognition as well as specific cognitive processes) and motivation; a "behavioral" level; and an interaction among biological, molar, and behavioral levels.

It is on the behavioral level that Sternberg's model incorporates the concept of SI. This level emphasizes the types of content to which one's intelligence is applied. Sternberg identified three general types of intelligence, which he termed *academic*, *social*, and *practical*. Sternberg used the term *academic intelligence* to refer to the kinds of behavior carried out within school settings, and which are tapped by IQ tests. Within the social domain of intelligence, he included interactions with people, although Sternberg (like Gardner) also included intrapersonal awareness under this rubric. Within the practical domain of intelligence, Sternberg (1988) included "behavior exhibited in one's occupation and in one's daily living" (p. 7). The distinction between social and practical intelligence breaks down somewhat in Sternberg's model, because he included under the practical domain such aspects of interpersonal functioning as "knowing how to get ahead in one's job" (Sternberg, 1986, p. 7), along with such nonsocial talents as "knowing how to perform one's job effectively" (Sternberg, 1988, p. 7). That Sternberg included within the practical domain many activities that are more typically thought of as social was reflected in his use of the term *tacit knowledge* in measures of the construct (Wagner & Sternberg, 1986). An example would be tapping understanding among junior professors at research universities of the unwritten rule that publishing proficiency is valued far more highly in tenure decisions than is teaching excellence.

In the one paper Sternberg (1984) devoted to exploring implications of his model for understanding MR, he used a two-part typology to refer to the content or behavioral domain: *everyday intelligence,* in which he included social and practical aspects; and *academic intelligence.* Sternberg argued, in line with the dual criteria approach to defining MR, that the notion of everyday intelligence is useful in identifying as non-MR those individuals in which quite low IQ co-occurs with average everyday intelligence. Although finding this substitution of everyday intelligence for the muddled concept of adaptive behavior useful (thus keeping the historic connection between MR and low intelligence), Greenspan, Switzky, and Granfield (1996) suggested a radical alternative: using deficit in everyday intelligence not as a secondary criterion but as the primary, or even sole criterion, in making the diagnosis.

The importance of SI within a broader model of intelligence, although not a prevalent theme in writing about intelligence, was noted by several prominent theorists who are represented in two important books co-edited by Sternberg. The first is a collection of essays under the title *What is Intelligence?* (Sternberg & Detterman, 1986). Another book (Sternberg & Wagner, 1986) specifically dealt with what Sternberg termed *practical intelligence* but which we have noted also dealt with what is more typically termed *social intelligence.* In the first volume, two authors who dealt with this topic in interesting ways are John Carroll and Jacqueline Goodnow.

Carroll (1986) posited a tripartite model of intelligence that is highly similar to those of Thordike, Guilford, and Sternberg. He divided intelligence according to the kinds of problems dealt with, and argued that there are three domains of intelligence: academic and technical, practical, and social. Academic and technical intelligence deals with the kinds of problems "arising in schoolwork, and later, in many fields of science, the professions and occupational specialties" (p. 51). Practical intelligence deals with problems "arising in managing one's daily affairs, making a living and planning one's course of action" (p. 51). Social intelligence deals with problems "encountered in dealing with others—individuals, groups, or even alien cultures" (p. 51). Carroll described intelligence as the cognitive capacity, applied either consciously or unconsciously, to think about problems encountered in these areas; that is, to "consider different alternative courses of action, to create strategies of solution, and to predict consequences" (p. 52).

Goodnow (1986) addressed the general tendency to assume that intelligence exists as a construct only to the extent to which it can be assessed by psychometrically adequate tests. She noted that we do not require objective test evidence to conclude that someone is gregarious or shy, or attractive or ugly, and she wondered why we cannot feel free to make similar global social judgments about someone's relative smartness or stupidity. Goodnow thus argued that intelligence should be viewed as a judgment or attribution about someone's behavior in the world, rather than as some quality that exists primarily within the individual. Following from this argument is the implication that one's intelligence can be best assessed in those everyday situations in which one attempts to solve problems, with many of these situations involving interaction with people. Goodnow noted that this point is an elaboration of arguments made by Rogoff and colleagues in the context of work on everyday cognition (Rogoff & Lave, 1984) and social mediation of cognition (Rogoff & Wertsch, 1984). Goodnow (1988) elaborated on this theme in more detail in a chapter in the Sternberg and Wagner (1986) volume dealing with practical intelligence.

Although the theoretical formulations described previously are driven by an interest in the role of SI within the broad areas of intelligence and learning, there is a related but substantially different body of work on SI (often under the rubric of social cognition) as an aspect of social and personality psychology. This work represents a larger shift within the field of personality psychology away from a conception of personality that is rooted primarily in the notion of fixed dispositions or traits (such as anxiety) and toward a conception of personality that takes account of abilities and cognitive processes (such as social intelligence) in explaining why people behave the way they do. One major difference between the intelligence and personality approaches to SI is that the former is more tactical (e.g., processing of particular social stimuli), whereas the latter is more strategic (e.g., development of life plans). Because of space limitations, the reader is referred to an excellent review in Cantor and Kihlstrom (1987) of the personological approach to SI.

In this section, we pointed out the dramatic growth of recent interest in SI among scholars interested in normative aspects of intellectual development. This work has contributed to a growing understanding that intelligence: involves more than just academic potential, and must be viewed in important social and cultural contexts. In the next section, we explore implications of the SI construct for the disability field.

SI AND DISABILITY

Possible reasons for deficits in SI among people with disabilities at present are still speculative. Although there is considerable variation among individuals with disabilities as to the expression of SI deficits, reasons for these deficits may be grouped into three categories: (a) social inexperience with age-appropriate relationships, stemming from segregated residential or educational placements, parental overprotection, or other forms of differential socialization; (b) limitations in sensory or expressive modalities such as vision, hearing, speech, and motor systems that are involved in receiving or sending social messages; and (c) organically based deficits in cognitive and/or perceptual capabilities, of a general nature (that affect processing of both social and nonsocial information) or of a specific nature (that affect mainly processing of social information). These three possible reasons for SI deficit are applicable in individualized ways in any particular case of disability. Although we do not, for the most part, address the issue of causality in this chapter, our primary emphasis is on the third (constitutionally based) set of factors.

The first explanation (socialization and experience) is obviously an important factor in many cases. It sometimes manifests itself more as a motivational factor (as in the case of those children whose inept behavior is a defense against feelings of academic inadequacy) or as a secondary factor, complicating the social skill deficits that are attributable to a primary organically based deficit in ability to decode or encode social cues.

The second set of factors—sensory or motor deficits—is mainly applicable in explaining demonstrated social skill deficits of people with disorders such as blindness, deafness, and cerebral palsy, although one must keep in mind that people in these categories often have constitutional cognitive deficits as well. For these people, the sensory deficit often leads to the same social inexperience that is postulated as a cause of the SI deficits in people without sensory impairment.

Although we are primarily reviewing research that focuses on processing deficits and assumes an organic basis for these deficits, the specific nature of these organic causes is still poorly understood. The one area in which such speculation has occurred, however, is in the area of LD subtyping, particularly those subtypes (such as nonverbal LD) where social skill deficit is attributed to brain injury or abnormal brain development. We discuss some of that literature, although much of this research is contradictory and highly preliminary in nature.

Although individual factors—attributable to specific or general processing deficits—are emphasized in this chapter, we do not mean to minimize the contribution of environmental factors to the amelioration of SI deficits and to the tremendous variability in SI levels and adaptive outcomes that may be found in any particular disability subgroup.

It should, of course, be noted that any particular social outcome, including behavior that might be considered unintelligent, is a function not only of the interaction of SI with one's environment, but of the interaction of SI with other aspects of personality and social competence. For example, one's temperament (e.g., impulsivity, emotionality) and character (e.g., perseverance, general niceness) are obvious contributors to success or failure in social roles and activities. One could imagine an individual who clearly understands that a particular action (e.g., calling someone an insulting name) is likely to elicit some negative reaction, but is so carried away with uncontrollable affect (temperament) or so uninterested in others' feelings (character) that he or she engages in that action anyway. It is this difficulty in separating out the causes of any particular action for a given individual that makes definition and measurement of social competence so difficult. In this chapter we deal with socially unintelligent behavior (i.e., behavior that has some interpersonal consequence that is both negative and undesired) as indicative of SI deficit, without denying the likely contribution of personality factors in any particular incident. For a fuller discussion of other aspects of social/personal competence, see Greenspan (1981a) and Greenspan and Driscoll (in press).

Mental Retardation and Social Intelligence

In line with developments in the disability field generally, there has been increasing interest since 1980 in studying aspects of social functioning in people with MR. In part, this interest in social behavior reflects a trend toward looking at the whole person, and understanding that social and emotional factors are often critical in determining the extent of an individual's adaptation to challenges faced in normative educational and community settings (Zigler & Balla, 1982).

Research relevant to SI and MR has been conducted under two rubrics: social skills, and social cognition. The former is largely conducted within a social learning paradigm, and focuses on assessing and intervening around behaviors believed to be critical to social competence outcomes. The latter is largely conducted within a cognitive–developmental paradigm, and has emphasized understanding social behavior in people with MR more than changing it.

The concept of social skills has been used with increasing frequency in various areas of disability, including MR. Although the term is somewhat broader than SI, there is no doubt that SI is a central aspect of social skills, as reflected in the statement by Matson and Fee (1991) that "social skills training is based on the theory that poor social competence is often the result of deficits in specific verbal and/or nonverbal skills necessary for effective interaction" (p. 468). In our view, SI should be understood as the cognitive underpinning of social skills. Where the social skills approach to SI differs, however, from the social–cognitive approach (see next subsection) is that practitioners—in line with their generally behaviorist orientation—tend to focus on promoting skillful behaviors without specifically invoking intervening cognitive processes or theories. Researchers interested in social skills generally eschew debates about the meaning of this or related constructs, and focus on specific target behaviors (e.g., asking, grunting, smiling, conversing, eye contact, hygiene, aggression, turn taking) and techniques (e.g., reinforcement, modeling, learning games, self-monitoring) likely to prove effective in increasing or decreasing the frequency of these behaviors (Matson & Fee, 1991).

Interest in social skills in MR has been widespread, with particular emphasis on utilizing operant and social learning techniques to increase social skills and the likelihood of success of persons with MR in a variety of settings. Particular attention has been paid to application of the social skills concept in two settings from which people with MR were until recently largely excluded: competitive employment and regular education classes.

The shift in the vocational habilitation of people with MR from sheltered settings to supported employment has placed increased priority on identifying and changing those behaviors that are seen as critical for success or failure in competitive work settings (Ellis & Rusch, 1991). Previously, emphasis in the vocational literature has been on physical or practical skills such as speed and work efficiency, reflecting the predominance of piece-work in sheltered workshop settings. Competence in more diverse and normalized work settings must, obviously, be defined in a manner that places greater emphasis on ability to understand and comply with the often unstated and complex social expectations of employers, coworkers, and the public.

Support for the idea that social competence should be a major target of vocational interventions for people with MR came from a number of studies that examined factors contributing to vocational success (or, more typically, failure) of people with MR in competitive work settings. Greenspan and Shoultz (1981), in one of the first such studies, found that socially incompetent behaviors—including behaviors that were palpably socially unintelligent (such as a chambermaid telling a late-sleeping hotel guest to "get your ass out of bed")—had as much or more to do with involuntary terminations from competitive employment of a sample of adults with mild MR as did actual work competence. The general truth of this finding has been confirmed by various scholars (cf. Martin, Rusch, Lagomarcino, & Chadsey-Rusch, 1986; Salzberg, Agran, & Lignuris-Kraft, 1986). Although the finding may be unsurprising, in that social incompetence has a lot to do with why anyone—including people with high IQ—lose their jobs, it served to focus attention by vocational professionals on the critical importance of social skills for the acceptance and success of people with MR in the new world of work outside of sheltered workshops (Chadsey-Rusch, 1992).

There are obvious parallels between the role of social skills in work settings and in school settings. Just as competitive employment until recently was not an option for most people with MR, so too segregated class or school placements were until recently the norm for children with MR, including children with mild MR. Just as deviant or highly inept behaviors are less likely to be tolerated in a competitive work setting than in a sheltered workshop, so too expectations for nondeviant or minimally skillful behaviors in a mainstream educational setting are likely to be much higher than in a self-contained classroom or special school. Research on factors contributing to successful educational "mainstreaming" of people with mild handicaps (LD as well as MR) has proliferated in recent years (Gottlieb, Alter, & Gottlieb, 1991). In line with results from vocational outcome studies, social skills have been found to be problematic for most MR students and quite critical for acceptance by peers and teachers (Gresham, 1983; Guralnick, 1992). Recent research (e.g., Leffert & Siperstein, 1996) suggests that social–cognitive processes, particularly those that involve executive function (i.e., coordination and sequencing of social cognitive operations), may be especially problematic for MR children in normative classroom settings. This finding parallels work done in the vocational area, in which it was found that ability to evaluate appropriateness of social problem-solving tactics discriminated MR from physically handicapped workers and was apparently related to successful job performance (Greenspan, Shoultz, & Weir, 1981).

A considerable amount of research on SI in MR has been stimulated by a neo-Piagetian paradigm, drawing inspiration from Piaget's early work on egocentric thinking. In Piaget's writing, the term *egocentrism* referred to perspective taking, particularly the ability to take someone's perspective when it differs from one's own. Three forms of perspective taking have been explored by researchers: perceptual perspective taking (knowing what someone is seeing), cognitive perspective taking (knowing what someone is thinking, and affective perspective taking (knowing what someone is feeling). Greenspan (1979) located perspective taking within social sensitivity, the first of the three domains of SI contained in his model. Another aspect of social sensitivity identified by Greenspan (1979) was termed *social inference* and involves the ability to make sense of social gestalts (e.g., by inferring that a social gathering in a workplace is a formal meeting rather than an informal lunch break). Social sensitivity is the aspect of SI that is most perceptual in nature, and involves relatively automatic reading of social cues. As such, it may be considered to be a developmental precursor of more abstract or cognitive aspects of SI. Much of the interest in SI in people with cognitive disability (not just MR, but autism and LD as well) has focused on this aspect, for two reasons: (a) because it is a skill attained fairly early in nonhandicapped people, and lack of it is a fairly dramatic distinguishing feature; and (b) because the construct of egocentrism appears to be a good qualitative descriptor of the unsophisticated and inept social behavior of many people with cognitively based disorders.

Two other aspects of SI, in addition to social sensitivity, were identified by Greenspan (1979): social insight and social communication. Social insight involves the ability to evaluate and analyze social phenomena, and contains three components: social comprehension (ability to reflect on social institutions and processes), psychological insight (ability to understand personal characteristics and processes), and moral judgment (ability to reflect on ethical issues). Social communication involves ability to evaluate and utilize effective interpersonal tactics, and includes two components: referential communication (ability to convey what one is thinking, perceiving or feeling) and social problem solving (understanding of how to handle difficult situations).

Simeonsson and colleagues (Simeonsson, Monson, & Blacher, 1982; Simeonsson & Rosenthal, 1991) comprehensively reviewed research on social–cognitive variables in persons with MR, covering most of the seven variables identified in Greenspan's (1979) typology of SI research. In approaching this literature, they were particularly interested in examining the applicability to persons with MR of the developmental stage sequences identified by Piaget, Kohlberg, and other cognitive–developmental researchers, including aspects of cognition (such as causality, conservation, and concrete operations) that involve nonsocial stimuli.

Generally, Simeonsson and colleagues noted, in line with the "developmental" position of Zigler (Zigler & Balla, 1982), that persons with MR, although deficient in social–cognitive abilities, progress through the same invariant social–cognitive and nonsocial–cognitive developmental stages as do nonhandicapped persons, and in a manner roughly congruent with their developmental age. Building on the work of Inhelder (1966), in which levels of MR severity were translated from IQ-deviation terms into Piagetian stage-fixation (*decalage*) terms (e.g., mild MR equals fixation in concrete operations, moderate MR in preoperations, and severe or profound MR in the sensory-motor stage), Simeonsson and Rosenthal (1991) noted that social cognitive and other Piagetian tasks may be particularly useful in assessing individuals with very severe levels of cognitive impairment, for which traditional intellectual assessment measures may have limited discriminatory or descriptive utility.

That persons with MR have deficits in social–cognitive variables is hardly surprising, because it is well established that persons with MR perform less adequately than do CA-matched nonhandicapped persons on a wide range of cognitive tasks. If SI were nothing more than a reflection of IQ (i.e., academic intelligence), however, then it would be difficult to make a case for developing separate measures of SI or establishing SI as a separate diagnostic criterion. (This topic is addressed in the next major section.) The critical question of whether SI is, in fact, a separate aspect of cognitive functioning in persons with MR has just begun to be addressed.

Research relevant to this question was conducted in Australia by Mathias (1990; Mathias & Nettelbeck, 1992a, 1992b) and in the United States by McGrew and Bruininks (1990; McGrew, Bruininks, & Johnson, 1996). Both research programs found general support for Greenspan's (1979, 1981a) model of personal competence, but Mathias and Nettelbeck (1992a) found SI and practical intelligence (PI) to form a single factor. McGrew et al. (1996) noted that this study utilized only a single measure of PI and failed to recognize correlated measurement error in their data. More appropriate analysis of the Mathias and Nettelbeck data using confirmatory methods provided support for the view that SI and PI comprise factorially separate domains (Greenspan & McGrew, 1996). This has particular implications for the definition of MR, as McGrew et al. (1996) reported more support for the tripartite model of intelligence than for the lumping of SI and PI in the model of adaptive skills contained in the new American Association on Mental Retardation definition (Luckasson et al., 1992).

In this section, we explored the implications of research on SI for understanding, definition, and habilitation in the field of MR. The emphasis in the SI research in MR has been on exploring implications of SI for outcomes in different contexts. This emphasis is reflective of the historical tendency to approach MR from a sociological perspective. In the following section, we review research on SI in persons with learning disabilities (LD). As becomes clear, there is a much greater emphasis in the LD literature on etiological factors, particularly brain development, in explaining why some individuals with LD exhibit significant SI deficits.

LD and SI

Although LD has been defined primarily as a disorder marked by problems in academic performance—in individuals who have otherwise normal intellectual and social functioning—there has been considerable recent interest in the fact that many LD individuals have significant problems in the area of social competence in general and SI in particular. Interest in social competence in persons with LD owes much, undoubtedly, to the pioneering work by Tanis Bryan and her colleagues (Bryan, 1982; Bryan & Bryan, 1990; Pearl, Donahue, & Bryan, 1986). This large body of research, which for several years was virtually the only work done on social aspects of LD—has focused on two aspects of social competence: outcomes (such as peer rejection) and social skills (particularly inept communications). Although Bryan and colleagues favored a motivational explanation (secondary reaction to academic rejection), she recently (Bryan, 1991) became quite interested in social cognition (i.e., SI) deficit as a primary explanation for the demonstrated social incompetence of many students with LD.

With respect to outcome-oriented studies of social incompetence in persons with LD, numerous studies have demonstrated that students with LD score lower on a variety of sociometric measures than do non-LD students of the same age (Bryan, 1991). Swanson and Malone (1992), in the first quantitatively based meta-analysis of that literature, however, noted that there is considerable variability in the social acceptance literature, with some studies (e.g., Sabornie, Kauffman, Ellis, & Marshall, 1988) finding that many students with LD are quite well accepted by peers. Attributing variation among studies to differences in measurement approaches, Swanson and Malone (1992) concluded that "Overall, results indicate that children with learning disabilities are more likely to be rejected than average achieving peers" (p. 434), reporting a mean effect size (ES), expressed in differences in standard deviation (SD) units between LD and non-LD samples, of .79. Stone and La Greca (1994), in a more recent review, supported this conclusion, but pointed out that there is considerable variability, with some LD youngsters experiencing rejection and others neglect by peers. They noted, furthermore, that LD girls and LD children who also have attention deficit disorders appear to be most at risk for peer difficulties.

Studies have also examined differences between LD and non-LD students on a number of social skill variables, most of them involving the use of effective verbal or nonverbal communication tactics. A typical study involved asking subjects to role play a situation in which they have to deliver bad news (Pearl, Donahue, & Bryan, 1985). Overall, LD students have been found to perform at approximately a full *SD* below their peers on various measures of tact, nonverbal sensitivity, and empathy (Swanson & Malone, 1992).

Explanations for peer rejection, and demonstrated social ineptness, of LD individuals has been sought in two areas: personality variables (temperament and character) and social cognition and social perception deficits. LD students have been found to be moderately more aggressive than are non-LD students, although this has not always been found to be the case (Swanson & Malone, 1992). More substantial differences have been found to occur in the area of immaturity and personal inadequacy variables (mean ES = .87) and attentional and on-task difficulties (mean ES = .83).

An interesting juxtaposition of a motivational and social cognitive explanation for the social ineptness of many LD youth was made by Wagner and Kistner (1990). Utilizing Sternberg's distinction between academic intelligence and PI, Wagner and Kistner (1990) considered whether deficits in practical intelligence (which, in Sternberg's typology, is largely synonymous with what others term *social intelligence*) might explain impairments in academic performance of LD children, and vice versa. They concluded that LD children are, as a group, relatively deficient in two types of tacit knowledge: understanding that academic performance is largely dependent on effort, and the use of spontaneously applied strategies for cognitive tasks. Wagner and Kistner (1990) further argued that demands on use of PI may be greater for LD children than on non-LD children, because of the greater difficulty in maintaining adaptive beliefs about themselves in the face of frequent failure, and in the need to constantly devise new strategies and compensatory mechanisms rather than rely on largely automatic schemas. They also noted that parents and teachers are more likely to foster dependence, to provide excessive direction, and to allow fewer opportunities for LD children to model their behavior after competent peers. Although this is interesting from a speculative standpoint, an obvious limitation of this line of speculation is the confounding of PI and SI with motivation, by defining the former largely in terms of possession of a positive motivational orientation.

Recently, there has been increasing interest in exploring more directly the role of social cognitive deficits as a possible primary explanation for the social incompetence of LD children and youth (see Jackson, Enright, & Murdock, 1987). In an excellent review, Bryan (1991) examined those studies that compared LD and non-LD subjects (both nonlabeled and those with mild MR) on a number of social–cognitive measures. Results were complex, reflecting in part the variation in difficulty level and psychometric adequacy of the instruments that were used. On some measures, no group differences in LD and non-LD subjects were found, on others significant differences occurred but covaried significantly with IQ differences, whereas in other studies such differences were found to be both significant and independent of IQ.

Among the studies that found LD subjects to do less well than do nonlabeled peers are ones that tapped aspects of what Greenspan (1979) termed "social sensitivity" (i.e., reading of social cues). Wong and Wong (1980), using the Chandler (1973) measure of cognitive perspective taking, found third- and fourth-grade LD children to be more egocentric than were their nonhandicapped peers. Most of these differences were attributable to deficits found in LD girls. Bryan (1991) found this interesting because of the reports in the literature that LD girls are more likely to be seen as socially incompetent than are LD boys. In one of the few studies exploring aspects of what Greenspan (1979) termed "social insight," Hoyle and Serafica (1988) found LD children to be significantly less sophisticated than non-LD peers (ES of approximately .8, according to Swanson &

Malone, 1992) in their conceptions of friendship and their thoughtfulness about conflict resolution issues.

Several studies have used the Test of Social Inference (Edmonson, deJung, Leland, & Leach, 1974), one of the few commercially published measures of SI and originally developed for use primarily with persons with mild MR. This measure taps the ability to make correct interpretations of what is happening in pictorially depicted social situations. As noted by Bryan (1991), LD subjects have been found to do considerably more poorly than do age-matched peers on this measure of SI. Other studies finding social sensitivity deficits in LD subjects have utilized the Four Factor Test of Social Intelligence (O'Sullivan & Guilford, 1966), a measure utilizing cartoon stimuli, and the Profile of Nonverbal Sensitivity, or PONS (Rosenthal, Archer, DiMatteo, Hall, & Rogers, 1979), a measure utilizng videotape stimuli.

Congruent with the observation (Greenspan, 1979) that videotape appears to be crucial to the development of adequate measures of SI, several studies have begun to utilize videotape to tap the ability of LD persons to understand and interpret interpersonal stimuli. In one study (Maheady, Maitland, & Sainato, 1984) using fairly static and obvious stimuli (e.g., two women with a baby, with the task being to pick which woman is the mother), no group differences were found. On the other hand, in two other studies that depicted more complex, subtle, and affectively charged situations (e.g., soap opera situations involving conflict, insecurity, and jealousy), LD middle school subjects were found to be significantly less skilled than were non-LD subjects in their interpretations of situations and feelings (Pearl & Cosden, 1982; Weiss, 1984).

More recently, Bryan herself conducted research on social intelligence of LD students, using the social information processing model of Dodge (1986). In a study with third-, fourth-, seventh-, and eighth-grade LD students, and matched groups of normal-achieving and low-achieving students, Tur-Kaspa and Bryan (1994) used an adaptation of Dodge's assessment procedure. Five videotapes were developed portraying common social situations such as peer rejection and conflict. Interviews probed such social information skills as correct decoding of situations, insight into motives of portrayed characters, evaluation of alternate problem-solving tactics, and encoding of social communications. Results found LD students to score significantly lower than did average-achieving students at all grades on all five components of Dodge's social information processing measure. Furthermore, discriminant function analysis was extremely effective in classifying the LD students based on these variables. Tur-Kapsa and Bryan were able to largely rule out low achievement as an explanation for this finding, in that the LD students differed significantly on most of the variables from the low-achieving but not-LD group. They conclude that "LD students are likely to exhibit a unique social information-processing pattern" (1994, p. 21).

A striking feature of most of the research on social competence of LD children, a feature that especially characterizes the work of Bryan and colleagues, is an almost exclusive reliance on a group comparison analysis of variance (ANOVA) main-effects research design, in which a clinically defined LD sample is compared with a non-LD sample (typically normal-achieving, but recently likely to include those who are low-achieving but not LD). Although such a research design is useful in preliminary identification of a population's risk status, continued reliance on a group comparison model may have contributed to the tendency of LD researchers to discuss social incompetence in LD as a unitary phenomenon, rather than to turn attention to the possibility that LD youth vary considerably in their levels of social incompetence. In fact, there is reason to think that the LD population falls into at least two distinct subgroups, those with normal SI and those with substantial SI deficits (Speece, 1993). It is highly possible that the consistent finding of group differences in social competence between LD and non-LD persons may reflect the lumping of these two subgroups together, and that it is a gross overgeneralization to conclude that all LD students are at risk for social rejection and failure.

In this section, we reviewed the research on SI in persons with LD. This research reflects the growing interest in SI as a core feature of the everyday behavior of many people with LD. SI is particularly important in issues of classification in LD, as is made clear later in this chapter. Although concern over SI deficits in persons with LD is relatively recent, it has historically held a central role in conceptualizations of autism.

Autism and SI

Despite the historical focus on social impairment that has been characteristic of autism since the disorder was first described by Kanner, researchers have only recently begun to direct their attention to the specific nature and possible causes of that social impairment (Hobson, 1984; Howlin, 1986; Lord, 1993). Initially, the dramatic lack of normal social attachments in autistic individuals was attributed to motivational factors believed to result from abnormalities in parenting. The shift toward a view of autism as a biologically based disorder was reflected in a search for cognitive deficits in areas such as communication (Rutter & Garmezy, 1983) and information processing (Ozonoff, Pennington, & Rogers, 1993). As pointed out by Fein, Pennington, and Waterhouse (1987), the heavy emphasis, until recently, on cognitive as opposed to social conceptions of autism reflected the nature of neuropsychological research and practice, in which cognitive measures and variables continue to play a dominant role. The current renewed interest in social behavior in autism reflects a growing awareness that extreme social ineptness (or what we have termed *low SI*) is a central aspect of the disorder, an increasing understanding of the link between brain pathology and social behavior, and a growing understanding that the study of cognition includes the study of social cognition.

There has been considerable interest recently in studying the manner in which persons with autism process social information. Although some of this research has utilized traditional measures such as role taking (Oswald & Ollendick, 1989) and affect comprehension (Fein, Lucci, Braverman, & Waterhouse, 1992), most of the SI-related research in autism recently has focused on the concept of "theory of mind." As summarized by Tager-Flusberg, Baron-Cohen, and Cohen (1993), the study of theory of mind was stimulated by the publication of Premack and Woodruff's (1978) seminal paper on the apparent understanding of human intentions in chimpanzees. In this and other papers, Premack (1988) suggested that animals such as chimpanzees show a fair amount of conscious SI in their manipulations of peers to achieve particular outcomes. Child development researchers were fascinated by the likelihood that if animals exhibited such perspective-taking ability, then it stood to reason that young children at comparable stages of cognitive development did also.

Following the suggestion of Dennett and others that theory of mind cannot be demonstrated until one can explain false belief (i.e., what is in another's head is wrong), Wimmer and Perner (1983) published an equally seminal paper on the understanding by 3- and 4-year-olds of false belief. In that study children were asked to predict where a character thinks a marble—moved while she was out of the room—is located, a problem that is only solved by children approaching their fourth birthday or older. This paper stimulated a tremendous flurry of ingenious experimentation, intended to explore the development in young children of the ability to take into account the intentions and thoughts of other people.

The theory of mind line of research represents an extension of, as well as a corrective to, research on normative social–cognitive development associated with Piaget and neo-Piagetian developmental psychologists. It is an extension of that research, in the sense that it deals with similar phenomena, particularly the phenomenon of egocentrism, and utilizes methods that are structurally similar to some of those (such as the three mountains experiment) used by Piaget, Flavell, Chandler, and others (Shantz, 1983). It is a corrective to that research in that it demonstrates a qualitative stage shift occuring at least 2 years earlier than was generally believed to be the case. It has long been known that use of more salient cues and probes in perspective-taking experiments can allow younger children to give more mature-appearing social cognitive responses (Chandler & Greenspan, 1972; Chandler, Greenspan, & Barenboim, 1973). Unlike the previous view of such findings as experimental artifacts, however, the results of theory of mind experimentation have demonstrated that important qualitative shifts in the cognitive underpinnings of social skills are in fact occuring during the early childhood period.

As noted by Rutter and Bailey (1993), interest in applying the concept of theory of mind to autism was stimulated by a widely read paper by Baron-Cohen, Leslie, and Frith (1985), in which they "reported evidence that autistic children lacked the ability to appreciate that other people's beliefs might differ from their own, and went on to argue that a theory of mind deficit might constitute the core of autism" (Rutter & Bailey, 1993, p. 481). The best overview of recent research on the theory of mind explanation of autism is contained in a comprehensive volume edited by Baron-Cohen, Tager-Flusberg, and Cohen (1993). In a central chapter in that volume, Baron-Cohen (1993) provided an authoritative review of recent research on theory of mind in individuals with autism. The following discussion of that research parallels, and borrows liberally from, the review by Baron-Cohen.

As noted by Baron-Cohen (1993), work on theory of mind can be divided into the following categories: understanding beliefs, understanding desire, understanding knowledge, understanding pretense, understanding perception, understanding emotion, understanding attention, and understanding goals. Although all three levels of the typology of SI presented by Greenspan (1979)—social sensitivity, social insight, and social comprehension—are involved in these forms of understanding, the first category of understanding (social sensitivity) is the one that is most closely related to the construct of theory of mind. This is because theory of mind relates primarily to that portion of SI that involves understanding of mental states of others. Social sensitivity is that aspect of SI that focuses on such states, whereas the other two major categories of SI, particularly social insight, focus on aspects of social understanding that go beyond (and frequently do not even involve) understanding of individual mental states.

The first of Baron-Cohen's subcategories—understanding beliefs—is critical to theory of mind research. This is because of the influential argument by Dennett (1978) that false belief might constitute a litmus test for theory of mind, in that it allows one to engineer a situation in which one can distinguish between the child's (true) belief and the child's awareness of someone else's different (false) belief. Wimmer and Perner (1983) devised a test (described previously) based on that argument, and Baron-Cohen, Leslie, and Frith (1985) used that test to argue that children with autism lack understanding of the mental state of belief, when compared on both chronological age (CA) and mental age (MA) to both nonhandicapped children as well as children with Down syndrome. This last finding was especially important in supporting the view that persons with autism possess specific SI deficits that are not explainable by more general information processing deficits. This pattern of results has been replicated in a number of studies reported on by Baron-Cohen (1993), including studies using a variety of methods such as puppets, real people, computer graphics, and experimenters (including mothers, to control for stranger anxiety), and difficulty levels. As noted by Baron-Cohen (1993): "The robustness of this finding suggests that in autism there is a general inability to understand other people's different beliefs" (p. 61).

Critical to the theory of mind hypothesis was the demonstration (Baron-Cohen, Leslie, & Frith, 1985) that many autistic individuals who are unable to understand mental states are able to understand both nonsocial stimuli as well as social stimuli where the task does not require understanding of mental states. Thus, the theory of mind hypothesis not only argues against a general cognitive deficiency as explaining theory of mind deficits, it also argues against a more general social–cognitive deficiency. Examples of this finding can be found in studies showing persons with autism demonstrating relatively normal competencies in such areas as perceptual perspective taking (understanding both of what someone sees and how something will appear to someone with a different perspective) as well as in studies of such concepts as person permanence, recognition of self versus others, recognition of features in others, and understanding of conceptual differences between animate and inanimate objects. Baron-Cohen (1993) concluded that "This body of evidence points to the intact nature of many aspects of social cognition in autism, and highlights the specificity of the deficits these subjects show in the development of their theory of mind" (p. 68). It should be noted, however, that these kinds of findings have not been universally replicated, and some researchers (e.g., Hobson, 1993) argued that SI deficits in individuals with autism go beyond limitations in theory of mind.

Although a complete review of the theory of mind literature is beyond the scope of this chapter, two other aspects of theory of mind research that have special importance for understanding autism are mentioned briefly. These involve studies of understanding of emotion and studies involving understanding of attention. Studies involving emotion have special importance because of the long tradition in autism scholarship of viewing autism as an emotionally based disorder. In his early work in this area, Hobson (1984) found persons with autism to perform more poorly than did control groups on emotion–expression matching tasks. In later studies, these differences were not found when subjects were matched on verbal mental age (Baron-Cohen, 1993). Other studies have focused on emotion prediction, as opposed to emotion recognition. These studies (which tap some aspects of psychological insight) assessed subjects' ability to understand the situational and personal causes of broad classes of feelings. Recent research has indicated that autistic children do have deficiencies in understanding and predicting affective responses, compared to both normal and mentally retarded controls, but that these differences are most likely to emerge with respect to those emotions (e.g., surprise) or circumstances (when emotions are affected by belief states) when ability to represent (as opposed to perceptually label) affective states is required to succeed in a given task (Baron-Cohen, 1993).

Understanding of attentional processes is a particularly interesting area of theory of mind research, in that it appears to be an early antecedent both of the development of theory of mind as well as of the development of early deficits in theory of mind. Studies of attentional understanding in infants have focused on such behaviors as gaze monitoring, declarative (as opposed to imperative) pointing, and shared attention. Mundy and Sigman (1989; Mundy, Sigman, & Kasari, 1993) found infants diagnosed as autistic (obviously, a limited population, given that autism is typically diagnosed in early or middle childhood) to be strikingly deficient in these competencies. Baron-Cohen (1993) interpreted these findings as generally supportive of the theory of mind hypothesis, merely seeing them as early manifestations of later theory of mind deficits. Mundy, Sigman, and Kasari (1993) suggested, however, that these findings may indicate that inability to represent internal states of others (i.e., theory of mind deficits) may be later developmental manifestations of more fundamental constitutional limitations, which in infancy manifest themselves in nonverbal communication limitations involving attention sharing. Under this interpretation, theory of mind deficit is viewed as a behavioral marker of the profound social incompetence of persons with autism rather than the cause of such incompetence.

Various other contributors to the Baron-Cohen, Tager-Flusberg, and Cohen (1993) volume, although acknowledging the tremendous contribution of the theory of mind hypothesis to research and speculation about the nature of autism, expressed a similar reluctance to embrace theory of mind as the "magic bullet" for which researchers and clinicians have been searching. Hobson (1993), one of the first researchers to call attention to the importance of studying the role of SI deficit in persons with autism, appears to have suggested that autism is a complex phenomenon and that there are multiple pathways by which children come to manifest that disorder which we term *autism*. Given that persons with autism function with different levels of competence and impairment, it may be that the kinds of conceptual limitations inherent in theory of mind may be more relevant for understanding some cases of autism and less relevant for others. Central to all cases of autism, for Hobson, is a biologically based impairment in the capacity for affective relatedness, and this incapacity manifests itself in a wide variety of SI-related phenomena that include, but by no means are limited to, the notion of theory of mind. This view was seconded by Klin and Volkmar (1993), who argued, in line with Kanner's original report, that "the social disability [in autism] is *general* in nature, i.e., that it affects basically all fundamentally social processes" (p. 321). They took exception to Baron-Cohen's suggestion that the social skill deficit in autism is selective and limited to situations where reading minds is involved. Such a conclusion, according to Klin and Volkmar (1993), is contrary to the clinical picture presented by many if not most individuals with autism.

Other researchers, although also acknowledging that theory of mind deficits contribute to the social incompetence of persons with autism, argued, as did Bruner and Feldman (1993), that these deficits are "a *consequence* of a more pervasive (and perhaps ultimately even more maladaptive) deficit in general cognitive functioning" (p. 286). Bruner and Feldman (1993) speculated that this general cognitive deficit consists of "a sharply reduced ability to encode experience (or create meaning) in a narrative mode" (p. 286). Fein (personal communication, 1994), taking a different tack, pointed out that differences between autistic and nonautistic samples on various SI measures, including theory of mind, are too weak to be the basis for creating a model of autism. She suggested that such findings can be explained by the fact that autistic individuals have a difficult time attending (or knowing how to attend) to social stimuli, and that social attentional processes may prove to be more important than social comprehension processes in explaining the social behavior of persons with autism.

Mayes, Cohen, and Klin (1993) presented a psychodynamic interpretation of the theory of mind phenomenon, and "suggest that the *desire to be with others* is a necessary precursor to knowing about the mind of the other" (p. 450). The fundamental deficit in persons with autism, according to these researchers, lies in the fact that the "capacity to experience desire for another, to experience the full depth of love in their inner psychic lives is either absent or distorted" (p. 460). They suggested that the competence model implicit in Baron-Cohen's formulation must be complemented by drawing attention to the intrapsychic experiences and affective or motivational context in which social–cognitive development takes place. The fundamental deficit in autism, according to this view, therefore, is the failure to develop the understanding that others (particularly mothers) "appreciate and return their desire for them" (p. 462).

Rutter and Bailey (1993) answered the question of "why the theory of mind hypothesis created such a stir?" (p. 481) by acknowledging the appeal in believing that a disorder with as wide a range of symptomotology as autism "might be explicable in terms of a single narrowly defined psychological process, albeit one with widely pervasive effects" (p. 481). They noted further that "The theory of mind hypothesis was important because it claimed to account for the social abnormality [of autism] in terms of a cognitive deficit" (p. 481). Finally, Rutter and Bailey (1993) noted that "One of the attractions of the theory of mind hypothesis was the possibility that it might provide a lead to the neurobiological basis of autism" (p. 497), because of the evidence suggesting a substantial degree of modularity, that is, of independence from other aspects of cognition. Rutter and Bailey (1993) pointed out that the jury is still very much out on the role and cause of theory of mind deficit in autism. Nevertheless, they acknowledged that the theory of mind hypothesis has contributed greatly to an increased awareness of the role of social cognition in human adaptation, and of the extent to which autism is a disorder in which lack of capacity for social reciprocity is the principal defining characteristic.

In this section, we reviewed the research on SI in persons with autism. Recent work on SI has been useful in fostering a richer understanding of the nature and severity of the interpersonal deficits constituting the disorder. It has also contributed to a better appreciation of the biological, as opposed to functional, basis of this disorder. Under the rubric of "theory of mind," work on SI in autism has been notable for the considerable degree of collaboration among researchers interested in both normative and atypical development. As becomes apparent in the following section, interest in SI has also contributed to ongoing debates over the heterogeneous nature of autism and other developmental disorders.

SI AND DEFINITIONS OF DISABILITY

A basic problem in the construction of classification schemes in the human services is that classification is, to a certain extent, an arbitrary process. In this process, political and economic pressures, along with often unclear scientific findings, contribute to definitions that for the most part use indirect functional criteria to diagnose conditions (such as mild MR or LD) that are in large part social inventions reflecting particular historical conditions that may no longer be operative (Kirk & Kutchins, 1992; Sleeter, 1986; Trent, 1994). As Reynolds (1991) pointed out, classification in the biomedical sciences is based on naturally occuring taxa, that is, relatively clear-cut distinctions ("nature carved at the joints") that typically reflect underlying organic (genotypic or etiological) causes.

The key to devising adequate and acceptable definitions of classes in education and the human services is to ground them, as much as possible, on empirically based (and, therefore, natural) as opposed to politically based (and, therefore, artifical) criteria. This is easier said than done, however, as reflected in the considerable amount of recent journal space devoted to definitional controversies in all three disability areas. Such controversy is a reflection of the confused nature of the empirical literature, the differing political or value agendas that are invoked, and the realities that people often exhibit characteristics that cut across more than one disability category, and the dividing line between normality and disability is often fuzzy and imprecise.

The construct of SI (under various names) has been discussed by scholars and committees seeking to devise better definitions for MR, LD, and autism. Relevant literature is reviewed briefly in this section, with emphasis placed on the extent to which SI might contribute to providing a closer congruence between the artifical class and the natural taxon for each of the categories or (in the case of LD) subcategories addressed.

Implications for Defining MR

Social intelligence has obvious relevance to the definition of MR. Before the invention of the Binet–Simon intelligence scale early in this century, MR was diagnosed informally, mainly on the basis of social behavior, or the perception by others that an individual lacked age-appropriate competence and needed special protection (Bialer, 1973). This emphasis on intelligent social and everyday functioning was replaced in the second decade of the 20th century by an emphasis on subaverage functioning on the various intelligence tests that were modeled on the Binet–Simon measure (Trent, 1994). This measure, as several commentators pointed out, was developed for the French educational authorities during the initial period of compulsory public education, to enable them to identify slow learners. As a result, the initial intelligence tests and their successors are mainly measures of what Sternberg (1984) termed *academic intelligence*, as reflected in the finding that measures of aptitude and achievement are largely isomorphic (Anastasi, 1976).

MR, like other disability categories, is a politically constructed class which utilizes functional rather than biological or etiological definitional criteria, and that is affected by economic and public policy considerations concerning how a given society wishes to treat people considered to be incompetent (Reynolds, 1991; Seltzer & Seltzer, 1991). Membership in this class grew substantially in the early part of this century through the application of vague and rather liberal criteria inspired in large part by the eugenics movement and the enthusiasm for the IQ measure as a basis for combatting crime and other social ills (Trent, 1994). That exclusive reliance on IQ resulted in many false positives in diagnosing MR (with devastating consequences for individuals' lives) was pointed out in this country many decades ago by Doll (1936), who argued that "social competence" should be used in combination with IQ in making the diagnosis. In England, Tredgold (1922) made a similar argument, but carried it a step further in arguing that social competence should be the primary diagnostic criterion. These suggestions finally bore fruit in the United States in the late 1950s, with the adoption by the American Association on Mental Deficiency (AAMD, now AAMR) of a widely emulated dual criteria definition of MR based on low IQ and significant deficits in adaptive behavior (Heber, 1961). Later, this step was supplemented by the elimination of the borderline category, which reduced the IQ cutoff score from 85 to 70, a move that drastically reduced the numbers of people eligible for being considered to have mild MR (Grossman, 1973).

The adaptive behavior construct was operationalized as having two components: relative competence in activities of daily living (or what we have termed *practical intelligence*), and relative absence of maladaptive behavior or psychopathology. Opposition to the use of the adaptive behavior criterion stemmed from those who felt it was a conceptually muddled construct, the inclusion of which would be likely to increase, rather than decrease, confusion regarding the definition of MR (Clausen, 1972; Zigler, Balla, & Hodapp, 1984). Specifically, it was pointed out that adaptive behavior was not defined in a manner that had clear connection to the traditional view of MR as a disorder of the intellect, or to the kinds of activities and challenges likely to face persons in community settings. Dissatisfaction with the adaptive behavior criterion is reflected in the frequent finding that it is often ignored in the field by agencies and professionals, who continue to rely largely on IQ as the sole diagnostic criterion for MR (Adams, 1973; Borthwick-Duffy, 1994).

The potential contribution of SI to the redefinition of MR was pointed out by Greenspan (1979) in the second edition of this volume, and in subsequent publications (Greenspan, 1981b; Greenspan & Granfield, 1992; Greenspan, Switzky, & Granfield, 1996). Specifically, it was argued that where the AAMD (now AAMR) erred in 1961 was in failing to ground the construct of adaptive behavior in what Sternberg (1984) termed *everyday intelligence* and Greenspan termed *adaptive intelligence*; namely, in the two nonacademic components of the tripartite intelligence model: SI and PI. Because PI is typically included as part I of most current adaptive behavior measures, this recommendation essentially calls for substituting social intelligence for the maladaptive behavior component of adaptive behavior. The recommendation to substitute SI and PI for adaptive behavior (or to simply redefine adaptive behavior in those terms) was justified on the basis that it would clarify the construct of MR, by bringing the definition of the class into congruence with the intuitive taxon—namely that of "everyday stupidity"—that was in use (and misuse) long before the invention of the IQ scale.

This recommendation was partially adopted by the AAMR in its most recent effort at revising the definition of MR (Luckasson et al., 1992). Citing Greenspan's (1979, 1981b) earlier theoretical work, the 1992 AAMR manual substituted the construct of *adaptive skills* for the earlier concept of *adaptive behavior*, and noted that these were intended to tap aspects of adaptive intelligence. Although maladaptive behavior, or psychopathology, was noted in a supplementary chapter as a problem for which people with MR are at increased risk, the new manual clearly dropped it from the definition of MR and from the list of adaptive skills. As noted by Greenspan, Switzky, and Granfield (1996), however, the revised definition of MR is not as heavily reliant on the tripartite model of intelligence as the theoretical chapter of the 1992 manual leads one to believe.

The new AAMR definition eases restrictions against entry into the class of MR. This is accomplished in two ways: raising the upper cutoff score from 70 to 75 (justified on the basis of standard error of widely used IQ scales) more than doubles the number of eligible individuals; and establishing a criterion of adaptive skills deficits in only 2 out of 10 skill areas, instead of the more stringent (even if often ignored) requirement of global deficits in adaptive behavior will presumably be a fairly easy hurdle for most service aspirants to clear. Easing restrictions was motivated apparently by concern that elimination of the borderline category in the 1970s disenfranchised some individuals whose needs are similar to those still eligible for services.

Although the tripartite model is used as justification for the shift to adaptive skills, the definition still refers to IQ as the primary criterion and adaptive skills as a secondary means of confirming normality or abnormality in the presence of sufficiently low IQ scores. (However, adaptive skills profile cannot in itself confirm abnormality in the presence of a too-high IQ score.) The list of adaptive skills is derived from an atheoretical community skills curriculum (Ford et al., 1989). As noted by Greenspan et al. (1996), 8 of the 10 skills largely tap practical intelligence, one taps conceptual intelligence, and only one (social skill) taps social intelligence, although other aspects of social competence (i.e., temperament and character) are mixed in with it. Thus, although the 1992 AAMR definitional manual is described as influenced by the tripartite model of intelligence, the role of SI continues to be minimal, at best.

Although there is much to recommend the new definition and classification scheme, it has engendered considerable opposition. Among the provisions objected to are: a move toward increasing eligibility at a time when trends in education and human services are in the opposite direction (MacMillan, Gresham, & Siperstein, 1993); the dropping of the (pre-IQ test) tradition of specifying levels of MR severity; and reliance on a policy agenda (the "support revolution" in disability services) to base definition of a scientific field (Jacobson & Mulick, 1992). To these arguments, Greenspan et al. (1996) made the additional point that the adoption of the construct of adaptive skills continues the pattern of using invented or artifical criteria. They argued that a more adequate approach would be to define MR as a condition marked by significant deficits in everyday (i.e., social and practical) intelligence reflected in the perception by professionals and laypeople that a person needs special services or supports in order to succeed in everyday life. Although such an approach could be abused (as was the case in the days of arbitrary decisions to institutionalize "mental defectives"), it could—with appropriate safeguards—allow for a more person-centered understanding of individual needs and potential than is typically obtained through the use of more "objective" methods.

Implications for Classifying LD

Increased awareness of research indicating that SI deficit is a primary problem for many individuals with LD caused the Interagency Committee on Learning Disabilities (ICLD, 1987) to propose to Congress a revised definition of LD as "a heterogeneous group of disorders manifested by significant difficulties in the acquisition and use of listening, speaking, reading, writing, reasoning, or mathematical abilities, or of social skills" (p. 222). In contrast, the National Joint Committee on Learning Disabilities (NJCLD, 1988) rejected the idea of social intelligence deficit as a primary basis for the diagnosis by stating that "problems in self-regulatory behaviors, social perception, and social interaction may exist with learning disabilities but do not by themselves constitute a learning disability" (p. 1). The ICLD effort to make it possible for a socially inept person to be diagnosed as LD without deficits in one or more academic disciplines stimulated much controversy in the literature. Key points made in this exchange follow.

Conte and Andrews (1993) summarized the arguments in favor of the ICLD proposal, arguing that there is an integral relationship between LD and social skills, noting that the rejection of LD children ". . . is related to inefficient and deficient use of language in social contexts" (p. 147), with such poor language use being a central problem for most people with LD. They went on to argue that "there may be a specific neural substrate underlying social skills deficit" (p. 148), and that even if many children with LD have normal social skills, "no one learning problem would be expected to affect all individuals who are diagnosed as learning disabled" (pp. 148–149).

Returning to the theme of social skill deficit as reflecting language deficits, Conte and Andrews (1993) pointed out that the two major aspects of communication—listening and speaking—are obviously related to social skills and can be considered to occur only within a social context. Addressing the political objection that the ICLD proposal would increase eligibiity under PL 94-142, they noted that scientific criteria, not political ones, should be used to create the basis for a scientific discipline. They asserted that LD should be based on deficits in domains that are central to functioning and success in important life settings, with few domains being more critical to life success than social skills.

Finally, Conte and Andrews argued that LD should be redefined in a manner that emphasizes deficits in intentional—but not in incidental—learning, within instructional contexts, as central to the diagnosis. Although social skill deficits may not necessarily meet this criterion, none of the proposed definitions of LD do either. Therefore, the notion of social skill LD should be supported because it is congruent with existing definitions, and because it is a problem that appears to underly much of the school-related difficulties of many students for whom LD would appear to be an appropriate diagnosis.

An opposing position was taken by Gresham (1992, 1993; Gresham & Elliot, 1989). Although a leading researcher in the area of social incompetence of persons with LD, Gresham tends to view such incompetence as a secondary phenomenon, rather than reflecting primary aspects of the disability. The main points made by Gresham in opposition to the position of the ICLD and the defense by Conte and Andrews are: (a) *social skills* is a highly confused construct, the meaning of which is not clear, and it is undesirable to attempt to clarify a muddled construct like LD by embedding within it a construct that is even more confused; (b) the ICLD position that social skills deficits are caused by neurologic dysfunctions is based on weak evidence, most of which is descriptive rather than causal; (c) although many LD children experience social skill difficulty, evidence suggests these difficulties—which are common, and not unique to LD—may reflect attentional or conduct disorders rather than academic disorders; (d) although children with LD are more likely to be socially incompetent, this correlation probably reflects intellectual differences, as indicated in the fact that low-achieving (but non-LD) individuals are also more likely to be socially incompetent; and (e) there is little support for the view that social skill deficits (which are related to pragmatic aspects of language use) are reflective of a general language disorder.

Forness and Kavale (1991) also weighed in against the ICLD position, and made several additional arguments, the main one being that it would make it possible to diagnose someone as LD with a social skill deficit but no academic deficits. This would hopelessly muddle the distinction between LD and other categories of exceptionality—particularly severe emotional disturbance—and would undermine the traditional view of LD as a primarily academic disorder. Forness and Kavale also questioned the empirical basis for the assertion that social skill deficit is an inevitable by-product of LD, and noted that many studies found significant numbers of LD persons to have normal social skills.

Although the arguments against accepting the ICLD position are compelling, the tendency (on both sides) to focus on whether or not social skill deficit is an inevitable consequence of LD begs the question of whether it is appropriate to construct a subtypology of LD in which existence or nonexistence of social skill (or SI) deficit is a legitimate classificatory question. It may, furthermore, be inappropriate to use findings of research conducted within the existing model of LD to argue against a proposed new way of defining the disorder. Little mention is made by either side in this controversy of what would appear to be the most compelling reason for establishing a new subtypology of LD utilizing SI criteria, namely that large numbers of such individuals may be falling between the cracks of existing service systems.

A significant literature has developed addressing social incompetence issues within the context of LD subtyping. For the most part, this literature differs from the ICLD position in that such social incompetence is usually seen as an accompaniment of academic difficulty (although of an atypical nature) rather than as something that exists in the absence of any academic difficulty. In the remainder of this section, we review briefly some of the recent literature on SI deficit as a subtype of LD.

Undoubtedly, a portion of the socially incompetent subpopulation of system-identified LD children is made up of individuals who might at one time have qualified for the label of educably mentally retarded (EMR). As noted by Zetlin and Murtaugh (1990), with the elimination in the 1970s of the borderline category of MR, large numbers of academically and socially incompetent children have been disenfranchised from educational services. The fact that 30% or more of students identified by school systems as LD fit better the profile of students with borderline or mild MR suggests a likely spillover effect from exclusionary trends in MR eligibility (MacMillan, 1993).

Most of the literature on SI deficit as a subtype of LD has, however, focused on individuals of relatively normal IQ, and who have some specific difficulty in processing social information. Early mention of this phenomenon was made by Johnson and Myklebust (1971) and Myklebust (1975), who focused on what they termed "social imperception." A variety of terms have been used since then to describe individuals who manifest such problems as lack of finesse and impaired pragmatic communication skills in relationships with others. These include social misperception syndrome (Spafford & Grosser, 1993), developmental learning disabilities (Tranel, Hall, Olson, & Tranel, 1987), comportmental learning disabilities (Price, Daffner, Stone, & Mesulam, 1990), right hemisphere deficit syndrome (Voeller, 1986), pragmatic disability (McTear & Conti-Ramsden, 1992) and social–emotional learning disabilities (Voeller, 1991).

One of the most interesting features of recent writing about SI deficits is the increasing emphasis on the possible contribution of brain-related structural and chemical abnormalities to the problem of social ineptness. Such interest reflects a growing awareness that environment and learning history alone cannot explain the failure of some individuals to develop normal social competence, and that social functioning, in line with other areas of functioning, may be affected by specific neurological dysfunctions. Although this literature has implications for a broad range of disabilities, including traumatic brain injury as well as autism, we are discussing it under the rubric of LD because of the continuing view of LD by most practitioners as reflective of underlying (even if minor or unknown) brain pathology and because of the already-mentioned tendency of many neuropsychological investigators to refer to such disorders as variations of LD.

Undoubtedly, the best-known body of scholarship relating to this topic is the work of Byron Rourke and colleagues on nonverbal learning disabilities (NLD; Rourke, 1989; Rourke & Fuerst, 1992). In a review of prominent research programs in LD, Torgesen (1993) wrote that "the two most completely developed current causal theories of learning disabilities are the nonverbal learning disabilities syndrome . . . and the theory of reading disabilities involving limitations in phonological processing" (pp. 158–159). Rourke and colleagues noted that persons with NLD are at high risk for being socially imperceptive and ineffective; for example, it is noted that there are "significant deficits in social perception, social judgment, and social interaction skills" (Harnadek & Rourke, 1994, p. 145), and that there is excessive verbosity with poor prosody and pragmatics. As a result of marginalization and isolation in social settings and roles, such individuals are considered to be at risk in adolescence and adulthood for emotional problems, including suicide (Rourke, Young, & Leemars, 1989). However, in spite of a clear claim for NLD as a condition having both academic and interpersonal manifestations, assessment and diagnosis of NLD in Rourke's writings is based solely on profiles of IQ subscale, educational achievement, and neuropsychological measures, and there is no mention in these writings of measuring social behavior or SI directly, as part of the diagnostic process. Although there is some limited amount of research aimed at validating the claims for a link between NLD and poor social competence (e.g., Ozols & Rourke, 1985), much more research is needed in establishing implications of NLD for everyday functioning in nonacademic contexts.

Rourke and Fuerst (1992) noted that NLD children exhibit "significant problems in visual–spatial–organizational, tactile–perceptual, psychomotor and nonverbal problem-solving skills, within a context of clear strengths in psycholinguistic skills. . . . [They] experience their major academic learning difficulties in mechanical arithmetic, while exhibiting advanced levels of word recognition and spelling" (p. 363). Harnadek and Rourke (1994) noted that children with NLD have "extreme difficulty in adapting to novel and otherwise complex situations" (p. 144) and, in the capacity to benefit from both positive and negative feedback, to appreciate incongruities (such as in humor) and to understand cause–effect relationships. Given that social situations are often novel, complex, and involve feedback and incongruity, deficits in these cognitive areas would appear to have obvious relevance to interpersonal functioning. Although, as Torgesen (1993) noted, "Rourke's theory does not identify specific processing deficits of children with NLD within an information-processing model . . ." (p. 159), there has been considerable theorizing, both by Rourke and others about the neuropsychological and neurodevelopmental factors that would appear to explain the identified pattern of academic and social difficulties.

Specifically, Rourke focused on "the destruction or dysfunction of white matter that is required for intermodal integration" (Rourke, 1989, p. 312), a condition that "interferes substantally with 'access' to right hemisphere systems" (p. 312) essential for such intermodal integration. Although destruction of white matter is presumed to most often reflect "developmental" (e.g., prenatal) causes, note was made of such postnatal factors as right hemisphere tissue damage occuring due to hydrocephalus, head injury, or other pathological causes (Harnadek & Rourke, 1994). The nature and severity of particular impairment depends, according to Rourke, on amount, location, and developmental timing of white matter destruction or damage. All persons with NLD are presumed, however, to have deficits in the right hemisphere-based area of intermodal integration of (otherwise routinized) schemas, with this deficit cited as the central factor underlying the various academic and social manifestations of the disorder. Although depression and suicidal ideation associated with NLD was assumed by Rourke and others writing about NLD to be secondary outcomes of increasing social marginalization in adulthood, Semirud-Clikeman & Hynd (1990) implied that such depression may have a similar primary grounding in right-brain pathology.

It was noted (Voeller, 1991) that psychiatric and other nosologies are not yet adequate for describing people with NLD or social deficit aspects of LD. However, slang terms, of a somewhat cruel nature, such as nerd or dork are widely used for that purpose. In a highly interesting and, in spite of its title, scholarly paper, Putnam (1990) discussed the possibility that youth identified by their (typically adolescent) peers as nerds (i.e., as socially inept individuals with poor pragmatic communication skills) have an unrecognized mild form of pervasive developmental disorder similar to Asperger's syndrome. He gave the example of a young man, "Michael," who suffers major depression as a result of unrelenting teasing and rejection by peers. In one episode, Michael fails at "phatic" communication (establishment of an atmosphere of sociability) when he attempts to befriend a peer coming out of a swimming pool by saying in a mechanical tone, "My, you certainly are wet" rather than the more appropriate (and relaxed) "Hey dude, how're you doing?" Michael has no idea why the other young man threw him (fully clothed) into the pool, with the comment "Of course I'm wet. I just got out of the pool, dork."

Putnam pointed out that such young people (typically male) are often diagnosed inappropriately as "schizoid" (suggesting lack of interest in socializing), whereas they want desperately to have social acceptance but lack the SI to attain it. In the case of Michael (who invited 20 people to his birthday party only to have 2 show up) he was incorrectly diagnosed as a depressive, a condition that was actually an outcome of his history of social failure. Putnam's paper lent support to Rourke's argument that individuals with NLD (a concept closely related to nerdism) are at much higher than average risk of suicide. Putnam suggested, however, an alternative neurological explanation for nerdism, based on Brothers' (1989) hypothesis—stemming from animal studies—about the connection between the amygdala and the capacity for empathy.

The term *comportmental learning disabilities* was coined by Price et al. (1990) to describe individuals who demonstrate "a specific type of learning disability in the realms of insight, foresight, social judgment, empathy, and complex reasoning" (p. 1383). The authors presented two case studies involving individuals who suffered severe bilateral frontal lobe damage in infancy or early childhood. These individuals, now in their 20s, were found to have significant impairments on a battery of role-taking and moral judgment tasks. Price et al. (1990) suggested, based on these and other cases in the literature, that this type of brain damage may contribute to delinquency (of a particularly clumsy and immature nature) and other forms of social incompetence. They attempted to differentiate this syndrome from the kind associated with right hemisphere damage, which they characterized as involving "shyness, chronic emotional difficulties, poor paralingustic abilities, and impaired visuospatial skills" (p. 1390), a form of learning disability that was also described by Weintraub and Mesulam (1983). Although such a differentiation is not really justified by their (rather weak) data, this case report provides further evidence of the growing interest in the connection between brain injury and social ineptness and social cognition deficit.

An obvious complication in any effort to identify SI deficit as a distinct subtype of LD is the likelihood of some overlap with the category of attention deficit-hyperactivity disorders (ADHD). Voeller (1991) commented on the large numbers of children with "right hemisphere deficit syndrome" who also were identified as having attention deficit disorders. Greenspan, Apthorp, and Williams (1991) noted that college students with LD who manifested characteristics of extreme SI deficit were more likely to have been diagnosed earlier as having ADHD. Several studies have reported social ineptness as a characteristic of many ADHD children, and there is considerable overlap between NLD and ADD without hyperactivity (Epstein, Shaywitz, Shaywitz, & Woolston, 1991; Fletcher, Morris, & Francis, 1991). Such overlap reflects two realities: (a) that neurologically based disorders manifest themselves in many ways, with attentional problems cutting across a number of brain-based disorders, and (b) that the ADHD category is often used, perhaps inappropriately, as a convenient dumping ground for such individuals, given the absence of any more suitable nosological category.

The possiblility that a common neurological cause may underlie the SI deficits noted in a number of disability categories was pointed out by McTear and Conti-Ramsden (1992), Semirud-Clikeman and Hynd (1990), Voeller (1991), and others. In addition to citing ADHD as a condition that overlaps considerably with NLD and other postulated SI-based LD subtypes, it was pointed out that LD and autism (particularly Asperger's syndrome or higher-functioning autism) may in fact be different points on the same continuum (Schopler, 1985; Shea & Mesibov, 1985). Conversely, as pointed out by Taylor and Cadet (1989), the common forms of social ineptness found in many people whose behavior—although exasperating—is considered normal, may reflect a benign form of this disorder.

Implications for Defining Autism

As with mental retardation and learning disabilities, debate over the proper definition and classification of autism centers around the effort to uncover a core deficit common to all who qualify for the label. Without necessarily using the term, scholars are converging on a severe absence of SI as the central defining characteristic of the disorder. As recounted by Borden and Ollendick (1992), there is increasing conviction that a lack of reciprocity in social relationships (terminology used by Rutter & Garmezy, 1983) is the central defining feature of autism and pervasive developmental disorders (PDD).

This view of autism is reflected in the recently released fourth edition of the *Diagnostic and Statistical Manual of Mental Disorders* (*DSM–IV*; American Psychiatric Association, 1994). The first criterion listed in the conceptual definition of PDD is a severe and pervasive impairment in "reciprocal social interaction skills" (APA, 1994, p. 65). This is also the first criterion mentioned with regard to two major subtypes of PDD: autistic disorder and Asperger's disorder. Two rarer PDD subtypes involving more overt biological symptoms—Rett's disorder and childhood disintegrative disorder—are not as clearly defined in SI deficit terms, whereas a residual "atypical" category is not as reliant on any particular symptom pattern.

The inclusion of Asperger's disorder (more commonly referred to as Asperger's syndrome) in *DSM–IV* reflects an obvious need to differentiate between the approximately 75% of people with PDD whose low IQ qualifies them for the secondary label of mild or moderate MR, and the 25% with relatively normal academic intelligence and PI. In terms of the tripartite model of intelligence discussed earlier, Asperger's disorder represents a form of pure SI deficit, whereas autistic disorder typically involves deficits in other areas of intelligence as well (Volkmar & Cohen, 1988). In stating, however, that both of these disorders involve problems in SI, one should not lose sight of the possibility of qualitative differences in the nature of SI deficit across disorders and individuals. These qualitative differences reflect the specific nature of SI-related skills and deficits. That Asperger's disorder (and, even more so, nonverbal LD) is less severely disabling than autistic disorder is due to two things: greater competence in academic and practical areas of intelligence, and greater likelihood (this is speculative) that SI deficits will manifest themselves more in situations of ambiguity or stress, and that individuals would demonstrate competence in developmentally more primitive SI skills (such as perceptual perspective taking).

In terms of the first author's broader model of personal–social competence, it should be noted that both forms of PDD can be conceptualized not only in terms of areas of intellectual deficit, but also in aspects of temperament and character. A major factor that distinguishes both autism and Asperger's disorder from related cognitive disorders such as nonverbal LD (a sister to Asperger's disorder) and MR (a sister to autistic disorder) is the presence in the two varieties of PDD of repetitive behavior patterns of an obsessional or stereotypic nature. Although obsessional behavior is characteristic of both varieties of PDD, a likely distinction between people with Asperger's disorder and people with "high functioning autism"—two terms that have largely been used interchangeably—is that these compulsions may be even more dramatic in people with Asperger's disorder (Tantam, 1991). In addition to this difference in temperament, there are differences in character as well. As noted in *DSM–IV* and in the literature (Borden & Ollendick, 1992), people with autistic or Asperger's disorder typically lack interest in interacting with others, a quality that—in spite of their often limited success in such interactions—does not characterize the majority of people with NLD or MR.

As with other disability categories, however, one must resist the temptation to overgeneralize about the extent to which persons with autism all share the same behavioral characteristics and patterns. Wing and her colleagues (Wing & Atwood, 1987; Wing & Gould, 1979) identified three "social subtypes"—based on degree and type of social impairment—that she believed characterized the behavioral patterns exhibited by the vast majority of persons with autistic and autisticlike symptoms (she also identified a fourth social subtype, which she considered characteristic of individuals with MR). These are: (a) aloof individuals who avoid interaction with others, (b) passive individuals who accept interactions initiated by others but who do not actively seek such interactions, and (c) active but odd individuals who make social approaches, but who do so to meet their own repetitive and idiosyncratic interests.

The first of these categories has been found to be most common among autistic individuals and to best differentiate between persons with and without autism, although individuals with autism may be found in all three categories. Volkmar and his colleagues (Volkmar, Bregman, Cohen, Hooks, & Stevenson, 1989; Volkmar & Klin, 1993), although noting the reliability and clinical utility of this typology, presented evidence suggesting that MA is the variable most likely to predict into which social subtype an individual with autism is likely to fall. According to this explanation, the predominance of the aloof subtype in autistic individuals may be viewed as an artifact of the low-IQ status of the majority of individuals with autism (the confounding of social subtype and MA level may be explained in part by Wing's inclusion of IQ level as one of the several diagnostic criteria proposed by her for each of the three subtypes).

A problem with the Wing typology is that it appears to focus primarily on relative lack of interest in socializing, with relative capacity for socializing (or SI) given little prominence. Although relative lack of interest in socializing is certainly a characteristic of persons with autism, most scholars today would probably consider this lack of interest to be reflective of (or, at the least, an accompaniment to) significant limitations in intuitive as well as reflective aspects of social intelligence. An alternative typology, which would be closer in spirit to the emphasis on social reciprocity in *DSM–IV* and current thinking about autism, would emphasize relative degree of SI deficit in social relations rather than relative degree of interest in such relations. Such a typology would be congruent with the assertion of Volkmar and his colleagues about the underlying role of MA (given that SI level and MA level are probably closely correlated in persons with autism) and would form a more logical basis for the development of a continuum having some of the characteristics of developmental stages.

CONCLUSION

In this chapter, we have discussed social intelligence as what Wellman (1990), writing about theory of mind, termed a "broad framework theory." Recent interest in SI reflects the growing awareness that development of social skills is a critical mediator between impairment as an input and disability as an outcome, regardless of the nature of one's handicapping condition. MR and autism may be considered severely disabling conditions precisely because of the greatly diminshed likelihood of developing levels of SI adequate for successful independent life. LD is generally considered a mildly disabling condition, precisely because most people with this label develop normal (or at least minimally adequate) SI, and are therefore able to "pass" as normal. However, some people with LD (informally, but with increasing frequency referred to as "severely LD") have serious problems in the area of SI—either because they "really" have MR or because they have specific deficits in the ability to process interpersonal information—and these people are reported to be at increased risk for living marginal, isolated, and unhappy lives.

Excessive reliance on a main effects model for conducting research on social competence in all three disability areas has tended to exaggerate the extent of homogeneity within disability categories, and distinctness from other categories (including "normality"). Considerable variability in level of SI, and other more personological aspects of social competence, may be found among individuals in all three of these categories. Implications of this heterogeneity for everyday life appear to be substantial, although more research in this area is badly needed. Fascinating work on the neuropsychology of SI, although preliminary and inconclusive in nature, suggests that SI deficit may be organically based to an extent that has been insufficiently appreciated. Although such research should be encouraged, validation of any neurological model of social incompetence must be carried out in a manner that attends to the meaning of social behavior and the contexts in which social behavior occurs.

Interest in SI is part of an increased awareness of the interactive nature of disability and of the limitations inherent in relying excessively on IQ (or what we have termed *academic intelligence*). The construct of SI provides an opportunity to view individuals with disabilities in a broader and more meaningful way. Research in SI is potentially useful in promoting a greater understanding of how persons with disabilities fit in with the new community contexts in which they are increasingly living, working, and studying.

REFERENCES

Adams, J. (1973). Adaptive behavior and measured intelligence in the classification of mental retardation. *American Journal of Mental Deficiency, 78*, 77–81.

American Psychiatric Association. (1994). *Diagnostic and statistical manual of mental disorders* (4th ed.). Washington, DC: Author.

Anastasi, A. (1976). *Psychological testing* (4th ed.). New York: Macmillan.

Baron-Cohen, S. (1993). From attention-goal psychology to belief-desire psychology: The development of a theory of mind and its dysfunction. In S. Baron-Cohen, H. Tager-Flusberg, & D. J.

Cohen (Eds.), *Understanding other minds: Perspectives from autism* (pp. 59–82). Oxford, England: Oxford University Press.

Baron-Cohen, S., Leslie, A. M., & Frith, U. (1985). Does the autistic child have a "theory of mind"? *Cognition?, 21*, 37–46.

Baron-Cohen, S., Tager-Flusberg, H., & Cohen, D. J. (Eds.). (1993). *Understanding other minds: Perspectives from autism*. Oxford, England: Oxford University Press.

Bialer, I. (1973). Mental retardation as a diagnostic construct. In I. Bialer & M. Sternlicht (Eds.), *The psychology of mental retardation: Issues and approaches* (pp. 67–123). New York: Psychological Dimensions, Inc.

Binet, A., & Simon, T. H. (1976/1905). The necessity of establishing the scientific diagnosis of inferior states of intelligence. In M. Rosen, G. Clark, & M. Kivitz (Eds.), *History of mental retardation: Collected papers* (Vol. 1, pp. 329–354). Baltimore, MD: University Park Press.

Borden, M. C. & Ollendick, T. H. (1992). The development and differentiation of social subtypes in autism. In B. B. Lahey & A. E. Kazdin (Eds.), *Advances in clinical child psychology* (Vol. 14, pp. 61–106). New York: Plenum.

Borthwick-Duffy, S. (1994). Review of 1992 AAMR manual. *American Journal of Mental Retardation, 98*, 541–544.

Brody, N. (1992). *Intelligence* (2nd ed.). San Diego, CA: Academic Press.

Brothers, P. (1989). A biological perspective on empathy. *American Journal of Psychiatry, 146*, 10–19.

Bruner, J., & Feldman, C. (1993). Theories of mind and the problem of autism. In S. Baron-Cohen, H. Tager-Flusberg, & D. J. Cohen (Eds.), *Understanding other minds: Perspectives from autism* (pp. 267–291). Oxford, England: Oxford University Press.

Bryan, T. H. (1982). Social skills of learning disabled children and yout: An overview. *Learning Disability Quarterly, 5*, 332–333.

Bryan, T. (1991). Assessment of social cognition: Review of research in learning disabilities. In H. L. Swanson (Ed.), *Handbook on the assessment of learning disabilities: Theory, research, and practice* (pp. 285–311). Austin, TX: Pro-Ed.

Bryan, T., & Bryan, J. (1990). Social factors in learning disabilities: An overview. In H. L. Swanson & B. Keogh (Eds.), *Learning disabilities: Theoretical and research issues* (pp. 131–140). Hillsdale, NJ: Lawrence Erlbaum Associates.

Cantor, N., & Kihlstrom, J. F. (1987). *Personality and social intelligence*. Englewood Cliffs, NJ: Prentice-Hall.

Carroll, J. B. (1986). What is intelligence? In R. J. Sternberg & D. K. Detterman (Eds.), *What is intelligence?: Contemporary viewpoints on its nature and definition* (pp. 51–54). Norwood, NJ: Ablex.

Chadsey-Rusch, J. (1992). Toward defining and measuring social skills in employment settings. *American Journal of Mental Retardation, 96*, 405–418.

Chandler, M. J. (1973). Egocentrism and antisocial behavior: The assessment and training of social perspective-taking skills. *Developmental Psychology, 9*, 326–337.

Chandler, M. J., & Greenspan, S. (1972). Ersatz egocentrism: A reply to H. Borke. *Developmental Psychology, 7*, 104–106.

Chandler, M. J., Greenspan, S., & Barenboim, C. (1973). Judgments of intentionality in response to videotaped and verbally presented moral dilemmas: The medium is the message. *Child development, 44*, 315–320.

Clausen, J. (1972). Quo vadis, AAMD? *Journal of Special Education, 6*, 51–60.

Conte, R., & Andrews, J. (1993). Social skills in the context of learning disability definitions: A reply to Gresham and Elliot and directions for the future. *Journal of Learning Disabilities, 26*, 146–153.

Dennett, D. (1978). *Brainstorms: Philosophical essays on mind and psychology*. Bennington, VT: Harvester Press.

Dodge, K. A. (1986). A social information-processing model of social competence in children. In M. Perlmutter (Ed.), *Cognitive perspectives on children's social and behavioral development: The*

Minnesota Symposia on Child Psychology (Vol. 18, pp. 77–125). Hillsdale, NJ: Lawrence Erlbaum Associates.

Doll, E. A. (1936). President's address: Current thoughts on mental deficiency. *Journal of Psycho-Asthenics, 18*, 40–41.

Edmonson, B., deJung, J. E., Leland, H., & Leach, E. (1974). *The test of social inference.* Freeport, NY: Educational Activities, Inc.

Ellis, W. K., & Rusch, F. R. (1991). Supported employment: Current practices and future directions. In J. L. Matson & J. A. Mulick (Eds.), *Handbook of mental retardation* (2nd ed., pp. 478–488). New York: Pergamon.

Epstein, M. A., Shaywitz, S. E., Shaywitz, B A. & Woolston, J. L. (1991). The boundaries of attention deficit disorder. *Journal of Learning Disabilities, 24*, 78–86.

Fein, D., Lucci, D., Braverman, M., & Waterhouse, L. (1992). Comprehension of affect in context in children with pervasive developmental disorders. *Journal of Child Psychology and Psychiatry, 33*, 1157–1167.

Fein, D., Pennington, B., & Waterhouse, L. (1987). Implications of social deficits in autism for neurological dysfunction. In E. Schopler & G. B. Mesibov (Eds.), *Neurobiological issues in autism* (pp. 127–144). New York: Plenum.

Fletcher, J. M., Morris, R. D., & Francis, D. J. (1991). Methodological issues in the classification of attention-related disorders. *Journal of Learning Disabilities, 24*, 72–77.

Ford, A., Schnorr, R., Meyer, L. Davern, L., Black, J., & Dempsey, P. (1989). *The Syracuse community-referenced curriculum guide.* Baltimore, MD: Brookes.

Forness, S. R., & Kavale, K. A. (1991). Social skills deficits as primary learning disabilities: A note on problems with the ICLD diagnostic criteria. *Learning Disabilities Research & Practice, 6*, 44–49.

Gardner, H. (1983). *Frames of mind.* New York: Basic Books.

Gardner, H. (1993). *Multiple intelligences: The theory in practice.* New York: Basic Books.

Goodnow, J. J. (1986). A social view of intelligence. In R. J. Sternberg & D. K. Detterman (Eds.), *What is intelligence?: Contemporary viewpoints on its nature and definition* (pp. 85–90). Norwood, NJ: Ablex.

Goodnow, J. J. (1988). Some lifelong everyday forms of intelligent behavior: Organizing and reorganizing. In R. J. Sternberg & R. K. Wagner (Eds.), *Practical intelligence: Nature and origins of competence in the everyday world* (pp. 143–162). Cambridge, England: Cambridge University Press.

Gottlieb, J., Alter, M., & Gottlieb, B. W. (1991). Mainstreaming mentally retarded children. In J. L. Matson & J. A. Mulick (Eds.), *Handbook of mental retardation* (2nd ed., pp. 63–73). New York: Pergamon.

Greenspan, S. (1979). Social intelligence in the retarded. In N. R. Ellis (Ed.), *Handbook of mental deficiency, psychological theory and research* (2nd ed., pp. 483–531). Hillsdale, NJ: Lawrence Erlbaum Associates.

Greenspan, S. (1981a). Defining childhood social competence: A proposed working model. In B. K. Keogh (Ed.), *Advances in Special Education* (Vol. 3, pp. 1–39). Greenwich, CT: JAI.

Greenspan, S. (1981b). Social competence and handicapped individuals: Implications of a proposed model. In B. K. Keogh (Ed.), *Advances in Special Education* (Vol. 3, pp. 41–82). Greenwich, CT: JAI.

Greenspan, S., Apthorp, H., & Williams, P. (1991). Social competence and work success of college students with learning disabilites. *Journal of Postsecondary Education and Disability, 9*, 227–234.

Greenspan, S., & Driscoll, J. (in press). The role of intelligence in a broad model of personal competence. In D. P. Flanagan, J. L. Genshaft & P. L. Harrison (Eds.), *Beyond traditional intellectual assessment: Contemporary and emerging theories, tests, and issues.* New York: Guilford.

Greenspan, S., & Granfield, J. M. (1992). Reconsidering the construct of mental retardation: Implications of a model of social competence. *American Journal on Mental Retardation, 96*, 442–453.

Greenspan, S., & McGrew, K. (1996). Reply to Mathias and Nettelbeck on the structure of competence: Need for theory-based methods to test theory-based questions. *Research in Developmental Disabilities, 17,* 145–152.

Greenspan, S., & Shoultz, B. (1981). Why mentally retarded adults lose their jobs: Social competence as a factor in work adjustment. *Applied Research in Mental Retardation, 2,* 23–38.

Greenspan, S., Shoultz, B., & Weir, M. M. (1981). Social judgment and work success of mentally retarded adults. *Applied Research in Mental Retardation, 2,* 335–346.

Greenspan, S., Switzky, H., & Granfield, J. (1996). Everyday intelligence and adaptive behavior. In J. Jacobson & J. Mulick (Eds.), *Manual of diagnosis and practice in mental retardation* (pp. 127–135). Washington, DC: American Psychological Association.

Gresham, F. M. (1983). Social skills assessment as a component of mainstreaming placement decisions. *Exceptional Children, 49,* 331–338.

Gresham, F. M. (1992). Social skills and learning disabilities: Causal, concomitant, or correlational? *School Psychology Review, 21,* 348–360.

Gresham, F. M. (1993). Social skills and learning disabilities as a type III error: Rejoinder to Conte and Andrews. *Journal of Learning Disabilities, 26,* 154–158.

Gresham, F. M., & Elliot, S. N. (1989). Social skills deficits as a primary learning disability. *Journal of Learning Disabilities, 22,* 120–124.

Grossman, H. (Ed.). (1973). *Manual on terminology and classification in mental retardation* (Special Publication No. 2). Washington, DC: American Association on Mental Deficiency.

Guilford, J. P. (1967). *The nature of human intelligence.* New York: McGraw-Hill.

Guralnick, M. J. (1992). A hierarchical model for understanding children's peer-related social competence. In S. L. Odom, S. R. McConnell, & M. A. McAvoy (Eds.), *Social competence in young children with disabilities* (pp. 37–64). Baltimore, MD: Brookes.

Harnadek, M. C. S., & Rourke, B. P. (1994). Principal identifying features of nonverbal learning disabilities in children. *Journal of Learning Disabilities, 27,* 144–154.

Heber, R. A. (1961). A manual on terminology and classification in mental retardation. *American Journal on Mental Retardation,* Monograph Supplement.

Hobson, P. (1984). Early childhood autism and the question of egocentrism. *Journal of Autism and Developmental Disorders, 14,* 85–104.

Hobson, P. (1993). Understanding persons: The role of affect. In S. Baron-Cohen, H. Tager-Flusberg, & D. J. Cohen (Eds.), *Understanding other minds: Perspectives from autism* (pp. 204–227). Oxford, England: Oxford University Press.

Howlin, P. (1986). An overview of social behavior in autism. In E. Schopler & G. B. Mesibov (Eds.), *Social behavior in autism* (pp. 103–131). New York: Plenum.

Hoyle, S. G., & Serafica, F. C. (1988). Peer status of children with and without learning disabilities: A multimethod study. *Learning Disability Quarterly, 11,* 322–332.

Inhelder, B. (1966). Cognitive-developmental contributions to the diagnosis of some phenomena of mental deficiency. *Merrill-Palmer Quarterly, 12,* 299–319.

Interagency Committee on Learning Disabilities. (1987). *Learning diabilities: A report to the Congress.* Washington, DC: U.S. Department of Health and Human Services.

Jackson, S. C., Enright, R. D., & Murdock, J. Y. (1987). Social perception problems in adolescents with learning disabilities: Developmental lags versus perceptual deficit. *Journal of Learning Disabilities, 20,* 361–364.

Jacobson, J. W., & Mulick, J. A. (1992). A new definition of MR or a new definition of practice? *Psychology in Mental Retardation and Developmental Disabilities, 18,* 9–14.

Johnson, D. J., & Myklebust, H. R. (1971). *Learning disabilities.* New York: Grune & Stratton.

Kirk, H., & Kutchins, S. (1992). *The selling of DSM: The rhetoric of science in psychiatry.* Hawthorne, NY: Aldine de Gruyter.

Klin, A., & Volkmar, F. (1993). The development of individuals with autism: Implications for the theory of mind hypothesis. In S. Baron-Cohen, H. Tager-Flusberg & D. J. Cohen (Eds.), *Understanding other minds: Perspectives from autism* (pp. 317–334). Oxford, England: Oxford University Press.

Leffert, J. S., & Siperstein, G. N. (1996). Assessment of social-cognitive processes in children with mental retardation. *American Journal on Mental Retardation, 100,* 441–455.

Lord, C. (1993). The complexity of social behavior in autism. In S. Baron-Cohen, H. Tager-Flusberg, & D. J. Cohen (Eds.), *Understanding other minds: Perspectives from autism* (pp. 292–316). Oxford, England: Oxford University Press.

Luckasson, R., Coulter, D. L., Polloway, E. A., Reiss, S., Schalock, R. L., Snell, M. E., Spitalnik, D. M., & Stark, J. A. (1992). *Mental retardation: Definition, classification, and systems of support* (9th ed.). Washington, DC: American Association on Mental Retardation.

MacMillan, D. (1993). Broadening the scope of classification research: Conceptual and ecological perspectives. In G. R. Lyon, D. B. Gray, J. F. Kavanaugh, & N. A. Krasnegor (Eds.), *Better understanding learning disabilities: New views from research and their implications for education and public policies* (pp. 117–152). Baltimore, MD: Brookes.

MacMillan, D. L., Gresham, F. M., & Siperstein, G. N. (1993). Conceptual and psychometric concerns over the 1992 AAMR definition of mental retardation. *American Journal on Mental Retardation, 98,* 325–335.

Maheady, L., Maitland, G., & Sainato, D. (1984). The interpretation of social interactions by mildly handicapped and nondisabled children. *Journal of Special Education, 18,* 151–159.

Martin, J. E., Rusch, F. R., Lagomarcino, T., & Chadsey-Rusch, J. (1986). Comparison between nonhandicapped and mentally retarded workers: Why they lose their jobs. *Applied Research in Mental Retardation, 7,* 467–555.

Mathias, J. L. (1990). Social intelligence, social competence, and interpersonal competence. *International Review of Research in Mental Retardation, 16,* 125–160.

Mathias, J. L., & Nettelbeck, T. (1992a). Validity of Greenspan's models of adaptive and social intelligence. *Research in Developmental Disabilities, 13,* 113–129.

Mathias, J. L., & Nettelbeck, T. (1992b). Reliability of seven measures of social intelligence in a sample of adolescents with mental retardation. *Research in Developmental Disabilities, 13,* 131–143.

Matson, J. L., & Fee, V. E. (1991). Social skills difficulties among persons with mental retardation. In J. L. Matson & J. A. Mulick (Eds.), *Handbook of mental retardation* (2nd ed., pp. 468–478). New York: Pergamon.

Mayes, L., Cohen, D., & Klin, A. (1993). Desire and fantasy: A psychoanalytic perspective on theory of mind and autism. In S. Baron-Cohen, H. Tager-Flusberg, & D. J. Cohen (Eds.), *Understanding other minds: Perspectives from autism* (pp. 450–465). Oxford, England: Oxford University Press.

McGrew, K., & Bruininks, R. (1990). Defining adaptive and maladaptive behavior within a model of personal competence. behavior. *School Psychology Review, 19,* 53–73.

McGrew, K., Bruininks, R. H., & Johnson, D. R. (1996). Confirmatory factor analysis investigation of Greenspan's model of personal competence. *American Journal on Mental Retardation, 100,* 533–545.

McTear, M. F., & Conti-Ramsden, G. (1992). *Pragmatic disability in children.* San Diego, CA: Singular Publishing Group.

Mundy, P., & Sigman, M. (1989). Specifying the nature of the social impairment in autism. In G. Dawson (Ed.), *Autism: Nature, diagnosis and treatment* (pp. 3–21). New York: Guilford.

Mundy, P., Sigman, M., & Kasari, C. (1993). The theory of mind and joint attention in autism. In S. Baron-Cohen, H. Tager-Flusberg, & D. J. Cohen (Eds.), *Understanding other minds: Perspectives from autism* (pp. 181–203). Oxford, England: Oxford University Press.

Myklebust, H. R. (1975). Nonverbal learning disabilities: Assessment and intervention. In H. R. Myklebust (Ed.), *Progress in learning disabilities. Vol. 3* (pp. 231–301). New York: Grune & Stratton.

National Joint Committee on Learning Disabilities. (1988, April). (Letter to NJCLD member organizations). Washington, DC: Author.

O'Sullivan, M., Guilford, J. P. (1966). *Six factor tests of social intelligence: Manual of instructions and interpretations.* Beverly Hills, CA: Sheridan Psychological Services.

O'Sullivan, M., Guilford, J. P., & DeMille, R. (1965). The measurement of social intelligence. *Reports from the Psychological Laboratory, University of Southern California, 34,* 1–44.

Oswald, D. P., & Ollendick, T. H. (1989). Role taking and social competence in autism and mental retardation. *Journal of Autism and Developmental Disorders, 19,* 119–127.

Ozols, E. J., & Rourke, B. P. (1985). Dimensions of social sensitivity in two types of learning-disabled children. In B. P. Rourke (Ed.), *Neuropsychology of learning disabilities: Essentials of subtype analysis* (pp. 281–301). New York: Guilford.

Ozonoff, S., Pennington, B., & Rogers, S. (1991). Executive function deficits in high-functioning autistic children: Relationship to theory of mind. *Journal of Child Psychology and Psychiatry, 32,* 1081–1106.

Pearl, R., & Cosden, M. (1982). Sizing up a situation: LD children's understanding of social interactions. *Learning Disability Quarterly, 5,* 371–373.

Pearl, R., Donahue, M., & Bryan, T. H. (1985). The development of tact: Children's strategies for delivering bad news. *Journal of Applied Developmental Psychology, 6,* 141–149.

Pearl, R., Donahue, M., & Bryan, T. H. (1986). Social relationships of learning-disabled children. In J. K. Torgeson & B. Y. L. Wong (Eds.), *Psychological and educational perspectives on learning disabilities* (pp. 193–224). San Diego, CA: Academic Press.

Premack, D. (1988). "Does the chimpanzee have a theory of mind?" revisited. In R. W. Byrne & A. Whiten (Eds.), *Machiavellian intelligence: Social expertise and the evolution of intellect in monkeys, apes and humans* (pp. 112–127). Oxford, England: Oxford University Press.

Premack, D. G., & Woodruff, G. (1978). Does the chimpanzee have a theory of mind? *Behavioral and Brain Sciences, 1,* 515–526.

Price, B. H., Daffner, K. R., Stowe, R. M., & Mesulam, M. M. (1990). The comportmental learning disabilities of frontal lobe damage. *Brain,* 1383–1393.

Putnam, N. (1990). Revenge or tragedy: Do nerds suffer from a mild pervasive developmental disorder? *Adolescent Psychiatry, 17,* 51–68.

Reynolds, M. C. (1991). Classification and labeling. In J. W. Lloyd, N. N. Singh, & A. C. Repp (Eds.), *The regular education initiative: Alternative perspectives on concepts, issues, and models* (pp. 29–41). Sycamore, IL: Sycamore.

Rogoff, B., & Lave, J. (1984). *Everyday cognition: Its development in social context* (pp. 220–237). Cambridge, MA: Harvard University Press.

Rogoff, B., & Wertsch, J. (Eds.). (1984). *The zone of proximal development.* San Francisco, CA: Jossey-Bass.

Rosenthal, R., Archer, D., DiMatteo, M. R., Hall, J., & Rogers, P. L. (1979). *Profile of nonverbal sensitivity test.* New York: Irvington.

Rourke, B. P. (1989). *Nonverbal learning disabilities: The syndrome and the model.* New York: Guilford.

Rourke, B. P., & Fuerst, D. R. (1992). Psychosocial dimensions of learning disability subtypes: Neuropsychological studies in the Windsor laboratory. *School Psychology Review, 21,* 361–374.

Rourke, B. P., Young, G. C., & Leemars, A. A. (1989). A childhood learning disability that predisposes those affected to adolescent and adult depression and suicide risk. *Journal of Learning Disabilities, 22,* 169–175.

Rutter, M., & Bailey, A. (1993). Thinking and relationships: Mind and brain (some reflections on theory of mind and autism). In S. Baron-Cohen, H. Tager-Flusberg, & D. J. Cohen (Eds.), *Understanding other minds: Perspectives from autism* (pp. 481–504). Oxford, England: Oxford University Press.

Rutter, M., & Garmezy, N. (1983). Developmental psychopathology. In M. E. Hetherington (Ed.), *Handbook of child psychology* (Vol. 4, pp. 775–911). New York: Wiley.

Sabornie, E. J., Kauffman, J. M., Ellis, E. S., & Marshall, K. J. (1988). Bidirectional and cross-categorical social status of learning disabled, behaviorally disordered and nonhandicapped adolescents. *Journal of Special Education, 21,* 39–56.

Salzberg, C. L., Agran, M., & Lignuris-Kraft, B. (1986). Behaviors that contribute to entry-level employment: A profile of five jobs. *Applied Research in Mental Retardation, 7,* 299–312.

Schopler, E. (1985). Convergence of learning disability, higher-level autism, and Asperger's syndrome. *Journal of Autism and Developmental Disorders, 15*, 359.

Seltzer, M. M., & Seltzer, G. B. (1991). Classification and social status. In J. L. Matson & J. A. Mulick (Eds.), *Handbook of mental retardation* (2nd ed., pp. 150–165). New York: Pergamon.

Semirud-Clikeman, M., & Hynd, G. W. (1990). Right hemisphere dysfunction in nonverbal learning disabilities: Social, academic, and adaptive functioning in adults and children. *Psychological Bulletin, 107*, 196–209.

Shantz, C. U. (1983). Social cognition. In J. H. Flavell & E. M. Markham (Eds.), *Handbook of child psychology: Vol. 3. Cognitive development* (pp. 629–649). New York: Wiley.

Shea, V., & Mesibov, G. B. (1985). Brief report: The relationship of learning disabilities and higher-level autism. *Journal of Autism and Developmental Disorders, 15*, 425.

Simeonsson, R. J., Monson, L., & Blacher, J. (1982). Social understanding and mental retardation. In P. H. Brooks, R. Sperber & C. McCauley (Eds.), *Learning and cognition in the mentally retarded* (pp. 389–417). Hillsdale, NJ: Lawrence Erlbaum Associates.

Simeonsson, R. J., & Rosenthal, S. L. (1991). Qualitative developmental processes. In J. L. Matson & J. A. Mulick (Eds.), *Handbook of mental retardation* (2nd ed., pp. 529–538). New York: Pergamon.

Sleeter, C. E. (1986). Learning disabilities: The social construction of a special education category. *Exceptional Children, 53*, 46–54.

Spafford, C. S., & Grosser, G. S. (1993). The social misperception syndrome in children with learning disabilities: Social causes versus neurological variables. *Journal of Learning Disabilities, 26*, 178–189.

Speece, D. L. (1993). Broadening the scope of classification research: Conceptual and ecological perspectives. In G. R. Lyon, D. B. Gray, J. F. Kavanaugh, & N. A. Krasnegor (Eds.), *Better understanding learning disabilities: New views from research and their implications for education and public policies* (pp. 57–73). Baltimore, MD: Brookes.

Sternberg, R. J. (1984). Macrocomponents and microcomponents of intelligence: Some proposed loci of mental retardation. In P. H. Brooks, R. Sperber, & C. McCauley (Eds.), *Learning and cognition in the mentally retarded* (pp. 89–114). Hillsdale, NJ: Lawrence Erlbaum Associates.

Sternberg, R. J. (1986). A framework for understanding conceptions of intelligence. In R. J. Sternberg & D. K. Detterman (Eds.), *What is intelligence?: Contemporary viewpoints on its nature and definition* (pp. 3–15). Norwood, NJ: Ablex.

Sternberg, R. J. (1988). *The triarchic mind: A new theory of human intelligence*. New York: Viking.

Sternberg, R. J., & Detterman, D. K. (Eds.). (1986). *What is intelligence?: Contemporary viewpoints on its nature and definition*. Norwood, NJ: Ablex.

Sternberg, R. J., & Wagner, R. K. (Eds.). (1986). *Practical intelligence: Nature and origins of competence in the everyday world*. Cambridge, England: Cambridge University Press.

Stone, W. L., & La Greca, A. M. (1994). Social deficits in children with learning disabilities. In A. J. Capute, P. J. Accardo, & B. K. Shapiro (Eds.), *Learning disabilities spectrum: ADD, ADHD and LD* (pp. 155–175). Baltimore, MD: York Press.

Swanson, H. L., & Malone, S. (1992). Social skills and learning disabilities: A meta-analysis of the literature. *School Psychology Review, 21*, 427–443.

Tager-Flusberg, H., Baron-Cohen, S., & Cohen, D. J. (1993). An introduction to the debate. In S. Baron-Cohen, H. Tager-Flusberg & D. J. Cohen (Eds.), *Understanding other minds: Perspectives from autism* (pp. 3–9). Oxford, England: Oxford University Press.

Tantam, D. (1991). Asperger syndrome in adulthood. In U. Frith (Ed.), *Autism and Asperger syndrome* (pp. 147–183). Cambridge, England: Cambridge University Press.

Taylor, E. H., & Cadet, J. L. (1989). Social intelligence: Aneurological system? *Psychological Reports, 64*, 423–444.

Thorndike, E. L. (1920). Intelligence and its uses. *Harper's Magazine, 140*, 227–235.

Torgesen, J. K. (1993). Variations on theory in learning disabilities. In G. R. Lyon, D. B. Gray, J. F. Kavanaugh, & N. A. Krasnegor (Eds.), *Better understanding learning disabilities: New views from research and their implications for education and public policies* (pp. 153–170). Baltimore, MD: Brookes.

Tranel, D., Hall, L. E., Olson, S., & Tranel, N. N. (1987). Evidence for a right-hemisphere developmental learning disability. *Developmental Neuropsychology*, *3*, 113–127.

Tredgold, A. J. (1992). *Mental deficiency.* New York: Wood.

Trent, J. W. (1994). *Inventing the feeble mind: A history of mental retardation in the United States.* Berkeley: University of California Press.

Tur-Kaspa, H., & Bryan, T. (1994). Social information-processing skills of students with learning disabilities. *Learning Disabilities Research and Practice*, *9*, 12–23.

Voeller, K. S. (1986). Right hemisphere deficit syndrome in children. *American Journal of Psychiatry*, *143*, 1004–1009.

Voeller, K. S. (1991). Social-emotional learning disabilities. *Psychiatric Annals*, *21*, 735–741.

Volkmar, F. R., Bregman, J., Cohen, D. J., Hooks, M., & Stevenson, J. (1989). An examination of social typologies in autism. *Journal of the American Academy of Child and Adolescent Psychiatry*, *28*, 82–86.

Volkmar, F. R., & Cohen, D. J. (1988). Classification and diagnosis of childhood autism. In E. Schopler & G. B. Mesibov (Eds.), *Diagnosis and assessment in autism* (pp. 71–90). New York: Plenum.

Volkmar, F. R., & Klin, A. (1993). Social development in autism: Historical and clinical perspectives. In S. Baron-Cohen, H. Tager-Flusberg, & D. J. Cohen (Eds.), *Understanding other minds: Perspectives from autism* (pp. 40–55). Oxford, England: Oxford University Press.

Wagner, R. K., & Kistner, J. A. (1990). Implications of the distinction between academic and practical intelligence for learning-disabled children. In H. L. Swanson & B. Keogh (Eds.), *Learning disabilities: Theoretical and research issues* (pp. 75–92). Hillsdale, NJ: Lawrence Erlbaum Associates.

Wagner, R. K., & Sternberg, R. J. (1986). Tacit knowledge and intelligence in the real world. In R. J. Sternberg & R. K. Wagner (Eds.), *Practical intelligence: Nature and origins of competence in the everyday world* (pp. 51–83). Cambridge, England: Cambridge University Press.

Wechsler, D. (1974). Cognitive, conative, and non-intellective intelligence. In D. Wechsler (Ed.), *Selected papers of David Wechsler* (pp. 36–38). New York: Academic.

Weintraub, S., & Mesulam, M. M. (1983). Developmental learning disabilities of the right hemisphere: Emotional, interpersonal, and cognitive components. *Archives of Neurology, Chicago*, *40*, 463–468.

Weiss, E. (1984). Learning disabled childrens' understanding of social interactions of peers. *Journal of Learning Disabilities*, *17*, 612–614.

Wellman, H. M. (1990). *The child's theory of mind.* Cambridge, MA: MIT Press.

Wimmer, H., & Perner, J. (1983). Beliefs about beliefs: Representation and constraining function of wrong beliefs in young children's understanding of deception. *Cognition*, *13*, 103–128.

Wing, L., & Attwood, A. (1987). Syndromes of autism and atypical development. In D. J. Cohen & A. M. Donnellan (Eds.), *Handbook of autism and pervasive developmental disorders* (pp. 3–19). New York: Wiley.

Wing, L., & Gould, J. (1979). Severe impairments of social interaction and associated abnormalities in children: Epidemiology and classification. *Journal of Autism and Developmental Disorders*, *9*, 11–30.

Wong, B. Y. L., & Wong, R. (1980). Role-taking skills in normal achieving and learning disabled children. *Learning Disability Quarterly*, *3*, 11–18.

Zetlin, A., & Murtaugh, M. (1990). Whatever happened to those with borderline IQs? *American Journal on Mental Retardation*, *95*, 463–469.

Zigler, E., & Balla, D. (Eds.). (1982). *Mental retardation: The developmental-difference controversy.* Hillsdale, NJ: Lawrence Erlbaum Associates.

Zigler, E., Balla, D., & Hodapp, R. (1984). On the definition and classification of mental retardation. *American Journal of Mental Retardation*, *89*, 215–230.

› 13 ‹

Individual Differences in Personality and Motivational Systems in Persons with Mental Retardation

Harvey N. Switzky
Northern Illinois University

Conceptions of personality and motivational processes in persons with mental retardation prior to the 1960s were only loosely related to theoretical models derived from mainstream psychological thought, and virtually none of the available knowledge was based on any sustained systematic study of the behavior of mentally retarded persons. Researchers were concerned primarily with identifying the cognitive deficits that characterized persons with mental retardation. Personality and motivational processes were deliberately ignored because they were viewed as confounding variables that should be controlled in studies on cognitive and learning processes (Haywood, 1971; Haywood & Switzky, 1986; Hobbs, 1963; Hodapp, Burack, & Zigler, 1990; Lipman, 1963). Over the past 30 years there has been a veritable explosion of research on persons with mental retardation (Balla & Zigler, 1979; Haywood & Switzky, 1986; Merighi, Edison, & Zigler, 1990; Zigler & Hodapp, 1991) that has described the complex interplay of personality and motivational processes with cognitive processes within a developmental perspective (Borkowski, Carr, Rellinger, & Pressley, 1990; Borkowski et al., 1992; Haywood, 1977; Haywood, Brooks, & Burns, 1986; Haywood, Meyers, & Switzky, 1982; Haywood & Switzky, 1992; Switzky & Haywood, 1984; Switzky & Heal, 1990). This new conceptualization of mental retardation is consistent with mainstream psychological thought concerning the development of human beings as active problem solvers (Leeper & Hodell, 1989; McCombs & Marzano, 1990; Paris & Newman, 1990; Sternberg & Berg, 1992; Stipek, 1993; Zimmerman & Schunk, 1989), and reflects the accelerating integration of a psychology of mental retardation and a developmental psychology of human growth for all human beings (Borkowski et al., 1990; Feuerstein & Feuerstein, 1991; Feuerstein, Klein, & Tannenbaum, 1991; Haywood & Tzuriel, 1992; Nicholls, Cheung, Lauer, & Pastashnick, 1989; Pintrich & Schrauben, 1992). This chapter begins with an overview of motivational research in mental retardation over the past 30 years. A second section reviews contemporary theories of personality and self-system processes of relevance to mental retardation. A final section provides a synthesis of available research with a view toward future research.

INDIVIDUAL DIFFERENCE VARIABLES IN MENTAL RETARDATION RESEARCH: A BRIEF HISTORY AND CRITIQUE

Attempts to explain the initiation, direction, intensity, and persistence of goal-directed behavior of persons with mental retardation have generally followed the dominant theoretical constructs of the day. A major limitation of many approaches has been that they were derived primarily from the behavior of nonretarded persons and were often forced, extended, or revised in order to incorporate and explain motivated behavior in persons with mental retardation. Although some attempts led to dead ends, others were quite systematic and fruitful in terms of psychological theory building and research related to a better understanding of the behavior of persons with mental retardation (Haywood & Switzky, 1986). The following sections provide a concise review of five theoretical models that have guided research in this area since 1960.

Rigidity Hypothesis

The rigidity hypothesis was one of the earliest formulations regarding the personality structure of persons with mild mental retardation. It was derived from the work of Lewin (1936) and Kounin (1941a, 1941b), who viewed the structure of personality as developmentally dynamic and consisting of inner-personal regions of needs, skills, and habits of behavior. As the individual developed there was an increase in the number and the complexity of these inner-personal regions, a process called *differentiation* that corresponded with the mental age of the individual. The boundaries of each inner-personal region were viewed as also varying in permeability, which allowed information to communicate and flow throughout the whole personality structure. As an individual matured it was believed that the boundaries between inner-personal regions became less permeable, a quality referred to as *rigidity*. To account for the deficient performance of persons with psychosocial mental retardation compared to persons without mental retardation even when matched on mental age (which controlled for the amount and degree of differentiation of cognition) on different laboratory learning tasks, Lewin and Kounin believed that the personality structure of persons with mental retardation was fundamentally different from that of nonretarded persons. The boundaries between the inner-personal regions of mentally retarded persons were believed to be less permeable and more rigid, accounting for the greater perseveration, concreteness, and stereotypical performance observed in the mentally retarded samples. In general, mentally retarded persons appeared to be less inclined to abandon unproductive ideas or unsuccessful strategies in favor of potentially more productive ones than were nonretarded persons (Haywood & Switzky, 1986).

The Lewin–Kounin studies provided a springboard for the most systematic, successful, and sustained series of studies over the last 30 years, emphasizing that the behavior of persons with mental retardation is not primarily due to a fundamentally different and defective personality structure, but to overlooked motivational and environmental variables existing between persons with and without mental retardation. The work of Edward Zigler and his colleagues from Yale University, the Yale Group (reviewed by Hodapp and Zigler in chap. 5 of this volume), systematically demonstrated the interaction of experiential, motivational, and personality processes in persons with mental retardation as it affects all aspects of their daily life experiences. Their work emphasized the operation of motivational processes and attempted to provide some counterbalance to the field's historic research preoccupation with the role of cognitive processes in accounting for the behavior of mentally retarded persons.

Social Learning Theories

Social learning theories were initially developed in order to explain the acquisition of socially relevant behaviors mediated by the operation of a set of internal cognitive processes rather than through the operation of isolated stimulus–response externally reinforced behavioral contingencies. Rotter (1954), one of the early social learning theorists, emphasized the individual's cognitive expectancies (beliefs) concerning the occurrence of reinforcing events (the contingencies of reward) in the individual's social world as well as the perceived value of these reinforcing events as determinants of behavior. Expectancies were determined not only by beliefs about the occurrence of reinforcing events in a particular situation, but also by generalized expectancies concerning the occurrence of reinforcing events in other similar situations (e.g., locus of control). This generalized expectancy for success became manifest in Rotter's notion of success-striving versus failure-avoiding motivational expectancies in individuals.

Rotter's (1954) perspective greatly influenced the work of Rue Cromwell (1963, 1967) and his colleagues (Bialer, 1961; Miller, 1961; Moss, 1958) in their application and extension of social learning theory to the personality and motivational processes of persons with mental retardation. In general, mentally retarded persons were found to: (a) have an external locus of control and failure-avoiding motivational expectancies compared to nonretarded persons (i.e., mentally retarded persons had stronger tendencies to be failure avoiders than success strivers); (b) enter a novel situation with a performance level that was depressed below what would be expected in terms of their psychometric mental age and intelligence; (c) have fewer tendencies than do nonretarded persons to increase effort following a mild failure experience; (d) have fewer tendencies to be "moved" by failure experiences than do nonretarded persons; and (e) blame themselves for lack of task completion rather than blaming their failure to complete the task on external causes (Cromwell, 1963; Haywood & Switzky, 1986). Later research using this theory conducted by Horai and Guarnaccia (1975) showed that contrary to Cromwell's (1963) generalization that mentally retarded persons expect failure and have fewer tendencies to be "moved by it" than do nonretarded persons, mentally retarded persons in this study showed great individual differences in their responses to success and failure. Furthermore, Hoffman and Weiner (1978) showed that the state of being mentally retarded does not inevitably lead to a failure-prone cognitive orientation and that one must be cognizant of the variety of individual differences existing in mentally retarded persons. Only a subset of persons with mental retardation have been found to make attributions (Weiner, 1986) that are counterproductive to achievement strivings (Zoeller, Mahoney, & Weiner, 1983).

Self-Concept Theories

Self-concept theories have increasingly dominated mainstream psychological research from 1940 (Rogers, 1947; Snygg & Combs, 1949) to the present period (Harter, 1983; Leahy, 1985; McCombs, 1988, 1989; McCombs & Marzano, 1990; McCombs & Whisler, 1989; Zimmerman & Schunk, 1989), in spite of the lack of research instruments having adequate reliability and construct validity to test the theory. Research on the self-concept of mentally persons has been sparse and the findings has been inconsistent because of the lack of appropriate instruments, particularly given the limited verbal abilities of people with mental retardation (Balla & Zigler, 1979; Haywood & Switzky, 1986). It might be expected that persons with mental retardation, because of their long history of failure and lack of success, stigmatization, rejection, and cognitive deficiencies, would have lower self-concepts and extreme negative self-perceptions compared to nonretarded persons (Balla & Zigler, 1979; Call, 1968; Covington, 1987; Haywood & Switzky, 1986; Merighi et al., 1990). This expectation has only been partially supported by empirical research. Contrary findings may be the result of unrealistically high self-concepts reported by subjects or unreliable measures. Zigler and his colleagues (Glick & Zigler, 1985) developed a developmental theory of self-concept (see the section on the rigidity hypothesis) that has been applied successfully to persons with mental retardation (Leahy, Balla, & Zigler, 1982; Zigler, Balla, & Watson, 1972) and may give self-concept research new vigor and thrust.

Anxiety Theories

Anxiety theories have also long dominated mainstream psychological research (Cantor, 1963; Covington, 1987; Hill, 1984; Hill & Wigfield, 1984; Sarason, Davidson, Lighthall, Waite, & Ruebusch, 1960; Spielberger, 1972), but have not been successful in increasing our understanding of the motivational systems operating in mentally retarded persons. It could be that the issues discussed previously regarding the self-concept theories (e.g., limited verbal ability of the mentally retarded group, and the lack of suitable research instruments having adequate reliability and construct validity in mentally retarded populations) may be hampering research in this area.

It might be expected that mentally retarded persons, because of their history of failure, social deprivation, and cognitive deficiencies, may have higher levels of anxiety regarding their ability to cope with their life experiences compared to nonretarded persons, and that these higher levels of anxiety may depress even more their competence to solve problems in school, at work, and in the community. Research has shown that persons with mental retardation have higher levels of anxiety than do mental age and chronological age nonretarded matches, with institutionalized mentally retarded samples being more anxious than retarded samples living in the community (Balla & Zigler, 1979). Consistent with the theory, greater anxiety has been associated with lower performance on a test of verbal abstraction (Lipman & Griffith, 1960).

Effectance Motivation and Intrinsic Motivation Theories

Effectance motivation and intrinsic motivation theories have greatly influenced our understanding of exploration, curiosity, mastery, and play behavior both in persons who are mentally retarded and in nonretarded persons (Harter, 1981a, 1987; Harter & Zigler, 1974; Haywood, 1992; Haywood & Switzky, 1986, 1992; Switzky & Haywood, 1974, 1984, 1991, 1992; Switzky & Heal, 1990; Switzky, Haywood, & Isett, 1974; Switzky, Ludwig, & Haywood, 1979; Zigler & Balla, 1982; Zigler & Hodapp, 1991). This area of research has been one of the most fruitful and productive areas of experimentation in aiding us to understand personality and motivational processes in persons with mental retardation. Much of this work in the field of mental retardation has been done by two research groups: the Yale Group and the Peabody-Vanderbilt Group. Both groups were deeply influenced by White's (1959) formulation of effectance motivation or mastery motivation, which theorized that everyone has an intrinsic need to feel competent in his or her world, a need that is associated with the pleasure and sustained performance individuals derive from using their own cognitive resources for their own sake and that is independent from environmentally derived external reinforcement, especially in the domains of exploration, play, curiosity, and mastery of the environment.

The Yale Group conceptualized the motivational problems of persons with mental retardation as due in part to deficient effectance motivation and lack of concern for the intrinsic motivation that inheres in being correct, regardless of whether or not an external agent dispenses the reinforcer for such correctness. This lack of effectance motivation is characterized by being heavily dependent on receiving environmentally derived external reinforcement feedback in order to perform a task (i.e., task extrinsic motivation) and an overreliance on cues from the external environment to help guide behavioral performance (i.e., outerdirectedness) with a concomitant increase in extrinsically motivated behavior. Generally, persons with mild mental retardation—because of their socially depriving life histories, their greater cognitive deficiencies, and related failure experiences, compared to nonretarded persons of the same mental age—have less effectance motivation and more of an extrinsic motivational orientation, leading to different patterns of incentives and reinforcement hierarchies compared to nonretarded persons (Balla & Zigler, 1979; Hodapp et al., 1990, Merighi et al., 1990; Zigler & Balla, 1981, 1982; Zigler & Hodapp, 1991).

Harter (1978, 1983) presented a general model of effectance motivation that could have implications for the development of extrinsic and intrinsic motivational orientations in persons with mental retardation. According to her basic model, the developmental pathways that lead to an intrinsic orientation are associated with positive reinforcement or approval by socialization agents for independent mastery attempts early in children's development. Additionally, socialization agents may model this approval and not reinforce children for dependency on adults. As a result, children internalize two critical self-systems: a self-reward system and a system of standards or mastery goals that diminishes the children's dependency on external extrinsic social reinforcement. This leads to feelings of competence and feelings of being in control of one's successes and failures, and increases children's effectance motivation and intrinsic motivation. This increased sense of intrinsic pleasure enhances one's motivation to engage in subsequent mastery behavior. Thus, children's social environments support their inherent need for mastery over their worlds, with the result that their behavior and incentive systems may be characterized as intrinsically motivated.

The developmental pathways that lead to an extrinsic orientation consist of negative outcomes such as lack of reward for or disapproval of independent mastery attempts, modeling of such disapproval, as well as reinforcement for dependency by adults. Children in these environments increasingly manifest strong needs for external approval and dependence on externally defined behavioral goals. This leads to feelings of low perceived competence and perceptions that external agents and events are controlling what is happening. These feelings of not being in control of one's successes and failures lead to feelings of anxiety in mastery situations and attenuate the motivation to be engaged in mastery behavior. Thus, such a child's effectance motivation is blocked and reduced, resulting in an extrinsic motivational orientation. Children who have experienced early failure and disapproval by socialization agents become children whose behavior is extrinsically motivated. This latter pattern may be especially characteristic of retarded and behaviorally incompetent children (e.g., those who are behaviorally disordered, learning disabled, or have motoric or sensory handicaps), leading them to display ever-greater behavioral deficits than would have been predicted on the basis of their initial incompetence (i.e., the MA deficit). Indeed, given a lifetime exposure to failure experiences, psychosocially retarded children may be more susceptible to the clinical condition known as *learned helplessness*. This analysis is very similar to models derived and extended from the Peabody-Vanderbilt Group (Haywood, 1992; Haywood & Burke, 1977; Haywood & Switzky, 1986, 1992; Haywood et al., 1982; Schultz & Switzky, 1990, 1993; Switzky & Haywood, 1984, 1991; Switzky & Heal, 1990; Switzky & Schultz, 1988), as well as models derived and extended from the Yale Group (Hodapp et al., 1990; Weisz, 1979, 1981, 1990).

The Peabody-Vanderbilt Group has studied the operation of intrinsic motivation as the primary concept in a cognitive theory of motivational orientation (Haywood, 1992; Haywood & Burke, 1977; Haywood & Switzky, 1986, 1992; Schultz & Switzky, 1990; Switzky & Haywood, 1974, 1984, 1991, 1992; Switzky & Schultz, 1988; Switzky et al., 1974, 1979), in which the central idea is behavior for its own sake and its own reward, and in the view that using one's cognitive resources to the fullest is intrinsically gratifying and motivating. The theory of motivational orientation and its key concept of *intrinsic motivation* is related to White's (1959) theory of effectance motivation but was more directly influenced by Hunt's (1963, 1965, 1966, 1971) conception of motivation inherent in information processing and action, the two-factor theory of work motivation formulated by Herzberg (Herzberg, 1966; Herzberg & Hamlin, 1961, 1963; Herzberg, Mausner, & Snyderman, 1959), and later by Bandura's social cognitive learning theories, especially his formulation of the self-system in reciprocal determinism (Bandura, 1977, 1978, 1986a), and Feuerstein's theory of mediational learning experiences (MLE) (Feuerstein, Klein, & Tannenbaum, 1991; Feuerstein & Rand, 1974; Feuerstein, Rand, Hoffman, & Miller, 1980).

The Peabody-Vanderbilt Group investigated individual differences, both in mildly handicapped and in nonhandicapped persons, in task-intrinsic and task-extrinsic motivation, and how these differences affect behavior under specified conditions. Accordingly, they believe that the processes of thinking, learning, and problem solving develop transactionally with task-intrinsic motivation, and related attitudes about learning and thinking, self-concept variables, and habits of working, thinking, and learning (Haywood, 1992; Haywood & Burke, 1977; Haywood & Switzky, 1986, 1992; Haywood, Tzuriel, & Vaught, 1992; Switzky & Haywood, 1984; Tzuriel, 1991). Moreover, they propose that there is a transactional relationship among fluid intelligence, cognitive development, and the development of motivational orientation. (See Borkowski et al., 1990, 1992, for a related theory concerning the relationship among cognitive development, motivation, and problem-solving behavior.) Accordingly, the Peabody-Vanderbilt Group suggests that all children, regardless of their level of fluid intelligence, are born with a general motive to explore and gain mastery over their worlds (i.e., with both curiosity and competence motives; Switzky et al., 1974, 1979). What happens to these motives is a direct function of the consequences both direct and social, of their successive attempts to explore and to gain mastery.

Beginning with the Pavlovian orienting reflex, children's exploratory and mastery behaviors are supported with relative success or failure experiences, and these consequences constitute reinforcing conditions that lead to acceleration or deceleration of these behaviors. Parents' responses to the exploratory and mastery behaviors of their childrens' performance provide feedback regarding the success or failure of the outcomes. Exploratory behaviors of relatively incompetent children (e.g., mentally retarded, learning disabled, behaviorally disordered, motoric or sensory impaired), meeting often with failure, become increasingly less frequent, resulting in less inclination of these relatively incompetent children to: expose themselves to novel stimuli; derive information from their encounters with their environments; and accumulate basic knowledge about their worlds to evaluate, to understand, and to elaborate subsequent new information to induce generalizations about the rules and structures of their worlds. The deficient cognitive development of these children is directed toward the development of the personality trait of task-extrinsic motivation (i.e., the tendency to attend to nontask and therefore non-failure producing aspects of the environment in order to avoid dissatisfaction and failure rather than to seek satisfaction and success).

In contrast, relatively competent children engage similarly in initial attempts to explore and gain mastery; however, these attempts are met by successful feedback by parents and other socializing agents thereby strengthening exploratory and curiosity behaviors and resulting in a greater inclination of these relatively competent children: to expose themselves to novel stimuli; to derive more and more information from their encounters with their environments; to accumulate more basic knowledge about their worlds in order to understand, and to elaborate subsequent new information to induce generalizations about the rules and structures of their worlds; and to develop the personality trait of task-intrinsic motivation (i.e., the tendency to seek success and satisfaction by attending to task-intrinsic aspects of the environment such as, creativity, increased responsibility, new learning, psychological excitement, and task-intrinsic aesthetics). This personality trait of task-intrinsic motivation is later expressed as a greater frequency of choices of activities in response to task-intrinsic incentives than in response to task-extrinsic incentives. On the other hand, the personality trait of task-extrinsic motivation is later expressed as a greater frequency of choices of activities in response to task-extrinsic incentives than in response to task-intrinsic incentives.

The cognitive and motivational aspects of individuals thus develop in a transactional way. For less competent individuals (e.g., mentally retarded, learning disabled, behaviorally disordered, motoric or sensory impaired), lack of external and social feedback of successful exploratory behavior by parents and other socializing agents results in fewer attempts at exploration and knowledge acquisition and the creation of an extrinsic-motivational orientation that creates the conditions of even less exploration and knowledge acquisition and a further slowing of cognitive development, and an increasing extrinsic-motivational orientation, which is known as the "poor get poorer" phenomenon (Haywood, 1992; Haywood & Switzky, 1992; Haywood et al., 1992), which is related to the earlier concept of the "MA deficit" (Haywood & Switzky, 1986; Haywood et al., 1992). The MA deficit refers to the phenomenon that even if retarded persons are matched on mental age with nonretarded younger persons, the retarded persons do less well on a variety of measures of learning and behavioral effectiveness (Lipman, 1963; Stevenson & Zigler, 1958; Zigler, 1971). For more competent individuals, the presence of external and social feedback of successful exploratory behavior by parents and other socializing agents results in accelerating increasing attempts at exploration and knowledge acquisition and the creation of an intrinsic-motivational orientation that creates the conditions of even more exploration and knowledge acquisition and an increasing intrinsic-motivational orientation (the "rich get richer" phenomenon; Haywood, 1992; Haywood & Switzky, 1992; Haywood et al., 1992). Generally, having an intrinsically motivated orientation is an increasing function of chronological age, mental age, psychometric intelligence, and social class. Usually, mentally retarded persons as a group are more extrinsically motivated (EM) compared with nonretarded persons of similar age. However, some mentally persons are found to be intrinsically motivated (IM). See Switzky and Heal (1990) for an extensive discussion of the construct validity of The Picture Motivation Scale (Kunca & Haywood, 1969), the primary instrument used by the Peabody-Vanderbilt Group to assess motivational orientation.

The theory of motivational orientation would predict:

1. That having an IM orientation is helpful to both mentally retarded and nonretarded learners compared to having an EM orientation in terms of learning more effectively. However, having an IM orientation may have more impact on mentally retarded and other dysfunctional and at-risk learners. Generally, these predictions have been confirmed. IM

learners work harder and longer on a task compared to EM learners. IM learners learn more effectively and have higher school achievement (Dobbs, 1967; Haywood, 1968a, 1968b; Haywood & Switzky, 1986; Haywood & Wachs, 1966; Schultz & Switzky, 1993; Wooldridge, 1966; Zewdie, 1995).

2. That there is an interaction between motivational orientation and incentives, such that one must match incentive systems to the unique motivational orientations of individuals, that is, the performance of IM individuals will be optimally reinforced by task-intrinsic incentives, whereas the performance of EM individuals will be optimally reinforced by task-extrinsic incentives. Generally, these predictions have been strongly confirmed (Gambro & Switzky, 1988, 1991; Haywood & Switzky, 1975, 1985, 1986, 1992; Haywood, Tzuriel, & Vaught, 1992; Haywood & Weaver, 1967; Schultz & Switzky, 1990, 1993; Switzky, 1985; Switzky & Haywood, 1974, 1984, 1991, 1992; Switzky & Heal, 1990; Switzky & Schultz, 1988).

3. IM persons may be characterized by self-monitored reinforcement systems that make them less dependent on external reinforcement conditions, whereas EM persons may be characterized by dependence on external reinforcement systems. IM children are more sensitive to task-intrinsic incentives, have high performance standards of internal self-reward, and are more likely to self-reinforce their own behavior, whereas EM children are intensively outer-directed, have very low performance standards of internal self-reward, and are extremely sensitive to the external reinforcement environment. These predictions have been strongly confirmed (Gambro & Switzky, 1988, 1991; Haywood & Switzky, 1975, 1985, 1986, 1992; Switzky & Haywood, 1974, 1991, 1992).

The research of the Peabody-Vanderbilt Group has been most productive in helping us understand the influence of effectance motivation and motivational orientation (intrinsic and extrinsic motivation) on the performance of retarded and nonretarded persons ranging from nonhandicapped preschoolers, school-age, and middle school children and mildly mentally retarded adults. There is much overlap between the ideas and constructs of the Yale Group and the Peabody-Vanderbilt Group regarding the operation of personality and motivational processes in persons with mental retardation. Together the ideas of these research groups form a complimentary tapestry of overlapping ideas which in concert help us understand those historically overlooked motivational and environmental variables regarding individual differences in behavior in both mentally retarded and nonhandicapped persons.

The concept of motivational orientation has evolved systematically over the last 30 years, recognizing the complex interplay of personality and motivational processes with cognitive processes within a developmental perspective that has brought it ever close to current ideas deriving from mainstream psychological thought concerning self-system self-regulatory processes. In the next section of the chapter a brief review of some of these current concepts is presented, and their implications for understanding individual differences in personality and motivational systems in persons with mental retardation are explored.

IMPLICATIONS OF CURRENT THEORETICAL CONCEPTIONS OF PERSONALITY AND SELF-SYSTEM PROCESSES FOR PERSONS WITH MENTAL RETARDATION

Theories of IM and EM

Modern theories of IM and EM are complex structures, each employing their own definition of intrinsic motivation, and each concentrating on very specific aspects of the learning process (i.e., goal setting/goal value, expectations, efficacy, competence, autonomy, curiosity), although there is much conceptual overlap among theories.

The study of motivation has been confounded with the field of learning; indeed, motivation often is inferred from learning, and learning is the indicator of motivation for the motivational researcher, for good or for ill (Weiner, 1990). The period of the 1970s was focused on individual differences among learners independent from any broad concern about personality structure. Motivational theorists each created their own measures of IM and EM, and ignored how their theoretical model related to or fit in with other personality structures or with other operational definitions of IM and EM invented by other motivational theorists. The creation of the individual difference measure followed the successful manipulation of a situational variable that captured a particular motivational phenomenon. This was true both for the Yale Group and the Peabody-Vanderbilt Group of motivational researchers in the field of mental retardation as well as for researchers in mainstream psychology.

The period of the 1980s emphasized that cognitions have motivational significance, and that self-system processes may be useful for understanding behavior, a set of ideas profoundly influencing the theoretical models of the Peabody-Vanderbilt Group. The period of the 1990s is dominated by varieties of cognitive approaches to motivation; the main theories today are based on the interrelated cognitions of casual ascriptions, efficacy and control beliefs, helplessness, and thoughts about the goals for which one is striving within the context of a theory of self-system processes, and how these models related to intrinsic/extrinsic motivation. The period of the 1990s is the period of "the Self," not as a cross-situational personality trait but as a domain-specific variable. (The success of the motivational models of the Peabody-Vanderbilt group have to do with the relatively undifferentiated state of self-system processes in mentally retarded and in the low mental age populations studied, whose self-system processes behave more like personality traits and show more cross-situational generality than in nonretarded and older populations). However, current theories of IM and EM are not highly focused or developed within a concise system of interrelated concepts, as we see in this section. The vagueness and lack of theoretical elaborations reduces both the generality and precision of these intertwined approaches, both in mainstream psychology and even more in the less developed area of IM and EM in the area of mental retardation.

Goal Setting/Goal Value. Currently, motivational researchers have focused on the perception of the reasons for task engagement; that is, goal setting and goal value. Individuals may perceive that they engage in tasks for extrinsic reasons (i.e., to achieve some goal unrelated to the task itself) or that they engage in tasks for intrinsic reasons (for enjoyment or to develop competency). This difference relates to the distinction current motivational theorists make between learning goals, mastery goals, and task goals, which motivate individuals to engage in tasks in order to develop mastery, understanding, increased competence, and learning new things; and performance goals and ego goals, which motivate individuals to validate their competence by obtaining positive judgments of ones' abilities (or avoid negative ones) by engaging in tasks in order to do better than others, to demonstrate more intelligence than others, or to win approval from others (Dweck & Leggett, 1988; Elliot & Dweck, 1988; Nicholls, 1984, 1989, 1990).

According to the Dweck and Leggett (1988) model, which is an extension of Atkinson's expectancy-value theory of achievement motivation (Atkinson, 1964), learning goals and performance goals have very different implications for how students behave in achievement settings and how they interpret performance outcomes. Motivational processes reflect an interplay of cognitive and affective factors that influence the initiation and maintenance of goal-directed striving (Dweck, 1989). Motivational patterns can be conceptualized as: *goal value*, the salience and attractiveness of achievement goals; *goal expectancy*, the subjective probability of goal attainment; and *means value*, the attractiveness or aversiveness of the activities necessary for goal attainment. The child enters an achievement situation with a repertoire of cognitive skills and a motivational set of self-system processes consisting of: *beliefs*—favored views about the nature of competence, the level of one's competence, and beliefs about what variables influence outcome; *inference rules*—favored modes of computing task difficulty, and deciding the causes of outcomes; *salient representations*—tendencies to focus on aversive or pleasurable means or on desirable or undesirable outcomes; and *values and interests*—one's personal hierarchy of what is important and enjoyable. Environmental-demand situational characteristics (e.g., about the task, the evaluator, the reward) are interpreted through one's cognitive skill repertoire and one's motivational set (one's self-system processes) in terms of goal value, goal expectancy, and means value leading to a course of action concerning which achievement goals to pursue and how to pursue them. The performance and outcomes of the individual feed back into the cognitive–motivational self-system possibly altering the goal value and/or the goal expectancy and/or the means value, thus altering the performance of the individual.

Students with learning goals, independent of their perceptions of their intellectual abilities, seek challenging tasks that provide opportunities to develop new competencies and perceive their teacher as a mentor in the learning process rather than as an evaluator. When these students have difficulties solving problems, they assume that their current strategy of problem solving is inappropriate and needs to be changed, or that they are not trying hard enough. Accordingly, they analyze their problem-solving strategy and try harder. For students with learning goals, judgments of competence are based on the amount of effort expended and the real learning or mastery achieved. Students with performance goals are motivated to validate their competence, or at least to not appear incompetent. These students perceive the teacher as a judge or rewarder–punisher, rather than as a mentor, and their validations of competence are based on performance relative to others or to external feedback, not on real gains in understanding, competence, or mastery. Those who are confident in their ability choose moderately difficult tasks to allow themselves to validate their competence and, because they are confident that they will succeed when they encounter difficulty in solving problem-solving tasks, they will engage in effective strategy behaviors. However, because their goal is to be perceived (validated) as competent (as opposed to be truly competent), they may use shortcuts that achieve their immediate goals but do not actually foster real learning. Students who have performance goals but lack confidence in their ability choose easy tasks to avoid displaying incompetence. When these students encounter difficulty in solving problems, they either engage in self-defeating strategies to avoid being perceived as low in ability, or give up entirely because they don't perceive themselves as demonstrating competence.

All individuals pursue learning and/or performance goal structures. The primary question is what variables determine which goal structures are operational when choices have to be made? Dweck (1985) believed that the particular goal structure chosen is a function of environmental-demand situational characteristics and individual differences among learners regarding one's motivational set. In situations when normative standards of success, as opposed to personal or autonomous standards, are made more salient, children will ignore learning opportunities and pursue performance goal structures, such as selecting tasks that will allow them to validate high ability or conceal low ability. When, instead, the value of the task for its own sake is made more salient, stressing the personal progress of each learner, children will choose the learning goal structure; that is, they will select a task that maximizes learning but involves the risks of errors and confusion. Children under this environmental-demand condition, regardless of their perceived level of ability, will choose to forego the chance to validate their high ability or conceal their low ability in favor of the learning opportunity (Elliott & Dweck, 1981).

There also appear to be strong individual differences in children's tendency to be motivated to pursue "learning" or "performance" goals in situations where the environmental-demand situation is ambiguous, that is, situations that do not emphasize one learning goal structure over the other (Bandura & Dweck, 1981; Dweck & Bempechat, 1983). Students were introduced to experimental tasks or asked to think about classroom situations in which the teacher is about to present new material. Students were then asked to indicate their preference for the type of problem or materials they would like to work on, with each choice representing a learning goal (e.g., "Problems that I'll learn something from, even if they're so hard that I'll get a lot wrong") or a performance goal ("Problems that aren't too hard, so I don't get many wrong," "Problems that are hard enough to show that I'm smart"). Children demonstrated strong individual differences in their choice of goal structures that were independent of the students' level of ability at the task or of the level of their school achievement. Children with learning goals were more likely than were children with performance goals to say that they would feel smarter after a high-effort mastery experience than after a low-effort mastery experience. When asked to indicate their affective reactions to low-effort mastery, children with learning goals were more likely than children with performance goals to choose "bored" or "disappointed" over "proud" or "relieved."

Performance goals and learning goals are differentially associated with a kind of weariness or lack of stamina in the face of obstacles. The more a child is focused on learning or progress, the greater the likelihood of maintaining effective strategies (or improving one's strategies) under failure experiences (Elliott & Dweck, 1981). A challenging task in which one exerts high effort with few apparent obstacles is a potent builder of competence. For those children operating under a performance-goal orientation, low expectancies of success may lead them to avoid the very tasks that foster learning (i.e., mastery experiences) and build competence, or at the least pursue them in ineffective ways. Elliott and Dweck (1981) also found that in spite of obstacles to learning, children with learning goals did not attribute outcomes to lack of ability, to show disruption in performance, or to exhibit negative affect, even if they perceived themselves as having low ability relative to others in contradiction to children with performance goals who showed the opposite types of responses.

The evidence suggests (Bandura & Dweck, 1981; Elliott & Dweck, 1981) that the characteristics of the learning situation have a lot to do with fostering and maintaining interest in the task. Challenging tasks and ones that pose obstacles are less likely to create negative affect (and more likely to create positive affect) for children with learning goals as compared to children with performance goals. High effort is itself more likely to be experienced as pleasurable in a learning situation (where effort engenders pride in one's work) than in a performance situation (where effort can be associated with the shame of displaying low ability). Learning goals may foster a greater sense of personal control, which is associated with greater intrinsic motivation, greater task interest, and enjoyment. Performance goals may involve situations that imply that others control outcomes or constrain behavior, conditions associated with a decline in intrinsic motivation, and a concomitant increase in extrinsic motivation.

In contrast, Nicholls' theory of goal setting (Nicholls, 1979b, 1984, 1989) distinguishes between task goals and learning goals where students are focused on completing the task that they are motivated to learn or master in terms of a self-referenced definition of success as the gaining of insight or skill or accomplishing something that is personally challenging (i.e., task involvement and task orientation), and ego goals and performance goals (i.e., ego involvement) where students are focused on themselves and especially on external evaluation of the self in terms of a definition of success where students must establish their ability as superior to those of others (i.e., ego involvement and ego orientation). Ego orientation means that although one might seek to learn, to gain insight, or to perform one's best, these efforts would not be ends in themselves (as they are in task orientation), but means to the end of establishing one's ability as superior.

In adult through junior high school populations (Maehr & Braskamp, 1986; Nicholls, Patashnick, & Nolen, 1985), the goal dimensions of task and ego orientation are independent of each other and do not form a single bipolar dimension. A third orientation, work avoidance, is negatively related to task orientation and unrelated or positively related to ego orientation (Nicholls et al., 1985; Thorkildsen, 1988). To ego-oriented students, it might be expected that the concept of ability would be very important and that success as they define it would be viewed as dependent on superior ability. To task-oriented students, concepts of learning, understanding, and effort would be important, and attempts to make sense of instructional domains would appear to be essential for success. Ego involvement is increased by situations that are testlike, where interpersonal competition is emphasized, and by feedback that focuses attention on one's standing relative to others. Such situations tend to undermine intrinsic involvement (IM in learning situations).

Negative effects on performance and level of aspiration of low perceived ability are more evident in such ego-involving contexts than in neutral or task-involving contexts. In ego-involving contexts, students with low perceived ability generally show more unrealistic levels of aspiration and more impaired performance. When this pressure is absent, students with low and high perceived ability (academic self-concept) generally perform similarity. Therefore, rather than asking how we can we increase students' self-concepts of ability, we might ask how can we encourage students to be task involved rather than ego involved; to focus on the work at hand and on the problem to be solved; to create classrooms where students perceive success as dependent on collaborative attempts to construct meaning, rather than on how able they are because task and ego orientations are not significantly correlated with perceived ability (academic self-concept). Research supporting this analysis has been obtained with older students with reference to general school instruction (Nicholls, 1984, 1989; Nicholls, Cheung, Lauer, & Patashnick, 1989; Nolen, 1988; Thorkildsen, 1988) and in second graders (Nicholls, Cobb, Wood, Yackel, & Patashnick, 1990; Nicholls, Cobb, Yackel, Wood, & Wheatley, 1990) with reference to mathematics instruction.

What learning environments or beliefs concerning the purposes of education support a task orientation (Nicholls, 1989; Nicholls et al., 1989; Thorkildsen, 1988)? Task orientation was associated with the view that the school should help one to do work that will be socially useful, to be an informed citizen, and to work hard and creatively despite obstacles, and the belief that academic success is achieved by working collaboratively, being interested, and trying to understand rather than merely memorize; that is, task orientation is associated with a tendency to perceive oneself as having social responsibilities and to perceive others as resources for learning. Work avoidance was negatively associated with these views and positively associated with the view that the purpose of school is to help one gain wealth and social status. Ego orientation was strongly associated as well with wealth and status as the aims of education and the beliefs that success depends on trying to beat others and having teachers think you will do well. Nicholls (1989) and Nicholls et al. (1989) maintained that to understand the academic motivation of students requires that researchers study students in a holistic perspective, taking into consideration the self-sustaining philosophies of students, their ethical and political values, and their idiosyncratic interpretations of the purposes of education and of curriculum content (i.e., the meaning of life in school, and the meaning of life in general) in an ecological approach to social cognition where thought and action are interpreted in terms of the thinker's purpose. The task of changing the motivation of students involves the changing of their self-sustaining philosophies concerning their views about society and themselves. For Nicholls and his colleagues (Nicholls, Cobb, Yackel, et al., 1990), the ideal classroom involves "conflict of ideas without a conflict of egos which is the essence of progressive, constructivist education and life" (p. 145).

The main strategy in maintaining positive achievement-related beliefs is to develop an incremental concept of ability and a task orientation for all students, because students learn optimally when they concentrate on mastering the skill to be learned rather than on their normative performance compared to other members of the class. This will lead to feelings of competence, personal responsibility, and pride, even in students who believe that their academic ability is lower than their classmates' (Nicholls et al., 1989).

Self-Efficacy. Bandura (1986a, 1986b, 1991, 1992, 1993) more recently has written about the idea of personal agency, that is, the idea that individuals take responsibility for their actions and impute success and failure to the goals they choose, the resources they mobilize, and the effort they expend. Perceived self-efficacy, that is, beliefs concerning one's capabilities to organize and implement actions necessary to attain designated levels of performance, is one of the most important constructs in Bandura's (1986a, 1991, 1992, 1993) social–cognitive approach and a critical component of personal agency, because self-perceptions of one's ability to behave in a particular way establish one's expectations and motivation.

Three different theoretical models of cognitive motivators influencing the self-regulation of motivation involving perceived self-efficacy can be distinguished (Bandura, 1991, 1992, 1993): attribution theory and casual attributions, expectancy-value theory and outcome expectancies, and goal theory and cognized goals. Self-efficacy beliefs operate in each of these theoretical models of cognitive motivation. Self-efficacy beliefs influence individual's casual attributions regarding the perceived causes of success and failure. Individuals who regard themselves as highly efficacious ascribe their failures to insufficient effort; those who regard themselves as inefficacious attribute their failures to low ability (Alden, 1986; Collins, 1982; McAuley, Duncan, & McElroy, 1989). Casual attributions affect motivation, performance, and affective reactions mainly through beliefs of self-efficacy (Chwalisz, Altmaier, & Russell, 1992; McAuley, 1991; Schunk & Gunn, 1986; Schunk & Rice, 1986). In expectancy-value theory, motivation is controlled by the individual's expectation that his or her behavior will result in certain outcomes with particular values. The motivating potential of outcome expectancies is partly the results by the self-beliefs of individuals regarding what they can do, as well as their beliefs about the likely outcomes of performance (i.e., their perceived self-efficacy). The usefulness of expectancy-value theory is increased by including self-efficacy determinants (de Vries, Dijkstra, & Kuhlman, 1988; Dzewaltowski, Noble, & Shaw, 1990; Madden, Ellen, & Ajzen, 1992; McCaul, O'Neill, & Glasgow, 1988; Wheeler, 1983). Goal theory is based on the motivational aspects of cognitized personal and evaluative goals operating in the present (Locke & Latham, 1990), mediated through self-influence processes. Motivation based on goal setting involves a cognitive comparison process. Individuals make their self-satisfaction conditional on matching adopted goals, thus giving direction to their behavior and creating incentives to persist in their efforts until they fulfill their goals and are prompted to intensify their efforts when discontented with substandard performances. Proactive control of motivation is possible as well (Bandura, 1993).

Students' efficacy beliefs influence achievement behaviors, including choice of task, persistence, effort expenditure, skill acquisition, and the selection and construction of the individual's environment. Students' behaviors and the demand conditions of the environment can modify their efficacy beliefs in a reciprocal fashion, according to the principle of reciprocal determinism. A strong belief in one's ability to use specific actions effectively (high perceived self-efficacy) enhances successful performance, and enhances feelings of pride, satisfaction, and self-respect, whereas a weak belief in one's ability to use specific actions effectively (low perceived self-efficacy) depresses performance and enhances feelings of guilt, failure, dissatisfaction, and low self-respect (Schunk, 1989a, 1989b, 1990). Efficacy beliefs influence how individuals feel, think, motivate themselves, make casual ascriptions, and behave (Bandura, 1993).

Students who have a low sense of self-efficacy are especially vulnerable to achievement anxiety. Meece, Wigfield, and Eccles (1990) showed that former academic successes and failures arouse achievement anxiety via their effects on students' perceived self-efficacy. Failure may decrease students' sense of efficacy, and they become anxious about scholastic demands made on them. If their perceived self-efficacy is strong, it can withstand academic failure experiences and the students can remain optimistic and calm. Students' beliefs in their capabilities to master academic subjects predict their subsequent academic attainments. Their level of scholastic anxiety is unrelated to subsequent academic performances.

In Bandura's (1986a) social cognitive learning theory, "Learning is largely an information-processing activity in which information about the structure of behavior and about environmental events is transformed into symbolic representations that serve as guides for action" (p. 51), and inform and motivate the individual so that expectations about future outcomes can be created. Learning occurs enactively by the consequences of the individuals' own actions (behaviors associated with successful consequences are retained, those that yield failure are discarded), or vicariously in the absence of overt behavior by individuals, usually by observing models (by watching actual events, or through the media by reading books, seeing movies, listening to the radio, or watching television). Response consequences from enactive and vicarious sources inform and motivate the observers. Vicariously observed behavior that leads to success and is deemed useful to learners is retained, whereas vicariously observed behavior that leads to failure or is deemed useless is not retained. Most learning is a combination of enactive and vicarious sources operating through enhancement or diminishment of the individuals' outcome expectations, which influence perceived self-efficacy.

Individuals acquire information about their self-efficacy in a given content domain from their enactive performances, vicarious experiences, social persuasion from others, and physiological states (e.g., physiological signs of anxiety: increased heart rate, gastric distress, headache, increased sweating). One's own performance provides the most valid information concerning one's self-efficacy (success raises it, whereas failure lowers it). Vicarious normative experiences (Marshall & Wienstein, 1984; Rosenholtz & Simpson, 1984) provide information regarding one's ability compared to others in the group (e.g., if one believes one is better than others in the group, self-efficacy is increased; if one believes one is worse than others in the group, self-efficacy plummets; observing individuals similar to oneself succeed increases self-efficacy; if similar persons fail, self-efficacy decreases). Social persuasion from others providing positive supportive informational feedback (e.g., "You can do the task") can increase perceived self-efficacy. Performance feedback that emphasizes achieved progress can enhance perceived self-efficacy. Performance feedback that emphasizes deficient progress underscores personal deficiencies and decreases performance (Bandura, 1993).

Bandura's (1993) expanded model can be summarized as follows. Individuals who have a low sense of personal efficacy in a given domain avoid difficult tasks, which are perceived as threatening. These individuals have both low aspirations and weak commitment to the goals they wish to undertake. They maintain a self-diagnostic focus rather than concentrate on how to perform the task successfully. Individuals, when confronted with difficult tasks, dwell on their personal deficiencies, on the obstacles, and on all sorts of adverse outcomes. These individuals are very slow to recover their sense of efficacy following failure. Because they perceive insufficient performance as deficient intellectual competence, it does not require much failure for them to lose faith in their capabilities. They are also overly sensitive to stress and depression.

A strong sense of efficacy enhances personal accomplishments in many ways. Individuals with high self-efficacy approach difficult tasks as challenges to be mastered rather than as threats to be avoided, with a strong sense of intrinsic motivation and task engagement. These individuals seek out challenging tasks and maintain strong commitment to them. They maintain a task-diagnostic focus that guides effective performance. These individuals heighten and sustain their efforts under failure. They attribute failure to insufficient effort or deficient knowledge and skills that are acquirable. They quickly recover their sense of efficacy after failures. They approach threatening situations with assurance that they can control them. Their sense of personal efficacy results in feelings of personal accomplishments, reduced stresses, and lowered vulnerability to depression.

Self-efficacy beliefs are a product of a complex process of self-persuasion that relies on the cognitive processing of diverse sources of efficacy information conveyed enactively, vicariously, socially, and physiologically (Bandura, 1986a). Once established, these self-efficacy beliefs contribute significantly to the quality and level of successful and optimal human functioning.

The extension of the study of personal agency and establishment of perceived self-efficacy to mentally retarded populations and preschool children may clarify our understanding of the operation of intrinsic and extrinsic motivation within a framework that has been very successful in understanding self-regulation of behavior in older and more normative populations.

Autonomy and Self-Determination. Decharms (1968, 1976, 1984), Deci and his colleagues (Deci, 1975; Deci & Ryan, 1985, 1991; Ryan & Connell, 1989; Ryan, Connell, & Deci, 1985), and Leeper and his colleagues (Leeper & Hodell, 1989) maintained that individuals have an inborn need to feel self-determining (to engage in activities by their own volition and endorsed by their sense of self) rather than to achieve some external reward or to avoid some external punishment or be controlled by intrapsychic forces such as guilt or a sense of obligation. Individuals are intrinsically motivated when they perceive themselves as the cause of their own behavior (i.e., as possessing personal causation, having an internal locus of causality, having a feeling of choice), through which they can experience themselves as causal agents and view themselves as the originators of their own behaviors rather than as pawns of external forces (DeCharms, 1968, 1976, 1984). Additionally, intrinsically motivated individuals have strong needs for a sense of competence, self-determination, and challenge (Deci, 1975; Deci & Chandler, 1986; Deci & Ryan, 1985; Deci, Vallerand, Pelletier, & Ryan, 1991). Individuals are extrinsically motivated when they believe they are engaging in behavior because of controlling external environmental demand conditions, that is, having an external locus of causality (e.g., external reinforcers, external constraints, and pleasing another person).

Many factors affect the perceived locus of causality, including the level of control exerted by others and the availability of rewards. Thus, someone who chooses to engage in an activity and is not rewarded for doing so is more likely to have an internal locus of causality than is someone who is required or forced to engage in the activity for external reinforcement. Despite the important effects of these and other variables, it is an individual's perception of causality that is more important than any objective index of causality.

The facilitation of learning which is intrinsically motivating and free from externally controlling teacher practices and extrinsic motivational control ideally should be the primary goal of American education for both handicapped and nonhandicapped students. However, because students show large individual differences in the degree to which they are intrinsically or extrinsically motivated, these internal self-system characteristics need to be considered, and educational practices need to be matched to the particular motivational orientation of each student, at least in the short term to encourage optimal learning. This author believes, however, that in the future educational techniques will be needed to change more extrinsically motivated students into intrinsically motivated ones.

One of the most important elements for promoting intrinsically motivated learning in students is the approach of the teacher. Whether teachers extinguish or nurture IM for learning depends on how rewards and punishments are used: as controlling or as informational feedback. Deci, Nezlek, and Scheinman (1981), and Deci, Schwartz, Scheinman, and Ryan (1981) reported that fourth-through sixth-grade teachers who believe in dealing with children in a way that encourages them to be autonomous, who use rewards informationally, tend to facilitate IM and self-determination in their students, whereas teachers who are controlling tend to discourage the IM and self-determination of their pupils. Deci described the controlling classroom approach as involving the teacher's mandating what the child must or should do; sanctions are used to ensure that tasks are completed. Informational classroom styles are described as supporting autonomy; the teacher encourages a self-determined competence by asking the students to compare their behavior with others and by encouraging students to arrive at a problem solution that seems right for themselves.

IM and Cognitive Processes. Even those persons who enter the world predestined to have the highest endowment of native fluid intelligence must learn a set of fundamental cognitive functions in order to have ready access to their intelligence and to behave in consistently intelligent ways (Feuerstein, Klein, & Tannenbaum, 1991; Hamers, Sijtsma, & Ruijssenaars,1993; Haywood & Switzky, 1986; Haywood & Tzuriel, 1992; Vye, Delclos, Burns, & Bransford, 1988). These cognitive functions include learned information processing components of intelligence, the internal or mental processes that underlie intelligent behavior: metacomponents, performance components, and knowledge acquisition components (Borkowski, Carr, & Pressley, 1987; Borkowski, Johnson, & Reid, 1987; Bransford & Stein, 1984; Brown, 1978; Pressley, Borkowski, & Schneider, 1990; Sternberg, 1987).

Metacomponents are the executive processes that coordinate, plan, monitor, and evaluate procedures used to solve problems. Examples of metacomponents include defining the problem, selecting mental representations, selecting strategies, monitoring solutions, and allocating attentional and other mental resources. *Performance components* implement the plans that metacomponents formulate. These include inferring relations among stimuli in terms of their similarities and differences, applying previously inferred relations to new situations, mapping higher-order relationships among stimuli, and comparing attributes to stimuli. *Knowledge acquisition components* are processes that enable one to learn new information. These are strategies that learners use to identify important information and to combine and compare new information with existing knowledge so as to increase and determine meaning. Processes used to determine meaning may include selective encodings or locating relevant new information, selective combinations, combining this relevant new information into meaningful wholes, and selective comparisons, interrelating information with what is already known as to maximize the connectedness of the newly formed knowledge structures to the previously formed knowledge structures.

In addition, knowledge acquisition components include instructing the learner to meaningful contextual cues.

Other components of cognitive processes that must be taught include experiential components of cognitive functioning for coping with novelty, and automatization of information processing components. The metacomponents, performance components, and knowledge acquisition components of information processing do not operate in an experiential vacuum. On the contrary, they are applied to tasks and in situations that vary in terms of their familiarity to the individual. Initially, tasks and situations may be quite novel. As the individual gains experience with tasks and situations, task performance may shift from being quite controlled to partially or fully automatic. Automatization frees mental resources for coping with novelty. The teaching of thinking may be useful when the problems to which the processes are applied are relatively but not wholly novel. Other things being equal, individuals who are able to use and acquire insight from new information, and who are able to perform operations smoothly and without much conscious effort, are likely to be more successful in learning and in problem-solving tasks than are those who do not have these abilities. Processes assumed to contribute to insightful acquisition of new knowledge are the three information processing knowledge acquisition processes of selective encoding, selective combination, and selective comparison.

The cognitive processing components of intelligence are operational, at varying levels of experience, in tasks of varying levels of contextual relevance to one's life. Behavior that occurs in highly relevant contexts is more pertinent to the use of cognitive processing components than is behavior that has no actual or even potential contextual relevance. Intelligent performance can only be meaningful in terms of the real-world context in which cognitive processes operate. Individuals must learn to manipulate the environment by adapting to the environment, by shaping or restructuring the environment, or by selecting new environments relevant to their own lives. Individuals usually attempt first to adapt to the environment in which they live. Adaptation consists of trying to achieve a good fit between oneself and the environment. If adaptation fails, due to a lack of congruence among one's interests, abilities, motives, or values, then one must try to restructure the environment or select a new environment. Shaping involves an attempt to restructure one's environment to increase the fit between oneself and one's environment. If and when shaping fails, it is time to search for new environments that are more congruent with one's needs and values. Virtually all persons need to learn cognitive processes that will be relevant to these aspects of practical intelligence. Cognitive development consists in large part of a process of successive discovery and applications of these understandings, processes, rules, and elementary logic systems. Exactly how cognitive functions are acquired, or why they fail to be acquired, is not completely clear, but it is highly likely that mediated teaching is an important contributor (Brown & Palinscar, 1987; Feuerstein et al., 1991; Haywood & Switzky, 1992; Haywood & Tzuriel, 1992; Schultz & Switzky, 1990; Switzky & Schultz, 1988).

Since the 1960s, educators and psychologists have tried to understand why mentally retarded and other learning deficient children often failed to generalize a newly trained skill to new similar learning contexts (Borkowski & Cavanaugh, 1979). The basic paradigm was the use of strategy instruction, which was viewed as being inefficient in these learning deficient students. Some positive effects were found following strategy instruction, but performance gains were ephemeral and transient and usually were restricted to tasks similar to the ones trained on (near transfer but little far transfer). Even the development of metacognitively driven models of strategy generalization (Borkowski, Johnston, & Reid, 1987; Pressley, Borkowski, & Schneider, 1990), which enhanced strategy generalization through: providing repeated practice with instructed strategies, using multiple problem types, informing children why strategies are useful, asking children to contrast their performance using different strategies, and teaching self-control procedures (e.g., planning, monitoring, and checking); all techniques that stressed that strategies become integrated into a coherent metacognitive network guided by self-regulatory processes in order to become stable and generalizable, did not lead to dramatic generalization effects.

It became apparent that the efficient operation of cognitive processes and ability systems is vitally linked to motivational processes. Only when personal-motivational processes are included in strategy training interventions will strategy generalization become facilitated. Strategy-based actions directly influence the self-concept, attitudes about learning, and attributional beliefs about personal control. In turn, these personal-motivational states determine the course of new strategy acquisition and, more important, the likelihood of strategy transfer and the quality of self-understanding about the nature and function of mental processes. Most metacognitively based strategy training interventions have failed because researchers falsely assumed that students automatically found pleasure in using their problem-solving skills and ignored the students' cognitive and emotional perspectives about learning and the learning task (Bandura, 1993; Borkowski et al., 1990; Borkowski, Johnston, & Reid, 1987; Borkowski & Kurtz, 1987; Carr, Borkowski, & Maxwell, 1991; Day, Borkowski, Dietmeyer, Howsepian; & Saenx, 1992; Dweck, 1986; Haywood & Switzky, 1992; Maehr & Pintrich, 1991; McCombs & Marzano, 1990; Nicholls, 1989, 1990; Paris & Byrnes, 1989; Paris & Newman, 1990; Pintrich & De Groot, 1990; Schiefele, 1991; Schunk, 1991; Sternberg, 1985; Wigfield & Karpathian, 1991).

Borkowski and his collaborators (Borkowski et al., 1992) developed a new model of strategy-based intervention based on the idea that interventions that enhance students' task involvement (Nicholls, 1989, 1990) or that promote the adoption of learning goals (Dweck, 1986) should result in greater generalization because they reduce comparisons between one's own performance and those of peers. Interventions that emphasize task involvement highlight the benefits rather than the liabilities associated with effortful achievement. Borkowski et al. (1992) realized that the students' definition of success (getting better vs. being the best) and failure (making understandable mistakes vs. being stupid) change under circumstances of task involvement, as do the students' attributions about the causes of success and failure (ability, effort, or appropriate strategy choice). Borkowski et al. (1992) stressed that increased task involvement and/or the adoption of learning goals are associated with motivational growth (e.g., an internal locus of control, mastery-oriented attributional patterns, positive feelings of self-efficacy, greater intrinsic motivation) as well as metacognitive development (e.g., accurate performance predictions, good choice of strategies, active planning and monitoring). These personal-motivational factors energize the self-regulating executive skills necessary for strategy selection, implementation, and monitoring. Individual differences among learners in task performance, problem solving, and strategy generalization are the result of deficiencies in the metacognitive system or the personal-motivational self-system, or in both systems.

Borkowski et al. (1990, 1992) believed that general strategy knowledge, and its associated motivational factors, are bidirectionally reciprocally related, each contributing to the other component. High self-esteem, an internal locus of control, and the tendency to attribute success to effort are the consequences of a history of consistent, successful, strategy-based habits of responding to learning and memory tasks. Good performance following strategy use strengthens general strategy knowledge, which promotes positive self-esteem and attributions of success to effort rather than to uncontrolled factors such as ability or luck. Positive self-esteem and effort-related attributional beliefs enhance the likelihood of strategy generalization. Ineffective motive systems can impair children's basic abilities to develop specific strategy knowledge, especially if children have doubts about their learning abilities. Furthermore, such self-doubts may lead to an impoverished general strategy knowledge base, which may limit the acquisition of new learning strategies and higher-level processes that guide the implementation of lower-level strategies. Motivational factors play a pivotal role in subsequent spontaneous strategy use by providing incentives necessary for deploying strategies, especially on challenging transfer tasks.

McCombs and her colleagues (McCombs, 1988; McCombs & Marzano, 1990) have long suggested that the self-system promotes children's progress toward self-determination by influencing the processing, transformation, and encoding of information. Children with positive self-concepts, along with effort-related attributions (among other self-system constructs), are likely to store and use newly learned information in such a way as to maximize the later usefulness of that information. Children with dysfunctional self-systems, on the other hand, are unlikely to take full advantage of new information. Harter (1986) found that individuals develop good or poor self-concepts depending on the amount of discrepancy between their actual performance and their perceptions of the importance of the task. Thus, the self-system and cognitive system are closely intertwined.

One way the self-system alters information processing is by determining how children perceive and integrate new information with existing knowledge in the same (and related) domains. Although perceptions of information may reflect certain global traits of the child, it also appears that children process new information in terms of task-specific relationships in concert with other self- and metacognitive system constructs. Marsh (1990) found that math and reading self-concepts were unrelated despite correlations between math and reading achievement scores. Abhalter and Switzky (1992) found similar results in their sample of elementary-aged nonhandicapped children. Such task-specific perceptions may be due to a maturing self-system that makes it easier for the child to develop positive self-esteem, and accompanying metacognitive knowledge about specific tasks and strategies. (The results of the Peabody-Vanderbilt group with mentally retarded and preschool-aged children have shown that these populations show much less domain-specificity in the organization of their self-systems, which is to be expected in individuals with less developed and less matured self-systems.)

Weiner (1990) commented on the renaissance of research between affect and cognitive processes. Affective responses to task demands and task outcomes are a product of, and reinforce the development of, the self- and metacognitive systems by modifying affective states, such as joy, pride, or sadness. Pride is enhanced by perceptions of personal causality (Weisz, 1978), when success is perceived to be the result of a combination of high ability and effort (Covington, 1987). Shame, guilt, and anxiety are enhanced when one believes that one's performance is indicative of low effort and low ability (Covington, 1987). Affective responses to success and failure are another cognitively linked component to the information processing system. Children respond emotionally to their performance outcomes, which either support or undermine their metacognitive and cognitive development, depending on the resultant self-perceptions. Attributional beliefs regarding success and failure also affect emotions and the subsequent development of metacognitive and cognitive processes. Attributing success to internal factors promotes pride and happiness (Stipek & Weisz, 1981). Failure attributions (i.e., the belief that one is personally unable to manage events that others seem able to control) following failure performance despite high effort influence one's self-worth and causes such emotions as self-blame, humiliation, and self-derogation (Covington, 1987), which in turn leads to decreasing expectancies and the avoidance of failure, resulting in an inhibited and deficient development of metacognitive and cognitive processes.

Borkowski et al. (1990, 1992), building on the older information processing models of Pressley, Borkowski, and O'Sullivan (1985) and Borkowski et al. (1987), developed a model of performance integrating metacognitive and motivational constructs. From the perspective of the Borkowski et al. (1990) metacognitive model, children who feel good about themselves and their ability (e.g., those who are intrinsically motivated to learn and who have effort-related attributions), are more likely to believe in strategic behavior and to develop complex, mature strategy knowledge. Self-system constructs energize metacognition by giving children the resolve to learn. Attributional beliefs are of particular importance for metacognitive development because children must first believe in the utility of their strategy-related effort (Clifford, 1984) before they will apply those efforts in situations that demand strategic behavior. Effort is actualized in the form of well-chosen strategies that are carefully and thoughtfully applied to difficult tasks. Children with positive self-systems are more likely to acquire specific strategy knowledge, and to apply this knowledge on new tasks because they have a general belief in the utility of strategies and effort (i.e., they have a well-developed general strategy knowledge component in their metacognitive system).

Emotional responses to success or failure also influence the development of metacognition. Children who have a sense of pride in their work and who seek success as a function of their effort are more likely to acquire and use metacognitive knowledge, and seek challenging experiences to increase these feelings of pride and self-fulfillment because of early successful strategic behavior that leads to positive attributional patterns. Later, these attributional patterns concerning controllability (self-determination) influence whether these children persist in strategic behaviors when they initially are unsuccessful. Thus, children who feel good about themselves as learners are more likely to continue to be strategic and to increase their metacognitive knowledge, because these behaviors have been successful in the past, enhancing performance and increasing self-esteem. Although it is the self-system that provides the motivational thrust in order for the child to become self-determining, it is the metacognitive system that provides the processes to reach that goal. For the metacognitive system to function efficiently, children must have adequate information about both general and specific strategy knowledge (about why, when, where, and how to use strategies). Personal-motivational processes (e.g., IM, self-determination, effort-related attributions) are useless to individuals who do not have the necessary accompanying specific strategic knowledge. Such individuals will be highly motivated to use the appropriate strategies, but will not know how to select the ones to use for particular task demands. Intervention programs for deficient and mentally retarded learners must have a dual focus: the development of personal-motivational self-system processes as well as the development of the metacognitive system in order to maximize learning and performance.

A SYNTHESIS OF MOTIVATIONAL THEORIES FOR MENTALLY RETARDED PERSONS: AN AGENDA FOR FUTURE RESEARCH

Both the Yale Group and the Peabody-Vanderbilt Group of mental retardation researchers have demonstrated that the performance of persons with mental retardation is a function of the complex interplay of personality and motivational processes within a developmental perspective, as well as the conception of persons with mental retardation as active problem solvers reflecting current mainstream psychological thought. This has facilitated the accelerating integration between a psychology of mental retardation and an overall developmental psychology of human growth applicable to both retarded and nonretarded persons. It can be argued that mental retardation researchers have been historically more sensitive to the impact of personality and motivational processes on the performance of learners with mental retardation, and have developed more elaborate models of motivational systems and self-system processes of individual differences compared to other developmental psychologists studying nonhandicapped learners. However, over the last 10 to 15 years these developmental psychologists as reviewed here have become more concerned with motivational and self-system processes in nonhandicapped learners and have developed very extensive and thoughtful models of motivational self-system processes. These new models of motivation and self-system processes need to be considered by mental retardation researchers to help them refine their models of motivation and their future research endeavors.

As Weiner (1990) thoroughly documented, the study of motivation has been confounded with the study of learning, without any real interest in developing any cohesive, generalizable models of personality structure. Motivational theorists studying handicapped and nonhandicapped populations have created their own unique measures of their motivational constructs and flatly ignored how their theoretical models related to the theoretical models of other motivational researchers or with other operational definitions of motivation created by other motivational theorists. Currently, developmental motivational theorists studying nonhandicapped populations have seen the error of their ways and have developed more cognitively based theories of motivation based on the interrelated cognitions of casual ascriptions, efficacy and control beliefs, learned helplessness, and the goals for which one is striving within the context of a theory of self-system processes and a theory of IM and EM. Bandura's (1993) most recent formulation of his theoretical model of self-efficacy, in this author's opinion, is one of the better attempts to deal with the concerns expressed by Weiner (1990). Motivational researchers in the field of mental retardation have to make the same attempts as their colleagues in mainstream psychology to develop more cohesive, more generalizable, more highly focused, more theoretically elaborate, and more precise models of motivational systems applicable to persons with mental retardation.

The work of Dweck and Leggett (1988) and the related work of Nicholls (1984, 1989, 1990) concerning the perceptions of the reasons for task engagement—that is, goal setting/goal values as a distinction among learning goals, mastery goals, and task goals that motivate individuals to engage in tasks in order to develop mastery, understanding, increased competence, and learning new things; and performance goals, and ego goals that motivate individuals to validate one's competence by obtaining positive judgments of ones' abilities (or avoid negative ones) by engaging in tasks in order to do better than others, to demonstrate more intelligence than others, or to win approval from others—must be evaluated by motivational researchers in the field of mental retardation as to their theoretical applicability to the motivational systems of mentally retarded persons. Do the belief systems of mentally retarded learners concerning the nature of intelligence, that is, smartness as an incremental theory in which intelligence is viewed as something one can increase or as an entity theory in which intelligence is viewed as a fixed static trait, operate the same way to change goal structures in mentally retarded individuals as they do in nonhandicapped individuals (Bandura & Dweck, 1981; Dweck, 1989; Nicholls, 1979a, 1979b, 1984, 1989; Nicholls et al., 1989; Stipek, 1984)?

Bandura's (1991, 1992, 1993) expansion of his social cognitive theory emphasizing the construct of personal agency and perceived self-efficacy stresses the ideas that individuals take responsibility for their actions and impute success and failure to the goals they choose, the resources they mobilize, and the efforts they expend, as well as the idea that beliefs concerning one's self-perceptions of one's capabilities to organize and implement actions necessary to attain designated levels of performance establish one's expectations and motivation, have tremendous implications for motivational researchers in mental retardation. The Peabody-Vanderbilt group has been heavily influenced by more preliminary versions of Bandura's social cognitive theory and this author expects that the Peabody-Vanderbilt group will attempt to refine its models of motivation in persons with mental retardation by integrating aspects of Bandura's expanded theory, which has been so successful in accounting for behavioral outcomes in both nonhandicapped children and adults in so many different domains of performance. Additionally, Bandura (1993) tried to integrate his social cognitive theory of self-regulation of motivation to the major mainstream psychological motivational theories dominating the current zeitgeist—attribution theory and causal attributions, expectancy-value theory and outcome expectancies, and goal theory and cognitized goals—in an attempt to lead the way to develop cohesive, generalizable models of personality structure and self-regulation. These attempts by Bandura surely need to be considered by all motivational researchers in the field of mental retardation in order to develop better motivational theories for persons with mental retardation.

Motivational theorists such as DeCharms (1976, 1984), Deci and his colleagues (Deci, 1975; Deci & Ryan, 1985, 1991; Ryan & Connell, 1989; Ryan, Connell, & Deci, 1985), and Leeper and his colleagues (Leeper & Hodell, 1989) focused on motivational constructs such as autonomy and self-determination. They maintained that individuals engage in activities initiated by their own volition and endorsed by their sense of self, rather than do things specifically to achieve some external reward or avoid some external punishment. Individuals are intrinsically motivated when they perceive themselves as the cause of their own behavior (i.e., as possessing personal causation, having an internal locus of causality, having a feeling of choice), where they can experience themselves as causal agents and view themselves as the originators of their own behaviors rather than pawns of external forces. Additionally, intrinsically motivated individuals have strong needs for a sense of competence, self-determination, and challenge. Individuals are extrinsically motivated when they believe they are engaging in behavior because of controlling external environmental demand conditions (e.g., external reinforcers, external constraints, pleasing another person, and having an external locus of causality).

These researchers have found that the demand conditions of the environment influence the individual's IM. Informational environments convey relevant information to the individual about competence at a task, thus supporting self-autonomy and intrinsic motivation. Controlling environments designed to bring about a particular behavioral outcome, usually by the use of extrinsic rewards, support dependency and EM in the individual by shifting the individual's perception away from autonomy and personal causation and toward a perception of external causation that undermines intrinsic motivation. Motivational researchers in the field of mental retardation need to apply these principles to mentally retarded persons and the environments that mentally retarded persons inhabit to determine the degree of informational and controlling components of the environment and ways in which one can facilitate the development of intrinsic motivation. Can one increase the informational qualities of the environment and decrease the controlling qualities of the environment to increase IM in persons with mental retardation?

Both the Yale Group and the Peabody-Vanderbilt Group of mental retardation researchers (Haywood & Switzky, 1986, 1992; Merighi et al., 1990; Zigler & Hodapp, 1991), very early in the development of their theoretical models, believed strongly that the performance of mentally retarded persons reflected the interaction of IM and cognitive processes. Over the last 10 years this theme has increasingly dominated both motivational researchers and cognitive researchers deriving from the mental retardation tradition (Borkowski et al., 1992; Feuerstein et al., 1991; Haywood & Tzuriel, 1992) as well as motivational and cognitive researchers from developmental psychology (Bransford & Stein, 1988; Brown, 1978; Brown & Palinscar, 1987; Dweck, 1986; Hamers et al., 1993;

Maehr & Pintrich, 1991; Nicholls, 1989, 1990; Paris & Byrnes, 1989; Paris & Newman, 1990; Pressley, Borkowski, & O'Sullivan, 1984, 1985; Sternberg, 1985; Vye et al., 1988; Wigfield & Karpathian, 1991; Zimmerman, 1990). The efficient operation of cognitive processes and ability systems is vitally linked to motivational processes.

Only when personal-motivational processes are included in strategy training interventions will strategy generalization become facilitated. Strategy-based actions directly influence the self-concept, attitudes about learning, and attributional beliefs about personal control. In turn, these personal-motivational states determine the course of new strategy acquisition and, more important, the likelihood of strategy transfer and the quality of self-understanding about the nature and function of mental processes. Borkowski and his collaborators (Borkowski et al., 1992) developed a new model of strategy-based intervention strongly linked to self-regulatory motivational and personality processes, which has great relevance for both handicapped and nonhandicapped learners. These models provide a foundation and a new agenda for research regarding problem-solving acquisition and usage in persons who are mentally retarded. Most interesting is the view of Markus and her colleagues (Cantor, Markus, Niedenthal, & Nurius, 1986; Markus, Cross, & Wurf, 1990; Markus & Nurius, 1986) and their theory of possible selves, which are individuals' visions of themselves in future states. In Borkowski's new theory (Borkowski et al., 1992), these hoped-for and feared possible-selves provide the impetus for achieving important short-term and long-term goals. In this way, the self-system takes on a futuristic perspective providing incentives for the operation of the entire metacognitive system. This author looks forward to the further testing and refinement of these models for mentally retarded learners.

A major problem for mental retardation researchers who study motivational, personality, and self-system processes in mentally retarded and low-mental-age persons has been the dearth of psychometric instruments and techniques with adequate construct validity. The author argued vigorously for the construct validity of the picture motivation scale as a measure of IM and EM in mentally retarded and low-mental-age populations (Switzky & Heal, 1990) and documented in this chapter the evidence to support these claims. The Yale Group invented operational definitions for their major motivational constructs of positive reaction tendencies and overdependency, negative reaction tendencies and wariness, expectancies of success and failure, outerdirectedness, effectance motivation, self concept deficiencies, and high anxiety. However, better measures of personality, self-regulatory, and motivational processes are needed to develop more fine-grained and refined theoretical models applicable to mentally retarded and low-mental-age populations that are better integrated with motivational and personality theories of self-system processes derived from mainstream developmental psychology.

There are very few instruments for nonhandicapped children below 8 years of age that have even moderate predictive validity: Piers and Harris's Children's Self-Concept Scale (Piers & Harris, 1964): The Children's Manifest Anxiety Test (Castaneda, McCandless, & Palermo, 1956); The Test Anxiety Scale for Children (Sarason et al., 1960); The Scale of Intrinsic Versus Extrinsic Orientation in the Classroom (Harter, 1981b) and its revision for mildly mentally retarded children (Silon & Harter, 1985); The Perceived Competence Scale for Children (Harter, 1982; Harter & Pike, 1984); and The Children's Academic Intrinsic Motivational Inventory (Gottfried, 1985) and its downward extension, The Young Children's Academic Intrinsic Motivation Inventory (Gottfried, 1990). Nicholls developed a set of instruments to measure task goal and learning goals (Nicholls, 1989, 1990; Nicholls et al., 1990) in children that may have application to low-mental-age and mentally retarded individuals. Bandura and his colleagues developed new measures of self-efficacy (Bandura, 1993; Capara, Pastorelli, & Bandura, 1992) that may also be very promising for mental retardation researchers. Deci and his collaborators (Deci, Eghrari,

Patrick, & Leone, 1991; Deci & Ryan, 1985; Ryan, 1991; Vallerand, 1991) expanded their theory of self-determination by developing measures of an autonomous continuum of extrinsic/intrinsic motivation (e.g., external regulation, introjected regulation, identified regulation, and integrated regulation) related to how successfully an optimal self-regulatory style of intrinsic motivation has been internalized and integrated into the self. Ryan and Connell (1989) designed The Academic-Self-Regulation Questionnaire (ASRQ) for students in elementary and middle school. These measures of regulatory style may also be fruitful for mental retardation researchers to adapt for lower-mental-age populations.

Zigler and his colleagues (Burack, Hodapp, & Zigler, 1988; Merighi et al., 1990; Zigler & Burack, 1989; Zigler & Glick, 1986; Zigler & Hodapp, 1991) raised the question concerning the interaction of different motivational and cognitive patterns in familial, organic, dually diagnosed psychiatric disordered, and genetic (i.e., etiology-specific) populations of developmentally disabled learners and argued that etiology, independent of psychometric intelligence, is an important predictor of performance. There may exist etiology-specific motivational behavioral profiles that need to be investigated by mental retardation motivational researchers (Dykens, Hodapp, & Finucane, 1993; Hodapp & Dykens, 1994; Stoel-Gammon, 1990). Individual differences have been identified concerning the behavior and development of persons with Down syndrome (Cicchetti & Beeghly, 1990; Dykens, Hodapp, & Evans, 1994; Wagner, Ganiban, & Cicchetti, 1990), fragile X syndrome (Dykens & Leckman, 1990; Pennington, O'Connor, & Sudhalter, 1991), autism (Cohen & Donnellan, 1987), Smith-Magenis syndrome (Greenberg et al., 1991; Van Haneghan, Switzky, & Baxter, in press), Prader-Willi Syndrome (Taylor & Caldwell, 1988), and Adrenoleukodystrophy (Moser, Smith, & Moser, 1995; Switzky, Van Haneghan, & Baxter, in press). There may exist dramatic differences in motivational and personality self-system processes in these different etiologic groups as well (Bregman, 1991; Bregman, Dykens, Watson, Ort, & Leckman, 1987; Bybee & Zigler, 1992; Dykens, Hodapp, & Leckman, 1994; Yando, Seitz, & Zigler, 1989).

Motivational mental retardation researchers need to develop a theoretical model of the ontology of personality and motivational self-system processes and their relationship to learning and achievement in persons with mental retardation. A social developmental theory and perspective needs to be developed and refined to ensure that every mentally retarded child and adult acquires and uses his or her optimal problem-solving strategies and total fluid intelligences. A running start to achieve these goals has been made by both the Yale Group and Peabody-Vanderbilt Group of mental retardation researchers. Future mental retardation researchers building on the models of both mainstream developmental psychologists and developmental psychologists deriving from the mental retardation tradition are in a strong position to further accelerate the integration between a psychology of mental retardation and an overall developmental psychology of individual differences in human growth and development applicable to both retarded and nonretarded individuals.

REFERENCES

Abhalter, D., & Switzky, H. N. (1992, February). *Measures of intrinsic and extrinsic motivation in elementary school students: A test of construct validity.* Paper presented at the Third Conference of the International Association for Cognitive Education, University of California at Riverside.

Alden, L. (1986). Self-efficacy and casual attributions for social feedback. *Journal of Research in Personality, 20,* 460–473.

Atkinson, J. (1964). *An introduction to motivation.* Princeton, NJ: Van Nostrand.

Balla, D., & Zigler, E. (1979). Personality development in retarded persons. In N. R. Ellis (Eds.), *Handbook of mental deficiency* (2nd ed., pp. 143–168). Hillsdale, NJ: Lawrence Erlbaum Associates.

Bandura, A. (1977). *Social learning theory.* Englewood Cliffs, NJ: Prentice-Hall.

Bandura, A. (1978). The self-system in reciprocal determinism. *American Psychologist, 33,* 344–358.

Bandura, A. (1986a). *Social foundations of thought and action: A social cognitive theory.* Englewood Cliffs, NJ: Prentice-Hall.

Bandura, A. (1986b). From thought to action: Mechanisms of personal agency. *New Zealand Journal of Psychology, 15,* 1–17.

Bandura, A. (1991). Self-regulation of motivation through anticipatory and self-regulatory mechanisms. In R. A. Dienstbier (Ed.), *Perspectives on motivation: Nebraska symposium on motivation* (Vol. 38, pp. 69–164). Lincoln: University of Nebraska Press.

Bandura, A. (1992). Exercise of personal agency through self-efficacy mechanism. In R. Schwartzer (Ed.), *Self-efficacy: Thought control of action* (pp. 3–38). Washington, DC: Hemisphere.

Bandura, A. (1993). Perceived self-efficacy in cognitive development and functioning. *Educational Psychologist, 28*(2), 117–148.

Bandura, M., & Dweck, C. S. (1981). *Children's theories of intelligence as predictors of achievement goals.* Unpublished manuscript, Harvard University, Cambridge, MA.

Bialer, I., (1961). Conceptualization of success and failure in mentally retarded and normal children. *Journal of Personality, 29,* 303–320.

Borkowski, J. G., Carr, M., & Pressley, M. (1987). Spontaneous strategy use: Perspectives from metacognitive theory. *Intelligence, 11,* 61–75.

Borkowski, J. G., Carr, M., Rellinger, E., & Pressley, M. (1990). Self-regulated cognition: Interdependence of metacognition, attributions, and self-esteem. In B. F. Jones & L. Idol (Eds.), *Dimensions of thinking and cognitive instruction.* (pp. 53–92). Hillsdale, NJ: Lawrence Erlbaum Associates.

Borkowski, J. G., & Cavanaugh, J. (1979). Maintenance and generalization of skills and strategies by the retarded. In N. Ellis (Ed.), *Handbook of mental deficiency* (2nd ed., pp. 569–617). Hillsdale, NJ: Lawrence Erlbaum Associates.

Borkowski, J. G., Day, J. D., Saenz, D., Dietmeyer, D., Estrada, T. M., & Groteluschen, A. (1992). Expanding the boundaries of cognitive interventions. In B. Y. L. Wong (Ed.), *Contemporary intervention research in learning disabilities.* (pp. 1–21). New York: Springer-Verlag.

Borkowski, J. G., Johnston, M. B., & Reid, M. K. (1987). Metacognition, motivation and controlled performance. In S. Ceci (Ed.), *Handbook of cognitive, social, and neurological aspects of learning disabilities* (Vol. 2, pp. 147–174). Hillsdale, NJ: Lawrence Erlbaum Associates.

Borkowski, J. G., & Kurtz, B. E. (1987). Metacognition and executive control. In J. G. Borkowski & J. D. Day (Eds.), *Cognition in special children* (pp. 123–152). Norwood, NJ: Ablex.

Bransford, J. D., & Stein, B. S. (1984). *The IDEAL problem solver.* New York: Freeman.

Bregman, J. (1991). Current developments in the understanding of mental retardation. Part II. Psychopathology. *Journal of the American Academy of Child and Adolescent Psychiatry, 30,* 861–872.

Bregman, J., Dykens, E., Watson, M., Ort, S., & Leckman, J. (1987). Fragile X syndrome: Variability in phenotypic expression. *Journal of the American Academy of Child and Adolescent Psychiatry, 26,* 463–471.

Brown, A. L. (1978). Knowing when, where, and how to remember: A problem of metacognition. In R. Glaser (Ed.), *Advances in instructional psychology* (Vol. 1, pp. 77–165). Hillsdale, NJ: Lawrence Erlbaum Associates.

Brown, A. L., & Palinscar, A. S. (1987). In J. D. Day & J. G. Borkowski (Eds.), *Intelligence and exceptionality* (pp. 81–132). Norwood, NJ: Ablex.

Burack, J. A., Hodapp, R. M., & Zigler, E. (1988). Issues in the classification of mental retardation: Differentiating among organic etiologies. *Journal of Child Psychology and Psychiatry, 29,* 765–779.

Bybee, J., & Zigler, E. (1992). Is outerdirectedness employed in a harmful or beneficial manner by students with and without mental retardation? *American Journal of Mental Retardation, 96,* 512–521.

Call, R. J. (1968). *Motivation-hygiene orientation as a function of socioeconomic status, grade, race, and sex.* Unpublished master's thesis, Tennessee State University, Nashville.

Cantor, G. N. (1963). Hull-Spence behavior theory and mental deficiency. In N. R. Ellis (Ed.). *Handbook of mental deficiency* (pp. 90–133). New York: McGraw-Hill.

Cantor, N., Markus, H., Niedenthal, P., & Nurius, P. (1986). On motivation and self-concept. In R. M. Sorrentino & E. T. Higgins (Eds.), *Motivation and cognition: Foundations of social behavior* (pp. 99–127). New York: Guilford.

Caprara, G. V., Pastorelli, C., & Bandura, A. (1992). *Impact of perceived academic self-efficacy on interpersonal and emotional behavior.* Unpublished manuscript, Stanford University, Stanford, CA.

Carr, M., Borkowski, J. G., & Maxwell, S. E. (1991). Motivational components of underachievement. *Developmental Psychology, 27,* 108–118.

Castaneda, A., McCandless, B. R., & Palermo, D. S. (1956). The Children's Form of the Manifest Anxiety Scale. *Child Development, 27,* 317–326.

Chwalisz, K. D., Altmaier, E. M., & Russell, D. W. (1992). Causal attributions, self-efficacy cognitions, and coping with stress. *Journal of Social and Clinical Psychology, 11,* 377–400.

Cicchetti, D., & Beeghly, M. (Eds.). (1990). *Children with Down Syndrome: A developmental perspective.* New York: Cambridge University Press.

Clifford, M. M. (1984). Thoughts on a theory of constructive failure. *Educational Psychologist, 19,* 108–120.

Collins, J. L. (1982, March). *Self-efficacy and ability in achievement behavior.* Paper presented at the annual meeting of the American Educational Research Association, New York.

Cohen, D., & Donnellan, A. (Eds.). (1987). *Autism and pervasive developmental disabilities.* New York: Wiley.

Covington, M. V. (1987). Achievement motivation, self-attributions and exceptionality. In J. D. Day & J. G. Borkowski (Eds.), *Cognition in special children* (pp. 173–213). Norwood, NJ: Ablex.

Cromwell, R. L. (1963). A social learning approach to mental retardation. In N. R. Ellis (Ed.), *Handbook of mental deficiency* (pp. 41–91). New York: McGraw-Hill.

Cromwell, R. L. (1967). Success–failure reactions in mentally retarded children. In J. Zubin & G. A. Gervis (Eds.), *Psychopathology of mental development.* New York: Grune & Stratton.

Day, D. D., Borkowski, J. G., Dietmeyer, D. L., Howsepian, B. A., & Saenz, D. S. (1992). Possible selves and academic achievement. In L. T. Winegar & J. Valsiner (Eds.), *Children's development within social context: Research and methodology* (Vol. 2, pp. 181–201). Hillsdale, NJ: Elbaum.

DeCharms, R. (1968). *Personal causation: The interval affective determinants of behavior.* New York: Academic Press.

DeCharms, R. (1976). *Enhancing motivation: Change in the classroom.* New York: Irvington.

DeCharms, R. (1984). Motivating enhancement in educational settings. In R. Ames & C. Ames (Eds.), *Research on motivation in education, Vol 1: Student motivation* (pp. 275–310). Orlando, FL: Academic Press.

Deci, E. L. (1975). *Intrinsic motivation.* New York: Plenum.

Deci, E. L., & Chandler, C. L. (1986). The importance of motivation for the future of the LD field. *Journal of Learning Disabilities, 19,* 587–594.

Deci, E. L., Eghrari, H., Patrick, B. C., & Leone, D. R. (1991). *Facilitating internalization: The self-determination theory perspective.* Unpublished manuscript, University of Rochester, Rochester, NY.

Deci, E. L., Nezlek, J., & Scheinman, L. (1981). Characteristics of the rewarder and the intrinsic motivation of the rewardee. *Journal of Personality and Social Psychology, 40,* 1–10.

Deci, E. L., & Ryan, R. M. (1985). *Intrinsic motivation and self-determination in human behavior.* New York: Plenum.

Deci, E. L., & Ryan, R. M. (1991). A motivational approach to self: Integration in personality. In R. Dienstbier (Ed.), *Nebraska symposium on motivation, Vol. 38: Perspectives on motivation* (pp. 237–288). Lincoln: University of Nebraska Press.

Deci, E. L., Schwartz, A. J., Scheinman. L., & Ryan, R. M. (1981). An instrument to assess adults' orientation toward control versus autonomy with children. *Journal of Educational Psychology, 73*, 642–650.

Deci, E. L., Vallerand, L. G., Pelletier, L. G., & Ryan, R. M. (1991). Motivation and education: The self-determination perspective. *Educational Psychologist, 26*, 325–346.

de Vries, H., Dijkstra, M., & Kuhlman, P. (1988). Self-efficacy: The third factor besides attitude and subjective norm as a predictor of behavioral intentions. *Health Education Research, 3*, 273–282.

Dobbs, V. (1967). *Motivational orientation and programmed instruction achievement gains of educable mentally retarded adolescents*. Unpublished doctoral dissertation, George Peabody College, Nashville, TN.

Dweck, C. S. (1985). Intrinsic motivation, perceived control, and self-evaluation maintenance: An achievement goal analysis. In C. Ames & R. Ames (Eds.), *Research on motivation: The classroom milieu* (Vol. 2, pp. 289–305). Orlando, FL: Academic Press.

Dweck, C. S. (1986). Motivational processes affecting learning. *American Psychologist, 41*, 1040–1048.

Dweck, C. S. (1989). Motivation. In A. Lesgold & R. Glaser (Eds.), *Foundations for a psychology of education* (pp. 87–136). Hillsdale, NJ: Lawrence Erlbaum Associates.

Dweck, C. S., & Bempechat, J. (1983). Children's theories of intelligence: Impact on learning. In S. G. Paris, G. M. Olson, H. W. Stevenson (Eds.), *Learning and motivation in the classroom* (pp. 239–281). Hillsdale, NJ: Lawrence Erlbaum Associates.

Dweck, C. S., & Leggett, E. L. (1988). A social–cognitive approach to motivation and personality. *Psychological Review, 95*, 256–273.

Dykens, E. M., Hodapp, R. M., & Evans, D. W. (1994). Profiles and development of adaptive behavior in children with Down syndrome. *American Journal of Mental Retardation, 98*, 580–587.

Dykens, E., Hodapp, R., & Finucane, B. (1993, June). *How do persons with genetic disorders differ in their behaviors? Provocations from the "new genetics."* Paper read at the National Conference of the American Association on Mental Retardation, Washington, DC.

Dykens, E. M., Hodapp, R. M., & Leckman, J. F. (1994). *Behavior and development in fragile X syndrome, Vol. 28*. Thousand Oaks, CA: Sage.

Dykens, E. M., & Leckman, J. F. (1990). Developmental issues in fragile X. In R. M. Hodapp, J. A. Burack, & E. Zigler (Eds.), *Issues in the developmental approach to mental retardation* (pp. 226–245). New York: Cambridge University Press.

Dzewaltowski, D. A., Noble, J. M., & Shaw, J. M. (1990). Physical activity participation: Social cognitive theory versus the theories of reasoned action and planned behavior. *Journal of Sport and Exercise Psychology, 12*, 388–405.

Elliott, E. S., & Dweck, C. S. (1981). *Children's achievement goals as determinants of learned helplessness and mastery-oriented achievement patterns: An experimental analysis*. Unpublished manuscript, Harvard University, Cambridge, MA.

Elliot, E. S., & Dweck, C. S. (1988). Goals: An approach to motivation and achievement. *Journal of Personality and Social Psychology, 54*, 5–12.

Feuerstein, R., & Feuerstein, S. (1991). Mediated learning experience: A theoretical review. In R. Feuerstein., P. S. Klein, & A. J. Tannenbaum (Eds.), *Mediated learning experience (MLE): Theoretical, psychosocial and learning implications* (pp. 3–51). London: Freund.

Feuerstein, R., Klein, P. S., & Tannenbaum, A. J. (Eds.). (1991). *Mediated learning experience (MLE): Theoretical, psychosocial and learning implications*. London: Freund.

Feuerstein, R., & Rand, Y. (1974). Mediated learning experiences: An outline of the proximal etiology for differential development of cognitive functions. *International Understanding, 9–10*, 7–37.

Feuerstein, R., Rand, Y., Hoffman, M. B., & Miller, R. (1980). *Instrumental enrichment: intervention program for cognitive modifiability.* Baltimore, MD: University Park Press.

Gambro, J. S., & Switzky, H. N. (1988). Motivational orientation and self-regulation in young children. *Reflections of Learning Research, 3*, 6–7.

Gambro, J. S., & Switzky, H. N. (1991). Motivational orientation and self-regulation in young children. *Early Child Development and Care, 70*, 45–51.

Glick, M., & Zigler, E. (1985). Self-image: A cognitive-developmental approach. In R. Leahy (Ed.), *The development of the self* (pp. 1–53). New York: Academic Press.

Gottfried, A. E. (1985). Academic intrinsic motivation in elementary and junior high school students. *Journal of Educational Psychology, 20*, 205–215.

Gottfried, A. E. (1990). Academic intrinsic motivation in young elementary school children. *Journal of Educational Psychology, 82*, 525–538.

Greenberg, F., Guzzetta, V., Montes-de Oca-Luna, R., Magenis, R. E., Smith, A. C., Richter, S. F., Kondo, I., Dobyns, W. B., Patel, P. I., & Lupski, J. R. (1991). Molecular analysis of the Smith-Magenis syndrome: A posible contiguous-gene syndrome associated with del(17) (p11.2). *American Journal of Medical Genetics, 49*, 1207–1218.

Hamers, J. H. M., Sijtsma, K., & Ruijssenaars, A. J. J. M. (Eds.). (1993). *Learning potential assessment.* Amsterdam: Swets & Zeitlinger.

Harter, S. (1978). Effectance motivation reconsidered: Toward a developmental model. *Human Development, 6*, 34–64.

Harter, S. (1981a). A model of intrinsic motivation in children. In W. A. Collins (Ed.), *Minnesota Symposium on Child Psychology* (Vol. 14, pp. 215–255). Hillsdale, NJ: Lawrence Erlbaum Associates.

Harter, S. (1981b). A new self-report scale of intrinsic versus extrinsic orientation in the classroom: Motivational and informational components. *Developmental Psychology, 17*, 300–312.

Harter, S. (1982). The Perceived Competence Scale for Children. *Child Development, 53*, 87–97.

Harter, S. (1983). Developmental perspectives on the self-system. In E. M. Hetherington (Ed.), *Handbook of child psychology: Socialization, personality and social development* (Vol. 4, pp. 278–386). New York: Wiley.

Harter, S. (1986). Processes underlying the construction, maintenance, and enhancement of the self-concept in children. In S. Suls & A. Greenwald (Eds.), *Psychological perspectives on the self* (Vol. 3, pp. 136–182). Hillsdale, NJ: Lawrence Erlbaum Associates.

Harter, S. (1987). The determinants and mediational role of global self-worth in children. In N. Eisenberg (Ed.), *Contemporary topics in developmental psychology.* (pp. 219–241). New York: Wiley.

Harter, S., & Pike, R. (1984). The pictorial scale of perceived competence and social acceptance for young children. *Child Development, 55*, 1969–1982.

Harter, S., & Zigler, E. (1974). The assessment of effectance motivation in normal and retarded children. *Developmental Psychology, 10*, 169–180.

Haywood, H. C. (1968a). Motivational orientation of overachieving and underachieving elementary school children. *American Journal of Mental Deficiency, 72*, 662–667.

Haywood, H. C. (1968b). Psychometric motivation and the efficiency of learning and performance in the mentally retarded. In B. W. Richards (Ed.), *Proceedings of the First Congress of the International Association for the Scientific Study of Mental Deficiency* (pp. 276–283). Reigate, England: Michael Jackson.

Haywood, H. C. (1971). Individual differences in motivational orientation: A trait approach. In H. I. Day, D. E. Berlyne, & D. E. Hunt (Eds.), *Intrinsic motivation: A new direction in education.* Toronto: Holt, Rinehart & Winston.

Haywood, H. C. (1977). A cognitive approach to the education of retarded children. *Peabody Journal of Education, 54*, 110–116.

Haywood, H. C. (1992). The strange and wonderful symbiosis of motivation and cognition. *International Journal of Cognitive Education & Mediated Learning, 2*, 186–197.

Haywood, H. C., Brooks, P., & Burns, S. (1986). Stimulating cognitive development at developmental level: A tested, non-remedial preschool curriculum for preschool and older retarded children. In M. Schwebel & C. A. Maher (Eds.), *Facilitating cognitive development: Principles, practices, and programs* (pp. 127–147). New York: Haworth.

Haywood, H. C., & Burke, W. P. (1977). Development of individual differences in intrinsic motivation. In I. C. Uzgiris & F. Weizman (Eds.), *The structuring of experience* (pp. 235–263). New York: Plenum.

Haywood, H. C., Meyers, C. E., & Switzky, H. N. (1982). Mental retardation. *Annual Review of Psychology, 33*, 309–342.

Haywood, H. C., & Switzky, H. N. (1975). Use of contingent social reinforcement to change the verbal expression of motivation in children of differing motivational orientation. *Perceptual and Motor Skills, 86*, 356–365.

Haywood, H. C., & Switzky, H. N. (1985). Work response of mildly mentally retarded adults to self versus external regulation as a function of motivational orientation. *American Journal of Mental Deficiency, 90*, 151–159.

Haywood, H. C., & Switzky, H. N. (1986). Intrinsic motivation and behavioral effectiveness in retarded persons. In N. Ellis & N. Bray (Eds.), *International review of research in mental retardation* (Vol. 14, pp. 1–46). New York: Academic Press.

Haywood, H. C., & Switzky, H. N. (1992). Ability and modifiability: What, how and how much? In J. S. Carlson (Ed.), *Advances in cognition and educational practice: Theoretical issues: Intelligence, cognition, and assessment* (Vol. 1–Part A, pp. 25–85). Greenwich, CT: JAI.

Haywood, H. C., & Tzuriel, D. (Eds.). (1992). *Interactive assessment.* New York: Springer-Verlag.

Haywood, H. C., Tzuriel, D., & Vaught, S. (1992). Psychoeducational assessment from a transactional perspective. In H. C. Haywood & D. Tzuriel (Eds.), *Interactive assessment* (pp. 38–63). New York: Springer-Verlag.

Haywood, H. C., & Wachs, T. D. (1966). Size discrimination learning as a function of motivation-hygiene orientation in adolescents. *Journal of Educational Psychology, 57*, 279–286.

Haywood, H. C., & Weaver, S. J. (1967). Differential effects of motivational orientation and incentive conditions on motor performance in institutionalized retardates. *American Journal of Mental Deficiency, 72*, 459–467.

Herzberg, F. (1966). *Work and the nature of man.* Cleveland, OH: World.

Herzberg, F., & Hamlin, R. M. (1961). A motivation-hygiene concept of mental health. *Mental Hygiene, 47*, 384–397.

Herzberg, F., & Hamlin, R. M. (1963). The motivation-hygiene concept and psychotherapy. *Mental Hygiene, 47*, 384–397.

Herzberg, F., Mausner, B., & Snyderman, B. B. (1959). *The motivation to work.* New York: Wiley.

Hill, K. (1984). Debilitating motivation and testing: A major educational problem, possible solutions, and policy applications. In R. Ames & C. Ames (Eds.), *Research on motivation in education, Vol 1: Student motivation* (pp. 245–272). Orlando, FL: Academic Press.

Hill, K., & Wigfield, A. (1984). Test anxiety: A major educational problem and what can be done about it. *The Elementary School Journal, 85*, 105–126.

Hobbs, N. (1963). Foreword. In N. R. Ellis (Ed.), *Handbook of mental deficiency* (pp. ix–x). New York: McGraw-Hill.

Hodapp, R. M., Burack, J. A., & Zigler, E. (Eds.). (1990). *Issues in the developmental approach to mental retardation.* New York: Cambridge University Press.

Hodapp, R. M., & Dykens, E. M. (1994). Mental retardation's two cultures of behavioral research. *American Journal on Mental Retardation, 98*, 675–687.

Hoffman, J., & Weiner, B. (1978). Effects of attributions for success and failure on the performance of retarded adults. *American Journal of Mental Deficiency, 82*, 449–452.

Horai, J., & Guarnaccia, V. J. (1975). Performance and attributions to ability, effort, task, and luck of retarded adults after success or failure feedback. *American Journal of Mental Deficiency, 79*, 690–694.

Hunt, J. M. (1963). Motivation inherent in information processing and action. In O. J. Harvey (Ed.), *Motivation and social interaction: Cognitive determinants* (pp. 35–94). New York: Ronald.

Hunt, J. M. (1965). Intrinsic motivation and its role in psychological development. In D. Levine (Ed.), *Nebraska symposium on motivation* (Vol. 13, pp. 189–282). Lincoln: University of Nebraska Press.

Hunt, J. M. (1966). The epigenesis of intrinsic motivation and early cognitive learning. In R. N. Haber (Ed.), *Current research in motivation* (pp. 355–370). New York: Holt.

Hunt, J. M. (1971). Toward a history of intrinsic motivation. In H. I. Day, D. E. Berlyne, & D. E. Hunt (Eds.), *Intrinsic motivation: A new direction in education* (pp. 1–32). Toronto: Holt.

Kounin, J. (1941a). Experimental studies of rigidity: I. The measurement of rigidity in normal and feebleminded persons. *Character and Personality, 9*, 251–272.

Kounin, J. (1941b). Experimental studies of rigidity: II. The explanatory power of the concept of rigidity as applied to feeblemindedness. *Character and Personality, 9*, 273–282.

Kunca, D. F., & Haywood, N. P. (1969). The measurement of motivational orientation in low mental age subjects. *Peabody Papers in Human Development, 7*(Whole No.2).

Leahy, R. L. (Ed.). (1985). *The development of the self.* Orlando, FL: Academic Press.

Leahy, R., Balla, D., & Zigler, E. (1982). Role taking, self-image and imitativeness in mentally retarded and nonretarded individuals. *American Journal of Mental Deficiency, 86*, 372–379.

Leeper, M. R., & Hodell, M. (1989). Intrinsic motivation in the classroom. In C. Ames & R. Ames (Eds.), *Research on motivation in education.* (Vol. 3, pp. 73–105). San Diego, CA: Academic Press.

Lewin, K. (1936). *A dynamic theory of personality.* New York: McGraw-Hill.

Lipman, R. S. (1963). Learning: Verbal, perceptual-motor, and classical conditioning. In N. R. Ellis (Ed.), *Handbook of mental deficiency.* (pp. 391–423). New York: McGraw-Hill.

Lipman, R. S., & Griffith, B. C. (1960). Effects of anxiety level on concept formation: A test of drive theory. *American Journal of Mental Deficiency, 65*, 342–348.

Locke, E. A., & Latham, G. P. (1990). *A theory of goal setting and task performance.* Englewood Cliffs, NJ: Prentice-Hall.

Madden, T. J., Ellen, P. S., & Ajzen, I. (1992). A comparison of the theory of planned behavior and the theory of reasoned action. *Personality and Social Psychology Bulletin, 18*, 3–9.

Maehr, M. L., & Braskamp, L. A. (1986). *The motivation factor: A theory of personal investment.* Lexington, MA: Lexington.

Maehr, M., & Pintrich, P. R. (1991). *Advances in motivation and achievement: Goals and self-regulatory processes* (Vol. 7). Greenwich, CT: JAI.

Markus, H., Cross, S., & Wurf, E. (1990). The role of the self-system in competence. In R. J. Sternberg & J. Kolligan, Jr. (Eds.), *Competence considered* (pp. 205–225). New Haven, CT: Yale University Press.

Markus, H., & Nurius, P. (1986). Possible selves. *American Psychologist, 41*, 954–969.

Marsh, H. W. (1990). The structure of academic self-concept: The Marsh/Shavelson model. *Journal of Educational Psychology, 82*, 623–636.

Marshall, H. H., & Wienstein, R. S. (1984). Classroom factors affecting students' self-evaluations: An interactional model. *Review of Educational Research, 54*, 301–325.

McAuley, E. (1991). Efficacy, attributional, and affective responses to exercise participation. *Journal of Sport and Exercise Psychology, 13*, 382–393.

McAuley, E., Duncan, T. E., & McElroy, M. (1989). Self-efficacy cognitions and causal attributions for children's motor performance: An exploratory investigation. *The Journal of Genetic Psychology, 150*, 65–73.

McCaul, K. D., O'Neill, K., & Glasgow, R. E. (1988). Predicting the performance of dental hygiene behaviors: An examination of the Fishbein and Ajzen model and self-efficacy expectations. *Journal of Applied Social Psychology, 18*, 114–128.

McCombs, B. L. (1988). Motivational skill training: Combining metacognitive, cognitive, and affective learning strategies. In C. E. Weinstein, E. T. Goetz, & P. A. Alexander (Eds.), *Learning and study strategies: Issues in assessment, instruction, and evaluation* (pp. 141–169). New York: Academic Press.

McCombs, B. L. (1989). Self-regulated learning and academic achievement: A phenomenological view. In B. J. Zimmerman & D. H. Schunk (Eds.), *Self-regulated learning and academic achievement* (pp. 51–82). New York: Springer-Verlag.

McCombs, B. L., & Marzano, R. J. (1990). Putting the self in self-regulated learning: The self in regulating will and skill. *Educational Psychologist, 25,* 51–69.

McCombs, B. L., & Whisler, J. S. (1989). The role of affective variables in autonomous learning. *Educational Psychologist, 24,* 277–306.

Meece, J. L., Wigfield, A., & Eccles, J. S. (1990). Predictors of math anxiety and its influence on young adolescents' course enrollment intentions and performance in mathematics. *Journal of Educational Psychology, 82,* 60–70.

Merighi, J., Edison, M., & Zigler, E. (1990). The role of motivational factors in the functioning of mentally retarded individuals. In R. M. Hodapp, J. A. Burack, & E. Zigler (Eds.), *Issues in the developmental approach to mental retardation* (pp. 114–134). New York: Cambridge University Press.

Miller, M. B. (1961). *Locus of control, learning climate, and climate shift in serial learning with mental retardates.* Ann Arbor, MI: University Microfilms.

Moser, H. W., Smith, K. B., & Moser, A. B. (1995). X-linked Adrenoleukodystrophy. In C. R. Scriver, A. L. Beaudet, W. S. Sly, & D. Valle (Eds.), *The metabolic and molecular bases of inherited disease* (pp. 2325–2348). New York: McGraw-Hill.

Moss, J. W. (1958). *Failure-avoiding and success-striving behavior in mentally retarded and normal children.* Ann Arbor, MI: University Microfilms.

Nicholls, J. G. (1979a). Development of perception of own attainment and casual attributions for success and failure in reading. *Journal of Educational Psychology, 71,* 94–99.

Nicholls, J. G. (1979b). Quality and equality in intellectual development. *American Psychologist, 34,* 1071–1084.

Nicholls, J. G. (1984). Achievement motivation: Conceptions of ability, subjective experience, task choice, and performance. *Psychological Review, 91,* 328–346.

Nicholls, J. G. (1989). *The competitive ethos and democratic education.* Cambridge, MA: Harvard University Press.

Nicholls, J. G. (1990). What is ability and why are we mindful of it? A developmental perspective. In R. Sternberg & J. Kolligen, Jr. (Eds.), *Competence considered* (pp. 11–40). New Haven, CT: Yale University Press.

Nicholls, J. G., Cheung, P. G., Lauer, J., & Patashnick, M. (1989). Individual differences in academic motivation: Perceived ability, goals, beliefs, and values. *Learning and Individual Differences, 1,* 63–84.

Nicholls, J. G., Cobb, P., Wood, T., Yackel, E., & Patashnick, M. (1990). Assessing students' theories of success in mathematics: Individual and classroom differences. *Journal for Research in Mathematics Education, 21,* 109–122.

Nicholls, J. G., Cobb, P., Yackel, E., Wood, T., & Wheatley, G. (1990). Students' theories about mathematics and their mathematical knowledge: Multiple dimensions of assessment. In G. Kulm (Ed.), *Assessing higher order thinking in mathematics* (pp. 137–154). Washington, DC: American Association for the Advancement of Science.

Nicholls, J. G., Patashnick, M., & Nolen, S. B. (1985). Adolescents' theories of education. *Journal of Educational Psychology, 77,* 683–692.

Nolen, S. B. (1988). Reasons for studying: Motivational orientations and study strategies. *Cognition and Instruction, 5,* 269–287.

Paris, S. G., & Byrnes, J. P. (1989). The constructivist approach to self-regulation and learning in the classroom. In B. J. Zimmerman & D. H. Schunk (Eds.), *Self-regulated learning and academic achievement* (pp. 169–200). New York: Springer-Verlag.

Paris, S. G., & Newman, R. S. (1990). Developmental aspects of self-regulated learning. *Educational Psychologist, 25,* 87–102.

Pennington, B., O'Connor, R., & Sudhalter, V. (1991). Toward a neuropsychology of fragile X syndrome. In R. J. Hagerman & A. C. Silverman (Eds.), *Fragile X syndrome: Diagnosis, treatment and research* (pp. 173–201). Baltimore, MD: Johns Hopkins University Press.

Piers, E. V., & Harris, D. B. (1964). Age and other correlates of self-concept in children. *Journal of Educational Psychology, 55*, 91–95.

Pintrich, P. R., & De Groot, E. V. (1990). Motivational and self-regulated learning. *Journal of Educational Psychology, 82*, 33–40.

Pintrich, P. R., & Schrauben, B. (1992). Students' motivational beliefs and their cognitive engagement in classroom academic tasks. In D. Schunk & J. Meece (Eds.), *Student perceptions in the classroom: Cause and consequences* (pp. 149–183). Hillsdale, NJ: Lawrence Erlbaum Associates.

Pressley, M., Borkowski, J. G., & O'Sullivan, J. T. (1984). Memory strategy instruction is made of this: Metamemory and durable strategy use. *Educational Psychologist, 19*, 94–107.

Pressley, M., Borkowski, J. G., & O'Sullivan, J. T. (1985). Children's metamemory and the teaching of memory strategies. In D. L. Forrest-Pressley, G. E. MacKennon, & T. G. Waller (Eds.), *Metacognition, cognition, and human performance* (pp. 111–153). San Diego, CA: Academic Press.

Pressley, M., Borkowski, J. G., & Schneider, W. (1990). Good information processing: What it is and how education can promote it. *International Journal of Educational Research, 2*, 857–867.

Rogers, C. (1947). Some observations on the organization of personality. *American Psychologist, 2*, 358–368.

Rosenholtz, S. J., & Simpson, C. (1984). The formation of ability conceptions: Developmental trend or construction? *Review of Educational Research, 54*, 31–63.

Rotter, J. (1954). *Social learning and clinical psychology.* New York: Prentice-Hall.

Ryan, R. M. (1991). The nature of the self in autonomy and relatedness. In G. R. Goethals & J. Strauss (Eds.), *Multidisciplinary perspectives on the self* (pp. 208–238). New York: Springer-Verlag.

Ryan, R., & Connell, J. (1989). Perceived locus of causality and internalization: Examining reasons for acting in two domains. *Journal of Personality and Social Psychology, 57*, 749–761.

Ryan, R. M., Connell, J. P., & Deci, E. L. (1985). A motivational analysis of self-determination and self-regulation. In C. Ames & R. Ames (Eds.), *Research on motivation in the classroom: Vol. 2, The classroom milieu* (pp. 13–51). Orlando, FL: Academic Press.

Sarason, S., Davidson, K., Lighthall, F., Waite, R., & Ruebusch, B. (1960). *Anxiety in elementary school children.* New York: Wiley.

Schiefele, U. (1991). Interest, learning, and motivation. *Educational Psychologist, 26*(3 & 4), 299–323.

Schultz, G. F., & Switzky, H. N. (1990). The development of intrinsic motivation in students with learning problems. *Preventing School Failure, 34*, 14–20.

Schultz, G. F., & Switzky, H. N. (1993). The academic achievement of elementary and junior high school students with behavior disorders and their nonhandicapped peers as a function of motivational orientation. *Learning & Individual Differences, 5*, 31–42.

Schunk, D. H. (1989a). Self-efficacy and cognitive skill learning. In C. Ames & R. Ames (Eds.), *Research on motivation in education, Vol. 3: Goals and cognitions* (pp. 13–44). San Diego, CA: Academic Press.

Schunk, D. H. (1989b). Social cognitive theory and self-regulated learning. In B. J. Zimmerman & D. H. Schunk (Eds.), *Self-regulated learning and academic achievement* (pp. 83–119). New York: Springer-Verlag.

Schunk, D. H. (1990). Goal setting and self-efficacy during self-regulated learning. *Educational Psychologist, 25*(1), 71–86.

Schunk, D. H. (1991). Self-efficacy and academic achievement. *Educational Psychologist, 26*(3 & 4), 207–231.

Schunk, D. H., & Gunn, T. P. (1986). Self-efficacy and skill development: Influence of task strategies and attributions. *Journal of Educational Research, 79*, 238–244.

Schunk, D. H., & Rice, J. M. (1986). Extended attributional feedback: Sequence effects during remedial reading instruction. *Journal of Early Adolescence, 6,* 55–66.

Silon, E. L., & Harter, S. (1985). Assessment of perceived competence, motivational orientation, and anxiety in segregated and mainstreamed educable mentally retarded children. *Journal of Educational Psychology, 77,* 217–230.

Snygg, D., & Combs, A. V. (1949). *Individual behavior: A new frame of reference for psychology.* New York: Harper.

Spielberger, C. (1972). Anxiety as an emotional state. In C. Spielberger (Ed.), *Anxiety: Current trends in theory and research, Vol. 1* (pp. 23–49). New York: Academic Press.

Sternberg, R. J. (1985). *Beyond IQ: A triarchic theory of human intelligence.* Cambridge, England: Cambridge University Press.

Sternberg, R. J. (1987). A unified theory of intellectual exceptionality. In J. D. Day & J. G. Borkowski (Eds.), *Intelligence and exceptionality* (pp. 135–172). Norwood, NJ: Ablex.

Sternberg, R. J., & Berg, C. A. (Eds.). (1992). *Intellectual development.* New York: Cambridge University Press.

Stevenson, H. W., & Zigler, E. (1958). Probability learning in children. *Journal of Experimental Psychology, 56,* 185–192.

Stipek, D. J. (1984). The development of achievement motivation. In R. Ames & C. Ames (Eds.), *Research on motivation in education, Vol. 1: Student motivation* (pp. 145–174). Orlando, FL: Academic Press.

Stipek, D. J. (1993). *Motivation to learn* (2nd. ed). Boston: Allyn and Bacon.

Stipek, D. J., & Weisz, J. R. (1981). Perceived personal control and academic achievement. *Review of Educational Research, 51,* 101–137.

Stoel-Gammon, C. (1990). Down Syndrome: Effects on language development. *Journal of the American Speech and Hearing Association, 32,* 42–44.

Switzky, H. N. (1985). Self-reinforcement schedules in young children: A preliminary investigation of the effects of motivational orientation and instructional demands. *Reflections of Learning Research, 1,* 3–18.

Switzky, H. N., & Haywood, H. C. (1974). Motivational orientation and the relative efficacy of self-monitored and externally imposed reinforcement schedules. *Journal of Personality and Social Psychology, 30,* 360–366.

Switzky, H. N., & Haywood, H. C. (1984). Bio-social ecological perspectives on mental retardation. In N. S. Endler & J. M. Hunt (Eds.), *Personality and the behavior disorders* (2nd ed., Vol 2, pp. 851–896). New York: Wiley.

Switzky, H. N., & Haywood, H. C. (1991). Self-reinforcement schedules in persons with mild mental retardation: Effects of motivational orientation and instructional demands. *Journal of Mental Deficiency Research, 35,* 221–230.

Switzky, H. N., & Haywood, H. C. (1992). Self-reinforcement schedules in young children: Effects of motivational orientation and instructional demands. *Learning and Individual Differences, 4,* 59–71.

Switzky, H. N., Haywood, H. C., & Isett, R. (1974). Exploration, curiosity, and play in young children: Effects of stimulus complexity. *Developmental Psychology, 10,* 321–329.

Switzky, H. N., & Heal, L. (1990). Research methods in special education. In R. Gaylord-Ross (Ed.), *Issues and research in special education* (Vol. 1, pp. 1–81). New York: Teachers College Press.

Switzky, H. N., Ludwig, L., & Haywood, H. C. (1979). Exploration, curiosity, and play in young children: Effects of object complexity and age. *American Journal of Mental Deficiency, 86,* 637–646.

Switzky, H. N., & Schultz, G. F. (1988). Intrinsic motivation and learning performance implications for individual educational programming for the mildly handicapped. *Remedial and Special Education, 9,* 7–14.

Switzky, H., Van Haneghan, J., & Baxter, A. (in press). Adrenoleukodystrophy. In L. Phelps (Ed.), *Handbook of health-related disorders in children.* Washington, DC: NASP.

Taylor, R., & Caldwell, M. (Eds.). (1988). *Prader-Willi Syndrome: Selected research and management issues.* New York: Springer-Verlag.

Thorkildsen, T. A. (1988). Theories of education among academically precocious adolescents. *Contemporary Educational Psychology, 13,* 323–330.

Tzuriel, D. (1991). Cognitive modifiability, mediated learning experience and affective motivational processes: A transactional approach. In R. Feuerstein, P. S. Klein, & A. J. Tannenbaum (Eds.), *Mediated learning experience (MLE): Theoretical, psychosocial and learning implications* (pp. 95–120). London: Freund.

Vallerand, R. J. (1991). *A motivational analysis of high school dropout.* Unpublished manuscript, University of Quebec at Montreal, Montreal, Canada.

Van Haneghan, J., Switzky, H., & Baxter, A. (in press). Smith-Magenis Syndrome. In L. Phelps (Ed.), *Handbook of health-related disorders in children.* Washington, DC: NASP.

Vye, N. J., Delclos, V. R., Burns, M. S., & Bransford, J. D. (1988). Teaching thinking and problem solving: Illustrations and issues. In R. J. Sternberg & E. E. Smith (Eds.), *The psychology of human thought* (pp. 337–365). Cambridge, England: Cambridge University Press.

Wagner, S., Ganiban, J., & Cicchetti, D. (1990). Attention, memory, and perception in infants with Down Syndrome: A review and commentary. In D. Cicchetti & M. Beeghly (Eds.), *Children with Down Syndrome: A developmental perspective* (pp. 302–328). New York: Cambridge University Press.

Weiner, B. (1986). *An attributional theory of motivation and emotion.* New York: Springer-Verlag.

Weiner, B. (1990). History of motivational research in education. *Journal of Educational Psychology, 82,* 616–622.

Weisz, J. R. (1978). Choosing problem-solving rewards and Halloween prizes: Delay of gratification and preference for symbolic reward as a function of development, motivation, and person of investment. *Developmental Psychology, 14,* 66–78.

Weisz, J. R. (1979). Perceived control and learned helplessness among mentally retarded and nonretarded children: A developmental analysis. *Developmental Psychology, 15,* 311–319.

Weisz, J. R. (1981). Learned helplessness in black and white children identified by their schools as retarded and nonretarded: Performance deterioration to failure. *Developmental Psychology, 17,* 499–508.

Weisz, J. R. (1990). Cultural–familial mental retardation: A developmental perspective on cognitive performance and "helpless" behavior. In R. M. Hodapp, J. A. Burack, & E. Zigler (Eds.), *Issues in the developmental approach to mental retardation* (pp. 137–168). New York: Cambridge University Press.

Wheeler, K. G. (1983). Comparisons of self-efficacy and expectancy models of occupational preferences for college males and females. *Journal of Occupational Psychology, 56,* 73–78.

White, R. H. (1959). Motivation reconsidered: The concept of competence. *Psychological Review, 66,* 297–333.

Wigfield, A., & Karpathian, M. (1991). Who am I and what can I do? Children's self-concepts and motivation in achievement situations. *Educational Psychologist, 26*(3 & 4), 233–261.

Wooldridge, R. (1966). *Motivation-hygiene orientation and school achievement in mentally subnormal children.* Unpublished EdS Study, George Peabody College, Nashville, TN.

Yando, R., Seitz, V., & Zigler, E. (1989). Imitation, recall, and imitativeness in children with low intelligence of organic and familial etiology. *Research in Developmental Disabilities, 10,* 225–240.

Zewdie, A. (1995). *Work performance of Afro-American adults with mild and moderate mental retardation to self versus external regulation as a function of intrinsic versus extrinsic motivation.* Unpublished doctoral dissertation, Northern Illinois University, DeKalb, IL.

Zigler, E. (1971). The retarded child as a whole person. In H. E. Adams & W. K. Boardman III (Eds.), *Advances in experimental clinical psychology* (Vol. 1, pp. 47–121). New York: Pergamon Press.

Zigler, E., & Balla, D. (1981). Issues in personality and motivation in mentally retarded persons. In M. J. Begab, H. C. Haywood, & H. L. Garber (Eds.), *Psychosocial influences in retarded performance* (Vol. 1, pp. 197–218). Baltimore, MD: University Park Press.

Zigler, E., & Balla, D. (Eds.). (1982). *Mental retardation: The developmental-difference controversy.* Hillsdale, NJ: Lawrence Erlbaum Associates.

Zigler, E., Balla, D., & Watson, N. (1972). Developmental and experiential determinants of self-image disparity in institutionalized and noninstitutionalized retarded and normal children. *Journal of Personality and Social Psychology, 23,* 81–87.

Zigler, E., & Burack, J. (1989). Personality development in the dually diagnosed person. *Research in Developmental Disabilities, 10,* 225–240.

Zigler, E., & Glick, M. (1986). *A developmental approach to adult psychopathology.* New York: Wiley.

Zigler, E., & Hodapp, R. M. (1991). Behavioral functioning in individuals with mental retardation. *Annual Review of Psychology, 42,* 29–50.

Zimmerman, B. J. (1990). Self-regulating academic learning and achievement: The emergence of a social cognitive perspective. *Educational Psychological Review, 2,* 173–201.

Zimmerman, B. J., & Schunk, D. H. (Eds.). (1989). *Self-regulated learning and academic achievement.* New York: Springer-Verlag.

Zoeller, C., Mahoney, G., & Weiner, B. (1983). Effects of attribution training on the assembly task performance of mentally retarded adults. *American Journal of Mental Deficiency, 88,* 109–112.

› 14 ‹

Communication, Language, and Mental Retardation

Steven F. Warren
Paul J. Yoder
Peabody College, Vanderbilt University

Communication and language development are central to our definitions of human intelligence (e.g., Gardner, 1983; Thurstone, 1938). Linguistic skills distinguish individuals who are gifted intellectually from those who are average intellectually and those with mental retardation more consistently than do other cognitive or social abilities. General intelligence tests such as the Wechsler Scales and the Stanford–Binet Intelligence Scale are weighted heavily toward linguistic abilities. Language serves as the input mode for acquiring and producing most other forms of abstract symbol use such as reading, writing, and math and serves as the output mode for a substantial portion of our social behavior. Our communication and language abilities are basic to how we define ourselves, and to how we perceive and evaluate others.

The fundamental role of communication and language in human social and cognitive functioning becomes starkly evident when these domains of activity fail to develop normally or are impaired in some way due to accident or disease. Delayed or deviant language and communication development are implicit in our definitions of mental retardation (Rosenburg & Abbeduto, 1993) and autism (Frith, 1989). Underlying language and communication problems also are likely to be one of the factors contributing to some learning disabilities and/or behavior disorders (Ceci, 1986). Communication and language-related developmental disorders affect several million school-age children in this country and account for the vast majority of children receiving special education services (Casby, 1989). These figures do not begin to tell the whole story. In an increasingly high-tech society, people's communication abilities will determine their job prospects, their social and educational opportunities, and their overall quality of life. Individuals who fail to acquire effective communication skills will likely endure lives of undue dependency, social isolation, and restriction, irrespective of other abilities they may have.

The central role of communication and language development in mental retardation was recognized in the earliest attempts at remediation, including Itard's famous attempt to educate and enculturate the so-called wild boy of Aveyron (Itard, 1962). However, serious scientific inquiry aimed at unraveling the relation of language and mental retardation, and at the prevention and remediation of language and communication problems, did not get underway until the 1960s. Investigators in the 1960s and 1970s were polarized (and to some extent paralyzed) by the great nature–nurture debate fueled by disparate theories of B. F. Skinner (1957), Noam Chomsky (1965), and others. Fortunately, a heightened interest in pragmatics (i.e., the study of how language is used in social contexts) and a realization that vocal language is only one form of communication emerged in the 1970s (e.g., Bates, 1976) and substantially broadened the focus of investigators studying both typical and atypical development. The notion that "form follows function" (Nelson, 1973) and a reemphasis on the social bases of language (cf. Bruner, 1975) created some common ground for researchers from seemingly divergent theoretical perspectives (Golinkoff & Hirsh-Pasek, 1990). This expanded focus allowed researchers to set aside radical nativist or behaviorist perspectives and move forward on a variety of important questions, with clear implications for understanding and remediating atypical development (cf. Warren, 1993).

Over the past 15 years, we have seen important advances in both the theory and methods guiding the study of typical and atypical language development and intervention. For example, progress has been made on identifying some of the causes of early language delay (e.g., Lonigan, Fischel, Whitehurst, Arnold, & Valdez-Menchaca, 1992), on developing increasingly effective early intervention approaches (e.g., Kaiser, Yoder, & Keetz, 1992), on understanding the relation of brain and language development (e.g., Bates, Thal, & Janowsky, 1992; Locke, 1993) and cognition and language development (e.g., Mervis & Bertrand, 1993); on the provision of valid, multidimensional assessments (e.g., Wetherby & Prizant, 1990); and on understanding the relation between communication and aberrant behavior (e.g., Reichle & Wacker, 1993). Nevertheless, many of the fundamental questions asked two decades ago (cf. Schiefelbusch & Lloyd, 1974) have only been partially answered to date. These include how language and cognitive development relate; how to optimally facilitate communication and language development; and how genetic, neurological, historical, and contextual factors interact to produce language.

Our goal in the present chapter is not to review all of the progress that has been made in understanding the relationship between language and mental retardation nor to identify all the challenges that lie ahead. These would be impossible goals to achieve in one chapter. Here, we describe the progress that has been made on several important issues of development and intervention and the implications of this work. Then we discuss some continuing problems that serve to undermine progress in understanding and/or remediating language delays related to mental retardation. Finally, we offer our perspective on what we see as the most promising avenues for further progress.

DEVELOPMENT

Because intelligence obviously includes both nonverbal and verbal components, one expects communication and language development of children with mental retardation to be delayed compared to chronological age-matched, typically developing children. On the whole, children with mental retardation tend to display a later onset of language; slower but not deviant development; a lower final level of achievement; and substantial variation in onset, rate of development, and final level of achievement (Rosenburg & Abbeduto, 1993). It has become increasingly clear that some of this variation is due to genetic differences associated with specific etiologies. For example, children with Down syndrome tend to show weaknesses in expressive language skills and grammar, and strengths in receptive language, pragmatics, and, eventually, vocabulary (Chapman, 1995;

Fowler, 1990). On the other hand, males with fragile X syndrome tend to show a wide range of pragmatic problems and dysfluencies (e.g., Sudhulter, Cohen, Silverman, & Wolf-Schein, 1990; Wolf-Schein et al., 1987). Meanwhile, as we discuss later in this chapter, some individuals with Williams syndrome display striking lexical, grammatical, and pragmatic abilities that appear to far exceed their general cognitive abilities (e.g., Bellugi, Marks, Bihrle, & Sabo, 1988).

Progress in understanding the genetic contributions to language development as well as the contributions of neurological, environmental, and contextual variables has been substantial in recent years. We have chosen to focus our discussion on three developmental questions of enduring importance. First, what is the relationship between language and cognition? Second, what role does the social environment play in the language development of children with mental retardation? Third, is there evidence of critical or optimal periods after which language development might be increasingly difficult?

Disentangling Cognition and Language

Piagetian theory links language to the development of other aspects of cognition. From this perspective, language develops as part of a more general ability to internalize, represent, and symbolize external reality. It is assumed that cognitive development leads the way for language development and that most language skills have cognitive prerequisites (Rice & Kemper, 1984).

Consistent with a Piagetian perspective, within the population of children considered mentally retarded, one typically finds that language skills are either consistent with or lag behind sensorimotor development. This is true for at least 75% of children with Down syndrome, who have been the subject of the vast majority of studies on language development in children with mental retardation (Miller, 1988). However, in recent years what has come to be known as the strong cognitive hypothesis (the notion that cognitive development is prerequisite to and proceeds language development; Rice & Kemper, 1984) has come under attack because of the discovery of substantial and varied sets of exceptions—children and adults in whom language skills are either superior to cognitive skills (e.g., most children with Williams syndrome, some children with spina bifida or brain injuries) or children with commensurate skills despite being severely impaired with cerebral palsy and unable to obtain more than a very minimal level of sensorimotor experience (assumed by Piaget to be crucial for cognitive development).

Some children with Williams syndrome have provided perhaps the strongest challenge to the notion that language development is dependent on general cognitive development. Williams syndrome is a rare genetic disorder that typically results in moderate mental retardation and poor visuospatial functioning. Although their language abilities are not consistent with their chronological age levels, some children with Williams syndrome score substantially higher on standardized language tests than they perform on nonlanguage cognitive tasks. These children also tend to be loquacious and highly social, with large complex vocabularies that they use spontaneously, appropriately, and meaningfully.

Mervis and Bertrand (1993) examined four previously proposed specific links between particular aspects of early cognitive development and particular aspects of early language development in typically developing children, children with Down syndrome, and children with Williams syndrome. The children with Williams syndrome demonstrated that two of these proposed links are not universal—that is, not prerequisite to the development of the language skills to which they were hypothesized to be linked. Specifically, they found that referential production of object labels need not be related to the comprehension and production of pointing gestures, and that spontaneous exhaustive sorting of objects (i.e., the spontaneous sorting of a set of objects into groups based on membership in a basic category) is not necessarily linked to the onset of the vocabulary spurt. Other researchers have demonstrated that children with Williams syndrome can typically comprehend affirmative and negative comparative and equative relational expressions, which supposedly require the ability to seriate (Shaffer & Ehri, 1980), in the absence of this cognitive skill. They can also comprehend and use full reversible passives appropriately in the absence of being able to conserve on Piagetian tasks (Bellugi, Marks, Bihrle, & Sabo, 1988).

The data on children with Williams syndrome, various sensory disorders (Bishop, 1988; Mills, 1988), some cases of autism and spina bifida, as well as disorders like Broca's aphasia, Alzheimer's, and schizophrenia (which often spare certain linguistic abilities while disrupting general cognitive abilities), suggest that linguistic functions can develop and occur separately from cognitive functions.

What are the implications of this finding? One obvious implication is that the Piagetian model of development may substantially overstate the role of cognition in language development (Mogford & Bishop, 1988). Pinker (1994) went so far as to argue that these disparities are evidence of a genetically derived language instinct that is separate from general cognitive abilities. But such a sweeping conclusion seems premature until the extent to which specific language abilities can be learned by alternative cognitive or social paths can be determined (Locke, 1994; Nelson, 1991). Another question of fundamental importance is the extent to which relatively advanced language abilities might be used by some children with mental retardation to mediate deficits in cognitive abilities. To date there has been very little research on this topic.

What Role Does Language Input Play in Language Development?

This question is important because of the possibility that inadequate input might cause or contribute to language delay and even mental retardation, and, conversely, that enhanced input might have a remedial effect on development. The role of language input in language development has been of fundamental interest since the philosophers first began to speculate on the nature and origin of language (e.g., St. Augustine). It became a particularly hot topic in the 1960s with the publication of Chomsky's theory of transformational grammar (Chomsky, 1957, 1965), which implies that neither the quantity nor quality of input have much effect on language development. This argument spurred a great deal of research. Consequently, we know much more about which environmental factors seem to effect language development and which factors do not.

Since the 1970s, proponents of the social interactionist perspective of language development (e.g., Bohannon, MacWhinney, & Snow, 1990; Bruner, 1975; Gallaway & Richards, 1994; Nelson, 1989; Snow, 1984; Tomasello, 1992) have been building the case that adult input does play an important role in children's language acquisition. They noted that from birth onward an ocean of language flows through the child's head. Fourteen hours a day, 365 days a year, the child is exposed to the "curriculum." It has been estimated that by age 4, the typical child will have uttered 10 to 20 million words and will have actively listened to 20 to 40 million words (Chapman et al., 1992). These are not just undifferentiated sounds. Much of this curriculum is specifically adjusted and fine tuned (Bruner, 1975; Sokolov, 1993) to the child's language level. A wide range of teaching devices have been detected in common use by parents and other adults, including expansions, models, contingent imitations, growth recasts, use of concrete, simplified vocabulary, slower rate of articulation, use of higher pitch and exaggerated intonation, a focus on objects and events to which the child is attending, and so on (Hoff-Ginsburg,

1986; Hoff-Ginsburg & Shatz, 1982; Menyuk, 1988; Nelson, 1991; Snow, Perlmann, & Nathan, 1987; van Kleeck, 1994). These adjustments, termed *motherese*, are assumed to simplify the task of acquiring linguistic and communication competence. The rate at which adults talk to children (Huttenlocher, Haight, Bryk, Seitzer, & Lyons, 1991) and the rate at which children themselves talk (e.g., Hart & Risley, 1980; Nelson, 1973; Schacter, 1979) have both been shown to correlate with faster acquisition of language.

A correlational analysis published by Hart and Risley (1992) on the language learning environments (i.e., homes) inhabited by young, typically developing children in 40 families suggests that both the type and quantity of input a child receives may have substantial effects on their subsequent IQ. Finally, although the strength of effects of conversationally based language interventions remains unclear, these interactions do appear to have some effect on learning and use (Fey, 1986; Kaiser, Yoder, & Keetz, 1992; Whitehurst et al., 1988). In summary, there is substantial evidence that adult input can affect the rate and quality of language development in both typically and atypically developing children.

Whatever the merits of the theory and data that have been offered by the social interactionalists, a strong argument that input is relatively unimportant has persisted for several reasons. First, irrespective of what sort of input the average young child receives, there is evidence that a significant proportion of children acquire language even when the verbal input they receive is severely limited in quantity (Schiff-Myers, 1988), degraded or inconsistent in quality (Klein & Rapin, 1988), inconsistent in linguistic characteristics (Genesee, 1988), or presented with limited contextual cues (Mills, 1988). Second, there is little evidence that mothers of children with mental retardation differ from mothers of nondisabled children in terms of the quantity of talk to their children, or in terms of the quality of their talk when the child's developmental age is considered (Rosenburg & Abbeduto, 1993). Also, there appears to be a great deal of variability in how parents from various cultures interact with their children during the language-learning years, with no apparent seminal effects on language development (van Kleek, 1994). Finally, most research on motherese is correlational in nature. Thus, it remains unclear what the actual effects of these modifications might be on the child's language acquisition (Rosenburg & Abbeduto, 1993).

The argument that input is relatively unimportant has been based largely on the fact that most children ultimately learn language irrespective of their circumstances. However, perhaps this argument misses the point, at least for children with mental retardation. There is clear evidence that language input can affect the rate and quality of language development for both children with disabilities and children without disabilities (Galloway & Richards, 1994). Furthermore, development can clearly be enhanced for any child via modifications of the input he or she receives. Optimal input may have a far greater impact on the ultimate language development of children with developmental disabilities than on typically developing children (Snow, 1994). Beyond the question of whether quality and quantity typically matter, two other questions remain to be answered. First, can it be made to matter? That is, can the environment be designed in such a way that input is optimized to compensate for the nature of the child's learning problem? This is the fundamental question facing intervention researchers, and one that we discuss later in this chapter. Second, are there certain points in development when external input might have a relatively powerful effect? This is the question to which we now turn.

Is There a Critical Period for Language Development?

A long-established general principle of neurological development states that while a neurological system is still immature, the nature of the input to that system determines how it develops, but once biological maturity is achieved then the system is unlikely to be modified by environmental influences. The term *critical period* has been used to refer to that window of time during which the environment should have its most significant effect on behavior. Penfield (1965) and Lenneburg (1967) both proposed that a critical period may exist for language development up to puberty, after which the ability to learn language probably diminishes.

In the nearly three decades that have transpired since Penfield and Lenneburg made their proposals, no strong evidence of a rigid, deterministic critical period for language acquisition has been uncovered, despite a thorough examination of several types of evidence (Newport, 1990). One set of studies investigated whether an alteration of the environment early in life has any permanent consequences after the environment is restored to normal. This approach included studies concerned with the effects of severe neglect and deprivation, conductive hearing loss, and tracheostomy (Mogford & Bishop, 1988). A second set of studies examined the extent to which language learning is possible beyond what has been typically regarded as the upper limit of the hypothesized critical period—puberty. The studies have included people with profound deafness and individuals with Down syndrome. A detailed longitudinal study of adolescents with Down syndrome by Chapman (1995) recently found no evidence of a critical language learning period in this population.

A third line of research investigated recovery from aphasia at different points in life. There is some evidence in the aphasia studies of a gradually diminishing facility for recovery throughout childhood. However, the data are highly variable, with some children showing poor recovery from unilateral lesions as early as age 5 or 6 and others recovering well from aphasia at 10 years of age or older (Mogford & Bishop, 1988). A fourth line of research examined the influence of maturational state on second language learning (Johnson & Newport, 1989). The data clearly demonstrated that second language learning is much easier and more successful for children than for adults and that it becomes generally more difficult throughout childhood. Finally, research has examined the acquisition of American Sign Language (ASL) by deaf children who typically have received no exposure to it before the age of 4 to 6 years. This research generally demonstrates that the later a language is learned, the less fluent and grammatically sophisticated its final form will be (Newport, 1990).

Although there is little evidence of a rigid, deterministic critical period, the issue of whether there is an *optimal* period for language acquisition—a period during which acquisition proceeds more quickly and easily than at other times—has received increasing theoretical and empirical support from the research summarized previously. From approximately age 7 onward through adulthood, there is a general, gradual linear decline in language learning performance (Johnson & Newport, 1989; Newport, 1990; Patkowski, 1980). Furthermore, the possibility that the first 3 to 4 years of life are an optimal period for language learning is supported by our growing understanding of early brain development. For example, between 9 and 24 months of age, the density of short-range synaptic connections within and across the cerebral cortex reaches approximately 150% of levels observed in human adults. This growth, which is termed *synaptogenesis*, corresponds closely to the primary milestones of early language development.

Synaptogenesis appears to peak at two points that correspond closely with two well-known bursts in normal language development—the so-called vocabulary burst between 16 and 20 months and the passage from single word to multiword speech between 18 and 20 months (Bates, Thal, & Janowsky, 1992). During this period each step in cognitive and linguistic development may open new paths and close others, an automatic consequence of the selection and increasing differentiation of the neural structures that support language and cognition, continuing the processes of tissue differentiation that originated in the embryo (Studdert-Kennedy, 1991). These neural correlates of language acquisition are intriguing. For example, if they do not occur on schedule, what effect does this have on the vocabulary burst? Can synaptogenesis be triggered, delayed, or enhanced by environmental events? Is it typically delayed or distorted in children with various forms of mental retardation?

Locke (1994) went so far as to argue that linguistic capacity develops in critically timed phases that occur gradually and sequentially under normal conditions. He theorized that when language does not develop at the usual rate (as with developmental language delays and mental retardation), it may be because too few lexical items were acquired earlier, a possible secondary consequence of the slow maturation of certain neural specializations related to the peaks in synaptogenesis. He suggested that the rapid accumulation of prosodically organized utterances may normally trigger the activation of analytic mechanisms in the left hemisphere of the brain necessary for the acquisition of grammar. But for children who have acquired too few utterances to generate the pressure necessary to trigger this activation, a critical period may come and go. This may lead to compensatory activity by the right hemisphere, which appears less suitable to support several of the specific operations required in language (e.g., phonological analysis). Although acquisition proceeds in this scenario with the right hemisphere carrying a larger burden than is typical, it may also set the stage for long-term problems with both acquisition and use (Aram, Ekelman, & Nation, 1987; Lewis & Friebairn, 1992).

Locke's (1994) theory suggests that neuromaturational delay is responsible for social cognitive deficits that delay the storage of words and phrases and subsequently the development of grammar. His theory also assumes that these neural maturational delays may be responsible for other types of deficits (e.g., auditory, visual, tactile, etc.) typically associated with mental retardation and various developmental disabilities.

Brain development peaks by 48 months, about the same time that most grammatical structures have been acquired and concurrent with the onset of a period of stabilization and automatization in linguistic and cognitive events. After 4 years there is a slow monotonic decline in synaptic density, and overall levels of brain metabolism corresponding with a gradual increase in the accessibility of complex grammatical forms and a slow decrease in the capacity for second language learning and recovery from aphasia (Bates, Thal, & Marchman, 1991). Is this first 48 months a period of optimal development? A period when the environment can have the greatest impact on a child's language abilities at the least cost? Because most language intervention does not begin until children are 3 years old or older and because there has been so little research to date on the effects of prelinguistic intervention implemented in the first 2 years of a child's life (Yoder & Warren, 1993), we have no answer for these questions. But they are surely tantalizing. Locke (1994) noted that, "Behavior constantly pushes the young brain around, and it is eminently reasonable to suppose that remediation—undertaken early and pursued rigorously—reorganizes the brain" (p. 614). What if we had effective intervention strategies that would allow us to optimize input to children with mental retardation during their first 3 years of life? Would these children have different developmental outcomes as a result?

Much of the research to date on the communication and language development of children with mental retardation has substantial implications for intervention. Among other things, this research suggests that language is not a mere by-product of cognition, although it is obviously directly impacted by it. Furthermore, although language input may not typically be the cause of later language problems, it may nevertheless serve as a means to enhance development, particularly during an optimal period for language acquisition that seems to occur during the first 48 months of life. These findings argue strongly for the continuing development of intervention procedures aimed at very early communication and language development.

INTERVENTION

Relative to language intervention research conducted in the 1960s and 1970s, research over the past 15 years has focused more on teaching lexical and pragmatic skills, on measuring and facilitating generalization, and on the development of more naturalistic intervention strategies. Research settings have shifted from residential institutions to schools, homes, and community settings, and subjects have become much younger (Gazdag & Warren, 1992). As with development, research on effective intervention strategies has progressed on many fronts. We have chosen to describe the progress that has been made in three areas that, in aggregate, demonstrate the still-unrealized potential of communication and language intervention. First, we discuss alternative and augmentative communication approaches. Next, we describe initial efforts to facilitate prelinguistic communication development in very young children. Finally, we describe the emergence of a developmentally appropriate continuum of intervention approaches.

The Development of Alternative and Augmentative Communication Approaches

Alternative and augmentative communication approaches refer to methods of communicating outside the standard vocal and written modalities. These approaches can include gestural (e.g., signs), or graphic (e.g., braille, communication boards) modes and include both nonsymbolic (e.g., eye gaze) and symbolic communication.

Alternative and augmentative communication systems have a long history. For example, braille was first invented in 1853. However, since the mid-1970s, research, development, and use of augmentative and alternative systems has expanded rapidly for several reasons. First, in the 1970s, interest in the pragmatics and use of language rapidly increased due to an expanded focus on the social and instrumental functions of communication (Dore, 1975; Halliday, 1975); an enhanced awareness that virtually any human behavior, regardless of form or intention, can be potentially communicative; and a realization that sophisticated communication is quite possible in modalities other than spoken language.

A second force in the rapid expansion of alternative and augmentative communication has been the microtechnology revolution that overtook the general area of communication technologies in the late 1980s (Mirenda & Iacono, 1990). The availability of relatively inexpensive, lightweight microcomputers and microswitches has influenced the rapid development of all types of communication devices and communication boards (e.g., Romski & Sevick, 1988) that can allow an individual with severe cerebral palsy to write a novel or carry on a conversation.

A third influence has been the discovery that sign languages used by individuals who are deaf (e.g., American Sign Language) are in fact full fledged languages, not simply gestural versions of, for example, English (Klima & Bellugi, 1979). That is, most sign languages (exceptions are systems such as signed English) are not like graphic representations of vocal language (e.g., braille, written English) that simply transform the mode of expression but preserve the syntax. Instead, they are living, evolving languages. This discovery has many implications, not the least of which has been the realization that the vocal modality, although it is extraordinarily efficient, is but one of several modes of sophisticated communication that are possible for humans.

Finally, research on the effects of total communication approaches (the simultaneous use of oral and gestural communication modalities) with children with hearing impairments generally indicates that this method often enhances overall communication development and in no way retards oral development (Quigley & Paul, 1987). Signing is now being increasingly used with children who have no significant hearing problem (e.g., young children with Down syndrome; individuals with autism) but who have difficulty (for varied reasons and at least temporarily) learning and/or using oral communication. For example, Miller and his colleagues (Miller, Sedey, Miolo, Rosin, & Murray-Branch, 1991; Sedey, Rosin, & Miller, 1991) reported that approximately 75% of the children with Down syndrome whom they have studied were first exposed to manual sign systems sometime between the ages of 2 and 4 years in an attempt to improve initial communication when their early verbal attempts were unintelligible. Miller's data show that children acquire unique signed vocabularies that expand their total (oral and signed) vocabularies. Besides consistent parent reports that early signing reduces their children's frustration, Miller also reported no evidence that early signing inhibits the development of oral language skills in this population.

Despite all the advances made in the past 20 years, the study of augmentative and alternative communication is very much in its infancy (Reichle, Mirenda, Locke, Piche, & Johnston, 1992). The rapid spread of signing, communication boards, and more sophisticated technologies, although opening up the communication process for many individuals, has also raised a large and varied set of research questions (e.g., what is the relationship between comprehension and production for augmentative system users), development challenges (e.g., how to design a feasible set of selection techniques to accommodate a learner's level of progress or deteriorating medical status), social and ethical questions (e.g., the intense debate of issues relating to the emerging deaf culture), and funding and service issues (e.g., how to ensure the provision of appropriate communication technologies to people, and how to ensure the provision of appropriately trained personnel to support alternative and augmentative communication users in community-based settings, schools, and homes).

Many of the issues facing researchers in this area are similar to issues facing researchers working with oral language speakers with mental retardation. For example, a review of research by Franklin and Beukelman (1990) noted that augmented communicators primarily respond rather than initiate, tend to produce a limited number of turns within a topic exchange, produce a limited number of communicative functions, and often fail to produce communicative repair strategies. Franklin and Beukelman concluded that speaking partners dominate conversations and structure interactions to require minimal responses from users of augmentative communication systems. Light, Collier, and Parnes (1985) reported that children who use augmentative and alternative communications systems act on as few as 50% of the available conversational opportunities during the course of an interaction. In short, the provision of an appropriate mode to communicate, although obviously essential, by itself is no panacea. A better understanding of the effect that a slower rate of communication (e.g., the latency between an initiation and a response—the time between the beginning of a message and its end) has on discourse could lead to the development of more effective interventions and devices.

The Extension of Assessment and Intervention to Prelinguistic Communication

The history of research on communication and language intervention with individuals with mental retardation has not progressed in a particularly logical manner at times. For example, even though language is typically acquired in the first few years of life in nonstructured, noninstitutional contexts and settings, much of the language intervention research in the 1960s and 1970s was carried out with older children, adolescents, and adults in residential institutions (Gazdag & Warren, 1992). Emphasis finally turned to younger children in the late 1970s as legislation opened school doors to all children. Research on language intervention has reflected this trend and a relatively large number of studies with preschool and primary grade children have been published since 1980 (cf. Kaiser & Gray, 1993; Warren & Reichle, 1992). We are just now beginning to see intervention research carried out during the period of development when children typically acquire the bulk of the system—their first 3 years.

The irony in the field's historic lack of interest in the communication and language development of very young children is rich. During the time period when typically developing children are making the most rapid and startling advances, and during which the brain seems optimally suited to being sculpted and shaped by the input of the environment, we wait. Specific language intervention efforts for a child who is having significant problems acquiring language typically get underway when the child is at least 3 years old, or older. But a nonspeaking 3-year-old may already be at least a year and a half behind his or her peers developmentally.

There are many reasons why we have essentially ignored the earliest period of development. First, until the last 10 years, infancy (birth to 2 years of age) was viewed too often as a period of biological unfolding during which there was little to do except sit back and wait (conversely, now it is seen by some researchers as a time of greatest environmental impact). Second, assessments during this period were the least valid and reliable. Thus, pediatricians and others were hard pressed to predict whether problems a child seemed to be experiencing were evidence of a significant underlying delay, or temporary variance that would wash out in time. Finally, even if it was known a child was certain to have problems with communication development, it was unclear how to intervene beyond ensuring that the child was in a warm, stable, nurturing environment. Each of these reasons for our lack of activity during the prelinguistic period have disappeared. We now know that the young infant begins actively learning almost at birth (Johanson & Terry, 1988), we know the environment can have a big impact on early brain and behavioral development, we are now developing assessments that allow us to reliably identify communication delays by 12 to 15 months of age (Wetherby & Prizant, 1990), and we now have some promising intervention approaches (e.g., Wilcox, 1992).

The importance of prelinguistic communication development became a focus of the child language literature in the 1980s (e.g., Bates, 1979; Bruner, 1981; Dore, 1986). However, it was not until 1990, when Wetherby and Prizant published an initial version of the Communication and Symbolic Behavior Scales (CSBS), that the field had a comprehensive and reliable means of examining the communicative, social-affective, and symbolic abilities of children whose functional communication abilities range from preintentional to early language use. This assessment instrument has two goals: to identify very young children with communication impairments; and to establish a communicative and symbolic profile to provide directions for further assessment, to plan intervention goals, and to chart changes in these abilities over time.

Paralleling the publication of the CSBS was the publication of the first prelinguistic intervention studies (e.g., Mahoney & Powell, 1988; Rosenburg & Robinson, 1985). To date, there are only a handful of these studies, but some of them, particularly the work of Wilcox (1992), Warren (Warren, Yoder, Gazdag, Kim, & Jones, 1993), and Yoder (Yoder, Warren, Kim, & Gazdag, 1994) reported unusually strong effects in terms of generalization of targeted skills and of general developmental gains (Wilcox, 1992).

There are some intriguing reasons why interventions that teach children to communicate—that teach them how to comment and request prelinguistically and thus move the child from preintentional to intentional communication—might have unusually strong effects. First, during their initial acquisition of intentional communication forms, children are actually acquiring basic communication functions (i.e., requesting, commenting, protesting, questioning), not simply new forms for expressing old functions (i.e., saying "more" as a request form or "no" as a protest), which is much of what later acquisition is really about. Acquiring these basic functions provides children with their first effective means of intentional communication.

Second, these functions are acquired against the backdrop of a very restricted repertoire of intentional behavior. This small repertoire makes it relatively easy for parents to recognize and respond differentially to new behaviors. In contrast, it is obviously difficult for even sensitive, attentive parents and teachers to recognize and respond to most new instances of behavior by a 3-year-old child who is learning 10 new words a day on average and has a large, frequently used complex repertoire of intentional behavior and sophisticated language. Yoder and Warren (Warren et al., 1993; Yoder et al., 1994) reported data showing that teachers and parents do respond differently to the display of prelinguistic requests by young children with mental retardation. For instance, they more frequently supply a label contingent on whatever the child has requested (in addition to fulfilling the request). That is, the onset of intentional requests by the child appears to trigger a substantial increase in linguistic mapping by most adults. This transactional effect may be potentially important because linguistic mapping is thought to be one of the devices used by adults to teach vocabulary to children (Nelson, 1989). Thus, one compelling question is: If we turn on prelinguistic intentional communication via intervention, does this also turn on the environment in ways (such as linguistic mapping) that support further language development?

Research on prelinguistic communication intervention is truly in its infancy. We have little idea what the ultimate effect of comprehensive prelinguistic intervention might be on language development in general. However, given our emerging knowledge of brain development during the first few years of life, the importance of studying this period can hardly be understated.

The Emergence of a Developmentally Appropriate Continuum of Intervention Approaches

Historically, language intervention approaches have been developed almost independent of a concern about how they might best match up to different phases in the child's development, or different characteristics of the language skills to be mastered (e.g., pragmatics vs. syntactic rules). Twenty-five years ago virtually all approaches were highly didactic in nature, irrespective of a child's intervention goals (e.g., Guess, Sailor, & Baer, 1974; Miller & Yoder, 1972; Risley, Hart, & Doke, 1972). Since 1980 there has been increasing emphasis on developing more naturalistic approaches that are based on following the child's attentional lead and that teach communication skills episodically across a child's day in the actual settings they typically inhabit (Fey, 1986; MacDonald, 1989; Warren & Rogers-Warren, 1985). As an increasingly wide array of approaches and techniques have become available, the question of relative efficacy has begun to be asked by a few researchers (e.g., Cole & Dale, 1986; Yoder, Kaiser, & Alpert, 1991). Research on relative efficacy is still preliminary. Nevertheless, the findings to date are both interesting and congruent with other developmental data. The following is a very circumscribed summary of what these data seem to indicate.

There are no comparative studies of intervention effectiveness during prelinguistic development yet because so little research has been done on this area. On the other hand, a modest amount of research has been done on early language intervention, beginning at the one word stage. Yoder and his colleagues (Yoder et al., 1991, 1995) compared the relative efficacy of three different intervention approaches with developmentally delayed children who ranged from Stage 1 to Stage 5 (mean length of utterance, MLU, 1.0 to 4.0). They found that an approach that utilizes primarily expansions and growth recasts as teaching techniques (termed the *responsive-interaction approach*; MacDonald, 1989) was more effective than milieu teaching (a very similar approach that uses elicited production prompts, including prompts for imitation in addition to expansions and recasts; Warren, 1991) with children who have an MLU above 2.5 morphemes, but less effective than milieu teaching with children who have an MLU under 1.5. The milieu approach may be relatively more effective than is responsive-interaction during the early period precisely because it uses elicited imitation and other production prompts at the time in development when imitation appears to be the most functional for children (Spiedel & Nelson, 1989). However, the value of imitation as a learning strategy recedes as children move into more complex language (Sokolov, 1992). Growth recasts and expansions that allow the child to "compare" their own utterance with one that is slightly advanced but preserves the semantic content and immediately follows theirs seem to become increasingly valuable to children as they move to more complex language (Nelson, 1989).

As children's language becomes increasingly complex, so do their attentional and memory resources and their ability to learn from a wide range of input expands (Rogoff, 1990). Most important, their ability to alter their attentional focus and simultaneously learn substantially improves (Rogoff, 1990). Thus, the necessity of teaching to their attentional lead declines and the usefulness of direct teaching techniques that maintain child attention by using well-organized materials, rapid pacing, and immediate contingent feedback appears to increase. Direct teaching techniques can be used to ensure that specific language skills and concepts (e.g., syntactic rules and grammar) that are difficult to make salient through other interaction strategies are actually taught to children with mental retardation. Indeed, the effectiveness of direct instruction may increase as skills become more abstract (i.e., linguistic) in nature (Connell, 1988). This hypothesis may explain why efficacy studies show direct instruction to be relatively more effective than milieu procedures in teaching more advanced skills (Yoder et al., 1991) and more effective than mediated teaching strategies, another approach in which teaching is based on following the child's lead but in which some direct instruction techniques are also used (Cole & Dale, 1986; Cole, Dale, & Mills, 1990).

Our intention in this brief overview is to suggest the following: An overreaching goal for intervention researchers should be the specification of a continuum of optimally effective, developmentally appropriate communication and language intervention procedures. We assume that no single approach currently available is appropriate to cover the range of development beginning with prelinguistic communication and proceeding to sophisticated language and then reading. Based on studies of typical development and the few comparative intervention studies, it appears that a rough continuum of approaches suitable for use with mentally retarded children is beginning to emerge. This continuum favors naturalistic approaches that utilize elicited imitation and other production prompts up to MLU 2.5, then switches to naturalistic approaches that utilize expansion and growth recasts and minimize imitation. Then, as children move to increasingly sophisticated syntax, it may utilize direct teaching and/or expansion-recasting approaches, perhaps in combination with additional techniques intended to enhance generalization and make language learning more meaningful for the child (e.g., whole language approaches).

To achieve the goal of an integrated continuum of optimally effective procedures, at least two things must happen. First, more hybrid approaches that integrate components of particularly effective techniques need to be designed, because many intervention approaches are needlessly narrow at present. One example of such a hybrid is Kaiser's "enhanced milieu teaching," which represents a combination of milieu teaching and responsive-interaction techniques (Kaiser, 1993). Second, more large-scale longitudinal comparative efficacy studies must be conducted. Until it can be determined if the efficacy of treatments changes over time within the same set of children, we will not know for certain whether the presently available aptitude-by-treatment results reflect individual differences or general developmental differences. At present there are less than a half-dozen comparative language intervention studies in the literature.

The development of optimally effective communication and language intervention approaches has proceeded steadily for the past three decades. Much of the emphasis during this period has been on the construction and evaluation of specific techniques, procedures, and technologies. This technology building period has relied on studies with limited numbers of subjects and of relatively short duration. With the possible exception of the prelinguistic period, the field may be nearing the end of this phase in its evolution. If further progress is to be made, researchers will need to increasingly turn their efforts to conducting comparative, longitudinal intervention studies that are complicated, expensive, and lengthy in nature. The prelinguistic period represents a different kind of challenge. It is possible that interventions during this period could have substantial payoffs in terms of a child's long-term developmental outcome. But, at present, the availability of appropriate, validated assessment and intervention procedures remains quite restricted.

UNDERLYING PROBLEMS

There are many problems impeding efforts to understand the relation between language and mental retardation as well as our efforts to enhance communication and language development. Some of these problems are perennial and similar to the problems faced by many fields. These include insufficient quality and quantity of research, insufficient research funding, ineffective transfer of research findings to practice, and so on. Although these are in fact real problems, we have chosen to focus this section on two other problem areas that might exist no matter how much research is being done and no matter how much research funding is available. Furthermore, these are problems that could be addressed, albeit over a lengthy period of time, without necessarily infusing more than a small amount of additional funds into the field. The first problem is the lack of sufficient generalization analyses and longitudinal research in the intervention literature. The second problem is the use of dubious practices lacking any scientific basis.

Insufficient Generalization Analyses

The extraordinary importance of measuring and analyzing the generalization resulting from communication and language intervention efforts was noted early on (Schiefelbusch & Lloyd, 1974). In the 1960s and early 1970s, formal generalization analyses were omitted from the majority of behavioral research studies (Stokes & Baer, 1977; Warren, 1977). Since then the trend has reversed itself. Generalization analyses are now included in the vast majority of published language intervention studies (Gazdag & Warren, 1992; Goldstein & Hockenberger, 1991). Although this trend is obviously good news, generalization is a multifaceted concept that can be measured on many levels, some relatively trivial.

Gazdag and Warren (1992) conducted an analysis of 23 studies of language intervention with children with mental retardation published between 1979 and 1989. To be included in this analysis, a study had to include an experimental analysis of stimulus generalization. In this case, stimulus generalization referred to the use of targeted verbal responses across five dimensions: persons, settings, materials, peers, and interaction style. The 23 studies yielded a total of 64 separate tests of stimulus generalization. The number of stimulus generalization tests was calculated by determining the number of tests that varied from each other (within a study) in terms of the five stimulus dimensions assessed.

Of the 64 tests analyzed, 44% reported a strong generalization effect (i.e., occurrence of the target form on 67% or more of the possible occurrences) and 41% reported moderate generalization (i.e., occurrence of the target form between 33% and 66% of the possible occurrences). In sum, 85% of the tests revealed strong to moderate stimulus generalization—a very encouraging result.

The data reported by Gazdag and Warren are obviously susceptible to a "publication bias." That is, positive results tend to be published, failures do not. However, a more significant factor may have been the fact that 52% of the reported generalization tests differed from the training context on only a single stimulus dimension (e.g., the person doing the test), whereas an additional 36% differed in only two dimensions. In sum, 88% of the tests differed from the intervention on only one or two of the possible five stimulus dimensions.

The analysis reported by Gazdag and Warren admittedly was conducted at a very gross level. It did not include all the stimuli that are likely influential in generalization, most important the dimension of time. Also, there was no attempt to weight the five stimulus dimensions—they were all considered equal. Nevertheless, the primary point of this analysis, that many reported stimulus generalization successes constitute relatively superficial analyses, is difficult to avoid. Moreover, it corresponds with other recent analyses of subsets of the intervention literature (e.g., Kaiser et al., 1992; Tannock & Girolametto, 1992) that, although reporting positive effects, have also noted that the majority of studies reviewed assessed generalization in very limited ways making it difficult to estimate overall intervention effects.

Reports of insufficient generalization resulting from initial language intervention efforts have been credited with influencing researchers to develop more naturalistic, pragmatically oriented approaches because of the assumption that these approaches will yield better generalization (Spradlin & Siegel, 1982; Warren & Rogers-Warren, 1985). When combined with rigorous experimental methods, a focus on generalization and maintenance may act as a self-correcting or self-righting mechanism that can guide researchers over time to increasingly effective intervention approaches. However, such a focus can work only if the generalization and maintenance analyses are appropriately challenging, ecologically valid, and meaningful.

Prevalence and Persistence of Dubious Practices

The effort to provide appropriate public education for all children, including children with disabilities, spurred the rapid development and deployment of educational, therapeutic, and clinical practices without an opportunity to empirically validate most of the practices. Over the past 20 years, much applied research has been aimed at determining which practices are effective and which are not. Some practices that have taken root in the field are based on faulty premises and are not just ineffective but potentially harmful to individuals with disabilities. In these cases the value of research has been to show the fallacies in these practices. We discuss two examples of dubious practices that recent research has called into question.

Cognitive Profiling. The theorists who formulated the cognitive hypothesis discussed earlier in this chapter never directly suggested that it be used to determine who should receive language intervention or who should be denied it. Nevertheless, diagnostic and service eligibility decisions are widely made on the basis of the relation between assessments of cognitive ability and assessments of language ability (Casby, 1989). A discrepancy between cognitive and language performance, with cognitive performance being higher, is thought to be a positive predictor of ability to benefit from intervention. On the other hand, a flat profile in which cognitive and language skills are judged to be equal is used to deny specific intervention services. This discrepancy model assumes that cognition sets the upper limit for development (Rice & Kemper, 1984). Based on this model, speech–language pathologists often consider children to be poor candidates for specific intervention services if they have equal delays in cognitive and language development (Chapman & Miller, 1980; Owens & House, 1984; Shane, 1981).

The discrepancy model of service eligibility has been challenged on many fronts. First, in addition to the argument regarding the relation of language and cognitive development presented earlier in this chapter, investigators questioned the adequacy of the theoretical basis of the model (e.g., Kemp, 1983; Notari, Cole, & Mills, 1992). Others noted a variety of additional weaknesses with the model across domains of development. These problems include the fact that IQ may not be independent of the contrasting skill area (Rice, 1983; Siegel, 1989), that IQ is a poor predictor of intervention progress (Cole, Dale, & Mills, 1990; Cole, Mills, & Harris, 1991; Stanovich, 1991), and that individuals with cognition higher than a delayed skill area may not have different causal factors for the delay than do individuals with less discrepant skill profiles (e.g., Leonard, 1987).

In addition to its theoretical weaknesses, the discrepancy model assumes that we can accurately measure the relationship between cognitive skills and other performance areas and that this testing will be reliable. Although test reliability is an important consideration in the assessment of any single skill area, it is critical in discrepancy modeling because the reliability of the difference between two different instruments is inherently worse than the reliability of either instrument (Anastasi, 1976).

A recent study by Cole, Dale, and Mills (1992) evaluated the stability, over 1- and 2-year periods, of the relation between a cognitive measure and two language measures with 125 children between 3 and 7 years of age enrolled in a special education school program. They examined whether the cognitive-language relation for these measures changed significantly over time and whether children remained in the same service eligibility category based on the discrepancy model over time. Their results indicated large changes in the cognitive-language relation over time. Thus, the children's eligibility for service, based on the discrepancy model, also fluctuated greatly over time.

Another recent study by Cole and his colleagues (Cole, Mills, & Kelley, 1994) examined the agreement of various measurement practices used to develop cognitive profiles. They administered a battery of cognitive and language measures to 26 preschool children with delayed language development and examined the agreement of combinations of cognitive-language profiles in determining service eligibility. They found substantial disagreement among profiles with different measures. Eligibility for service ranged from a high of 22 out of 26 children to a low of 3 out of 26 children, depending on the specific measures used. This analysis further undercuts the validity of cognitive profiling.

Based on their results and the findings of others, Cole et al. (1992) recommended that "discrepancy modeling, or cognitive referencing as it is sometimes known, based on global measures of cognition and language, be discontinued as a means of allocating services to children on the basis of predictions of who should be able to benefit from intervention. Services should be provided to students who have delayed language performance relative to CA and environmental demands regardless of IQ" (Cole et al., 1992, p. 142).

Discrepancy profiling provides a convenient way for administrators and practitioners to ration scarce services. However, as the research by Cole and others indicates, it has no empirical basis and its theoretical basis is shaky at best. It is likely to be inaccurate and may frequently result in speech–language services being withheld from children who would benefit from them while other children may be getting inappropriate interventions due to misdiagnoses.

Facilitated Communication. Facilitated communication (FC) is a technique for physically assisting an individual with autism or mental retardation to communicate via computer, typewriter, or a communication board. A person who is not disabled (the facilitator) holds the hand or arm of a disabled partner in order to isolate an index finger, while they jointly select letters on a keyboard or other display to spell words. Proponents of FC have suggested that this method is appropriate for individuals who are not yet able to access a communication aid independently and meaningfully (Biklen, 1993). Biklen (1990) hypothesized that FC aids individuals in overcoming undetected neuromotor difficulties (e.g., apraxia) and that it also enhances the confidence of people with autism to a level that enables them to communicate effectively.

FC was developed by Rosemary Crossley in Australia in the 1980s and was introduced by Douglas Biklen to the United States in 1989. Uncontrolled, qualitative descriptions of FC (Biklen, 1990) suggested that this technique allowed individuals previously thought to be severely autistic to communicate using words and sentences, often of a highly literate, truly surprising nature. Based on these findings, Biklen (1992) concluded that:

> In their typed facilitated communication, students demonstrate literacy ability free of the pronoun reversals and incorrect verb tense often associated with autism. Indeed, the language revealed through facilitation suggests that we must rethink the notion of autism as a social cognitive disability. The literacy skills and thinking abilities of people using facilitated communication challenge prior assumptions about their cognitive abilities and suggest that in the main they experience difficulties with expression. (p. 17)

The amazing success of FC quickly caught the attention of mass media, and its use rapidly spread throughout North America. However, within 2 years of its introduction in the United States, controlled studies began to question the validity of FC. These studies were designed to answer a critical question: Who is actually doing the communicating, the facilitator or the client? That is, is the facilitator biasing or manipulating the apparent FC output? By 1994, a large number of investigations that controlled facilitator's access to information necessary to produce messages via FC provided compelling evidence that the facilitators are the actual authors of most "facilitated" messages (see Green, 1994, for a comprehensive review of these studies). These studies revealed that FC is not an effective intervention and that its validity and reliability are highly questionable (Cummins & Prior, 1992; Green, 1994; Jacobson et al., 1994; Mulick, Jacobson, & Kobe, 1992; Smith & Belcher, 1994). Given the extraordinary claims of FC proponents and the way the technique was initially introduced in this country through the mass media (e.g., *60 Minutes*, *PrimeTime*, *20/20*) it is hardly surprising that it has been referred to as the "cold fusion of the social sciences" (Wolfensberger, 1994).

The FC debacle contains many lessons. For one thing, it demonstrates the overwhelming importance of communication in human interaction and our perception of an individual's underlying competence and potential. With an effective communication mode, people thought to have severe autism suddenly appear capable of highly literate acts including poetry, political actions, and compelling charges of sexual and physical abuse. Unfortunately, it also demonstrates how easily communication can be manipulated even by well-intentioned individuals—how easily we can put words in the mouths of people who cannot speak for themselves. Finally, the FC debacle reveals the extraordinary power of wishful thinking and the vulnerability of many family members and professionals associated with individuals with severe autism and mental retardation.

FUTURE DIRECTIONS

Much of what we believe the field needs to do in the future has been stated in the preceding pages of this chapter. That is, the field needs to continue research aimed at (a) disentangling the relationship of cognition and language relative to various genetic endowments (e.g., Williams syndrome); (b) determining the role that environmental input plays in shaping language development; (c) delineating the presence (or absence) of a critical early period of language acquisition, which has obvious implications for when (and perhaps how) intervention efforts are initiated. The field also needs to support (d) the further development of alternative and augmentative communication approaches; (e) the development of prelinguistic assessment and intervention procedures; (f) the further development of a continuum of effective, developmentally appropriate intervention procedures; (g) the institutionalization of more rigorous generalization analyses; and (h) continued efforts to expose and remove dubious clinical and educational practices. Sustained efforts focused on these issues surely will lead to more effective practice and better outcomes for individuals with mental retardation.

For the remainder of this chapter we focus on two superordinate issues that may determine on a much broader scale the ultimate efficacy of efforts to understand and remediate communication and language skills. These issues are the infusion of a broader systems perspective into the research and practice of the field, and the infusion of a transdisciplinary perspective throughout the field.

A Systems Perspective

It has become increasingly clear that a further expansion of our knowledge of language acquisition and intervention will depend to a large degree on the extent to which language is reintegrated with behavior and biology (Bates & Carnevale, 1993). There are many indications that we are steadily moving toward a systems approach that begins to account for the bidirectional influences of genes, cells, organs, behavior, context, and history (see Warren, 1993, for an extended discussion of these). These indicators include: the recent publication of relatively sophisticated general systems theories such as Gottlieb's theory of behavioral canalization (Gottlieb, 1991); enhanced interest in processes that enable and guide development as reflected by the specification of dynamical systems theory (Thelen & Ulrich, 1991) and connectionist models of neural activity and development (Plunkett, 1992); the recent publication of several papers that attempt to directly relate early neural development to communication and language impairment (e.g., Bates, Thal, & Janowsky, 1992; Locke, 1994); an increasing number of studies in which the independent variable represents a traditional domain of behavior (e.g., motor development) and at least one of the dependent variables represents another domain (e.g., communication). Good examples of such work includes Miller's analysis of the causes of early expressive communication delay in children with Down syndrome (Miller, Miolo, Sedey, Pierce, & Rosin, 1989) and Durand and Carr's (1991) research on the relationship of severe aberrant behavior to functional communication. A fifth indicator is research that attempts to directly relate communication and language problems to specific neurological or genetic problems. For example, Dawson and her colleagues (Dawson, Finley, Phillips, Galpert, & Lewy, 1988; Dawson & Lewy, 1989) showed through studies of cortical-event-related potentials that deficiencies in the arousal modulation of children with autism may selectively affect attention to and processing of social information at the neural level.

We are presently witnessing a rapid expansion of knowledge about the genetic and neural bases of behavior (stimulated by the explosive development of the neurosciences and work in genetics, such as the attempt to map the human genome). Breakthroughs in these areas will increase the necessity for a formal systems theory of human behavior if we are to understand how activity at these levels influences operations of the whole system (Gottlieb, 1991). As understanding of these levels of the human system increases, interest in the contributions of actual behavior, history, and immediate context should correspondingly increase. This coalescence should bring many of the issues discussed in this chapter into sharper focus. For example, whether a critical period of language acquisition exits, how it is characterized, and how it is triggered or suppressed should become clearer, as should the relative impact of genetic heritage and early environmental input. New and/or more precise methods of identifying and remediating (or preventing) communication and language disorders may be outcomes of these developments (Warren, 1993).

A Transdisciplinary Perspective

The extent to which a true systems perspective can be infused into research and practice on the communication and language of children with mental retardation may depend on the acceptance of a transdisciplinary perspective by both researchers and practitioners (Warren & Reichle, 1992). Communication and language play central roles in human development and behavior across the life span. However, their complexity encourages conceptual and clinical fragmentation—which strongly characterizes the study of communication and language development and intervention (Warren & Reichle, 1992). The human communication system emerges out of the complex interaction of sensorimotor, phonological, lexical, morphological, semantic, syntactic, auditory, and pragmatic subsystems influenced by genetic, cellular, neural, historical, and contextual factors. This inherent complexity naturally spawns scientists and clinicians who are expert in only one or two of these many interacting subsystems. These individuals may lack an understanding of how their particular component fits into the overall development of an individual's communication system. The fragmentation is obvious at all levels of the field, including theory, practice, and professional identification and training. This fragmentation, despite representing an artificial division of the human language system, is understandable from a historical perspective. Nevertheless, its continuation over the long term may pose a serious obstacle to efforts to bring a systems perspective to both research and practice.

CONCLUSION

In this chapter we have described a number of areas in which substantial progress has been made in understanding communication and language development in children with mental retardation and in developing effective means to enhance language acquisition and use. If we compare our present knowledge base to that which existed 20 years ago (cf. Schiefelbusch & Lloyd, 1974), we can see that significant and important gains have been made. On the other hand, our belief is that even more substantial, definitive gains should be made over the next two decades, particularly in the areas we have described in this chapter. Such gains will depend on the continuation of sufficient research support of course. Given that difficulties in acquiring and using language are central to the definition of mental retardation, further developments in these areas hold promise for an increased understanding of the general phenomenon of mental retardation and its effective prevention and remediation.

ACKNOWLEDGMENTS

Support for preparation of this manuscript was provided in part by grants from the National Institute of Child Health and Human Development (RO1 HD27594) and the Office of Special Education Programs of the U.S. Department of Education (HO23C20152). However, opinions expressed in this chapter are those of the authors and no endorsement by supporting agencies should be inferred.

REFERENCES

Anastasi, A. (1976). *Psychological testing* (4th ed.). New York: Macmillan.

Aram, D. M., Ekelman, B. L., & Nation, J. E. (1987). Preschoolers with language disorders: 10 years later. *Journal of Speech and Hearing Research, 27*, 232–244.

Bates, E. (1976). *Language and context: The acquisition of pragmatics.* New York: Academic Press.

Bates, E. (1979). *The emergence of symbols.* New York: Academic Press.

Bates, E., & Carnevale, G. F. (1993). New directions in research on language development. *Developmental Review, 13*, 436–470.

Bates, E., Thal, D., & Janowsky, J. S. (1992). Early language development and its neural correlates. In I. Rapin & S. Segalowitz (Eds.), *Handbook of neuropsychology: Vol. 7: Child neuropsychology* (pp. 107–179). Amsterdam: Elsevier.

Bates, E., Thal, D., & Marchman, V. (1991). Symbols and syntax: A Darwinian approach to language development. In N. Krasnegor, D. Rumbaugh, R. L. Schiefelbusch, & M. Studdert-Kennedy (Eds.), *Biological and behavioral determinants of language development* (pp. 67–88). Hillsdale, NJ: Lawrence Erlbaum Associates.

Bellugi, U., Marks, S., Bihrle, A., & Sabo, H. (1988). Dissociation between language and cognitive functions in Williams syndrome. In D. Bishop & K. Mogford (Eds.), *Language development in exceptional circumstances* (pp. 177–189). Edinburgh: Churchill Livingstone.

Biklen, D. (1990). Communication unbound: Autism and praxis. *Harvard Education Review, 60*, 291–315.

Biklen, D. (1992, January). Typing to talk: Facilitated communication. *American Journal of Speech and Language Pathology*, pp. 15–17.

Biklen, D. (1993). *Communication unbound: How facilitated communication is challenging traditional views of autism and ability/disability.* New York: Teachers College Press.

Bishop, D. (1988). Language development after focal brain damage. In D. Bishop & K. Mogford (Eds.), *Language development in exceptional circumstances* (pp. 203–219). Edinburgh: Churchill Livingstone.

Bohannon, J. N., III, MacWhinney, B., & Snow, C. E. (1990). No negative evidence revisited: Beyond learnability or who has to prove what to whom. *Developmental Psychology, 26*, 221–226.

Bruner, J. (1981). The social context of language acquisition. *Language and Communication, 1*, 155–178.

Bruner, J. S. (1975). The ontogenesis of speech acts. *Journal of Child Language, 2*, 1–19.

Casby, M. W. (1989). National data concerning communication disorders and special education. *Language, Speech, and Hearing Services in the Schools, 10*, 22–30.

Ceci, J. J. (Ed.). (1986). *Handbook of cognitive, social and neuropsychological aspects of learning disabilities.* Hillsdale, NJ: Lawrence Erlbaum Associates.

Chapman, R., & Miller, J. (1980). Analyzing language and communication in the child. In R. Schiefelbusch (Ed.), *Nonspeech language and communication: Acquisition and intervention* (pp. 159–196). Baltimore, MD: University Park Press.

Chapman, R. S. (1995). Language development in children and adolescents with Down syndrome. In P. Fletcher & B. MacWhinney (Eds.), *Handbook of child language* (pp. 641–663). Oxford, England: Blackwell.

Chapman, R. S., Streim, N., Crais, E., Salmon, D., Strand, E., & Negri, N. A. (1992). Child talk: Assumptions of a development process model for early language learning. In R. S. Chapman (Ed.), *Child talk: Processes in language acquisition and disorders* (pp. 3–19). St. Louis, MO: Mosby-Year Book.

Chomsky, N. (1957). *Syntactic structures*. The Hague, Netherlands: Mouton.

Chomsky, N. (1965). *Aspects of the theory of syntax*. Cambridge, MA: MIT Press.

Cole, K., Dale, P., & Mills, P. (1990). Defining language delay in young children by cognitive referencing: Are we saying more than we know? *Applied Psycholinguistics, 11*, 291–302.

Cole, K., Mills, P., & Harris, S. (1991). Retrospective analysis of physical and occupational therapy progress in young children: An examination of cognitive referencing. *Pediatric Physical Therapy, 3*, 185–189.

Cole, K. N., & Dale, P. S. (1986). Direct language instruction and interactive language instruction with language delayed preschool children: A comparison study. *Journal of Speech and Hearing Research, 29*, 206–217.

Cole, K. N., Dale, P. S., & Mills, P. E. (1992). Stability of the intelligence quotient–language quotient relation: Is discrepancy modeling based on myth? *American Journal on Mental Retardation, 97*(2), 131–143.

Cole, K. N., Mills, P. E., & Kelley, D. (1994). Agreement of assessment profiles used in cognitive referencing. *Language, Speech, and Hearing Services in Schools, 25*, 25–31.

Connell, P. J. (1988). Induction, generalization, and deduction: Models for defining language generalization. *Language, Speech, and Hearing Services in the Schools, 19*, 282–291.

Cummins, R. A., & Prior, M. P. (1992). Autism and assisted communication: A response to Biklen. *Harvard Educational Review, 62*, 228–241.

Dawson, G., Finley, C., Phillips, S., Galpert, L., & Lewy, A. (1988). Reduced P3 amplitude of the event-related brain potential: Its relationship to language ability in autism. *Journal of Autism and Developmental Disorders, 18*, 493–504.

Dawson, G., & Lewy, A. (1989). Reciprocal subcortical-cortical influences in autism: The role of attentional mechanisms. In G. Dawson (Ed.), *Autism: Nature, diagnosis, and treatment* (pp. 144–173). New York: Guilford.

Dore, J. (1975). Holophrases, speech acts, and language universals. *Journal of Child Language, 2*, 21–41.

Dore, J. (1986). The development of conversational competence. In R. Schiefelbusch (Ed.), *Language competence: Assessment and intervention* (pp. 3–59). San Diego, CA: College Hill Press.

Durand, V. M., & Carr, E. G. (1991). Functional communication training to reduce challenging behavior: Maintenance and application in new settings. *Journal of Applied Behavior Analysis, 24*, 251–264.

Fey, M. E. (1986). *Language intervention with young children*. San Diego, CA: College Hill Press.

Fowler, A. (1990). Language abilities in children with Down syndrome: Evidence for a specific syntactic delay. In D. Cicchetti & M. Beeghly (Eds.), *Children with Down syndrome: A developmental perspective* (pp. 302–328). Cambridge, England: Cambridge University Press.

Franklin, K., & Beukelman, D. (1990). Augmentative communication: Directions for future research. In J. Miller (Ed.), *New directions in research on child language disorders* (pp. 321–338). Austin, TX: PRO-ED.

Frith, U. (1989). *Autism: Explaining the enigma*. Cambridge, MA: Basil Blackwell.

Gallaway, C., & Richards, B. J. (Eds.). (1994). *Input and interaction in language acquisition*. Cambridge, England: Cambridge University Press.

Gardner, H. (1983). *Frames of mind*. New York: Basic Books.

Gazdag, G., & Warren, S. F. (1992, March). *An analysis of stimulus generalization reported in language intervention studies with mentally retarded children.* Paper presented at the 25th Annual Gatlinburg Conference on Research and Theory on MR/DD, Gatlinburg, TN.

Genesee, F. (1988). Bilingual language development in preschool children. In D. Bishop & K. Mogford (Eds.), *Language development in exceptional children* (pp. 62–79). Edinburgh: Churchill Livingstone.

Goldstein, H., & Hockenberger, E. H. (1991). Significant progress in child language intervention: An 11-year retrospective. *Research in Developmental Disabilities, 12,* 401–425.

Golinkoff, R. M., & Hirsh-Pasek, K. (1990). Let the mute speak: What infants can tell us about language acquisition. *Merrill-Palmer Quarterly, 36,* 67–92.

Gottlieb, G. (1991). Experiential canalization of behavioral development: Theory. *Developmental Psychology, 27,* 4–13.

Green, G. (1994). The quality of evidence. In H. C. Shane (Ed.), *Facilitated communication: The clinical and social phenomenon* (pp. 157–226). San Diego, CA: Singular Press.

Guess, D., Sailor, W., & Baer, D. M. (1974). To teach language to retarded children. In R. L. Schiefelbusch & L. L. Lloyd (Eds.), *Language perspectives: Acquisition, retardation, and intervention* (pp. 431–468). Baltimore, MD: University Park Press.

Halliday, M. A. K. (1975). Learning how to mean. In E. Lenneberg & E. Lenneberg (Eds.), *Foundations of language development* (Vol. 1, pp. 17–32). New York: Academic Press.

Hart, B., & Risley, T. (1980). In vivo language intervention: Unanticipated general effects. *Journal of Applied Behavior Analysis, 13,* 407–432.

Hart, B., & Risley, T. (1992). American parenting of language-learning children: Persisting differences in family–child interactions observed in natural home environments. *Developmental Psychology, 28*(6), 1096–1105.

Hoff-Ginsberg, E. (1986). Function and structure in maternal speech: Their relation to the child's development of syntax. *Developmental Psychology, 22*(2), 155–163.

Hoff-Ginsberg, E., & Shatz, M. (1982). Linguistic input and the child's acquisition of language. *Psychological Bulletin, 92,* 3–26.

Huttenlocher, J., Haight, W., Bryk, A., Seltzer, M., & Lyons, T. (1991). Early vocabulary growth: Relation to language input and gender. *Developmental Psychology, 27*(2), 236–248.

Itard, J. M. G. (1962). *The wild boy of Aveyron* (G. Humphrey & M. Humphrey, Trans.). Englewood Cliffs, NJ: Prentice-Hall.

Jacobson, J. W., Eberlin, M., Mulick, J. A., Schwartz, A. A., Szempruch, J., & Wheeler, D. L. (1994). Autism and facilitated communication and future directions. In J. L. Matson (Ed.), *Autism in children and adults: Etiology, assessment, and intervention* (pp. 59–83). New York: Brooks/Cole.

Johanson, I. B., & Terry, L. M. (1988). Learning in infancy: A mechanism for behavioral change during development. In E. M. Blass (Ed.), *Handbook of behavioral neurobiology: Developmental psychobiology and behavioral ecology* (Vol. 9, pp. 47–61). New York: Plenum.

Johnson, J., & Newport, E. (1989). Critical period effects in second language learning: The influence of maturational state on the acquisition of English as a second language. *Cognitive Psychology, 21,* 60–99.

Kaiser, A. P. (1993). Parent-implemented language intervention: An environmental system perspective. In A. P. Kaiser & D. B. Gray (Eds.), *Enhancing children's communication: Research foundation for intervention* (pp. 63–84). Baltimore, MD: Brookes.

Kaiser, A. P., & Gray, D. B. (Eds.). (1993). *Enhancing children's communication: Research foundation for intervention.* Baltimore, MD: Brookes.

Kaiser, A. P., Yoder, P., & Keetz, A. (1992). Evaluating milieu teaching. In. S. F. Warren & J. Reichle (Eds.), *Causes and effects in communication and language intervention* (pp. 9–47). Baltimore, MD: Brookes.

Kemp, J. (1983). The timing of language for a pediatric population. In J. Miller, D. Yoder, & R. Schiefelbusch (Eds.), *Contemporary issues in language intervention* (pp. 183–195). Rockville, MD: American Speech-Language-Hearing Association.

Klein, S. K., & Rapin, I. (1988). Intermittent conductive hearing loss and language development. In D. Bishop & K. Mogford (Eds.), *Language development in exceptional children* (pp. 96–109). Edinburgh: Churchill Livingstone.

Klima, E. S., & Bellugi, U. (1979). *The signs of language.* Cambridge, MA: Harvard University Press.

Lenneberg, E. (1967). *Biological foundations of language.* New York: Wiley.

Leonard, L. (1987). Language learnability and specific language impairment in children. *Applied Psycholinguistics, 10,* 179–202.

Lewis, B. A., & Friebairn, L. (1992). Residual effects of preschool phonology disorders in grade school, adolescence, and adulthood. *Journal of Speech and Hearing Research, 35,* 819–831.

Light, J., Collier, B., & Parnes, P. (1985). Communicative interaction between young nonspeaking physically disabled children and their primary caregivers: Part I, Discourse patterns. *Augmentative and Alternative Communication, 1,* 74–83.

Locke, J. L. (1993). *The child's path to spoken language.* Cambridge, MA: Harvard University Press.

Locke, J. L. (1994). Gradual emergence of developmental language disorders. *Journal of Speech and Hearing Research 37,* 608–616.

Lonigan, C. J., Fischel, J. E., Whitehurst, G. J., Arnold, D. S., & Valdez-Menchaca, M. C. (1992). The role of otitis media in the development of expressive language disorders. *Developmental Psychology, 28,* 430–440.

MacDonald, J. (1989). *Becoming partners with children: From play to conversation.* San Antonio, TX: Special Press.

Mahoney, G., & Powell, A. (1988). Modifying parent–child interaction: Enhancing the development of handicapped children. *Journal of Special Education, 22,* 82–96.

Menyuk, P. (1988). *Language development: Knowledge and use.* Glenview, IL: Scott, Foresman.

Mervis, C. B., & Bertrand, J. (1993, March). *General and specific relations between early language and early cognitive development.* Paper presented at the biennial meeting of the Society for Research in Child Development, New Orleans, LA.

Miller, J., Miolo, G., Sedey, A., Pierce, K., & Rosin, M. (1989, November). *Predicting lexical growth in children with Down syndrome.* Paper presented at the annual convention of the American Speech–Language–Hearing Association, St. Louis, MO.

Miller, J., Sedey, A., Miolo, G., Rosin, M., & Murray-Branch, J. (1991, November). *Spoken and sign vocabulary acquisition in children with Down syndrome.* Poster presented at the American Speech–Language–Hearing Association Convention, Atlanta, GA.

Miller, J. F. (1988). The developmental asynchrony of language development in children with Down syndrome. In L. Nadel (Ed.), *The psychobiology of Down syndrome* (pp. 167–198). Cambridge, MA: MIT Press.

Miller, J. J., & Yoder, D. E. (1972). A syntax teaching program. In J. E. McLean, D. E. Yoder, & R. L. Schiefelbusch (Eds.), *Language intervention with the retarded* (pp. 115–134). Baltimore, MD: University Park Press.

Mills, A. (1988). Visual handicap. In D. Bishop, & K. Mogford (Eds.), *Language development in exceptional circumstances* (pp. 150–164). Edinburgh: Churchill Livingstone.

Mirenda, P., & Iacono, T. (1990). Communication options for persons with severe and profound disabilities: State of the art and future directions. *Journal of The Association for Persons with Severe Handicaps, 15,* 3–21.

Mogford, K., & Bishop, D. (1988). Five questions about language acquisition considered in the light of exceptional circumstances. In D. Bishop & K. Mogford (Eds.), *Language development in exceptional circumstances* (pp. 239–260). Edinburgh: Churchill Livingstone.

Mulick, J. A., Jacobson, J. W., & Kobe, R. H. (1993). Anguished silence and helping hands: Miracles in autism with facilitated communication. *Skeptical Inquirer, 17,* 270–280.

Nelson, K. (1973). Structure and strategy in learning to talk. *Monographs of the Society for Research in Child Development, 38*(1–2, Serial No. 149).

Nelson, K. E. (1989). Strategies for first language teaching. In M. L. Rice & R. L. Schiefelbusch (Eds.), *The teachability of language* (pp. 263–310). Baltimore, MD: Brookes.

Nelson, K. E. (1991). On differentiated language-learning models and differentiated intervention. In N. Krasnegor, D. Rumbaugh, R. Schiefelbusch, & M. Studdert-Kennedy (Eds.), *Biological and behavioral determinants of language development* (pp. 399–428). Hillsdale, NJ: Lawrence Erlbaum Associates.

Newport, E. (1990). Maturational constraints on language learning. *Cognitive Science, 14*, 11–28.

Notari, A., Cole, K., & Mills, P. (1992). Cognitive referencing: The (non)relationship between theory and application. *Topics in Early Childhood Special Education, 11*, 22–28.

Owens, R., & House, L. (1984). Decision-making processes in augmentative communication. *Journal of Speech and Hearing Disorders, 49*, 18–25.

Patkowski, M. (1980). The sensitive period for the acquisition of syntax in a second language. *Language Learning, 30*, 449–472.

Penfield, W. (1965). Conditioning the uncommitted cortex for language learning. *Brain, 88*, 787–798.

Pinker, S. (1994). *The language instinct.* New York: Morrow.

Plunkett, K. (1992). Connectionism and developmental theory. *British Journal of Developmental Psychology, 10*, 209–254.

Quigley, S. P., & Paul, P. V. (1987). Deafness and language development. In S. Rosenberg (Ed.), *Advances in applied psycholinguistics: Vol. 1. Disorders of first-language development* (pp. 180–219). Cambridge, England: Cambridge University Press.

Reichle, J., Mirenda, P., Locke, P., Piche, L., & Johnston, S. (1992). Beginning augmentative communication systems. In S. F. Warren & J. Reichle (Eds.), *Causes and effects in communication and language intervention* (pp. 131–156). Baltimore, MD: Brookes.

Reichle, J., & Wacker, D. P. (Eds.). (1993). *Communicative alternatives to challenging behavior: Integrating functional assessment and intervention strategies.* Baltimore, MD: Brookes.

Rice, M. (1983). Contemporary accounts of the cognition/language relationship: Implications for speech–language clinicians. *Journal of Speech and Hearing Disorders, 48*, 347–359.

Rice, M. L., & Kemper, S. (1984). *Child language and cognition.* Austin, TX: PRO-ED.

Risley, T. R., Hart, B. M., & Doke, L. (1972). Operant language development: The outline of a therapeutic technology. In R. L. Schiefelbusch (Ed.), *Language of the mentally retarded* (pp. 177–198). Baltimore, MD: University Park Press.

Rogoff, B. (1990). *Apprenticeship in thinking: Cognitive development in social context.* New York: Oxford University Press.

Romski, M. A., & Sevcik, R. A. (1988). Augmentative and alternative communication systems: Considerations for individuals with severe intellectual disabilities. *Augmentative and Alternative Communication, 4*, 83–93.

Rosenberg, S., & Abbeduto, L. (1993). *Language and communication in mental retardation: Development, processes, and intervention.* Hillsdale, NJ: Lawrence Erlbaum Associates.

Rosenberg, S., & Robinson, C. (1985). Enhancement of mothers' interactional skills in an infant education program. *Education and Training of the Mentally Retarded, 20*(2), 163–169.

Schachter, F. F. (1979). *Everyday mother talk to toddlers.* New York: Academic Press.

Schiefelbusch, R. L, & Lloyd, L. L. (Eds.). (1974). *Language perspectives: Acquisition, retardation, and intervention.* Baltimore, MD: University Park Press.

Schiff-Myers, N. (1988). Hearing children of deaf parents. In D. Bishop & K. Mogford (Eds.), *Language development in exceptional children* (pp. 4–61). Edinburgh: Churchill Livingstone.

Sedey, A., Rosin, M., & Miller, J. (1991, November). *The use of signs among children with Down syndrome.* Poster presented at the American Speech–Language–Hearing Association Convention, Atlanta, GA.

Shaffer, T., & Ehri, L. (1980). Seriators' and nonseriators' comprehension of comparative adjective forms. *Journal of Psycholinguistic Research, 9*, 177–204.

Shane, H. (1981). Decision making in early augmentative communication system use. In R. Schiefelbusch & D. Bricker (Eds.), *Early language: Acquisition and intervention* (pp. 389–425). Baltimore, MD: University Park Press.

Siegel, L. (1989). IQ is irrelevant to the definition of learning disabilities. *Journal of Learning Disabilities, 22*, 469–478.

Skinner, B. F. (1957). *Verbal behavior.* New York: Appleton-Century-Crofts.

Smith, M. D., & Belcher, R. G. (1994). Facilitated communication and autism: Separating fact from fiction. *Journal of Vocational Rehabilitation, 4*, 66–74.

Snow, C. (1984). Parent-child interaction and the development of communicative ability. In R. L. Schiefelbusch & J. Pickar (Eds.), *The acquisition of communicative competence* (pp. 69–108). Baltimore, MD: University Park Press.

Snow, C. (1994). Beginning from baby talk: Twenty years of research on input in interaction. In C. Gallaway & B. J. Richards (Eds.), *Input and interaction in language acquisition* (pp. 1–12). Cambridge, England: Cambridge University Press.

Snow, C., Perlmann, R., & Nathan, D. (1987). Why routines are different: Toward a multiple factors model of the relation between input and language acquisition. In K. E. Nelson & A. van Kleeck (Eds.), *Child language* (Vol. 6, pp. 65–97). Hillsdale, NJ: Lawrence Erlbaum Associates.

Sokolov, J. L. (1992). Linguistic imitation in children with Down syndrome. *American Journal on Mental Retardation, 97*(2), 209–221.

Sokolov, J. L. (1993). A local contingency analysis of the fine-tuning hypothesis. *Developmental Psychology, 29*(6), 1008–1023.

Spiedel, G., & Nelson, K. E. (1989). *The many faces of imitation in language learning.* New York: Springer-Verlag.

Spradlin, J. E., & Siegel, G. M. (1982). Language training in natural and clinical environments. *Journal of Speech and Hearing Disorders, 47*, 2–6.

Stanovich, K. (1991). Discrepancy definitions of reading disability: Has intelligence led us astray? *Reading Research Quarterly, 26*, 7–29.

Stokes, T., & Baer, D. M. (1977). An implicit technology of generalization. *Journal of Applied Behavior Analysis, 10*, 349–367.

Studdert-Kennedy, M. (1991). Language development from an evolutionary perspective. In N. Krasnegor, D. Rumbaugh, R. L. Schiefelbusch, & M. Studdert-Kennedy (Eds.), *Biological and behavioral determinants of language development* (pp. 5–28). Hillsdale, NJ: Lawrence Erlbaum Associates.

Sudhalter, V., Cohen, I., Silverman, W., & Wolf-Schein, E. (1990). Conversational analyses of males with fragile X, Down syndrome, and autism: Comparison of the emergence of deviant language. *American Journal on Mental Retardation, 94*, 431–441.

Tannock, R., & Girolametto, L. (1992). Reassessing parent-focused language intervention programs. In S. F. Warren & J. Reichle (Eds.), *Causes and effects in communication and language intervention* (pp. 49–79). Baltimore, MD: Brookes.

Thelen, E., & Ulrich, B. D. (1991). Hidden skills. *Monographs of the Society for Research in Child Development, 56*(1, Serial No. 223).

Thurstone, L. D. (1938). *Primary mental abilities.* Chicago: University of Chicago Press.

Tomasello, M. (1992). *First verbs.* Cambridge, England: Cambridge University Press.

van Kleeck, A. (1994). Potential cultural bias in training parents as conversational partners with their children who have delays in language development. *American Journal of Speech-Language Pathology, 3*(1), 67–78.

Warren, S. F. (1977). A useful ecobehavioral perspective for applied behavior analysis. In A. K. Rogers-Warren & S. F. Warren (Eds.), *Ecological perspectives in behavior analysis* (pp. 173–196). Baltimore, MD: University Park Press.

Warren, S. F. (1991). Enhancing communication and language development with milieu teaching procedures. In E. Cipani (Ed.), *A guide for developing language competence in preschool children with severe and moderate handicaps* (pp. 68–93). Springfield, IL: Thomas.

Warren, S. F. (1993). Early communication and language intervention: Challenges for the 1990s and beyond. In A. Kaiser & D. Gray (Eds.), *Enhancing children's communication: Research foundations for intervention* (pp. 375–395). Baltimore, MD: Brookes.

Warren, S. F., & Reichle, J. (Eds.). (1992). *Causes and effects in communication and language intervention*. Baltimore, MD: Brookes.

Warren, S. F., & Rogers-Warren, A. K. (Eds.). (1985). *Teaching functional language*. Austin, TX: PRO-ED.

Warren, S. F., Yoder, P. J., Gazdag, G. E., Kim, K., & Jones, H. A. (1993). Facilitating prelinguistic communication skills in young children with developmental delay. *Journal of Speech and Hearing Research, 36*, 83–97.

Wetherby, A., & Prizant, B. (1990). *Communication and Symbolic Behavior Scales–research edition*. Chicago: Riverside.

Whitehurst, G. J., Falco, F. L., Lonigan, C. J., Fischel, J. E., DeBaryshe, B. D., Valdez-Menchaca, M. C., & Caulfield, M. (1988). Accelerating language development through picture book reading. *Developmental Psychology, 24*(4), 552–559.

Wilcox, M. J. (1992). Enhancing initial communication skills in young children with developmental disabilities through partner programming. *Seminars in Speech and Language,13*(3), 194–212.

Wolf-Schein, E., Sudhalter, V., Cohen, I., Fisch, G., Hanson, D., Pfadt, A., Hagerman, R., Jenkins, E., & Brown, W. T. (1987). Speech–language and the fragile X syndrome: Initial findings. *Journal of the American Speech and Hearing Association, 29*, 35–38.

Wolfensberger, W. (1994). The "facilitated communication" craze as an instance of pathological science: The cold fusion of human services. In H. C. Shane (Ed.), *Facilitated communication: The clinical and social phenomenon*. San Diego, CA: Singular Publishing.

Yoder, P. J., Kaiser, A. P., & Alpert, C. (1991). An exploratory study of the interaction between language teaching methods and child characteristics. *Journal of Speech and Hearing Research, 24*, 155–167.

Yoder, P. J., Kaiser, A., Goldstein, H., Alpert, C., Mousetis, L., Kaczmarek, L., & Fischer, R. (1995). An exploratory comparison of milieu teaching and responsive interaction in classroom application. Manuscript submitted for publication. *Journal of Early Intervention, 19*, 218–242.

Yoder, P. J., & Warren, S. F. (1993). Can developmentally delayed children's language development be enhanced through prelinguistic intervention? In A. Kaiser & D. Gray (Eds.), *Enhancing children's communication: Research foundations for intervention* (pp. 35–61). Baltimore, MD: Brookes.

Yoder, P. J., Warren, S. F., Kim, K., & Gazdag, G. E. (1994). Facilitating prelinguistic communication skills in young children with developmental delay II: Systematic replication and extension. *Journal of Speech and Hearing Research, 37*, 841–851.

› 15 ‹

Mental Retardation and Family Adaptation

Zolinda Stoneman
The University of Georgia

The study of families is one of the most active and vibrant areas of mental retardation research. Perusal of any of the mental retardation journals leads to the clear conclusion that the study of families is dynamic and energetic, both nationally and internationally. Family research has developed from a narrow historic focus on identifying family pathology and dysfunction to a theoretically driven field of research examining complex reciprocal family processes that are affected by the presence of a family member with mental retardation. The purpose of this chapter is to provide a review of mental retardation family research. The information presented in the chapter is organized according to the theory that guided the research effort. For those family studies that are not clearly aligned with one theoretical position, findings are grouped according to the theoretical position that they best illuminate. As such, multifaceted findings from some studies may be found across different sections of the chapter. Although the focus is on mental retardation, studies of families with members who have autism and certain other disabilities associated with mental retardation are also included. Family mental retardation researchers have overwhelmingly focused their efforts on the childhood period. Only a few researchers have studied families of adults with mental retardation. Accordingly, although this chapter takes a life-span perspective, the emphasis is on families who have a child who has mental retardation.

FAMILY STRESS THEORIES

Do Families of Children With Mental Retardation Experience Heightened Stress?

Stress models (i.e., Lazarus, DeLongis, Folkman, & Gruen, 1985; Pearlin, Liberman, Menaghan, & Mullan, 1981; Selye, 1956) have been the most widely used conceptual frameworks for guiding the study of families with a member who has mental retardation. Researchers have been intrigued by the notion that the presence of a child with mental retardation in the family would result in increased stress for other family members. In an early study, Fowle (1969) compared families who had institutionalized their child with families who were providing in-home care, assuming that those families who had placed their child had done so in order to diminish family stress. Contrary to expectations, the groups did not differ. Among parents who had placed, however, marital integration was higher for families who had placed 2 years or more before the interview, causing the authors to suggest that placement may have caused an alleviation of stress with the passage of time. Fotheringham, Skelton, and Hoddinott (1972) followed families longitudinally for 1 year after they placed their child and found that, contrary to their expectations, family functioning did not improve in the year following placement. In a similar study, Holroyd, Brown, Wikler, and Simmons (1975) found that among families of children with autism, stress levels were similar in families who had and had not placed their children out of home. Caldwell and Guze (1960) also found no differences in mothers or siblings based on placement status. Thus, evidence supporting a reduction in family stress following out-of-home placement is weak at best.

Numerous researchers have tried to document increased family stress by comparing families of children with mental retardation to families of typically developing children. Cummings (Cummings, 1976; Cummings, Bayley, & Rie, 1966) reported that mothers and fathers of children with mental retardation had higher depressive affect, enjoyed their children less, and had a lower sense of parenting competence than did comparison parents. The authors concluded that these negative effects resulted from increased stress. In other studies, parents reported increased malaise and depression (Fisman, Wolf, & Noh, 1989; Romans-Clarkson et al., 1986; Smith, Innocenti, Boyce, & Smith, 1993; Wallander et al., 1989; Wishart, Bidder, & Gray, 1981), greater stress (Dyson, 1991, 1993; Friedrich & Friedrich, 1981; Kazak, 1987; Singhi, Goyal, Pershad, Singhi, & Walia, 1990; Wilton & Renaut, 1986), less psychological well-being (Friedrich & Friedrich, 1981), and increased fatigue and anxiety (Romans-Clarkson et al., 1986). Others found family stress to be limited to issues directly related to the child with a disability, with little to no spillover into other areas of family life (Boyce, Behl, Mortensen, & Akers, 1991; Dyson & Fewell, 1986; McKinney & Peterson, 1987; Walker, Van Slyke, & Newbrough, 1992; Wolf, Noh, Fisman, & Speechley, 1989).

Many studies, however, failed to find increased stress in families of children with mental retardation and related disabilities (Bristol, Gallagher, & Schopler, 1988; Cameron, Dobson, & Day, 1991; Dumas, Wolf, Fisman, & Culligan, 1991; Dyson & Fewell, 1986; Gamble & McHale, 1989; Gowen, Johnson-Martin, Goldman, & Appelbaum, 1989; Harris & McHale, 1989; Houser & Seligman, 1991a; Kazak, 1988; Koegel, Schreibman, O'Neill, & Burke, 1983; McKinney & Peterson, 1987; Salisbury, 1987; Van Riper, Ryff, & Pridham, 1992; Walker, Ortiz-Valdes, & Newbrough, 1989; Wishart, Bidder, & Gray, 1980). Older mothers providing care for a son or daughter with mental retardation actually were in better health than other women their age and had higher morale, and perceived less burden and stress than other older caregivers (Seltzer & Krauss, 1989). Certain families may be particularly vulnerable to stress, including families of children with autism (Bouma & Schweitzer, 1990; Dumas et al., 1991; Fisman et al., 1989; Holroyd & McArthur, 1976; Wolf et al., 1989) and single-parent families (Beckman, 1983; Boyce et al., 1991; Salisbury, 1987; Schilling, Kirkham, Snow, & Schinke, 1986; Sherman, 1988), although McCubbin (1989) failed to find increased stress for single-parent mothers. Hispanic families reported less burden than did non-Hispanic White families (Heller, Markwardt, Rowitz, & Farber, 1994).

Overall, although a large number of studies have tried to determine whether families with children with mental retardation experience increased stress, findings are contradictory and lead to no clear conclusions. This can, in part, be explained by the observation that researchers have used a variety of stress measures to study heterogeneous groups of families, with children with different types and levels of mental retardation, at very different chronological ages. Selection of appropriate comparison groups has been a major design problem (see Stoneman, 1989). Theoretically, researchers have often failed to differentiate between stressor events and the stress response (i.e., depression, decreased self-esteem) of the individual or family (McKinney & Peterson, 1987; Wallander, Pitt, & Mellins, 1990). Perhaps part of the problem lies in the research question itself. Asking if families, on average, experience more stress when a member with mental retardation is present may never prove to be genuinely enlightening, regardless of the rigor of the research design. Examining within-group variability using theoretically driven research questions would seem to be a more promising approach. In other words, why do some families with children who have mental retardation experience heightened stress whereas others do not?

ABCX Family Stress Model

Hill (1949, 1958) proposed the ABCX model as a framework to understand the effects of stress on families. In this model, the stressor/crisis event (A), the resources of the family (B), and the family's meaning or definition of the stressful event (C) interact to determine the impact of the event on the family (X). McCubbin and Patterson (1983) proposed the Double ABCX model, which adds a longitudinal component to the original ABCX conceptualization. It incorporates the pileup of multiple stresses, the resources and coping strategies that the family develops over time, and the meaning that the family attributes to the stressor as they adjust to the event.

Using the original formulation of the model (Hill, 1949, 1958), Minnes (1988) investigated perceived stress associated with a child with mental retardation, using internal and external family resources (B) and characteristics of the child (A) as predictors of perceived stress (X). She found the quality of the family climate (B) to be the most consistent predictor of stress, with severity of disability (A) also accounting for additional variance. The finding of an uneven pattern of predictors for different stress outcomes caused her to question the ABCX model and to suggest that researchers use the Double ABCX formulation. Bristol (1987) used the Double ABCX stress model to examine the predictors of healthy functioning in families of children with autism and severe communication disorders. She found that the model successfully predicted substantial variance in three targeted outcomes: quality of parenting, maternal depression, and maternal marital adjustment. Willoughby and Glidden (1995) found that the link between father participation in child care and marital satisfaction, posited by their conceptualization of the ABCX model, existed for both mothers and fathers.

McCubbin (1989) examined whether an expansion of the Double ABCX model was as applicable for single parents of children with disabilities as for two-parent families. In general, the model was appropriate for both family forms. This adaptation of the ABCX model has also proved valuable in studying the predictors of health and health care consultation (McCubbin & Huang, 1989). Orr, Cameron, and Day (1991) used path analysis to test the Double ABCX model among parents of children who had moderate mental retardation. Rather than conceptualizing severity of disability as the stressful event (A), as has generally been done by researchers using this model, Orr et al. (1991) focused on the stressful impact of child behavior problems. As predicted, the more severe the behavior problems, the more stress the family experienced. Overall support for the conceptual model, however, was modest. Smaller paths existed from stressor to resources (A to B), from stressor to perception of the event (A to C), and from resources to outcomes (B to X). Other predicted paths were not significant.

Child Characteristics and Stress

As a result of the work of Bell (i.e., Bell & Harper, 1977), reciprocal, bidirectional influences in the development of children and families are now almost universally accepted. Consistent with this emphasis on the importance of child effects, mental retardation researchers have attempted to identify child characteristics associated with increased family stress. The most consistent association has been between child behavior problems and increased parent stress and depression (Beckman, 1983; Cameron & Orr, 1989; Chetwynd, 1985; Dumas et al., 1991; Heller & Factor, 1993; Orr et al., 1991; Sloper, Knussen, Turner, & Cunningham, 1991; Walker, Ortiz-Valdez, & Newbrough, 1989; Walker, Van Slyke, & Newbrough, 1992). Severe stress from challenging behavior can lead to out-of-home placement (Black, Cohn, Smull, & Crites, 1985; Heller & Factor, 1993; Heller et al., 1994; Sherman, 1988; Tausig, 1985).

Emotional problems of children with mental retardation also have been related to increased parent stress (Cameron & Orr, 1989), as have difficult temperamental attributes, including hyperirritability, hyperactivity, and lack of responsivity (Affleck, Allen, McGrade, & McQueeney, 1982; Beckman, 1983, 1991; Cameron & Orr, 1989; Chetwynd, 1985; Konstantareas & Homatidis, 1989; Shonkoff et al., 1992). Repetitive behavior patterns (Beckman, 1983) and self-abusive behavior (Konstantareas & Homatidis, 1989) also create parent stress. Hoppes and Harris (1990) found that the diminished responsiveness of a child with autism decreased maternal gratification and hence created stress.

Stress also results when children create increased care demands because of their dependence on parents for activities of daily living (Beckman, 1983; Breslau, Staruch, & Mortimer, 1982; Cameron & Orr, 1989; Walker et al., 1992) and their need for increased supervision because of an inability to play with others or keep themselves occupied (Chetwynd, 1985). The general relationship between severity of the child's cognitive disability and parent stress is less clear. Researchers have found that diminished child competence or independence is associated with certain aspects of stress (Boyce et al., 1991; Cameron & Orr, 1989; Frey, Greenberg, & Fewell, 1989; Minnes, 1988; Seltzer & Krauss, 1989).

Other child attributes noted in the literature as stressful include multiple disabilities (Cameron & Orr, 1989), motor impairments (Shonkoff et al., 1992), male gender (Boyce et al., 1991; Farber, 1959; Frey, Greenberg, & Fewell, 1989), older child age (Donovan, 1988; Konstantareas & Homatidis, 1989), and poor physical health (Barrera, Watson, & Adelstein, 1987; Seltzer & Krauss, 1989). Recent findings suggest that parents of children with Down syndrome experience less stress and greater well-being than parents of children with other types of mental retardation (Goldberg, Marcovitch, MacGregor, & Lojkasek, 1986; Seltzer & Krauss, 1989; Seltzer, Krauss, & Tsunematsu, 1993), although the reason for this effect is not clear.

Stress Differences Between Mothers and Fathers

Researchers have generally found that, compared to fathers, mothers of children with mental retardation experience more depression and stress (Bristol et al., 1988; Fisman et al., 1989; Moes, Koegel, Schreibman, & Loos, 1992; Shonkoff, Hauser-Cram, Krauss, & Upshur, 1992; Wolf et al., 1989), more symptoms of distress (Goldberg et al., 1986; Sloper et al., 1991), poorer emotional and physical health (Beckman, 1991; Dunst, Trivette, & Cross, 1986; Krauss, 1993), greater marital role tension (Fowle, 1969), greater burden (Weinhouse, Weinhouse, & Nelson, 1992), less personal well-being (McLinden, 1990), and more pessimism (Rousey, Best, & Blacher, 1992). These findings are probably related to the differential family roles assumed by mothers and fathers, reviewed in a subsequent section of this chapter as a part of the discussion of research sponsored by role theory.

Transitions and Family Stress

Although it is generally accepted that both normative and nonnormative transitions are stressful, the research elucidating the relationship between disability-related transitions and family stress has yielded inconsistent and somewhat fragmented findings. Early childhood transitions accompanied by increased family stress include diagnosis, the point at which help is first sought, and the transition from infant to preschool programs (Bernheimer, Young, & Winton, 1983). Wikler (1986) identified the onset of adolescence and of adulthood as periods of high family stress, whereas Orr, Cameron, Dobson, and Day (1993) found higher stress during middle childhood than during either the preschool or adolescent years. Others suggested that stress follows a chronological progression from infancy through adolescence, increasing as children age (Haldy & Hanzlik, 1990). Flynt and Wood (1989), however, failed to find differences in stress across key transitional periods of childhood, whereas Glidden, Kiphart, Willoughby, and Bush (1993) found decreases in maternal depression across early childhood. Thorin and Irvin (1992) studied families of children with severe disabilities during the transition to adulthood and found stress strongly related to concern about future residential placement.

What Is Stressful?

Although stress research has traditionally focused on the impact of major life events, more recently stress researchers have emphasized an alternate conceptualization, namely that of life hassles (Kanner, Coyne, Schaefer, & Lazarus, 1981). Hassles are the irritating events and demands that characterize a person's everyday life. Larger life events, such as the presence of a child with a disability in the family, are believed to operate by influencing the pattern of daily hassles. Hassles relating to parenting a child with a disability include time demands, fatigue, or restricted freedom (Bouma & Schweitzer, 1990; Chetwynd, 1985; Harris & McHale, 1989; Holmes & Carr, 1991; McLinden, 1990), behavior management (Harris & McHale, 1989; Holmes & Carr, 1991; Weiss, 1991), family strains and conflicts involving the child (Harris & McHale, 1989; Weiss, 1991), expenses (Harris & McHale, 1989), and family relocation because of the child (Chetwynd, 1985).

Community attitudes, as well as interactions with programs and professionals, create hassles (Baxter, 1989; Harris & McHale, 1989; Koegel et al., 1992; Weiss, 1991), as do negative community reactions to children's speech, appearance, and behavior (Baxter, 1989; Weiss, 1991), children's sleep problems (Konstantareas & Homatidis, 1989), self-stimulatory or self-destructive behavior, screaming (Weiss, 1991), and dependency demands (Bouma & Schweitzer, 1990; Holmes & Carr, 1991; Koegel et al., 1992). Some parents fear for the future, anticipating the possible need for life-long care (Bouma & Schweitzer, 1990; Harris & McHale, 1989; Koegel et al., 1992; Weiss, 1991). Other hassles are quite practical, such as extra washing and ironing (Holmes & Carr, 1991) and difficulties in finding child care (Palfrey, Walker, Butler, & Singer, 1989). Maternal stress, as measured by daily hassles and disability-related problems, has been found to contribute to compromised maternal mental health (Wallander et al., 1990). Yet, Blackard and Barsh (1982) found that professionals consistently underestimate family stress from ongoing practical issues, or hassles, related to rearing a child with a disability.

MODELS OF SOCIAL SUPPORT AS A BUFFER OF STRESS

The Amount and Type of Social Support Available to Families

It has been widely documented that the effects of stress on individuals and families can be buffered by social support (Cohen & Wills, 1985; Gottlieb, 1983). This body of work has led researchers to focus attention on the social support available to families of children with mental retardation and on the impact of social support on their well-being. Researchers have been interested in comparing the social support available to families of children with mental retardation to that experienced by other families. Kazak's studies are representative of this research approach (Kazak, 1987, 1988; Kazak & Marvin, 1984; Kazak & Wilcox, 1984). In general, her studies suggested some degree of disruption in the social support systems of parents of children with disabilities, with their networks tending to be smaller in size and more dense (network members knew and interacted with one another) than those in comparison families. McAllister, Butler, and Lei (1973) found that parents of children with behavioral retardation, particularly mothers, experienced some degree of social isolation.

Using a nationally representative sample from the 1970 birth cohort in Bristol, England, Cooke, and Lawton (1984) found that, in general, relatives, friends, and neighbors of families of children with disabilities were available in times of crisis but did not provide day-to-day help to the family. Support received by parents of children with mild, moderate, and severe disabilities was comparable, leading the authors to suggest that families with the greatest needs do not receive more support. Some studies have not found differences in social support between parents of children with mental retardation and comparison families (Beckman, 1991; Rodrigue, Morgan, & Geffken, 1990; Waisbren, 1980).

Other researchers have found social support strengths. Mothers of children with disabilities have been found to view their social support as being more helpful (Gowen et al., 1989) and express more satisfaction with support from friends and community groups than do comparison mothers (Erickson & Upshur, 1989). Older women providing care for adult sons or daughters with mental retardation have been found to have smaller support networks than do the standardization samples (Seltzer & Krauss, 1989), but these networks seemed to be very effective in enhancing well-being of the older mothers. In a Canadian study, Trute and Hauch (1988b) studied the social networks of well-adjusted families of young children with developmental delays. Parents had smaller than expected social networks, but, similar to the findings of Seltzer and Krauss (1989), these networks appeared to be quite effective. Families expressed high satisfaction with their social support. These successful families were viewed by the researchers as actively constructing their social support networks.

A few researchers have found etiological differences in social support. For example, mothers (Shonkoff et al., 1992) and fathers (Goldberg et al., 1986) of children with Down syndrome have been found to be the more satisfied with their social support than families of children with other forms of mental retardation. Similar findings have emerged for older caregivers of individuals with Down syndrome (Seltzer et al., 1993). As with similar findings for family stress, the reasons behind these etiological differences are not yet known. In a somewhat idiosyncratic finding, Rodrigue et al. (1992) found that fathers of autistic girls reported receiving less social support than did fathers of sons with autism or fathers of children of either gender with mental retardation.

The Effects of Social Support on Families

Research by Dunst and colleagues has provided strong evidence for the facilitative effects of social support in families of children with mental retardation. Dunst et al. (1986) found that preschool children with mental retardation, physical disabilities, and developmental risk were more likely to make developmental progress and to be more accepted and integrated into the community if their parents had supportive social networks. Families with more supportive informal networks were less likely to use community resources. In a subsequent study, Dunst, Leet, and Trivette (1988) found that intra- and extrafamily support were positively related to maternal well-being. Family social support networks remained stable at different stages of transition into an early childhood program (Dunst, Trivette, & Cornwell, 1989). Families with larger personal support networks had fewer unmet needs and better problem-solving capabilities.

Other researchers have found high levels of social support to be associated with reduced stress (Beckman, 1991; Boyce et al., 1991; Kazak, 1988; Konstantareas & Homatidis, 1989; Seltzer & Krauss, 1989; Shonkoff et al., 1992), less depression (Frey et al., 1989b; Gowen et al., 1989), happier marriages (Friedrich, Cohen, & Wilturner, 1987), positive family functioning (Brotherson et al., 1988), a greater sense of parenting competence (Haldy & Hanzlik, 1990), positive adjustment to the parental role (Jones, 1991), reduced caregiving burden (Heller & Factor, 1993; Heller et al., 1994; Seltzer & Krauss, 1989), greater life satisfaction (Seltzer & Krauss, 1989), and fewer parent–child problems (Floyd & Phillippe, 1993).

The effects of social support are not always beneficial. Konstantareas and Homatidis (1989) found that many sources of social support were seen by parents as being sources of aggravation rather than constructive support. Jones (1991) suggested that grandmothers and relatives may intrude into parenting decisions, over time potentially undermining the mother's self-confidence. Waisbren (1980) found both positive and negative social support effects. When fathers of young children with disabilities perceived that their own parents were highly supportive, they engaged in more activities with their child, saw themselves as changing for the better over time, and were more willing to make plans for the future. However, these fathers were also more negative about the child's influence on their marriages and experienced more symptoms of stress. Mothers who viewed their in-laws as being highly supportive had more positive feelings about their child and consulted fewer doctors, but they listed more symptoms of stress. Results indicate the importance of husbands' parents in providing support, but they also suggest that social support carries with it both benefits and costs.

Social Support Differences Between Mothers and Fathers

There is some evidence that patterns of social support may differ for mothers and fathers of children with mental retardation. Mothers express a greater need than do fathers for family and social support (Bailey, Blasco, & Simeonsson, 1992), and mothers report more support from outside the family than do fathers (Goldberg et al., 1986). Fathers report receiving more support from their wives than wives do from their husbands (Goldberg et al., 1986). Konstantareas and Homatidis (1989) found that mothers reported both higher levels of support and higher levels of social aggravation than did fathers. Not all researchers, however, found differences between mothers and fathers in their degree of social support or social isolation (Beckman, 1991; Brotherson et al., 1988; Krauss, 1993; McLinden, 1990).

Relationships between social support and wellness outcomes also have been found to differ by parent gender. Romans-Clarkson et al. (1986), studying families of preschool children with disabilities in New Zealand, found no relationship between social support and health symptoms for mothers; for fathers, poor health was related to unavailable and inadequate supports. Similarly, Beckman (1991) found formal support to be correlated with less general life stress for fathers, but not for mothers. For mothers, the association between depression and child-related stress has been found to be suppressed when social support was present (Wolf et al., 1989); for fathers, social support acted as a moderator (a stress × social support interaction), rather than as a suppressor, in the relationship between stress and depression. Frey et al. (1989) found that social support was positively related to family and marital adjustment for both mothers and fathers. For fathers, criticism from the social support network was strongly negatively related to perceived family adjustment, parenting stress, and psychological distress. For mothers, the amount of assistance contributed by the social network (rather than criticism) seemed to be the most important factor.

Developmental Changes in Social Support

There is a question as to whether the social support available to families with members who have mental retardation changes in predictable ways across transition periods and over the life course. Suelzle and Keenan (1981) found that the use of personal support networks by families of children with disabilities declined from the birth of a child through the child's 21st birthday; need for family support assumed a U-shaped relationship, being highest during the preschool and young adult years. Shonkoff et al. (1992) found that social support helpfulness and number of supports increased across the period of infancy. In a contrary finding, Flynt, Wood, and Scott (1992) detected no differences in social support available to families of children with mental retardation between infancy and young adulthood.

Grant (1986), in a North Wales study, found that as caregivers age they are more likely to be the lone caregivers in the household. Older caregivers had more restricted social networks, with fewer friends and neighbors to draw on for help and assistance. Similarly, Heller and Factor (1993) found that as parents age, support from relatives decreases. Older parents tend to have more difficulty in leaving their son or daughter in the care of others (Englehardt, Lutzer, & Brubaker, 1987). Grant (1986) documented a reversal in the expected social support relationship for a subsample of caregivers. In these families, the adult with mental retardation was providing care for their aging parent, rather than vice versa. In some cases, the older parent was able to remain independent because a son or daughter with mental retardation lived in the home and provided them with critical daily support.

Siblings as Sources of Social Support

Siblings have been studied as important components of the social support networks of older caregivers. Only a small percentage of adults with mental retardation received instrumental support from their siblings; most, however, received affective sibling support (Seltzer, Begun, Seltzer, & Krauss, 1991). The most involved sibling was more likely to be a sister; that sibling was also generally older and lived close to the family home. When siblings were involved, caregiver health and morale were higher, and less burden and stress associated with caregiving were experienced by the parent. In an interesting finding, Seltzer et al. (1991) noted that maternal well-being was not related to the support exchanged between the mother and her adult children. Rather, the important factor was the support provided by siblings to the sibling with mental retardation.

Formal Sources of Social Support

Researchers have found that the social networks of families of individuals with mental retardation contain more professionals than do those of comparison families (Gowen et al., 1989; Kazak, 1988; Seltzer & Krauss, 1989; Young & Roopnarine, 1994). There is not consistent evidence, however, that this formal support positively contributes to family well-being. Waisbren (1980) found that formal support made little impact on the well-being of families of infants with disabilities, whereas Vadasy, Fewell, Schell, and Greenberg (1984) found some improvement in social support. Participation by mothers in group early intervention programs was unrelated to the stress experienced by the women (McKinney & Peterson, 1987), even though involved mothers listed more peers as sources of support. In their longitudinal study of families receiving early intervention services, Shonkoff et al. (1992) found that mothers who attended professionally organized parent groups had an increase in the size and helpfulness of their support networks, but they also experienced increased strains within the family. The greater the mothers' participation in parent groups, the greater the increase in stresses in family relationships and maternal personal strain. Similarly, mothers who received family-oriented supports in addition to general early intervention services had greater change in the size (but not the helpfulness) of their support networks and greater increases in parenting stress. Increased home visits, on the other hand, were associated with decreased parenting stress.

High caregiver stress and burden has been associated with greater utilization of formal services (Heller et al., 1994; Seltzer & Krauss, 1989). It is possible that families experiencing greater stress make more use of services (Heller et al., 1994). It is also possible that interacting with the formal service system can increase family stress. Families receiving early intervention services primarily from a single discipline have been found to have significant decreases in parenting stress compared to those who received their services through a multidisciplinary approach (Shonkoff et al., 1992). Brinker, Seifer, and Sameroff (1994) also found that for mothers of infants with developmental delays, contact with a greater number of agencies was associated with greater stress, whereas the frequency of attendance at one comprehensive program was associated with less stress.

The research strongly suggests that social support is often of great benefit to families with members who have mental retardation. There is a note of caution, however, that arises from studies documenting that social support can also have negative effects on families, or that similar supports can have positive effects on some families and negative effects on others. There is a great need to better understand what types of social supports are effective in buffering which specific stressors, for which families, living in what particular circumstances. This is a research agenda for the future.

THEORIES OF COPING

Coping Strategies Used by Families

Along with an interest in the stresses experienced by families of children with mental retardation has come a small, but growing, interest in the strategies that these families use to successfully cope with their life circumstances. The cognitive coping model developed by Folkman and Lazarus (Folkman, Schaefer, & Lazarus, 1979; Lazarus & Folkman, 1984) has been the most influential in guiding this research. In this model, coping is defined as efforts to manage environmental demands, including competing demands, that go beyond the person's resources (Folkman et al., 1979). The person appraises his or her current situation, determines whether a stressor exists, and then decides what resources and strategies to employ in order to address the stressful situation. Lazarus and Folkman (1984) identified two major types of coping strategies: emotion focused and problem focused. Emotion-focused strategies, used to regulate emotional reactions to stress, are more likely to be used when the person believes that nothing can be done to change the stressful event. Problem-focused strategies, on the other hand, directly deal with the problem and are more likely to be used when the person believes that he or she has at least some control over the situation or event.

Rodrigue et al. (1990, 1992) found that coping strategies of wish-fulfilling fantasy and information seeking were used more frequently by mothers and fathers of children with autism and Down syndrome than by comparison mothers. Information seeking is an active, problem-focused coping response. The authors noted that even escape into fantasy may be adaptive when paired with other more active coping strategies. Mothers and fathers of children with Down syndrome also were more likely to use cognitive restructuring, a cognitive reappraisal in which the presence of the child with a disability is made to seem less distressing. Other researchers have found mothers of adolescents with autism and mental retardation to cope by actively seeking advice and help outside the family system (Donovan, 1988). Single parents of children with disabilities seem to be less able than parents in intact families to use coping strategies that enhance family togetherness, unity, and a positive outlook on their total situation (McCubbin & Patterson, 1983).

Houser and Seligman (1991a, 1991b) examined the use of emotion-focused coping (distancing, self-control, positive reappraisal, accepting responsibility, escape avoidance) and problem-focused coping (confrontive coping, problem solving) by fathers of adolescents with mental retardation. The fathers were asked to focus on a stressful encounter involving their adolescent during the past month. These fathers were more likely than comparison fathers to use emotion-focused coping; no group differences were found on the use of problem-focused strategies. The authors suggested that the fathers perceived less control when their adolescents had mental retardation, leading to use of emotion-focused coping. Fathers may have increased their use of emotion-focused coping strategies in order to maintain hope, at the same time utilizing problem-focused strategies to directly confront their family situation.

Effectiveness of Different Coping Strategies

Frey, Greenberg, and Fewell (1989) studied three coping resources identified by Folkman et al. (1979), namely social networks, problem-solving skills, and self-appraisals. These coping resources were examined in relation to characteristics of the child with a disability and three targeted family outcomes: parent's response to the child, quality of family interaction, and parent psychological functioning. Parent beliefs, including self-comparisons with other parents in similar circumstances and perceived control over life events, were strongly related to all three family outcomes, providing support for the role of cognitive appraisal in successful coping. Mothers who received high levels of criticism from their social networks had minimal psychological distress as long as they had a relatively positive belief system. The authors concluded that the frame of reference used by parents to evaluate themselves and their child is an important moderator of parent stress. Use of problem-focused coping strategies was associated with less parenting stress and less psychological distress for mothers and fathers, as well as better family adjustment for fathers. Conversely, avoidant coping strategies were related to greater psychological distress for both mothers and fathers and to poorer family adjustment for fathers; wishful thinking was associated with more psychological distress and poorer family adjustment for mothers and more psychological distress and more parenting stress for fathers. Each of the Lazarus and Folkman (1984) coping resources significantly contributed to the prediction of the key family outcomes. Each predictor exhibited a different pattern of associations with the outcome domains, suggesting that the coping processes involved are complex and multifaceted.

Other evidence exists for the association between coping strategies and important life outcomes. British parents of children with Down syndrome have been found to have greater life satisfaction and less malaise when they use practical coping strategies (Knussen, Sloper, Cunningham, & Turner, 1992; Sloper et al., 1991). On the other hand, heightened feelings of malaise and lesser life satisfaction accompany greater use of wishful thinking as a coping strategy. Religiosity has been found to buffer the stressors of pessimism, child behavior problems, and physical incapacitation, whereas an internal locus of control buffers the stresses associated with children's physical disabilities (Friedrich et al., 1988). Harris and McHale (1989), using Lazarus, Kanner, and Folkman's (1980) coping model, examined whether appraisals of family stressors were related to psychological well-being in a group of mothers of children with mental retardation. As predicted, negative maternal problem appraisals were related to maternal depression. Among mothers of infants with severe perinatal complications, mothers who blamed others for their infant's condition reported more mood disturbances (depression, anxiety, confusion) and anticipated greater caretaking difficulty than did mothers who blamed themselves or who attributed the problem to chance (Affleck et al., 1982). The authors concluded that assigning personal responsibility is a more positive coping strategy than blaming others. Coping through the use of self-directed cognitions (self-instructions as to how to respond to stress) was effective for siblings of children with disabilities, helped minimize depression, and was associated with greater satisfaction with the sibling relationship and more positive interactions with their sibling (Gamble & McHale, 1989).

Coping Differences Between Mothers and Fathers

Several authors have noted differences between men and women in their use of coping strategies. For example, mothers of children with Down syndrome are more likely than are fathers to cope using expressions of negative affect, self-blame, information seeking, and communication of feelings (Damrosch & Perry, 1989). McLinden (1990) found that fathers of young children with disabilities used fewer coping strategies or resources than did mothers. In a study conducted in Israel, Kravetz, Nativitz, and Katz (1993) asked mothers and fathers of children with mental retardation to describe how they dealt with their child's mental retardation. Mothers used emotion-focused coping strategies more than fathers did, but no parent gender differences were found on problem-focused coping. For fathers, use of emotion-focused coping was positively related to children's school achievement; for mothers, problem-focused coping was associated with positive school behavior and fewer behavior disturbances. Frey, Fewell, Vadasy, and Greenberg (1989) found that cognitive coping strategies such as problem solving were more important to the adjustment of fathers than that of mothers.

To date, findings concerning coping have not been entirely consistent with the Folkman and Lazarus coping model (Folkman, Schaefer, & Lazarus, 1979; Lazarus & Folkman, 1984) that has guided the majority of the research. As with research on family stress, the process of coping is complex and multifaceted and has proved difficult to operationalize. The data collected on coping strongly suggests that this is a fertile area for future research, as well as for refined model building related to families with members who have mental retardation.

FAMILY SYSTEMS AND ECOLOGICAL THEORIES

Family systems theory (Broderick & Smith, 1979) has had a major impact on the way researchers approach the study of families. This theoretical perspective emphasizes the interconnectedness of family members, positing that when events impact one member of a family, all family members are changed in some way. Similarly, multiple-family subsystems are interrelated, such that a change in the parent–child subsystem, for example, would be expected to also affect the marriage and the relationship between siblings. Following this line of reasoning, the presence of a child with mental retardation in the family would be expected to affect all aspects of the family system, including the marriage, the sibling relationship, and the interactions between parents and children. Ecological theory (Bronfenbrenner, 1979) is compatible with this approach, focusing on the person and family in relation to the ecological settings that they experience, and the larger environmental contexts in which these settings are embedded. Changes in the individual are to be understood in the context of the family, and changes in the family are to be understood in relation to the wider social contexts surrounding the family. As with family systems theory, family members are believed to mutually influence each other, as well as to both directly and indirectly influence all other family subsystems.

Marital and Family Adjustment

Researchers interested in family systems have examined the impact that a child with mental retardation has on the marital relationship and the overall family climate. This research often has been guided by an assumption that marriages and families would suffer from the presence of a child with a disability. Only a few researchers, however, have found this to be the case. Although there is some evidence to suggest that families of children with disabilities have lower marital adjustment (Bristol et al., 1988; Friedrich & Friedrich, 1981; Trute, 1990), less positive communication, and higher negative reciprocity (Floyd & Zmich, 1991), a large number of researchers found the marriages of these families to be similar to comparison families (Abbott & Meredith, 1986; Fisman et al., 1989; Gath & Gumley, 1984, 1986; Kazak, 1987; Rodrigue et al., 1992; Van Riper et al., 1992; Waisbren, 1980; Williams & McKenry, 1981). Similarly, family functioning has not been found to differ from comparison families (Abbott & Meredith, 1986; Bouma & Schweitzer, 1990; Rodrigue et al., 1992; Trute, 1990; Van Riper et al., 1992). Wives tend to report greater marital stresses than do husbands (Beckman, 1991; Floyd & Zmich, 1991; Krauss, 1993).

Cooke, Bradshaw, Lawton, and Brewer (1986), studying a 1970 British birth cohort, found that children with disabilities, particularly those with severe disabilities, were more likely than comparison children to spend time in a one-parent household. These data are consistent with Gath's (1978) finding that the birth of a child with Down syndrome "was not as likely to mar a good marriage as to turn a moderate or somewhat shaky marriage into a poor one" (p. 66). The high proportion of single parents is important because these families seem to be particularly at risk for compromised functioning (Beavers, Hampson, Hulgus, & Beavers, 1986; Hampson, Hulgus, Beavers, & Beavers, 1988).

Although much research emphasis has focused on trying to identify detrimental effects of a child with mental retardation on the marriage and family, many studies have painted a more optimistic picture. Abbott & Meredith (1986), for example, found that parents of children with mental retardation were less critical of each other and perceived fewer family problems than did comparison parents; 88% of the parents reported that family strengths developed as a result of having a child with mental retardation. Numerous others have found families of children with mental retardation to be relatively healthy, well-organized units with high cohesion and spousal closeness (Beavers et al., 1986; Brotherson et al., 1988; Hampson et al., 1988; Konstantareas & Homatidis, 1989; O'Connor & Stachawiak, 1971; Rodrigue et al., 1990; Young & Roopnarine, 1994).

Child Characteristics and Marital and Family Functioning

Characteristics of the child with mental retardation have been studied in relation to marital adjustment and family functioning. Rodrigue et al. (1990) found that mothers of children with autism reported less marital satisfaction than did mothers of children with Down syndrome or comparison mothers. Somewhat different patterns of family strengths were also found for the two disability groups. Among older parents, families of adult sons and daughters with Down syndrome have been found to be less conflicted than are families of adults with other types of mental retardation (Seltzer, Krauss, & Tsunematsu, 1993). Blacher, Nihira, and Meyers (1987) reported that children with more severe cognitive disabilities had greater negative impact on family adjustment, but marital adjustment did not differ by level of disability. Others did not find the type or degree of the child's disability to be related to marital adjustment (Trute, 1990; Williams & McKenry, 1981) or level of family functioning (Krauss, 1993; Trute, 1990; Trute & Hauch, 1988a).

As can be seen, the findings concerning the impact of a child with mental retardation on marital and family functioning are inconsistent. One plausible reason for this inconsistency is the wide variation among families of children with mental retardation. Ecological and systems theories are being drawn upon to explain that within-group variability. These approaches hold promise for moving beyond the rather simplistic group-difference questions that have dominated the field to address the complex family processes that culminate in one family becoming stronger as a result of their family situation, whereas another family is compromised.

Marriage, Parent Psychological Resources, and Parenting

One research question of theoretical interest has been the degree to which a strong, positive marital relationship serves to buffer the family against the stresses accompanying the presence of a child with a disability. Friedrich (1979; Friedrich, Wilturner, & Cohen, 1985) found that mothers with high marital satisfaction reported less stress and a more positive family emotional climate. Spousal support has been associated with less depression and a greater sense of parental control and competence (Gowen et al., 1989; McKinney & Peterson, 1987), whereas higher marital satisfaction has been associated with better maternal mental health (Wallander et al., 1989) and greater life satisfaction (McKinney & Peterson, 1987; Sloper et al., 1991).

Positive family functioning has also been related to decreased stress and increased well-being. Among parents of young children with disabilities, higher family resources, adaptability, and cohesion have been associated with lower stress (Boyce et al., 1991; Shonkoff et al., 1992); higher family cohesion also has been related to greater life satisfaction (Sloper et al., 1991). Similarly, mothers of adults with mental retardation perceived less burden when their families were more cohesive, less conflicted, and more organized (Seltzer & Krauss, 1989).

Parent psychological resources also affect the response of the family system to the child with mental retardation. For example, depressed, externally oriented mothers reported the lowest quality family relationships (Friedrich, Cohen, & Wilturner, 1987). Paternal depression was associated with more coercive father–child interactions; maternal depression was associated with general underinvolvement (Floyd & Phillippe, 1993). Both mothers and fathers experienced greater parenting stress when they had less belief in their own control over the development of the child with a disability and ascribed greater control to professionals (Shonkoff et al., 1992). For mothers, an external locus of control predicted decreases in the quality of mother–child interaction over time.

The marital relationship has been implicated as an important source of support for parenting. Bradley, Rock, Whiteside, Caldwell, and Brisby (1991) tested an adaptation of Belsky's (1984) model of the determinants of parenting, focusing on families of children with disabilities. Parenting quality was positively related to marital quality and negatively related to family stress. Expressive spousal support has been found to be a strong predictor of observed quality of parenting (Bristol et al., 1988). Utilizing a systems model, Floyd and Zmich (1991) found that, for families of children with mental retardation, self-report measures of marital adjustment were strongly related to parenting confidence. Observed marital negativity was related to observed parent–child negativity. Thus, evidence exists to link marital quality with positive parenting of children with disabilities.

Family Effects on Children and Siblings

Researchers employing a systems approach have studied family correlates of behavior problems in children with mental retardation. Lower marital adjustment has been related to the presence of child behavior problems (Floyd & Zmich, 1991; Gath & Gumley, 1984, 1986), as have authoritarian and narcissistic parenting (Floyd & Phillippe, 1993). In general, negative child outcomes have been found to be more likely when the family has a control-oriented atmosphere and high conflict (Meyers, Nihira, & Mink, 1984; Nihira, Meyers, & Mink 1983). It is likely that lower marital and family adjustment compromise parenting, which then exacerbates the presence of behavior problems. In turn, challenging behaviors probably serve as stressors that further compromise marital and family functioning.

The well-being of siblings, and of the sibling relationship, also has been linked to the family context, including family climate, marital satisfaction, emotional resources of the parents, childrearing approaches, and sibling socialization practices (Stoneman & Brody, 1993). In the least healthy families, taboos against expressing negative feelings inhibit siblings from being open about thoughts and feelings (Hampson et al., 1988). Being in a family in which parents have a warm marriage seems to protect siblings of children with mental retardation from adverse effects (Gath & Gumley, 1987); a positive family climate and low stress seem to have similar protective effects on siblings (Dyson, Edgar, & Crnic, 1989). Conflict between mothers and nondisabled siblings has been related to conflict between the siblings, as well as to depression and anxiety in the nondisabled sibling (McHale & Gamble, 1989), whereas parent favoritism fosters negative sibling relationships (McHale & Pawletko, 1992; McHale, Sloan, & Simeonsson, 1986). When families are characterized by high levels of cohesion and expressiveness, and high levels of family organization, adult siblings are more involved with their brothers and sisters with mental retardation (Seltzer et al., 1991). Seltzer et al. suggested that a strong relationship exists between family climate and sibling relations, even during adulthood.

Social Context Effects

Other ecological and systems researchers have focused on relationships between the family and external sources of influence, such as intervention and education service providers. Marital adjustment, stress, and level of family functioning determine, in part, those parents who will complete parent intervention programs and who will successfully utilize the skills learned (Baker, Landen, & Kashima, 1991; Clark & Baker, 1983; Robbins, Dunlap, & Plienis, 1991). Children make greater intervention gains when families are better adjusted (Frey, Fewell, et al., 1989). Brinker, Seifer, and Sameroff (1994), studying mothers of infants with developmental delays, found that the effects of early intervention on children and families were not consistent across income levels. For example, when middle-income mothers were experiencing high levels of stress, participation in early intervention programs had a positive impact on child developmental gains, whereas, for poor families, the impact was a negative one. Changes in parent stress over time were related to a complex three-way interaction among income level, child competence, and parent involvement in early intervention.

Compared to research on family stress, the use of ecological and family systems theories is quite new in mental retardation family research. The focus on the interrelatedness of different family subsystems and the acknowledged importance of the social context make research efforts using these models more complex and laborious, but also more promising, than many other approaches.

FAMILY RESEARCH GUIDED BY ROLE THEORY

Roles Within the Family

Role theorists (Burr, Leigh, Day, & Constantine, 1979; Nye, 1976; Sarbin, 1954; Sarbin & Allen, 1968) have sought to understand the pattern of social norms, beliefs, and expectations that people hold for themselves and for each other (roles). These include the roles that members of a family enact as they define their position and responsibilities within the family system. Roles provide predictability to behavior and to social exchanges among family members. Farber's classic studies (Farber, 1959, 1960; Farber & Jenné, 1963) introduced role theory concepts into the study of families of children with mental retardation. He posited that these families would experience an arrest in role changes that accompany the family life cycle, attributable to the slow development of the family member with mental retardation (Farber, 1959). In the face of this life-cycle arrest, Farber posited that nondisabled children in the family would progressively assume an older child role in relation to the child with mental retardation, regardless of the actual birth order of the children (Farber, 1959, 1960). Role shifts were thought to be particularly problematic for sisters, whose roles were expanded with increased housework and child care (Farber & Jenné, 1963).

Farber studied 240 Chicago families who had a child with mental retardation. Although much of Farber's theoretical framework was not directly addressed by his research, findings tended to support his predictions. For example, sisters, but not brothers, who interacted more frequently with their sibling with mental retardation experienced greater role tension (Farber, 1960). When children with mental retardation had fewer adaptive skills, older sisters, in particular, had higher role tension (Farber, 1959). Although Farber assumed that these findings resulted from the older sister's assumption of a parent surrogate role, no data were presented in direct support of sibling role shifts or role expansion. Others, particularly sisters, however, have confirmed the expansion of parentlike, caregiver roles for older siblings (Hampson et al., 1988; Holmes & Carr, 1991; McHale & Gamble, 1989; Stoneman, Brody, Davis, & Crapps, 1987, 1988,1989; Wilson, Blacher, & Baker, 1989). Role reversals in which younger siblings of children with mental retardation assume dominant roles have also been documented (Brody, Stoneman, Davis, & Crapps, 1991; O'Connor & Stachawiak, 1971; Stoneman, Brody, Davis, Crapps, & Malone, 1991). The presence of an older child willing to assume child-care roles can ease parental time demands and diminish parent stress (Smith, 1986).

In an early study of marital roles, Tallman (1965) found that mothers of school-age children with severe mental retardation demonstrated more role adaptability than did fathers, altering roles, actions, and attitudes in response to problem situations. Maternal (but not paternal) role adaptability was found to be associated with children's gains in competence over a 2-year period. Stoneman, Brody, and Abbott (1983) observed roles assumed during parent–child play, finding that parents of Down children assumed a manager role more frequently, whereas comparison parents were more likely to engage their children as playmates. Floyd and Phillippe (1993) reported a similar elevation in parental manager roles. In general, parent interactions with children who had Down syndrome were characterized by asymmetrical role relationships, whereas role relations in comparison families were more equalitarian. When mothers were present, fathers tended to withdraw from interaction with their child; mothers remained actively involved (Floyd & Phillippe, 1993; Stoneman et al., 1983).

Parental Caregiving Roles

Mothers of children with mental retardation not only tend to take the lead roles in play interactions with their children, they also assume a disproportionate share of added caregiving roles. These role responsibilities are accentuated because the family member with mental retardation is often not able to stay alone, without supervision, for even a short period of time (Hirst, 1985; Holmes & Carr, 1991). Children with disabilities place heavy time demands and role restrictions on families, including feeding, bathing, and dressing; these added role responsibilities fall disproportionately on mothers (Beckman, 1991; Breslau, 1983; Bristol et al., 1988; Carey, 1982; Cooke & Lawton, 1984; Dunlap & Hollinsworth, 1977; Dunst et al., 1986; Dupont, 1986; Eheart & Ciccone, 1982; Erickson & Upshur, 1989; Gumz & Gubrium, 1972; Harris & McHale, 1989; Hirst, 1985; Holmes & Carr, 1991; Konstantareas & Homatidis, 1992; Krauss, 1993; Levy-Shiff, 1986; McConachie, 1989; McLinden, 1990; Rodrigue et al., 1990; Smith, 1986; Vadasy et al., 1984; Waisbren, 1980; Willoughby & Glidden, 1995). One of the few studies not to find increased maternal caregiving was conducted by Gallagher, Scharfman, and Bristol (1984). Comparison group problems, however, compromise interpretation of this study (see Stoneman, 1989).

Some children with disabilities place greater demands on maternal and sibling caregiving roles. Konstantareas and Homatidis (1992) found that maternal involvement was greater when the child had seizures and was younger. Similarly, children with physical disabilities place greater demands when they are younger and less able to perform tasks of daily living (Smith, 1986). When children have fewer adaptive skills, mothers are relieved of supervision of the child less often (Lucca & Settles, 1981), sibling role asymmetries are accentuated (Stoneman et al., 1987, 1989), and sibling caretaking is greater (McHale & Gamble, 1989; Stoneman et al., 1988).

Research concerning father involvement in the care of children with mental retardation has yielded a less clear pattern of findings. Rodrigue et al. (1992), for example, found that fathers of children with Down syndrome reported greater caretaker burden than did comparison fathers. Conversely, fathers of children with autism and severe communication disabilities were less involved in the child care and did fewer household tasks than did comparison fathers (Bristol et al., 1988). Young & Roopnarine (1994) found no difference between fathers of preschool children with disabilities and comparison fathers in their involvement in a variety of child care tasks. There is some suggestion that the most involved fathers are those in manual occupations (Cooke & Lawton, 1984), those who have other children requiring care (McConachie, 1989), and those who are retired or not working (Holmes & Carr, 1991), although Hirst (1985) found that employment status was not associated with fathers' participation.

When fathers are involved with their children with disabilities, they are more likely to entertain the children by playing with them than by being actively engaged in child care (Cooke & Lawton, 1984; McConachie, 1989; Willoughby & Glidden, 1995). In general, mothers receive more help with child minding than with other aspects of child care; they receive more assistance with child care than with housework (Carey, 1982; Cooke & Lawton, 1984). Fathers assist with lifting and moving when needed (Hirst, 1985), as well as shaving, feeding, and general supervision (Holmes & Carr, 1991). Fathers were more likely to provide personal care for sons than for daughters (Hirst, 1985). Less father involvement was predicted for families having a child with autism and having a firstborn or only child (Konstantareas & Homatidis, 1992). Bristol et al. (1988) found that fathers were the least involved in care when children had severely atypical language, affect, and behavior. Competence of the child with a disability seems to be less related to the caregiving roles of fathers than that of mothers (Hirst, 1985).

Konstantareas and Homatidis (1989) and Vadasy et al. (1984) reported that mothers desired greater assistance from their husbands in caring for the child with a disability. Assistance from spouse has been rated as the most important resource in keeping a child with severe mental retardation at home (Cole & Meyer, 1989). Assumption of increased caretaking roles has been associated with negative outcomes for mothers. Beckman (1991) found that greater caregiving requirements were related to greater maternal parenting stress; no similar relationship was found for fathers. The more dependent the child is on the parent for activities of daily living, the greater the mother's psychological distress is (Breslau, Staruch, & Mortimer, 1982). The time mothers spend in caregiving and child activities has been related to their ratings of the difficulties in family life (Harris & McHale, 1989).

Milgram and Atzil (1988) utilized an Israeli sample of families of children with autism to examine the relationship between what they believed to be objective stressors (low adaptive behavior in the child, child symptoms) and subjective stressors related to role distribution (parents' appraisals of difficulty, share of the parenting burden, fairness of this share, and satisfaction with this share). Parents agreed that fathers did about one third of the caregiving tasks, whereas mothers did two thirds. In addition, both parents perceived that, to be fair, fathers should do more. As might be expected, mothers who assumed a greater burden found it less fair and were less satisfied with the distribution of work. Maternal satisfaction was correlated with their share of the parenting burden and the difference between their current share and what they perceived to be a fair distribution. Similar correlations were found for fathers, but the strength of relationship was somewhat lower. Bristol et al. (1988) found that the best predictor across areas of family maladaptation (depression, marital adjustment, parenting) was disharmony between current and desired spousal support. Paternal participation in child care has been associated with marital satisfaction for both parents (Willoughby & Glidden, 1995).

Work Roles

In addition to affecting roles within the family, work roles also are impacted by the presence in the family of a child with a disability. Numerous researchers have found that women delay their entry into the workforce after giving birth to a child with a disability (Beckman, 1991; Dunlap & Hollinsworth, 1977; Dupont, 1986), whereas men's work roles are also occasionally affected (Dunlap & Hollinsworth, 1977; Dupont, 1986). Others, such as Landis (1992) and Carr (1988), suggested that the impact on women's work roles comes less from a delay in entry into the workforce than from working fewer hours once workforce reentry has taken place. Carr (1988) found that mothers could work only during the time that their child was attending a program; the women's work hours were therefore affected, as well as the type of job they could hold. For married mothers, a child with a disability has a greater negative effect on work roles when those mothers are African-American or live in low-income families (Breslau, Salkever, & Staruch, 1982). On the other hand, Breslau et al. (1982) found that the labor market participation of single mothers does not seem to be affected by child disability, either alone or in interaction with income or race. Employed mothers of children with disabilities have been found to be less depressed (Walker et al., 1989), suggesting that employment may provide respite from the demands of caretaking, provide access to other sources of social support and accomplishment, and buffer stress. Of course, it is also possible that when depression is high, mothers are less likely to return to work.

It is clear that a family member with mental retardation affects the role structures of parents and siblings, both within the family and in the world of work. Much is yet to be learned, however, about the processes through which families implement and adapt to these role shifts, as well as about the positive and negative implications of long-term role reorganization for the well-being of the family, and the individuals who comprise the family.

ETHNOGRAPHIC APPROACHES AND ECOCULTURAL THEORY

Ethnographic approaches attempt to understand human behavior in the context of culture. Such research often features extensive observation and interviews, with strong personal involvement by the researcher (Weisner, 1993). Zetlin and Turner (1985) conducted participant observations and interviews with a group of adults with mild mental retardation. Issues that emerged included independence struggles with parents, resistance to parent rules and restrictions, perceived parent partiality to siblings, peer rejection, and lack of friends. Focusing on parent relationships, Winik, Zetlin, and Kaufman (1985) conducted an ethnographic study of adults with mild mental retardation living independently. Three types of relationships with parents emerged: supportive, dependent, and conflict ridden. All of the adults required extensive support from their families to remain independent.

Ecocultural theory proposes that one of the major tasks for families is to construct and maintain adaptive daily routines and activities (Gallimore, Weisner, Kaufman, & Bernheimer, 1989; Weisner, 1993). These routines reflect the culture and how it is experienced by families. Gallimore et al. (1989) studied how families of young children with developmental delays construct and modify ecocultural niches, routines, and activities. They found that parents prioritized the construction of a satisfying daily routine, balancing resources to achieve that goal. Social support provided assistance to families, but it sometimes had costs that outweighed its benefit. Parental beliefs about their child and about disability were powerful influences because parents used these beliefs to guide decision making.

In a follow-up study, Gallimore, Weisner, Bernheimer, Guthrie, and Nihira (1993) studied changes the family made in order to accommodate their child with a delay. They found that the earlier the child entered early intervention, the greater the accommodations made by the family, including modifying or changing residences, adjusting domestic roles, and arranging child care. Frequent accommodations involved time reallocation, scheduling, family division of labor, child care, and employment. Nihira, Weisner, and Bernheimer (1994) found that important ecocultural factors that predicted child outcomes included the family's attempt to seek information and services, help available in the family, and career orientation of the parents. Parents expressed concerns about mediating sibling conflict, burdening siblings with child care and household tasks, and equitably dividing their attention (Weisner, 1993).

In another study drawn from the same research, Weisner, Beizer, and Stolze (1991) examined how parents' religious beliefs can provide meaning to their experiences. They compared nonreligious and highly religious families, finding that religious families were characterized by family connectedness, joint family activities, and companionate couple relationships. These families were more likely to emphasize family support, seek child care from family members, and value child nurturance. They received more material help from neighbors and friends, more positive feedback from professionals, and participated more in social activities with friends. The groups did not differ in their acceptance of the child with a delay, self-blame, peace of mind, chronic disappointment, or level of depression.

Weisner (1993) argued that the single most important thing for researchers to know in understanding families of children with mental retardation is the "cultural place" (p. 51) in which the family lives. Ethnographic researchers have documented that mental retardation has strong, culturally tied meanings (Harry, 1992). The study of family processes in the context of the cultural setting is one of the most important scientific contributions of this body of work.

MODELS OF GRIEF AND CHRONIC SORROW

Solnit and Stark's (1961) conceptualization of the family's mourning for the loss of a wished-for, perfect child, while simultaneously adjusting to the child with a disability, has been widely cited. Olshansky (1962, 1966) described the family's sadness as being lifelong in nature, terming this grief reaction "chronic sorrow." The classic grief model of Kübler-Ross (1969) has been adapted to explain the stages inherent in the grief reaction of families to the diagnosis of disability in a child. Drotar, Baskiewicz, Irvin, Kennell, and Klaus (1975) used this conceptualization to explain family adaptation, describing five grief stages: shock, denial, sadness and anger, adaptation, and reorganization. Fortier and Wanlass (1984) proposed a similar five-stage model.

Gath (1978) found that, without exception, parents of infants with Down syndrome experienced grief and shock. Other emotions reported by researchers include loss, hopelessness, anger, guilt, denial, disbelief, shame, depression, sorrow, confusion, loneliness, isolation, and helplessness (Cameron, Snowdon, & Orr, 1992; Childs, 1985; Mary, 1990; Mölsä & Ikonen-Mölsä, 1985; Waisbren, 1980). Eden-Piercy, Blacher, and Eyman (1986) found that parent grief reactions fit a three-category (shock or despair, denial, acceptance) rather than a five-category model.

Other researchers have examined whether grief is chronic or timebound. Wikler, Wasow, and Hatfield (1981) found that parents of children with mental retardation reported a series of emotional ups and downs, with no general upward course across time. Damrosch and Perry (1989) found that almost all fathers depicted their adjustment from infancy to adulthood as steady improvement over time, whereas a majority of mothers perceived their adjustment to have a more erratic course, with peaks and valleys over time.

Bruce, Schultz, Smyrnios, and Schultz (1994), using the Kübler-Ross (1969) grief model, found no evidence for age-related grief stages. Mothers scored higher than did fathers on all grief measures, except wishful thinking; for mothers, more intense grief persists over time. Hodapp, Dykens, Evans, and Merighi (1992) presented data suggesting that development of a disability-specific model of grief may be warranted. This model might include, for example, a differential pattern for parents of children with Down syndrome, who tend to be aware of the diagnosis much earlier than are other parents (Gath & Gumley, 1986). In her 1984 review of grief and disability, Blacher concluded that scientific validation of grief models was lacking. More than a decade later, this is still true.

FAMILY TYPOLOGIES

Researchers interested in family typologies attempt to identify subgroupings of families who share similar interactional or lifestyle patterns. The research objective is to develop a system that classifies families into meaningful types (Mink, Nihira, & Meyers, 1983). Farber (1960) proposed three family typologies (child oriented, home oriented, and parent oriented), focusing on strategies that families might use for counteracting what he believed to be negative effects of a child with mental retardation on the marriage. As Farber had expected, families using one of the three strategies had higher marital integration than did parents that could not be classified into a strategy. Mink et al. (1983) used cluster analysis to identify five typologies among families of children with moderate mental retardation. These typologies differed along dimensions of cohesion, harmony, control, child orientation, disclosure, morale, and expressiveness. Children with Down syndrome were more likely to live in the healthiest families. In a subsequent study (Mink, Meyers, & Nihira, 1984), seven types of families of children with mild mental retardation were identified. Mink and Nihira (1986, 1987) found that the direction of causative effects was different for each of the family typologies identified by Mink et al. (1983, 1984).

Shulman, Margalit, Gadish, and Stuchiner (1990) used typologies developed by Reiss (1981) to examine the impact of a child with mental retardation on the family system. The three dimensions of interest were: configuration (adaptability), coordination, and closure (flexibility). In this Israeli sample, most families fell into one of two "faulty" family types. The authors suggested that chronic stress contributes to the development of negative family patterns. In a contrasting study, Koller, Richardson, and Katz (1992) used cluster analysis in an Aberdeen, Scotland, population sample. Most families of children with mental retardation were well functioning and clustered with comparison families. Mink et al., (1984) noted that identifying clusters of families serves as the beginning of the research process, not the end. After family typologies have been identified, the challenge is to understand the processes that created the different family types and to identify why each set of typologies is important.

CIRCUMPLEX MODEL

The Circumplex Model (Olson, Sprenkle, & Russell, 1979) has enjoyed only modest use as a theory to guide research on families of children with mental retardation. The Circumplex Model posits the existence of two underlying family process dimensions: cohesion (emotional bonding) and adaptability (ability to change). These two dimensions have curvilinear relations to family health. Moderate cohesion and adaptability are considered functional and balanced; too little or too much of either dimension is considered to be pathological. Florian (1989) used the Circumplex model to study Israeli Jews and Israeli Arabs who had children with disabilities. Parents of children with a disability had lower cohesion and adaptability than did comparisons, but findings differed for the two cultural groups studied. Using the Circumplex model to compare parent–child and marital relations in families of children with disabilities, Martin and Cole (1993) found that fathers who were involved in cohesive marital relationships were also involved in cohesive father–child relationships; mother–child relationships were less closely related to the marital relationship.

Barnes and Olson (1985) argued that family communication is an important component in understanding family relations, positing that good communication facilitates both family cohesion and adaptation. Using the Barnes and Olson (1985) Circumplex Model, Morrison and Zetlin (1992) employed cluster analytic techniques to identify distinct family groups. They found five patterns of family adaptability, cohesion, and communication; all but one cluster was split almost evenly between families with and without a child with a disability. The authors concluded that patterns of family dynamics are not specific to disability. The data on the Circumplex Model are still too sparse to evaluate its usefulness in understanding families with members who have mental retardation.

HARDINESS

Another infrequently utilized theoretical construct is that of hardiness. Hardiness is posited to be a personality attribute that protects individuals against stress (Maddi & Kobasa, 1984). Dimensions of the hardy personality are commitment (viewing stressful situations as meaningful and interesting), control (perceiving that stressors can be changed or altered), and challenge (viewing change as a positive aspect of life). Studying families of children with autism, Gill and Harris (1991) found that mothers who were high in the commitment dimension of hardiness had the fewest depressive symptoms. There was a strong positive correlation between hardiness and social support.

McCubbin, McCubbin, and Thompson (1987) incorporated the construct of hardiness into family stress theory, focusing on the family's typical manner of perceiving, processing, and coping with stressful situations. Failla and Jones (1991) utilized this family hardiness model to examine the relationship among family hardiness, stressors, family appraisal, social support, coping, and family adaptation in mothers with a young child with a developmental disability. Family hardiness was related to maternal satisfaction with family functioning, social support, and positive appraisal of family stressors. The authors concluded that family hardiness acts as a resistance resource, diminishing the negative effects of stress, increasing access to social support, and facilitating adaptation. Although infrequently used in the family literature, hardiness and family hardiness appear to be promising constructs to guide future research.

CONCLUDING COMMENTS

The opening comments to this chapter noted that the field of family mental retardation research is vibrant and energetic. The body of work reviewed here proves that to be the case. Although this field of study is not as mature as many of the others reviewed in this volume, it has experienced enormous growth in the past decade and is on a dramatically expanding course. Over time, the work has become more theoretically driven and has increased in methodological sophistication. The number of ongoing longitudinal studies has expanded, promising that the next decade will reveal a wealth of additional information about families and family processes.

Several challenges still remain, however. Most of what is known about families has been learned by studying White middle-class families whose children have Down syndrome or autism. Etiological differences among children with mental retardation have only begun to be addressed, often without theoretical guidance (Stoneman, in press). Very little is known about the role of culture. Similarly, race and ethnicity have seldom been addressed. The largest population of children with mental retardation live in poverty, often living in families who face multiple stressors and life challenges; family researchers have ignored these children and their families almost totally (Stoneman, 1990).

Methodological issues still prove troublesome for family researchers. Important constructs, such as family stress, are often studied using inadequate measurement tools (Glidden, 1993). For other key family process constructs, measurement tools are totally lacking. Use of inappropriate or poorly selected comparison groups distort findings of studies focusing on group differences (Stoneman, 1989). Difficulties in recruiting participating families often compromise sampling parameters and yield heterogeneous groups where more homogeneity would be preferred. Yet, these and other problems notwithstanding, the field of mental retardation family research is undergoing a knowledge explosion in which both the quality and the quantity of information about families are rapidly increasing. This increased information will benefit families and the professionals who provide them with support.

ACKNOWLEDGMENTS

Partial support for preparation of this manuscript was provided by grant No. 04-DD-000-58 from the Administration on Developmental Disabilities, U.S. Department of Health and Human Services to the Georgia University Affiliated Program for Persons with Developmental Disabilities, The University of Georgia.

REFERENCES

Abbott, D. A., & Meredith, W. H. (1986). Strengths of parents with retarded children. *Family Relations*, *35*, 371–375.

Affleck, G., Allen, D., McGrade, B. J., & McQueeney, M. (1982). Maternal causal attributions at hospital discharge of high-risk infants. *American Journal of Mental Deficiency*, *86*, 575–580.

Bailey, D. B., Jr., Blasco, P. M., & Simeonsson, R. J. (1992). Needs expressed by mothers and fathers of young children with disabilities. *American Journal on Mental Retardation*, *97*, 1–10.

Baker, B. L., Landen, S. J., & Kashima, K. J. (1991). Effects of parent training on families of children with mental retardation: Increased burden or generalized benefit? *American Journal on Mental Retardation*, *96*, 127–136.

Barnes, H., & Olson, D. H. (1985). Parent–adolescent communication and the circumplex model. *Child Development*, *56*, 438–447.

Barrera, M. E., Watson, L. J., & Adelstein, A. (1987). Development of Down's syndrome infants with and without heart defects and changes in their caretaking environment. *Child: Care, Health, and Development*, *13*, 87–100.

Baxter, C. (1989). Investigating stigma as stress in social interactions of parents. *Journal of Mental Deficiency Research*, *33*, 455–466.

Beavers, J., Hampson, R. B., Hulgus, Y. F., & Beavers, W. R. (1986). Coping in families with a retarded child. *Family Process, 25*, 365–378.

Beckman, P. (1983). Influence of selected child characteristics on stress in families of handicapped infants. *American Journal of Mental Deficiency, 88*, 150–156.

Beckman, P. (1991). Comparison of mothers' and fathers' perceptions of the effect of young children with and without disabilities. *American Journal on Mental Retardation, 95*, 585–595.

Bell, R. Q., & Harper, L. V. (1977). *The effect of children on parents*. Hillsdale, NJ: Lawrence Erlbaum Associates.

Belsky, J. (1984). The determinants of parenting: A process model. *Child Development, 55*, 83–96.

Bernheimer, L. P., Young, M. S., & Winton, P. J. (1983). Stress over time: Parents with young handicapped children. *Developmental and Behavioral Pediatrics, 4*, 177–181.

Blacher, H. (1984). Sequential stages of parental adjustment to the birth of a child with handicaps: Fact or artifact. *Mental Retardation, 22*, 55–68.

Blacher, J., Nihira, K., & Meyers, C. E. (1987). Characteristics of home environment of families with mentally retarded children: Comparison across levels of retardation. *American Journal of Mental Deficiency, 91*, 313–320.

Black, M. M., Cohn, J. F., Smull, M. W., & Crites, L. (1985). Individual and family factors associated with risk of institutionalization of mentally retarded adults. *American Journal of Mental Deficiency, 90*, 271–276.

Blackard, M. K., & Barsh, E. T. (1982). Parents' and professionals' perceptions of the handicapped child's impact on the family. *Journal of the Association for People with Severe Handicaps, 17*, 62–70.

Bouma, R., & Schweitzer, R. (1990). The impact of chronic childhood illness on family stress: A comparison between autism and cystic fibrosis. *Journal of Clinical Psychology, 46*, 722–730.

Boyce, G. C., Behl, D., Mortensen, L., & Akers, J. (1991). Child characteristics, family demographics and family processes: Their effects on the stress experienced by families of children with disabilities. *Counseling Psychology Quarterly, 4*, 273–288.

Bradley, R. H., Rock, S. L., Whiteside, L., Caldwell, B. M., & Brisby, J. (1991). Dimensions of parenting in families having children with disabilities. *Exceptionality, 2*, 41–61.

Breslau, N. (1983). Care of disabled children and women's time use. *Medical Care, 21*, 620–629.

Breslau, N., Salkever, D., & Staruch, K. S. (1982). Women's labor force activity and responsibilities for disabled dependents: A study of families with disabled children. *Journal of Health and Social Behavior, 23*, 169–183.

Breslau, N., Staruch, K. S., & Mortimer, E. A. (1982). Psychological distress in mothers of disabled children. *American Journal of Disease in Children, 136*, 682–686.

Brinker, R. P., Seifer, R., & Sameroff, A. J. (1994). Relations among maternal stress, cognitive development, and early intervention in middle- and low-SES infants with developmental disabilities. *American Journal on Mental Retardation, 98*, 463–480.

Bristol, M. M. (1987). Mothers of children with autism or communication disorders: Successful adaptation and the Double ABCX model. *Journal of Autism and Developmental Disorders, 17*, 469–485.

Bristol, M. M., Gallagher, J. J., & Schopler, E. (1988). Mothers and fathers of young developmentally disabled and nondisabled boys: Adaptation and spousal support. *Developmental Psychology, 224*, 441–451.

Broderick, C., & Smith, J. (1979). The general systems approach to the family. In W. R. Burr, R. Hill, F. I. Nye, & I. L. Reiss (Eds.). *Contemporary theories about the family* (Vol. II, pp. 112–129). New York: The Free Press.

Brody, G. H., Stoneman, Z., Davis, C. H., & Crapps. J. M. (1991). Observations of the role relations and behavior between older children with mental retardation and their younger siblings. *American Journal on Mental Retardation, 95*, 527–536.

Bronfenbrenner, U. (1979). *The ecology of human development*. Cambridge, MA: Harvard University Press.

Brotherson, M. J., Turnbull, A. P., Bronicki, G. J., Houghton, J., Roeder-Gordon, C., Summers, J. A., & Turnbull, H. R. (1988). Transition into adulthood: Parental planning for sons and daughters with disabilities. *Education and Training in Mental Retardation, xx*, 165–174.

Bruce, E. J., Schultz, C. L., Smyrnios, K. X., & Schultz, N. C. (1994). Grieving related to development: A preliminary comparison of three age cohorts of parents of children with intellectual disability. *British Journal of Medical Psychology, 67*, 37–52.

Burr, W. R., Leigh, G. K., Day, R. D., & Constantine, J. (1979). Symbolic interaction and the family. In W. R. Burr, R. Hill, F. I. Nye, & I. L. Reiss (Eds.), *Contemporary theories about the family* (Vol. II, pp. 42–111). New York: The Free Press.

Caldwell, B. M., & Guze, S. B. (1960). A study of the adjustment of parents and siblings of institutionalized and noninstitutionalized retarded children. *American Journal of Mental Deficiency, 64*, 845–861.

Cameron, S. J., Dobson, L. A., & Day, D. M. (1991). Stress in parents of developmentally delayed and non-delayed preschool children. *Canada's Mental Health, 39*, 13–17.

Cameron, S. J., & Orr, R. R. (1989). Stress in families of school-aged children with delayed mental development. *Canadian Journal of Rehabilitation, 2*, 137–144.

Cameron, S. J., Snowdon, A., & Orr, R. R. (1992). Emotions experienced by mothers of children with developmental disabilities. *Child Health Care, 21*, 96–102.

Carey, G. E. (1982). Community care—care by whom? Mentally handicapped children living at home. *Public Health, 96*, 269–278.

Carr, J. (1988). Six weeks to twenty-one years old: A longitudinal study of children with Down's syndrome and their families. *Journal of Psychology and Psychiatry, 29*, 407–431.

Chetwynd, J. (1985). Factors contributing to stress on mothers caring for an intellectually handicapped child. *British Journal of Social Work, 15*, 295–304.

Childs, R. E. (1985). Maternal psychological conflicts associated with the birth of a retarded child. *Maternal-Child Nursing Journal, 14*, 175–182.

Clark, D. B., & Baker, B. L. (1983). Predicting outcome in parent training. *Journal of Consulting and Clinical Psychology, 51*, 309–311.

Cohen, S., & Wills, T. A. (1985). Stress, social support, and the buffering hypothesis. *Psychological Bulletin, 98*, 310–357.

Cole, D. A., & Meyer, L. H. (1989). Impact of needs and resources on family plans to seek out-of-home placement. *American Journal on Mental Retardation, 93*, 380–387.

Cooke, K., Bradshaw, J., Lawton, D., & Brewer, R. (1986). Child disablement, family dissolution and reconstitution. *Developmental Medicine and Child Neurology, 28*, 610–616.

Cooke, K., & Lawton, D. (1984). Informal support for the carers of disabled children. *Child: Care, Health and Development, 10*, 67–79.

Cummings, S. T. (1976). Impact of the child's deficiency on the father: A study of fathers of mentally retarded and chronically ill children. *American Journal of Orthopsychiatry, 46*, 246–255.

Cummings, S. T., Bayley, H. C., & Rie, H. E. (1966). Effects of the child's deficiency on the mother: A study of mothers of mentally retarded, chronically ill, and neurotic children. *American Journal of Orthopsychiatry, 36*, 595–608.

Damrosch, S. P., & Perry, L. A. (1989). Self-reported adjustment, chronic sorrow, and coping of parents of children with Down syndrome. *Nursing Research, 38*, 25–30.

Donovan, A. M. (1988). Family stress and ways of coping with adolescents who have handicaps: Maternal perceptions. *American Journal on Mental Retardation, 92*, 502–509.

Drotar, D., Baskiewicz, A., Irvin, N., Kennell, J., & Klaus, M. (1975). The adaptation of parents to the birth of an infant with a congenital malformation: A hypothetical model. *Pediatrics, 56*, 710–717.

Dumas, J. E., Wolf, L. C., Fisman, S. N., & Culligan, A. (1991). Parenting stress, child behavior problems, and dysphoria in parents of children with autism, Down syndrome, behavior disorders, and normal development. *Exceptionality, 2*, 97–110.

Dunlap, W. R., & Hollinsworth, J. S. (1977). How does a handicapped child affect the family? Implications for practitioners. *The Family Coordinator, 26*, 286–293.

Dunst, C. J., Leet, H. E., & Trivette, C. M. (1988). Family resources, personal well-being, and early intervention. *The Journal of Special Education, 22*, 108–116.

Dunst, C. J., Trivette, C. M., & Cornwell, J. (1989). Family needs, social support, and self-efficacy during a child's transition to school. *Early Education and Development, 1*, 7–18.

Dunst, C., Trivette, C. & Cross, A. (1986). Mediating influences of social support: Personal, family and child outcomes. *American Journal of Mental Deficiency, 90*(4), 403–417.

Dupont, A. (1986). Socio-psychiatric aspects of the young severely mentally retarded and the family. *British Journal of Psychiatry, 148*, 227–234.

Dyson, L. L. (1991). Families of young children with handicaps: Parental stress and family functioning. *American Journal of Mental Retardation, 95*, 623–629.

Dyson, L. L. (1993). Response to the presence of a child with disabilities: Parental stress and family functioning over time. *American Journal on Mental Retardation, 98*, 207–218.

Dyson, L., Edgar, E., & Crnic, K. (1989). Psychological predictors of adjustment by siblings of developmentally disabled children. *American Journal on Mental Retardation, 94*, 292–302.

Dyson, L., & Fewell, R. F. (1986). Stress and adaptation in parents of young handicapped and nonhandicapped children: A comparative study. *Journal of the Division for Early Childhood, 10*, 25–34.

Eden-Piercy, G. V. S., Blacher, J. B., & Eyman, R. (1986). Exploring parents' reactions to their young child with severe disabilities. *Mental Retardation, 24*, 285–292.

Eheart, B. K., & Ciccone, J. (1982). Special needs of low-income mothers of developmentally delayed children. *American Journal of Mental Deficiency, 87*, 26–33.

Englehardt, J. L., Lutzer, V. D., & Brubaker, T. H. (1987). Parents of adults with developmental disabilities: Age and reasons for reluctance to use another caregiver. *Lifestyles: A Journal of Changing Patterns, 8*, 47–54.

Erickson, M., & Upshur, C. C. (1989). Caretaking burden and social support: Comparison of mothers of infants with and without disabilities. *American Journal of Mental Retardation, 94*, 250–258.

Failla, S., & Jones, L. C. (1991). Families of children with developmental disabilities: An examination of family hardiness. *Research in Nursing and Health, 14*, 41–50.

Farber, B. (1959). Effects of a severely mentally retarded child on family integration. *Monographs of the Society for Research in Child Development, 24*(2).

Farber, B. (1960). Family organization and crisis: Maintenance of integration in families with a severely mentally retarded child. *Monographs of the Society for Research in Child Development, 25*(1).

Farber, B., & Jenné, W. C. (1963). Family organization and parent–child communication: Parents and siblings of a retarded child. *Monographs of the Society for Research in Child Development, 28*(7) (Serial No. 91).

Fisman, S. N., Wolf, L. C., & Noh, S. (1989). Marital intimacy in parents of exceptional children. *Canadian Journal of Psychiatry, 34*, 519–525.

Florian, V. (1989). The cultural impact on the family dynamics of parents who have a child with a disability. *Journal of Comparative Family Studies, 20*, 97–111.

Floyd, F. J., & Phillippe, K. A. (1993). Parental interactions with children with and without mental retardation: Behavior management, coerciveness, and positive exchange. *American Journal on Mental Retardation, 97*, 673–684.

Floyd, F. J., & Zmich, D. E. (1991). Marriage and the parenting partnership: Perceptions and interactions of parents of mentally retarded and typically developing children. *Child Development, 62*, 1434–1448.

Flynt, S. W., & Wood, T. A. (1989). Stress and coping of mothers of children with moderate mental retardation. *American Journal on Mental Retardation, 94*, 278–283.

Flynt, S. W., Wood, T. A., & Scott, R. L. (1992). Social support of mothers of children with mental retardation. *Mental Retardation, 30*, 233–236.

Folkman, S., Schaefer, C., & Lazarus, R. S. (1979). Cognitive processes as mediators of stress and coping. In V. Hamilton & D. M. Warburton (Eds.), *Human stress and cognition* (pp. 265–298). New York: Wiley.

Fortier, L. M., & Wanlass, R. L. (1984). Family crisis following the diagnosis of a handicapped child. *Family Relations*, *33*, 13–24.

Fotheringham, J. B., Skelton, M., & Hoddinott, B. A. (1972). The effects on the family of the presence of a mentally retarded child. *Canadian Psychiatric Association Journal*, *17*, 283–288.

Fowle, C. M. (1969). The effect of the severely mentally retarded child on his family. *American Journal of Mental Deficiency*, *73*, 468–473.

Frey, K. S., Fewell, R. F., Vadasy, P. F., & Greenberg, M. T. (1989). Parental adjustment and changes in child outcome among families of young handicapped children. *Topics in Early Childhood Special Education*, *8*, 38–57.

Frey, K. S., Greenberg, M. T., & Fewell, R. F. (1989). Stress and coping among parents of handicapped children: A multidimensional approach. *American Journal on Mental Retardation*, *94*, 240–249.

Friedrich, W. N. (1979). Predictors of the coping behavior of mothers of handicapped children. *Journal of Consulting and Clinical Psychology*, *47*, 1140–1141.

Friedrich, W. N., Cohen, D. S., & Wilturner, L. T. (1987). Family relations and marital quality when a mentally handicapped child is present. *Psychological Reports*, *61*, 911–919.

Friedrich, W. N., Cohen, D. S., & Wilturner, L. T. (1988). Specific beliefs as moderator variables in maternal coping with mental retardation. *Child Health Care*, *17*, 40–44.

Friedrich, W. N., & Friedrich, N. (1981). Psychosocial assets of parents of handicapped and nonhandicapped children. *American Journal of Mental Deficiency*, *85*, 551–553.

Friedrich, W. N., Wilturner, L. T., & Cohen, D. S. (1985). Coping resources and parenting mentally retarded children. *American Journal of Mental Deficiency*, *90*, 130–139.

Gallagher, J. J., Scharfman, W., & Bristol, M. (1984). The division of responsibilities in families with preschool handicapped and nonhandicapped children. *Journal of the Division for Early Childhood*, *8*, 3–11.

Gallimore, R., Weisner, T. S., Bernheimer, L., Guthrie, D., & Nihira, K. (1993). Family responses to young children with developmental delays: Accommodation activity in ecological and cultural context. *American Journal on Mental Retardation*, *98*, 185–206.

Gallimore, R., Weisner, T. S., Kaufman, S. Z., & Bernheimer, L. P. (1989). The social construction of ecocultural niches: Family accommodation of developmentally delayed children. *American Journal on Mental Retardation*, *94*, 216–230.

Gamble, W. C., & McHale, S. M. (1989). Coping with stress in sibling relationships: A comparison of children with disabled and nondisabled siblings. *Journal of Applied Developmental Psychology*, *10*, 353–373.

Gath, A. (1978). *Down's syndrome and the family: The early years*. London: Academic Press.

Gath, A., & Gumley, D. (1984). Down's syndrome and the family: Follow-up of children first seen in infancy. *Developmental Medicine & Child Neurology*, *26*, 500–508.

Gath, A., & Gumley, D. (1986). Family background of children with Down's syndrome and of children with a similar degree of mental retardation. *British Journal of Psychiatry*, *149*, 161–171.

Gath, A., & Gumley, D. (1987). Retarded children and their siblings. *Journal of Child Psychology and Psychiatry and Allied Disciplines*, *28*, 715–730.

Gill, M. J., & Harris, S. L. (1991). Hardiness and social support as predictors of psychological discomfort in mothers of children with autism. *Journal of Autism and Developmental Disorders*, *21*, 407–416.

Glidden, L. M. (1993). What we do *not* know about families with children who have developmental disabilities: Questionnaire on Resources and Stress as a case study. *American Journal on Mental Retardation*, *97*, 481–495.

Glidden, L. M., Kiphart, M. J., Willoughby, J. C., & Bush, B. A. (1993). Family functioning when rearing children with developmental disabilities. In A. P. Turnbull, J. M. Patterson, S. K. Behr, D.

L. Murphy, J. G. Marquis, & M. J. Blue-Banning (Eds.), *Cognitive coping, families, and disability* (pp. 183–194). Baltimore, MD: Brookes.

Goldberg, S., Marcovitch, S., MacGregor, D., & Lojkasek, M. (1986). Family responses to developmentally delayed preschoolers: Etiology and the father's role. *American Journal of Mental Deficiency, 90*, 610–617.

Gottlieb, B. H. (1983). Social support as a focus for integrative research in psychology. *American Psychologist, 38*, 278–287.

Gowen, J. W., Johnson-Martin, N., Goldman, B. D., & Appelbaum, M. (1989). Feelings of depression and parenting competence of mothers of handicapped and nonhandicapped infants: A longitudinal study. *American Journal on Mental Retardation, 94*, 259–271.

Grant, G. (1986). Older carers, interdependence and the care of mentally handicapped adults. *Ageing and Society, 6*, 333–351.

Gumz, E. J., & Gubrium, J. (1972). Comparative parental perceptions of a mentally retarded child. *American Journal of Mental Deficiency, 77*, 175–180.

Haldy, M. B., & Hanzlik, J. R. (1990). A comparison of perceived competence in child-rearing between mothers of children with Down syndrome and mothers of children without delays. *Education and Training in Mental Retardation, xx*, 132–141.

Hampson, R. B., Hulgus, Y. F., Beavers, W. R., & Beavers, J. S. (1988). The assessment of competence in families with a retarded child. *Journal of Family Psychology, 2*, 32–53.

Harris, V. S., & McHale, S. M. (1989). Family life problems, daily caregiving activities, and the psychological well-being of mothers of mentally retarded children. *American Journal on Mental Retardation, 94*, 231–239.

Harry, B. (1992). Making sense of disability: Low-income, Puerto Rican parents' theories of the problem. *Exceptional Children, 59*, 27–40.

Heller, T., & Factor, A. (1993). Aging family caregivers: Support resources and changes in burden and placement desire. *American Journal on Mental Retardation, 98*, 417–426.

Heller, T., Markwardt, R., Rowitz, L., & Farber, B. (1994). Adaptation of Hispanic families to a member with mental retardation. *American Journal on Mental Retardation, 99*, 289–300.

Hill, R. (1949). *Families under stress*. New York: Harper.

Hill, R. (1958). Social stresses on the family. *Social Casework, 39*, 139–150.

Hirst, M. (1985). Dependency and family care of young adults with disabilities. *Child: Care, Health and Development, 11*, 241–257.

Hodapp, R. M., Dykens, E. M., Evans, D. W., & Merighi, J. R. (1992). *Developmental and Behavioral Pediatrics, 13*, 118–123.

Holmes, N., & Carr, J. (1991). The pattern of care in families of adults with a mental handicap: A comparison between families of autistic adults and Down syndrome adults. *Journal of Autism and Developmental Disorders, 21*, 159–176.

Holroyd, J., Brown, N., Wikler, L., & Simmons, J. Q., III. (1975). Stress in families of institutionalized and noninstitutionalized autistic children. *Journal of Community Psychology, 3*, 26–31.

Holroyd, J., & McArthur, D. (1976). Mental retardation and stress on the parents: A contrast between Down's syndrome and childhood autism. *American Journal of Mental Deficiency, 80*, 431–436.

Hoppes, K., & Harris, S. L. (1990). Perceptions of child attachment and maternal gratification in mothers of children with autism and Down syndrome. *Journal of Clinical Child Psychology, 19*, 365–370.

Houser, R., & Seligman, M. (1991a). A comparison of stress and coping by fathers of adolescents with mental retardation and fathers of adolescents without mental retardation. *Research in Developmental Disabilities, 12*, 251–260.

Houser, R., & Seligman, M. (1991b). Differences in coping strategies used by fathers of adolescents with disabilities and without disabilities. *Journal of Applied Rehabilitation Counseling, 22*, 7–10.

Jones, C. W. (1991). Role adjustment among low-income, single parents with a retarded child: Patterns of support. *Journal of Family Psychology, 4*, 497–511.

Kanner, A. D., Coyne, J. C., Schaefer, C., & Lazarus, R. S. (1981). Comparison of two modes of stress measurement: Daily hassles and uplifts versus major life events. *Journal of Behavioral Medicine, 4,* 1–23.

Kazak, A. E. (1987). Families with disabled children: Stress and social networks in three samples. *Journal of Abnormal Child Psychology, 15*(1), 137–146.

Kazak, A. E. (1988). Stress and social networks in families with older institutionalized retarded children. *Journal of Social and Clinical Psychology, 6,* 448–461.

Kazak, A. E., & Marvin, R. S. (1984). Differences, difficulties and adaptation: Stress and social networks in families with a handicapped child. *Family Relations, 33,* 67–77.

Kazak, A. E., & Wilcox, B. L. (1984). The structure and function of social support networks in families with handicapped children. *American Journal of Community Psychology, 12,* 645–661.

Knussen, C., Sloper, P., Cunningham, C. C., & Turner, S. (1992). The use of the Ways of Coping (Revised) questionnaire with parents of children with Down's syndrome. *Psychological Medicine, 22,* 775–786.

Koegel, R. L., Schreibman, L., Loos, L. M., Dirlich-Wilheim, H., Dunlap, G., Robbins, F. R., & Plienis, A. J. (1992). Consistent stress profiles in mothers of children with autism. *Journal of Autism and Developmental Disorders, 22,* 205–216.

Koegel, R. L., Schreibman, L., O'Neill, L., & Burke, J. C. (1983). The personality and family interaction characteristics of parents of autistic children. *Journal of Consulting and Clinical Psychology, 51,* 683–692.

Koller, H., Richardson, S. A., & Katz, M. (1992). Families of children with mental retardation: Comprehensive view from an epidemiologic perspective. *American Journal on Mental Retardation, 97,* 315–332.

Konstantareas, M. M., & Homatidis, S. (1989). Assessing child symptom severity and stress in parents of autistic children. *Journal of Child Psychology and Psychiatry, 30,* 459–470.

Konstantareas, M. M., & Homatidis, S. (1992). Mothers' and fathers' self-report of involvement with autistic, mentally delayed, and normal children. *Journal of Marriage and the Family, 54,* 153–164.

Krauss, M. W. (1993). Child-related and parenting stress: Similarities and differences between mothers and fathers of children with disabilities. *American Journal on Mental Retardation, 97,* 393–404.

Kravetz, S., Nativitz, R., & Katz, S. (1993). Parental coping style and the school adjustment of children who are mentally retarded. *British Journal of Developmental Disabilities, 29,* 51–59.

Kübler-Ross, E. (1969). *On death and dying.* New York: Macmillan.

Landis, L. J. (1992). Marital, employment, and childcare status of mothers with infants and toddlers with disabilities. *Topics in Early Childhood Special Education, 12,* 496–507.

Lazarus, R. S., DeLongis, A., Folkman, S., & Gruen, R. (1985). Stress and adaptational outcomes. *American Psychologist, 40,* 770–779.

Lazarus, R. S., & Folkman, S. (1984). *Stress, appraisal, and coping.* New York: Springer.

Lazarus, R. S., Kanner, A., & Folkman, S. (1980). Emotions: A cognitive-phenomenological analysis. In R. Plutchik & H. Kellerman (Eds.), *Theories of emotion* (pp. 189–217). New York: Academic Press.

Levy-Shiff, R. (1986). Mother–father–child interactions in families with a mentally retarded young child. *American Journal of Mental Deficiency, 91,* 141–149.

Lucca, J. A., & Settles, B. H. (1981). Effects of children's disabilities on parental time use. *Physical Therapy, 61,* 196–201.

Maddi, S. R., & Kobasa, S. C. (1984). *The hardy executive: Health under stress.* Homewood, IL: Dow Jones-Irwin.

Martin, J. M., & Cole, D. A. (1993). Adaptability and cohesion of dyadic relationships in families with developmentally disabled children. *Journal of Family Psychology, 7,* 186–196.

Mary, N. L. (1990). Reactions of black, Hispanic, and white mothers to having a child with handicaps. *Mental Retardation, 28,* 1–5.

McAllister, R. J., Butler, E. W., & Lei, T. J. (1973). Patterns of social interaction among families of behaviorally retarded children. *Journal of Marriage and the Family, 35*, 93–100.

McConachie, H. (1989). Mothers' and fathers' interactions with their young mentally handicapped children. *International Journal of Behavioral Development, 12*, 239–255.

McCubbin, M. A. (1989). Family stress and family strengths: A comparison of single- and two-parent families with handicapped children. *Research in Nursing and Health, 12*, 101–110.

McCubbin, M. A., & Huang, T. T. (1989). Family strengths in the care of handicapped children: Targets for intervention. *Family Relations, 38*, 436–443.

McCubbin, M. A., McCubbin, H. I., & Thompson, A. I. (1987). Family hardiness index. In H. I. McCubbin & A. I. Thompson (Eds.), *Family assessment inventories for research and practice* (p. 123–130). Madison: University of Wisconsin.

McCubbin, H. I., & Patterson, J. (1983). The family stress process: The double ABCX model of adjustment and adaptation. In H. I. HcCubbin, M. B. Sussman, & J. M. Patterson (Eds.), *Social stress and the family: Advances and developments in family's stress theory and research* (pp. 7–37). New York: Halworth.

McHale, S. M., & Gamble, W. C. (1989). Sibling relationships of children with disabled and nondisabled brothers and sisters. *Developmental Psychology, 25*, 421–429.

McHale, S. M., & Pawletko, T. M. (1992). Differential treatment of siblings in two family contexts. *Child Development, 63*, 68–81.

McHale, S. M., Sloan, J., & Simeonsson, R. J. (1986). Sibling relationships of children with autistic, mentally retarded, and nonhandicapped brothers and sisters. *Journal of Autism and Developmental Disorders, 16*, 399–413.

McKinney, B., & Peterson, R. A. (1987). Predictors of stress in parents of developmentally disabled children. *Journal of Pediatric Psychology, 12*, 133–150.

McLinden, S. E. (1990). Mothers' and fathers' reports of the effects of a young child with special needs in the family. *Journal of Early Intervention, 14*, 249–259.

Meyers, C. E., Nihira, K., & Mink, I. T. (1984). Predicting retarded students' short-term growth from home environment. *Applied Research in Mental Retardation, 5*, 137–146.

Milgrim, N. A., & Atzil, M. (1988). Parenting stress in raising autistic children. *Journal of Autism and Developmental Disorders, 18*, 415–424.

Mink, I. T., Meyers, C. E., & Nihira, K. (1984). Taxonomy of family life styles: II. Homes with slow-learning children. *American Journal of Mental Deficiency, 89*, 111–123.

Mink, I. T., & Nihira, K. (1986). Family life-styles and child behaviors: A study of direction of effects. *Developmental Psychology, 22*, 610–616.

Mink, I. T., & Nihira, K. (1987). Direction of effects: Family life styles and behavior of TMR children. *American Journal of Mental Deficiency, 92*, 57–64.

Mink, I. T., Nihira, K., & Meyers, C. E. (1983). Taxonomy of family life styles: I. Homes with TMR children. *American Journal of Mental Deficiency, 87*, 484–497.

Minnes, P. M. (1988). Family resources and stress associated with having a mentally retarded child. *American Journal on Mental Retardation, 93*, 184–192.

Moes, D., Koegel, R. L., Schreibman, L., & Loos, L. M. (1992). Stress profiles for mothers and fathers of children with autism. *Psychological Reports, 71*, 1272–1274.

Mölsä, P. K., & Ikonen-Mölsä, S. A. (1985). The mentally handicapped child and family crisis. *Journal of Mental Deficiency Research, 29*, 309–314.

Morrison, G. M., & Zetlin, A. (1992). Family profiles of adaptability, cohesion, and communication for learning handicapped and nonhandicapped adolescents. *Journal of Youth and Adolescence, 21*, 225–240.

Nihira, K., Meyers, C. E., & Mink, I. T. (1983). Reciprocal relationship between home environment and development of TMR adolescents. *American Journal of Mental Deficiency, 88*, 139–149.

Nihira, K., Weisner, T. S., & Bernheimer, L. P. (1994). Ecocultural assessment in families of children with developmental delays: Construct and concurrent validities. *American Journal on Mental Retardation, 98*, 551–566.

Nye, I. (1976). *Role structure and analysis of the family.* Beverly Hills, CA: Sage.

O'Connor, W. A., & Stachowiak, J. (1971). Patterns of interaction in families with high adjusted, low adjusted, and mentally retarded members. *Family Process, 10*, 229–241.

Olshansky, S. (1962). Chronic sorrow: A response to having a mentally defective child. *Social Casework, 43*, 190–193.

Olshansky, S. (1966). Parent responses to a mentally defective child. *Mental Retardation, 4*, 21–23.

Olson, D. H., Sprenkle, D. H., & Russell, C. S. (1979). Circumplex model of marital and family systems: I. Cohesion and adaptability dimensions, family types, and clinical applications. *Family Process, 18*, 3–28.

Orr, R. R., Cameron, S. J., & Day, D. M. (1991). Coping with stress in families with children who have mental retardation: An evaluation of the double ABCX model. *American Journal on Mental Retardation, 95*, 444–450.

Orr, R. R., Cameron, S. J., Dobson, L. A., & Day, D. M. (1993). Age-related changes in stress experienced by families with a child who has developmental delays. *Mental Retardation, 31*, 171–176.

Palfrey, J. S., Walker, D., Butler, J. A., & Singer, J. D. (1989). Patterns of response in families of chronically disabled children: An assessment in five metropolitan school districts. *American Journal of Orthopsychiatry, 59*, 94–104.

Pearlin, L. I., Lieberman, M. A., Menaghan, E. G., & Mullan, J. T. (1981). The stress process. *Journal of Health and Social Behavior, 22*, 337–356.

Reiss, D. (1981). *The family's construction of reality.* Cambridge, MA: Harvard University Press.

Robbins, F. R., Dunlap, G., & Plienis, A. J. (1991). Family characteristics, family training, and the progress of young children with autism. *Journal of Early Intervention, 15*, 173–184.

Rodrigue, J. R., Morgan, S. B., & Gefken, G. R. (1990). Families of autistic children: Psychological functioning of mothers. *Journal of Clinical Child Psychology, 19*, 371–379.

Rodrigue, J. R., Morgan, S. B., & Gefken, G. R. (1992). Psychosocial adaptation of fathers of children with autism, Down syndrome, and normal development. *Journal of Autism and Developmental Disorders, 22*, 249–263.

Romans-Clarkson, S. E., Clarkson, J. E., Dittmer, I D., Flett, R., Linsell, C., Mullen, P. E., & Mullin, B. (1986). Impact of a handicapped child on mental health of parents. *British Medical Journal, 293*, 1395–1397.

Rousey, A. M., Best, S., & Blacher, J. (1992). Mothers' and fathers' perceptions of stress and coping with children who have severe disabilities. *American Journal on Mental Retardation, 97*, 99–109.

Salisbury, C. L. (1987). Stressors of parents with young handicapped and nonhandicapped children. *Journal of the Division for Early Childhood, 11*, 154–160.

Sarbin, T. R. (1954). Role theory. In G. Lindzey (Ed.), *Handbook of social psychology* (Vol. 1, pp. 223–258). Reading, MA: Addison-Wesley.

Sarbin, T. R., & Allen, V. L. (1968). Role theory. In G. Lindzey & E. Aronson (Eds.). *Handbook of social psychology* (pp. 488–567). Reading, MA: Addison-Wesley.

Schilling, R., Kirkham, M., Snow, W., & Schinke, S. (1986). Single mothers with handicapped children: Different from their married counterparts? *Family Relations, 35*, 69–77.

Seltzer, G. B., Begun, A., Seltzer, M. M., & Krauss, M. W. (1991). Adults with mental retardation and their aging mothers: Impacts of siblings. *Family Relations, 40*, 310–317.

Seltzer, M. M., & Krauss, M. W. (1989). Aging parents with adult mentally retarded children: Family risk factors and sources of support. *American Journal on Mental Retardation, 94*, 303–312.

Seltzer, M. M., Krauss, M. W., & Tsunematsu, N. (1993). Adults with Down syndrome and their aging mothers: Diagnostic group differences. *American Journal on Mental Retardation, 97*, 496–508.

Selye, H. (1956). *The stress of life.* New York: McGraw-Hill.

Sherman, B. R. (1988). Predictors of the decision to place developmentally disabled family members in residential care. *American Journal on Mental Retardation, 92*, 344–351.

Shonkoff, J. P., Hauser-Cram, P., Krauss, M., W., & Upshur, C. (1992). Development of infants with disabilities and their families: Implications for theory and service delivery. *Monographs of the Society for Research in Child Development, 57*(6).

Shulman, S., Margalit, M., Gadish, O., & Stuchiner, N. (1990). The family system of moderately mentally retarded children. *Journal of Mental Deficiency Research, 34*, 341–350.

Singhi, P. D., Goyal, L., Pershad, D., Singhi, S., & Walia, B. N. S. (1990). Psychosocial problems in families of disabled children. *British Journal of Medical Psychology, 63*, 173–182.

Sloper, P., Knussen, C., Turner, S., & Cunningham, C. (1991). Factors related to stress and satisfaction with life in families of children with Down's syndrome. *Journal of Child Psychology and Psychiatry, 32*, 633–676.

Smith, R. (1986). Physically disabled children and parental time use. *Journal of Leisure Research, 18*, 284–299.

Smith, T. B., Innocenti, M. S., Boyce, G. C., & Smith, C. (1993). Depressive symptomatology and interaction behaviors of mothers having a child with disabilities. *Psychological Reports, 73*, 1184–1186.

Solnit, A. J., & Stark, M. S. S. (1961). Mourning and the birth of a defective child. In. R. S. Essler, A. Freud, H. Hartmann, & M. Kris (Eds.), *The psychoanalytic study of the child* (Vol. XVI, p. 523–537). New York: International Universities Press.

Stoneman, Z. (1989). Comparison groups in research on families with mentally retarded members: A methodological and conceptual review. *American Journal on Mental Retardation, 94*, 195–215.

Stoneman, Z. (1990). Conceptual relationships between family research and mental retardation. In N. W. Bray (Ed.), *International review of research in mental retardation* (Vol. 6, pp. 161–202). Orlando, FL: Academic Press.

Stoneman, Z. (in press). Research on siblings of children with mental retardation: Contributions of developmental theory and etiology. In J. Burack, E. Zigler, & R. M. Hodapp (Eds.), *Handbook of mental retardation and development.* New York: Cambridge University Press.

Stoneman, Z., & Brody, G. H. (1993). Sibling relations in the family context. In Z. Stoneman & P. W. Berman (Eds.), *The effects of mental retardation, disability, and illness on sibling relationships* (pp. 3–30). Baltimore, MD: Brookes.

Stoneman, Z., Brody, G. H., & Abbott, D. (1983). In-home observations of young Down syndrome children with their mothers and fathers. *American Journal of Mental Deficiency, 87*, 591–600.

Stoneman, Z., Brody, G. H., Davis, C. H., & Crapps, J. M. (1987). Mentally retarded children and their older siblings: Naturalistic in-home observations. *American Journal on Mental Retardation, 92*(3), 290–298.

Stoneman, Z., Brody, G. H., Davis, C. H., & Crapps, J. M. (1988). Childcare responsibilities, peer relationships, and sibling conflict: Older siblings of mentally retarded children. *American Journal of Mental Retardation, 93*(2), 174–183.

Stoneman, Z., Brody, G. H., Davis, C. H., & Crapps, J. M. (1989). Role relations between mentally retarded children and their older siblings: Observations in three in-home contexts. *Research in Developmental Disabilities, 10*, 61–76.

Stoneman, Z., Brody, G. H., Davis, C. H., Crapps, J. M., & Malone, D. M. (1991). Ascribed role relations between children with mental retardation and their younger siblings. *American Journal on Mental Retardation, 95*, 537–550.

Suelzle, M., & Keenan, V. (1981). Changes in family support networks over the life cycle of mentally retarded persons. *American Journal of Mental Deficiency, 86*, 267–274.

Tallman, I. (1965). Spousal role differentiation and the socialization of severely retarded children. *Journal of Marriage and the Family, 27*, 37–42.

Tausig, M. (1985). Factors in family decision-making about placement for developmentally disabled individuals. *American Journal of Mental Deficiency, 89*, 352–361.

Thorin, E. J., & Irvin, L. K. (1992). Family stress associated with transition to adulthood of young people with severe disabilities. *Journal of the Association for Persons with Severe Handicaps, 17*, 31–39.

Trute, B. (1990). Child and parent predictors of family adjustment in households containing young developmentally disabled children. *Family Relations, 39*, 292–297.

Trute, B., & Hauch, C. (1988a). Building on family strengths: A study of families with a positive adjustment to the birth of a developmentally disabled child. *Journal of Marital and Family Therapy, 14,* 185–193.

Trute, B., & Hauch, C. (1988b). Social network attributes of families with positive adaptation to the birth of a developmentally disabled child. *Canadian Journal of Community Mental Health, 7,* 5–16.

Vadasy, P. F., Fewell, R. F., Meyer, D. J., Schell, G., & Greenberg, M. T. (1984). Involved parents: Characteristics and resources of fathers and mothers of young handicapped children. *Journal of the Division for Early Childhood, 8,* 13–24.

Van Riper, M., Ryff, C., & Pridham, K. (1992). Parental and family well-being in families of children with Down syndrome: A comparative study. *Research in Nursing and Health, 15,* 227–235.

Waisbren, S. E. (1980). Parents' reactions after the birth of a developmentally disabled child. *American Journal of Mental Deficiency, 84,* 354–366.

Walker, L. S., Ortiz-Valdes, J. A., & Newbrough, J. R. (1989). The role of maternal employment and depression in the psychological adjustment of chronically ill, mentally retarded, and well children. *Journal of Pediatric Psychology, 14,* 257–370.

Walker, L. S., Van Slyke, D. A., & Newbrough, J. R. (1992). Family resources and stress: A comparison of families of children with cystic fibrosis, diabetes, and mental retardation. *Journal of Pediatric Psychology, 17,* 327–343.

Wallander, J. L., Pitt, L. C., & Mellins, C. A. (1990). Child functional independence and maternal psychosocial stress as risk factors threatening adaptation in mothers of physically or sensorially handicapped children. *Journal of Consulting and Clinical Psychology, 58,* 818–824.

Wallander, J. L., Varni, J. W., Babani, L., DeHaan, C. B., Wilcox, K. T., & Banis, H. T. (1989). The social environment and the adaptation of mothers of physically handicapped children. *Journal of Pediatric Psychology, 14,* 371–387.

Weinhouse, D., Weinhouse, M., & Nelson, J. G. (1992). Stress factors in families of young children with exceptional educational needs. *School Psychology International, 13,* 51–59.

Weisner, T. S. (1993). Ethnographic and ecocultural perspectives on sibling relationships. In Z. Stoneman & P. W. Berman (Eds.), *The effects of mental retardation, disability, and illness on sibling relationships: Research issues and challenges* (pp. 51–83). Baltimore, MD: Brookes.

Weisner, T. S., Beizer, L., & Stolze, L. (1991). Religion and families of children with developmental delays. *American Journal on Mental Retardation, 95,* 647–662.

Weiss, S. J. (1991). Stressors experienced by family caregivers of children with pervasive developmental disorders. *Child Psychiatry and Human Development, 21,* 203–216.

Wikler, L., Wasow, M., & Hatfield, E. (1981). Chronic sorrow revisited: Parent vs. professional depiction of the adjustment of parents of mentally retarded children. *American Journal of Orthopsychiatry, 51,* 63–70.

Wikler, L. M. (1986). Periodic stresses of families of older mentally retarded children: An exploratory study. *American Journal of Mental Deficiency, 90,* 703–706.

Williams, R. G., & McKenry, P. C. (1981). Marital adjustment among parents of mentally retarded children. *Family Perspective, 3,* 175–178.

Willoughby, J. C., & Glidden, L. M. (1995). Fathers helping out: Shared child care and marital satisfaction of parents of children with disabilities. *American Journal of Mental Retardation, 99,* 399–406.

Wilson, J., Blacher, J., & Baker, B. L. (1989). Siblings of children with severe handicaps. *Mental Retardation, 27,* 167–173.

Wilton, K., & Renaut, J. (1986). Stress levels in families with intellectually handicapped preschool children and families with nonhandicapped preschool children. *Journal of Mental Deficiency Research, 30,* 163–169.

Winik, L., Zetlin, A. G., & Kaufman, S. Z. (1985). Adult mildly retarded persons and their parents: The relationship between involvement and adjustment. *Applied Research in Mental Retardation, 6,* 409–419.

Wishart, M. C., Bidder, R. T., & Gray, O. P. (1980). Parental responses to their developmentally delayed children and the South Glamorgan Home Advisory Service, *Child: Care, Health, and Development*, *6*, 361–376.

Wishart, M. C., Bidder, R. T., & Gray, O. P. (1981). Parents' reports of family life with a developmentally delayed child. *Child: Care, Health and Development*, *7*, 267–279.

Wolf, L. C., Noh, S., Fisman, S., & Speechley, M. (1989). Brief report: Psychological effects of parenting stress on parents of autistic children. *Journal of Autism and Developmental Disabilities*, *19*, 157–166.

Young, D. M., & Roopnarine, J. L. (1994). Fathers' childcare involvement with children with and without disabilities. *Topics in Early Childhood Special Education*, *14*, 488–502.

Zetlin, A. G., & Turner, J. L. (1985). Transition from adolescence to adulthood: Perspectives of mentally retarded individuals and their families. *American Journal on Mental Retardation*, *89*, 570–579.

› 16 ‹

Severe Behavior Problems Among People With Developmental Disabilities

Stephen R. Schroeder
Richard E. Tessel
Pippa S. Loupe
Christopher J. Stodgell
The University of Kansas

In our corresponding chapter on severe behavior problems of people with mental retardation published in the second edition of this volume (Schroeder, Mulick, & Schroeder, 1979), we noted a dramatic shift from group outcome studies of etiology and nosological classification toward single-subject experimental and applied behavior analytic studies across the full range of mental retardation (MR). Once again in the past 15 years there has been a revolution in our thinking about behavior problems of people with developmental disabilities. At least 80% of the research literature on this topic has been published since 1979, (i.e., over 2,000 research studies and more than 100 reviews). Our purpose in this chapter is not to make an exhaustive review of all of these papers, but to highlight major findings and future trends and then to propose an integrated approach to assessment, diagnosis, and treatment.

Definition of Terms

The term *behavior problems* was chosen to reflect a pretheoretical approach to etiology. This functional approach, which was first proposed by Bijou (1966), simply views behavior problems as deviant behavior patterns related to impaired current functioning and progressive changes in interactions between the individual, "as a totally functioning biological system," and the environment. *Severe* means having consequences that are correlated with tissue damage requiring medical treatment or that result in exclusion from social and educational activities appropriate to one's adaptive level. Other names that have come into vogue are "challenging" behaviors or "people with severe reputations" (Smull & Harrison, 1992). Such terms appear to have their origins in advocacy for people with developmental disabilities and have little support from a scientific analysis at present. A Chinese proverb says, "Wisdom begins with calling things by their right name."

Taxonomy of Severe Behavior Problems

What behaviors usually are considered in the literature on behavior problems of people with developmental disabilities (DD)? The list developed in a review by Bates and Wehman (1977) still holds today: aggressive behaviors, including destruction, biting others, verbal aggression, choking, throwing, and hitting others; self-injurious behaviors (SIB), including headbanging, biting self, scratching, gouging, and voluntary falling; stereotyped behaviors, including bizarre gestures, hand flicking, hand staring, mouthing, body rocking, headweaving, and verbal repetitions; classroom disruptive behaviors, including impulsive behavior, hyperactivity, talking out, arguing, obscene vocalizations, and out-of-seat behaviors; noncompliance, including bickering, jumping on furniture, persistent crawling, and playing inappropriately with objects; other inappropriate behaviors, including pica, stealing, enuresis, coprophagy, encopresis, nasal discharge, self-exposure, and chronic ruminative vomiting. This is a fairly representative list of severe behavior problems studied. It is likely that a modern-day list would also include a list of psychiatric disorders such as the *Diagnostic and Statistical Manual of Mental Disorders* (*DSM–IV*; APA, 1994).

Assessment Procedures for Severe Behavior Problems

These behaviors usually are assessed by three classes of methods: functional assessment, psychometric assessment, and clinical diagnostic assessment.

Functional Assessment. A recent entire issue of the *Journal of Applied Behavior Analysis* (1994) was devoted to this topic. Functional assessment refers to a range of strategies used to identify the antecedents and consequences that control problem behavior, such as informant questionnaires, checklists, experimental hypothesis testing in the natural environment, and experimental analyses in environments analogous to the natural environment with systematic observation of behavior. The latter form of assessment is termed *functional analysis* (Horner, 1994). Although it was frequently practiced by many applied behavior analysts in the 1960s and 1970s, functional analysis was first published as a standardized procedure by Iwata, Dorsey, Slifer, Bauman, and Richman (1982) and has since had a significant impact on behavioral approaches that match assessment to treatments for behavior problems.

Functional assessment technology is an important advance because it focuses on finding out the variables that control a behavior problem rather than solely on a technical application of procedures that produce change (Mace, 1994). Treatments for behavior problems in the past have frequently been chosen or rejected based on their least intrusiveness, as defined by governmental regulatory or ethical guidelines, without regard for adjusting their parameters or matching their operant functions to treatment efficacy. Functional analysis gives a method for asking why a certain behavior problem is occurring and why a procedure is or is not working.

Psychometric Assessment. In the past there have been very few standardized psychometric measures available for assessing severe behavior problems among people with DD. It was usually necessary to adapt measures that had been standardized on nondisabled populations. This situation has changed dramatically in the past 15 years. There are now a variety of instruments suited for different populations with different behavior problems. Aman (1991) performed a thorough review and analysis of 46 of these measures. Among some of the most widely used scales are: the Vineland Adaptive Behavior Scales (Sparrow, Balla, & Cicchetti, 1984); American Association on Mental Retardation (AAMD) Adaptive Behavior Scales (Lambert, Windmiller, Tharinger, & Cole, 1981; Nihira, Foster, Shellhaas, & Leland, 1975); Aberrant Behavior Checklist (Aman & Singh, 1986); Psychopathology Instrument for Mentally Retarded Adults (PIMRA; Matson, 1988); and Reiss Screen for Maladaptive Behavior (Reiss, 1988a, 1988b).

Clinical Diagnostic Assessment. Clinical diagnostic assessment differs from functional assessment and psychometric assessment, in that the goal is to assign a differential classification (e.g., depression, schizophrenia) based on differential etiology with a view to differential treatment and prognosis for outcomes. Diagnosticians are likely to use a variety of biological (e.g., genetic, neurological, psychiatric, etc.) assessments in addition to behavioral and psychometric assessments in an interdisciplinary manner to identify relevant diagnostic symptoms and irrelevant ones related to differential treatment.

Advances in clinical diagnostic approaches from psychiatry and psychology have been slow to have an impact on the field. Early psychodynamic approaches were of use mostly for higher functioning clients only. For years Menolascino's compendium, *Psychiatric Approaches to Mental Retardation* (1970), was the main sourcebook for clinical diagnosis. Since then, three trends have coalesced to change the approach to clinical diagnosis of behavior problems: the publication of *DSM–III* (APA, 1980), the advent of the concept of dual diagnosis, and the increased attention to the psychopharmacology of behavior problems in MR.

The need for classification of disorders in both mental illness and MR has been recognized since the turn of the century. Manuals of terminology and classification by the American Psychiatric Association (APA) and the American Association on Mental Retardation (AAMR) have undergone many revisions since their beginnings. In the 1983 AAMR revision, maladaptive behavior was made an integral part of the definition of MR through the inclusion of the AAMD Adaptive Behavior Scales (Nihira, Foster, Shellhaas, & Leland,1975) in the assessment protocol. The newly revised AAMR definition (Luckasson et al., 1992) is a radical departure from previous definitions in which the AAMD Adaptive Behavior Scales had been emphasized. The new definition is characterized by significantly subaverage functioning plus limitations in at least 2 of 10 adaptive skill areas. Specific behavior problems such as those mentioned in this chapter are not discussed.

In contrast, *DSM–III* (APA, 1980) introduced a number of important methodological innovations, including explicit diagnostic criteria, a multiaxial system, and a descriptive approach that attempted to be neutral with respect to theories of etiology. This approach encouraged empirical work on validation of diagnostic criteria for developmental disorders and their relationship to mental disorders. *DSM–IV* (APA, 1994) is a further refinement of this process.

Work on *DSM–III* set the stage for a serious treatment of the concept of *dual diagnosis*, that is, the presence of mental disorders among people with MR. One of the first books to publish prevalence figures of 25% to 30% of the population with MR and a *DSM–III* diagnosis of mental disorders was Szymanski and Tanguay (1980). Several other studies set similar prevalence figures for schizophrenia and mental retardation (Eaton & Menolascino, 1982) and affective disorders (Sovner & Hurley, 1983). Reiss, Levitan, and Szyszko (1982) also demonstrated "a phenomenon in which the presence of mental retardation decreases the diagnostic importance of abnormal behavior" (p. 572). This "diagnostic overshadowing" has been replicated several times over the past decade. It therefore appears to be well established. Of course, questions remain as to how valid the diagnoses of mental disorders among people with severe and profound retardation really are. Menolascino, Wilson, Golden, and Ruedrich (1986) claimed to be able to diagnose schizophrenia among nonverbal people with severe retardation. Benavidez and Matson (1993), comparing children without retardation with those who had mild–moderate or severe retardation, using traditional rating scales, found mixed results for the lower functioning group (IQ = 33–69). They suggested that depressive symptoms of this group may differ from those in higher functioning ranges. Sovner and Lowry (1990) published a behavioral methodology for diagnosing affective disorders in all people with MR—even profound MR. They also published a study of successful treatment of depression and self-injurious behavior in two adults with severe and profound MR using their diagnostic scheme (Sovner, Fox, Lowry, & Lowry, 1993). These results remain to be replicated by other groups.

The validation of *DSM–IV* diagnostic schemes of mental disorders among subgroups of people with MR is an important area for future research not only for classification and epidemiology but also for behavioral and differential pharmacological treatment. Existing practices leave a great deal to be desired. For instance, Macmann and Barnett (1993), in a study of 126 dually diagnosed clients, found chance-corrected agreement between psychiatric diagnosis and psychological case reports to average .47. Rojahn, Borthwick-Duffy, and Jacobson (1993) found no compelling correlation between psychiatric diagnoses and severe behavior problems recorded on instruments used in their statewide client databases in New York (N = 45,683) and California (N = 89,419). Thus, neither self-injurious behavior, aggression, destruction, nor stereotypy determined whether a person received a psychiatric diagnosis or not.

Although modern-day psychopharmacology is often dated as beginning in 1937 with the treatment of hyperactive children with Benzedrine by Bradley and in the 1950s with the discovery of chlorpromazine for treatment of schizophrenia (Werry, 1993), in MR a good starting point would be Lipman's review (1970). In this review he showed that the use of psychotropic drugs, especially neuroleptics, among people with MR, was very widespread (i.e., over 50% among institutionalized populations). Sprague and Werry's (1971) classic review showed that there was a paucity of well-designed studies of the effectiveness of these drugs in treating major mental illness or severe behavior problems in MR. Sprague and Werry set methodological standards that still serve as a benchmark today.

Interest and sophistication in the psychopharmacology of MR grew rapidly in the late 1970s and early 1980s, although its practice was still based on a trial-and-error strategy rather than on a neurobiological rationale. In the early 1980s, however, drug studies began to appear that were specifically based on rationales underlying dual diagnoses or specific behavior problems like self-injurious behavior (see Aman, 1993, for a review). Aman (1993) cited over 250 studies involving psychopharmacology and mental retardation. Baumeister, Todd, and Sevin (1993) performed an excellent analytical review of those studies that contained satisfactory experimental designs. The prospect of developing a rational pharmacotherapy with effective and specific effects for distinct behavioral disorders of persons with MR has greatly increased the importance of improved clinical diagnostic approaches to behavior problems in MR.

EPIDEMIOLOGICAL TRENDS

In the last 15 years there has been a fivefold increase in the number of prevalence studies of behavioral and mental disorders in people with mental retardation. Jacobson (1990) reviewed 23 studies published between 1975 and 1987. Prevalence estimates varied widely from 7% to 70%, depending on the methodology, type of setting, level of MR, and age of the population. Over this period there was also a dramatic shift in living environments away from larger congregate residential settings to small, homelike settings with 15 persons or less. This shift has also affected the prevalence rates of behavior problems that restrict residential options (Bruininks, Olson, Larson, & Lakin, 1994).

As Scott (1988) noted, the tools of modern epidemiology have not been applied very systematically to most prevalence studies of developmental disability in the United States. Few epidemiologists have been interested in this field. Indeed, there is no national study based on a truly representative sampling strategy for persons with MR and behavior disorders in the United States, nor is there likely to be such an expensive study in the near future. Such a study would be very important for discovering risk factors, case definition, and clustering of disorders with interrelated topographies based on their biological and behavioral origins and functions, their developmental time course, and a host of other variables necessary for prevention programs. Nevertheless, there have been national survey studies, studies of statewide databases, and smaller scale point prevalence studies that have been extremely informative on a number of risk factors related to behavior problems in MR. The main points are summarized in this chapter.

Since the classic Isle of Wight study by Rutter, Tizard, and Whitmore (1970), which is still the best epidemiological study in the field, there has been a broad consensus that the presence of psychiatric disturbances among people with mental retardation is on average about five times as high as among their age-matched peers. As Jacobson (1990) pointed out, however, the actual estimates vary greatly from study to study. A major reason for such wide variation is that these disorders are multiply caused and multiply effected (Schroeder, Mulick, & Rojahn, 1980) by a combination of many risk factors and their covariates, whose influence change over the course of one's life. For instance, type of residence may be a probable cause of behavior problems at one time and a probable effect at another. Thus, the possibility of confounded misinterpretation of residential data is high.

A second major difficulty with interpreting these prevalence studies is that it is unclear how *DSM–IV* diagnoses of psychiatric disorders such as schizophrenia, depression, pervasive developmental disorders, and so on overlap with behavior problems such as aggression, self-injury, property destruction, and the host of other problems mentioned in this chapter. Matson (1986) called for behaviorists to attempt to apply *DSM* diagnoses to their cases of behavior problems in MR. It is very important for an understanding of both the biological substrates and their behavioral manifestations that are the basis for rational pharmacological and behavioral intervention. This biobehavioral rapprochement is a promising future direction of research.

Risk Factors for Behavior Problems

The interest in risk factors for behavior problems in MR grew with the publication of two prevalence studies of SIB among institutional populations (Maisto, Baumeister, & Maisto, 1978; Schroeder, Schroeder, Smith, & Dalldorf, 1978), both of which found comparable results. The Schroeder et al. (1978) results can be summarized as follows: A combined informant questionnaire and interview survey of SIB at a large state facility for persons with MR was conducted independently three times over a 3-year period. Prevalence consistently was about 10% of the population. SIB cases tended to be younger and institutionalized longer than were the rest of the population. Severe cases had a longer history of chronic SIB. SIB cases had more seizure disorders, severe language handicaps, visual impairments, and severe or profound retardation than the rest of the population.

They appeared to fulfill most of the Rutter (1966) criteria for autism. However, unlike the severely autistic, there was little relation of gender to incidence of SIB. SIB frequency was actually higher among women in the Maisto et al. (1978) study. Over 90% of SIB cases changed status over 3 years, suggesting that SIB was amenable to behavior modification in most cases (94%). Psychotropic behavior control medications helped in some intervention programs (32%). SIB remitted spontaneously in 21% of SIB cases where there had been no behavioral or drug intervention. These early studies have been replicated and extended frequently across cultures and to include several other behavior problems, mainly aggression and property destruction. The best summaries by the four main research groups in the United States are Borthwick-Duffy (1994); Bruininks, Olson, Larson, and Lakin (1994); Jacobson (1990); and Rojahn (1994). Their work is summarized next.

Level of Mental Retardation. There is good agreement that the prevalence of SIB, aggression, and property destruction increases with severity of MR. However, in the case of profound MR, there may be subgroups, such as nonambulatory or medically fragile people who lack the physical capacity to be aggressive or to display destructive behavior, but their SIB maybe higher.

Chronological Age. The occurrence of self-injury may begin as early as 6 months of age. It tends to increase rapidly between 3 and 25 years and then decrease just as rapidly into old age. Data beyond the age of 65 years are fragmentary. This is not due to high mortality rate among SIB cases compared to matched control cases (Borthwick-Duffy, 1994; Wieseler, Hanson, & Nord, 1994). Frequency of aggressive and destructive behavior similarly tends to increase rapidly into the 20s and 30s and stabilizes until it declines in the 50s and 60s.

Gender. No clear relationship between gender and SIB has been found. There may be gender preference for certain SIB topographies (Rojahn, 1994). On the other hand, aggression and destruction are nearly twice as frequent among males compared to females (Borthwick-Duffy, 1994). This result is similar to the frequency of externalizing behaviors by people without MR (Achenbach & Edelbrock, 1981).

Medical Problems. The presence of medical problems is associated with higher rates of self-injury, aggression, and destruction. In the Schroeder et al. (1978) study, SIB cases had significantly more seizures than did a matched control group. Whether this relationship represents a cause, an effect, or simply collinear correlation with level of MR is uncertain. A multivariate approach would be needed to sort out all of the medical factors thought to precipitate SIB. Such an epidemiological study has not yet been published. There is no dearth of hypotheses, however. For instance, Gedye (1989) argued that SIB may be caused by frontal lobe seizures. Coulter (1990) debated her views. The investigation of specific biomedical risk factors and behavior problems will be one of the most important areas of research in the next decade.

Residential Setting. There is general agreement that the prevalence of SIB, aggression, and destruction is related positively to the restrictiveness of the residential setting. The order is: (a) institution, (b) group homes, (c) foster homes, (d) family homes, and (e) semi-independent living (Bruininks et al., 1994). These results are largely due to placement decisions and placement failures (Eyman, Borthwick, & Miller 1981; Hill & Bruininks, 1984). The contention that placement in large residential facilities produces maladaptive behavior was not supported in these studies. Thus, the size of the facility of itself is not a risk factor. There is ample evidence that environmental impoverishment and the lack of choice for activities alternative to behavior problems in MR is a strong risk factor, whatever the residential setting (see Schroeder, Rojahn, & Oldenquist, 1991, for a review).

Psychiatric Disorders. Self-injury, aggression, and destruction are all related to the presence of psychiatric disorders in MR (Nihira, Price-Williams, & White, 1988), but the nature of these relationships is as yet unclear. For instance, it is not known whether SIB in MR is like suicidal depression in mental illness.

Sensory and Communication Deficits. Visual, auditory, and language impairments were all found to be risk factors for SIB by Schroeder et al. (1978). This result was replicated for expressive communication among people with SIB, aggression, and/or destruction (Borthwick-Duffy, 1994; Griffin, Williams, Stark, Altmeyer, & Mason, 1986; Gunter 1984). Communication deficits may be risk factors for behavior problems in some people with MR. Indeed Carr (Carr & Durand, 1985; Carr et al., 1994) developed a whole line of intervention procedures based on replacing problem behaviors with appropriate communication skills.

In summary, a considerable amount of research on problem behaviors in MR has been gleaned from prevalence studies in the past 15 years, and there is reasonable agreement as to what they are. This research will become increasingly important as intervention procedures focus more and more on prevention (Schroeder, Bickel, & Richmond, 1986).

TRENDS IN ETIOLOGICAL THEORIES

Since the previous review in 1979, a number of new behavioral and biological theories of behavior problems have emerged. These new theories were posited for several reasons. Much of the behavioral research to date had been based on the premise that these behavior problems were learned and therefore could be changed by merely manipulating their consequences. Their antecedents and the environmental context had been largely ignored. Those researchers who looked for generalization and maintenance of the behaviors, however, found that they were poor irrespective of the behavior procedures used. These generalization and maintenance data have been reviewed extensively at the Consensus Development Conference sponsored by the National Institute for Child Health and Human Development (NICHD, 1991).

Research on functional analyses in the 1980s and 1990s made it clear that problem behaviors are comprised of much more complex response classes than were previously envisioned, and the stimuli that evoked them were multiple and organized in a hierarchical conditional probabilistic fashion (Schroeder & MacLean, 1987). Problem behaviors are exhibited in a wide variety of behavioral topographies and environmental settings. There exist several conditions reputedly conducive to its development: failure to inhibit infantile self-stimulatory patterns; suffering a lesser pain to avoid a more aversive experience; stimulus discrimination of a positive reward (e.g., attention); self-stimulation following disruption of homeostasis; frustration or stress; elicited aggression; failure to communicate, and so on (Schroeder et al., 1979). None of these explanations is mutually exclusive, and none alone accounts satisfactorily for the development of these problem behaviors. It is likely that some or all of these conditions could be present in a single case. Much more research must be done that determines how the variety of identifiable antecedents contributes to the development of behavior problems before an adequate choice among treatments can be made.

Biological theories of etiology prior to 1980 consisted mostly of searches for medical syndromes, for example, Lesch–Nyhan syndrome (Nyhan, 1967), which had a high incidence of a problem behavior like SIB (see Harris, 1992, for a review). Several syndromes were found, but all of them were rare and could account for only a small portion of cases of problem behaviors known to exist. It was not until animal models suggested that syndromes such as Lesch–Nyhan syndrome might be a window on a much broader array of SIB (Baumeister, Frye, & Schroeder, 1983) that neurobiological models of problem behaviors in MR generated considerable interest.

Next we review two new behavioral and six new neurobiological theories of stereotypy and SIB. We are not aware of any new hypotheses on aggression or destruction except Gedye's (1989) frontal lobe seizure hypothesis previously mentioned. This hypothesis lacks sufficient supporting data as yet. Neurobiological theories of SIB (e.g., serotonergic theories) often view stereotypy SIB and aggression as have overlapping biological substrates. Although this assumption is not universally accepted, we treat these theories of stereotypy, SIB, and aggression together, although we are not prejudging the issues.

Guess and Carr's Behavior State Model for Emergence of Stereotypy and SIB

Guess and Carr (1991) proposed a three-level model to explain the emergence and maintenance of rhythmic stereotypy and self-injury. Level I consists of rhythmic behaviors as internally regulated states common in normally developing infants, but delayed in onset among children with handicapping conditions. Level II is homeostasis, wherein stereotypy and self-injury are viewed as adaptations to under- or overstimulating environments. Level III represents stereotypy and self-injury as learned behaviors emitted to control the behavior of others. Behavior develops in a sequence from Levels I to III. There are fluid transitions between levels. Delayed or arrested development represents a risk factor for pathology. Interventions that facilitate the transitions to age-appropriate levels are likely to prevent behavior problems. Premature inhibitory interventions of Level I behavior states may be counterproductive.

The Guess and Carr model is a very interesting descriptive model that integrates a variety of diverse findings about stereotypy. Although it has its critics (Lovaas & Smith, 1991; Mulick & Meinhold, 1991), it is the first attempt to show how self-injury may develop from rhythmic behavior states. Chaos theory (Guess & Sailor, 1993) is used to analyze phase changes and differentiation of behavior response classes. This is a very innovative idea. Thus far, however, Guess and colleagues (Guess et al., 1993) have concentrated on differentiating Level I state conditions among people with severe and profound MR. They have not as yet demonstrated the emergence of SIB as implied by their theory, but this is certainly a promising future research direction.

King's Compulsive Behavior Hypothesis for SIB

The compulsive behavior hypothesis holds that for some individuals, self-injury is a compulsive behavior that occurs in the context of cerebral damage (King, 1993). It is based on four observations: cerebral damage sometimes causes compulsive behavior; severity of mental retardation may reflect the degree of underlying cerebral impairment; persons with self-injurious or compulsive behavior susceptibility react similarly to stress, anxiety, and task demands; and some serotonergic drugs (e.g., clomipramine, fluoxetine, buspirone) appear to ameliorate obsessive–compulsive disorders (OCD) and self-injury.

The compulsive behavior hypothesis is almost entirely speculative and without conclusive empirical support. Although it is interesting, like all other existing hypotheses of SIB, it has had no disjunctive or exclusive test to prove its specificity. Nevertheless, it may be correct for a given subpopulation of SIB cases. Several of the neurobiological and behavioral histories of OCD and SIB may overlap; in others they do not. How and to what degree they overlap are the big questions. For instance, King (1993) cited self-restraint among SIB cases as evidence of compulsive behavior. Yet the survey by Fovel, Lash, Barron, and Roberts (1989), which he also cited shows that 80% of their SIB cases did not exhibit self-restraint. Furthermore, for their self-restrainers, 90% performed SIB, but also 50% performed aggression, 60%—property destruction, 45%—tantrums, 35%—oral behaviors, 30%—stripping; and 15%—smearing feces. This profile does not look much like the symptom profile for obsessive compulsive behavior in *DSM–IV* (APA, 1994).

King (1993) also cited as evidence the high incidence of self-injury and compulsive tics in Gilles de la Tourette syndrome, which is not related to MR level as it is in the case for SIB in MR (Robertson, Trimble, & Lees, 1989). It remains to be shown how much overlap there is between these two SIB populations and how similarly they respond to the same psychopharmacological interventions. For instance, haloperidol, pimozide, and fluphenazine, the most effective drugs for treating motor and verbal tics in Tourette disorder (Robertson, 1992), have had a much more inconsistent effect on SIB in the MR population (Aman, 1993).

Neonatal Dopamine Depletion Hypothesis of SIB

Breese and Traylor (1970) found that injecting an adult rat with the neurotoxin 6-hydroxydopamine (6-OHDA) in the corpus striatum created a selective lesion of dopamine neurons resulting in supersensitivity. If the rats were then challenged with a dopamine agonist such as L-DOPA or apomorphine, they became aggressive and hyperactive. If, however, this lesion was performed at age 5 to 15 days and then the rats as adults were challenged with a dopamine agonist, they began biting themselves severely. Breese and Baumeister recognized this as a potential model for self-biting in Lesch–Nyhan syndrome (Breese et al., 1984a, 1984b). Examination of postmortem brain tissues of Lesch–Nyhan cases by Lloyd et al. (1981) indeed showed a large depletion of dopamine in the corpus striatum and elevated serotonin levels in the substantia nigra, as would be predicted by the Breese–Baumeister model.

The question then arose as to why dopamine blockers such as haloperidol and chlorpromazine do not decrease SIB among humans very well (Aman, 1993). Breese posited that these drugs blocked primarily D_2 dopamine receptor subtypes, whereas SIB is primarily a D_1 dopamine receptor phenomenon. Using the experimental drug SCH23390, a specific D_1 receptor antagonist, he was able to block SIB in neonatal dopamine-depleted rats who had been challenged with apomorphine.

Unfortunately, there is no pure D_1 receptor antagonist available for clinical use as yet in the United States to test the neonatal dopamine depletion model in human SIB cases. Clinical trials with D_1 and D_2 receptor blockers fluphenazine (Gualtieri & Schroeder, 1989) and clozapine (Hammock, Schroeder, & Levine, 1995) have both been successful, but all of these drugs have serious side effects. Clozapine also has an affinity for other dopamine (D_4) and serotonin receptors in addition to D_1 and D_2 dopamine receptors. These drugs are, therefore, not an unambiguous test of the neonatal dopamine depletion hypothesis, even though Criswell, Mueller, and Breese (1989) showed that clozapine at low doses was a relatively selective D_1 blocker in the Breese animal model.

Serotonin Hypothesis for SIB and Aggression

Serotonin is another major central nervous system (CNS) neurotransmitter that often acts in a reciprocal relationship with dopamine. Mizuno and Yugari (1974) found that giving 5-hydroxtryptophan (5-HTP), a serotonin agonist, to four Lesch–Nyhan boys had a dramatic effect for a few weeks. Other investigators failed to replicate this finding until Nyhan, Johnson, Kaufman, and Jones (1980) gave 5-HTP along with carbidopa, and imipramine to prevent rapid excretion in the urine. They also found a dramatic effect that disappeared after 3 months and could not be recovered.

More recently there have been a number of serotonin reuptake inhibitors used in uncontrolled clinical trials for which suppression of SIB and aggression in persons with MR has been found. Examples of these drugs are fluoxetine, trazodone, buspirone, sertraline, and related drugs (see Baumeister et al., 1993, for review). Because none of these studies was methodologically sound, they do not offer unequivocal support for the specificity of the serotonin hypothesis. But they do merit a closer examination in future research (Schroeder & Tessel, 1994). Lewis, Bodfish, Powell, and Golden (1995) recently found in a double-blind comparison with placebo that clomipramine reduced stereotypy, hyperactivity, and irritability among people with severe and profound mental retardation. Serotonin dysregulation also occurs in many psychiatric disorders in persons without mental retardation.

Opioid Peptide Hypotheses of SIB

Two hypotheses by Sandman et al. (1983) were based on the clinical observation that some SIB cases appear to be insensitive to pain or even to seek painful stimuli. Perhaps their pain regulatory system is not working normally. Perhaps stimulation of their pain receptors results in production of excessive amounts of opioid peptides, that is, neurotransmitters involved in pain regulation.

The first hypothesis, the pain hypothesis, proposes that SIB is a symptom of general sensory depression, including hypoalgesia, caused by chronic elevation of endogenous opiates. If a person has elevated pain threshold, the SIB might be a form of self-stimulation to reach it. Opiate blockers, such as naloxone and naltrexone, on the other hand, reduce the pain threshold and thereby lower self-stimulatory SIB rate.

The second hypothesis, the addiction hypothesis, suggests that SIB subjects are addicted to their opiate system and that they engage in SIB to secure pain-induced release of opiates, producing a reinforcing opiate "high." Opiate blockers might attenuate SIB by increasing pain and reducing the subsequent "high."

Sandman (1990–1991) reviewed 16 studies of naloxone and naltrexone involving 45 subjects, most of whom had autism and 28 of whom had SIB. Of the SIB cases, 24 had varied positive responses averaging about 50%. These studies varied widely in methodological quality. Two recent large-scale well-conducted studies are discussed in further detail.

Sandman et al. (1993) performed a 10-week double-blind crossover study of naltrexone among 24 adults with SIB and mental retardation at Fairview Developmental Center. Out of the institutional population of 1,200 there were 129 SIB cases, out of which 24 with the highest SIB rates were chosen. Other psychoactive medications (used in 43% of these cases) were kept constant during the trial. Different orders of weekly treatments of placebo, 0.5, 1.0, and 2.0 mg/kg of naltrexone, were assigned randomly to subjects. Videotaped observations, neurological examinations, ratings of adaptive and maladaptive behavior, and a discrimination learning task were conducted. Only the videotaped observations and the discrimination task yielded significant results. There was a dose response effect of naltrexone on change scores of SIB ranging from 10% to 90% reduction in 18 of 21 cases. The median was 50% at optimal dose. There was also improvement on the discrimination task secondary to reduction of SIB while on naltrexone. Use of change scores did not allow one to see the absolute baseline SIB levels, nor were potential drug–drug interactions between psychoactive medications that subjects were using studied. Nevertheless, this is an impressive study.

An excellent double-blind crossover study of the effects of naltrexone on SIB in eight adults with severe or profound mental retardation was performed by Thompson, Hackenberg, Cerutti, Baker, and Axtell (1994). Five-minute behavioral samples were taken one per hour for 7 hours each day over four two-week phases (baseline, placebo, 50 mg, and 100 mg) in randomly assigned order. Half of the subjects also received .3 mg per day of clonidine along with naltrexone, in order to control for possible confounding due to opiatelike withdrawal symptoms that may accompany naltrexone administration. The results showed no psychotropic effects of clonidine, but naltrexone significantly reduced high-intensity headbanging and self-biting ranging from 23% to 100% in six of eight subjects. There was no improvement in eye-, nose-, or throat poking or face slapping. The largest effects were on hand-to-head hitting and head-to-object hitting. Few physiological side effects of naltrexone were observed except that sleep increased from 5.34 hours to 6.72 hours per night.

Taken together, the studies of naltrexone on SIB show a highly consistent dose effect averaging about a 50% reduction in SIB in 60% to 80% of cases, which is related to intensity and topography. This is the best documented selective neuropharmacological hypothesis to date for some types of SIB.

Isolate-Rearing Model of Destructive Behavior

Kraemer (1992) posited a comprehensive psychobiological attachment theory (PAT) in which disruptions between the infant and its caretaker set the stage in the central nervous system (CNS) for social dysfunction in later life. He summarized 25 years of research at the Harlow laboratories on isolate rearing of infant rhesus monkeys. This research shows that, if an infant monkey is separated from its mother for the first 22 months of life, it develops a variety of dysfunctional behaviors, for example, abnormal motor patterns, hyperphagia, hyperresponsivity to change, stereotyped rocking, self-injurious biting, and head-banging, and aggressive attacks when later confronted with normal monkeys (Kraemer & Clarke, 1990). These behaviors have been related to the decoupling in the brain of the tuning processes effected by the norepinephrine (NE) system, of the switching processes by the dopamine (DA) system, and the gatekeeping or enabling functions effected by the serotonin (5HT) system (Kraemer, Ebert, Schmidt, & McKinney, 1989). Social isolation is thought to produce cytoarchitectural changes in these brain biogenic amine systems that result in their dysregulation, such that the animal is not prepared to respond appropriately to normal social stimuli, but performs inappropriate behaviors instead.

PAT theory is a very heuristic model that attempts to integrate a wide variety of disparate findings from the animal literature and from human infant attachment theories by Bowlby (1969) and Ainsworth, Blehar, Waters, and Wall (1978). It also has many critics, as was evident from the open peer commentary following Kraemer's article. Probably the most controversial idea is that attachment systems alter neurobiological structures in the brain. This idea is supported only modestly by direct evidence. Most of it is indirect evidence inferred from assays of neurotransmitters, their precursors, and their metabolites in cerebrospinal fluid of live monkeys (Mason, 1992). Nevertheless, Kraemer's approach begins to reflect the complexity of the effects of environmental and biological interactions on the development of stereotypy, self-injury, and aggression, and points to future directions for research.

Neural Oscillator Model of Stereotyped Behavior, SIB, and Aggression

Lewis and Baumeister (1982), in their review of animal and human models of stereotypy, put forth a cohesive view first posited for infants by Wolff (1967) that stereotyped movements are the behavioral expression of a central motor program controlled by neural pattern generators or oscillators. This hypothesis is an outgrowth of extensive biological research (Delcomyn, 1980) showing that the CNS does not need sensory feedback to generate sequenced rhythmic movements. Such a theory fits well some other self-regulatory theories of stereotypy. For an excellent book on these theories, see Sprague and Newell (1996).

Support for the view comes from: the regularity of number of bouts, bout length, and periodicity of much stereotyped bodyrocking, head weaving, and so on; presence of ultradian rhythms in people who perform stereotypies; the apparent lack of discrete environmental stimulus control over stereotypy; and the fact that, once triggered, stereotyped action patterns appear to run to completion independent of environmental stimulus control. This holds not only for moment-to-moment fluctuations (Lewis et al., 1984) but also for longer periods of time (Lewis, MacLean, Johnson, & Baumeister, 1981). In fact, Lewis, Silva, and Gray-Silva (1995) extended this analysis to stereotypy SIB, and aggression occurring over three- and five-month cycles in large institutional populations. Lewis interpreted these rhythmic cycles as representing a shift from environmental stimulus control to internal self-regulation primarily under CNS control.

The presence of cyclicity in the occurrence of aberrant behaviors is certainly noteworthy and important to caregivers. The theoretical explanations for cyclicity and stereotyped behavior are still a matter of much speculation (Sprague & Newell, 1996). There have been no direct observations of neural pattern generators in the CNS. They must be inferred indirectly from behavioral or neurophysiological methods. This will be a growing area for research in the future.

Genetic and Perinatal Risk Factors and Rodent Models of Stress-Induced Destructive Behavior

Tessel and colleagues (Loupe, Schroeder, & Tessel, 1995; Stodgell, Schroeder, Hyland, & Tessel, 1994; Tessel, Schroeder, Loupe, & Stodgell, 1995) have combined the effects of isolate rearing with three rodent models for stress-induced destructive behavior. They are a genetic model of aggression using the Spontaneously Hypertensive Rat, a model of stereotyped behavior using methylazoxymethanol (MAM) injected prenatally to induce microcephaly in rat offspring, and a model of SIB using the Breese–Baumeister neonatal dopamine depletion model in rats.

Tessel and colleagues found that, under conditions when rats were administered periodic unavoidable shock, members of the SHR group initially demonstrated aggressive responses by biting the bars of the chamber; soon after, within the same session, SHR animals displayed marked increases in freezing behavior. MAM animals under the same conditions became hyperactive and engaged in stereotypic rearing behavior. No self-injurious behavior was observed in any group during shock sessions. However, when 6-OHDA animals who had experienced shock were exposed to apomorphine, self-injurious biting did occur. Periodic food delivery to food-deprived animals induced nonrearing stereotypies among SHR animals, and rearing and hyperactivity among both SHR and MAM animals. Together these data suggest that there are specific aberrant behavior patterns associated with the different models. Now a question arises: Will drug or other treatments serve to reduce the aberrant behavior associated with the various models?

Another set of fascinating data derives from observations related to fixed ratio (FR) discrimination training. Initially, subjects were taught to discriminate between FR-1 and FR-16 schedules. This procedure involved having subjects respond to a center lever and then, when that lever was retracted and one of two side levers was presented, the subjects responded to the left lever if the center lever had one ratio requirement and to the right lever if the center lever had another ratio requirement. When the discrimination started with the easy FR-1 versus FR-16 discrimination and then gradually progressed to FR-8 versus FR-16, all groups learned the discriminations and their learning curves were essentially identical. However, when the discrimination was reversed, MAM rats reversed more slowly than did the subjects of the other three groups. Moreover, when the fixed ratio discrimination started with the FR-8 versus FR-16 discrimination, MAM and SHR rats learned the discrimination at a significantly slower rate than did controls.

Analysis of brain structures and chemicals, however, yielded the most exciting findings. The 6-OHDA animals who had been given fixed ratio training showed a reversal of cerebral and striatal catecholamine depletion. Similarly, MAM animals that had been given FR discrimination training showed a partial reversal of hippocampal hypoplasia (reversal of MAM-induced hippocampal weight and protein concentration reduction). These observations are the first to suggest the possibility that susceptibility to chronic aberrant behavior and the presence of cognitive deficits may not only be amenable to prevention, they may also be amenable to reversal. Although changes in behavior must be associated with changes in the brain, no one has previously shown such specific and massive changes related to training. Moreover, the fact that changes were in the direction of normality for animals with specific lesions was totally unexpected.

These changes raise a number of important questions. First, are the changes related to a specific kind of training involving progressive increase in problem difficulty, or would training on a simple repetitive task result in the brain changes? Second are such changes restricted to rats or do they occur in other animals including humans? Are these changes in brain structure and chemistry accompanied by more generalized changes in behavior? For example, do MAM animals who have been through fixed ratio discrimination training engage in less stereotyped rearing, or do 6-OHDA animals no longer engage in self-biting when administered apomorphine and electric shock? Is it possible that such training will have a more generalized effect?

The combined approach of isolate rearing in different risk models may help Tessel and colleagues to increase the specificity of their hypotheses related to animal models of the development of aberrant behavior. This promises to be a fruitful line of research for the future.

TRENDS IN THE TREATMENT OF SEVERE BEHAVIOR PROBLEMS IN MR AND DD

Research on assessment technology and etiological theories over the past 15 years has greatly changed treatment approaches to severe behavior problems in MR and DD. The 1980s witnessed the advent of politics, ideology, and advocacy into research in this field. The debate crystallized over the use of restrictive punishment, so-called "aversive procedures," for treatment. An excellent edited volume summarizing this debate is Repp and

Singh (1990). The debate also led to a consensus Development Conference on Destructive Behavior held at the National Institutes of Health in 1989 and published in 1991 (NICHD, 1991). Three dominant trends in treatment of behavior problems were noted: behavior-enhancing interventions, behavior-reducing interventions, and pharmacological interventions.

Regardless of one's view of the aversive controversy, it clearly accelerated the trend away from restrictive interventions aimed at controlling only the consequences of aberrant behaviors and toward an emphasis on their functional antecedents and giving the person choices of alternative behaviors with which to replace them. Research on functional analysis has dominated behavioral research on behavior problems since 1982, as we noted in an earlier section, but what the future holds is uncertain. Hopefully, an integration of this new knowledge into a new technology integrating antecedent-based and consequence-based treatments will occur. We only summarize the highlights of more than 1,000 studies and 100 reviews performed in this area over the last 15 years. The best, most exhaustive reviews are still the NICHD consensus conference background papers by Carr, Taylor, Carlson, and Robinson (1991), Cataldo (1991), and Thompson, Hackenberg, and Schaal (1991).

Positive Behavior Interventions

There are basically two types of positive behavioral interventions (Carr et al., 1991): reinforcement-based treatments and stimulus-based treatments. Both are aimed at replacing the problem behavior with a more appropriate behavior.

Reinforcement-based treatments try to accomplish this replacement by using: differential reinforcement of other behaviors (DRO); differential reinforcement of incompatible behavior (DRI), such as communication; and acquisition of alternative skills that reduce the occasion for behavior problems. Examples of the latter would be teaching compliance, cooperativeness, self-monitoring, self-reinforcement, functional independence skill, and so on.

In most cases the behavioral processes that explain how reinforcement-based treatments replace problem behaviors or how these behaviors can be maintained and generalize to new situations have not been well specified in the literature. An analysis of this problem by Saunders and Spradlin (1991) suggested a constructional approach in which enablement of the nonaberrant repertoire is the central component. Enablement means being provided with a chance to do something for oneself. Such skills are often present in people with severe behavior problems, but opportunities and adaptations to use them may be unavailable. By focusing on existing competent performances, training on specific deficits would be more successful. Skills to be taught should have a reasonable prognosis for acquisition, given the developmental level of the client. The focus should be on assisting the person to complete the task, so that it produces its intended function without interruption or delay, because interruptions and failure are strong stimuli for evoking problem behaviors. This approach emphasizes fluid and competent performance of existing skills to maximize reinforcement. Training new skills would occur in very small steps only after a careful functional analysis. Saunder's and Spradlin's definition of *competence* is functional performances initiated independently and performed fluently, with outside assistance sufficient only to maintain fluency, so as to encourage personal control and environmental mastery. They called their approach *supported routines*. The analogy to the supported employment model (Rusch, 1990) is obvious. Saunders applied this approach to large-scale modification of whole residential populations, and noted large decreases in stereotyped behavior and some SIB and aggression lasting over a 5-year period.

Stimulus-based treatments focus on making functional stimuli for appropriate behavior more probable or on changing the function of stimuli controlling the onset of SIB, or on removing a stimulus that sets the occasion for SIB. A modest amount of research has isolated five stimulus-based intervention strategies: introduce stimuli that control low rates rather than high rates of SIB, modify stimuli that control high rates of SIB, embed stimuli that control high rates of SIB among those that control low rates of SIB, modify educational curricula associated with SIB (e.g., reduce boring routines), and improve setting events for SIB (e.g., teach relaxation before a dental examination for a person with SIB; Carr et al., 1991).

Almost all of these stimulus-based treatments reduce behavior problems, but that reduction rarely is complete and durable or appropriately generalized beyond the treatment setting, especially if its functions are not determined in the natural setting. It is possible that such treatment failures occur because there had not been a complete analysis of all of the events that systematically evoked the aberrant behavior, but only a subset that happened to occur during the treatment program, which often may not be the main evokers outside of the treatment setting. Thus, a fine-grained conditional probability analysis of how the functional behavior repertoire is hierarchically organized might be needed in such cases (Schroeder & MacLean, 1987). This is a promising direction for future research on stimulus-based treatments for behavior problems.

Behavior-Reducing Interventions

The literature on these types of behavioral interventions is considerably larger (tenfold) than the literature on positive behavioral interventions. Hopefully, with the current emphasis on development of positive interventions, that imbalance will change. The techniques most frequently used are punishment, avoidance conditioning, overcorrection, contingent restraint, extinction, time out, visual and facial screening, and satiation (see Cataldo, 1991, for a review). All of them follow a punishment paradigm.

Punishment consists of delivering an intense stimulus immediately contingent on occurrence of behavior problems to suppress it. The stimulus need not be aversive, but its presence must result in response suppression. If an aversive stimulus, when presented, results in an increase in the target response, it is, by definition, not a punisher. This point is often confused in the literature, where aversive stimulation and punishment are considered synonymous. No stimulation is inherently aversive or punishing but is so only in relation to its consequences on behavior.

The suppressive effect of immediate contingent punishment is usually rapid and dramatic. When it occurs, it tends to be highly discriminated by the subject, and therefore generalization across settings is difficult to achieve. In practice, punishment often fails to work. If it does work, it often loses its effectiveness. There have been reports of long-term suppression if there is training of parents and teachers in the generalized setting. However, it is unlikely that behavior problems would be eliminated with punishment unless there were naturally reinforced alternative replacement behaviors readily available in the client's environment and continued surveillance of the problem behavior.

There has been a great deal of concern about negative side effects of punishment procedures (e.g., conditioned emotional responses, elicited aggression, avoidance of the punisher, etc.). Most of these side effects can be avoided with proper use of punishment procedures. In addition there are often many positive side effects observed (Cataldo, 1991). The essential problem with punishment is that it does not teach desirable or new behavior. It is not a habilitative procedure per se, but only an adjunct to habilitative treatment.

Pharmacotherapy for Severe Behavior Problems in MR and DD

As we noted in an earlier section, the psychopharmacology of developmental disabilities is an area that has come of age in the last 15 years. There are several textbooks specifically on this topic, for example, Aman and Singh (1990), Gadow and Poling (1987), Gualtieri (1991), and Ratey (1991). There also now exist several practitioners' guides, (e.g., Poling, Gadow, & Cleary, 1991; Werry & Aman, 1993), as well as several excellent reviews, the most thorough and exhaustive of which are Baumeister et al. (1993); Lewis, Schroeder, Aman, Gadow, and Thompson (in press), and Thompson et al. (1991). From these three reviews and our own reading of the literature, we constructed a summary table (Table 16.1) showing drugs for which there is some presumptive evidence (i.e., at least two well-conducted studies) that the drug had a significant effect on behavior problems.

It is true that no study in this area is without flaws. These flaws have been amply pointed out in previous reviews, especially Baumeister et al. (1993), and there is not space to treat each of them here. Studies using potentially lethal drugs in this high-risk group of people who have limited ability to consent are extraordinarily difficult to conduct and require

TABLE 16.1
Drugs for Which There Are at Least Two Well-Conducted Studies Showing Significant Positive or No Effects on Behavior Problems in MR/DD

Drug or Drug Class	*SIB*	*Aggression*	*Stereotypy*	*Hyperactivity*
Antipsychotics (neuroleptics)				
Phenothiazines	Yes	Yes	Yes	Yes
Butyrophenones	Yes	Yes	Yes	Yes
Antidepressants				
Heterocyclic antidepressants	Yes	Yes	Yes	Yes
Monoamine oxidase inhibitors	?	?	?	?
Antimanics				
Lithium	Yes	Yes	Yes	Yes
Stimulants				
Amphetamines	?	?	No	Yes
Methylphenidate	?	?	No	Yes
Anxiolytics				
Benzodiazepinies	Yes	Yes	?	?
Antihistimines	?	?	?	?
Anticholinergics	?	?	?	?
Narcotic Analgesics				
Opioid peptides	Yes	Yes	No	Yes
Antiepileptics (psychotropic)				
Carbemazepine	?	Yes	?	Yes
Valproic acid	?	?	?	?
Sedative Hypnotics	No	No	No	No
Miscellaneous				
Clonidine	?	Yes	?	?
5-hydroxytryptophan	No	?	?	?
Fenfluramine	?	?	No	Yes
β-adrenergic blockers	Yes	Yes	?	?

great caution. In most cases, trade-offs between experimental rigor and the clinical welfare of the subject must be made. Nevertheless, our technology is improving, and, when it does, the results become clearer, as can be seen in the case of naltrexone for SIB discussed previously.

There is great hope in the future for a rational pharmacotherapy for people with MR and DD and behavioral or psychiatric problems. There is a distinct trend away from the trial-and-error methods of the past (Gualtieri, 1991). But, in order for this trend to succeed, several challenges will have to be met: (a) Selectivity of drug response must be improved. Few drugs as yet can be shown to improve specific problem behaviors while not worsening learning or memory (Williams & Saunders, in press) with (b) minimal side effects at a given (c) dose in a given (d) set of circumstances. In order to succeed at this task, the (e) assessment technology and (f) psychiatric diagnoses must improve so that they are noninvasive and (g) ecologically valid. As knowledge accumulates about (h) drug–drug interactions and (i) drug–behavior interactions, it will be possible to better predict (j) who will be a drug responder. At that point (k) treatment acceptability on part of the consumers will increase. It is true that views of the use of psychotropic medication among people with MR and DD vary from positive (Wolfensberger & Menolescino, 1970) on the one hand to very negative (Wolfensberger, 1994) on the other. Rational pharmacotherapy lies somewhere between these extremes. Finally (l) basic research on neurobiological and behavioral models of the causes of severe behavior problems in MR and DD should improve our prediction of a selective drug response, as it has for people with depression and schizophrenia. Meeting these challenges is a tall order for future researchers.

Summary and Conclusions

Over the past 15 years there has been an incredible growth in basic and applied research on severe behavior problems in MR and DD in nearly every area: development of functional and structural taxonomies (Repp & Dietz, 1990; Rojahn, 1994; Van Houten & Axelrod, 1993); functional psychometric and clinical diagnostic assessment procedures (Lewis et al., in press; Reichle & Wacker, 1993); epidemiology (Borthwick-Duffy, 1994; Bruininks et al., 1994; Rojahn, 1994); etiological theories, both behavioral and biological, as discussed in this chapter; analysis of ecological setting factors (O'Neill, Horner, Albin, Storey, & Sprague, 1990); and treatment interventions (NICHD, 1991), both behavioral and pharmacological.

It is gratifying to note that all of these trends that were called for and discussed in our 1979 chapter in this handbook have reached the stage where we can design more effective settings and treatments for people with severe behavior problems (Horner, O'Neill, & Flannery, 1993). Nevertheless, behavior problems still remain the major barrier to school inclusion (U.S. Department of Education, 1992) and community inclusion (Bruininks et al., 1994). Much more research remains to be done. We would like to suggest some directions for the next 15 years that would promote a synthesis of the many disparate findings of the past 15 years.

An Integrative Developmental Biological and Behavioral Theory

It is a truism that severe behavioral problems in MR and DD are multiply caused and multiply affected (Schroeder et al., 1980). Although in 1979 there was a paucity of viable hypotheses supported by the available research, today there is a flood of new hypotheses to consider. All of them appear to be supportable to some extent in explaining the behavior of subsets of the population under study. Few of them attempt a broader integrated developmental approach. Only Guess and Carr's model (1991) appears to offer such a possibility. In the future, effort needs to be spent generating disjunctive tests that result in sorting our relevant hypotheses and discarding irrelevant ones. For example, behavioral studies must take into account drug effects and biological risk factors in their research; and, by the same token, psychopharmacological studies must do appropriate behavioral functional assessments (Schaal & Hackenberg, 1994). All research in this area must become more interdisciplinary if fragmentation is to be prevented in our future research and in our clinical applications. Any new theory should be judged not only for its heuristic value, but also for its ability to account for a broader array of findings.

An Improved Methodology

Considerable progress has been made over the past 15 years in behavioral and biological methodologies. In the future, studies need to be judged in a manner more critically based on reliability and validity of their methods. Many conflicting findings in the current literature appear to be the result of using faulty methods and measurement instruments.

Functional Analysis. Functional analysis techniques have been a major advance in the past 15 years. There still remain a large number of people (cf. 40%) whose behavior problems have not yielded to functional analysis. Perhaps for these people a more in-depth analysis of the stimulus class or classes that combine to evoke their aberrant behavior is needed. It is likely that a conditional probability analysis and a variety of methods will be required (Lerman & Iwata, 1993; Patterson, 1982). Perhaps there are some response classes that are spontaneous or state-dependent and relatively free of specific evocative control. Here, a functional diagnosis based on biological hypotheses (Van Praag et al., 1990) may be helpful.

Structural Analysis. Theorists differ greatly in how they view the developmental sequence of stereotyped behavior, SIB, aggression, and hyperactivity. At the neurobiological level the systems underlying them appear to overlap considerably, but their behavioral manifestations vary greatly. Pharmacotherapeutic interventions tend to be rather nonselective, whereas behavioral interventions tend to be highly specific. Often, behavioral interventions fail to generalize and maintain over time. Future research must be done to meld these two assessment strategies and resultant intervention strategies. The natural methodologies to do this are drug–behavior interaction studies. We reviewed this literature in 1983 (Schroeder, Lewis, & Lipton, 1983). Very little work of this type has been done since then on the MR population (Lewis et al., in press). These studies would likely have a higher yield in empirical findings than ever before. Many model studies are already available in the literature on combined pharmacological and behavioral interventions on hyperactivity.

Improved Designs That Are Also Clinically Valid. In our 1979 chapter, we proposed three criteria to judge the effectiveness of behavioral interventions: degree and rapidity of suppression, durability of suppression, and covariation (i.e., generalization of positive and negative side effects). These criteria have held up well over the years but, in addition, treatment acceptability and social validity have gained much more importance. Treatments unacceptable to consumers will not likely be used. The research on positive behavioral supports for people in the community with behavior problems has developed a variety of techniques and treatment packages for designing effective settings that make problem behaviors irrelevant, ineffective, and inefficient (Horner et al., 1993). This ecobehavioral technology is rendering behavioral research more clinically valid and acceptable to parents and consumers (Schroeder, 1990).

Research designs for pharmacotherapy have not advanced much since the classic article by Sprague and Werry (1971). Clinical validity has only been part of drug study designs as a follow up to an acute-dose study demonstrating an effect. The basic designs have been: Randomized group parallel dose designs, within-subjects crossover designs with randomized or counterbalanced order of placebo and several doses of a drug, and single-subject time-series design. The former two are not clinically valid; the latter lacks external validity and is often uncontrolled due to confounding of period and order effects resulting from a drug's main effect and its side effects.

Sheiner, Beal, and Sambol (1989) made an extensive analysis of these designs and made a strong argument for dose escalation designs. There are many variations of this design, but they all start with baseline, placebo, and raising a dose by a fixed amount at a fixed interval until a clinical endpoint is reached. Each subject stops at his or her clinical endpoint within the dose range studied. No dose reversals are permitted. Adverse responders are dropped. These procedures provide relatively unbiased data for least-squares or weighted least-squares group analysis. Sheiner et al. (1989) gave an analysis of the various problems in different dose ranging study designs, as shown in Table 16.2.

TABLE 16.2
Potential Problems for Various Dose-Ranging Study Designs

Problem	*Problem No.*	*Parallel-Dose Design*	*Crossover Design*	*Dose-Escalation Design*
Ethical	1	++	+++	0
Problems in study execution				
Number of patients (cost)	2	*N*	*N/M*	*N/M*
Time (cost)	3	1 unit	*M* units	*M* units
Need for many centers	4	++	+	+
Complexity of protocol	5	0	+	+/+++
Problems in study analysis				
Complexity	6	0	+	+
Reliance on modeling assumptions	7	0	+	+++
Carryover effects	8	0	++	+
Period effects	9	0	++	++
Center effects	10	++	+	+
Few doses examined	11	++	++	0
Biased parameter estimates	12	+++	0	+
Poor/no estimate of variability	13	+++	+	+
Problems in extrapolation				
Not representative of individual response	14	+++	0	0
Not representative of clinical practice	15	+	+++	0
Not representative of patient group	16	+	+++	0

Key: + = Mild ++ = Moderate +++ = Severe N = Number of subjects M = Number of units, (e.g., doses, time, etc.)

Note. From Sheiner, Beal, & Sambol (1989). Study designs for dose-ranging. *Clinical Pharmacology and Therpeutics, 46*, 63–77.

The dose escalation designs are the most clinically valid, the most like normal clinical practice, and they have the fewest ethical problems. These and other drug–behavior intervention designs need to be considered in future studies of behavior problems in MR and DD. Some new designs may be required to meet emerging research needs.

In conclusion, in the past 15 years we have witnessed substantial increases in knowledge and sophistication concerning behavior problems among people with mental retardation. There have been many advances in technology for assessment of the antecedents and probable causes of many types of behavior problems. Even more hopeful is the tendency toward an integration of behavioral and biological analyses of their potential causes, and toward interventions that last. This field is poised for some major breakthroughs in the next 15 years.

ACKNOWLEDGMENTS

We wish to acknowledge NICHD grants #HD 02528 and HD 26927 as well as MCH grant #MCJ 944 and ADD grant #07DD0365 for financial assistance during the writing of this chapter.

REFERENCES

Achenbach, T. M., & Edelbrock, C. S. (1981). Behavioral problems and competencies reported by parents of normal and disturbed children aged four through sixteen. *Monographs of the Society for Research in Child Development, 46*(1, Serial No. 188).

Ainsworth, M. D. S., Blehar, M. C., Waters, E., & Wall, S. (1978). *Patterns of attachment: A psychological study of the strange situation.* Hillsdale, NJ: Lawrence Erlbaum Associates.

Aman, M. G. (1991). *Assessing psychopathology and behavior problems in persons with mental retardation: A review of available instruments.* Rockville, MD: U.S. Department of Health and Human Services.

Aman, M. G. (1993). Efficacy of psychotropic drugs for reducing self-injurious behavior in developmental disabilities. *Annals of Clinical Psychiatry, 5,* 177–188.

Aman, M. G., & Singh, N. N. (1986). *Aberrant Behavior Checklist manual.* East Aurora, NY: Slosson.

Aman, M. G., & Singh, N. N. (Eds.). (1990). *Psychopharmacology of the developmental disabilities.* New York: Springer-Verlag.

American Psychiatric Association. (1980). *Diagnostic and statistical manual of mental disorders.* Washington, DC: American Psychiatric Press.

American Psychiatric Association (1994). *Diagnostic and statistical manual of mental disorders* (4th ed.). Washington, DC: American Psychiatric Press.

Bates, P., & Wehman, P. (1977). Behavior management with the mentally retarded: An empirical analysis of the research. *Mental Retardation, 15,* 9–12.

Baumeister, A. A., Frye, G., & Schroeder, S. R. (1984). Neurochemical correlates of self-injurious behavior. In J. A. Mulick & B. L. Mallory (Eds.), *Transitions of mental retardation: Advocacy, technology and science* (pp. 207–228). Washington, DC: American Association on Mental Deficiency.

Baumeister, A. A., Todd, M. E., & Sevin, J. A. (1993). Efficacy and specificity of pharmacological therapies for behavioral disorders of persons with mental retardation. *Clinical Neuropharmacology, 16,* 271–294.

Benavidez, D. A., & Matson, J. L. (1993). Assessment of depression in mentally retarded persons. *Research in Developmental Disabilities, 14,* 179–188.

Bijou, S. (1966). A functional analysis of retarded development. In N. R. Ellis (Ed.), *International review of research in mental retardation* (Vol. 1, pp. 1–18). New York: Academic.

Borthwick-Duffy, S. A. (1994). Epidemiology and ontogeny of destructive behavior. In T. Thompson & D. Gray (Eds.), *Destructive behavior in developmental disabilities* (pp. 13–23). Thousand Oaks, CA: Sage.

Bowlby, J. (1969). *Attachment and loss: Separation, anxiety, and anger.* New York: Basic Books.

Breese, G. R., Baumeister, A. A., McCowan, T. J., Emerick, S., Frye, G. D., Crotty, K., & Mueller, R. A. (1984a). Behavioral differences between neonatal- and adult-6– hydroxydopamine-treated rats to dopamine agonists: Relevance to neurological symptoms in clinical syndromes with reduced brain dopamine. *Journal of Pharmacology and Experimental Therapeutics, 231*, 343–354.

Breese, G. R., Baumeister, A. A., McCowan, T. J., Emerick, S., Frye, C. D., & Mueller, R. A. (1984b). Neonatal-6–hydroxydopamine treatment: Model of susceptibility for self-mutilation in the Lesch-Nyhan syndrome. *Pharmacology Biochemistry and Behavior, 21*, 459–461.

Breese, G. R., & Traylor, T. D. (1970). Effects of 6–hydroxydopamine on brain norepinephrine and dopamine: Evidence of selective degeneration of catecholamine neurons. *Journal of Pharmacology and Experimental Therapeutics, 174*, 413–420.

Bruininks, R. H., Olson, K. M., Larson, S. A., & Lakin, C. (1994). Challenging behaviors among persons with mental retardation in residential settings: Implications for policy, research, and practice. In T. Thompson & D. Gray (Eds.), *Destructive behavior in developmental disabilities* (pp. 24–48). Thousand Oaks, CA: Sage.

Carr, E. G., & Durand, V. M. (1985). Reducing behavior problems through functional communication training. *Journal of Applied Behavior Analysis, 18*, 111–126.

Carr, E. G., Levin, L., McConnachie, G., Carlson, J. I., Kemp, D. C., & Smith, C. E. (1994). *Communication-based intervention for problem behavior: A user's guide for producing positive change.* Baltimore, MD: Brookes.

Carr, E. G., Taylor, J. C., Carlson, J. I., & Robinson, S. (1991, July). *Reinforcement and stimulus-based treatments for severe behavior problems in developmental disabilities* (NIH Publication No. 91-2410). Paper presented at the Consensus Development Conference on Destructive Behavior, National Institutes of Health, Bethesda, MD.

Cataldo, M. F. (1991, July). *Effects of punishment and other behavior reducing procedures on the destructive behaviors of persons with developmental disabilities* (NIH Publication No. 91-2410). Paper presented at the Consensus Development Conference on Destructive Behavior, National Institutes of Health, Bethesda, MD

Coulter, D. A. (1990). Frontal lobe seizures: No evidence of self-injury. *American Journal on Mental Retardation, 96*, 81– 84.

Criswell, H. E., Mueller, R. A., & Breese, G. R. (1989). Clozapine antagonism of D-1 and D-2 dopamine receptor-mediated behaviors. *European Journal of Pharmacology, 159*, 141–147.

Delcomyn, F. (1980). Neural basis of rhythmic behavior in animals. *Science, 210*, 492–498.

Eaton, L., & Menolascino, F. (1982). Psychiatric disorders in the mentally retarded: Types, problems, and challenges. *American Journal of Psychiatry, 139*, 218–230.

Eyman, R. K., Borthwick, S. A., & Miller, C. (1981). Trends in maladaptive behavior of mentally retarded persons placed in community and institutional settings. *American Journal of Mental Deficiency, 85*, 473–477.

Fovel, J. T., Lash, P. S., Barron, D. A., Jr., & Roberts, M. S. (1989). A survey of self-restraint, self-injury, and other maladaptive behaviors in an institutionalized retarded population. *Research in Developmental Disabilities, 10*, 377– 382.

Gadow, K., & Poling, A. (1987). *Pharmacotherapy and mental retardation.* Boston: Little, Brown.

Gedye, A. (1989). Extreme self-injury attributed to frontal lobe seizures. *American Journal on Mental Retardation, 94*, 20–26.

Griffin, J. C., Williams, D. E., Stark, M. T., Altmeyer, B. K., & Mason, M. (1986). Self-injurious behavior: A state-wide prevalence survey of the extent and circumstances. *Applied Research in Mental Retardation, 7*, 105–116.

Gualtieri, C. T. (1991). *Neuropsychiatry and behavioral pharmacology.* New York: Springer-Verlag.

Gualtieri, C. T., & Schroeder, S. R. (1989). Pharmacotherapy of self-injurious behavior: Preliminary tests of the D-1 hypothesis. *Psychopharmacology Bulletin, 25*, 364–371.

Guess, D., & Carr, E. (1991). Emergence and maintenance of stereotypy and self-injury. *American Journal on Mental Retardation, 96*, 299–320.

Guess, D., Roberts, S., Siegel-Causey, E., Ault, M., Guy, B., & Thompson, B. (1993). Analysis of behavior state conditions and associated environmental variables among students with profound handicaps. *American Journal on Mental Retardation, 97*, 634–653.

Guess, D., & Sailor, W. (1993). Chaos theory and the study of human behavior: Implications for special education and developmental disabilities. *The Journal of Special Education, 27*, 16–34.

Gunter, P. L. (1984). Self-injurious behaviour: Characteristics, etiology, and treatment. *The Exceptional Child, 31*, 91–98.

Hammock, R. G., Schroeder, S. R., & Levine, W. R. (1995). The effect of clozapine for self-injurious behavior. *Journal of Autism and Developmental Disorders, 25*, 611–626.

Harris, J. C. (1992). Neurobiological factors in self-injurious behavior. In J. Luiselli, J. L. Matson, & N. Singh (Eds.), *Self injurious behavior: Analysis, assessment, and treatment* (pp. 59–92). New York: Springer-Verlag.

Hill, B. K., & Bruininks, R. H. (1984). Maladaptive behavior of mentally retarded individuals in residential facilities. *American Journal of Mental Deficiency, 88*, 380–387.

Horner, R. H. (1994). Functional assessment: Contributions and future directions. *Journal of Applied Behavior Analysis, 27*, 401–404.

Horner, R. H., O'Neill, R. E., & Flannery, K. B. (1993). Building effective behavior support plans from functional assessment information. In M. E. Snell (Ed.), *Systematic instruction of persons with severe handicaps* (4th ed., pp. 184–214). Columbus, OH: Merrill.

Iwata, B. A., Dorsey, M. F., Slifer, K. J., Bauman, K. E., & Richman, G. S. (1982). Toward a functional analysis of self-injury. *Analysis and Intervention in Developmental Disabilities, 2*, 3–20.

JABA. (1994). Special Issue on functional analysis approaches to behavioral assessment and treatment. *Journal of Applied Behavior Analysis, 27*, 196–418.

Jacobson, J. W. (1990). Assessing the prevalence of psychiatric disorders in a developmentally disabled population. In E. Dibble & D. B. Gray (Eds.), *Assessment of behavior problems with persons with mental retardation living in the community* (pp. 19–70). Rockville, MD: Department of Health and Human Services, National Institutes of Health, Public Health Service, Alcohol, Drug Abuse, and Mental Health Administration.

King, B. H. (1993). Self-injury by people with mental retardation: A compulsive behavior hypothesis. *American Journal on Mental Retardation, 98*, 93–112.

Kraemer, G. W. (1992). A psychobiological theory of attachment. *Behavioral and Brain Sciences, 15*, 493–541.

Kraemer, G. W., & Clarke, H. S. (1990). The behavioral neurobiology of self-injurious behavior in rhesus monkeys. *Progress in Neuropsychopharmacology and Biological Psychiatry, 14*, 141–168.

Kraemer, G. W., Ebert, M. H., Schmidt, D. E., & McKinney, W. T. (1989). A longitudinal study of the effect of different social rearing conditions on cerebrospinal fluid norepinephrine and biogenic amine metabolites in rhesus monkeys. *Neuropsychopharmacology, 2*, 175–189.

Lambert, N., Windmiller, M., Tharinger, D., & Cole, L. (1981). *AAMD Adaptive Behavior Scale—School edition, administration and instructional planning manual.* Austin, TX: Pro-Ed.

Lerman, D. C., & Iwata, B. A. (1993). Descriptive analyses of variables maintaining self-injurious behavior. *Journal of Applied Behavior Analysis, 26*, 293–319.

Lewis, M. H., & Baumeister, A. A. (1982). Stereotyped mannerisms in mentally retarded persons: Animal models and theoretical analyses. In N. R. Ellis (Ed.), *International review of research in mental retardation* (Vol. 12, pp. 123–161). New York: Academic Press.

Lewis, M. H., Bodfish, J. W., Powell, S. B., & Golden, R. N. (1995). Clomipramine treatment for stereotypy and related repetitive movement disorders in mental retardation: A double-blind comparison with placebo. *American Journal on Mental Retardation, 100*, 299–312.

Lewis, M. H., MacLean, W. E., Jr., Bryson-Brockmann, W., Arendt, R., Beck, B., Fidler, P. S., & Baumeister, A. A. (1984). Time-series analysis of stereotyped movements: Relationship of body rocking to cardiac activity. *American Journal on Mental Retardation, 89*, 287–294.

Lewis, M. H., MacLean, W. E., Jr., Johnson, W. L., & Baumeister, A. A. (1981). Ultradian rhythms in stereotyped and self-injurious behavior. *American Journal of Mental Deficiency, 85*, 601–610.

Lewis, M. H., Schroeder, S., Aman, M., Gadow, K., & Thompson, T. (in press). Psychopharmacology. In J. W. Jacobson & J. A. Mulick (Eds.), *Manual of diagnosis and professional practice in mental retardation*. APA Books.

Lewis, M. H., Silva, J. R., & Gray-Silva, S. (1995). Cyclicity of aggression and self-injurious behavior in individuals with mental retardation. *American Journal on Mental Retardation, 99*, 436–444.

Lipman, R. S. (1970). The use of psychopharmacological agents in residential facilities for the retarded. In F. Menolascino (Ed.), *Psychiatric approached to mental retardation* (pp. 387–398). New York: Basic Books.

Lloyd, K. C., Hornykiewicz, O., Davidson, L., Shannak, K., Farley, I., Goldstein, M., Shibuya, M., Kelley, W., & Fox, I. H. (1981). Biochemical evidence of dysfunction of brain neurotransmitters in the Lesch–Nyhan Syndrome. *The New England Journal of Medicine, 305*, 1106–1111.

Loupe, P., Schroeder, S. R., & Tessel, R. E. (1995). FR discrimination training effects in SHR and microcephalic rats. *Pharmacology, Biochemistry, and Behavior, 51*, 869–876.

Lovaas, O. I., & Smith, T. (1991). There is more to operant theory and practice: Comment on Guess and Carr. *American Journal on Mental Retardation, 96*, 324–326.

Luckasson, R., Coulter, D. L., Polloway, E. A., Reiss, S., Schalock, R. L., Snell, M. E., Spitalnik, D. M., & Stark, J. A. (1992). *Mental retardation: Definition, classification, and systems of supports*. Washington, DC: American Association on Mental Retardation.

Mace, F. C. (1994). The significance and future of functional analysis methodologies. *Journal of Applied Behavior Analysis, 27*, 385–392.

Macmann, G. M., & Barnett, D. W. (1993). Reliability of psychiatric and psychological diagnoses of mental retardation severity: Judgments under naturally occurring conditions. *American Journal on Mental Retardation, 97*, 559–567.

Maisto, C. R., Baumeister, A. A., & Maisto, A. A. (1978). An analysis of variables related to self-injurious behavior among institutionalized retarded persons. *Journal of Mental Deficiency Research, 22*, 27–36.

Mason, W. A. (1992). Does function imply structure? *Behavioral and Brain Sciences, 15*, 519–520.

Matson, J. L. (1986). Self-injury and its relationship to diagnostic schemes in psychopathology. *Applied Research in Mental Retardation, 7*, 223–228.

Matson, J. L. (1988). *The PIMRA Manual*. Orland Park, IL: International Diagnostic Systems, Inc.

Menolascino, F. J. (1970). *Psychiatric approaches to mental retardation*. New York: Basic Books.

Menolascino, F. J., Wilson, J., Golden, C. J., & Ruedrich, S. L. (1986). Medication and treatment of schizophrenia in persons with mental retardation. *Mental Retardation, 24*, 277–284.

Mizuno, T. L., & Yugari, Y. (1974). Self-mutilation in the Lesch–Nyhan syndrome. *Lancet, 1*, 761.

Mulick, J. A., & Meinhold, P. M. (1991). Evaluating models for the emergence and maintenance of stereotypy and self-injury. *American Journal on Mental Retardation, 96*, 327–384.

National Institute for Child and Human Development. (1991). *Treatment of destructive behaviors in persons with developmental disabilities* (NIH Publication No. 91-2410). Rockville, MD: Author.

Nihira, K., Foster, R., Shellhaas, M., & Leland, H. (1975). *AAMD Adaptive Behavior Scale Manual* (rev. ed.). Washington, DC: American Association on Mental Deficiency.

Nihira, K., Price-Williams, D. R., & White, J. F. (1988). Social competence and maladaptive behavior of people with dual diagnosis. *Journal of the Multihandicapped Person, 1*, 185–199.

Nyhan, W. L. (1967). The Lesch–Nyhan Syndrome: Self-destructive biting, mental retardation, neurological disorder and hyperuricemia. *Developmental Medicine and Child Neurology, 9*, 563–572.

Nyhan, W. L. Johnson, H. G., Kaufman, I. A., & Jones, K. L. (1980). Serotonergic approaches to the modification of behavior in the Lesch–Nyhan syndrome. *Applied Research in Mental Retardation, 1*, 25–40.

O'Neill, R. E., Horner, R. H., Albin, R. W., Storey, K., & Sprague, J. R. (1990). *Functional analysis of problem behavior: A practical assessment guide*. Pacific Grove, CA: Brooks/Cole.

Patterson, G. R. (1982). *Coercive family process: A social-learning approach*. Eugene, OR: Castalia.

Poling, A., Gadow, K., & Cleary, J. (1991). *Drug therapy for behavior disorders*. New York: Pergamon.

Ratey, J. J. (Ed.). (1991). *Mental retardation: Developing pharmacotherapies*. Washington, DC: American Psychiatric Press.

Reichle, J., & Wacker, D. (Eds.). (1993). *Communicative alternatives to challenging behavior: Integrating functional assessment and intervention strategies*. Baltimore, MD: Brookes.

Reiss, S. (1988a, September). *The development of a screening measure for psychopathology in people with mental retardation*. Paper presented at the joint National Institute of Mental Health–National Institutes of Health Workshop on The Assessment of the Mental Health Aspects of Mental Retardation. Bethesda, MD.

Reiss, S. (1988b). *Test manual for the Reiss Screen for Maladaptive Behavior*. Orland Park, IL: International Diagnostic Systems.

Reiss, S., Levitan, G. W., & Szyszko, J. (1982). Emotional disturbance and mental retardation: Diagnostic overshadowing. *American Journal of Mental Deficiency, 86*, 567–574.

Repp, A. C., & Dietz, D. (1990). Using an ecobehavioral analysis to determine a taxonomy of stereotyped responding. In S. R. Schroeder (Ed.), *Ecobehavioral analysis and developmental disabilities: The twenty-first century* (pp. 122–140). New York: Springer-Verlag.

Repp, A. C., & Singh, N. N. (Eds.). (1990). *Perspectives on the use of nonaversive and aversive interventions for persons with disabilities*. Sycamore, IL: Sycamore.

Robertson, M. M. (1992). Self-injurious behavior and Tourette syndrome. In T. N. Case, A. J. Friedhoff, & D. J. Cohen (Eds.), *Advances in neurology* (Vol. 58, pp. 105–114). New York: Raven.

Robertson, M. M., Trimble, M. R., & Lees, A. J. (1989). Self-injurious behavior and the Gilles de la Tourette syndrome: A clinical study and review of the literature. *Psychological Medicine, 19*, 611–625.

Rojahn, J. (1994). Epidemiology and topographic taxonomy of self-injurious behavior. In T. Thompson & D. Gray (Eds.), *Destructive behavior and developmental disabilities* (pp. 49–67). Thousand Oaks, CA: Sage.

Rojahn, J., Borthwick-Duffy, S., & Jacobson, J. (1993). The association between psychiatric diagnoses and severe behavior problems in mental retardation. *Annals of Clinical Psychiatry, 5*, 163–170.

Rusch, F. R. (Ed.). (1990). *Supported employment: Models, issues and methods*. Sycamore, IL: Sycamore.

Rutter, M. (1966). Behavioural and cognitive characteristics of a series of psychotic children. In J. K. Wing (Ed.), *Early childhood autism: Clinical, educational and social aspects* (pp. 1–22), London: Pergamon.

Rutter, M., Tizard, J., & Whitmore, K. (1970). *Education, health, and behavior*. New York: Wiley.

Sandman, C. A. (1990–1991). The opiate hypothesis in autism and self-injury. *Journal of Child and Adolescent Psychopharmacology, 1*, 237–248.

Sandman, C. A., Datta, P., Barron, J. L., Hoehler, F., Williams, C., & Swanson, J. (1983). Naloxone attenuates self-abusive behavior in developmentally disabled subjects. *Applied Research in Mental Retardation, 4*, 5–11.

Sandman, C. A., Hetrick, W. P., Taylor, D. V., Barron, J. L., Touchette, P., Lott, I., Crinella, F., & Martinazzi, V. (1993). Naltrexone redness self-injury and improves learning. *Experimental and Clinical Psychopharmacology, 1*, 242–258.

Saunders, R. R., & Spradlin, J. E. (1991). A supported routines approach to active treatment for enhancing independence, competence, and self-worth. *Behavioral Residential Treatment, 6*, 11–37.

Schaal, D. W., & Hackenberg, T. (1994). Toward a functional analysis of drug treatment for behavior problems of people with developmental disabilities. *American Journal on Mental Retardation, 99*, 123–140.

Schroeder, S., Mulick, J., & Schroeder, C. (1979). Management of severe behavior problems of the retarded. In N. Ellis (Ed.), *Handbook of mental deficiency* (2nd ed., pp. 341–366). Hillsdale, NJ: Lawrence Erlbaum Associates.

Schroeder, S. R. (Ed.). (1990). *Ecobehavioral analysis and developmental disabilities: The twenty-first century.* New York: Springer-Verlag.

Schroeder, S. R., Bickel, W. K., & Richmond, G. (1986). Primary and secondary prevention of self-injurious behavior. In K. Gadow & I. Bialer (Eds.), *Advances in learning and behavioral disabilities* (Vol. 5, pp. 65–87). Greenwich, CT: JAI.

Schroeder, S. R., Lewis, M. A., & Lipton, M. A. (1983). Interactions of pharmacotherapy and behavior therapy among children with learning behavioral disorders. In K. D. Gadow & I. Bialer (Eds.), *Advances in learning and behavioral disabilities* (Vol. 2, pp. 179–225). Greenwich, CT: JAI.

Schroeder, S. R., & MacLean, W. (1987). If it isn't one thing, it's another: Experimental analysis of covariation in behavior management data of severely disturbed retarded persons. In S. Landesman-Dwyer & P. Vietze (Eds.), *Living environments and mental retardation* (pp. 315–338). Washington, DC: AAMD Monograph Series.

Schroeder, S. R., Mulick, J. A., & Rojahn, J. (1980). The definition, taxonomy, epidemiology, and ecology of self-injurious behavior. *Journal of Autism and Developmental Disorders, 10,* 417–432.

Schroeder, S. R., Rojahn, J., & Oldenquist, A. (1991, July). *Treatment of destructive behaviors among people with mental retardation and developmental disabilities: An overview of the program* (NIH Publication No. 91-2410). Paper presented at the Consensus Development Conference on Destructive Behavior, National Institutes of Health, Bethesda, MD.

Schroeder, S. R., Schroeder, C., Smith, B., & Dalldorf, J. (1978). Prevalence of self-injurious behavior in a large state facility for the retarded. *Journal of Autism and Childhood Schizophrenia, 8,* 261–269.

Schroeder, S. R., & Tessel, R. (1994). Dopaminergic and serotonergic mechanisms in self injury and aggression. In T. Thompson & D. Gray (Eds.), *Treatment of destructive behavior in developmental disabilities* (pp. 198–212). Newbury Park, CA: Sage.

Scott, K. G. (1988). The need for a national epidemiological study. In J. Stark, F. J. Menolascino, M. Albarelli, & V. Gray (Eds.), *Mental retardation and mental health* (pp. 50–54). New York: Springer-Verlag.

Sheiner, L. B., Beal, S. L., & Sambol, S. C. (1989). Study designs for dose-ranging. *Clinical Pharmacology and Therapeutics, 46,* 63–77.

Smull, M., & Harrison, S. B. (1992). *Supporting people with severe reputations in the community.* Alexandria, VA: National Association of State Directors of Developmental Disabilities Services, Inc.

Sovner, R., Fox, C., Lowry, M. J., & Lowry, M. A. (1993). Fluoxetine treatment of depression and associated injury in two adults with mental retardation. *Journal of Intellectual Disability Research, 37,* 301–312.

Sovner, R., & Hurley, A. (1983). Do the mentally retarded suffer from affective illness? *Archives of General Psychiatry, 40,* 61–67.

Sovner, R., & Lowry, M. (1990). A behavioral methodology for diagnosing affective disorders in individuals with mental retardation. *The Habilitative Mental Healthcare Newsletter, 9,* 56–61.

Sparrow, S. S., Balla, D. A., & Cicchetti, D. V. (1984). *Interview edition. Expanded form manual. Vineland Adaptive Behavior Scales.* Circle Pines, MN: American Guidance Service.

Sprague, R. L., & Newell, K. M. (1996). *Stereotyped movements: Brain and behavior relationships.* Washington, DC: American Psychological Association.

Sprague, R. L., & Werry, J. S. (1971). Methodology of psychopharmacological studies with the retarded. In N. R. Ellis (Ed.), *International review of research in mental retardation* (Vol. 5, pp. 148–220). New York: Academic Press.

Stodgell, C. J., Schroeder, S. R., Hyland, J. M., & Tessel, R. E (1994). Effect of repeated footshock stress, apomorphine and their combination on the incidence of apomorphine (APO)-elicited self-injurious behavior (SIB) in juvenile neonatal 6–hydroxydopamine (6HD)-treated rats. *Neuroscience Abstracts, 20,* 1444.

Szymanski, L., & Tanguay, P. (1980). *Emotional disorders of mentally retarded persons.* Baltimore, MD: University Park Press.

Tessel, R. E., Schroeder, S. R., Loupe, P. S., & Stodgell, C. J. (1995). Reversal of 6HD-induced neonatalbrain catecholamine depletion after operant training. *Pharmacology Biochemistry and Behavior, 51,* 861–867.

Thompson, T., Hackenberg, T., Cerutti, D., Baker, D., & Axtell, S. (1994). Opioid antagonist effects on self-injury in adults with mental retardation: Response form and location as determinants of medication effects. *American Journal on Mental Retardation, 99,* 85–102.

Thompson, T., Hackenberg, T., & Schaal, D. (1991, July). *Pharmacological treatments for behavior problems in developmental disabilities* (NIH Publication No. 91-3410). Paper presented at the Consensus Development Conference on Destructive Behavior, National Institutes of Health, Bethesda, MD.

U.S. Department of Education. (1992). *Fourteenth annual report to congress on the implementation of public law 94–142: The education for all handicapped children act.* Washington, DC: Author.

Van Houten, R., & Axelrod, S. (1993). *Behavior analysis and treatment.* New York: Plenum.

Van Praag, H. M., Asnis, G. M., Kahn, R. S., Brown, S. L., Korn, M., Harkavy-Friedman, J. M., & Wetzler, S. (1990). Monoamines and abnormal behaviour: A multi-aminergic perspective. *British Journal of Psychiatry, 157,* 723–734.

Werry, J. S. (1993). Introduction: A guide for practitioners, professionals, and public. In J. S. Werry & M. G. Aman (Eds.), *Practitioner's guide to psychoactive drugs for children and adolescents* (pp. 3–21). New York: Plenum.

Werry, J. S., & Aman, M. G. (1993). *Practitioner's guide to psychoactive drugs for children and adolescents.* New York: Plenum.

Wieseler, N. H., Hanson, R. H., & Nord, G. (1995). An investigation of mortality and morbidity associated with self-injurious behavior. *Americaan Journal on Mental Retardation, 100,* 1–4.

Williams, D. C., & Saunders, K. J. (in press). Methodological issues in the study of drug effects on cognitive skills in mental retardation. In N. W. Bray (Ed.), *International review of research in mental retardation.* New York: Academic Press.

Wolfensberger, W. (1994). A personal interpretation of the mental retardation scene in light of "Signs of the Times." *Mental Retardation, 32,* 19–33.

Wolfensberger, W., & Menolascino, F. J. (1970). Methodological considerations in evaluating the intelligence-enhancing properties of drugs. In F. Menolascino (Ed.), *Psychiatric approaches to mental retardation* (pp. 399–421). New York: Basic Books.

Wolff, P. (1967). The role of biological rhythms in early psychological development. *Bulletin of the Menninger Clinic, 31,* 197–218.

Author Index

C

I

J

S

Subject Index

For Product Safety Concerns and Information please contact our EU
representative GPSR@taylorandfrancis.com
Taylor & Francis Verlag GmbH, Kaufingerstraße 24, 80331 München, Germany

www.ingramcontent.com/pod-product-compliance
Lightning Source LLC
LaVergne TN
LVHW011102300926
849160LV00008B/257
* 9 7 8 1 1 3 8 9 6 8 5 9 2 *